Social Stratification: Canada

Social Stratification: Canada

Second Edition

Edited by

James E. Curtis
University of Waterloo

William G. Scott
University of Waterloo

Prentice-Hall of Canada, Ltd., Scarborough, Ontario

Canadian Cataloguing in Publication Data

Main entry under title:

Social stratification, Canada

Bibliography: p.
ISBN 0-13-818633-2

1. Social classes —Canada—Addresses, essays,
lectures. I. Curtis, James E., 1942–
II. Scott, William G., 1919–

HN110.Z9S62 1979   301.44'0971   C79-094049-3

Prentice-Hall, Inc., Englewood Cliffs, New Jersey
Prentice-Hall of Australia, Pty., Ltd., Sydney
Prentice-Hall of India Pvt., Ltd., New Delhi
Prentice-Hall International, Inc., London
Prentice-Hall of Japan, Inc., Tokyo
Prentice-Hall of Southeast Asia (Pte.) Ltd., Singapore

Production Editors: Ernest Hillen, Irwin DeVries

Design: Gail Ferreira

ISBN 0-13-818633-2

1 2 3 4 5   83 82 81 80 79

Contents

III. Selected Correlates of Class, Power, and Status Differences

Preface

This volume of selections is intended for students of contemporary Canadian society, particularly as a text and supplement for courses in social stratification and Canadian society. All the selections were written after the mid-1960s and most are much more recent. The book, as did its first edition, emerged largely from our repeated use of particular Canadian research reports in supplemental reading lists for courses in social stratification, Canadian society, and introductory sociology. Our purpose here is to acquaint the reader with some of the current thought and research on structured social inequality in Canada.

Not all the interests of sociologists of social stratification can be acknowledged in a single volume. This area has been very active; a rich diversity of approaches, ideologies, assumptions, and research interests now co-exist in the current literature. We believe that our selections provide a cross-section of central areas of interest and approaches, although the treatment afforded these is not exhaustive.

This edition departs in several ways from its predecessor. The changes reflect some changing thought, on our part, about how social stratification in this society can best be understood; and, especially, reflect the richer array of studies now available. Of the 28 selections, most are new to (or revised for) this edition; only four are retained from the original edition. About one quarter of the selections are previously unpublished.

We have expanded the number of selections that focus on theoretical and conceptual materials. Each of these papers builds from reviews of Canadian and international research findings. This change was made possible by a profusion of materials on social stratification since our first edition, including several fine theoretical and state-of-the-field pieces. The appearance of the latter is one indicator of the development of a specialty area in sociology.

We have maintained, as an organizing tool, our *multidimensional* approach as described in the introduction and in Part I, but have lengthened the list of stratification dimensions. The new materials are on sex status and age status. Studies of class from a Marxian perspective have increased as well, because of the greater availability of such work now. These include, for example, two new historically oriented pieces by Leo Johnson, a Marxian scholar at the University of Waterloo.

We have also given new emphasis to the distinction between *distributive* and *relational* processes in social stratification. The first involve studying stratification as aspects of individuals and their status level placements; the latter concern actions and interactions of groups (such as classes or elites) and larger collectivities. We found it difficult to elect an approach that focuses more on one than on the other of these types of processes because it seems to us that structured inequality, the research problem of social stratification, entails both phenomena. We see little to be gained in a more specialized definition *if* both sets of problems are indeed pursued. We add this last caveat because, until recently, relational problems seemed to be getting less attention in the Canadian studies. It is clear, though, that the major change in the literature since our last edition has been the increase in studies dealing with relational issues.

Taken together, our selections in Parts II and III display a range of theoretical approaches. The approaches are reviewed and compared in Part I. We argue, however, that much of the research can be roughly organized in terms of the broad approaches—the conflict and the functionalist perspectives. Our collection also assumes the two theoretical (perhaps, more properly, definitional) claims referred to above: first, there seem to be two *broad* sets of problems to be pursued in social stratification studies — the distributive and the relational; second, evidence suggests that social stratification occurs along various dimensions. The evidence does not entirely compel us to adopt a single perspective as sufficient to handle the various concerns raised by any one definition of the field. As our choice of selections implies, we find one or another approach especially illuminating for certain phenomena.

Compared to other Canadian sociological specialty areas, social stratification is probably the most developed. There is a line of research on occupational stratification and ethnic group relations which began with the works of pioneers of the discipline in this country such as Carl Dawson, E. C. Hughes, Horace Miner, J. C. Falardeau, Oswald Hall, and S. D. Clark. Another research tradition was established by Harold Innis and his colleagues, and focused on macro-level problems of regional and international stratification processes. A central concern of these researchers, and of their successors, has been to describe and interpret the ways in which particular social inequalities occur and persist in society. Outstanding among contemporary scholars is John Porter, whose brilliant study *The Vertical Mosaic*[1] reflects his longstanding interest in macro-analysis of status and power. The magnitude of Porter's contribution alone distinguishes the study of stratification from other areas of sociological interest in Canada. Several of our contributors spell out their debts to Porter's work.

In the preface to our first edition we remarked as follows on Canadian Studies:

> In several sub-fields of sociology, including areas within social stratification, there is only a meager collection of available published works. . . . We should note in particular that there has been little investigation of such topics as the history of the

---

1. J. Porter, *The Vertical Mosaic* (Toronto: University of Toronto Press, 1965). See also J. Porter, "Research Biography of a Macrosociological Study: The Vertical Mosaic" in J. S. Coleman et al., *Macrosociology: Research and Theory* (Boston: Allyn and Bacon, 1970), pp. 149–181. The latter provides comments on the state of Canadian stratification studies, the situation with respect to available data and research funds in the 1950s, and traditions influencing Porter in his own work.

working and middle classes, class consciousness, community prestige, ... the role of religious status, and many social behavioral and social psychological correlates of social class. With a handful of exceptions, there are no large-scale local surveys or case study researchers on social class compared, for example, to those which exist for Great Britain or the United States.... Attention had only begun to turn to subjective and reputational research approaches to class.

The past few years have seen research in each of these areas, and we would therefore want to alter these appraisals. Much remains to be done, but the literature has developed enormously. The increase in the literature has meant laments for us as editors: numerous illuminating studies had to be set aside because of space constraints. We have tried to capture something more of the rich development of the field in our Further Readings section. This section, too, must be seen as quite selective.

Beyond being guided by the emphases mentioned above, we chose for this edition articles depicting significant sets of research findings and major theoretical hunches. For Parts II and III, we selected articles that (a) included both statements of empirically testable propositions and systematic reporting of Canadian data bearing on them, or (b) developed theoretical arguments while drawing on an extensive review of previous studies. Readability for undergraduates was also a consideration. Finally, we focused largely, but not exclusively, on studies of the contemporary social stratification scene or on socio-historical analyses that date to the present.

ACKNOWLEDGMENTS

We would like very much to thank our contributors. Obviously, the strengths of this book are largely their doing. We are also indebted to several people for help of various kinds, including thoughtful comments on our materials. These people include especially Ben Agger, Peter Archibald, Raymond Breton, Carl Cuneo, Edward Grabb, John Goyder, Hubert Guindon, Neil Guppy, Stephen Hawkins, Rick Helmes, Ronald Lambert, John Loy, Dennis Olsen, James Rinehart, and Irwin DeVries and Marta Tomins at Prentice-Hall.

Introduction: The Substance of Social Stratification

What accounts for success and failure in wealth and poverty, power, or different types of honor and disrepute? What are the consequences of different ranks in these regards for personal beliefs, values, and patterns of behavior? What are the relationships between categories and groups of people defined by their differing amounts of power, wealth, and prestige? What are the consequences of these relationships? These are questions scholars of social stratification attempt to answer. *Social stratification* is the branch of sociology concerned with the nature, social causes, and consequences of the unequal social evaluations and distribution of resources among different population categories.

Phrased more broadly, these questions are among the principal concerns of sociology itself: To what extent do members of a society have the same or different beliefs, values, and patterns of conduct? What accounts for similarities and differences? What are the patterns of relationships between different types of social groups? Since previous research has led us to see that social stratification differences have been significant sources of variability in many patterns of beliefs and social behavior, studies in the field of stratification must be viewed as of central importance in sociology.[1] This has meant, for example, that in the design of almost every sociological survey, various measures of the respondents' social status backgrounds are given important consideration as potential independent or control variables.[2] The same is true of research in which the behaviors or interrelationships of groups (as opposed to individuals) are studied.

THEORETICAL APPROACHES TO SOCIAL STRATIFICATION

Lipset's paper in Part I argues that much research on social stratification is directly guided by one of two general theoretical perspectives — the *Marxian* approach or, more generally, the conflict approach; and the *functionalist* approach. An even larger cross-section of research in this area is influenced less directly by these perspectives because this work pursues topics initially raised under them. Lipset describes these approaches as comparatively recent variants of conservative versus radical orientations to societal change. He deals with their differences in some detail, but a brief introduction to them might nevertheless be in order here.

1

In the nineteenth century a powerful critique of social inequalities was put forward, from a conflict perspective, by Karl Marx.[3] He focused on differences in economic power and, specifically, in relationships of groups of people to the means of production. These means were seen to be chiefly land, tools, and machinery. The historical process was viewed as the interactions — always conflictive, coercive, and exploitative — between groups differing in their relationship to the means of production. History, it was held, could be roughly divided into several periods, each of which had its characteristic mode of production that formed the basis of structures composed of the rulers of the instruments of production versus people under the influence of these rulers. These structures meant conflicts of interest, between those who controlled the productive instruments and those who did not. In the most recent period, the private ownership of the means of production had created an oppressive class system, divided largely between the exploitative owners, or the capitalist class, and the exploited workers. According to Marx, human freedom and equality required that the control of the means of production be widely shared among all who did productive work. He favored reform to a situation of "from each according to his ability, to each according to his need."[4]

Variants of this approach have been employed by many scholars since Marx's time. These include sociologists who are "non-Marxist" and who write from a more general "conflict" theoretical perspective. These writers make similar arguments on the centrality of conflict in social life and in social change. However, the competing actors focused on in their analyses are often groups other than classes — professional or business associations, unions, lobby groups, the elites of religious, political, or educational organizations, and so on. Examples of more contemporary proponents of the conflict approach in the international literature include Lewis Coser, Ralf Dahrendorf, Gerhard Lenski, Michael Mann, Ralph Miliband, C. Wright Mills, and Frank Parkin.[5] Canadian proponents of this perspective include, among our contributors, Archibald, Baldus, Guindon, Clement, Johnson, and Tepperman.

Conflict theorists see society as a set of groups and organizations (including classes, but more than classes) competing for the distribution of scarce resources. In a society such as ours these resources would include power, economic control, and wealth. Power is seen as a key factor in the distribution of all highly valued resources. Conflicts around group interests, and the control and coercion of one group by another, are emphasized in research.

Gerhard Lenski has elaborated on the principles subscribed to by conflict theorists as follows.[6] He assumes that persons must live in society with others, but that they will generally choose to promote their own and their group's interests over the interests of others. Also, he assumes that decisions of self-interest will frequently arise because the material and nonmaterial resources which people value and strive to achieve are in scarce supply. Finally, Lenski believes that people are always, to some extent, unequally equipped by nature to compete for scarce resources.

Lenski develops two laws of distribution. First, he believes that people share the resources gleaned from their labors to an extent required to ensure the survival and continued productivity of other persons whose actions are necessary or beneficial to themselves. In short, human cooperation and sharing are necessitated by the recognized need for human group support. Cooperation and sharing are said to dominate in technologically simple societies that have little surplus of goods. In these societies social stratification is most limited, with some distinctions of power and prestige, based often on differences in age, sex, skills, and abilities.

In situations where improved technology and more efficient division of labor provide for a surplus of goods, Lenski believes, power determines nearly all distribution of the surplus. Competition for surpluses occurs, and those with the greater power obtain the greater share. The powerful generally get what they can achieve. The exceptions here are acts of altruism. Lenski also suggests that the greater the surplus, the more this will be distributed according to differences in power.

The use of power in the pursuit of surplus does not always involve raw force or coercion, Lenski reminds us. For example, distributive systems, or rules for the allocation of resources, often become legitimized over time. The unequal distribution of rewards that power makes possible comes to be understood by "have nots" and "haves" as right, justified. Presumably, there is sometimes some negotiation between these groups over the rules of distribution, but, again, differences in power tend to take precedence. For example, legitimizing beliefs about the appropriateness of rules of private property, which support inequalities, may become widely accepted (see the selection by Clement in this volume). Or, beliefs about the superiority of skill levels and abilities of the highly educated may be used to justify inequalities in income, prestige, and power across educational statuses (see the selections by Rocher, and Lambert and Curtis on legitimizing beliefs around the educational system).

The functionalist perspective is especially indebted to the works of Emile Durkheim,[7] as Lipset's analysis shows. Other recent proponents include Bernard Barber, Kingsley Davis, Robert Merton, Wilbert Moore, and Talcott Parsons.[8] This perspective emphasizes that some statuses — largely jobs or occupations — are of greater importance for society's wellbeing than others. These positions also tend to require greater amounts of training and talent if they are to be successfully filled, it is argued. To ensure that highly qualified people will fill the more crucial positions, and will be motivated to perform well, there must be inequalities in the distribution of rewards to positions. Greater rewards must go to the more crucial positions, it is said. These rewards include the prestige of the position, income, and power. It is assumed that if all occupations carried equal rewards, most people would want to take on the least demanding ones for which the least training was required; and these tend to be the less crucial positions. According to this approach, social stratification is an "unconsciously evolved device by which societies ensure that the most important positions are conscientiously filled by the most qualified persons."[9]

Some writers emphasize that this approach does not accommodate exceptions which are frequent in societies such as Canada. Three types of problems have been singled out: First, there are occupations, such as those had by garbage collectors, sewage plant workers, or small farmers, which are essential to society, but for which rewards in prestige and power are low. Second, there are similar reward levels for occupations which differ markedly in skill and training requirements. Third, there are different reward levels for occupations which require similar skills and for which there are no apparent differences in importance to society. More generally, there is the problem that the relative "importance" of positions is difficult to measure, and no method has been agreed on.[10]

If power, control, and conflict are central to the conflict perspective, prestige is a highlight in the functionalist perspective. Occupations are viewed in a ladder-like fashion. There is said to be a generally understood prestige ordering of occupations in society. This is disputed, but some research suggests that prestige rankings of this sort occur (see Lipset in Part I, and Pineo and Porter in Part II).

The functionalist perspective has perhaps had its greatest influence by prompting many studies of the individual's attainment, and inheritance, of occupation prestige levels. Studies have been conducted by both proponents and skeptics of the functionalist approach (e.g., see Hunter in Part I and Guindon, and Goyder and Curtis in Part II). Sometimes such studies emphasize that occupational prestige deserves study in its own right because it is more difficult to inherit than economic control and wealth.[11] The exception is in instances of inherited business occupations (for example, sons becoming farm owners or pharmacy owners by inheriting these businesses, and occupations, from their fathers). Studies of occupational status attainment show the importance of the parent's occupation as a predictor of the offspring's occupation achievement (as in our selection by Goyder and Curtis). However, such findings are often interpreted as follows: Occupational prestige is not so much inherited from the parents as is a general socio-economic level, a cultural milieu within the home, a likely set of associates, and so on. The latter have implications for the quality and level of education that the offspring seeks and achieves (see Breton's study of students' educational plans here). Education has a strong effect on occupational attainment.

Another implication of the functionalist perspective, as well as of other theoretical traditions (see Lipset's chapter on the influence of Max Weber's work), is that prestige is not constrained to occupational statuses. Prestige is also accorded by society to differences between social positions such as educational statuses, sex statuses, and ethnic statuses (compare the selections by Labovitz and Lambert and Curtis, for example). Different prestige hierarchies may co-exist, with possibly loose inter-correlations, so that an individual or group may have high prestige on one dimension and low prestige on another. Where this is the case, the implication is that the system of inequalities is not as binding on persons as the conflict approach with its emphasis on fewer dimensions of inequality, might suggest.

Writers favoring a conflict approach and a unidimensional approach which emphasizes power or class inequalities would view this issue slightly differently. They would argue that the sociological significance of the dimension of social inequality (say, class) that they are interested in is obscured too much when it is seen to be embedded in context with various other types of inequality, some of them less important for explaining the way societies have developed and will develop.

For Lenski, though, prestige is largely a function of power wielded by status groups to attain recognition and evaluation. He emphasizes, for example, that much of the prestige of an occupation can be accounted for by the income and educational levels of persons holding it (see the selection by Pineo and Porter; compare similar arguments for ethnic status and sex status by Breton and McDonald). He argues that differences in education and income may be seen as rough indicators of the power wielded by members of the occupation.[12]

Hypotheses and research problems suggested by the conflict and the functionalist perspectives have informed our own work (compare the selections by Lambert and Curtis, and Goyder and Curtis). However, we see each of these perspectives as providing a partial interpretation of the complex reality of social stratification. The conflict perspective, especially as extended by Lenski, provides a more complete explanation of the social structural underpinnings of inequalities of power and wealth and of the sources of social change. We find it difficult to accept most of the principles of the functionalist perspective, because of the problems mentioned. Nonetheless, we see it as focusing attention on (1) the pervasive phenomena of prestige and its multiple bases and (2) factors in the status attainments of individuals. These problems are de-emphasized in the conflict perspective, in which the focus is on power and control, and on the actions of groups as opposed to the achievements of individuals of different social backgrounds. Though we continue to find merit in the research problems and issues raised by both approaches, we believe that currently the conflict perspective takes us much closer to a compelling general interpretation of the range of social stratification phenomena.

Because we see the need for additional development of general theoretical perspectives, we have incorporated research concerns and conceptual distinctions of both theoretical approaches in the organization of this volume. The studies by Johnson, Clement, Tepperman, Guindon, Baldus, Archibald, and Lambert and Curtis are from the conflict or Marxian perspectives. The selections by Pineo and Porter, Goyder and Curtis, Labowitz, and Segal are from the functionalist perspective, or deal with research issues raised by the perspective. There are also selections which deal with prestige in different forms.

TWO BROAD RESEARCH CONCERNS IN SOCIAL STRATIFICATION STUDIES

In order to present materials relevant to the two theoretical traditions we have included selections bearing on two broad research concerns. These are defined by the difference between *distributive* and *relational* aspects of social stratification.[13] Students of the conflict perspective generally give more attention to relational phenomena; those working from a functionalist perspective focus more on distributive phenomena.

In studies of *distributive phenomena* there is description and explanation of how the individual is placed in status levels or status groups. Attention is given to "the impact on individual careers of differences in parental resources, access to educational institutions and the like, or ... upon individual characteristics of people variously placed." Studies of *relational phenomena* describe and explain status groups and their activities and interactions. There is a "concern here with the ways in which differential class power and social advantage operate in predictable and routine ways, through specifiable social interactions between classes or interest groups, to give shape to determinate social structures and to create differential life chances."[14] Relational phenomena more often involve differences in power and economic control between groups, though conflict over the prestige given to different groups may be involved as well. Distributive phenomena can entail differences in various statuses and rewards — prestige, power, income and so on — acquired by individuals.

The relational and the distributive problems involve different *units of analysis*. Work on the two problems means a focus on *data on different types of social actors*. In the distributive approach, characteristics and actions (say, status attainment) of *individuals* are focused on. In the relational approach characteristics and actions of *groups* or organizations are emphasized.[15] In the first instance, the actor, or *decision-making unit*, is the individual. In the second it is the group. Researchers who study either problem often look to phenomena of the second type as well when they attempt to explain their findings (neither phenomenon exists in isolation). Illustrative of this latter point are studies of individuals' patterns of voting by their occupational status backgrounds, which find that these status differences predict voting poorly, if at all. Some have found partial explanations of these findings in the limited political party alternatives that have been made available to voters because of the historical interplay of political and economic elites. The parties have not focused on, and represented, the interests of given occupational statuses (compare the selections by Guindon and Ogmundson). Another example is in Clement's analysis, in this volume, wherein patterns of recruitment of individuals to the economic elite are explained in terms of class relations in Canada.

Both sets of phenomena are part of social stratification in any society, and must be understood for a full appreciation of structural inequalities. Social stratification involves the ways in which "individuals are assigned to their respective niches in terms of background and training."[16] It also, however, involves exchanges among various classes and interest groups differentially located within the social structure. It is a system, in which command and coercion play parts. Various status interest "groups use their resources so as to effectively maintain or advance their positions and to maximize the distribution of material and social benefits to their advantage." A focus on the distributive aspects of stratification would "direct attention away from the socio-political mechanisms through which members of different strata monopolize chances by reducing the chances of others."[17] It is one thing to study the extent to which, and how, individuals achieve access to high occupational status (see the selections by Goyder and Curtis and the first one by Clement in Part II). It is quite another to study how groups and organizations help to maintain patterns of occupational mobility and wealth differentials (compare, for example, our selections by Johnson and Clement). The two problems are related, but they may be analytically separated for study, as they often are.

SOME BASIC CONCEPTS

Social Stratification

Social stratification refers to a hierarchy of social inequality. As used here the term applies to hierarchies based on the possession by persons or groups of one or more of these scarce resources: (1) power, (2) economic control (ownership), (3) wealth or income, and (4) prestige. For this society, we see prestige to be based especially on widely understood *evaluations* of (1) occupational status, (2) educational status, (3) racial and ethnic status, (4) sex status, (5) age status, and (6) levels of power, economic control, wealth and income. As we will see, power, economic control, and wealth and income are also distributed according to these same factors (1 to 6). In short, we see social stratification as multi-faceted or *multi-dimensional*.[18]

Traditionally, social stratification has been used to signify phenomena at the local community level or at the societal level, but it also occurs in smaller groups. Most groups of some size and complexity involve stratification, especially in terms of power. An example of a stratification study within a smaller group, albeit a group embedded in the wider society, is given by Ball in Part II. Ball describes how race and nationality relate to the attainment of playing positions differing in leadership and control on professional football teams.

Stratification versus Differentiation

A distinction is often drawn between *social stratification* and *social differentiation*. Members of a society may be different in many respects — age, skin color, color of hair, hat size, ethnicity, job, educational status, wealth, type of clothing. When members of society respond to the differences of others, we say there is social differentiation. Such differences alone do not represent stratification. Social differentiation, when it involves, for example, a division of labor or occupational specialization, may provide a basis for stratification (compare the selections by Hunter, Pineo and Porter, and Goyder and Curtis and the two by Johnson). However, such differences do not *necessarily* imply differential evaluations of higher versus lower or superior versus inferior for the categories of persons or groups that are isolated, nor do they necessarily imply differences in attainment of the resources of power, ownership, and wealth. Witness, for example, the limited consequences in terms of evaluation and resources that different hair colors or hat sizes have in this country. The process of social stratification involves persons or groups being placed at different levels of evaluation or attainment of resources as a consequence of their characteristics. *Differences in evaluation* or *inequalities in access to valued resources* are involved in social stratification. Some sort of social differentiation is a necessary, but insufficient, condition for social stratification.

Social stratification may be viewed as having a social psychological basis in the two universal processes that we have alluded to: (1) the tendency for people to perceive and define differences in society and (2) individuals' tendencies to evaluate these differences. As Roach *et al.* have put it:

> A widely acknowledged universal disposition of humans is their capacity to notice things, to discern likenesses and differences, and to set apart one characteristic from another. This capacity leads them to separate sex and age groupings, to distinguish occupational and education roles, and to accept differentiation generally in social life. ... Another acknowledged universal disposition is the readiness to appraise the utility and significance of any object or experience which influences survival and enhancement of life. Men judge and evaluate their surroundings.[19]

To these perceptual and evaluative processes may be added persons' tendencies to pursue self-interest and the interests of their group — based on their perceptions and evaluations.

Status: Prestige and Role

A *status* is a culturally defined position in society. It is a set of shared ideas regarding how people are supposed to respond toward the person, and how the person should behave when in a particular position. Statuses consist of sets of rules — statements of rights and obligations — specifying how interaction is to take place. Statuses are often the unit part of different social groups and organizations, such as in the different occupations in a work organization. However, some statuses are based more on individuals' ascribed characteristics, such as age and race. Some statuses are ranked *vis à vis* other related ones on a given status dimension. They are given differences in *prestige*. This occurs, in large part, because of the social significance that has been historically attached to these rules of rights and obligations. An example is professional occupations versus unskilled workers, and the greater rank generally given the first. Another example is the differential evaluation given to the statuses man versus woman in many contexts. In other instances, there appears to be little such ranking, as in comparisons of adolescent versus infant. These statuses are simply seen as different. Compare, however, the statuses adult and aged in this society (see the selection by Abu-Laban and Abu-Laban). In addition, the rights and obligations specify whether different amounts of scarce resources should flow to persons occupying different statuses. Again, for some status comparisons there often is a differential flow, as in the differences in income and power between doctors and lawyers and unorganized, unskilled farm or urban laborers. In other cases, there may be little of this differential flow as, for example, in comparisons, other things being equal, of infants and other young children in Canadian society. Since social stratification is concerned with statuses which are *differentially evaluated* or otherwise *differentially rewarded* we limit our use of the term to these types of situations.

Statuses can be *ascribed* or *achieved*. An achieved status can be assumed only after a person acts in some way to assume it; i.e., the incumbent performs to meet particular requirements for the status. Movement into an achieved status is based on a person's accomplishments. What are relevant accomplishments, though, are typically prescribed. Examples in our society are attainment of educational statuses, occupational statuses, income statuses or positions differing in power.

An ascribed status is assigned to an individual irrespective of his or her accomplishments. This assignment is frequently, but not always, at birth (compare age statuses which "automatically" change in a lifetime). Examples in our society include racial and ethnic statuses, sex statuses, and age statuses. This ascription-achievement distinction requires specification for periods in the life cycle, however. For example, after birth some may successfully change ethnic and racial statuses by passing as a member of a different status (compare Breton's discussion in Part II). There are obvious changes in persons' age statuses through the life cycle. There is an initial placement at birth for the otherwise achieved statuses of class and income and wealth levels, in the sense that children are born into and acquire certain opportunities from the socio-economic circumstances of their families.[20]

In a complex society such as Canada, each person has several statuses at any one point in life because of memberships in various groups and organizations and because of different socially meaningful ascribed characteristics. All of a person's statuses taken together, at any time in the life cycle, are called his or her *status set*.

A distinction is also often drawn between statuses and *roles*. A role is performance in a given status or social position. *Esteem* frequently refers to evaluations of a person's performance in a position. An example of the distinctions between status and role and their evaluations in prestige and esteem would be as follows: Unskilled work, such as bricklayer's helper, has relatively low prestige compared with many other occupations, especially white-collar ones. However, the helper may have high esteem among co-workers because of work well done: The helper can have low prestige and high esteem.[21]

Strata, Status Groups, and Classes

A *stratum* consists of persons who have similar statuses along a given dimension of evaluation or resource allocation, such as persons of the same occupational status, income level, ethnicity, age, and so on. Sometimes *status category* refers to this status similarity. People in strata do not act in terms of their status similarity *as a social group* to any appreciable extent. This is not part of what people have learned in experiences with the culture which they share, their status rights and obligations, their beliefs about inequalities. When people have a shared status, consider themselves members of that status, and are inclined to act as a group, we speak of them as *status groups*. Examples are French Canadians or groups of native peoples who act politically out of a shared ethnic consciousness rather than as atomized individuals sharing an ascribed characteristic (a stratum or status category). This is a distinction which Breton emphasizes in his selection on theoretical approaches to ethnic stratification and group behavior. Guindon's selection shows the change in stratification of ethnic strata and status groups in Quebec, suggesting that at least the new middle class segment among francophones approximates a status group. The same distinction is applied to age and sex differences by Abu-Laban and Abu-Laban in this volume.

Classes are given varying definitions in the stratification literature, and in our selections in this volume. The student reader should not be dismayed by this, but should acknowledge it as a mark of a developing research area with contending approaches. What is important is that the referent for the concept be clearly determined in each instance.

All definitions of class refer to strata or status groups. Common definitional approaches include the following: (1) Classes are broad occupational strata or status groups, as in Guindon's description of the francophone new middle class of semi-professional, professional, and management employees in public bureau-cracies versus the urban lower classes of other lower occupational levels. (2) Classes are different levels of general socio-economic circumstances flowing from differences in occupations and wealth, as in Ossenberg's portrayal in this volume of Calgary's classes — the upper class of "the oil elite and ranching group," the middle class of "clerical workers, small businessmen, and generally middle-range employees of larger local firms," and the lower class of service personnel, laborers, and those more deprived. (3) Classes are economic or occupational groupings with a shared consciousness. This is Lipset's definition in this volume — classes "have developed or should develop some 'consciousness of kind,' that is, some sense of existence as a group attribute of society" (compare the research of Ogmundson and Goyder and Pineo on persons' identifications with broad social class labels and some correlates of these identifications). (4) Classes have different relationships to the means of produc-tion. This is the definition, used earlier, from the Marxian perspective, which is emphasized as well in the selections by Johnson and Clement.

We recommend that "class" be reserved for distinctions pointed out by Marx because, as Lipset will indicate, Marx's work provided the primary impetus for the study of class in the social sciences and much work closely follows the Marxian definition.

Classes in the Marxian perspective are somewhat related to occupational status levels, but with significant differences. "Occupation" designates positions within the *technical* division of labor; i.e., an occupation represents a set of activities fulfilling certain technically defined functions. "Class," on the other hand, designates positions within the *social* relations of production; i.e. it designates the "social relationship between actors."[22] A plumber who produces a set of results with pipes in buildings may have one of three different types of class placement. He or she could be a *worker* who does not own the means of production and, therefore, must sell labor power to capitalists. On the other hand, this person may be a small *capitalist*, who owns the means of production, purchases the labor of workers and does not sell labor. Another possibility within the Marxian approach is that of a *petty bourgeois producer*, who owns the means of production but does not purchase the labor of others or sell personal labor (see Lipset's discussion and Johnson's first selection in this volume).

Lipset writes that a class in the Marxian approach may also be a class "in itself" or "for itself." A class "in itself," though composed of members with common relations to production, does not have a high level of class consciousness. Its members do not see themselves in conflict with another class over different interests. A class "for itself" is the opposite in identity and political awareness: people within it have a shared identity and an understanding that they are part of a structure of conflicting class interests, and they tend to take collective action to promote their interests. A class "in itself" is an example of a stratum, as defined earlier, but with relationship to the means of production being the defining criterion. A class "for itself" has the characteristics of a status group with the same criterion of relationship to the means of production.

Ownership of the means of production, or economic control, is central to the way we view classes. Therefore, class differences are akin to differences in wealth and power. In this volume we have combined studies of classes in sections with studies of wealth and income. The unique conceptual domain of class, however, should be kept in mind.

Part of what is at issue between strata and status groups is whether stratification along the status dimension is along a *continuum* or involves *discrete groups*. On the one hand, we may conceptualize and study statuses along a continuum of gradual differences in terms of, for example, income (see Johnson's second study in Part II), occupational prestige (see Pineo and Porter's and Goyder and Curtis' studies), or power. Here, divisions between strata on the status dimension are drawn more or less arbitrarily. They may not correspond to qualitative differences in consciousness or actions of the strata but may depend on research purposes, available data, and how fine a set of distinctions is preferred. Presumably, people would be classified into such divisions in order (1) to determine how they achieve these levels or (2) to see what differences the categories make, raising such questions as the relationship of position on the continuum to life chances, use of leisure time, political behavior, and the like (see the selections in Part III by Anderson, Ossenberg, and Segal).

On the other hand, the status dimension may be seen as a hierarchical set of discrete groups. The divisions are not statistical constructs but, rather, results of the consciousness of inequalities and, perhaps, common actions of persons in the groups (see, for example, Clement's conclusions from his study of access to the corporate elite and Ogmundson's study of the relationship of social class identification and self-reported class vote in this volume). At issue here are both differing conceptual approaches and *empirical questions*. By the latter we mean that for any status dimension in any historical circumstance we should study the precise extents to which there are status consciousness and group action at different points along it.

When such research is done we sometimes find further complexity. There are situations in which one status level is like a group, characterized by consciousness and joint political actions, while counterpart levels on the stratification dimension lack these characteristics. For example, Clement's study of access to the Canadian elite, when juxtaposed with other selections in this volume, suggests that this is so for class relations in Canada; he shows the corporate elite to be far more organized, far more of a social group, than is suggested by other works on other status levels.

Major Status Dimensions in Canadian Society

Eight status dimensions of social stratification have been identified (Figure 1). We see these as the *major* ones in Canadian society. We believe that it is along these dimensions that society members make evaluations of differential worth and according to which the resources of power, ownership, and wealth flow. We make this judgment from reading widely in studies of social inequalities in this country. We do not see this as an exhaustive list of status dimensions, but these factors, for contemporary Canada, would be included in any reasonably detailed list. These dimensions may be seen as specifying basic *contradictions*, or sets of differing vested interests, because of the meanings conveyed in status rights and obligations in this society. These define interests with which wide segments of the population may get involved. These are either actual or potential points of conflict of interest. Hershel Hardin argues that "to get at the Canadian circumstance," or any other national circumstance, "is above all to see the country in terms of its *contradictions* — the contending forces that underlie the character of the people."[23] Hardin gives this illuminating example of the impact of one such contradiction:

> One poignant case sticks in my mind because it illustrates the leading Canadian contradiction at work on a man whose identity as a Canadian was still in the process of formation. It was during the St. Leonard controversy over whether all schools should be French-language, or whether there should be English-language instruction available as well. An ethnic spokesman caught in the cross fire protested with quiet emotion to CBC radio that his group was an innocent victim... because they had no ingrained hostility against French Canadians. 'We're not against the French Canadians,' he said. 'And we're not against the English Canadians. We just want to be Canadian.' It never occurred to him that having to explore this linguistic conflict and cope with it, and in intensely passionate, practical circumstances, would give him more insight into what it meant to be a Canadian than most Canadians would gather from a lifetime. Even while he was protesting, he probably had already realized there was no total escape from the contradiction other than by leaving the country. Wasn't that why he was protesting in the first place? And after going through that experience, would he ever agree that being a Canadian and an American involved more or less the same thing.[24]

The implication of our distinctions between strata, status groups, class "in itself," and class "for itself," is that such contradictions may vary over time and circumstances in people's thoughts. Status groups may have coalesced around one of these sets of contradictions and may be acting in terms of their shared interests, or people may be doing little of this. The contradictions of language groups and ethnicities that Hardin emphasizes now have high profile in this country for reasons that Guindon discusses in his selection. The contradictions of occupational, income, and class groupings have increased lately in peoples' consciousness with the experiences of high unemployment and high inflation, as the selection by Lambert and Curtis argues. The implementation and public judgments of the Anti-Inflation Board (AIB) have highlighted these distinctions. For example, the AIB used the "historical relationships" among groups of workers as one of its critera in assessing salary increase settlements. The women's rights movement has attempted to highlight and address still another set of contradictions.

Some of these sets of status contradictions may, of course, not help us understand stratification in other societal contexts. It depends on whether prestige, power, or economic resources are distributed along these lines. Thus Parkin claims:

> This "multi-dimensional" view of the reward system is perhaps useful in analyzing societies like the United States which are highly differentiated in terms of race or ethnicity, religious affiliation, and sharp regional variations (especially between north and south) as well as by social classes. But in societies like Britain and many other European countries, multiple cleavages of this kind tend to be rather less marked, so that the multi-dimensional model would seem to be less applicable.[25]

The order of the status dimensions in Figure 1 is not meant to imply their relative importance for Canadian society. There is disagreement in stratification literature on whether one, or some, status dimensions should be seen as more "primary," with the others derivative. There is also disagreement on how primary dimensions might be defined. We have mentioned the primacy, simply in choice of research topics or focus, that tends to be given to some dimensions by conflict theorists and by functionalists. Tepperman's study in Part II shows another strategy. He concludes, for one research setting, that economic power was more basic because it seemed to lead to prestige and not vice versa. Clement and Johnson conclude that class relations are most important in explaining trends in research problems—the distribution of wealth, income, and economic control. Other selections, such as Lipset's, indicate that this argument cannot be extended to a general proposition fitting all inequalities.

What would be a strong argument for the idea that one dimension of stratification, or two, should be seen as more "primary" for a given time? For us, it would have to be evidence that the range of problems pursued by students of social stratification can be largely explained by the effects of that one dimension. We believe this is impossible to do compellingly for any single dimension of contemporary Canadian society. Our answer on which status dimension is most basic, consistent with the selections in this volume, would be "it depends on what one is trying to explain, and in what socio-historical context." Several studies show the comparatively strong influence of class power and class relations (compare, for example, selections by Clement, Johnson and Archibald), or occupational statuses (compare, for example, selections by Goyder and Curtis, and Ossenberg) on particular phenomena. Lambert and Curtis, on the other hand, show a comparatively strong influence of educational status backgrounds, over other status factors, when the problem studied is various political attitudes.

When the range of phenomena to be explained is more narrowly defined, though, we believe compelling arguments can be made concerning the *comparatively strong* explanatory power of certain dimensions. It is clear that in explanations of current political and economic structures in Canada one finds that information on the historical interplay of economic and political groups is indispensable, and matters of other status dimensions add comparatively less. Focusing on the macro-level issues of stability and changes in Canada's economic and political arrangements, information suggests that the class power dimension takes us a long way, though it may not tell the whole story (compare selections by Clement, Johnson and Guindon). However, again, selections in Parts II and III argue other cases for the *comparatively high* explanatory import of *other* selected status dimensions, for *other* research problems.

To turn the issue around — away from what is required to support a uni-dimensional approach to stratification — what would be the appropriate criteria in assessing a multi-dimensional approach for a given societal case? These, we think, should include the following: First, there should be empirical evidence that social stratification is multi-dimensional. Second, we should be able to show, on theoretical grounds, that each dimension, while interdependent with others, has independent consequences for the social order. One should be able to show that the dimensions, while probably related to or affected by one another, have some autonomy in affecting other social phenomena. Third, there should be good measurement techniques for each of the dimensions.[26] In Parts I-III, there is support for each of these three points in data and theorizing on this one national case. By reviewing the selections, and perhaps other studies (see Further Readings), the reader should satisfy herself or himself as to how well the multi-dimensional approach meets the requirements just mentioned.

There are aspects of the issue which are not closed. There are additional data to come in. And, someone may yet generate a general theoretical formulation, relying on a central stratification dimension, that gives a compelling overall interpretation of the complex range of phenomena discussed in this volume.

Status Consistency, Inconsistency, and Interrelations of Status Dimensions

A primary concern, for those following the multi-dimensional approach, is to determine precisely how the dimensions interact, and the ways in which they relate to other variables. We must answer the following questions: (1) How are the different dimensions of stratification arranged and articulated with one another? (2) To what extent are various dimensions and combinations of these dimensions correlated (positively or negatively)? (3) How are the dimensions and their combinations related to patterns of belief and social conduct? (4) What are the existing forms of access and opportunities for change in rank on the dimensions?

Complex problems of *status consistency* and *status inconsistency* are among special concerns for analysis. *Status consistency* refers to a high correlation among the various dimensions of status which describe an individual or group. For example, the physician who is male, white, Anglo-Saxon, Anglican, and involved in the Canadian Medical Association will probably occupy a highly evaluated position on all counts in his community, among his colleagues and among civil servants and politicians who must pay attention when he represents the C.M.A. on questions of national health policy. He will also enjoy well above average income and education. *Status inconsistency*, on the other hand, is present when the individual's status set is such that there are significant discrepancies between his or her various ranks on the dimensions we have discussed; there will be a low correlation instead of high correlation between dimensions. For example, we can cite impoverished, well-educated aristocrats in England who must use their castles as tourist attractions to provide for their families. Other examples might be a Canadian physician of high income, education and occupational prestige who is female and a member of a non-Anglo-Saxon minority group, or the highly successful call girl who in income and perhaps influence may be among the highest in the community, but whose occupational prestige is less than respectable.

At present, available Canadian and cross-national research evidence does not enable us to say much about status consistency and status inconsistency. However, we can make these general points:[27] (1) Individuals in both simple and complex societies may experience less than perfect correlation among their rankings on several different dimensions of stratification. (2) Apparently there are social processes conducive to maintaining this lack of perfect correlation for a long time (e.g., unchanged patterns of power distribution and ethnic and racial prejudice), as well as processes for increasing the degree of status consistency (e.g., daughters of the *nouveaux riches* marry men of distinguished lineage). (3) An important question for stratification research concerns the various empirical tendencies toward status consistency or inconsistency in different societies and times. For comments on these tendencies in Canada, compare the selections by Johnson, Tepperman, Clement, Guindon, Segal, and Lambert and Curtis, and their interpretations of various ethnicity/education/power rank consistencies and discrepancies.

Social Mobility

Social mobility involves the movement, by an individual or a group, from one status level to another. Any of the status dimensions described may be involved. We can speak of *individual mobility* and *group mobility*. The former is illustrated by persons who move from one educational status (e.g., high school graduate) to another (e.g., university graduate) or from one occupational status (skilled labor) to another (unemployed skilled labor, or professional). Group mobility is illustrated by a successful class revolution, or a successful women's rights movement. Mobility can also be *intra-generational* (in an individual's career or a lifetime) or *inter-generational* (between parents and children).

There is an important distinction between the processes of mobility to statuses and the rewards accompanying statuses. Parkin describes it as follows:

> Inequalities associated with the class system are founded upon two interlocking, but conceptually distinct, social processes. One is the allocation of rewards attaching to different *positions* in the social system; the other is the process of *recruitment* to these positions.[28]

He points out that sociologists have evaluated these problems differently, in either *egalitarian* or *meritocratic* critiques:

> The egalitarian critique of the class system raises objections to the wide disparities of reward accruing to different positions. On what grounds, it is asked, is it morally legitimate to give greater economic and social benefits to one set of occupations than to another, when each in its own way contributes to the social good? Generally, egalitarians have espoused a view of social justice which asks that men be rewarded in accordance with their individual social needs, family responsibilities, and the like, rather than in accordance with their role in the division of labor. The meritocratic critique of the class system, on the other hand, is less concerned about inequalities of reward accruing to different positions than about the process of recruitment to these positions. The prime objection raised is against present restrictions on the opportunities for talented but lowly born people to improve their personal lot. Seen from this angle, social justice entails not so much the equalization of rewards as the equalization of opportunities to compete for the most privileged positions.[29]

Though there are exceptions, writers in the conflict theoretical tradition have been more likely to give the egalitarian critiques; scholars in the functionalist perspective have been more likely to give the meritocratic critique. Relational research problems concern positions and the groups defined by them. Distributive problems concern the mobility and recruitment of individuals to positions.

As with the differences between distributive and relational problems, the issues of mobility and recruitment versus positions are intertwined with the actual workings of stratification. Parkin emphasized this in his study of British society. Wallace Clement, in his study of the Canadian corporate elite, is among those making a similar point for this society. He focuses on stratification by class, or economic control, and argues for the slightly broader distinctions between *condition* and *opportunity*:

> Condition is the framework within which a society is organized and focuses on stable sets of social relations at the structural level. Opportunity focuses on the individual level but the individual as representing certain social types such as members of social classes, ethnic groups, different sexes, region of birth or other ascribed characteristics. Opportunity involves the freedom persons with particular characteristics have to move within settings created by the social structure.
>
> In liberal democracies, where the economic system is predominantly capitalist, condition parallels the class structure and opportunity corresponds to the ability of persons with different class origins to cope with the class structure. The way society is organized provides some with the advantage to accumulate power and privilege then transfer these to their children in the form of wealth, stockholdings, social

"position," access to education or "inside" contacts for job placements. The prerogatives of power within capitalism provide that private property and benefits which go along with it represent an important link between condition and opportunity. Private property is at the basis of the economic system in capitalist society and the advantages it affords some are the limits it imposes on others.[30]

Dominant and Counter Ideologies

We have spoken of statuses as aspects of culture; i.e., as ideas about rights and obligations of persons placed in specific situations in the society. We have also alluded to another aspect of culture, with a broader point of reference, which is important in studies of social stratification — legitimizing beliefs or *ideologies*. Ideologies are affectively held ideas which describe, explain, and justify the way in which society is organized. As Patricia Marchak writes, "ideologies are screens through which we perceive the social world. Their elements are assumptions, beliefs, explanations, values, and orientations. They are seldom taught explicitly and systematically. They are, rather, transmitted through example, conversation, and casual observation."[31]

There are *dominant* and *counter* ideologies. *Dominant ideologies* are sets of ideas which support, or do not question, existing arrangements of inequalities. Marchak gives this example of dominant ideologies in operation:

> The child asks the parent: "Why is that family poorer than us?" and receives an answer such as "because their father is unemployed." The accumulation of such responses provides a ready index to the organization of the society in occupational terms, and with reference to age and sex roles. The child is informed by such responses that some occupations provide higher material rewards than others, that an occupation is essential, and that fathers, not mothers, earn family incomes. The child is not provided with an explanation for the differential between postmen and sales managers, between the employed and the unemployed, between families in one income group and families in the other, but some children think to ask. There are, then, additional responses such as: :'If you work hard at school, you can go to the top," or "Sales managers are more important than postmen," or "Well, if people don't work, they can't expect to get along in the world."[32]

Counter ideologies are promoted by individuals and groups who contest the status quo and call for change. They question the assumptions, beliefs, and values in dominant ideologies. They ask: "Why is education related to occupations?" "What is meant by 'the top,' and why should people want to go there?" "Why is status associated with material wealth?" "What does a sales manager do that makes him important and to whom is his work important?" "Why would anyone not work when the penalties for unemployment are so severe?"[33]

Several of our selections speak to issues of stratification ideologies in Canadian society: Rocher discusses the widespread adoption of democratic and egalitarian educational systems; Clement emphasizes that class relations in Canada rest on ideas of a private property system of exchange; and Lambert and Curtis analyze the relationships between educational statuses and attitudinal support for major Canadian institutions.

THE SELECTIONS AND PLAN OF THE BOOK

The selections in this volume present data from Canadian social life which bear on the multi-dimensional approach to social stratification and on some of the phenomena referred to in our discussion of basic concepts. The selections make clear that we are only beginning to approach a full understanding of the causes, forms, and consequences of the social inequalities in this country, but several of our authors will argue that priorities are now established for fruitful pursuit of this understanding.

Part I

Part I begins with theoretical and research overviews of the field which provide further orientation for the readings that follow. We begin with S. M. Lipset's discussion of significant theoretical traditions and conceptual approaches. His analysis extends beyond our introductory materials in several directions. In particular, he describes the intellectual roots of the conflict and functionalist traditions and, thereby, the works of early students of relational and distributive stratification phenomena. There is attention given to the importance attached to distinction between class, power and prestige in the works of Marx, Durkheim, Weber, and American functionalists. The significance of distinctions between subjective, objective and accorded aspects of status is also discussed. Alfred Hunter's chapter describes patterns in Canadian studies of the distribution of power, occupational prestige, income, and so on. The findings are brought to bear on propositions from functionalist and conflict theories. Several issues touched on here are followed up in more specialized studies in Parts II and III. These first two articles provide a conspectus of the core data and approaches in the field.

Part II

Part II is divided into three sections to highlight the distinction between the scarce resources of *economic control*, *income and wealth*, *power*, and *prestige*, as part of the criteria for social stratification.

Section A contains four reports on class relations, income, and wealth. Leo Johnson describes the way in which the petite bourgeoise class, of farmers and other independent proprietors and commodity producers, has been declining in size and influence. The conceptualization of classes is Marxian, and the interpretations are in terms of the role played by class relations. The findings are said to occur because the capitalist mode of production requires an ever-growing, more complex and specialized, labor force. The implications of this are also discussed for the following: (1) the extent of absorption of the work potential of the Canadian population, (2) the participation rates of age groups in the labor force, (3) the participation rates of men and women. Next, Wallace Clement reports on an analysis of the social background characteristics of the Canadian corporate elite in 1972. Modelled after, if not directly replicating, John Porter's earlier study in 1951 (cf. Hunter's remarks) the findings suggest that access to high-level positions in dominant corporations may have become the preserve of members of the upper class. Mobility to the elite from working-class origins is shown to be minimal and, in fact, to have declined in comparison with 1951. Compradorization, the reflection at the elite level of foreign influence in Canada's economy, is also examined. Note that the problem in this study is distributive in part, dealing with the individual's access to elite positions. The conceptualization and measurement of class is not strictly Marxian, but the interpretations of the findings are in terms of class control. Scarce and valued elite positions are said to be controlled through selection procedures based on corporate elite members' activities in "private worlds." Tepperman studies status inconsistency in the Toronto elite of the 1920s. That fame and wealth are frequently inconsistent in the elite is taken as evidence against a given principle of the functionalist perspective. Tepperman argues in his study that wealth is a much more convertible, more dominant, resource than fame. Wealth seems to lead to fame rather easily, but not vice versa. The interpretations of the findings are consistent with, but not explicitly in, the conflict theory mode. Leo Johnson's second discussion looks at the disparities in the average incomes of deciles of Canadian income earners between 1948 and 1974. He attempts to explain why, contrary to what he takes to be the conventional wisdom, there has been no narrowing of the gap between the lower and the higher income groups. The status categories employed, deciles of earners, are not class categories, though they are, by *statistical* definition, relational. The theoretical interpretations are Marxian.

Section B of Part II includes three studies of power distribution. First, Hubert Guindon presents an updated version of his classic analysis of changes in power and status attainment among francophone Quebecers. He shows some of the complex ways in which developments in the political sector and in public bureaucracies, changes in the work settings of francophones, and changes in religious institutions were all related in the 1960s and 1970s. Changes in the power and control of institutions involved the decline of the church and the expansion of public bureaucracies. These are shown to have had the unanticipated consequences of the development of a francophone status group, particularly at the "new middle class" occupational levels, and the creation of an anglophone minority status group. The analysis involves a conflict perspective with a focus on the relations between institutions and status groups, and some attention to the dynamics of status inconsistency and status dissatisfaction.

The selection by Bernd Baldus breaks new theoretical ground. He calls for a conceptualization of power which is free from "interaction" and "resistance" criteria generally used in the literature. In a sweeping review of the theoretical and research literature, he shows that scholars in both the conflict and the functionalist traditions, as much as they differ on other counts, use similar conceptions of power. These conceptions lead to inattention to pervasive power phenomena where relations between social units are free of resistance, and where there is no direct interaction between the units. An alternative approach is proposed, which sees power as structured and manifested in the *maintenance* of inequalities over time. This approach makes it easier to give attention to control via socialization and ideology. Clement's second selection is from his new book,

Continental Corporate Power. It summarizes his findings in that project, which was a follow-up to his earlier study of access to the elite. The analyses and problems studied are in the conflict perspective and relational domain. He shows that there has been a fragmentation of the capitalist class in this country, that there has been a "compradorization" of the elite, that foreign direct investment has meant a flow of capital *out* of the country, and that class and regional inequalities are intertwined and based on rules of private property.

Section C of Part II contains ten studies of differences in the status dimensions of occupations, education levels, ethnicity and race, age, and sex. The studies show either how evaluation or prestige is accorded on the status dimension, how the statuses are attained, or how the status dimensions seem to condition the attainment of the resources of income and power.

In the material on occupational status, Peter Pineo and John Porter present findings from the most detailed Canadian study of the phenomenon of occupational prestige. Drawing on national survey data, they provide an account of respondents' rankings of the "social standings" of some 200-odd occupational titles, and give comparisons with similar findings from a U.S. study. The selection by John Goyder and James Curtis looks at mobility access to occupational statuses over three and four generations. The analysis tests hypotheses of "cumulative family ascription." Data are provided by male respondents' reports, in a recent national sample survey, of their own occupations plus those of their fathers, grandfathers, and eldest sons. Direct links between occupational status scores over three generations are found but, as would be expected, the effects here are relatively low compared to those between fathers and sons. Perhaps surprisingly, the occupations of great-grandfathers and great-grandsons are found to show no association. Among other findings, there is some evidence of a status consistency effect (for family status in two earlier generations) on respondents' status attainments. White collar respondents with white collar fathers and grandfathers are more numerous than would be expected. The results also suggest that the effect of grandfather's status on occupation in the third generation is channelled through the grandson's education. Implications of the findings for interpretations of the level of ascription versus achievement in Canadian society are discussed.

The next two papers are on educational stratification. Guy Rocher's selection reviews evidence on individuals' recruitment patterns to high schools and universities, by their parents' occupational statuses, their sex status, and their ethnicity and race, showing stratification on each of these counts. He discusses theoretical interpretations of these relationships. These interpretations, and his discussion of the ways in which the educational system mirrors economic and political organization in the wider society, are very much in the domain of relational phenomena. In his study, Raymond Breton is interested in showing how stratification within the organization of the education system is a crucial factor in educational advancement and opportunity through its impact on aspirations for advancement. Using data from a sample of secondary school students, he shows that two types of ranking — organization of school curricula into different programs of study and evaluation of students' performances — are closely related to educational aspirations. Both have substantial effects, but the former seems to have the stronger impact. In terms of distinctions that we made earlier, the different programs involve statuses and the performance measures involve a type of "esteem."

Next we have three papers on ethnic and racial stratification. Raymond Breton begins with a discussion of three theoretical perspectives on ethnic stratifications: "the individual competitive," "the class conflict," and "the social closure" approaches. The first and last of these are examples of what we have described as the distributive and relational approaches, applied to ethnicity. Breton's second approach is also relational, with its focus more on class dynamics which may overlap ethnic status categories. Breton's approaches, with some modifications, should have utility for analyses of racial stratification as well. Richard Joy follows with his study of languages in conflict, updating, through to the 1970s, the analyses in his earlier book by the same title. His title is misleading from the point of view of our discussion of theoretical approaches, because his study is less from the conflict and relational perspectives than it is on a distributive problem. Joy wonders what the inter-generational patterns of language transfers (and language assimilation) are, and whether or not these are specified by region, as he suspects they may be. He is able to get only approximate data on the problem from Canadian Census information on language categories. His findings include these: two thirds of the Canadian population live in English-dominated regions, within which minorities of all other languages are dwindling through assimilation. However, there is also an area, a French Canada, within which it is the use of the English language that is declining. The two languages, English and French, co-exist only within a narrow bilingual belt. As Guindon's analysis suggests, these demographic realities of language status changes have provided one of the bases for the development of ethnic status groups and ethnic conflict in this country. Donald Ball's study of Canadian professional football shows that mobility to team playing positions differing in control is associated with race and nationality. A hypothesis of differences in "training backgrounds" is tested, and rejected, as the explanation of these findings. Ball speculates that the findings might involve "stacking" whereby management and coaches give higher evaluations to Whites and Americans (over Blacks and Canadians) for highly central team positions.

Part II ends with three papers on sex and age stratification. Sharon and Baha Abu-Laban ask whether the concept of minority group can be applied to the aged and women. They review information and theory on sex and age differences and discuss arguments which address the extent to which women and the aged in North America can be said to be status groups versus social strata. Distributive and relational issues are, therefore, also discussed. Sanford Labovitz's study focuses on sexual, ethnic and racial evaluations. He uses a procedure of name evaluations to get at these evaluations in two samples from mid-western Canada. His findings include the following: The rank ordering of names on an evaluational scale ranging from highly favorable to highly unfavorable was (1) Edward

Blake (English-Canadian male), (2) Edith Blake (English-Canadian female), (3) Joseph Walking Bear (Canadian-Indian male) and Marcel Fournier (French-Canadian male). Lynn McDonald's study shows how the differences between the incomes of males and females have been widening over time. Theoretical interpretations of a conflict perspective variety are discussed, as are policy recommendations and their rationales.

Part III

In Part III we turn to studies concerned with social correlates and consequences of social stratification along the major status dimensions. Students have found hardly an area of social stratification where some aspects are not influenced by social strata or status groups. The selections in this section suggest the variety of social phenomena which are associated with social stratification. These phenomena range from mortality and survival to voting and bar behavior. Needless to say, many other facets of social life are affected by, or affect, social stratification. Some of these are covered in the materials in Further Readings.

We have grouped the studies in this section in three categories: "differences in life chances," "differences in political behavior," and "differences in styles of life and beliefs." In the first section there are two studies of "life chances," in the sense of living and dying and of options before the courts. Ursula Anderson reports on rates of infant mortality, stillbirths, and perinatal mortality across areas of Toronto differing in socio-economic characteristics. One of her findings was that 14 percent of the population was identified as having mortality rates two to two-and-a-half times as high as 11 percent of the population with low rates. High risk areas were low in educational attainment and income levels and high in over-crowding and recent migrants. The implication is that the social status characteristics identified as comparatively high and low in the high risk populations are associated, at the level of *individuals* and families, with mortality. That is, there is the assumption that it is the low-education and low-income parents in the areas who experience higher infant mortality. However, note that the information is for rates/characteristics of the *areas*; it is not keyed to individuals or families *per se*. Wynne and Hartnagel follow with a study of race and plea negotiation. Data in the files of a crown prosecutor's office in the Prairies showed that natives were less likely than whites to obtain a negotiated plea. Alternative interpretations, involving correlates of race, are carefully explored as well.

From studies of social stratification and political behavior we have included selections by Rick Ogmundson and David Segal. Ogmundson describes a consensus in the literature which says that Canada stands out sharply as a country in which the relationship of "social class" (in this case, educational, occupational, and income statuses) to party support in elections is almost non-existent. Using a new measure which takes into account voters' perceptions of the "class positions" of the political parties, he found a social class-voting relationship. These and other findings are interpreted to be a result of relations between voters and parties, where the latter give no clear electoral options in terms of class representation. Segal's study of public opinion polls looks at status inconsistency and its relationship to left of center party choice. A popular hypothesis in the literature, on this relationship, is tested. Note, though, that Segal's study uses the Liberal party as the left of center party, excluding the NDP from the analysis (compare Ogmundson's discussion).

Among our studies of life styles and beliefs is Peter Archibald's on the alienating effects of class in face-to-face interaction in and outside the workplace. A conflict perspective is applied to aspects of interpersonal behavior. It is argued that class-based conflicts of interest and coercion-induced threat are central in cross-class interactions. The article by Richard Ossenberg tests a hypothesis on the bar behavior of middle-class versus lower-class persons during festival time — the Calgary Stampede. Participation in the festival, and in aggressive-expressive behavior, was found to be highest among middle-class persons. Interpretations of these findings are drawn from the differences in life styles of the classes and from the social role of festivals.

We end with three studies of social status differences in beliefs. Ronald Lambert and James Curtis report findings on the relationships between expressed nonconfidence in seven major Canadian institutions and educational status and economic dissatisfaction, after controls. The data are from a national adult sample, with controls for income, occupation, language, and age. The analyses are guided by two variants of an "indoctrination interpretation" of the significance of people's exposure to higher levels of education for their political attitudes. The findings indicate that people treat education as an investment in the interest of future economic rewards and that this has differing consequences for the relationship between educational status and political attitudes among adults — depending on their level of economic dissatisfaction. There is a positive relationship between educational status and nonconfidence in institutions among people who are dissatisfied economically and no relationships, or the opposite type of relationship, among people satisfied economically. There is a discussion of theoretical and research implications of these findings for the study of subscription to dominant and counter ideologies. Jean Pierre Richert's study looks at interview and observational data on anglophone and francophone elementary school pupils. The children, it was found, overwhelmingly identified with historical symbols of their own culture, and such differences increased with age. The two groups also identified with different periods of history. Perhaps understandably, the francophone children identified more with the period pre-1760, when members of their ethnic group played a more powerful role. These findings may result from social psychological dynamics in school children, the actions of teachers, or the perspective provided by school textbook writers. The author discusses whether such findings suggest that history is a divisive rather than a binding force between ethnic groups.

John Goyder and Peter Pineo present research on subjective social class placements made by adult Canadians. Theirs is the most systematic study of this phenomenon done in this country. Using various survey data sources, they ask how Canadians of different types, different occupational backgrounds, and different ethno-religious groups, place themselves. There is also a discussion on methodological problems in survey approaches to this issue.

It is hoped that these studies will sharpen the reader's appetite for the wider body of literature, both Canadian and cross-national, that comes under the heading "sociology of social stratification." The ample notes to the articles, references, and the Further Readings section will serve as guides to other works.

FIGURE 1   Major Status Dimensions

Achieved statuses	*Ascribed statuses*
1. Income and wealth	6. Ethnic and racial statuses
2. Economic ownership	7. Sex status
3. Authority and power rankings	8. Age status
4. Occupational status	
5. Educational status	

Notes

1. See, for example, the discussion in J.L. Roach *et al.*, *Social Stratification in the United States* (Englewood Cliffs, N.J.: Prentice-Hall, 1969).

2. A variable is simply any individual or group characteristic which has different levels or categories (e.g., male versus female; high economic power versus low economic power). Control variables are dimensions on which the researcher wants to hold the effects constant (e.g., they may control for the sexes of respondents in a survey research study). A dependent variable is one whose differing levels the researcher attempts to explain and an independent variable is a factor which represents some prior influence on a dependent variable. For an example, consider the study by Richert in Part III. The variables to be explained (dependent variables) are children's different perceptions of historical heroes and symbols. The independent variable (or "cause") is the ethnic background of the children. Controls are made for age in this study.

3. See, for example, K. Marx and F. Engels, *Manifesto of the Communist Party* (New York: International Publishers, 1932) and K. Marx, *Capital*, Vol. 1 (New York: New World Paperbacks, 1967), or K. Marx, *Selected Writings in Sociology and Social Philosophy*, T. Bottomore and M. Rubel, eds. (New York: McGraw-Hill, 1964). These are among many good recent interpretations of the Marxian approach: E.O. Wright and L. Perrone, "Marxist Class Categories and Income Inequality," *American Sociological Review*, 42(1977), pp. 32–55; E.O. Wright, "Class Boundaries in Advanced Capitalist Societies," *New Left Review*, 98(1976), pp. 3–41; and N. Poulantzas, *Classes in Contemporary Capitalism* (London: New Left Books, 1975).

4. K. Marx, *Selected Writings, op. cit.*, p. 258.

5. See, for example, L.A. Coser, *The Functions of Social Conflict* (Glencoe, Ill.: The Free Press, 1956); R. Dahrendorf, *Class and Class Conflict in Industrial Society* (Stanford, Calif.: Stanford University Press, 1959); G. Lenski, *Power and Privilege: A Theory of Stratification* (New York: McGraw-Hill, 1966); M. Mann, *Consciousness and Action Among the Western Working Class* (London: Macmillan, 1973); R. Miliband, *The State in Capitalist Society* (London: Weidenfeld and Nicholson, 1969); C.W. Mills, *The Power Elite* (New York: Oxford Press, 1956); F. Parkin, *Class Inequality and Political Order* (London: Paladin Publishing, 1972).

6. Lenski, *op. cit.*, especially chapters 2–5.

7. See especially E. Durkheim, *The Division of Labour in Society* (Glencoe, Ill.: Free Press, 1960 [1893]).

8. B. Barber, *Social Stratification* (New York: Harcourt, Brace and World, 1957); K. Davis, *Human Society* (New York: Macmillan, 1949); K. Davis and W. Moore, "Some Principles of Stratification," *American Sociological Review*, 10(1945), pp. 242-49; R. Merton, *Social Theory and Social Structure* (Glencoe, Ill.: Free Press, 1957); T. Parsons, "A Revised Analytical Approach to the Theory of Social Stratification," in R. Bendix and S.M. Lipset, eds., *Class, Status and Power* (Glencoe, Ill;: Free Press, 1953), pp. 92-128.

9. Davis, *op. cit.*, p. 367.

10. See, for example, M.M. Tumin, "Some Principles of Stratification: A Critical Analysis," *American Sociological Review (ASR)* , 18(1953), pp. 387-93; "Reply to Tumin," *ASR*, 18(1953), pp. 394-97; "Reply to Kingsley Davis," *ASR*, 18(1953), pp. 672-73; A.L. Stinchcombe, "Some Empirical Consequences of the Davis-Moore Theory of Stratification," *ASR*, 28(1963), pp. 805-8; and W. Wesolowski, "Some Notes on the Functional Theory of Stratification," *The Polish Sociological Bulletin*, 3-4 (1962), pp. 28-38.

11. P.M. Blau and O.D. Duncan, *The American Occupational Structure* (New York: John Wiley and Sons, 1967), chapters 1, 2, and 12.

12. Lenski, *op. cit.*, pp. 430-31.

13. We take these terms from L.A. Coser, "Two Methods in Search of Substance," *American Sociological Review*, 40(1975), pp. 691-700 and J.H. Goldthorpe, "Class Status and Party in Modern Britain," *European Journal of Sociology*, 13(1972), pp. 342-72. Compare replies to Coser's paper and his rebuttal in *The American Sociologist*, 11 (February, 1976), pp. 4-38.

14. Coser, "Two Methods," *op. cit.*, p. 694.

15. Several works have argued that, while these different units of analysis are the primary ones in sociology in general, greater emphasis has been placed on the individual focus in North American sociology. See R.C. Hinkle and G.J. Hinkle, *The Development of Modern Sociology*, (New York: Random House, 1954); K.H. Wolff, "The Sociology of Knowledge and Sociological Theory," in L. Gross, ed., *Symposium on Sociological Theory* (New York: Harper and Row, 1959); K. Westhues, "Class and Organization as Paradigms in Social Science," *The American Sociologist*, 11(1976), pp. 38-49; J.E. Curtis and J.W. Petras, eds., "Introduction," in *The Sociology of Knowledge* (New York: Praeger, 1970); and J. Harp and J. Curtis, "Linguistic Communities and Sociology," in J.E. Gallagher and R.D. Lambert, eds., *Social Process and Institutions: The Canadian Case* (Toronto: Holt, Rinehart and Winston, 1971), pp. 57-70. In the latter piece we have pointed to ways in which francophone Canadian sociology focuses more on the group or the organization (or the society) as a unit of analysis, as compared with anglophone Canadian sociology. See also similar arguments by A.K. Davis, for example, in his Foreword to W.E. Mann and L. Wheatcroft, eds., *Canada: A Sociological Profile* (Toronto: Copp Clark, 1976), and by F.G. Vallee and D. Whyte, "Canadian Society: Trends and Perspectives" in B.R. Blishen *et al.*, eds., *Canadian Society: Sociological Perspectives* (Toronto: Macmillan, 1968), pp. 833-52. These francophone-anglophone differences obtain in social stratification studies as well.

16. Coser, "Two Methods," *op. cit.*, p. 694.

17. Coser, *ibid.*.

18. Definitional approaches to social stratification differ markedly, especially on the numbers and types of dimensions along which stratification takes place. In addition to similar definitions in some of our selections, compare the multidimensional positions in B. Barber, "Introduction to Social Stratification," in D. Sills, ed., *The International*

Encyclopedia of the Social Sciences (New York: Macmillan and Free Press, 1968), pp. 288–289; J. Kahl, *The American Class Structure* (New York: Holt, Rinehart and Winston, 1957), chapter 1; and Roach *et al.*, *op. cit.*, chapter 2.

19. Roach *et al.*, *op. cit.*, p.3.

20. Compare also our approaches to ascription and achievement of statuses in C.J. Cuneo and J.E. Curtis, "Social Ascription in Educational and Occupational Attainment Among Urban Canadians," *Canadian Review of Sociology and Anthropology*, 12(1975), pp. 6–24 and in the Goyder and Curtis selection in this volume.

21. For a similar definitional approach to the concepts dealt with in this section see R.K. Merton, *op. cit.*.

22. Wright and Perrone, *op. cit.*, p. 35.

23. H. Hardin, *A Nation Unaware* (Vancouver: J.J. Douglas Ltd., 1974), p. 10.

24. *Ibid.*, p. 13.

25. Parkin, *op. cit.*, p. 17.

26. See Barber, "Introduction," *op. cit.*, for a similar list.

27. Barber, "Introduction," *op. cit.*, p. 291 ff draws similar conclusions on the cross-national evidence on status consistency-inconsistency.

28. Parkin, *op. cit.*, p. 13.

29. *Ibid.*, p. 13.

30. W. Clement, *The Canadian Corporate Elite* (Toronto: McClelland and Stewart, 1975), p. 1–2.

31. M.P. Marchak, *Ideological Perspectives on Canada* (Toronto: McGraw-Hill Ryerson, 1975), p.1. Other studies which approach this concept in a similar way include W. Christian and C. Campbell, *Political Parties and Ideologies in Canada* (Toronto: McGraw-Hill Ryerson, 1974); J.E. Curtis and R.D. Lambert, "Educational Status and Reactions to Social and Political Heterogeneity," *Canadian Review of Sociology and Anthropology*, 13(1976), pp. 189–203; J. Huber and W.H. Form, *Ideology and Income* (New York: Free Press, 1973); M. Mann, "The Social Cohesion of Liberal Democracy," *American Sociological Review*, 35(1970), pp. 423–30; F. Parkin, *op. cit.*, and J. Porter, *The Vertical Mosaic* (Toronto: University of Toronto Press, 1965), chapters 15–16.

32. Marchak, *op. cit.*, p. 1.

33. Marchak, *ibid.*, p. 2.

PART ONE

The Study of Social Stratification

Approaches to Social Stratification*

Seymour M. Lipset

Concern with social class and social stratification is as old as social thought. The ancient Greek philosophers were extremely conscious of the effects of stratification, and propositions about stratification may be found throughout many of the writings of Aristotle and Plato. Thus Aristotle, in discussing the conditions for different types of political organization, suggested in essence that constitutional government—limitation on the powers of the political elite—is most likely to be found in societies with large middle classes, while city-states characterized by large lower classes and small middle and upper classes would be more likely to be governed as dictatorships based on mass support, or as oligarchies. This general approach has been elaborated in contemporary studies of the social requisites of democracy. Plato, in the *Republic*, discussed the conditions for a genuine equalitarian communist society and suggested that the family is the key support of inequality — that is, of social stratification. His argument, which is still followed by many contemporary sociologists, was that individuals are motivated to secure for other family members, for whom they feel affection, any privileges that they themselves enjoy. Hence, in every society there is a built-in pressure to institutionalize inequality by making it hereditary. Plato argued that the only way to create a communist society would be to take children away from their parents and to have the state raise them, so as to eliminate the tendency toward inherited social privilege.

Most contemporary sociological theory and research on social class, however, does not stem from the Greeks. The emphasis of the Enlightenment on the possibility of social laws and of their discovery through observation and comparative study must be taken as one of the principal methodological breakthroughs. Institutional regularities, such as those governing class, status, and political relationships, became objects of disinterested inquiry as things in themselves, thus reversing the notion, dominant in the Middle Ages, that the temporal sphere was nothing more than an auxiliary part of a supernatural plan, subject to the principles of natural law.

The Enlightenment served to erase the assumptions about hierarchy, class, and intergroup relationships that stemmed from the medieval model of an organic Christian civilization. Thus, the basis was being laid for a science of society.

* Reprinted with permission from *The International Encyclopedia of the Social Sciences*, David L. Sills, Editor. Volume 15, pages 296–316. © 1968 by Crowell Collier and Macmillan, Inc.

But it was Karl Marx, more than anyone else, who carried this scientific perspective into the study of social class, even going so far as to derive his idea of class from what he called the scientific laws of history. He then not only accepted the premise that social phenomena possess their own laws, but also set out to discover the underlying variables and how they are expressed under differing historical conditions. Thus, if one were to award the title of father of the study of social class to any individual, it would have to be to Marx. He made class the central aspect of his analysis of society and of his theory of social change. Though most latter-day sociologists have disagreed with Marx's assumptions about stratification, many of the non-Marxist or anti-Marxist ideas on the subject have come about in reaction to Marx's original formulations.

This does not mean, of course, that there were not other important eighteenth-century and nineteenth-century figures who used stratification concepts in a sophisticated manner. Marx obviously was a child of his times; many of his ideas, sometimes in almost identical form, can be found in the writings of others. The Marxist formulation, laid down in the chapter "Social Classes" in *Capital*, that there are three major economic classes in modern society — landlords receiving rent, capitalists profit, and workers wages — is derived directly from Ricardo's *Principles*, published in 1817, a work that also presented the labor theory of value. Adam Smith's great book, *The Wealth of Nations*, is an important work for the study of stratification, as are other writings of the school of Scottish philosophers of his day. The American founding fathers admitted that all complex societies are stratified and that there is an inherent basis of conflict among groups with diverse economic and class interests. Various American Marxist groups have, in fact, sought to legitimate Marxist doctrine as compatible with classic American thought by pointing to the similarities between the ideas presented in No. 10 of *The Federalist* and various writings of Marx (see especially De Leon 1889–1913). However, these precursors of Marxism influenced sociology primarily through their influence on Marx himself. It was he who formulated the theory of class so powerfully that he defined the terms of the argument for later sociological thinkers.

TYPES OF THEORETICAL APPROACH

Approaches to social inequality have differed in the extent to which they emphasize change or stability in social systems. These differences in theoretical orientation have to a considerable extent reflected political differences. Reformists or radicals have seen social inequality and social class differences as sources of social change, which they are inclined to favor. Theorists with more conservative political tastes have justified aspects of the existing order by trying to show the functions performed by hierarchy in all social systems. Concern with social change has generally been associated with interest in social classes; that is, groups within stratified collectivities that are said to act politically as agents of change. Those stressing the functional basis of inequality have been interested in social stratification and in the purposes served by differential rewards, particularly in prestige, to various positions in social systems.

Those using the concept of social class to interpret the dynamics of social change have assumed that the creation of new occupational or economic roles has often resulted in the emergence of groups that initially were outside the traditional hierarchical system. As these new groups attempt to stabilize their position within society, they come into conflict with older, privileged strata whose status, economic resources, or power they challenge. The new groups also often develop sets of values, both secular and religious, that enhance their position by undermining the stability of the prior value system and the structure of privilege it justified. Thus historical change is viewed basically as a consequence of the rise of new classes and the downfall of old ones; it is assumed that complete social systems are inherently unstable and that conflicts stemming from inequality cause pressure for changes in the system.

In contrast, functional theorists have assumed that social systems must be treated as if they were in equilibrium. From this point of view, it is necessary to relate the various attributes of the social hierarchy to the conditions for social stability. Class, therefore, has been seen by these theorists not as an intervening variable in the process of social change but, rather, as a set of institutions that provide some of the conditions necessary for the operation of a complex society. These conditions amount to the need for a system of differentiated rewards as a means of institutionalizing the division of labor: differentiation by status and income is posited as a necessary part of the system of motivation required to place individuals in the various positions that must be filled if society is to operate.

The interest of students of social change in why people rebel, why they want change, has led to an emphasis within the tradition of class analysis on the way in which inequality frustrates people and leads them to reject the *status quo*. Functional analysts, on the other hand, are much more concerned with how the social system gets people to conform, to seek and remain in various positions in society, including ones that are poorly rewarded or require onerous work. The former, in other words, often ask how systems of stratification are undermined; the latter seek to know how and why they hold together.

It is important to note that though any analysis of social class must necessarily deal with social stratification as well, these two terms are not synonymous. Theories of social class refer to the conditions affecting the existence of strata that have developed or should develop some "consciousness of kind," that is, some sense of existence as a group attribute of society. Stratification refers to the entire complex of hierarchical differentiation, whether group-related or not. Though this article is about social class, much of the discussion in it will involve stratification, since it is impossible to account for the way in which social classes are formed, change, and affect other aspects of society without referring to stratification systems as such.

I have distinguished two polar traditions of social thought that do not, of course, occur in pure form in real life. Marx, the foremost student of class and social change and the advocate, par excellence, of instability and revolution, was also aware of the functional aspects of social stratification. Many of his writings attempt to show how ideologies, values, and patterns of behavior — all at different class levels—maintain the stability of the social order. In fact, Marxian analysis is replete with functional propositions.

The functionalists, on the other hand, are of course aware that change and conflict occur and that people not only accept but also reject the given stratification system. Thus (as is noted in more detail below) the most influential stimulator of functional thought in sociology, Emile Durkheim, sought to show the way in which strains in value emphases within the same system lead individuals and groups to reject the dominant value system and to deviate from expected forms of behavior. Whereas Marx saw alienation as inherent in social inequality, Durkheim suggested that anomie, or rulelessness, is endemic in all complex social systems.

To see the way these concerns with stability and change, with alienation, and with the formation of class sentiments have evolved in modern social thought, it is necessary to turn to an examination of the work of some of the key theorists, particularly Marx, Weber, and Durkheim.

THE MARXIST THEORY OF CLASS

Marxist sociology starts from the premise that the primary function of social organization is the satisfaction of basic human needs — food, clothing, and shelter. Hence, the productive system is the nucleus around which other elements of society are organized. Contemporary sociology has reversed this emphasis by stressing the distribution system, the stratification components of which are status and prestige. To Marx, however, distribution is a dependent function of production.

Stemming from the assumption of the primacy of production is the Marxist definition of class: any aggregate of persons who play the same part in the production mechanism. Marx, in *Capital*, outlined three main classes, differentiated according to relations to the means of production: (1) *capitalists*, or owners of the means of production; (2) *workers*, or all those who are employed by others; (3) *landowners*, who in Marx's theory seemingly differ from capitalists and are regarded as survivors of feudalism ([1867–1879] 1925–1926, vol. 3, pp. 862–863). From Marx's various historical writings, it is clear that he had a more complex view than this of the hierarchical reality and that he realized, for instance, that there is differentiation within each of these basic categories. Thus, the small businessmen, or petty bourgeoisie, were perceived as a transitional class, a group that will be pressed by economic tendencies inherent in capitalism to bifurcate into those who descend to the working class and those who so improve their circumstances that they become significant capitalists.

Though Marx differentiated classes in objective terms, his primary interest was in understanding and facilitating the emergence of class consciousness among the depressed strata. He wished to see created among them a sense of identical class interests, as a basis for conflict with the dominant class. The fact that a group held a number of objective characteristics in common but did not have the means of reaching organized class consciousness meant for Marx that it could not play the role of a historically significant class. Thus, he noted in "The Eighteenth Brumaire of Louis Bonaparte" that the French peasants of that period possessed many attributes that implied a common class situation:

> The small-holding peasants form a vast mass, the members of which live in similar conditions, but without entering into manifold relations with one another. Their mode of production isolates them from one another, instead of bringing them into mutual intercourse. The isolation is increased by France's bad means of communication and by the poverty of the peasants.... In so far as millions of families live under economic conditions of existence that separate their mode of life, their interests and their culture from those of other classes, and put them in hostile opposition to the latter, they form a class. In so far as there is merely a local interconnection among these small-holding peasants, and the identity of their interests begets no community, no national bond and no political organization among them, they do not form a class. (Marx [1852] 1962, p. 334)

Nikolai Bukharin, one of the leading theoreticians of the Russian Communist party, who was more concerned with sociological theory and research than any other major Marxist figure, attempted to formalize the differences among the workers, the peasants, and the lumpenproletariat (unattached laborers), making the workers a class and the other two not classes. His analysis, based on the events of the early decades of the twentieth century, was elaborated beyond that of Marx (see Table I).

TABLE I   Bukharin's Analysis of Class Conditions

Class properties	Peasantry	Lumpen-proletariat	Proletariat
1. Economic exploitation	+	−	+
2. Political oppression	+	+	+
3. Poverty	+	+	+
4. Productivity	+	−	+
5. Freedom from private property	−	+	+
6. Condition of union in production and common labor	−	−	+

Source: Bukharin (1921) 1965, p. 289.

The working class is exploited by a visible common oppressor, is brought together by conditions of work that encourage the spread of ideas and organization among them, and remains in a structured conflict situation with its employers over wages and working conditions. Consequently, over time it can become a conscious class.

Marx, however, did not really anticipate a high correlation between objective class position and subjective revolutionary class consciousness until the point at which the social system in question broke down: if there was to be total class consciousness in any given society, then by definition it would be in the midst of revolution. In normal times, structural factors press deprived strata to become conscious, but the inherent strength of the ruling class prevents class consciousness. The dominant class possesses social legitimacy, controls the media of communication, is supported by the various mechanisms of socialization and social control, such as the school and the church, and, during its period of stability, is able to "buy off" those inclined to lead or participate in opposition movements. The Marxist term that characterizes the attitudes of the lower class in the period of the predominance of the other classes is "false consciousness."

Marx was not very concerned with analyzing the behavior of the capitalist upper class. Basically, he assumed that the powerful parts of such a class must be self-conscious and that the state as a vehicle of power necessarily serves the interests of the dominant class in the long run. But more important to Marx than the sociology of the privileged class was that of the workers; the important question for research and action concerned the factors that would bring about working-class consciousness.

The dilemma of the Marxist theory of class is also the dilemma of every other single-variable theory. We can locate a class member objectively, but this may tell us little about the subjective correlates (social outlook, attitudes, etc.) of class position. Marx never actually said that at any given point in history or for any individual there would necessarily have to be a relationship between class position and the attitudes of class members. He did believe, however, that common conditions of existence create the necessary base for the development of common class attitudes, but that at any point in time, sharp discrepancies may exist between class position and class attitudes or behavior. Marx attempted to deal with this problem by his theory of transitional stages in the development of class. The first stage, in which a class is a class "in itself" (the German *an sich*), occurs when the class members do not understand their class position, the controls over them, or their "true class interests." The proletariat, insofar as it is simply fighting for higher wages without recognizing that this is part of a necessary class struggle between themselves and the bourgeoisie that will end in the victory of one or the other, is a class *an sich*. In ideal-type terms the opposite of the class in itself is the class "for itself" (*für sich*). The class *für sich* is a self-conscious class, a large proportion of whose members consciously identify with it and think in terms of the class's struggle with another class. As long as most persons in a lower class think in *an sich* terms, the behavior of class members will be characterized by intraclass competition in which individual members of the class strive to get ahead of other members. In such a period, class conflict will be weak. Only when *für sich* attitudes develop does the class struggle really emerge. Members of a lower class who do not yet identify with their class are, according to Marx, thinking in terms of values or concepts that are functional for the stability of the position of the dominant class. Any individual, therefore, though objectively a member of the lower class, may subjectively be identified with or may be acting in ways which correspond to the position of another class. At different periods varying portions of an underprivileged population may be either *an sich* or *für sich*. One of the purposes of Marxist analysis is the investigation of this discrepancy. In discussing the rise of the bourgeoisie, Marx suggested that the period during which the bourgeoisie was a class *an sich* was longer and required greater effort than the period during which it became self-conscious and took political class action to overthrow feudalism and monarchy ([1847] 1963, pp. 146–147). Implicit in this discussion of the development of the bourgeois class is the idea that the emergence of self-consciousness among the workers will also take a long time. Marx in fact suggested "making a precise study of strikes, combinations and other forms of class activity" in order to find out how the proletariat organizes itself as a class (*ibid.*, p. 147).

Alienation

A key element in the Marxist sociology of the exploited is the concept of alienation. Men are distinguished from animals — are, in fact, less animal and more human — insofar as they become increasingly self-conscious about and freely selective of their work and conditions of life. Insofar as men do not freely choose their work but, rather, do whatever tasks are set before them, simply in order to exist, they remain in a less than human state. If work (or leisure) is imposed on man, so far from being free, he is objectively exploited and alienated from the truly human, that is, autonomous, condition (Marx 1844, pp. 120–134 in the 1964 edition).

Alienation, for Marx, is an objective, not a subjective, condition. It signifies lack of autonomy, of self-control. The fact that workers may say that they like their work or social conditions does not mean that they are free actors, even if they think they are. Thus, in a slave society the fact that some slaves may have believed that they preferred to be slaves, and even that they were better off as slaves than as freed men, did not change the fact that objectively they were slaves. Similarly, the fact that a wage worker likes his conditions of work does not affect his position of being alienated and economically exploited or his potential as a free human being. In this sense, class society is akin to slavery. Class society must produce alienated individuals who are distorted, partial people. Marx therefore sought to document the facts about alienation and to understand the conditions under which estrangement, resentment, and, ultimately, political class consciousness would arise. Both class and alienation, he thought, would be eliminated by ending the private ownership of the means of production, for as long as people are working for others, they do not have conscious control over their life space and therefore are not truly human. Fully human society would come about when the production system could produce abundance in an absolute sense, when the machines produced enough food, clothing, and shelter for all men to have as much as they needed, so that they could then devote themselves not to fighting over the scarce fruits of production but to fostering the activities of the mind. In essence, he was arguing that all class societies were prehuman and that class must disappear.

THE WEBERIAN APPROACH TO STRATIFICATION

While Marx placed almost exclusive emphasis on economic factors as determinants of social class, Weber suggested that economic interests should be seen as a special case of the larger category of "values," which included many things that are neither economic nor interests in the ordinary sense of the term. For Weber, the Marxist model, although a source of fruitful hypotheses, was too simple to handle the complexity of stratification. He therefore sought to differentiate among the various sources of hierarchical differentiation and potential cleavage. The two most important sets of hierarchies for Weber were class and status ([1906-1924] 1946, pp. 180-195).

Class

Weber reserved the concept of class for economically determined stratification. He defined a class as being composed of people who have life chances in common, as determined by their power to dispose of goods and skills for the sake of income. Property is a class asset, but it is not the only criterion of class. For Weber, the crucial aspect of a class situation is, ultimately, the market situation.

The existence of large groups of people who can be located in a common class situation need not produce communal or societal action — that is, conscious, interest-determined activity — although it should produce *similar* reactions in the sense that those in the same class situation should exhibit similar behavior and attitudes without having a sense of class consciousness. These similarities, such as patterns of voting behavior or of drinking habits, reflect the effect of variations in life chances among the classes.

Weber, like Marx, was concerned with the conditions under which class consciousness arises. For him, however, there was no single form of class consciousness. Rather, which groups develop a consciousness of common interests opposed to those of another group is a specific empirical question; different groups acquire historical significance at different times and in different places. The extent of consciousness of kind depends to a considerable degree on the general culture of a society, particularly the sets of intellectual ideas current within it. Concepts or values that might foster or inhibit the emergence of class-conscious groups cannot be derived solely from knowledge about the objective economic structure of a society. The existence of different strata subjected to variations in life chances does not necessarily lead to class action. The causal relationship posited by Marx between the fact of group inferiority and other aspects of the structure that might be changed by action had to be demonstrated to people; consciousness of it need not develop spontaneously. The presence or absence of such consciousness is not, of course, a fortuitous matter. The extent to which ideas emerge pointing to a causal relationship between class position and other social conditions is linked to the transparency of the relationship — that is, to how obvious it is that one class will benefit by action directed against another.

An examination of the history of class struggles suggested to Weber that conflicts between creditors and debtors are perhaps the most visible form of conflict flowing from economic differentiation. The conflict between employers and workers is also highly visible under capitalism, but it is essentially a special case of the economic struggle between buyers and sellers, a form of interest tension normal within a capitalist market economy. It involves an act of creative imagination and perception to develop the idea that the tension between employer and worker requires an attack on the entire system of private ownership through the common action of all workers against the capitalist class. Such an act is much more likely to come from the intellectuals, who thereby present the workers with an ideological formula, than from the workers themselves. In this respect, Weber came to conclusions similar to those drawn by Lenin, who also argued that workers by themselves could only reach the stage of economism, of trade union consciousness — that is, of conflict with their employers over wages and working conditions. For Lenin, as for Weber, the emergence of revolutionary class consciousness requires leadership, much of which would be drawn from other strata — in Lenin's case, the elite or vanguard party (Lenin 1902). Weber explicitly formalized the conditions that facilitate the emergence of class consciousness in terms that incorporated the principal elements of the Marxist scheme almost intact, although he made the significant and important addition of common status:

> Organized activity of class groups is favored by the following circumstances: (a) the possibility of concentrating on opponents where the immediate conflict of interests is vital. Thus workers organize against management and not against security holders who are the ones who really draw income without working.... (b) The existence of a class status which is typically similar for large masses of people. (c) The technical possibility of being easily brought together. This is particularly true where large numbers work together in a small area, as in the modern factory. (d) Leadership directed to readily understandable goals. Such goals are very generally imposed or at least are interpreted by persons, such as intelligentsia, who do not belong to the class in question. (1922, p. 427–428 in the 1947 edition).

Weber's condition (a) is essentially a rephrasing of Marx's antagonism factor, though Weber made a distinction, not made by Marx, concerning the direction of the antagonism — in this case, toward the visible overseer. Condition (b) was never explicitly discussed by Marx. Condition (c) is borrowed directly from Marx. As for condition (d), in Marx's works it appears as the role of the party, although Marx never faced up to the problems that arise when a workers' party has a middle-class leadership.

Status

The second major dimension of stratification, status, refers to the quality of perceived interaction. Status was defined by Weber as the positive or negative estimation of honor, or prestige, received by individuals or positions. Thus it involves the felt perceptions of people. Those in a similar status position tend to see themselves as located in a comparable position on the social hierarchy. Since status involves perception of how much one is valued by others, men value it more than economic gain.

Weber argued that since status is manifest, consciousness of kind is more likely to be linked to status differentiation than to class. In other words, those who are in a higher or lower status group are prone to support status-enhancing activities, whether or not these activities can be classed as political. Those groups with high status will be motivated to support values and institutions that seemingly serve to perpetuate their status. Weber regarded economic class as important primarily because it is perceived as a cause of status. Since it is usually easier to make or lose money than it is to gain or lose status, those in privileged status positions seek to dissociate status from class, that is, to urge that status reflects factors such as family origin, manners, education, and the like — attributes that are more difficult to attain or lose than economic wealth.

There is, of course, as Weber pointed out, a strong correlation between status and class positions. However, once a group has attained high status through given achievements, its members try to limit the chances that others will replace them. And this is often done by seeking to deny the original source of individual or family status. The economic and class orders are essentially universalistic and achievement-oriented. Those who get, are. He who secures more money is more important than he who has less. The status order, on the other hand, tends to be particularistic and ascriptive. It involves the assumption that high status reflects aspects of the system that are unachievable. Thus it operates to inhibit social mobility, up or down. Weber, in his writings on status, echoed the functional analysis of the role of style presented by Veblen (1899). For Weber, as for Veblen, the function of conspicuous consumption — that is, of emphasis on pragmatically useless styles of consumption that take many years to learn — was to prevent mobility and to institutionalize the privileges of those who had risen to the top in previous years or epochs. Status groups are therefore identifiable by specific styles of life. Even though the original source of status was economic achievement, a status system, once in existence, operates independently of the class system and even seeks to negate its values. This, as Weber and Veblen both suggested, explains the seemingly surprising phenomenon that even in an industrial capitalist society, money-making is considered vulgar by many in privileged positions, and the children of those who have made money are frequently to be found in non-commercial activities.

Class Relations and Status Relations

The distinction between class and status is also reflected in the different nature of the key set of interactions that characterizes each. Class relations are defined by interaction among unequals in a market situation; status is determined primarily by relations with equals, even though there are many status contacts among unequals. The sanctions, in the case of status, are greater when violating the norms for relations with equals than those for relations with unequals.

One value of differentiating between class and status is that while these two dimensions of stratification are correlated, there are many cases in which they are discrepant. Thus individuals or groups may be higher in status than in class, or vice versa. Weber argued that such discrepancies are important aids to understanding the dynamics of social change and of conflict; he detected an inherent strain between the norms of the market and those of status systems. Markets are the dynamic source of tension for modern industrial society. Success or failure in the market constantly upsets the relative position of groups and individuals: groups high in status and wealth often lose their relative economic position because of market innovations, failure to adjust to change, and the like, while others rise suddenly on the scale of wealth. Those who had status and its frequent concomitant, legitimate access to political authority, exert their influence and power against the *nouveaux riches*. For example, a common interpretation of the behavior of the French bourgeoisie during the Revolution of 1789 is that they had not pressed for economic rights and power because they already possessed all they needed. Rather, they had wanted to force the monarchy and aristocracy to accord them high status. Similarly, Weber's disciple Robert Michels suggested that the political radicalism of many quite wealthy European Jews before World War I was a consequence of their having been denied a status position commensurate with their class level in society (1911, pp. 260–261 in the 1915 edition).

Social Structure and Political Conflict

An industrial society characterized by an elaborate, highly institutionalized status structure *combined* with the class tensions usually found in industrial societies is more likely to exhibit class-conscious politics than is one in which status lines are imprecise and not formally recognized. It has therefore been argued that Marxist, class-conscious parties have been stronger in societies, like the Wilhelmine Germany in which Weber lived most of his life, that maintain a very visible and fairly rigid status system derived from preindustrial society than in class societies, such as the United States, that lack a feudal tradition of estates. Moreover, insofar as the dynamics of a successful industrial society undermine the ascriptive status mechanisms inherited from the feudal precapitalist order, the amount of political conflict arising from class consciousness is reduced. Hence it would seem to follow from Weber's analysis that the growth of industrial capitalism, and the consequent imposition on the stratification system of capitalism's emphases on achievement and universalism, weaken rather than increase class-linked consciousness of kind.

This thesis of Weber's that stresses the consequences of structural changes on class relationships has been paralleled by T.H. Marshall's analysis of the relationship between citizenship and social class (1934–1962, pp. 71–134 in the 1965 edition). Citizenship, for Marshall, is a status that involves access to various rights and powers. In premodern times citizenship was limited to a small elite; social development in European states has consisted to a considerable extent in admitting new social strata — first the bourgeoisie and later the workers — to the status of citizen. The concept of the citizen that arose with the emergence of the bourgeoisie in the eighteenth century involved a claim to universalistic rights in the status order, as well as the political one. Marshall has suggested that class-conscious ideologies of the extreme sort are characteristic of new strata, such as the bourgeoisie or the working class, as they fight for the right to full social and political participation — that is, for citizenship. As long as they are denied citizenship, sizable segments of these classes endorse revolutionary ideologies. In turn, older strata and institutions seeking to preserve their ancient monopolies of power and status foster extreme, conservative doctrines.

From this point of view, the history of political ideologies in democratic countries can be written in terms of the emergence of new social strata and their eventual integration into society and the polity. In Europe, the struggle for such integration took the form of defining a place in the polity for the business strata and the working class alongside the preindustrial upper classes and the church. Unless class conflicts overlapped with continuing controversies concerning the place of religion, as they did in Latin Europe, or concerning the status of the traditional upper strata, as they did in Germany, intense ideological controversy declined soon after the new strata gained full citizenship rights.

Power, Status, and Bureaucracy

Power, which in the Marxist analysis derives from class position, is a much more complex phenomenon in the Weberian model. Weber defined power as the chance of a man or group to realize their will even against the opposition of others. Power may be a function of resources possessed in the economic, status, and political systems; both status and class are power resources. Since people want higher status, they tend to try to orient their behavior to that approved by those with the higher status which they value. Power resources can also be found in institutions that command the allegiance of people — religions, parties, trade unions, and the like. Anyone with followers or, like the military, with control of force, may have access to power. In large measure, the relative weight of different power resources is determined by the rules of the political game, whatever these may be in different societies. The structure of legal authority and its degree of legitimacy influence the way in which power is secured.

For Weber, the key source of power in modern society is *not* to be found in the ownership of the means of production. Rather, the increased complexity of modern industrial society leads to the development of vast bureaucracies that become increasingly interconnected and interdependent. The modern state, with its monopoly of arms and administration, becomes the dominant institution in bureaucratized society. Because of the increasing complexity of operating modern social institutions, even economic institutions are brought into a close, dependent relationship with the administrative and military bureaucracies of the state. Increasingly, therefore, as all social institutions become more bureaucratized and the centralized state gains control of other social institutions, the key power resources become rigidly hierarchical large-scale bureaucracies.

Bureaucratization and Alienation

This concern with bureaucracy as the key hierarchical power-related structure of the stratification system of industrial society (whether the society is formally capitalist or socialist is irrelevant) led Weber to formulate a source of alienation very different from that of Marx. For Weber, it was not only the wage worker who becomes alienated through his lack of control over his human needs; the bureaucrat is even more subject to obsessive demands. Bureaucracy, in fact, has an inherent tendency to destroy men's autonomy. It is characterized by formalism and it involves, in Weber's terms: (1) subordination; (2) expertise (and hence a rigid division of labor); (3) obeying rules ([1906–1924] 1946, pp. 196–198). Even members of small, nonbureaucratic structures have their freedom reduced if these structures are involved with bureaucracies. In this conclusion, Weber agreed with Marx. However, for Weber the key depersonalizing element is the expectation that the bureaucrat will give absolute loyalty to the organization. Loyalty within a bureaucracy is impersonal; no personal attachments are supposed to interfere with the functioning of the system. Thus the depersonalization of loyalty became the equivalent of what Marx called the alienation of man from his labor. Weber argued that, as a social mechanism, bureaucracy assumes absolute discipline and a high level of predictability. People in bureaucracies fulfill role requirements rather than their personal desires. Rational action in bureaucracies is not an end in itself but, rather, an aspect of the structure of social interaction. Individuals both judge others and interact on the basis of universalistic norms; personal motives are not considered. The bureaucratic structure functions for its own ends, not those of the people within it. In theory, all individuals in bureaucracies are expendable and only positions are important.

Preparation for a bureaucratic career involves increasing conformity. Bureaucracy requires that individuals become highly specialized. Success depends on the individual's ability to conform. As one enters a bureaucracy, he loses much of his freedom to change his life alternatives. He becomes highly specialized and therefore cannot move from one firm or type of job to another. Such specialization, such conformity to narrow role requirements — to the needs of the "machine" — means dehumanization, or alienation from true human choice.

The alienation inherent in bureaucracy is, for Weber, independent of the system of property relations. Socialism means more rather than less alienation, because it involves greater bureaucratization. There is little difference between capitalist and socialist societies in their class relations and their propensity to alienation. The source of alienation lies in bureaucracy, which is inherent in industrial society.

The growth of bureaucratization also has the effect of separating work roles from other activities, with socially destructive consequences. An individual within a bureaucracy has to conform to efficiency rules, production standards, and other impersonal goals that have no meaning in his life outside work, since they are the bureaucracy's goals, not his; he conforms to them while at work, but gets no guidance as to how to behave in other activities. Weber can be interpreted as having believed that the nonbureaucratic part of life was becoming increasingly normless while bureaucratic structures were becoming increasingly normative. As social institutions become more bureaucratized, individuals learn how to behave within bureaucracies but not outside of them.

In a sense, Weber raised Marx's ideas about the nature and consequences of stratification to a higher order of generalization. Marx's conclusions were based mainly on his analysis of social relations under capitalism; this analysis presupposed a social system in which the fruits of production were scarce and control over the means of production was inequitably distributed. Weber, by using more general analytical categories, sought to deal with issues that cut through all complex social systems. Thus he characterized every complex system according to the distribution of economic and honorific life chances in it. While Marx stressed that social stratification is a result of economic scarcity, Weber emphasized that honor and prestige are themselves scarce: economic goods could increase, and everyone could gain in an absolute sense, but, since prestige is determined by relative ranking, if one went up, another went down. The latter form of stratification involves a zero-sum game, and consequently occasions continual tensions in any society with unrestricted social mobility.

Alienation also is presented as a broader category in Weber's work than in that of Marx. Basically, alienation from self involves compulsive conformity to norms: the alienated individual is role-bound. Since such compulsive conformity is inherent in bureaucracy, which Weber saw as the dynamic element in modern society, he was much more pessimistic about the future of society than was Marx.

Much of contemporary writing by intellectuals and social scientists about alienation is derived more from Weber than from Marx. For instance, the ideas advanced by Erich Fromm, David Riesman, William H. Whyte, Robert K. Merton, Arnold Green, and C. Wright Mills concerning the "bureaucratic," "marketeer," or "other-directed" personality, the "organization man," and, in general, the individual who seeks to get ahead by selling his personality, are all related to the effects of bureaucracy on individuals. Weber is the intellectual father of these and all similar discussions. His ideas, therefore, constitute not only a contribution to sociological analysis but also a basic source for the moral criticism of society. They usually have not been perceived as such because Weber's empirical conclusion, that all complex societies will be both stratified and alienative, leads to no positive moral solution. This is because for Weber (as for C. Wright Mills), the only society that really makes individual autonomy possible is the nonbureaucratized society of small producers, and societies of this type are rapidly vanishing.

FUNCTIONALIST APPROACHES

Although the ideas generated by Marx and Weber remain the most fruitful sources of theory on social stratification, much contemporary sociology accepts the so-called functionalist approach to the subject. This approach is associated with the names of Emile Durkheim, Kingsley Davis, Talcott Parsons, and Robert K. Merton.

Durkheim and subsequent functionalists have assumed that since modern society has a complex and highly differentiated system of roles, which must be performed, different men must be motivated to perform different roles (Durkheim 1893). They see man as a social animal whose needs are not primarily physical and satiable but, rather, culturally determined and potentially unlimited. However, if all individuals had the same set of unlimited desires, no complex social structure would be possible. Consequently, some social or moral force must shape and limit these potentially unlimited desires. Society prescribes varying goals for different individuals and groups, sets limits on these goals, and prescribes the means that may legitimately be used to attain them.

In analyzing the function of stratification, functionalists see it as the mechanism through which society encourages men to seek to achieve the diverse positions necessary in a complex social system. The vast variety of positions that must be filled differ in their requirements for skill, education, intelligence, commitment to work, willingness to exercise power resources against others, and the like. Functionalist theory posits that in an unstratified society—that is, one in which rewards are relatively equal for all tasks—those positions which require more work, postponement of gratification, greater anxiety, and the like will not be filled by the most able people. The stratification system is perceived, therefore, as a motivation system; it is society's mechanism for encouraging the most able people to perform the most demanding roles in order to have the society operate efficiently.

The theory also suggests that status—honorific prestige—is the most general and persistent form of stratification because what human beings as social animals most require to satisfy their ego needs is recognition from others. Beyond a certain point, economic rewards and power are valued, not for themselves but because economic or power positions are symbolic indicators of high status. Hence, the functionalist school of stratification agrees with Weber that stratification, or differential hierarchical reward, is an inherent aspect of complex society and that status as a source of motivation is inherently a scarce resource.

The emphasis in functional analysis on the need for hierarchical differentiation does not, of course, explain how men evaluate different individuals in the stratification system. Parsons has pointed to three sets of characteristics which are used as a basis of ranking. These are *possessions*, or those attributes which people own; *qualities*, belonging to individuals and including traits that are ascribed, such as race, lineage, or sex, or that are attributed as permanent characteristics, such as a specific ability; and *performances*, or evaluations of the ways in which individuals have fulfilled their roles—in short, judgments about achievements. Societies, according to Parsons, vary considerably in the degree to which their central value systems emphasize possessions, qualities, or performances in locating people on the social hierarchy. Thus, ideally, a feudal social system stresses ascribed qualities, a capitalist society emphasizes possessions, and a pure communist system would assign prestige according to performance. Parsons has stated that no actual society has ever come close to any of these three "ideal-type" models; each society has included elements of all three. However, the variation in the core ideal value does inform the nature of the stratification system, patterns of mobility, and the like (1953).

If we assume, as most functionalists do, that the function of stratification is to act as a system of role allocation, then it follows that a key requisite for an operating social system is a relatively stable system of social rankings. That is, there must be consensus in a society about what sorts of activities and symbols are valued; without such consensus, the society could not operate. Given this assumption, an ongoing system of stratification requires a general set of ideological justifications. There must be various mechanisms which explain, justify, and propagate the system of inequality, and which cause men to accept as legitimate the fact of their own inequality. From an ideal-typical point of view, a system of stratification that is stable would set for various groups within societies goals that could be achieved by all within each group. Feudal societies, which theoretically separate the population from birth into distinct hierarchical strata which cannot be crossed, but within which men may succeed and gain social recognition for doing a good job, represent perhaps the extreme form of stratification as something that adjusts men to the needs of society. Theoretically, in a society in which individuals were socialized to accept attainable positions as the proper and necessary fulfillment of their role in life, men would feel "free" and satisfied. The sense of freedom, of being one's own master and of achieving what one thinks one wants to achieve, exists only where the means-ends relationship defined by society is stable — that is, where men do in fact get what they have been taught to want.

But it is extremely doubtful whether any such system of balanced means-ends relationships within a stratification system ever existed or could exist. The assumption that individuals seek to maximize the esteem in which they are held implies that those who are in low-valued positions are subject to punishment. To be valued negatively means to be told that one is no good, that one is bad. Consequently, it may be argued that there is an inherent tension between the need to maximize esteem and the requirements of a stratification system.

In actual stratification systems, this tension appears to be alleviated by various transvaluational mechanisms. That is, there seems in all societies to be a reverse stratification system, the most enduring form of which is usually found in religion. Inherent in many religions is the belief that wealth and power are associated with sin and evil, while virtue is associated with poverty. Christianity and Hinduism, for example, both posit that righteousness will somehow be rewarded in the hereafter, so that the virtuous poor will ultimately be able to look down upon the wicked rich. This mechanism, which holds out the hope of subsequent reward for adhering to the morality of the present, does not, of course, challenge the existing secular distribution of privilege. It does, however, reflect the inherent tension within stratified society: that there is both acceptance and rejection of the value system by the underprivileged.

Empirical Studies

A considerable amount of the research on stratification by American sociologists has stemmed directly from functional analysis. Perhaps the most extensive single set of studies is contained in the many volumes by W. Lloyd Warner and his associates reporting on the "social class" (i.e., status) system of a number of American communities (see, for example, Warner 1941–1959). Warner, an anthropologist by training and originally a follower of Durkheim, has argued that any effort to deal in functional terms with the social system of a modern community must relate many of the institutional and behavioral patterns of the community to the needs of the classes within them rather than to the larger system as such. Using the method of reputational analysis (asking people in the community to rank others and seeing who associated with whom as status equals), Warner located five or six social classes ranging from "upper-upper" to "lower-lower." Each of them was found to possess a number of distinct class characteristics, such as intrafamily behavior, associational memberships, and attitudes on a variety of issues. On the whole, Warner sees class divisions as contributing to social stability rather than to conflict, because the strata are separated into relatively distinct elements that have a more or less balanced and integrated culture. He has interpreted his data as indicating that those in lower positions tend to respect those above them in the status hierarchy and to follow their lead on many issues. While most sociologists would agree with Warner concerning the existence of the sort of status groupings that he has described (Weber presented a picture of American status relations in much the same terms), many would disagree with him concerning the degree of consensus within the system as to where individuals are located and would tend to agree more with Merton that tensions and conflicts are inherent in any hierarchical order. It is interesting to note, however, that while the various community studies of the accorded status system do suggest considerable ambivalence about where various individuals or families rank, particularly if they are not close to the very top or bottom of the system, investigations concerning the prestige rankings of occupations indicate considerable consensus both within and among a variety of nations. The prestige studies would seem to be in line with the assumption of functionalist theory that consensus in the desirability of different occupational roles is necessary in order to motivate the most competent individuals to seek those positions which are valued most.

Criticism of the Functionalist Approach

Functionalist theory has been sharply criticized by a number of sociologists who argue that while systems of widespread inequality characterize all existing complex societies, this fact does not demonstrate that inequality is a social requisite for a stable society, as many functionalists argue. Rather, these critics urge that systems of stratification persist and take the varying forms they do because the privileged strata have more power and are able to impose their group interests on the society. The greater rewards in income and status received by various positions reflect greater power than the need to motivate individuals to secure them. The value systems related to stratification therefore reflect the functional needs of the dominant strata, not those of the social system as such (Tumin 1953; Buckley 1958). A Polish sociologist, Wlodzimierz Wesolowski (1962), has suggested that functionalist sociologists, particularly Davis and Moore (1945), who have written the most comprehensive contemporary statement of the functionalist position, are wrong when they emphasize the need for stratification as a system of motivation in the form of material advantage or prestige. He has contended that there are alternative systems of social organization that can sharply reduce inequality in prestige and income while motivating people to seek higher education and fill responsible positions. Hence, class differences that derive from such forms of inequality may decline greatly. Wesolowski, however, agrees with the functionalists that complex social systems will continue to be organized on hierarchical lines, because systems of authority and command are necessary. People will continue to be divided between those who occupy "positions of authority ... who have the right (and duty) to give orders, while the others have the duty to obey them" ([1962] 1966. p. 68). He has noted that Friedrich Engels, Marx's closest intellectual collaborator, "said that in a communist system the State as a weapon of class domination would wither away ... [and yet] declared that it would be impossible to think of any great modern industrial enterprise or of the organization of the future communist society without authority — or superiority-subordination relationships" (*ibid.*).

Wesolowski agrees with the functionalists that stratification is inevitable because differentials in authority relationships, not variations in income or prestige, are necessary. As he put it, "if there is any functional necessity for stratification, it is the necessity of stratification according to the criterium of authority and not according to the criterium of material advantage or prestige. Nor does the necessity of stratification derive from the need to induce people for the acquirement of qualifications, but from the very fact that humans live collectively" (p. 69).

Wesolowski has presented in general terms a formulation very similar to that of the German sociologist Ralf Dahrendorf, who has tried to reformulate Marx's theoretical assumptions so as to deal more adequately with certain structural changes in Western society — especially those which have resulted in the divorce of ownership from management that is characteristic of the modern corporation (Dahrendorf 1957). Many have argued that this separation negates Marx, since it means the disappearance of the class of private capitalists as a powerful stratum. Dahrendorf, however, has suggested that the only significant difference this change makes is that it is now more meaningful to speak of the differential distribution of *authority* as the basis of class formation than it is to speak of the ownership of the means of production. It is differential access to authority positions and, therefore, to power and prestige that gives rise to contemporary class conflict, for those who are excluded from authority in "imperatively co-ordinated associations" (a term Dahrendorf borrowed from Weber) will be in conflict with those who have command over them. Articulation of manifest interest and organization of interest groups then become the dynamite for social-structural change.

Functionalism and Marxism

In urging that the universality of stratification, or hierarchical differentiation — though not, it should be noted, of social class — is linked to the functional requirements for a power hierarchy, Wesolowski has built an interesting theoretical bridge between Marxist and functionalist sociology. For his and Dahrendorf's lines of reasoning ultimately are not greatly different from the functionalist approach to power presented by Parsons. The latter, of course, does not emphasize the theme of power as self-interested, which is found in the Marxian tradition, or that of coercion, which was stressed by Weber. Rather, Parsons has suggested that power—in his terms, the ability to mobilize resources necessary for the operation of the system — should be viewed in value-neutral terms, as follows. Inherent in the structure of complex society, especially in the division of labor, is the existence of authority roles, holders of which are obligated to initiate acts that are socially necessary. Most of the things done by those at the summits of organizations or societies are necessary. If individuals and groups are to achieve their goals within the division of labor, it must include a complex system of interactions. The more complex the system, Parsons has argued, the more dependent individuals are on others for the attainment of their goals, that is, the less free or powerful they are. And power is basically control over the allocation of resources and roles so as to make a given system operative. Power, under any system of values, resides in having what people desire, because they will obey for the sake of getting what they desire. Finally, unless the capacity to organize the behavior of those in a system existed, sharply differentiated societies could not operate (1963).

It should be noted that there is a coincidence of the Marxist and functionalist approaches to political power. Both approaches view it as a social utility—as the means, par excellence, through which societies attain their objectives, including the expansion of available resources. Elite theories of power, on the other hand, see it in "zero-sum" terms, that is, they assume a fixed amount of power, so that the gain of one group or individual necessarily involves the loss of others. Two reviews of C. Wright Mills's analysis of the American power elite (Mills 1956) — one by a functionalist, Parsons (1957), and the other by the student of stratification who, among leading American sociologists, stands closest to Marxism, Robert S. Lynd (1956; 1957)—criticized Mills for having a zero-sum game approach to power and for identifying it with domination. That is, both Lynd and Parsons agreed that power should be viewed, both sociologically and politically, in the light of its positive functions as an agency of the general community and that it is erroneous to view power, as Mills did, solely or even primarily in terms of powerholders seeking to enhance their own interests.

There is, of course, a link with stratification theory in Parsons' analysis of power, since he has assumed that what people value most are economic advantage and esteem. It follows from this that those who possess the qualities which place them at the upper levels of the economic and status hierarchies also have the most power. Money and influence, Parsons has noted, are exchangeable for power, since power is the ability to mobilize resources through controlling the action of others.

DIMENSIONS OF STRATIFICATION

The foregoing discussion of the Marxist, Weberian, and functionalist approaches to social class analysis has distinguished a number of issues that continue to concern sociologists. Instead of moving toward one concept of social class, students of stratification have generally reacted to an awareness of the complexity of the subject by differentiating a large number of apparently relevant concepts, most of which are directly derivable from the three traditions discussed above. The differences in approach have, in large measure, reflected variations in the intellectual concerns of the scholars involved.

Contemporary students of stratification continue to be divided into two groups: those who urge that there is a single dimension underlying all stratification and those who believe that stratification may best be conceptualized as multidimensional. That is, they disagree as to whether economic class position, social status, power, income, and the like are related to one underlying factor in most societies, or whether they should be considered as distinct although related dimensions of the stratification system. To some degree this controversy may be perceived as a continuation on a more formal level of the differences between the approaches of Marx and Weber. However, some of those who uphold the single attribute position are far from being Marxists. They do not believe that position in the economic structure determines all other aspects of status; rather, they would argue that statistical analysis suggests the presence of a basic common factor. For analytic purposes, however, the controversy cannot be resolved by statistical manipulation, since some of those who favor a multidimensional approach would argue that even if it turns out that these various aspects of stratification do form part of a single latent attribute, there is enough variation among them to justify the need to analyze the cases in which individuals or groups are ranked higher on certain dimensions than on others.

If we assume, as most contemporary sociologists do, that stratification may most usefully be conceptualized in multidimensional terms, we are confronted with the issues of which dimensions the various theorists emphasize. The dimensions they have suggested may be grouped into three categories: (1) *objective* status, or aspects of stratification that structure environments differently enough to evoke differences in behavior; (2) *accorded* status, or the prestige accorded to individuals and groups by others; (3) *subjective* status, or the personal sense of location within the social hierarchy felt by various individuals. These approaches in turn may be further broken down in terms of important variables, as follows.

Objective Class Concepts

Perhaps the most familiar component of objective status is power position within the economic structure. This is essentially Marx's criterion for class: persons are located according to their degree of control over the means of production. In the first analysis this serves to distinguish owners from employees. Owners, however, may vary in their degree of economic security and power, as important businessmen differ from unimportant ones, and workers also may vary according to the bargaining power inherent in the relative scarcity of the skills they possess.

Another important concept in this area is extent of economic life chances. Weber perceived economic status not only in terms of ownership but also in terms of the probability of receiving a given economic return, or income. Thus an employee role, such as engineer or lawyer, which gave someone a higher probability of earning high income than a small businessman, would place him in a higher class position. Essentially, this dimension refers to power in the market.

Indeed, the simple difference in income received has been suggested as the best way to measure economic class.

Variation in the relative status of different occupations has also been seen as an important criterion for differentiating positions in the economic hierarchy. This approach has increasingly come to be used in studies of social mobility. Occupational prestige is, of course, a form of accorded status, except that what are being ranked are occupations, not individuals or groups.

Another aspect of stratification that is sometimes perceived as an objective one is power, which may be defined as the ability to affect the life chances of others, or conversely as the amount of freedom from control by others. Power may also be conceptualized as the set of probabilities that given role relationships will allow individuals to define their own will—that is, to impose their version of order even against the resistance of others. This dimension is extremely difficult to describe in operational terms: how, for instance, does one compare the different amounts and types of power possessed by labor leaders, Supreme Court justices, factory owners, and professors? It is also argued that power should not be regarded as an aspect of stratification in itself, as if it were comparable with economic class, but, rather, as the dynamic resultant of the forces brought into play in different types of social situations. Authority—legitimate power within a formal structure—is clearly hierarchical, but the rank order of authority usually applies only to a given authority structure within a society, not to the society itself.

Finally, a number of sociological studies have treated education as a major determinant of objective status and as a dimension of stratification. The differences in behavior and attitudes of those who are higher or lower in educational attainments have been demonstrated by empirical research. On the theoretical level, it is argued that education, like the various economic dimensions, affects the life chances of individuals — their degree of security, their status, and their ability to interact with others. People are given differential degrees of respect and influence according to their level of education.

Accorded Status

The dimension of accorded status is the one most sociologists tacitly or overtly refer to when they use the term "social class." This dimension involves the amount of status, honor, or deference that a given position commands in a society. Various methods are used to study accorded status, but in any case the location of individuals or groups in the status system depends on the opinion of the individuals who go to make up the system rather than the opinion of the sociologist who observes it. Accorded status, then, is a result of the felt perceptions of others, and a social class based on accorded status is composed of individuals who accept each other as equals and therefore as qualified for intimate association in friendship, marriage, and the like.

Since this concept depends on rankings by others, it is difficult to apply it to large-scale social systems, particularly nations, except at the level of the small uppermost social class. Individuals from different communities cannot rank each other unless they rely on criteria more objective than social acceptability. The social class consisting of individuals who have, roughly speaking, the same attributes will vary with size of community; for instance, the type of individual who may be in the highest social class of a small town will probably be in the middle class of a large city. It has, in fact, been argued that the larger the community, the more likely it is that accorded status will correspond to objective status. In other words, individuals who live in large communities are more prone to make status judgments about others on the basis of knowledge about their jobs, how much their homes are worth, how many years of education they have had, and the like.

Accorded status tends to become an ascribed characteristic, that is, one that can be inherited. "Background," which usually means family identification, is the way in which people define the source of accorded status. This implies that in addition to specific lineage, other visible ascribed characteristics, such as race, ethnicity, and religion, often constitute elements in status placement. In all societies that contain a variety of racial, ethnic, or religious groups, each such group is differentially ranked in honorific or status terms. Those groups which were present first and retain the highest economic and political positions tend to have the highest status. Thus in the United States, such traits as being white, Anglo-Saxon, and Protestant (preferably of the historically earliest American denominations, such as Episcopal, Congregational, or Quaker) convey high status on those possessing them. The status attributes of various socially visible groups are also determined by various typical characteristics of their members. Thus religious or ethnic groups which are poor on the average are of low status, and wealthy members of such groups tend to be discriminated against socially by comparably well-to-do members of more privileged groups (for instance, a well-to-do Baptist will have lower status in most American communities than a comparably affluent Episcopalian).

Status, it should be noted, is a power resource in much the same way as economic position or political authority. Since status involves being accepted by those in high positions, and since the desire for status is universal, men seek to accommodate their actions to those who can confer status on them.

Subjective Status

Unlike objective and accorded class concepts, which locate individuals in the stratification hierarchy according to the judgments of analysts or of the community, subjective status categories involve efforts to discover the way in which the individual himself perceives the stratification hierarchy. In sociology there are essentially two main traditions of dealing with subjective positions, one based on the methodological device of self-identification and the other on reference group theory.

Self-Identification

The technique of self-identification is used to determine the extent to which given individuals or portions of specific groups see themselves as members of a given class or other group that may be located in terms of stratification. Efforts to locate individuals have involved asking them to place themselves in one of a number of class categories furnished by the investigator in such questions as "Do you think of yourself as a member of the upper, middle, working, or lower class?" (Centers 1949). The number of alternatives furnished respondents may, of course, be larger or smaller than this. Other investigators, instead of following this procedure, have sought to find out what categories people use to describe the social hierarchy (Manis & Meltzer 1963).

Reference Group Theory

The groups that individuals use as reference points by which to evaluate themselves or their activities are known in sociology as reference groups. They can be, but need not be, groups to which an individual belongs. Thus a person may judge his degree of occupational achievement by comparing his attainments with those which preponderate among his fellow ethnic, racial, or religious group members, people he went to school with, neighbors, or those who are more privileged than he is and whose position he would like to attain.

Reference group theory assumes that individuals rarely use the total social structure as a reference group but, rather, that they judge their own status by comparison with smaller, more closely visible groups. The extent of satisfaction or dissatisfaction with status is held to depend on one's reference groups.

Reference groups are often derivable from structural factors; thus neighborhoods, factories, employers, schoolmates, and the like often constitute relevant reference groups. On the other hand, relevant reference groups may be manipulated, as when organized groups that are competing for support seek to affect the reference groups of those whose support they want so as to increase their sense of satisfaction or dissatisfaction (Lipset & Trow 1957). The formation of class consciousness may be seen as a process in which members of the lower social strata change their reference groups: while class consciousness is dormant or incipient, the lower-class individual relates himself to various small groups; with the full emergence of class consciousness, he relates himself to aspects of the larger social structure.

OBJECTIVE AND SUBJECTIVE ORIENTATIONS

The fact that social class may be conceptualized both objectively and subjectively does not mean that these are in any sense mutually exclusive ways of looking at the social hierarchy. Almost all analysts, regardless of which approach they choose to stress, are interested in examining the interrelations between their conception of class and other factors, which they view either as determinants or as consequences of class variations. Thus, as has been noted, Marx was intensely interested in the subjective reactions of people to their location in the class structure.

It is significant that Richard Centers, who is most identified with the social-psychological approach to class as involving self-definition, initiated his study of the subject as a way of finding out to what extent American workers were class-conscious in the Marxist sense. In fact, Centers' work is more directly inspired by Marx than is that of many sociologists, who are more wont to approach the subject in objective terms.

It should also be noted that there are close links between elements in Marx's thought and contemporary reference group theory. In seeking to suggest hypotheses that would explain the relationship between objective position and anticipated subjective reactions, Marx advanced a theory of relative deprivation. He suggested that although objective improvement in the economic position of the workers could take place under capitalism, this would not prevent the emergence of "true" class consciousness, since the position of the capitalists would improve more rapidly than that of the workers. As he put it, the "material position of the worker has improved, . . . but at the cost of his social position. The social gulf that divides him from the capitalist has widened" ([1849] 1962, p. 98). In another work Marx illustrated this generalization with the story of a man who was very happy with a small house in which he lived until a wealthy man came along and built a mansion next door: then, wrote Marx, the house of the worker suddenly became a hut in his eyes (1898, pp. 268–269 in the 1936 edition).

Similarly, although Marx never dealt with the distinction between class and status on a conceptual level, there are frequent references in his historical writings to distinctions among social strata in various countries. These distinctions actually reflect what would now be called variations among status groups. Perhaps the most interesting formulation related to this question may be found in a major Marxist classic by Engels. In discussing political life in nineteenth-century England, Engels pointed out in very clear terms that status may be an independent source of power, more important in a given situation than economic power:

> In England, the bourgeoisie never held undivided sway. Even the victory of 1832 left the landed aristocracy in almost exclusive possession of all the leading government offices. The meekness with which the wealthy middle class submitted to this remained inconceivable to me until the great Liberal manufacturer, Mr. W. A. Forster, in a public speech implored the young men of Bradford to learn French, as a means to get on in the world, and quoted from his own experience how sheepish he looked when, as a Cabinet Minister, he had to move in society where French was, at least, as necessary as English! The fact was, the English middle class of that time were, as a rule, quite uneducated upstarts, and could not help leaving to the aristocracy those superior government places where other qualifications were required than mere insular narrowness and insular conceit, seasoned by business sharpness....
>
> The English bourgeoisie are, up to the present day, so deeply penetrated by a sense of their social inferiority that they keep up, at their own expense and that of the nation, an ornamental caste of drones to represent the nation worthily at all state functions; and they consider themselves highly honoured whenever one of themselves is found worthy of admission into this select and privileged body, manufactured, after all, by themselves. ([1880] 1935, pp. 25–26)

Clearly, what Engels was describing is a situation in which an old upper class, which had declined in economic power, continued to maintain its control over the governmental machinery because it remained the highest status group in the society. Those with less status but more economic resources conformed to the standards set up by the higher status group.

Stable and Unstable Status Systems

The relationships among the different dimensions of stratification vary in different types of societies and different periods; they are probably at their weakest during periods of rapid social change involving the rise of new occupational strata, shifts from rural to urban predominance, and changes in the status and authority of key institutions, such as religion and education. Of all the relatively stable types of society, the ones in which the various dimensions of stratification are most closely correlated are rural, caste, and feudal societies. The growth of industrial and urban society in Europe and America has resulted in a system of stratification characterized by wide discrepancies between class and objective status, and between both of these and the subjective attributes of status. Currently, as Western society moves into a "postindustrial" phase characterized by a considerable growth in the white-collar, technological, and service sectors of the economy and a relative decline in employment in manufacturing, the relationships between the dimensions have become more tenuous. Status, economic reward, and power are tied to educational achievement, position in some large-scale bureaucracy, access to political authority, and the like. In a predominantly bureaucratic society, property as such has become a less important source of status and social mobility. Complaints about alienation and dehumanization are found more commonly among students, intellectuals, and other sectors of the educated middle classes than among the working class. Most recently, sections of the communist movement have openly discussed the revolutionary role of university students and the petite bourgeoisie, and have seen the organized proletariat in Western society as a relatively conservative group, unavailable for radical politics.

These developments may reflect the fact that some of the most politically relevant discontent in the bureaucratic "affluent society" of the 1960s seems to be inherent in social tensions induced by *status inconsistencies*. However, the bulk of resentment against the stratification system is still rooted in objective deprivation and exploitation. The concept of status inconsistency introduced by Lenski (1954), who derived it from Weber, refers to the situation of individuals or groups that are differentially located on various dimensions of stratification. Persons in such a situation are exposed to conflicting sets of expectations: for instance, those who are high in educational attainments but are employed in relatively low-paid occupations tend to be more dissatisfied than those whose stratification attributes are totally consistent. As evidence in support of this assumption it is possible to cite research findings that among the relatively well-to-do, those with discrepant status attributes are more likely to favor change in the power structure and to have more liberal or leftist attitudes than those with status attributes that are mutually consistent (Goffman 1957). Consequently, the increase in status discrepancy inherent in situations of rapid social change should result in an increase in overall discontent and, among those in the more ambiguous status positions (which in the 1960s occurred largely in the well-educated middle strata) in greater receptivity to the myths justifying rebellion. In industrialized societies those who form the underprivileged strata but who have consistent status attributes remain politically on the left but show little interest in radical change. Because all social change generates status discrepancies, rebellious and extremist mass movements are more likely to be found during periods of rapid industrialization and economic growth, and in areas where immigration has caused sudden population growth, than in industrially mature urbanized areas.

Analysis of the consequences of status discrepancies has yielded seemingly contradictory results, largely because some researchers treat all discrepancies as necessarily equal in their effects. For example, institutionalized discrepancies, such as those which result when a member of a minority group becomes rich but is still discriminated against, are equated with inconsistencies between education and occupation, or between occupation and income. Highly visible institutionalized discrepancies should result in more active expression of resentment and more efforts to bring about *social* change than do loosely structured personal inconsistencies. The latter are more likely to be reflected in efforts by the individual to change his personal situation through various forms of mobility, including change in occupation, residence, or organization. The consequences of status discrepancies should therefore be investigated within broad status categories rather than for total societies. For instance, discrepancies among the poor may have effects very different from those they have among the well-to-do. A manual worker with a claim, based on good education or family background, to higher status than his occupational position allows him is more likely to be politically conservative than workers whose status attributes are consistent. Among the well-to-do, however, status inconsistency will impair claims to high positions and will induce favorable attitudes toward liberal or egalitarian ideologies. The effects of status inconsistencies in societies with relatively rigid status lines are quite different from their effects in societies that have relatively fluid stratification systems. Clearly, the concept of status inconsistency, though potentially a useful tool in class analysis, presupposes some systematic treatment of how the relationship between the various dimensions of status varies from one type of stratification to another.

The Future of Social Class

To conclude on a note of irony, it may be observed that in a certain sense history has underwritten one of Marx's basic assumptions, which is that the cultural superstructure, including political behavior and status relationships, is a function of the underlying economic and technological structure. As Marx put it in the Preface to *Capital*: "The country that is more developed industrially only shows, to the less developed, the image of its own future" ([1867–1879] 1925–1926,

Vol. 1, pp. 8–9). Hence, the most economically developed society should also have the most advanced set of class and political relationships. Since the United States is the most advanced society economically, its class system, regarded as part of its cultural superstructure, should be more appropriate to a technologically advanced society than the class systems of the less developed economies of Europe. In addition, one might argue that the United States, since it lacks a feudal past, should evolve the institutions of a highly developed society in their purest form. Hence, an unpolitical Marxist sociology would expect the social class relationships of the United States to present an image of the future of other societies that are moving in the same general economic direction. Characteristic of such a social system is a decline in emphasis on social class, that is, a decline of distinct visible strata with a "felt consciousness of kind" (Lipset 1964a; 1964b); the various dimensions of stratification are more likely to operate in a criss-crossing fashion, increasing the numbers who are relatively high on some components of status and low on others. Highly developed societies of this kind, whether variants of the communist or the capitalist model, are more likely to possess systems of social stratification — varied rankings — than social classes.

These comments suggest the need to view stratification in international as well as national terms (Horowitz 1966). The differences between the average per capita income of the poorest and wealthiest nations are on the order of 40 or 50 to 1, that is, much greater than the differences among social strata within the industrially advanced nations. The variations in national wealth constitute structural parameters that greatly affect the "class" relationships between nations. A Chinese communist has already advanced the thesis that the significant class struggle is between the predominantly rural nations, which are underdeveloped and very poor, and the urbanized, wealthy ones (Piao 1965). He has also argued that the wealth of the latter has to a considerable degree reduced the political expression of class tensions within them, but that this should be seen as a result of exploitation by the economically advanced countries of the underdeveloped ones. Whether this thesis is warranted by the facts of international trade relationships or not, it does seem true that any analysis of class structures and their political consequences must in the future consider the impact of variation in national incomes. Many in the elite of the poorer part of the world see themselves as the leaders of oppressed peoples; the radicalism of the intellectuals, university students, military officers, and the like in the less developed nations can be related to the social and economic inferiority of their countries, rather than to their position in the class structure. Such considerations take us far afield from the conventional Western sociological concerns with class relationships, but they clearly are relevant to any effort at specifying the sources of class behavior and ideologies. As sociology becomes more comparative in outlook and research, we may expect efforts to link class analysis of individual nations to the facts of international stratification.

References

BELL, DANIEL
(1960) 1962 *The End of Ideology: On the Exhaustion of Political Ideas in the Fifties.*
2d ed., rev. New York: Collier.

BUCKLEY, WALTER
(1958) 1961 Social Stratification and the Functional Theory of Social Differentiation.
Pages 478–484 in Seymour M. Lipset and Neil Smelser (editors), *Sociology: The
Progress of a Decade.* Englewood Cliffs, N.J.: Prentice-Hall. First published in
Volume 23 of the *American Sociological Review.*

BUKHARIN, NIKOLAI I.
(1921) 1965 *Historical Materialism: A System of Sociology.* Translated from the 3d
Russian edition. New York: Russell. First published as *Teoriia istoricheskogo
materializma.*

CENTERS, RICHARD
(1949) 1961 *The Psychology of Social Classes: A Study of Class Consciousness.* New
York: Russell.

DAHRENDORF, RALF
(1957) 1959 *Class and Class Conflict in Industrial Society.* Rev. & enl. ed. Stanford
Univ. Press. First published in German.

DAVIS, KINGSLEY; AND MOORE, WILBERT E.
(1945) 1966 Some Principles of Stratification. Pages 47–53 in Reinhard Bendix and
Seymour M. Lipset (editors), *Class, Status, and Power: Social Stratification in
Comparative Perspective.* 2d ed., rev. New York: Free Press. First published in
Volume 10 of the *American Sociological Review.*

DE LEON, DANIEL
(1889–1913) 1932 *James Madison and Karl Marx: A Contrast and a Similarity.* 3d ed.
New York: Labor News Co.

DURKHEIM, EMILE
(1893) 1960 *The Division of Labor in Society.* Glencoe, Ill.: Free Press. First published
as *De la division du travail social.*

DURKHEIM, EMILE
(1897) 1951 *Suicide: A Study in Sociology.* Glencoe, Ill.: Free Press. First published in
French.

ENGELS, FRIEDRICH
(1880) 1935 *Socialism: Utopian and Scientific.* New York: International Publishers.
First published in French.

GOFFMAN, IRWIN W.
1957 Status Consistency and Preference for Change in Power Distribution. *American
Sociological Review* 22:275–281.

HODGE, ROBERT W.; TREIMAN, DONALD J.; AND ROSSI, PETER H.
1966 A Comparative Study of Occupational Prestige. Pages 309–321 in Reinhard
Bendix and Seymour M. Lipset (editors), *Class, Status, and Power: Social Stratification in Comparative Perspective.* 2d ed., rev. New York: Free Press.

HOROWITZ, IRVING LOUIS
1966 *Three Worlds of Development: The Theory and Practice of International
Stratification.* New York: Oxford Univ. Press.

LENIN, VLADIMIR I.
(1902) 1961 What Is to Be Done? Volume 5, pages 347–529 in Vladimir I. Lenin,
Collected Works. 4th ed. Moscow; Foreign Languages Publishing House. First
published as "Chto delat'?"

LENSKI, GERHARD E.
(1954) 1961 Status Crystallization: A Non-vertical Dimension of Social Status. Pages

485–494 in A Non-vertical Dimension of Social Status. Pages 485–494 in Seymour M. Lipset and Neil Smelser (editors), *Sociology: The Progress of a Decade*. Englewood Cliffs, N.J.: Prentice-Hall. First published in Volume 19 of the *American Sociological Review*.

LIPSET, SEYMOUR M.
1964*a*, The Changing Class Structure and Contemporary European Politics. *Daedalus* 93:271–303.

LIPSET, SEYMOUR M.
1964*b*, Political Cleavages in "Developed" and "Emerging" Polities. Pages 21–55 in Erik Allardt and Yrjö Littunen (editors), *Cleavages, Ideologies and Party Systems: Contributions to Comparative Political Sociology*. Transactions of the Westermarck Society, Vol. 10. Helsinki: The Society.

LIPSET, SEYMOUR M.; AND TROW, MARTIN
1957 Reference Group Theory and Trade-union Wage Policy. Pages 391–411 in Mirra Komarovsky (editor), *Common Frontiers of the Social Sciences*. Glencoe, Ill.: Free Press.

LYND, ROBERT S.
1956 Power in the United States. *Nation* 182:408–411. A review of C. Wright Mills's *The Power Elite*.

LYND, ROBERT S.
1957 Power in American Society as Resource and Problem. Pages 1–45 in Arthur Kornhauser (editor), *Problems of Power in American Democracy*. Detroit, Mich.: Wayne State Univ. Press.

MANIS, JEROME G.; AND MELTZER, BERNARD N.
1963 Some Correlates of Class Consciousness Among Textile Workers. *American Journal of Sociology* 69:177–184.

MARSHALL, T. H.
(1934–1962) 1964 *Class, Citizenship, and Social Development: Essays*. Garden City, N.Y.: Doubleday. A collection of articles and lectures first published in England in 1963 under the title *Sociology at the Crossroads, and Other Essays*. A paperback edition was published in 1965.

MARX, KARL
(1844) 1963 *Early Writings*. Translated and edited by T. B. Bottomore. London: Watts. First published in German. Contains "On the Jewish Question," "Contribution to the Critique of Hegel's Philosophy of Right," and "Economic and Philosophic Manuscripts." A paperback edition was published in 1964 by McGraw-Hill.

MARX, KARL
(1847) 1963 *The Poverty of Philosophy*. With an introduction by Friedrich Engels. New York: International Publishers. First published in French. A paperback edition was published in 1964.

MARX, KARL
(1849) 1962 Wage Labour and Capital. Volume 1, pages 70–105 in Karl Marx and Friedrich Engels, *Selected Works*. Moscow: Foreign Language Publishing House. First published in German in the *Neue Rheinische Zeitung*.

MARX, KARL
(1852) 1962 The Eighteenth Brumaire of Louis Bonaparte. Volume 1, pages 243–344 in Karl Marx and Friedrich Engels, *Selected Works*. Moscow: Foreign Languages Publishing House. First published in German in the journal *Die Revolution*. A paperback edition was published in 1964 by International Publishers.

MARX, KARL
(1867–1879) 1925–1926 *Capital: A Critique of Political Economy*. 3 vols. Chicago: Kerr. Volume 1: *The Process of Capitalist Production*. Volume 2: *The Process of Circulation of Capital*. Volume 3: *The Process of Capitalist Production as a Whole*.

Volume 1 was published in 1867. The manuscripts of volumes 2 and 3 were written between 1867 and 1879 and first published posthumously in German in 1885 and 1894.

MARX, KARL
(1898) 1962 Wages, Price, and Profit. Volume 1, pages 398–447 in Karl Marx and Friedrich Engels, *Selected Works*. Moscow: Foreign Languages Publishing House. First published in German.

MERTON, ROBERT K.
(1949) 1957 *Social Theory and Social Structure*. Rev. & enl. ed. Glencoe, Ill.: Free Press.

MICHELS, ROBERT
(1911) 1959 *Political Parties: A Sociological Study of the Oligarchical Tendencies of Modern Democracy*. New York: Dover. First published as *Zur Soziologie des Parteiwesens in der modernen Demokratie*. A paperback edition was published in 1966 by Collier.

MILLS, C. WRIGHT
1956 *The Power Elite*. New York: Oxford Univ. Press.

PARSONS, TALCOTT
1953 A Revised Analytical Approach to the Theory of Social Stratification. Pages 92–128 in Reinhard Bendix and Seymour M. Lipset (editors), *Class, Status, and Power: A Reader in Social Stratification*. Glencoe, Ill.: Free Press.

PARSONS, TALCOTT
1957 The Distribution of Power in American Society. *World Politics* 10:123–143.

PARSONS, TALCOTT
(1963) 1966 On the Concept of Political Power. Pages 240–265 in Reinhard Bendix and Seymour M. Lipset (editors), *Class, Status, and Power: Social Stratification in Comparative Perspective*. 2d ed., rev. New York: Free Press. First published in Volume 107 of the American Philosophical Society *Proceedings*.

PIAO, LIN
1965 Long Live the Victory of the People's War. *Peking Review* 8, no. 36:9–39.

TUMIN, MELVIN M.
(1953) 1966 Some Principles of Stratification: A Critical Analysis. Pages 53–58 in Reinhard Bendix and Seymour M. Lipset (editors), *Class, Status, and Power: Social Stratification in Comparative Perspective*. 2d ed., rev. New York: Free Press. First published in Volume 18 of the *American Sociological Review*.

VEBLEN, THORSTEIN
(1899) 1953 *The Theory of the Leisure Class: An Economic Study of Institutions*. Rev. ed. New York: New American Library. A paperback edition was published in 1959.

WARNER, W. LLOYD
(Editor) 1941–1959 *Yankee City Series*. 5 vols. New Haven: Yale Univ. Press. An abridged edition was published in 1963 as *Yankee City*.

WEBER, MAX
(1906–1924) 1946 *From Max Weber: Essays in Sociology*. Translated and edited by Hans H. Gerth and C. Wright Mills. New York: Oxford Univ. Press.

WEBER, MAX
(1922) 1957 *The Theory of Social and Economic Organization*. Edited by Talcott Parsons. Glencoe, Ill.: Free Press. First published as Part 1 of *Wirtschaft und Gesellschaft*.

WESOLOWSKI, WLODZIMIERZ
(1962) 1966 Some Notes on the Functional Theory of Stratification. Pages 64–69 in Reinhard Bendix and Seymour M. Lipset (editors), *Class, Status, and Power: Social Stratification in Comparative Perspective*. 2d ed., rev. New York: Free Press. First published in the *Polish Sociological Review*.

Studies of Class, Power, and Status*

Alfred A. Hunter

SOME BASIC CONCEPTS IN SOCIAL STRATIFICATION

Inequalities in power and prestige define, respectively, hierarchies of *class* and *status*. While these terms are often used interchangeably, they will not be so here. As two major dimensions of stratification systems, power and prestige are analytically distinct, though theoretically and empirically related. A failure to distinguish clearly between class and status would be to confound whatever separate importance power and prestige might have for social relations.

If the young in a society tend to inherit the status of their parents, clearly defined *social strata* may develop, with clusters of people at some prestige levels and none at others. Such a development would facilitate the development of *status groups*, that is, aggregates of persons similar in prestige who are capable of acting in concert to achieve shared goals. There is nothing in the concept of a status hierarchy, however, which implies the existence of identifiable social strata, and the existence of such strata need not mean that there are status groups. People might be distributed in continuous array up and down the status hierarchy. And members of a social stratum might be unaware of their commonalities or, even if aware of them, they might be socially divided by competing ethnic, religious, or other loyalties, or physically separated from one another.

With class hierarchies, the issues are somewhat different, since the class structure within any domain of power (for example, a business firm, a labor union, or a nation state) in its most basic form consists of those who control the resources that permit them to make decisions, and those who do not (Dahrendorf, 1959: 169–71). Power, then, is discontinuous in a way that prestige is not, and the potential exists for only two classes: a *dominant class* and a *subordinate class*. In the economic division of labor in a society such as Canada, this distinction corresponds to those who own (or at least control) the means of production, as opposed to those who exchange their labor for a wage or salary (Marx and Engels, 1932; Miliband, 1969). As in the case of social strata, the existence of social classes need not imply that they are organized.

* Abridged from "Class and Status in Canada" by Alfred A. Hunter, in *Introduction to Canadian Society*, edited by G. N. Ramu and S. D. Johnson. Reprinted by permission of The Macmillan Company of Canada Limited.

    The author would like to thank Rita Bienvenue, Carl Cuneo, Jane Synge, Sharon Thompson, and two anonymous reviewers for their useful comments and suggestions.

To the extent that the status and class positions of members of a society are fixed by their status and class origins, that society has an *impermeable* stratification system (Svalastoga, 1965). Typically this means that individuals tend to inherit positions similar to those previously occupied by their parents. In so far as class and status inheritance do not occur, a society is said to have a degree of *vertical mobility*.

Often, a distinction is made between power exercised as a recognized right, termed *authority* or *legitimate power*, and other varieties of power (Weber, 1947). Thus, for example, one way in which the relationship between a major and a private can be distinguished from that between an armed robber and a victim is that the former is based on legitimate power, while the latter is not. In general, legitimate power in one domain loses legitimacy when exercised in another.

TWO MAJOR THEORIES OF SOCIAL STRATIFICATION

According to the *functional theory* of social stratification (Davis and Moore, 1945), all societies are stratified, since all societies, if they are to survive, must have essential positions occupied, and the occupants must perform their duties adequately. Consequently, members of a society must be motivated to occupy these positions and, once in them, to discharge their obligations faithfully. No special problem would exist if social positions did not differ from one another in inherent pleasantness, importance to society (functional importance), and skill requirements. Since some are more pleasant, important, and demanding in skills than others, it matters who occupies them. In order to ensure that the duties of each position are performed with a diligence appropriate to its importance, rewards must be available as inducements, and these rewards must be distributed unequally according to the pleasantness, importance, and skill requirements of each position. Thus, it is argued, the position of medical doctor carries with it substantial economic rewards and considerable prestige because of the necessarily lengthy, difficult, and expensive training, while that of waitress, an unskilled position of little importance, brings few material or symbolic benefits.

In functional theory, then, stratification arises out of the social division of labor, and is both necessary and inevitable if group life is to be maintained. Unfortunately, there seem to be no convincing examples of societies that have ceased to survive as a clear consequence of the failure of the stratification system to maintain an effective division of labor.[1] Also, the idea that positions are rewarded according to their importance to society would be much more persuasive if it could be demonstrated that some positions are functionally more important than others. A further criticism of the functional theory is that it more convincingly explains stratification as it applies to societies where location in the system is *achieved* largely through open competition with others on the basis of merit, than as it applies to societies where location tends to be fixed or *ascribed* at birth. Indeed, in the latter system, stratification would seem, if anything, to threaten the survival of group life by placing restrictions on the recruitment of persons of talent and training. Finally, functional theory seems best adapted to an analysis of inequalities in prestige and material benefits. It provides no consistent treatment of the phenomenon of power, or of its role in social stratification, even though it can be argued that inequalities in power are the very essence of stratification, and that inequalities in prestige and material rewards are at once derivative and secondary in importance (Dahrendorf, 1959; Lenski, 1966).

In the Marxian tradition (Marx, 1935, 1965; Marx and Engels, 1932) social stratification is regarded as neither necessary nor inevitable. In fact, it is viewed as the major source of social conflict and human suffering. According to Marx[2] each period in history can be described in terms of its characteristic form of economic production, which constitutes the supporting infrastructure for the legal, religious, political, and other superstructures of society. The form of production — of which modern, bourgeois capitalism is one example and feudalism another — provides the basis for a class structure, consisting ultimately of a dominant and a subordinate class, although a variety of other classes may appear and disappear from time to time before the characteristic mode of production reaches full development. For Marx, a social class is an aggregate of persons who perform a similar function in the organization of production. The crucial element in this function is not income or prestige, or even occupation as such, but whether one owns and controls the means of production, or exchanges labor for an income with someone who does. Even though two men might be engineers by occupation, if one owns a business firm and employs the other in it, the employer is a member of the dominant class, and his employee a member of the subordinate one.

Modern capitalism is distinguished by a form of production involving machines, materials, labor, and money paid in exchange for labor. In this era, there are those who own only capital, those who own only land, and those who own only their labor power. The first two combined constitute the dominant class, or *bourgeoisie*, and the third the subordinate class, or *proletariat*. If commodities produced under a capitalist system are sold at cost, no surplus value would remain for the capitalist (Marx, 1935). Since workers must provide for themselves by exchanging their labor for a wage or salary, capitalists can demand that they work extra hours for no extra pay or the same number of hours for less. By such means, the capitalist system creates surplus value and a source of profit. This profit can be consumed by members of the capitalist or bourgeois class, or it can be reinvested in equipment and materials in order to remain competitive.[3] As profits are accumulated and reinvested, wealth gathers in the hands of fewer and fewer capitalists who are able to take over the businesses of poorer capitalists, thereby increasing efficiency and eliminating competition. As a result, wages fall, unemployment rises, and business cycles become increasingly severe. At the same time, members of the working class or proletariat become more and more dissatisfied with their inability to acquire an equitable share of the available economic rewards, and are increasingly aware that together they form an oppressed, exploited class. Their dissatisfaction and class consciousness promote organization for political action, culminating in the overthrow of the bourgeoisie and the creation of a communist society devoid of private property, class, inequality, and conflict. Devoid also of any division of labor:

> In communist society where nobody has one exclusive sphere of activity but each can become accomplished in any branch he wishes, society regulates the general production and thus makes it possible for me to do one thing today and another tomorrow, to hunt in the morning, fish in the afternoon, rear cattle in the evening, criticize after dinner... without ever becoming hunter, fisherman, shepherd or critic (Marx 1965: 45).

Marx identified the locus of social stratification primarily in class structures generated by the existence of private property, and only secondarily in such factors as the occupational structure. Class, defined in relation to the means of production, was the central issue. While he scarcely denied the existence of inequalities in material rewards and prestige, he saw them as ultimately the consequence of property relations.

Marxian analysis has been the object of much debate (Bottomore, 1966; Dahrendorf, 1959: Part One). One potentially major difficulty lies in its characterization of the relationship between ownership and control, which Marx originally viewed as inseparable in capitalism. The emergence of the joint stock corporation in more recent times, however, has created the possibility of the separation of ownership and control and, thus, the possibility of eliminating the very basis of class and class conflict. If ownership is widely diffused among the population in the form of stock ownership, and if control resides in a group of managers who run the affairs of corporations for the stockholders' benefit, then Marx's analysis could be a historical anachronism, or at least in need of fundamental revision. The evidence does suggest that relatively little separation of ownership and control has occurred in Canada (Porter, 1965: 242). At the same time, the possibility of separation has prompted a re-analysis of the entire issue, with the result that some theorists now hold the position that it is control, not ownership, which provides the basis for class formation (Dahrendorf, 1959: 136–41; Miliband, 1969: 23–45).

CANADIAN CLASS STRUCTURE

In Canada, a substantial and increasing proportion of women and the overwhelming majority of men are employed or self-employed outside the home. If only those between 25 and 54 years of age are considered, since many of those younger still attend educational institutions of various kinds, and large numbers of those who are older have retired, virtually all men in Canada are gainfully employed, temporarily laid off, or in search of employment. While almost 40 percent of all women 15 years of age and over were in the labor force in 1971, single women have higher participation rates than the widowed and divorced, who, in turn, have higher rates than married women. In fact, most single women are gainfully employed, along with a majority of widowed and divorced women. An increasing minority of married women are in the labor force. During the child-bearing years, labor-force participation among married women is lower than it is either before or after (Allingham, 1967).

What kinds of occupations do the more than nine million Canadians in the labor force pursue? They are occupations in which income is earned through employment, rather than self-employment. Fully 86 percent of the work force in 1971 received a wage or salary through employment, while the remaining 14 percent received income from self-employment (Department of National Revenue, 1973: 13). In that same year, about 63 percent of all Canadians reporting an income received a wage or salary through employment in a business firm, about 12 percent through direct employment in federal, provincial, or municipal government, and most of the remainder through indirect governmental employment (hospitals, prisons, schools, and universities). Approximately four percent were self-employed as business proprietors, and eight percent as investors, property owners, farmers, and fishermen.

Perhaps the most significant factor is that, in the brief period of Canadian history, the nation has been transformed from one in which the majority were self-employed to one in which they are now in the employ of others. Where once small businessmen, independent craftsmen, and farmers — the Marxian petite bourgeoisie — were numerically dominant, the labor force has been, in Marxian terms, proletarianized, and the class structure greatly simplified (Johnson, 1972). Beginning in the late nineteenth century the development of modern capitalism, with its large-scale, centralized production and distribution facilities, placed small businessman and independent commodity producer alike at a competitive disadvantage from which they were unable to recover. As a result, a numerically large class of small businessmen, independent craftsmen, and farmers were replaced by a small class of owners and managers presiding over large corporate enterprises, often employing many thousands of workers, and with assets in the millions of dollars. As Johnson observes, "With the decline of the petite bourgeoisie and the consolidation and maturation of capitalism, a new situation — one more closely resembling Marx's delineation of a capitalist economy — has emerged" (1972: 178).

Working-Class Structure and Organization[4]

While the overall size of the labor force has grown enormously since the turn of the century, this growth has not touched all occupational categories equally. Some categories have actually experienced large, numerical declines. During this period there has been a substantial increase in the proportion of persons employed in white-collar occupations, while by contrast the proportion involved in primary occupations has declined sharply. The representation of blue-collar workers has remained quite stable during this 60-year span, while that of transportation and communication workers, as well as those in service occupations, has increased.

Among white-collar occupations, there has been some proportional growth, with clerical occupations, especially in the 1941–61 period, leading the way. The proprietary and managerial category as a whole has grown least rapidly, but growth patterns for occupations within this category have been far from uniform. In general, independent proprietors have declined as a proportion of the labor force, while managers have increased (Ostry, 1967: 11). The professional category increased fairly steadily in the period 1901–41, and rather more rapidly since that time. Commercial-financial occupations have continued to grow steadily, if not rapidly. Among blue-collar occupations, the construction category has varied little since the turn of the century in its proportion of the labor force, while the other two categories have been more volatile. The proportion of the labor force in the laborer category increased quite sharply in the early years of the twentieth century in Canada, only to begin a decline which has continued to the present. Except for a sharp decline between 1901 and 1921, the manufacturing-mechanical category has more or less maintained its proportional share of the labor force. The greatest change which has occurred in the occupational structure since the turn of the century has been the decline in the agricultural sector. In 1901 fully 40.3 percent of the labor force were engaged in agricultural pursuits. By 1961 this figure had dropped to 10.0 percent. In fact, the actual number of persons engaged in agricultural occupations increased in the period 1901–31. Since 1941 the representation of the agricultural sector has decreased both proportionally and in absolute numbers to the point that, as of 1951, the manufacturing-mechanical category replaced the agricultural as the largest in the occupational structure. The remaining occupational categories — transportation-communication and service — have displayed slow and generally steady growth since 1901.

Table I shows the percentage distribution of the labor force by broad occupational categories for 1971. The introduction of a new occupational classification scheme for the 1971 Census of Canada precludes any precise comparisons between 1971 and earlier years at the present time.

While there has been a great increase in the proportion of the labor force employed (as opposed to self-employed), only a minority of paid workers belong to labor unions, and the labor movement in Canada is dominated by a small number of large, politically conservative, international unions with headquarters in the United States (Lipton, 1972). About one-third of all non-agricultural, paid workers in Canada are members of labor unions, up from less than one-sixth in 1921. Very few agricultural workers belong to unions. Unionization is most advanced in transportation, storage, and communication (53.0 percent in 1961), logging (51.4 percent), public utilities (50.2 percent), and mining (49.1 percent), and least advanced in service (15.2 percent), fishing (12.7 percent), and trade (4.8 percent). The manufacturing and construction sectors were 39.7 percent and 35.7 percent unionized in 1961 (Porter, 1969: 99). In general, blue-collar workers are more highly unionized than are white-collar workers, although union membership has grown more rapidly among the latter than among the former in recent years.

As Johnson (1972) points out, labor unions have been most successful in organizing workers and exacting relatively high wages from employers in monopolistic industries with expensive production facilities, such as automobile manufacturing, steel, and chemicals. This has happened partly because of the

TABLE I   Percentage Distribution of Labor Force, 15 Years and over, by Occupation Division, for Canada, 1971

Occupation division	Percentage
Managerial, administrative, and related	4.3
Natural sciences, engineering, and mathematics	2.7
Social sciences and related	0.9
Religion	0.3
Teaching and related	4.1
Medicine and health	3.8
Artistic, literary, recreational, and related	0.9
Clerical and related	15.9
Sales	9.5
Service	11.2
Farming, horticultural, and animal husbandry	5.9
Fishing, hunting, trapping, and related	0.3
Forestry and logging	0.8
Mining and quarrying	0.7
Processing	3.9
Machining and related	2.8
Product fabricating, assembling, and repairing	7.4
Construction trades	6.6
Transport equipment operating	3.9
Materials handling, not elsewhere classified	2.4
Other crafts and equipment operating	1.3
Not elsewhere classified	1.9
Not stated	8.6
Total	100.0

Source: Derived from *1971 Census of Canada*, Cat. 94-717.

considerable expense that would be involved were these industries to relocate in a low-wage area, and partly because increased labor costs can generally be passed on to the consumer in the form of higher prices. Competitive industries requiring relatively little in the way of capital investment are more likely to relocate or to cease operations when faced with rising labor costs, making a union's task much more difficult. Consequently, workers in such industries (textiles, furniture manufacturing, and garment manufacturing) receive much lower wages and are much less likely to be organized. The result has been a major division between two large classes of paid workers, which, combined with the conservative politics and international structure of most large labor unions, makes it unlikely that the Canadian labor movement in its present form will provide a vehicle for organized class action. Nor is it likely that organized labor's voice in Parliament or the New Democratic Party will provide that vehicle. As Teeple has argued, "The reason why the Canadian Labour Congress — in essence, the coalition of American-based unions in Canada — has affiliated with the NDP is to win political concessions in the form of 'better' labor legislation" (1972: 246).

Elite Structure and Organization

If access to power in Canadian society is gained through positions that provide effective control of productive private property, then it is clear from the data presented above that only a tiny minority of Canadians could possibly be described as members of the dominant class or economic elite. Who, then, constitute this minority? And to what extent, if any, might they be described as taking on the character of an organized group?

To date, there have been three major studies of the Canadian economic elite: a little-known one by Libbie and Frank Park (1962, 1973), a celebrated one by Porter (1965), and a partial replication and extension of Porter's work by Clement (1975).

The Parks address themselves to the question of "who owns Canada," and analyze in detail what they see as "the structure of Canadian monopoly and the alliance of Canadian and U.S. capital that is bringing about U.S. domination of Canada" (p. xv). Beginning with the premise that "control is based on ownership and that without ownership control vanishes" (p. 11), they attempt to identify the members of Canada's dominant class "that owns and controls the mines and mills and factories of Canada" (p. 10). These persons, they argue, form a tightly knit group, who, on the basis of an ideology of corporate internationalism, are selling the country out to United States financiers (see Levitt, 1970). They note that "at the centre of this financial and industrial corporate structure lie the chartered banks, the members of whose boards of directors make up the 'Who's Who' of the dominant financial groups" (p. 71), and then try to show how the same group of financiers dominates both industry and the banks through the mechanism of overlapping board memberships. While the Parks agree in retrospect that their analysis was too narrowly economic (p. ix), their work provides an effective theoretical counterbalance to Porter's and, especially in its focus on the extensive and increasing penetration of United States-based multinational corporations into the Canadian economy, a useful supplement as well.

Porter identified the "economic elite of Canada ... as the 985 Canadian residents holding directorships in the 170 dominant corporations, the banks, insurance companies, and numerous other corporations" (p. 274). The 760 of these persons for whom relevant additional information was available held 82 percent of the directorships in the dominant corporations held by Canadian residents. Porter points out two striking aspects of the careers of these persons: a very high proportion had fathers who were members of the elite before them, and almost all achieved their positions of dominance within established corporations. Only a tiny minority came from non-elite families and went on to establish business firms which prospered and grew to dominance.

The homogeneity of background among members of the economic elite was quite remarkable. Not only did many come from elite backgrounds, but the majority were university-educated, Protestant, Anglophone males, and better than one-third had attended private schools, such as Upper Canada College. Virtually absent were Jews and Francophones. Totally absent were women. Among those elite members whose political preferences could be determined, approximately one-half supported the Progressive Conservatives, and the other half the Liberals. No New Democratic Party supporters were found.

As Porter showed, "Economic power belongs almost exclusively to those of British origin" (p. 286). Even though over 30 percent of the Canadian population are Francophone, they made up only 6.7 percent of the economic elite. Jews made up 0.78 percent of the elite and 1.4 percent of the population as a whole. Given the over-representation of Jews in upper-level, white-collar occupations (to be discussed below), their virtual absence among the elite is all the more notable.

The Royal Commission on Bilingualism and Biculturalism (1969: 53–60) found that, even within Quebec, Francophone entrepreneurs do not operate on a scale comparable to that of Anglophone Canadians in that province. Francophone business firms are concentrated in the agricultural and service fields, whereas those owned by Anglophones are more evenly distributed across industrial sectors of the economy. Moreover, Francophone manufacturing firms employ fewer persons, yield less added value, are less productive, pay lower wages, and are more localized in the distribution of their products than are Anglophone manufacturing firms.

The high degree of homogeneity in social background among elite members, Porter argues, has produced a group of persons very similar in belief and attitude. It is a similarity reinforced through informal social contact, kinship, and membership in certain exclusive clubs. Porter observes that "the elite world appears as a complex network of small groupings interlocked by a high degree of cross-membership" (p. 304). This cross-membership is important in the degree that it permits and facilitates co-operation and internal co-ordination among members of the economic elite, particularly in the conduct of business. As unrelated individuals, each controls enormous economic resources. Were they able to operate as a group, their pooled resources would, of course, be many times larger. In fact, "the boards of the dominant corporations...are...woven by the interlocking directorship into a fabric not unlike the web of kinship and lineage which provides cohesion to primitive life" (p. 304). Of the 907 elite members for whom the relevant data could be obtained, about 22 percent held directorships in more than one dominant corporation, and most sat on the boards of other corporations not classified as dominant. One person held ten director-ships. The majority of those sitting on the boards of the nine chartered banks were also directors of dominant corporations. Likewise, there was considerable overlap in membership among the boards of directors of dominant corporations and the major life insurance companies. In aggregate, this evidence suggests a high degree of potential co-ordination among members of the economic elite (pp. 578–80).

From a Marxian point of view, the economic elite *is* the dominant class. For Porter, the economic elite happened to be the first among several, including elites from politics, the federal bureaucracy, the ideological system (mass media, higher learning, and the clergy), and labor. He found that in general the social backgrounds of members of the various elites were very similar, with the exception of the labor elite. Many friendship and kinship ties also bound members of different elites together, and there was even considerable movement in membership among elites—all of which is conducive to a degree of inter-elite co-ordination, although Porter is careful to point out that conflict does occur. Among the several elites, in Porter's judgment, labor was probably the least powerful, the most isolated from other elites, and the most distinctive in the relatively modest social origins of its members.

Following Porter's lead, Clement located the economic elite in those who through a "corporate mirage... preside over the corporate world, using as their means of power, the central institutions of the Canadian economy — 113 dominant corporations, their subsidiaries, affiliates, investments, interlocking directorships with smaller corporations, family ties and shared class origins" (p. 125). These 113 corporations had 1,454 directorships held by Canadian residents, and an additional 306 held by persons living outside the country—mainly in the United States and the United Kingdom (p. 167). Those holding multiple directorships, his data revealed, held among them 54 percent of the total number of directorships, with 29 percent of the 946 members of the elite holding more than one directorship, and one member holding a total of eight. In comparing these findings with Porter's, Clement concludes that "there has been ... an increasing centralization and concentration of capital into fewer and larger firms" (p. 168), and that there has been "a further concentration of power at the top of the economic elite over the past twenty years" (p. 168). It should be pointed out, however, that differences in the manner in which Porter and Clement define such critical terms as "dominant corporation" and consequently "economic elite" render *any* comparisons between the two studies problematic. Clement's conclusions may be true, but they do not follow directly from the data he presents.

CANADIAN STATUS STRUCTURE

According to the functional theory of stratification, "a man qualifies himself for occupational life by obtaining an education; as a consequence of pursuing his occupation he obtains income" (Duncan, 1961: 116). In addition to material benefits, he or she also receives symbolic rewards in the form of prestige. The next section is devoted to an analysis of how material and symbolic benefits are distributed among Canadians, and in particular how they are tied to positions in the occupational structure. A discussion of recruitment patterns will follow and finally some comments will be offered on inter-generational mobility in Canada.

Positional Stratification

In 1971, 82 percent of all income reported in tax returns came from employment (wages, salaries, and commissions), six percent was business and professional income, and an additional six percent came from investments (Department of National Revenue, 1973). Only those with very low incomes depend heavily upon transfer payments for their income, while investment income forms a significant part of the total incomes of the very poor and the very well-to-do, but not of the majority of people. Only those in the very highest income brackets receive large amounts of money from investments (Podoluk, 1968: 146).

In 1970, 24 percent of the population 15 years of age and over reported no money income from any source, and 12 percent of those reporting at least some income received less than $1,000. The average individual income for that year was $5,033, and slightly more than eight percent of the population reported an income of $10,000 or more. Information on individual incomes does not provide a complete picture of the financial resources to which most persons have access, however, since most belong to family units in which more than one person receives income. Indeed, about nine out of ten persons in Canada belong to a family unit, and the approximately five million families in the country reported an average income of $9,600 for 1970. About three percent of these families reported less than $1,000 in income for the year, and 39 percent reported $10,000 or more. Of those persons not attached to families, some one million in all, 19 percent received less than $1,000, and five percent received $10,000 or more. The average income in 1970 for unattached persons was $3,261.

Between one-quarter and one-third of all non-farm families with both a husband and a wife present have both in the labor force. In 1961 the labor-force participation of wives had the overall effect of increasing family income by about 13 percent. As Podoluk notes, "Obviously, the presence of the wife in the labor force is, for many families, the means by which families can move into middle-income brackets" (1968: 132–33).

In analyzing incomes, the concept of poverty is frequently used and variously defined. A Special Senate Committee, organized to study poverty in Canada, established a series of poverty lines for family units of different sizes, then estimated the number of units falling below the poverty line, as shown in Table II. In 1969 it was estimated that

> the overall poverty rate for that year was approximately 25.1 percent; that is, one Canadian in four was a member of a family unit whose income was below the poverty line.... the incidence of poverty... was highest among unattached individuals, two-person families, and families with five or more members. The lowest incidence was among families with three and four members (Special Senate Committee, 1971: 11).

These estimates are based on the incomes of Canadians *including* government transfer payments.

In a variation on the poverty line theme, Porter considered the proportion of families able to achieve a "middle class life-style" (1965: 129–32). He estimated that, in the mid- to late 1950s, this life-style (which included, at the time, an automobile, some equity in a suburban home, a television set, central heating, regular dental checkups, and children bound for university — all paid for by a single wage-earner) was certainly beyond the means of 50 percent, and perhaps available to no more than 10 percent, of all Canadian families.

Of course, poverty lines are always arbitrary, however carefully they might be chosen. For this reason, and because it is more consistent with the general approach taken in this chapter, it is probably more useful to consider how equally or unequally the available income is distributed within the population. It is difficult to summarize inequalities in the overall distribution of incomes simply

TABLE II Poverty Rates by Family Size, Canada, 1969

Family unit size	Poverty line (dollars)	Number of family units below poverty line (thousands)	Poverty rate (per cent)
1	2,140	629	38.7
2	3,570	408	28.4
3	4,290	161	16.8
4	5,000	157	15.6
5 or more*	6,570	416	28.5

*Figures based on average unit size of 6.2.
Source: Table adapted from Special Senate Committee, 1971: 12.

or neatly, but some measure of them can be gained from knowing, for example, that approximately 40 percent of all non-farm-family income after transfer payments goes to the top 20 percent of all non-farm families, whereas the bottom 20 percent of these families receive less than seven percent of all income (Adams *et al.*, 1971: 21). Postwar changes in the income distribution, especially in very recent years, seem generally to have been to the benefit of the top one third of income earners in Canada, and to the detriment of the rest (Johnson, 1973).

It is important to note that these income inequalities seem to persist and increase partly as a result of the income tax structure, rather than in spite of it. Drawing on the work of Maslove (1972), Clement argues that "in Canada the overall tax structure is regressive at the under-$6,000 level (that is, the lower the income the higher the taxation rate) and only proportional above $6,000 (the same rate over a range of incomes)" (1975: 122). Not only does Canada apparently have a regressive income-tax structure, but federal and provincial income-tax revenues have been drawn increasingly from individuals, and less and less from corporations (Deaton, 1972).

The amount of income received is a function of whether or not one is in the labor force to begin with and just what occupations those who are pursue. Table III gives the average incomes of males and females in different occupations for 1970. As these data reveal, even when very broad categories of occupations are considered, the economic rewards attached to different categories vary enormously.

When specific occupations are considered, the contrasts in income from occupation to occupation are often far greater than those reported above, as can be seen from Table IV.

The relative income levels for different occupational categories have varied a good deal over time. Between 1931 and 1951, the incomes of professionals and managers declined relative to those of occupational groups generally (Meltz, 1968: 17), while this trend was reversed in the decade 1951–61. The relative earnings of manufacturing and construction occupations, as well as of laborers, increased in the period 1931–51, and then decreased between 1951 and 1961. In the years between 1931 and 1941, the relative incomes of those employed in

TABLE III   Average Incomes for Males and Females, 15 Years and over, Who Worked in 1970, by Occupational Division, for Canada, 1971

Occupation division	Average income	
	Males	Females
Managerial, administrative, and related	$13,407	$6,135
Natural sciences, engineering, and mathematics	8,905	4,750
Social sciences and related	10,971	4,441
Religion	4,738	3,065
Teaching and related	9,014	5,401
Medicine and health	14,175	4,135
Artistic, literary, recreational, and related	6,545	3,274
Clerical and related	5,823	3,391
Sales	7,120	2,285
Service	5,276	1,954
Farming, horticultural, and animal husbandry	3,321	1,541
Fishing, hunting, trapping, and related	3,340	1,669
Forestry and logging	4,544	1,668
Mining and quarrying	6,966	4,577
Processing	5,957	2,563
Machining and related	6,695	3,263
Product fabricating, assembling, and repairing	6,402	2,828
Construction trades	6,175	3,708
Transport equipment operating	6,190	2,722
Materials handling, not elsewhere classified	5,141	2,551
Other crafts and equipment operating	7,528	3,122
Not elsewhere classified	4,496	2,603
Not stated	5,418	2,794
Total	6,574	3,199

Source: *1971 Census of Canada*, Cat. 94-768.

agricultural and service occupations decreased, and then increased in the years 1941–61. The relative incomes of clerical, communications, and transportation occupations have declined continuously since 1931.

Occupations are not only the source of most people's incomes, they are also a source of prestige (Pineo and Porter, 1967). A variety of empirical studies conducted in Canada and elsewhere show that people can rank occupations in terms of their "social standing" or prestige, and that there is a certain amount of agreement in their rankings.

Interestingly, the prestige scores accorded different occupations in Canada and the United States are, with few exceptions, virtually identical (Pineo and Porter, 1967). An analysis of Anglophone-Francophone differences in occupational prestige evaluations in Canada conducted by the author revealed few substantial differences, and those which were found did not generally follow any obvious pattern.

Since all persons are not equally rewarded, and since the material and symbolic rewards most people receive are in large measure determined by their

TABLE IV   Average Incomes for Males and Females, 15 Years and over, Who Worked in 1970, 12 Selected Occupations, for Canada, 1971

Occupation	Average income	
	Males	Females
Physicians and surgeons	$26,900	$11,054
Veterinarians	14,912	6,731
Architects	14,405	5,391
University professors	13,667	7,608
Civil engineers	11,417	7,481
Commercial travelers	8,935	4,030
Insurance agents	8,680	4,485
Funeral directors	8,155	3,392
Bartenders	4,213	2,388
Cooks	4,000	2,299
Fishermen	3,141	1,992
Newsvendors	901	1,142

Source: *1971 Census of Canada*, Cat. 94-768.

occupations, it is reasonable to inquire why some occupations are more highly rewarded than others. According to the functional theory of stratification, the two major factors in the stratification of positions are their functional importance and their skill requirements. If the idea of functional importance can be set aside on the grounds that it is too imprecise to be immediately useful, we are left with the notion that some occupations are more highly rewarded than others largely because powerful incentives must be made available before people will be willing to undergo the demanding period of training which they require.

Consistent with what one would expect from the functional theory, it is generally true that those occupations whose incumbents have high levels of educational attainment tend to bring with them substantial economic and prestige rewards. At the same time, the correspondence between educational levels and rewards is far from perfect. Some occupations, for instance, are grossly overpaid relative to their educational levels, while others are grossly underpaid. Physicians and surgeons, dentists, lawyers, and airline pilots all receive much higher incomes than one would expect on the basis of their education, as do proprietors and managers of businesses generally. University professors, architects, school teachers, and professional social workers, to name but a few, have traditionally received less income than their educational levels would seem to warrant.[6] What is the reason for such discrepancies?

One possibility is that members of some occupations whose educational requirements could entitle them to higher incomes, might accept lower remuneration in exchange for other benefits, such as an added occupational prestige. Conversely, members of other occupations might forgo a degree of prestige in exchange for extra income. Still, this compensatory-reward hypothesis does not adequately account for the lack of correspondence between educational levels and economic rewards. University professors, for example, on the average have as much education and occupational prestige as physicians and surgeons, but only about half the income.

Another possibility lies in the fact that many of the relatively overpaid occupations have organized their memberships into groups which actively seek to maintain a monopoly over the services they offer, and which attempt to restrict access to group membership in order to keep their numbers small. This combination of monopolistic control and restricted access can ensure that there will be limited competition for clients and fees: competition would mean reduced income levels. Medicine, dentistry, and law all afford good illustrations of this approach. The medical profession, for example, has done battle to restrict the activities of chiropractors, optometrists, naturopaths, and acupuncturists — all of whom have posed some threat to the profession's organized monopoly on what it defines as "medical practice." Indeed, to practise medicine without a licence is a legal offence, and the profession carefully supervises the processes by which licences are obtained.[7] Many of the relatively underpaid occupations, however, are conspicuous by their lack of monopolistic control and ability to restrict access to membership. University professors, for instance, are often reluctant to organize in this collective self-interest, preferring to regard the university as a benevolent community of scholars, each in pursuit of his or her own intellectual goals. Insofar as these processes operate in the fashion described, it is difficult to see how they could be explained in terms of the functional theory of stratification.

While occupations are generally rewarded according to their educational requirements, it seems clear that the bulk of the labor force are over-educated in relation to the skill demands of their occupations. And the degree to which they are over-educated continues to increase. Table V provides information on the rising levels of educational attainment of persons in different occupational categories. As Collins (1971) argues, competition for a small number of desired occupational positions has led to an increase in the general educational level of the population. This development has not been accompanied by a proportional increase in the number of elite jobs available, with the result that there has been a progressive increase in the educational requirements for jobs generally, independent of any changes in skill requirements. There seems to be no obvious way to explain the phenomenon of over-education in strictly functional terms.

In the functional theory of stratification, it is generally assumed that extended formal training is necessary to provide the skills that persons in most high-status occupations must have. Serious questions can often be raised, however, about the value of such training for the acquisition of job-related skills (Berg, 1970). Graduate engineers, for example, often find that their first job begins with a lengthy and intensive company-sponsored training program. Newly minted lawyers who join established law firms typically find that they spend their early years performing routine, almost clerical, duties. And Doctor X (Doctor X, 1965) did not feel that medical school equipped physicians adequately for the practice of medicine. It would not stretch the point too far to mention the many instances in which persons with little or no formal training have successfully masqueraded as physicians, dentists, engineers, and university professors, often

TABLE V   Percentage of Labor Force, 15 Years and over, with Nine Years or More Formal Education, by Occupation Division, for Canada, 1941, 1951, and 1961

Occupation division	Percentage			Change
	1941	1951	1961	1941–61
White collar	75.8	79.8	83.8	+ 8.0
Proprietary, managerial	56.9	66.5	73.6	+16.7
Professional	92.7	96.6	95.5	+ 2.8
Clerical	82.4	84.3	87.1	+ 4.7
Commercial, financial	65.8	69.0	73.6	+ 7.8
Blue collar	36.7	39.3	45.6	+ 8.9
Manufacturing, mechanical	41.7	41.9	47.2	+ 5.5
Construction	33.5	38.0	43.8	+10.3
Laborers*	24.3	26.3	33.8	+ 9.5
Primary	19.0	23.2	31.1	+12.1
Agricultural	19.4	24.0	31.9	+12.5
Fishing, hunting, trapping	12.1	15.8	22.0	+ 9.9
Logging	11.9	15.9	22.7	+10.8
Mining, quarrying	26.3	30.0	38.5	+12.2
Transportation, communication	36.3	41.6	48.4	+12.1
Service	37.3	40.4	47.2	+ 9.9

*Except those in Primary.
Source: Derived from Meltz, 1968: 221.

to have their very success lead to their discovery (for example, Crichton, 1959). While it would be misleading to infer from these examples that the educational requirements of occupations are wholly arbitrary, some of the reasons behind them should be explored further.

One reason would seem to be that employers find educational requirements useful in selecting employees who are likely to share their general values, attitudes, and life-style preferences (Collins, 1974). Employers are often willing to pay more for well-educated workers — even though the less well-educated might be just as capable of doing the work — because they are more likely to be socially acceptable persons in the employer's terms of reference.

Recruitment

Recruitment to positions in the division of labor in Canada takes place in a complex process of ascription, achievement, and random selection, only the outlines of which are presently understood.

Sex and Stratification

Perhaps the most fundamental and pervasive ascriptive criterion used in the assignment of persons to positions is sex. Generally, women are less likely to be employed outside the home than men, and those women who are employed are less likely to be employed full time. Podoluk notes that "the principal explanation given for not working a full year was staying home and keeping house" (1968: 37). When one member of a family withdraws from the labor force to manage a household, it is generally the wife who does so.[8]

Those women who are employed are highly concentrated in a relatively small number of occupations traditionally regarded as appropriate for women, many of which are extensions into the labor market of traditional household tasks (for example, maid, waitress, nurse, nursing assistant or aide, janitor or cleaner, hairdresser, and school teacher). In addition, women have increasingly moved into white-collar occupations, most notably stenographer and sales clerk, which accounted for about 17 percent of all women working outside the home in 1961 (Ostry, 1967: 27). Between 1901 and 1961, women's share of clerical occupations trebled, increasing from 20 to 60 percent, and their share of commercial occupations quadrupled, growing from about 10 to approximately 40 percent.

The considerable increase in labor-force participation among women, which was noted earlier, has not led to growth in all areas of the occupational structure. As Ostry points out, "The female share of the professional work force in 1961 was lower than at any period in this century except 1901" (1967: 28), and certain of the better-paid occupations dominated by women, such as school teaching, are increasingly being selected by men. Most women in blue-collar occupations are found in manufacturing and mechanical jobs, although their share of these has declined from 25 percent in 1901 to 17 percent in 1961. Since 1931 there has been a large increase in the representation of women in the agricultural sector, from about two percent in 1931 to over 10 percent in 1961. In the period 1901–61, the representation of women in transportation and communication occupations has increased from about one percent to nearly eight percent. Nearly 70 percent of the service occupations were held by women in 1901, but their representation had fallen to less than 50 percent by 1961. If personal service occupations alone are considered, however, the drop has not been quite so large.

In general, the occupations in which women are concentrated are lower in both prestige and income than the occupations of men. In 1970 women in the labor force earned on the average less than half of what their male counterparts earned. This discrepancy is partly due to differences in their occupations. Part of it is also due to the fact that men are more likely to be employed full time throughout the year. If we compare men and women employed full time in the same occupations, however, substantial income differences remain. Podoluk argues that continuity of employment and occupation "are likely to explain away less than half of the gap that exists" (1968: 69).

In their study of Canadian university teachers, Robson and Lapointe found that "at the same type of university . . . in the same field, with the same rank and with the same competence (measured by the highest earned degree) women earn, on the average, $1,199 less than men" (1971: 4). When this difference is projected over an entire career, and when we consider that many fringe benefits are based on earnings, the gap between males and females of apparently equivalent experience, competence, and occupational standing is very large indeed.

The gap is even larger when it is considered that men and women of equivalent competence or training do not generally work at the same jobs. Although women are concentrated in relatively low-paying, low-prestige occupations, on average, women in the Canadian labor force are not obviously less well educated than men as can be seen from Table VI.[9] Thus, equivalent educations do not yield equivalent jobs, and equivalent jobs do not yield equivalent incomes and related economic benefits.

If many women do not work outside the home at all, or if those who do find they are unable to compete on equal ground with men, it is neither an accident nor a law of nature which makes it so. It is a social fact. It can be seen most clearly, perhaps, in male-female occupational differences as these vary over time and from society to society. Films and stories of Soviet women working on road construction strike many as highly humorous, but what is revealed is a society

TABLE VI   Percentage of Males and Females, 15 Years and over, in the Labor Force, with Nine Years or More Schooling, by Occupation Division, for Canada, 1971

Occupation division	Percentage	
	Males	Females
Managerial, administrative, and related	93.7	94.3
Natural sciences, engineering, and mathematics	95.9	96.0
Social sciences and related	97.3	96.1
Religion	93.4	79.9
Teaching and related	98.8	98.7
Medicine and health	92.0	92.0
Artistic, literary, recreational, and related	89.2	93.4
Clerical and related	85.4	94.1
Sales	82.4	80.1
Service	65.2	61.7
Farming, horticultural, and animal husbandry	51.7	55.2
Fishing, hunting, trapping, and related	32.2	46.7
Forestry and logging	43.3	57.4
Mining and quarrying	55.4	61.8
Processing	56.8	46.7
Machining and related	62.4	57.3
Product fabricating, assembling, and repairing	63.7	44.7
Construction trades	55.0	61.6
Transport equipment operating	56.0	70.1
Materials handling, not elsewhere classified	60.1	56.6
Other crafts and equipment operating	75.1	71.8
Not elsewhere classified	59.3	58.6
Not stated	64.4	67.2
Total	69.2	79.3

Source: Derived from *1971 Census of Canada*, Cat. 94-729.

TABLE VII Percentage of Labor Force, 15 Years and over, by Ethnic Group and Occupation Division, for Canada, 1971

Occupation division	Ethnic group						
	British	French	German	Italian	Jewish	Ukrainian	Indian and Eskimo
Managerial, administrative, and related	6.9	4.6	4.5	2.3	14.2	3.8	1.6
Natural sciences, engineering, and mathematics	4.4	2.5	3.7	1.7	3.5	3.6	1.4
Social sciences and related	1.0	0.8	0.5	0.3	3.6	0.6	1.3
Religion	0.4	0.4	0.5	0.1	0.3	0.2	0.1
Teaching and related	2.5	2.5	2.3	1.1	3.5	2.4	0.7
Medicine and health	1.4	1.5	1.1	0.5	5.1	1.2	0.5
Artistic, literary, recreational, and related	1.1	1.0	0.8	0.7	2.2	0.8	1.1
Clerical and related	8.6	8.1	5.6	4.8	8.8	6.7	3.0
Sales	11.2	9.3	9.0	6.9	27.6	8.3	2.3
Service	9.1	9.1	7.3	11.2	4.9	9.0	7.3
Farming, horticultural, and animal husbandry	6.7	5.3	14.3	2.1	0.5	13.2	7.5
Fishing, hunting, trapping, and related	0.6	0.4	0.2	0.0*	0.0*	0.1	3.0
Forestry and logging	0.9	1.9	0.7	0.3	0.0*	0.6	8.9
Mining and quarrying	0.9	1.3	1.0	0.6	0.0*	1.3	1.5
Processing	4.1	6.1	4.7	6.7	1.8	4.8	4.8
Machining and related	3.4	4.0	4.9	6.9	0.8	4.0	2.6
Product fabricating, assembling, and repairing	7.7	9.0	9.4	12.0	7.8	8.7	4.1
Construction trades	8.6	10.1	11.8	22.2	2.6	10.0	13.7
Transport equipment operating	6.3	6.6	5.2	3.7	2.6	5.7	4.7
Materials handling, not elsewhere classified	3.1	2.6	2.9	3.2	0.9	3.6	3.9
Other crafts and equipment operating	2.0	1.7	1.4	0.9	0.8	1.4	0.9
Not elsewhere classified	2.3	3.0	2.1	4.4	1.3	2.7	4.4
Not stated	6.8	8.2	6.1	7.4	7.2	7.3	20.7
Total	100.0	100.0	100.0	100.0	100.0	100.0	100.0

*Less than 0.0 per cent, but not empty category.

Source: Derived from *1971 Census of Canada*, Cat. 94-734.

where such a role is not at all unnatural. Lane notes that "by 1967 women ... accounted for 52 percent of all professional employees in the USSR, including 72 percent of the doctors, 68 percent of the teachers, and 63 percent of the economists" (1971: 88). This situation, too, is in sharp contrast to the position of women in Canada. But few are likely to see these facts as whimsical, because they indicate that not only are women fully capable of working at physically demanding jobs that are generally regarded as undesirable, but they are also fully capable of working at very desirable jobs, many of which are more or less reserved for men in Canada.

Occupations are, of course, sex-typed, and even employment itself is viewed in Canada as more appropriate for men than for women. If women do not work outside the home, if they have discontinuous careers, or if they tend disproportionately to work at certain kinds of jobs, it is because of the social role assigned to them in our society. It is a social role defined in beliefs and values, learned in a process of childhood socialization, and buttressed by legal, economic, religious, and other institutional arrangements.

Ethnicity and Stratification

Ethnicity is another important ascriptive criterion used in recruitment. Table VII shows the degree to which the occupations pursued by members of different ethnic groups vary. In general, Jews are over-represented in high-prestige, high-paying occupations, along with those of British origin, while members of the other ethnic groups are under-represented in varying degrees. With some exceptions, differences in the occupational structures of these groups are constant from one province to another, but they have varied significantly over time. The overall thrust of these temporal changes has been in the direction of increasing inter-group differences, with those of Jewish and British origins strengthening their hold on occupations at the top of the hierarchy, at the expense of members of other ethnic groups.[10]

The relative positions of the British and the French in the occupational structures of the ten provinces are very similar — despite the fact that large numbers of French outside Quebec report English as their mother tongue. Another apparent anomaly occurs within Quebec, where the British enjoy an even larger advantage over the French through their grip on professional and managerial occupations than they do in the country as a whole. Moreover, within the city of Montreal itself, their advantage is greater yet. The evidence suggests that these varying disparities between the British and French occur more as a result of differences in the relative positions of the British in the occupational structures of Montreal and the Province of Quebec, than of the French (Royal Commission, 1969: 45).

Differences among Canada's ethnic groups in levels of educational attainment closely parallel differences among them in their occupational structures. Jews clearly stand out above the rest, followed at some distance by the British. Lowest of all are Indians and Eskimos. These differences are such that, "if the labour force of French origin had a level of education equivalent to the British, the observed differences in the occupational distribution of the two groups would be reduced by about 60 percent" (Royal Commission, 1969: 47).

No single factor seems sufficient to account for this pattern of educational disparities. In the case of the French, Porter notes that "the educational system was inappropriate for the kind of society that by 1950 Quebec was becoming. It was an outstanding example of institutional failure" (1965: 92). To be sure, there has long been a Francophone class of lawyers, physicians, and clergymen whose educational preparation is beyond criticism, but the educational system in Quebec until recent years was not equipped to turn out large numbers of persons capable of competing on equal grounds with the British for occupations in business and industry. Partly for this reason, those of French origin in Quebec are located disproportionately in unskilled and semi-skilled blue-collar jobs. Italian immigrants generally have entered the country with relatively low levels of educational attainment. Jews have a long tradition of faith in education, and their very high levels of educational attainment in Canada reflect a pattern found among Jews in the United States and elsewhere.

Although differences in levels of educational attainment seem in large measure to explain differences in occupational distributions among ethnic groups in Canada, they do not explain them entirely. Here again, equivalence in education does not seem to yield equivalence in occupation. One reason might lie in differences in educational quality which are obscured in a simple examination of educational attainment levels, but quality is a very difficult matter to assess (Beattie, 1975: 120 25). Occupational preferences might also play a role, although, as was noted earlier, there do not seem to be any strong and consistent differences between Anglophones and Francophones in the occupations they regard as prestigious (which is not the same, however, as occupations viewed as desirable). Another possibility is that lack of fluency in English places certain groups at a competitive disadvantage (Beattie, 1975: 134–38), although Armstrong (1970) argues that this is no longer the case for Francophone professionals, at least. Finally, all questions of educational quality and language aside, it seems that the failure of equivalency in education to yield equivalency in occupation is the result of ethnic discrimination rooted in stereotype and prejudice. Here too, Armstrong argues that in the case of young, well-educated Francophones ethnicity actually operates to their advantage — an argument which finds little support in Beattie's study of the federal public service. How these processes operate for other ethnic groups in Canada remains largely unknown.

The ethnic groups considered in this analysis differ considerably in their income levels. While ethnic income disparities vary somewhat from province to province, the general pattern remains more or less the same, with Jews having the highest income levels, followed at some distance by those of British origin. When levels of educational attainment, occupational distributions, under-employment (number of weeks worked in a year), age, region of residence, and industry are all taken into account as factors influencing relative ethnic income levels, persons of English-Scottish, Irish, and Northern European origins still seem to earn more than one would otherwise expect. Persons of French, Italian, and Eastern European origins earn less. And Jews and Germans earn just about what one would expect. Table VIII shows these ethnic income disparities before and after the extra explanatory variables have been introduced. Those disparities which remain have been described as "the expression of a complex phenomenon composed of many elements which are impossible to separate: among these are the quality of schooling; work attitudes; occupational choice; motivations and values; the quality, orientation, and effectiveness of institutions; obstacles to mobility; discrimination; and the weight of the past" (Royal Commission, 1969: 35).

TABLE VIII   Deviation of Income above (+) or below (−) Average for All Groups, and Deviation Remaining for All Groups after Education, Occupation, Under-Employment, Region, Age, and Industry Effects Removed, by Ethnic Origin, Montreal, 1961

Ethnic group	Deviation from average	Deviation remaining
English-Scottish	+$1,319	+$606
Irish	+ 1,012	+ 468
French	− 360	− 267
Northern European	+ 1,201	+ 303
Italian	− 961	− 370
Jewish	+ 878	+ 9
Eastern European	− 100	− 480
German	+ 387	+ 65

Source: Royal Commission on Bilingualism and Biculturalism, 1969: 77.

Since the collection and analysis of the above data, Lanphier and Morris (1974) and Beattie (1975) have studied Anglophone-Francophone income differentials using more recent information. Lanphier and Morris found evidence to suggest that the overall differential has probably diminished somewhat over time, although the income disparities for workers in some occupations, most notably the lesser skilled, seem actually to have increased. In commenting on the effects of the Quiet Revolution, the authors conclude:

> although it is now a commonplace that the middle class, and perhaps the skilled workers, are the main beneficiaries in terms of fresh employment opportunities, our data support the further argument that reductions in income inequality have been restricted to these same groups (p. 65).

Beattie, on the other hand, found that the Anglophone-Francophone salary differential for his sample of middle-level bureaucrats in the federal public service during this same period had actually increased (p. 188).

SOCIAL MOBILITY

In analyses of social mobility, the primary concern is with estimating the degree to which, and explicating the processes by which, individuals in a society inherit their class and status positions from their parents. A society in which there was complete inheritance of position (in which everyone ended up occupying positions identical to those occupied by his or her parents at an earlier time) would have no vertical mobility whatever and no permeability. One in which there was total anti-inheritance (in which everyone ended up occupying positions maximally different from those earlier occupied by his or her parents) would have the greatest possible vertical mobility, but still no permeability. Finally, a society in which the positions occupied by the parents bore no relation to those occupied by their children would have intermediate levels of mobility and maximal permeability. Each of these examples is, of course, hypothetical, useful for purposes of clarifying the concepts employed in mobility analyses, but corresponding to no known societies.

In his work, Porter found levels of internal recruitment among members of the economic elite which were far higher than one would expect on the basis of chance alone: "Of the 611 Canadian-born, 135 (22 percent) directly inherited their positions from near kin, principally the father" (1965: 291). If those with fathers from other elites, along with those whose wives were born into elite families are considered as well, this figure increases from 22 to 31 percent. And if still others from very wealthy, but non-elite, families are added to the total, it increases still further to 37.8 percent. Quite clearly, the Canadian class structure is considerably less than maximally permeable, but its permeability relative to the class structures of other countries is something which Porter does not analyze. Clearly, too, mobility into and out of the economic elite is severely constricted, although there is no way of knowing whether it is more or less so now than in the past, or more so in Canada compared to other countries. As noted above, Clement (1975) reports similar findings with regard to class permeability and mobility for a later point in time, but no strong inferences can be made about temporal trends, owing to differences in the methodologies he and Porter employed.

The Canadian status structure seems also to be characterized by less than maximal permeability and mobility, although the available evidence is remarkably sparse. Using data gathered on samples of Anglophone and Francophone males and females living in Toronto and Montreal, Cuneo and Curtis (1975) examined aspects of inter-generational status inheritance. For both samples of males, the higher his father's level of educational attainment and occupational prestige, the better educated a person was likely to be, and as a consequence of his education, the higher the prestige of both his first and current occupations. The same pattern of relationships held for Anglophone females. For Francophone females, the influence of father's occupation on their education was negligible, but father's occupation directly influenced both their first and their current job.

Perhaps the most frequently expressed view is that Canada stands somewhere between the United States and Great Britain in its tolerance of positional inequalities and social ascription — more tolerant than the former, and less so than the latter (Naegele, 1961; Lipset, 1963). It is a view which has not gone without serious challenge (Davis, 1971; Truman, 1971); for the data are limited and often open to alternative interpretation. Truman mounts a devastating attack on Lipset's analysis, pointing out methodological problems in his sources of information, documenting the arbitrary nature of many of his conclusions, and supplying additional information casting doubt on his rank ordering of the three nations. The debate on these issues is interesting, if inconclusive, but it suffers from a confusion between values relating to social stratification on the one hand and actual patterns of stratification on the other. It is entirely possible that the values people hold concerning inequality are only tenuously related, if related at all, to the presence or absence in a society of positional inequalities, permeability, and mobility.

In comparing their results with those reported in a major study conducted in the United States, Cuneo and Curtis were not able to conclude that the level of status inheritance in Canada was significantly different from that in the United States. The nature of the data, however, and the very difficult problems involved in making precise comparisons of this kind, prevented a more definitive statement.

At least prior to the Quiet Revolution, it was generally assumed that French Canada was a more traditional society than English Canada — late to industrialize, slow in rationalizing its system of education, less secular generally, and less mobility-oriented (Dofny and Rioux, 1964). In their study of Anglophone-Francophone mobility in Quebec, de Jocas and Rocher report evidence consistent with this characterization. They conclude that "the channels and barriers of mobility that we have observed for the French Canadians are not the same as for the English-speaking Canadians. The former go up the scale step by step, while the latter seem to move more rapidly to the top occupational levels" (1957: 66). It seems obvious that in the two decades since these data were gathered this situation has changed both within Quebec and in Canada generally, but the research necessary to demonstrate the changes remains to be done. Cuneo and Curtis's (1975) data on Montreal Francophones and Toronto Anglophones, for example, do not suggest any marked or consistent differences between the two groups in status inheritance, although it would be a mistake to generalize their findings beyond the confines of their samples.

Finally, important features of Canada's stratification system arise out of the interaction over time among migration, mobility, and the structure of class and status (Porter, 1965: 29–59). This century has seen high, if periodic, levels of immigration and emigration, largely confined to English Canada. Immigration has served as a source of recruits for occupations at all levels within the status hierarchy, although the bulk of immigrants have moved into lesser-skilled jobs (Department of Manpower and Immigration, 1974). At the same time, as Porter notes, "Canada ... has had to rely heavily on skilled and professional immigration to upgrade its labor force in periods of industrial growth" (1965: 43). We know rather less about the characteristics of emigrants from Canada, but they seem disproportionately to have been professionals — a loss which has been more than compensated for by the influx of the professionally trained from other countries. In the 1960s, immigration reached its lowest point in 1961 and its highest point in 1967 (higher than in any other postwar year except for 1957). New immigration regulations instituted in 1962 changed the bases of selection from ethnic origin (previously, immigrants from Great Britain and northern European countries had been favored) to education and occupation, with the result that the proportion of immigrants with high levels of educational attainment and high status occupations has apparently increased (Kalbach and McVey, 1971: 337). In this period, too, there have been rising numbers of highly qualified immigrants from the United States, while emigration from Canada to that country has declined, levels of unemployment are high, and unprecedented numbers of Canadians are enrolled in institutions of higher education. One can only guess at the long-term implications of these trends for the Canadian stratification system.

CONCLUDING REMARKS

This chapter has presented a highly selective description and analysis of social stratification in Canada. It has been selective not only because it would have been impossible to use more than a very small proportion of the available literature, but because theoretical judgments and personal preferences have led to the omission of entire topics and large bodies of material. In particular, I have deliberately not discussed many of the cultural and social psychological aspects of stratification in Canada in order to concentrate on matters of social structure and organization, with an emphasis, wherever possible, on temporal changes.

Notes

1. See Bendix and Lipset (1966) for critical commentary on functional theory.
2. Referring to Marx alone is for ease of exposition only.
3. This analysis is based on what was known to nineteenth-century economists as the *labour theory of value*.
4. The terms "subordinate class," "working class," and "proletariat" are used interchangeably throughout, as are "dominant class," "economic elite," and "bourgeoisie," except where they take on a very precise meaning within the context of a particular theory.
5. For critical commentary on Porter's work, see Heap (1974).
6. The situation for at least some of these occupations has undoubtedly changed in very recent years.
7. Note that members of these occupational groups are generally forbidden by their professional associations to advertise their services or be competitive in their fees.
8. For a more detailed analysis of women in the labor force, see Ostry (1968).
9. Proportionally more males than females have university degrees and other forms of advanced, post-secondary education. See 1971 *Census of Canada*, Cat. 92-743.
10. Mobility-permeability is the least understood sub-area of social stratification in Canada at the present time.

References

ADAMS, I., CAMERON, W., HILL, B., AND PENZ, P.
The Real Poverty Report. Edmonton: Hurtig, 1971.

ALLINGHAM, JOHN D.
Women Who Work: Part I. Special Labour Force Studies, No. 5. Ottawa: Dominion Bureau of Statistics, 1967.

ARMSTRONG, DONALD E.
Education and Economic Achievement. Documents of the Royal Commission on Bilingualism and Biculturalism, No. 7. Ottawa: Information Canada, 1970.

BEATTIE, CHRISTOPHER.
Minority Men in a Majority Setting. Toronto: McClelland and Stewart, 1975.

BENDIX, R., AND LIPSET, S.M., EDS.
Class, Status, and Power. New York: The Free Press, 1966.

BERG, IVAR.
Education and Jobs: The Great Training Robbery. Boston: Beacon Press, 1971.

BOTTOMORE, T. B.
Classes in Modern Society. London: Allen and Unwin, 1965.

CANADA.
Department of Manpower and Immigration. *Immigration and Population Statistics*. Ottawa: Information Canada, 1974.

Department of National Revenue. *Taxation Statistics*, 1971. Ottawa, 1973.

Special Senate Committee on Poverty. *Poverty in Canada: Report of the Special Senate Committee*. Ottawa: Information Canada, 1971.

CLEMENT, WALLACE.
The Canadian Corporate Elite: An Analysis of Economic Power. Toronto: McClelland and Stewart, 1975.

COLLINS, RANDALL
"Functional and Conflict Theories of Educational Stratification," *American Sociological Review* 36 (1971): 1002–19.

"Where Are Educational Requirements for Employment Highest?" *Sociology of Education* 47 (1974): 419–42.

CRICHTON, ROBERT.
The Great Imposter. New York: Random House, 1959.

CUNEO, C. J., AND CURTIS, J. E.
"Social Ascription in the Educational and Occupational Status Attainment of Urban Canadians," *Canadian Review of Sociology and Anthropology*, 1975, in press.

CURTIS, J. E., AND SCOTT, W. G.
Social Stratification in Canada. Scarborough: Prentice-Hall, 1973.

DAHRENDORF, RALF.
Class and Class Conflict in Industrial Society. Stanford: Stanford University Press, 1959.

DAVIS, ARTHUR K.
"Canadian Society and History as Hinterland Versus Metropolis," in Richard J. Ossenberg, ed., *Canadian Society: Pluralism, Change, and Conflict*. Scarborough: Prentice-Hall, 1971.

DAVIS, K., AND MOORE, W. E.
"Some Principles of Stratification," *American Sociological Review* 10 (1945): 242–49.

DEATON, RICK.
"The Fiscal Crisis of the State," *Our Generation*, Vol. 8, No. 4 (1972).

DOCTOR X.
  The Intern. New York: Harper and Row, 1965.

DOFNY, J., AND RIOUX, M.
  "Social Class in French Canada," in M. Rioux and Y. Martin, eds., *French-Canadian Society*, Vol. I. Toronto/Montreal: McClelland and Stewart, 1964.

DUNCAN, OTIS D.
  "A Socio-Economic Index for All Occupations," in Albert J. Reiss, ed., *Occupations and Social Status*. New York: The Free Press, 1961.

HAMBLIN, ROBERT L.
  "Mathematical Experimentation and Sociological Theory: A Critical Analysis," *Sociometry* 34 (1971): 423–52.

HEAP, JAMES L., ED.
  Everybody's Canada: The Vertical Mosaic Reviewed and Re-Examined. Toronto: Burns and MacEachern, 1974.

DE JOCAS, Y., AND ROCHER, G.
  "Inter-Generation Occupational Mobility in the Province of Quebec," *Canadian Journal of Economics and Political Science* 4 (September 1971): 346–66.

JOHNSON, LEO A.
  "The Development of Class in Canada in the Twentieth Century," in G. Teeple, ed., *Capitalism and the National Question in Canada*. Toronto: University of Toronto Press, 1972.
  Incomes, Disparity and Impoverishment in Canada Since World War II. Toronto: New Bytown Press, 1973.

KALBACH, W. E., AND MCVEY, W. W.
  The Demographic Bases of Canadian Society. Toronto: McGraw-Hill, 1971.

KUBAT, D., AND THORNTON, D.
  A Statistical Profile of Canadian Society. Toronto: McGraw-Hill Ryerson, 1974.

LANE, DAVID.
  The End of Inequality. Harmondsworth: Penguin, 1971.

LANPHIER, C. M., AND MORRIS, R. N.
  "Structural Aspects of Differences in Income Between Anglophones and Francophones," *Canadian Review of Sociology and Anthropology* 11 (February 1974): 53–66.

LENSKI, GERHARD E.
  Power and Privilege: A Theory of Social Stratification. New York: McGraw-Hill, 1966.

LEVITT, KARI.
  Silent Surrender: The Multinational Corporation in Canada. Toronto: Macmillan, 1970.

LIPSET, SEYMOUR M.
  The First New Nation: The United States in Historical and Comparative Perspective. New York: Basic Books, 1963.

LIPTON, CHARLES.
  "Canadian Unionism," in G. Teeple, ed., *Capitalism and the National Question in Canada*. Toronto: University of Toronto Press, 1972.

MARX, KARL.
  Value, Price and Profit. New York: International Publishers, 1935.
  The German Ideology. London: Lawrence and Wishart, 1965.

MARX, K., AND ENGELS, F.
  Manifesto of the Communist Party. New York: International Publishers, 1932.

MASLOVE, ALLAN M.
The Pattern of Taxation in Canada. Ottawa: Information Canada, 1972.

MELTZ, NOAH M.
Manpower in Canada, 1931 to 1961. Ottawa. Department of Manpower and Immigration, 1968.

MILIBAND, RALPH.
The State in Capitalist Society. London: Quartet, 1969.

NAEGELE, KASPAR D.
"Canadian Society: Some Reflections," in B. Blishen *et al.*, eds., *Canadian Society*. Toronto: Macmillan, 1961.

OSTRY, SYLVIA.
The Occupational Composition of the Canadian Labour Force. 1961 Census Monograph. Ottawa: The Queen's Printer, 1967.
The Female Worker in Canada. 1961 Census Monograph. Ottawa: The Queen's Printer, 1968.

PARK, L. C., AND PARK, F. W.
Anatomy of Big Business. Toronto: James Lewis and Samuel, 1962, 1973.

PINEO, P. C., AND PORTER, J.
"Occupational Prestige in Canada," *Canadian Review of Sociology and Anthropology* 4 (1967): 24–40.

PODOLUK, JENNY R.
Incomes of Canadians. 1961 Census Monograph. Ottawa: The Queen's Printer, 1968.

PORTER, JOHN.
The Vertical Mosaic: An Analysis of Social Class and Power in Canada. Toronto: University of Toronto Press, 1965.
Canadian Social Structure: A Statistical Profile. Toronto: McClelland and Stewart, 1969.

ROBSON, R. A. A., AND LAPOINTE, M.
A Comparison of Men's and Women's Salaries and Employment Fringe Benefits in the Academic Profession. Studies of the Royal Commission on the Status of Women, No. 1. Ottawa: Information Canada, 1971.

ROYAL COMMISSION ON BILINGUALISM AND BICULTURALISM.
Vol. III, *The Work World*. Ottawa: Information Canada, 1969.

SCHMITT, DAVID R.
"Magnitude Measures of Economic and Educational Status," *Sociological Quarterly* 6 (1965): 387–91.

SVALASTOGA, KAARE.
Social Differentiation. New York: McKay, 1965.

TEEPLE, GARY, ED.
Capitalism and the National Question in Canada. Toronto: University of Toronto Press, 1972.

TRUMAN, TOM.
"A Critique of Seymour M. Lipset's Article, 'Value Differences, Absolute or Relative: The English-Speaking Democracies,'" *Canadian Journal of Political Science* 4 (1971): 497–525.

WARNER, W.L., MEEKER, M., AND EELLS, K.
Social Class in America. New York: Harper, 1960.

WEBER, MAX.
The Theory of Social and Economic Organization. London: Hodge, 1947.

PART TWO

Studies in Canadian Social Stratification Dimensions

A. Class, Income, and Wealth

Precapitalist Economic Formations and the Capitalist Labor Market in Canada, 1911-71

Leo A. Johnson

Following the publication of "The Development of Class in Canada in the Twentieth Century,"[1] a number of questions arose concerning the degree to which the capitalist mode of production had actually dissolved precapitalist modes of production in Canada; when this dissolution had occurred; and what had been — or were — its consequences. The nature and status of two socio-economic entities, the petite bourgeoisie and the family, were scrutinized in particular. In both cases, there was considerable controversy among Marxists as to whether these formations were pre-capitalist or capitalist entities, and whether, therefore, they were anachronisms, destined to disappear, or permanent formations of capitalism in which certain contradictions allowed them to become the focus of revolutionary change.

From a left-wing political standpoint, the issue is important. If the petite bourgeoisie (by which was generally meant farmers and other independent proprietors or commodity producers) and the family are pre-capitalist formations, destined to be dissolved and to disappear as capitalism reaches its most mature stages, then any hope that the agony of their dissolution would provide the basis for a socialist revolution is either illusory or opportunist, and is destined to fail. If, on the other hand, these formations are integral and necessary to capitalism, and are exploited by capitalism in a manner analogous to the proletariat — to form, as it were, a modern proletariat — then it is conceivable that they might form the spearhead for revolutionary change. In general, little consensus has yet appeared on this issue.

This paper examines the dissolution of the petite bourgeoisie and family as productive entities, in the face of the capitalist mode of production's demands for an ever-growing, more complex and highly specialized labor force. What have been the timing and consequences of this process, and, if the process follows the Marxist paradigm, what future developments might we look for? As was the case with "The Development of Class in Canada" and *Poverty in Wealth*,[2] this paper is intended to open a discussion of these issues, not to provide the last word.[3]

Before the data are examined, a few of Marx's ideas and definitions related to the subject should be clarified. Just what constitutes the "capitalist mode of production" and how does it differ from other modes of production? Although Marx and Engels wrote extensively on the subject, there is still confusion among Marxist scholars as to what Marx meant.

Marx saw history as great epochs of human development characterized by particular modes of economic production. The modern era, which began about 1400, was one in which the feudal mode of production in Western Europe was gradually overthrown and supplanted by the bourgeois mode of production — which in turn evolved toward its highest stage, capitalism.[4] Marx said that the distinction between the bourgeois mode of production in general (the production of commodities for exchange for commodities) and capitalism was that in the latter stage the commodities were produced by human labor power which itself had become a commodity, bought and sold in the capitalist labor market. In Marx's words:

> In themselves money and commodities are no more capital than are the means of production and of subsistence. They want transforming into capital. But this transformation itself can only take place under certain circumstances that centre in this, viz., that two very different kinds of commodity-possessors must come face to face and into contact; on the one hand, the owners of money, means of production, means of subsistence, who are eager to increase the sum of values they possess, by buying other people's labor power; on the other hand, free laborers, the sellers of their own labor power, and therefore sellers of labor. Free laborers, in the double sense that neither they themselves form part and parcel of the means of production, as in the case of slaves, bondsmen, etc., nor do the means of production belong to them, as in the case of peasant proprietors; they are, therefore, free from, unencumbered by, any means of production of their own. With this polarization of the market for commodities, the fundamental conditions of capitalist production are given.[5]

For bourgeois production to reach its highest stage, capitalist production, it was necessary for previous forms of bourgeois labor relations (neo-feudalism, modern slavery, and independent commodity "petit bourgeois production") to be dissolved and displaced by capitalist labor relations.

Marx, however, always made it clear that the mode of production was something far more complex than merely the relations and activities that existed in the workplace. As he pointed out in the introduction to *A Contribution to the Critique of Political Economy*, the general method by which a society goes about creating the necessities and amenities of human social existence (Marx, by the way, would have rejected a distinction between necessities and amenities) profoundly affects every aspect of its life:

> In the social production of their existence, men inevitably enter into definite relations, which are independent of their will, namely relations of production appropriate to the material forces of production. The totality of these relations of production constitutes the economic structure of society, the real foundation, on which arises a legal and political superstructure and to which correspond definite

forms of social consciousness. The mode of production of material life conditions the general process of social, political and intellectual life. It is not the consciousness of men that determines their existence, but their social existence that determines their consciousness.[6]

Thus, when one mode of production overthrows another, or when evolution occurs within a general mode of production, whole sections of the social, political and ideological levels of society are rendered obsolete and must be swept away. Marx's description of the overthrow of independent commodity production (a form of bourgeois production in which the producers own and operate their independent means of production, and sell the objects that are the end products) by capitalist production indicates the painful nature of that process:

> The private property of the laborer in his means of production is the foundation of petty industry whether agricultural, manufacturing, or both.... This mode of production pre-supposes parcelling of the soil, and the scattering of the other means of production.... At a certain stage of development it brings forth the material agencies for its dissolution. From that moment new forces and new passions spring up in the bosom of society; but the old social organization fetters them and keeps them down. It must be annihilated; it is annihilated. Its annihilation, the transformation of the individualized and scattered means of production into socially concentrated ones, of the pigmy property of the many into the huge property of the few, the expropriation of the great mass of the people from the soil, from the means of labor, this fearful and painful expropriation of the mass of the people forms the prelude of the history of capital.... Self-earned private property, that is based, so to say, on the fusing together of the isolated, independent laboring individual with the conditions of his labor, is supplanted by capitalistic private property, which rests on exploitation of the nominally free labor of others, i.e., on wage labor.[7]

As the data will show, the destruction of independent commodity producers in Canada (the most important of which were farmers) has now reached its final stage.

In Marx's and Engels' treatment of the family, they saw a process occurring which was analogous to the destruction of other forms of pre-capitalist production. In their view, the family had originated as a socio-economic unit appropriate to a given mode of production and, as capitalism emerged as the dominant mode, it would be transformed appropriately, or be dissolved and its members absorbed.[8] Whether the process was transformation or dissolution depended on the needs of the stages of the capitalist mode of production as it evolved.

In commenting on the eventual proletarianization of women, Engels argued that during the transition period, prior to the dissolution of the family, women were caught in a contradictory situation, torn between the needs and social relations of two distinct and ultimately irreconcilable modes of production:

> In the old communistic household, which embraced numerous couples and their children, the administration of the household, entrusted to the women, was just as much a public, a socially necessary industry as the providing of food by the men. This situation changed with the patriarchal family, and even more with the monogamian individual family. The administration of the household lost its public

character. It was no longer the concern of society. It became a *private service*. The wife became the first domestic servant, pushed out of participation in social production. Only modern large-scale industry again threw open to her — and only to the proletarian women at that — the avenue to social production; but in such a way that, when she fulfils her duties in the private service of her family, she remains excluded from public production and cannot earn anything; and when she wishes to take part in public industry and earn her living independently, she is not in a position to fulfil her family duties. . . .[9]

If women were to be fully integrated into the capitalist mode of production, fundamental and painful alterations at every level of social existence would have to occur. For the thousands of Canadian women struggling valiantly to fulfil the demands of both the family and capitalist spheres of production, Engels' words must ring only too true.

In the data which follow, three specific questions are addressed: the degree to which the capitalist mode of production (with all its attendant formations) has absorbed the work potential of Canadians; how the changing nature of the labor demands of capitalism has affected the participation rates of specific age groups; and how both of these have affected the participation rates of men and women.

Between 1911 and 1971 Canada experienced dramatic and fundamental changes. Population tripled; birthrates fell, then rose and fell again; immigration dried to a trickle, then reached flood proportions after World War II; and during all this, depression, World War I, the booming 1920s, depression again, World War II, and the prosperous 1950s and 1960s all came and went, each with its own sweeping impact. And yet, through all this turmoil and change, as Table I[10] shows, there was, until 1971, little overall change in the desire and willingness of Canadians to work. For 50 years, the greatest variation in participation rates of working age adults was the 1.4 percent reduction between 1911 and 1921. Then, between 1961 and 1971, total participation jumped from 53.8 to 58.0 percent — three times the largest previous change — suggesting some significant alteration in labor force behavior.

When the working age population is trimmed to remove those who are not participants in the capitalist labor market (persons in active military service, inmates of institutions, Indians on reserves) a different pattern appears. Table II,[11] drawn from Statistics Canada estimates, suggests that among those *available* for competition in the labor market, there was a significant decline in participation between 1931 and 1951 (from 58.3 to 53.7 percent), then in 1961

TABLE I   Canada: Labor Force Participation, Number and Percent, among the Total Population Fifteen Years and up, 1911-71

	1911	1921	1931	1941	1951	1961	1971
Population '000s	4,819	5,756	7,086	8,297	9,742	12,023	15,190
Labor force '000s	2,698	3,144	3,908	4,498	5,277	6,458	8,813
Participation rate	56.0	54.6	55.1	54.2	54.2	53.8	58.0

TABLE II   Canada: Labor Force Characteristics of the Population Fourteen Years and Over, 1931–71, Statistics Canada Estimates (thousands of persons)

	1931	1941	1951	1961	1971
Population available	7,116	8,056	9,732	12,053	15,388
Labor Force	4,151	4,466	5,223	6,521	8,631
Unemployed	481	195	126	466	552
Employed	3,670	4,271	5,097	6,055	8,079
Participation rate	58.3	55.4	53.7	54.1	56.1
Unemployment rate	11.6	4.4	2.4	7.1	6.4
Percent of available population employed	51.6	53.0	52.4	50.2	52.5

and 1971 an increase again. Both of these movements, however, are virtually cancelled by decreases and increases in the level of unemployment. It would appear, on the basis of these data, that the absorption capacity of the capitalist labor market is a good deal less elastic than the laboring-age population's need or desire for employment. Given that capitalist investors must consider long range as well as short range factors, it is not surprising that demands for labor by employers are relatively inelastic.

By comparing the data contained in Tables I and II, several situations are revealed. First, the needs of the population (objective and subjective) for jobs, as reflected in the participation rate, were remarkably constant, on a national basis, between 1911 and 1961. Between 1961 and 1971, however, there was, in the laboring-age population, a major increase in the propensity to seek work. Second, because the institutionalized portion of the population fluctuated drastically (because of army service, etc.) the consistency of participation rate in the whole laboring-age population is not reflected in the participation rate of the labor-available population. For the latter, a good deal more volatility is exhibited. It seems that within the laboring-age population there is a compensation mechanism which operates to overcome changes in labor availability levels due to withdrawals because of institutional demands such as military service. Thus, for every individual who would normally be in the labor market, but is withdrawn, another individual, not previously in the market, begins to seek work. Mobilization of female workers in World War II to replace departing soldiers is the clearest example of such a compensatory mechanism at work. But whether this mechanism operates primarily at the ideological level (for example, the use of propaganda in World War II designed to motivate women to enter the labor force) or at the economic (the withdrawal of one income earner from the family earning unit forcing, where possible, the entry of another), or as a combination of the two, is, as yet, unclear. What is clear is that given the lack of correlation between participation rate and labor absorption levels since 1951, the mobilization factors now at work appear to stem more and more significantly from the needs and aspirations of the laboring-age population and less from the direct needs of employers.

TABLE III   Canada: Labor Force Participation in the Agricultural Sector, 1911–71

	1911	1921	1931	1941	1951	1961	1971
Total labor force	1,698	3,144	3,908	4,498	5,277	6,458	8,813
Agricultural labor force	928	1,025	1,118	1,075	826	649	512
Percent agricultural	34.4	32.6	28.6	23.9	15.7	10.0	5.8

Patterns of labor participation and labor absorption rates indicate important changes in Canada's social and economic life, but beneath the general levels even more significant events have been and are taking place. The most important one is the alteration and/or dissolution of the two major remaining pre-capitalist economic formations, independent commodity production and the family. Since 1911 the capitalist labor market has grown enormously and has also made huge inroads into the pre-capitalist sectors, incorporating those previously involved in independent or family production. The tempo of this process has, apparently, been increasing.

After 1900 the largest remaining independent commodity production activity in Canada was farming. Table III[12] shows how rapidly that sector has declined both in numbers and in proportion to the whole economy. Moreover, proletarianization has occurred even within the remaining agricultural sector. In 1911, 72.6 percent of the agricultural labor force were owners or managers; by 1971 this had declined to 50.4 percent.[13] The gradual collapse of hundreds of small urban agricultural service centers across Canada illustrates the social catastrophe the independent commodity producing sector experienced. Although there are less data, the decay of hundreds of Maritime fishing villages (or their conversion into tourist attractions where the sons and daughters of fishermen serve as waiters and chambermaids) suggests a similar experience for independent producers in the fishing sector. What collapsed is not merely an economic mode of existence, but a society with unique ideologies, values and social organizations. This process has been greatly facilitated by mass education and mass media purveying capitalist urban values.

The collapse of household production is more difficult to document statistically. Still, if the huge increase in sales of convenience foods and labor-saving appliances is evidence of the decline of household production, then the case is clear. What can be demonstrated is the enormous inroad the capitalist labor market has made into the ranks of working-age women. Table IV[13] shows that after very little increase in the female participation rate from 1911 to 1941 (from 16.2 to 20.7 percent), there was a sudden increase, climbing to 39.9 percent by 1971. Tables II and IV contain a striking parallel. In both it is after 1941 that the process of dissolution and absorption of pre-capitalist modes of production is most strongly felt. It is with the huge growth of industry and foreign investment during and after World War II that Canada matures as a capitalist economy.

One remarkable aspect of the large-scale movement of women into the labor market is that, between 1911 and 1961, an equal proportion of men left the labor force, resulting in the generally stable participation rate in Table I. Table V[14]

TABLE IV   Canada: Female Labor Force Participation, 1911–71

	1911	1921	1931	1941	1951	1961	1971
Women, 15 years and up	2,207	2,757	3,376	4,022	4,831	5,984	7,649
Female labor force, 15+	357	485	663	832	1,162	1,764	3,053
Participation rate	16.2	17.6	19.7	20.7	24.1	29.5	39.9

TABLE V   Canada: Labor Force Participation by Sex, 1911–71

	1911	1921	1931	1941	1951	1961	1971
Males 15 and up	2,612	2,999	3,710	4,274	4,911	6,039	7,540
Females 15 and up	2,207	2,757	3,376	4,022	4,831	5,984	7,649
Total 15 and up	4,819	5,576	7,086	8,297	9,742	12,023	15,189
Male labor force	2,341	2,658	3,245	3,666	4,114	4,694	5,760
Female labor force	357	485	663	832	1,162	1,764	3,053
Total labor force	2,698	3,144	3,908	4,498	5,277	6,458	8,813
Male participation rate	89.7	88.7	87.5	85.6	83.8	77.7	76.4
Female participation rate	16.2	17.6	19.7	20.7	24.1	29.5	39.9
Total participation rate	56.0	54.6	55.1	54.2	54.2	53.8	58.0

TABLE VI   Canada: Labor Force Participation Rate by Age Group, 1951–71

	Male			Female			Total		
	1951	1961	1971	1951	1961	1971	1951	1961	1971
15–19	57.1	39.5	46.6	37.2	33.0	37.0	47.2	36.3	41.9
20–24	92.2	86.6	86.5	46.8	49.3	62.8	69.2	67.8	74.7
25–34	96.4	93.9	92.6	24.2	29.5	44.5	59.6	62.2	68.9
35–44	96.7	94.2	92.8	21.8	31.0	43.9	59.9	62.4	68.8
45–54	94.5	91.8	90.3	20.4	33.3	44.4	58.8	63.1	67.1
55–64	85.7	81.7	80.1	14.5	24.4	34.4	51.3	53.5	56.9
65+	38.6	28.4	23.6	5.7	6.7	8.3	22.1	17.2	15.1
Total	83.8	77.7	76.4	24.1	29.5	39.9	54.2	53.7	58.0

TABLE VII   Canada: Ratio of Male Participation Rate to Female Participation Rate, 1951–71

	1951	1961	1971
15–19	1.53	1.19	1.25
20–24	1.97	1.75	1.37
25–34	3.98	3.18	2.08
35–44	4.43	3.03	2.11
45–54	4.63	2.75	2.03
55–64	5.91	3.34	2.32
65+	6.77	4.23	2.84
Total	3.47	2.63	1.91

shows that the sudden rise in total labor force participation in 1971 was due to the enormous increase in the female participation rate which was not complemented by a reduction in the male participation rate. For the first time since 1911 the inter-sexual compensation mechanism appears to have broken down. Women, in large numbers, are continuing to enter the labor market, whereas men have, it appears, stopped withdrawing. When the capitalist economy failed to expand proportionately to this oversupply, high unemployment resulted (Table II).

In regard to labor force participation by age groups, Table VI[15] shows that, between 1951 and 1961, there was a reduction in the male participation rate in every age category with the largest drops in the under-20 and over-65 groups. For women, except for those under 20, the situation was the opposite — a significant gain is shown, even for women over 65. For women under 20, there was a decline in participation. From 1951 to 1961 there occurred a general increase in participation for both men and women between the ages of 25 and 65, but decreases for younger and older groups.

Between 1961 and 1971, among both men and women under 20, the decline in participation rate experienced between 1951 and 1961 reversed (Table VII[16]), with men regaining about half the losses and women returning to the 1951 levels. For prime-aged males, the decline continued, but at a much slower rate. For men over 65, the decline continued at about half the rate of the previous decade. Among prime-aged women, the participation rate rose to the highest in history, with some age groups approaching a 50 percent increase. Even for women over 65, the increase was 24 percent of 1961 levels. These changes caused an equalization of labor participation rates between men and women: Whereas in 1951 there were 3.5 men employed for every woman, in 1971 there were only 1.9. The older the age group, the more noticeable the tendency toward equalization. If entry into the capitalist labor market is an important aspect of female liberation, then its effects are much more evident among older than younger women.

According to Marxist theory, however, the reproduction of the capitalist labor force is not merely concerned with the quantity of labor produced, but its quality as well, and a modern economy requires vast numbers of highly trained and educated employees. In examining the inroads of the capitalist labor market into the working-age population, those persons attending school should not, in general, be seen as part of the reserve army of labor. Rather, students should be viewed as an integral part of the labor force, albeit in training, indispensable in the long run.

When one combines labor force and school participation (Table VIII[17]) there appears in recent years, for both men and women, a huge overlap. Whereas in 1961 it appears that school attendance may have precipitated a large drop in labor force participation (Table VI[18]), in 1971 this was no longer the case. In assessing this overlap, it should be noted that most of it is caused by increased school attendance, not increased labor participation. For example, among males under 20 years of age, school attendance rose from 61.3 percent in 1961 to 73.8 percent in 1971, while labor force participation rose from 39.5 percent to 46.6.[19] The situation was similar for women in the same age group: in 1961, 55.8 percent attended school while 33.0 percent were in the labor force; in 1971 these proportions had risen to 71.3 and 37.0.[20] It would seem that broadening the school attendance into lower income groups did not result in removing them entirely from the labor force. However, most of the overlap for the under-20 group was compensated for by high rates of unemployment which exceeded 15 percent for men and ten percent for women.[21]

With geography and economic resources as diversified and regionalized as those in Canada, it is obvious that national transformations occur at different rates. The data show, however, that dissolution of pre-capitalist modes of production transcends regional economic differences; the rates of change vary, but the general process remains. As the independent commodity production sector dissolved across Canada, every region experienced the same process. Table IX[22] shows that the decline has been most severe in the Maritimes and Quebec where small-scale, capital-poor farmers have been particularly vulnerable to market competition. On a national basis the number of persons employed in the agricultural sector has declined by 52.4 percent since 1941; in the Maritimes and Quebec, 74.8 percent and 68.8 percent respectively. In contrast, the percent reduction in Ontario was 46.6 percent, the Prairies 42.9 percent, and British Columbia 31.7 percent.[23]

There are also significant differences in the degree that agriculture has become a capitalist rather than an independent commodity production sector. In Table X[24] Newfoundland, Nova Scotia and British Columbia show high proportions of proletarian labor in the agricultural sector, New Brunswick is close behind, Ontario appears to be a transition area with numbers of wage earners and owner-operators about evenly balanced, while in Prince Edward Island, Quebec, and the Prairies, agriculture is still dominated by independent commodity

TABLE VIII   Canada Labor Force and School Participation, Combined Rates by Age Group, 1951–71

	Male			Female			Total		
	1951	1961	1971	1951	1961	1971	1951	1961	1971
15–19	97.9	100.8	120.4	77.4	88.8	108.3	87.7	94.9	114.5
20–24	98.7	98.0	109.5	50.1	53.9	75.9	74.1	75.8	92.8
25–34	96.4*	93.9*	98.6	24.2*	29.5*	48.7	59.6*	62.2*	74.0
35–44	96.7	94.2	92.8	21.8	31.0	43.9	59.9	62.4	68.8
45–54	94.5	91.8	90.3	20.4	33.3	44.4	58.8	63.1	67.1
55–64	85.7	81.7	80.1	14.5	24.4	34.4	51.3	53.5	56.9
65+	38.6	28.4	23.6	5.1	6.7	8.3	22.1	17.2	15.1
Total	88.9	86.2	90.9	28.8	26.5	52.0	59.1	61.5	71.3

*Census does not give figures for school attendance.

TABLE IX   Number and Percent of the Population, Fifteen Years of Age and Over, Employed in Agriculture by Region, 1911-71

	1911	1921	1931	1941	1951*	1961*	1971*
	Number (in thousands)						
Maritimes	114	113	107	95	63	34	24
Quebec	203	213	223	250	193	133	78
Ontario	304	292	303	268	203	172	143
Prairies	282	372	442	420	336	284	240
B.C.	24	35	44	41	28	24	28
Canada	928	1025	1118	1075	826	649	512
	Percent						
Maritimes	18.4	17.3	16.1	12.1	6.0	2.9	1.7
Quebec	16.5	14.6	12.0	11.0	7.2	3.9	1.8
Ontario	17.0	14.3	12.3	9.4	6.0	4.1	2.6
Prairies	32.1	30.6	28.2	24.2	18.8	13.5	9.7
B.C.	8.1	9.3	8.3	6.5	3.3	2.2	1.8
Canada	19.3	17.8	16.8	13.0	8.5	5.4	3.4

*Includes Newfoundland.

producers. The differing importance of unpaid family workers from province to province is also noteworthy. In general, large proportions of wage laborers are offset by small proportions of unpaid family workers (e.g., Newfoundland, Nova Scotia, New Brunswick, and British Columbia). In contrast, Quebec shows an unusually high percentage of unpaid family workers, of whom almost 50 percent were males (as opposed to the national average of 38 percent). Agriculture in Quebec, it seems, has preserved the traditional family patterns of the independent commodity production society to a greater degree than any other province. The contrast between the Maritimes and Quebec, the regions most affected by the dissolution of independent commodity production agriculture, is interesting. In the Maritimes (except in Prince Edward Island) agriculture has moved the furthest toward the capitalist mode of production (the McCains of Florenceville, New Brunswick, are, perhaps, the epitome of this process), but in Quebec, while under equal pressure, agriculture has with government intervention managed to retain to a large degree the traditional forms and social relations.

Before examining regional aspects of the dissolution of family production and employment of females in capitalist labor relations, it is necessary to look at regional variations in the labor force and labor participation rates. Tables XI[25] and XII[26] show considerable difference in rates of increase of labor forces in different regions. For example, in the Maritimes there was little growth except between 1931 and 1941 when the Depression discouraged rural out-migration in all parts of Canada, and in 1961-71 when both federal and provincial economic development programs appear to have inhibited normal out-migration. In con-

TABLE X   Proportion of the Agricultural Labor Force Working as Wage Earners, on Own Account or as Unpaid Family Workers, 1971

	Wage earners	Own account	Unpaid family workers	Total
Newfoundland	65.8	21.9	12.3	100.0
Prince Edward Island	31.4	46.1	22.4	99.9
Nova Scotia	51.6	33.5	14.8	99.9
New Brunswick	46.4	36.4	17.2	100.0
Atlantic Provinces	45.7	36.9	17.4	100.0
Quebec	25.8	45.8	28.3	99.9
Ontario	39.2	39.4	21.4	100.0
Manitoba	24.4	51.8	23.9	100.1
Saskatchewan	20.5	58.6	20.9	100.0
Alberta	27.0	48.6	24.4	100.0
Prairie Provinces	23.7	53.5	22.8	100.0
British Columbia	54.0	28.5	17.5	100.0
Canada	31.0	46.3	22.7	100.0

TABLE XI   Total Labor Force by Region, 1911–71 (thousands)

	1911	1921	1931	1941	1951	1961	1971
Maritimes	323	347	351	413	530*	562*	715*
Quebec	645	771	1,014	1,231	1,467	1,768	2,243
Ontario	981	1,111	1,343	1,570	1,883	2,393	3,411
Prairies	545	695	894	941	953	1,158	1,495
British Columbia	205	219	306	343	444	578	930
Canada	2,698	3,144	3,908	4,498	5,277*	6,458*	8,813*

*Includes Newfoundland.

TABLE XII   Percentage Increase in Labor Force by Region, 1911–71

	1911–21	1921–31	1931–41	1941–51	1951–61	1961–71	1911–71
Maritimes	7.4	1.2	17.7	2.4*	6.0*	27.2*	121.4†
Quebec	19.5	31.5	21.4	19.2	20.5	26.9	247.8
Ontario	13.3	20.9	16.9	19.9	27.1	42.5	247.8
Prairies	27.5	28.6	5.3	1.3	21.5	29.1	174.3
British Columbia	6.8	39.7	12.1	29.4	30.2	60.9	353.7
Canada	16.5	24.3	15.1	14.9*	22.4†	36.5†	226.6†

* Does not include Newfoundland.
†Includes Newfoundland.

trast, growth rates in Quebec, Ontario and British Columbia went up faster than average, but with these differences: Quebec's labor force grew at above average rates from 1911 to 1951, then dropped sharply to below average levels while Ontario and British Columbia grew at below average levels before 1921 but at above average levels ever since. The Prairies show yet another pattern: high growth rates from agrarian settlement to 1931, stagnation during and after the Depression when large-scale out-migration occurred, and nearly average growth since 1951.[27]

Not surprisingly, given the large differences in growth rates of the labor force in the various regions, there are also significant differences in participation rates (Table XIII[28]). Particularly important is that although Maritime and Quebec participation rates remain close to the national average until 1951, between 1951 and 1961 Maritime rates for males drop well below average, and between 1961 and 1971 Quebec male rates follow suit. Similarly, Maritime female participation rates remain close to the national average until 1941, then drop behind the rapid

TABLE XIII   Male, Female, and Total Labor Force Participation Rates by Region, 1911–71

	1911	1921	1931	1941	1951*	1961*	1971*
				Male			
Maritimes	88.5	88.3	86.2	84.7	81.0	70.8	70.7
Quebec	87.3	86.9	87.2	85.4	85.0	76.7	71.4
Ontario	89.6	88.8	86.7	86.4	85.6	80.8	80.3
Prairies	92.3	90.4	89.4	86.6	83.0	79.2	78.7
British Columbia	91.9	88.8	87.8	83.1	88.5	74.2	77.6
Canada	89.6	88.7	87.5	85.8	83.8	77.7	76.4
				Female			
Maritimes	14.0	16.2	16.7	18.2	19.6	23.3	32.6
Quebec	16.2	18.7	21.9	22.9	24.9	27.9	35.0
Ontario	17.7	19.0	20.5	22.3	26.7	32.6	44.3
Prairies	13.6	14.5	16.6	16.6	21.1	29.7	42.5
British Columbia	18.1	16.2	19.4	18.7	23.4	28.3	40.5
Canada	16.2	17.5	19.6	20.7	24.1	29.5	39.9
				Total			
Maritimes	52.3	52.9	52.5	52.5	50.5	47.4	51.7
Quebec	52.3	52.8	54.7	54.2	54.6	52.1	52.8
Ontario	54.9	54.3	54.4	54.9	56.0	56.6	62.1
Prairies	61.9	57.1	57.0	54.3	53.4	55.2	60.7
British Columbia	68.1	58.4	58.5	53.4	51.6	51.6	59.1
Canada	56.0	54.6	55.1	54.2	54.2	53.8	58.0

*Includes Newfoundland.

TABLE XIV   Labor Force and Persons Employed, by Region, 1951-71

	Labor force (thousands)		Employed (thousands)		Percentage growth 1951-71	
	1951	1971	1951	1971	Labor force	Employed
Maritimes	513	676	491	618	31.8	25.9
Quebec	1,462	2,394	1,420	2,197	63.7	54.7
Ontario	1,870	3,249	1,838	3,079	73.7	67.5
Prairies	948	1,401	933	1,338	47.8	43.4
British Columbia	431	911	416	847	111.4	103.6
Canada	5,224	8,631	5,098	8,079	65.2	58.5

rise in national female labor force participation. In Quebec, female labor force participation rates tend to be at or above average until 1951; after that they begin to fall behind. In contrast, Prairie female labor force participation remains below average until 1951, then increases rapidly to above average levels in 1971.

In spite of the capacity of capitalism in Canada to dissolve pre-capitalist productive relations, since World War II it has not demonstrated an equal ability to absorb the working-age population looking for work. Table XIV,[29] based on Statistics Canada calculations, shows that, although there are enormous differences in the rates of labor participation and employment between regions, in every region labor force growth has outstripped job creation, with the result that high rates of unemployment have become endemic. In the Maritimes, where labor participation rates are dropping drastically behind national averages and where unemployment rates among those participating are the highest in the country, the capitalist sector is showing the least capacity to absorb labor. At current (1951-71) rates, for every 100 new jobs created, 128 persons enter the labor force. For Quebec the number is 120; Ontario, 111; the Prairies, 112; B.C., 111; and for Canada as a whole, 117. In other words, for the 3,407,000 Canadians who entered the labor force between 1951 and 1971, there were only 2,981,000 jobs available, leaving some 426,000 to join the 126,000 persons already unemployed.

In spite of these huge surpluses building up in the capitalist labor market, the pre-capitalist production sectors continue to be eroded (Table XV[30]). Between 1971 and 1976 employment in the agricultural sector fell by about ten percent, while the proportion of women working or seeking work increased by 14.9 percent. These changes were made in the face of a labor market which was becoming ever less inviting — where the proportion of unemployed men increased by 12.8 percent and of women by 22.5 percent. Dissolution of the pre-capitalist production sectors was, it appears, not the result of the demands of the capitalist labor market for labor — since 1951, there has been a growing

TABLE XV   Labor Force Participation and Employment, Selected Sectors, Canada 1971–76

	January 1971	January 1976	July 1971	July 1976
Employment in agriculture '000s	465	416	588	532
Percent of total labor force	5.6	4.2	6.5	4.9
Women in the labor force '000s	2,834	3,715	3,076	4,026
Female participation rate	38.0	43.5	40.7	46.9
Male participation rate	75.1	75.8	82.0	81.9
Total participation rate	56.3	59.6	61.1	64.2
Female unemployment rate	7.5	8.5	6.7	8.9
Male unemployment rate	7.5	7.8	5.7	6.1
Total unemployment rate	7.5	8.0	6.1	7.2

surplus of that commodity — but from other factors. Marx's grim predictions about the final dissolution of pre-capitalist forms of production arising from competition between modes of production appear to be coming true in Canada.

The dissolution of the material base of a social formation, Marx argued, ultimately caused the collapse of ideologies and social structures built on that base. With the decline of independent commodity production, therefore, one might expect the decay of ideologies and social structures based on individualism and resistance to interference or control by external agencies be they religious, governmental or societal in nature. Similarly, with the decline of household production, ideologies and structures based on monogamy, heterosexuality and superiority of the male may well be called into serious question. Those who intend to involve themselves in the moral, political and social issues arising from these changes should remember that, according to Marxist theory, the clock cannot be turned back unless the material basis for these social forms is re-established. Given the material superiority of the capitalist mode of production over pre-capitalist modes, that is unlikely.

Notes

1. Leo A. Johnson, "The Development of Class in Canada in the Twentieth Century," *Capitalism and the National Question in Canada*, Gary Teeple, ed. (Toronto, 1972), pp. 141–183.

2. Leo A. Johnson, *Poverty in Wealth* (New Hogtown Press, Toronto, 1974).

3. In general, it is my work style to keep coming back to these issues as the discussion and my own understanding and ideas develop. Thus *Poverty in Wealth* is the second look at the question of income disparity as it is related to the labor market, and a new version of "The Development of Class in Canada" is taking shape as research and study continue.

4. Karl Marx, *A Contribution to the Critique of Political Economy*, Maurice Dobb, ed. (London, 1970), preface by Marx, pp. 20–22.

5. Karl Marx, *Capital* (International Publishers, New York, 1967) Vol. I, p. 74. See especially chapters XXVI to XXXIII, pp. 713–765, for a clear exposition of this subject. Marx's comments in Vol. III, pp. 325 ff. also bear directly on the distinction between merchant and capitalism, and on the nature of pre-capitalist bourgeois modes of production.

6. Marx, *A Contribution to the Critique of Political Economy*, *op. cit.*, pp. 20–21.

7. Marx, *Capital* Vol. I, pp. 761–2.

8. Marx, *A Contribution to the Critique of Political Economy*, *op. cit.*, pp. 33, 50–51; Karl Marx and Frederick Engels, "Feuerbach: Opposition of the Materialistic and Idealistic Outlook" (Chap. I of *The German Ideology*) in *Karl Marx and Frederick Engels Selected Works* (Moscow, 1969), Vol. I, pp. 34ff.; Frederick Engels, "Origin of the Family, Private Property and the State," *Selected Works*, *op. cit.*, Vol. III, especially pp. 240–248.

9. Engels, *Selected Works*, *op. cit.*, p. 247.

10. The census data are drawn from the "occupations" tables in various years of the *Canada Census*. Calculations are my own. It should be noted that there is some variation in the manner in which the labor force data were collected. From 1911 to 1941 the basis was "gainfully occupied" which eliminated those young persons who had never held a paying job, although then seeking work. From 1951 on, this small group was included. It is thought that such a change had little impact on the overall data. It should be noted, as well, that "labor force" includes those persons who are unemployed, but looking for work, as well as those who are not working due to temporary illness, vacations, etc. Throughout the tables drawn from the census, the 1941 labor force includes persons on active service.

11. The data for unemployment are drawn from *Canadian Statistical Review, Historical Summary, 1970*, Statistics Canada, catalogue no. 11-505F, Tables 7 and 8, pp. 50–51. Calculations are my own. In this table Statistics Canada has manipulated the census data in the following manner: a) they excluded inmates of institutions, members of the armed forces, Indians living on reserves, and residents of the Yukon and Northwest Territories; b) estimates for 1931 and 1941 include persons on temporary lay-off as employed; c) estimates for 1931 and 1941 are for June 1 only, 1951 the average of four quarterly surveys, and 1961 and 1971, the average of 12 monthly surveys. Unemployment data for 1931 and 1941, therefore, are likely to be significantly underestimated.

12. *Canada Census*, see note 10.

13. *Ibid.*

14. *Ibid.*

15. *Ibid.*

16. *Ibid.*

17. *Ibid.*

18. *Ibid.*

19. *Ibid.*

20. *Ibid.*

21. Statistics Canada, *Facts about the Unemployed*, Catalogue no. 71-520 occasional, pp. 10–13.

22. *Canada Census*, see note 10.

23. *Ibid.*

24. *Ibid.*

25. *Ibid.*

26. *Ibid.*

27. For definitive treatments of labor force growth and composition, and of interprovincial migration, see Sylvia Ostry, *Geographic Composition of the Canadian Labour Force* (D.B.S., Ottawa, 1968); Sylvia Ostry, *Provincial Differences in Labour Force Participation* (D.B.S., Ottawa, 1968), and Leroy O. Stone, *Migration in Canada: Some Regional Aspects* (D.B.S., Ottawa, 1969). Also useful is Noah M. Meltz, *Manpower in Canada 1931–1961* (Manpower and Immigration, Ottawa, 1969).

28. *Canada Census*, see note 10.

29. *Canadian Statistical Review*, *op. cit.*, pp. 48–50, Tables 4:3–4:9. See note 11.

30. *Canada Census*, see note 10.

31. Data are from *Historical Labour Force Statistics – Actual Data, Seasonal Factors, Seasonally Adjusted Data*, Statistics Canada, Labour Force Survey Division, 1976. Calculations are my own.

Access to the Canadian Corporate Elite*

Wallace Clement

Embedded in the capitalist economic order of Canada and perpetuated through the sanctity of private property, the corporate elite during the post-World War II period has concentrated its base of power (Clement, 1974: 18–25) and consolidated avenues of access into its inner circles. Important transformations have occurred in the economic structure, and rapid industrialization has been evident, but the corporate elite remains as closed as it was in 1951, even tighter in some key respects. Contrary to liberal ideology, which holds that greater mobility will characterize "postindustrialism," Canada remains capitalist, industrial, and closed at the upper levels of corporate power. Many sociologists who celebrate existing structures assert that corporate capitalism, with time and industrialization, will reduce inequalities based on ascription. Talcott Parsons, for example,[1] argues that religion, ethnicity, regionalism, and social class based on ascriptive characteristics "have lost much of their force" (1970: 14–15). Evidence now exists which shows that this has not been the case for Canada between 1951 and 1972. Although only the upper levels of corporate power are examined in this study, other recent studies find that increasing inequality is a general phenomenon penetrating the entire social structure.

ELITES AND SOCIAL CLASS

Corporate elite positions reflect Marx's analysis of the accumulation and concentration of capital into fewer and larger units and the "Pareto principle" of "separating the trivial many from the vital few." The corporate elite are synonymous in many respects with the "big bourgeoisie." Within the 113 dominant corporations in Canada in 1972,[2] two dimensions of inequality are important. One involves positions within corporations, their stratification and power differentials, and the other, recruitment to these positions. The first is concerned with condition and the second with opportunity. In other words, the first is concerned about the structure of inequality, the second about the processes

* Abridged from the *Canadian Review of Sociology and Anthropology* 12 (1) 1975, pp. 33–52. Used with permission.

　This paper was an extension of an earlier paper (Clement, 1974) and the same acknowledgments to John Porter, Dennis Olsen, Leo Panitch, and Dennis Forcese (all of Carleton University) are in order. In addition, the advice of Raymond Breton has been important to the final form of this paper.

of maintaining inequality.[3] To show that a corporate elite exists demonstrates the existence of inequality of condition; to show that there is differential access to elite positions demonstrates that there is an unequal opportunity structure.

This dichotomy is similar to that outlined by Frank Parkin (1972) when he distinguished between the "egalitarian critique" and the "meritocratic critique." The first focuses on "objection to the wide disparities of reward accruing to different positions," while the second is concerned about "the process of recruitment to these positions... Seen from this angle, social justice entails not so much the equalization of rewards as the equalization of opportunities to compete for the most privileged positions"(13). Parkin suggests the importance of synthesizing the two critiques since they are analytically distinct aspects of inequality but actually closely related. One concept used to integrate the two is kinship, whereby families are able to pass on their accumulated advantages intergenerationally, thus perpetuating class continuity through the ascriptive institutions of kinship and inheritance.[4] Of course, it is not kinship per se that perpetuates existing class structures. This is accomplished by the persistence of an economic order organized on the basis of corporate capitalism which determines which types of occupations will be created, how many there will be, how the economy will expand, its direction and scope, and the level of technology which will exist. Class structures, therefore, are a product of the way a society's economy is organized and class continuity a product of the way privilege is transferred. In Canada, as with all capitalist societies, there is a high correlation between class structures and class continuity. Those with advantages are able to pass them on, while those without are not able to provide their offspring with the same privileges.

Hierarchies within economic organizations and the existence of dominant corporations create positions of power to which social classes are differentially recruited, thus perpetuating dominant classes and reinforcing power disparities. By examining inequalities of power associated with key corporate positions and the perpetuation of class advantages, a corporate elite with roots firmly embedded in the upper class will be illustrated.

OWNERS, DIRECTORS, AND MANAGERS

Ownership and control are not as widely separated as has sometimes been suggested (see Zeitlin, 1974). Family firms among the dominant corporations in Canada still have a very prominent place. However, within some corporations ownership has become dispersed, primarily within the upper levels of income earners, but controlling ownership typically remains concentrated. Dispersal of ownership, which does occur in some cases, is not spread evenly throughout the population. Indeed in 1968 only 10.3 percent of income earners owned even one share, and the top 10 percent of income earners owned about three-quarters of all shares (Statistics Canada, 1970: Tables 2 and 5). This results in a community of interest among a select group of large shareholders who provide binding ties transcending individual corporate entities. The small stockholder remains a rentier, whose capital is mobilized as an investment for dividend and capital appreciation but not for control. Controlling ownership is represented usually by a block of about ten percent or more of the voting shares, if the remainder of the stock is widely dispersed. In this situation, a block of shares is able to control corporations which exceed the value of the investment many times over. When this is combined with the fact that there are 1,848 interlocked positions among the boards of 113 dominant corporations in Canada (Clement, 1974:23–5), it becomes difficult to maintain an image of competitive capitalism. In fact, 60.3 percent of the executives in dominant corporations hold an outside directorship in at least one of the other 113 dominant corporations; moreover, members of the corporate elite also hold an additional 41 percent of the uppermost positions (senior management and directors) in the next 175 largest corporations, many of which are executive posts. In other words, the outside directors of one dominant company tend to be the executives of others. It is one thing to say a person is an outside director of a particular corporation and quite another to place that corporation within the entire network of large corporations where such persons are typically members of the executive of one or more other companies. Members of the corporate elite tend to have several roles simultaneously; many are owners, managers, and directors all at the same time. Consequently, by broadening the scope of study, the distinction between these three categories tends to lose much of its meaning.

Decision-making remains a collegial activity involving those within the arena of power. Although the corporate elite is being defined as senior executives and members of the boards of the 113 largest corporations in Canada, all within this group are not equal in their power. If share ownership were determined, the number of corporate elites would probably be substantially reduced. Senior executives and the boards of directors are, however, a strong indicator of stock ownership since those who hold controlling blocks of shares are able to select the boards of directors for the corporation and these in turn appoint senior management. Porter argues, "Directors control the resources of corporations through particular legal instruments which give them the right to do so" (1965:229). The board of directors represents directly the interests of dominant shareholders and makes decisions of importance about the policy and direction of the corporation. Managers deemed important by the controlling interests, outsiders of importance, and the controlling ownership itself, all sit on these boards.[5] It is the people who occupy these powerful positions in the 113 dominant corporations in Canada who are called the corporate elite.

SOCIAL CHARACTERISTICS OF CORPORATE ELITE

The findings of the present study show that access into elite positions has become more difficult for persons outside the upper class. Since 1951 there has been a crystallization of the upper levels of power beyond the already rigid power structure identified by Porter in 1951. Directors and senior executives were identified from the 113 dominant corporations operating in Canada, and it was shown that a total of 946 individuals resident in Canada hold 1,456 of the corporate directorships. Adequate biographical data were found for 775 persons

(81.9 percent) who between them account for 1,276 positions (87.8 percent). This compared favorably with Porter's coverage of 77.8 percent of the members and 82 percent of the positions for 1951.

Career Avenues into the Elite

Several important changes have occurred in the career patterns for members of the corporate elite. The proportion of members of the elite technically trained in science and engineering has declined. It would be expected that greater proportions of technical men would have made their way into the elite if specialized technical skills were now more central to decision-making as the "post-industrial" thesis would suggest, but this has not been the case.

Financial executives have remained stable, with one significant change occurring in terms of educational backgrounds for this group. While in 1951 only 45 percent had attended university, now 60 percent of the financiers, 70 percent of the insurance company executives, and 57 percent of the other financial executives have done so. While only a quarter of the banking executives have attended university, these seven represent a substantial increase from the one in twenty-three who had in 1951. Porter indicates that in 1951, 39 percent of the financiers had elite connections with such connections being most prevalent among the youngest group. This is borne out in the present set of financiers, 46 percent of whom have family connections in the elite. Bankers also have a high percentage (35 percent) of elite connections. A high proportion of individuals in this group attended private school. Enjoying this advantage were 23 (46 percent) financiers, nine (31 percent) bankers, seven (23 percent) insurance executives, and eleven (37 percent) other financial executives. Private schools have provided large numbers of the individuals in this category with common experiences at an early age, as well as allowing extensive contacts to be developed with other upper class peers. These initial contacts have been fostered in later life within the confines of one or more of the exclusive national men's clubs (Rideau, Mont Royal, St. James, York, Toronto, and National). Sixty-six percent of the financiers, 90 percent of the bank executives, 47 percent of the life insurance company executives, and 70 percent of the other financial executives belong to one or more of these six clubs.

Lawyers tend to be of upper class origin, and many have inherited law firms and directorships from their fathers. There has been a substantial increase in the proportion of lawyers entering the corporate elite. This change is due almost exclusively to those who have law degrees but choose to enter the elite via the corporation legal department rather than the law firm. While only nine percent of the lawyers came through the legal departments of corporations in 1951, 24 percent were internal recruits in 1972. This suggests an increasing number who have chosen law as a general education suited to the corporate world and not primarily as a means of entering private practice. Law partnerships, however, remain an important linking institution. Porter reports for 1951 that 13 sets of partners had more than one member in the elite. This number has increased to 23 in 1972. Together they include 60 partners and 106 dominant directorships.

Many lawyers share a common social experience in their educational careers; for example, four went to the University of Toronto Schools for their private schooling together, each going to the University of Toronto for their LLBs and then on to Osgoode Hall "finishing school." This included one pair of twins, John A. and James M. Tory, who followed their lawyer father's footsteps, together taking over five of his dominant corporate directorships. All the lawyers are trained in Canada, with half attending Osgoode Hall. About one-fifth go to the University of Toronto and one-fifth to McGill University. Private school education is not uncommon for lawyers in the elite; 46 percent of those in law practice and 29 percent of the internal lawyers have this advantage.

Similar proportions in both periods made it into the elite through the finance departments. Of the 44 Canadian-born, 33 are chartered accountants, nine have economics or administrative training, and two appear to be inside-trained, both of whom entered the corporate world after attending private schools. Only four of the 15 foreign-born are chartered accountants. The others worked their way up as treasurers or comptrollers. For the most part, those entering the elite through the finance department have entered as inside directors and remained there; they also have fewer interlocks with other dominant companies than do those with other career patterns.

Porter did not include commerce as a career pattern in 1951, noting that "comparatively few persons in the elite have been trained in commerce or business administration" (1957:381). Commerce careers have become more prevalent. Persons in commerce hold 5.1 percent of the directorships in dominant corporations, 5.5 percent of bank directorships, and 5.7 percent of those in insurance. An additional 30 members of the elite have also received commerce degrees but their main careers have been classified elsewhere.

More people have been classified in this study as having their main careers in another elite than was the case in 1951, but part of the reason for this is a redefinition in this study of what constitutes inclusion. Only 14 persons (1.8 percent) transferred to the corporate elite after having their main careers in the political, bureaucratic, or military elite, in 1951. In 1972, 5.8 percent of the corporate elite entered by way of another elite, including 18 from the bureaucratic elite and 17 from the political elite as defined by Porter (1965) and Olsen (1973). An additional ten are classified as coming from the academic elite, including university deans, presidents, and prominent professors, particularly from business schools. There are no members having their main careers in the military. Even using only the political and bureaucratic elite, the numbers when compared to Porter's findings have more than doubled, representing a greater degree of interlock between the corporate and state elites than existed 20 years earlier. Among the members of the political elite are eight former federal cabinet ministers, five former provincial premiers, one former prime minister, and three provincial political elites. "Career switchers" hold 6.2 percent of all dominant directorships.

The 133 individuals who have been characterized as gaining access to the elite through family firms have spent the majority of their business careers in corporations where their fathers, or in five cases maternal grandfathers, held key corporate positions. This does not include all those who began at or near the top of the class structure, nor does it include those who gained their access through their father-in-law's firms. There are 133 individuals in this category now, compared to the 113 in 1951. The current figure includes 126 of the Canadian-born (18.8 percent) and only seven foreign-born (6.8 percent). Within the current elite who are Canadian-born with their main careers in family firms, there are 24 father/son combinations, and thirty-two are brothers. In examining the entire group of 133 individuals who inherited their positions it becomes evident that private schools play a large part in their careers. Eighty-five attended private schools (64 percent of the group), and 108 attended university (81 percent). The power of this group extends further than does that of any other group in terms of interlocking directorships; they account for 18.7 percent of the directorships in all dominant companies, 23 percent in banks with 35 percent of the group holding dominant bank directorships, and 21.4 percent of the insurance directorships.

In contrast to those who enter the elite through family firms are those who manage to establish firms on their own account and gain the stature of becoming members of the elite in one generation. For 1951 Porter reports that 58 of the elite made it in this manner. A strong indicator that the structure of power in Canada has become more rigid over the past 20 years is the fact that only 26 members of the present elite have made it on their own account. They hold only two percent of the dominant directorships and 1.5 percent of the bank directorships.

Class Origins

Class origins are important from a number of perspectives. They show the extent of mobility existing at any given time and (if more than one time-frame is available, as in the present case) relative changes in class access to elite positions. When one is concerned with mobility one assumes that talent is distributed throughout all classes in society and if everyone had an equal chance at access to the elite the total society would be better served. From the perspective of liberal democratic theory, the concern is focused on the value that everyone should have equal opportunity to participate in the management and direction of a society's future. From the social structural perspective, class access is an important indicator of the degree of openness present in the flow between different classes or, put differently, the extent of class crystallization there is in a society. The more difficult it is for people outside the upper class to enter the elite, the greater the exclusiveness of power in a particular society. With greater crystallization of power there is less opportunity for those outside the inner circles of power to actualize their concerns and desires, thus stifling equality of opportunity which forms the basis of liberal democratic ideology.

Comparing over-all changes between 1951 and 1972 it is found for the Canadian-born members of the current elite that 28.5 percent had fathers, or, in a few cases, uncles, in the corporate elite at some time. This represents an increase of 6.5 percent from 1951 of the proportion of the elite enjoying the advantage of coming from a family directly in the inner circles of the corporate world in a previous generation. There is obviously a high degree of continuity when 192 members replicate their fathers' positions. Adding 16 members who had fathers either in the political or bureaucratic elite, gives an increase to 30.9 percent compared to 24 percent in 1951. A further 39 not already included married into elite families. This means that 247 members of the current elite embarked on their careers with the initial advantage of having elite connections. This represents about a six percent increase since 1951. Another 68 not thus far included had fathers who were in substantial businesses which, as far as could be determined, were not dominant but of sufficient size to provide an initial upper class avenue into the elite. This means that 46.8 percent of the present elite began at or near the top of the class structure.[6] The current figure for those who started with this initial advantage shows a full nine percent increase over the 1951 findings. Of the remainder, 85 had attended private schools. This brings to 400 or 59.4 percent of the elite, the number who had upper class origins, a significantly higher percentage than the 50 percent with the same origins in 1951.

A further 57 had fathers who were engaged in middle class occupations such as engineers, doctors, lawyers, ministers, or managers. This brings the total to 457, accounting for almost 68 percent of the elite. There are also 177 persons not included to this point who had attended university. The addition of this group brings the proportion accounted for to 94.2 percent, while the same indicators accounted for only 82 percent in 1951. The remaining percentage accounts for those who have made it into the elite from lower than middle class origins. While in 1951 18 percent of the elite were in this bottom classification, only 5.8 percent of the present elite are in the same position. The majority of the population, of course, has less than middle class origins as defined here, with over 80 percent of the male population engaged in other than managerial, technical, or professional occupations (see Kalbach and McVey, 1971:257). Each indicator shows that the current elite is of higher class origins than 20 years ago. The class structure of Canadian society has tightened in terms of gaining access into the corporate elite.

Particularly the upper class, but also the middle class, are over-represented compared to the general population. Moreover, this over-representation has increased over the last two decades. While there is no reason to believe that there have been any significant changes in the size of the upper class, the proportion of those of upper class origins in the elite has increased by 9.4 percent over the period. The number of persons in the current elite who are of middle class origin has increased by 2.8 percent, a change which could correspond to a change in the class composition of the population. Those with working class origins represent a significant decline of 12.2 percent. The major difference between the two periods can be found in the 6.5 percent increase in the proportion with fathers in the corporate elite, and particularly those whose careers are in family firms, as discussed earlier.

It is recognized that there is differentiation within the elite based on length of time in the elite, by corporate positions, by control exercised as in the case of comprador and indigenous elites, by corporate activities or functions, and between single and multiple directorship holders. These will now be examined.

Elite Continuity

Within the present elite there is a set of 76 members who appear in both the 1951 and 1972 elites, that is, they have survived over twenty years in the corporate elite. Analysis of this group showed a conservative bias in the method of data collection on social origins in favor of lower class origins. Based on this it can be asserted that the method employed by Porter and replicated here understates the extent of elite reproduction. This analysis also found that there is a dramatic difference between the class origins of the group which has been in the elite for twenty years and all members of the elite for 1951 and for 1972. Exactly one-half of the first group had fathers who were themselves in the economic elite in an earlier period. This involves 38 individuals, of whom thirty-five directly inherited directorships from their fathers. Inheritance is substantially more prevalent for those who have lasted twenty years or more than for either the 1951 or the 1972 elites. It is found that 68.5 percent of the core group had upper class origins compared to 50 percent and 59.4 percent of the 1951 and 1972 elites respectively. This suggests not only that upper class members move to the top at an earlier age but that they last longer, providing greater historical continuity than even their high numbers in the elite as a whole would imply. It also illustrates that private property in the form of inheritance is a major legal device members of the upper class have for staying in powerful positions and they use this to pass privileges on to their offspring. It is also important to note that within this group there is only one Jew and three French Canadians (less than four percent) and no one from other ethnic groups aside from Anglo-Saxons. This illustrates that only Anglo-Saxons have high continuity within the elite, most likely because they control capital in terms of ownership, which they are able to transfer intergenerationally.

Corporate Positions

Few members of the elite could be said to be selected *meritocratically* in the sense that they have worked their way up through the corporate bureaucracy without the advantages of middle or upper class origins. Even all inside directors are not meritocratic. They are rather of two types: first, sons learning the business, and secondly, those engaged in a long, or relatively long, crawl to the boardroom. Based on an analysis of the difference between the class origins of insiders and executives it can be said that even at the upper levels of power those with class advantages are more likely to make the break from the insider to executive level; 63.5 percent of the outside directors and 62 percent of the executives have upper class origins, while only 46.7 percent of the inside directors enjoyed this advantage. If the sons who have careers in family firms are separated, only 31 percent of the inside directors originated in the upper class. It is evident that it is primarily sons learning the business and those of high class origin who are able to make the shift into the executive ranks from within the bureaucracy and similarly into the circle of outside directors. Given this phenomenon, it is doubtful that many of the insider comprador elites will break into the executive ranks of multinational corporations they work for.

Comprador Elites and Mobility

The comprador elite[7] is made up of those members of the elite who identified their main corporate affiliation as a Canadian subsidiary of a foreign-controlled parent. In cases where the "principal occupation" was other than corporate, as in the case of a law firm, the designation was based on the country of control of the corporations in which the individual held the majority of his dominant directorships.

When the affiliations of all Canadian-born members are analyzed it is found that 76 percent are members of the indigenous Canadian elite, 15.8 percent are US-controlled comprador elites, 5.6 percent UK comprador elites, and 2.6 percent "other" comprador elites.[8] When the various elites are divided by age, an interesting pattern emerges. Of those born before 1905, 84.9 percent are members of the indigenous elite, with only 12.6 percent US comprador, 1.7 percent UK, and 0.8 percent "other." In contrast, of those born between 1905 and 1920, 73.2 percent are indigenous, a drop of over 10 percent from the older group, while 17 percent are US comprador, 5.6 percent UK, and 4.2 percent "other." The youngest group, born after 1920, begins to reverse the age relationship with 76 percent indigenous, 15.8 percent US, 5.6 percent UK, and 2.6 percent "other." The increasing compradorization of the corporate elite represented by the shift from the oldest to the middle group is counteracted by the youngest group which has the highest degree of inheritance and is consequently indigenous. In spite of the high degree of inheritance within the youngest age group, there are still 8.9 percent more comprador elites in this group than in the oldest, while an 11.7 percent difference between the middle and oldest group remains the greatest gap. Although the over-all trend in the past twenty years has been toward increased compradorization of the Canadian corporate elite, there still remains a strong and vigorous indigenous core, evident in the existence of the youngest group of indigenous capitalists.

A very interesting difference exists between comprador and indigenous elites with respect to class origins. While "only" 45 percent of the comprador elites started out with upper class advantages, 64 percent of the indigenous elites had this initial advantage. For the middle class, a reversal occurs, with the comprador elite having 50 percent of its members within the middle class while only 30 percent of the indigenous elite are in this category. Comprador elites are more middle class than indigenous elites. For the working class there is a greater proportion of members from the indigenous elite than comprador, accounted for predominantly by Canadian institutions such as banks which have tended in the past to have lower class recruitment through their ranks. For this reason it can be stated that compradorization is predominantly a phenomenon of the middle class.

Compradorization has permitted some members of the middle class, but not the working class, to participate in arenas of power, unlike the indigenous elite, who have higher class origins and tend to exclude even the middle class. The process of compradorization is primarily a phenomenon of the middle class and does not have the same extent of participation from the upper class. The implications of this will be developed in the conclusion. Although the comprador elite has power within the Canadian context, or at least represents the power outsiders exercise in Canada, within the continental or North Atlantic triangle framework this so-called elite has only secondary power since it is dependent upon the externally based parasite elite.

CLOSING AVENUES TO THE ELITE

A good deal of evidence arises from this study to indicate that the elite is becoming an increasingly closed group. This will be summarized here for banks, new corporate sectors and regionalism.

Banks

Traditionally, the long crawl through the banks was one institutional avenue leading to the elite for those starting near the bottom of the class structure. Many bank executives used to begin at a very young age as clerks in local banks and work their way up over an average of 40 years into the executive ranks. To some extent this is still possible, but over the past 20 years this avenue of mobility has become restricted. More current executives come from upper class families, go to private schools and university, and enter the executive ranks at a much earlier age. For example, nine of the twenty-nine bank executives (31 percent) attended private schools and ten (35 percent) have family connections in the elite. Three of the executives have gone to post-graduate training, two at Harvard and one at the London School of Economics. Seven have undergraduate degrees. The tightening up of the upper levels in the banks is part of a general trend in this direction. With more of the upper class being recruited into the elite and with this one avenue being closed off to the lower classes, there are indications that the future will see even greater monopolization of positions of power by the upper class.

New Sectors

Of interest from the perspective of social change is the effect that expanding the scope of activities covered by dominant corporations has on the composition of the elite. Three new sectors have been introduced to the analysis since 1951, including trust companies, mortgage companies, and sales finance and consumer loans corporations. By examining class origins of elite members from these "new" financial fields it is possible to determine if their presence has had an effect on class access to the elite. Those individuals with directorships *only* in one of these sectors and holding no other dominant directorships will be examined. It is expected that class origins would shift lower since virtually all those with multiple directorships are excluded by definition. In spite of these qualifications, a similar class distribution remains. Examining those from the upper class, 60.2 percent of the subset are included with 59.4 percent over-all, compared to 50 percent over-all in 1951. The evidence shows that no inroads have been made into the elite because of the increased importance of these new sectors; quite the contrary, nearly one-quarter of these "new" positions are filled by sons of previous corporate elite. At the other end of the class structure only eight percent of the new group started with working class origins, while 5.8 percent of the entire group were in the same situation compared to 18 percent in

1951. This suggests that expanding the scope of the elite does not mean new social types are necessarily recruited. They can, as this data indicates, be "captured" by the traditional power holders. In Canada this is facilitated by the fact that these "new" sectors are all in finance, the traditional preserve of the indigenous elite. Another potential source of lower class mobility is cut off and upper class control becomes more pervasive.

Regionalism

Analysis of regionalism in Canada also indicates that avenues leading to the elite are closing. By examining the disparity between birth place of elites and the distribution of population at the time of their birth, it is possible to establish that regional inequalities exist in terms of access possibilities into the elite. Of the Canadian-born members of the elite, 68 percent were born in Ontario or Quebec, 23 percent in the western provinces, and only nine percent in the Maritimes. When this is compared to the 1921 distribution of population, the census year closest to when most of the present elite were born, it is found that the central provinces are over-represented by about eight percent while the west is under-represented by five percent and the east by three percent. There is a 13 percent difference between the center and the western periphery and 11 percent between the center and the east, with the center over-represented in each case.

For present purposes it is important to analyze differential class access by regions as distinct from disparities in numerical representation. As would be expected, Ontario and Quebec, with their longer established and more crystallized class structures, have more elite members from the upper class with 62.7 percent than the Maritimes, which are next with 59.3 percent, and the west, which has the lowest number with only 50 percent of the present elite members born there having upper class origins. There is a substantially greater difference between the west and the center (about 13 percent at the upper level) compared to the east and the center (a difference of only 3.4 percent). The findings suggest a high degree of similarity between the center and the east, based on the older established class structure in these regions. The west, on the other hand, as an immigrant society, did not have a rigid class structure relative to the other parts of Canada when the present elites were growing up in the 20s and 30s, or even when they were embarking on their careers in the 40s. An important conclusion from this is that as social structures mature and become more established, the chances decrease of those from the working and even middle classes entering elite positions. The small difference between the center and the east also indicates that it is not so much the level of development within the region that determines mobility as the maturity of the class structure. Measured in terms of economic development the east would be more similar to the west than to Ontario and Quebec. The major determinant of mobility would then seem to be the length of time the class structure of a particular region is allowed to survive without encountering social upheavals rather than the level of economic development within the region. The more hierarchical the social structure, the less chance for mobility, regardless of the so-called opportunity structure, which is said to be correlated with the level of development in society. It can be argued that as the west begins to mature, another avenue of access to elite positions from lower class origins may also be cut off.

CAREER AVENUES AND CORPORATE SECTORS

Of the 673 Canadian-born members of the corporate elite, 63 percent, or 433, can be classified as having used one primary corporate sector as an avenue into the elite. This particular analysis is limited to those born in Canada because its purpose is to isolate indigenous avenues into the elite. Of the remaining 37 percent Canadian-born not classified, 127 used law as the main avenue and 35 came from other elites. A further 78 could not be classified as having entered the elite through one of the five sectors. These include some from construction, engineering firms, accounting firms, the media, architecture, real estate, advertising and other activites, including some who switched between sectors during their careers.

Sectors were divided into major divisions and separated by control in order to determine what main corporate avenues have been used by the Canadian-born elite to move into their present positions. Of those classified, 8.8 percent came through utilities, 38.8 percent through finance, 18.7 percent through resources, 22.2 percent through manufacturing, and 11.5 percent through trade. When separated by control this same group includes three-quarters who gained access to the elite through Canadian-controlled firms, about one-fifth through US-controlled companies, and three percent each through UK and "other" controlled companies.

The findings indicate that by far the greatest corporate avenue is through Canadian-controlled finance corporations. Within the transportation and utilities sector, 92 percent had their early careers in Canadian-controlled firms while the remainder were in US-controlled companies. This increases to 95 percent through Canadian-controlled finance companies. Canadian-controlled companies in trade were also the main avenue for 88 percent. In manufacturing the situation begins to change, with only 58 percent using Canadian-controlled companies and 57 percent of these are in food, beverages, and related products, while US-controlled manufacturing accounts for 27 percent. In the resource sectors, US companies have the greatest career avenues, accounting for 53 percent, over half of all those who have used US-controlled companies. Canadian-controlled resource firms account for only 38 percent of the avenues in this sector, with 68 percent of these in the pulp and paper field.

Aside from US resource companies which provide avenues for 10 percent of the Canadian-born classified and, to a lesser extent, US manufacturing which provides an avenue for about five percent of the total, foreign firms have not been a major avenue to the elite for Canadians. Canadian-controlled companies, particularly in finance, utilities, and trade, have been a more common avenue. The evidence would suggest that there remain independent Canadian-controlled avenues, open to at least upper class Canadians born in Canada. There is still a core of Canadian elites who very much control the access into their select ranks.

ETHNICITY AND INEQUALITY OF ACCESS[9]

In Canada, as in other societies built on conquest and immigration, ethnicity is interwoven into the class system so that it provides advantages for the conquerors while keeping the conquered and the newly arrived at the bottom of the so-called opportunity structure. Two elite systems based on the two charter groups provide their members with differential access to the corporate elite, while the "third force" of other ethnic groups does not even have an elite of its own to operate in the national arenas of economic power.

French Canadians

Although French Canadians constitute about one-third of Canada's population, only 65 members of the corporate elite could be classified as such, making the French component of the elite only 8.4 percent. For 1951, Porter found there were 51 French Canadians representing only 6.7 percent of the elite at that time. This represents a net increase of only 14 persons or 1.7 percent over the past 20 years. The slight changes evident between the two periods have not decreased Anglo-Saxon dominance since the slight decline in the total proportion of Anglo-Saxons in the corporate elite is totally offset by their decline in the total population over the same period. It has been shown elsewhere that the Anglo-Saxons "index of representation" remains identical for each period, that is, they are just as over-represented in 1972 as they were in 1951 when compared to their proportion in the population (see Clement and Olsen, 1974:25–6). Some may argue that while the French have not made it into the very top of the corporate world, they have made strong gains in middle range and smaller corporations. Once again the evidence is to the contrary. A recent study based on 12,741 names which appeared in the 1971 *Directory of Directors* (a much larger group than the 775 members of the corporate elite) found that only 9.48 percent of these directors were French Canadians (Presthus, 1973:56).

Other Ethnic Groups

Although over one-fifth of Canada's population is made up of ethnic groups other than the two charter groups, they have almost no representation in the corporate elite, Jews being a notable exception. From the non-charter groups, there are only 32 Jewish Canadians (4.1 percent) and ten individuals from other third ethnic groups (1.3 percent). In 1951 there were only six Jews (0.78 percent) in the elite, an indication that they have made significant inroads into the elite over the past 20 years. There are, however, several factors associated with their mobility worth noting. Most of their inroads have been on their "own account," that is, mobility into the elite has not been through established corporations but through firms which have been established and grown to national scope within one generation. A closer examination of these firms explains why Jewish Canadians account for 4.1 percent of the elite and only 1.3 percent of the population. Of the 32 Jews, 28 are associated with five corporations; one is a long-established firm in the beverage industry, three others are in trade, and a final one deals primarily in real estate. These are all tightly held family firms, with only six families accounting for 25 of the 32 Jewish members of the elite. Outside these family firms, Jews have very little power in the corporate elite, holding only five bank directorships (2.4 percent) and two insurance directorships (1.2 percent). They have gained access by creating a parallel structure alongside, and for the most part separate from, the indigenous Anglo-Saxon elite.

EDUCATION AS TRAINING AND SOCIAL NETWORKS

Less than 10 percent of the male population in the same age group as the corporate elite have any education past secondary school, and about five percent have university degrees; the few who did have the advantage of higher education were indeed privileged. Of course if females of the corresponding age were included the proportions who attended university would drop even lower since only about two percent of the women had the same advantage. The corporate elite, in contrast to the general population, has had two distinct advantages; it is almost exclusively male (only six women), and most of its members have graduated from university.

In 1951, 58.3 percent of the corporate elite were university-educated, with an additional 5.4 percent having some other higher education past the secondary level such as chartered accountancy degrees or technical training. By 1972, 80.5 percent of the elite had university training and an additional four percent had other post-secondary education. In other words, only 104 (15.5 percent) of the Canadian-born members of the elite do not have more than secondary education; in 1951, 36.3 percent of the elite were in this position.

The interesting question becomes, not how many were educated at university, but how those who were not managed to get into the elite. Of the 104 who did not have post-secondary education, one-quarter (26) attended private schools and a further one-fifth (21) inherited their positions. In other words, almost half had upper class advantages and did not require university training as an avenue to the elite. Of those remaining, 14 spent an average of 40 years in the banks before attaining an executive post, two through insurance or other finance companies, eight by becoming financiers, six on their own account, two from the political elite, and 18 from a variety of other routes.

Not only is university education important but it appears that post-graduate training and professional degrees are also rapidly becoming prerequisites of elite membership. Of the Canadian-born, 280 have additional training beyond their undergraduate degrees. This number accounts for 41.6 percent of the entire Canadian-born elite. Of these, 183 have law degrees, including 15 who have post-graduate degrees beyond law, with ten of them attending Harvard for MBAS. Altogether, 53 of those with post-graduate degrees went to the United States for their education and 34 of these to Harvard for MBAS. An additional 14 went to the United Kingdom and two to France for their post-graduate training, with the rest obtaining their degrees in Canada.

Age has an effect on whether or not members of the elite attended university, with 73.1 percent of those born before 1905, 79.3 percent of those born between 1905 and 1920, and 87.3 percent of those born after 1920 attending. Together with the difference for the entire elite between 1951 and 1972, this provides conclusive evidence of the increasing importance of university education for elite membership.

Not all universities in Canada are equally endowed with the ability to pass on elite membership. Actually, only four universities passed on three-fifths of the elite attending university. Of those attending university, 27.1 percent had their undergraduate education at the University of Toronto, while another 15.7 percent went to McGill. While almost half obtained their degrees in one of these two places, there are eight other universities that had between three percent and 5.4 percent of the elite passing through their gates at the undergraduate level, together accounting for 34.7 percent of those attending. Not only university attendance itself but which university is attended also makes a considerable difference for movement into the elite.

THE PRIVATE WORLD OF POWERFUL PEOPLE

The upper levels of power in Canada are surrounded by a society very different from that experienced by most Canadians; the elite are people who become involved at the executive level in a range of philanthropic and cultural activities. From private schools to private clubs, they lead a life quite apart from, although very much affecting, the existence of the vast majority of Canadians. Through a series of elite forums and political connections, they make decisions well beyond those confined to the dominant corporations where they gain their power.

Private Schools

Although they may be examined as educational institutions, private schools can also be seen as class institutions designed to create elite associations and maintain class values both by exclusion and socialization, that is, exclusion of the lower classes and socialization of the potential elite. Private school education is a lifelong asset for the select few who experience it. The thousands of dollars it costs to send their children pays off many times over in the "social capital" accumulated during these formative years. What Porter refers to as "Simply an item within the common experience of class" (1965:528) is the total package of upper class training which occurs not only in the private schools but through the experiences gained by living in exclusive residential areas of Canada's metropolitan centers (areas such as Forest Hill, Westmount, or Rockcliffe Park), by vacationing at exclusive resorts in Canada and abroad, and by being privy to a host of other experiences known only to the upper levels of the class structure.

Attending "Dad's" old school is another form of inheritance which preserves elite continuity. The fee-paying private schools of eastern Canada are institutions that stem well back into Canada's history, with some, like Upper Canada

College, founded in 1829 and Trinity College School, founded in 1865, providing common class experiences for many generations of Canada's upper class.

The pervasiveness of private school attendance is on the increase in the elite. While 34.2 percent of the Canadian-born elite attended in 1951, this figure has increased to 39.8 percent, or 267, of the elite in 1972. Included are 49 of the 65 French Canadians who attended classical colleges,[10] about the same proportion as the 42 who had in 1951. Of those attending English-speaking private schools, elite members went almost exclusively to one of the members of the Headmasters' Association and, within this group, primarily to the older schools of eastern Canada.

It is evident why 64 percent of the elite members who had careers in family firms attended private schools. Providing the aspiring elite with a total environment for usually eight of the most formative years, private schools teach the sons of the upper class values appropriate to their position; they have "strong characters built" and the opportunity to build lasting friendships with other upper class boys they later meet in the boardrooms of Canada's largest corporations. As was already illustrated, the pervasiveness of private school attendance within the elite has increased since 1951, but at the same time concentration in fewer of the finer schools has also been occurring. While 29 members of the elite had attended Upper Canada College (UCC) in 1951, by 1972 this number had increased to 38. Other elite schools include the University of Toronto Schools, which can account for the private school education of 28 members of the present elite, Trinity College School, accounting for 21 members, and ten others accounting for between seven and 13 members each. Since many of these schools were founded as extensions of the Anglican church, it is understandable that 38 percent of those Canadian-born members of the elite attending private schools would be Anglican, 47 percent if French Canadians are excluded.

Common private school attendance is only the beginning for many careers that lead to very similar career paths. For example, of five elite members who attended Appleby College at the same time, four went on to the University of Toronto, including two of them by way of Royal Military College. Five members of the elite followed a path which leads directly from UCC to the University of Toronto to Osgoode Hall, while another twelve stopped short of Osgoode and went directly into the corporate world. Three UCC alumni are on the board of Crown Life together, and two of these are also on the board of the Bank of Montreal, where they met a third former UCC graduate. There are also five UCC graduates on the board of National Trust, four of whom appear to have attended their alma mater at the same time. These are not uncommon occurrences within the boardrooms of dominant corporations: there are at least two former UCC students on no fewer than 18 dominant corporations. This is not unique to UCC by any means; for example, seven present members of the elite were at Ridley College at the same time and between them hold 25 dominant directorships.

After private school and typically the University of Toronto or McGill, sons of the upper class are ready for the corporate boardrooms. Like their fathers, they then enter another private world; that of the exclusive men's clubs.

Private Clubs, Bastions of the Elite

Providing more than simply status to the upper class male, the exclusive gentlemen's club is a meeting place, a social circle, where businessmen can entertain and make deals. It serves as more than a badge of "social certification" in that the club is a place where friendships are established and old relationships nourished. Especially in the six national exclusive men's clubs there is an opportunity for the corporate elite to come together socially at the national level, thus transcending the metropolitan or regional class systems. These six Canadian clubs are one of the key institutions which form an interacting, active, national upper class.

The high cost of club membership is typically borne by the corporation. Among a number of other benefits, a recent survey of company presidents in Canada found that "more than nine out of ten presidents hold a town club membership at company expense" (Heidrick and Struggles Inc. 1973:6).

Three of Canada's national clubs are located in Toronto, including, appropriately enough, the National, founded in 1874, the York, established in 1909, and the Toronto, whose origins are the oldest of all the national clubs, dating back to 1835. In Montreal are the Mount Royal (1899) and the St James (1857). The sixth is the Rideau of Ottawa, dating back to two years prior to Confederation and, although not central to the corporate elite, national because of its location and heritage. Over half the corporate elite (51.1 percent) belong to one or more of these six clubs, with members from all across Canada belonging to each of them. Between them, the 396 members of the corporate elite who belong to one or more of these six clubs hold 689 memberships, an average of almost two each. The total memberships of these clubs is not large, averaging 578 in 1947 and 644 in 1957, that being the last year for which total records are available. Based on projected growth, it is estimated that they average just over 700 members currently. In 1957 they ranged in size from 300 in the York Club to a high of 1,127 in the National Club.

CONCLUSION

In an earlier paper (Clement, 1974), it was shown historically that as the economic structure becomes more concentrated mobility declines, while new economic forces tend to bring new social types into positions of power. This paper has shown that this relationship also holds true for changes in the economy between 1951 and 1972. The traditional, established, indigenous Canadian elite based in finance, transportation, and utilities has concentrated and consolidated its power in these sectors, and as a result mobility has declined as evidenced in the over-all shift from 50 percent of the elite having upper class origins at the time of Porter's study to 60 percent with the same origins at the time of the present study. On the other hand, new social forces have emerged as a result of expanded foreign investment in manufacturing and resource sectors, which accounts for greater openness in the comprador elite. It was shown that 45 percent of the comprador elite have upper class origins, compared to 64 percent of the indigenous elite, while 50 percent of the compradors originate in the middle class, compared to only 30 percent of the indigenous elite. In other words, the over-all access to positions of economic power has become increasingly upper class in spite of the tendency for compradorization to be more middle class. Other structural transformations, such as the parallel structure created by a few Jewish Canadians and the effect of long-established social structures on limiting mobility, as was illustrated in the analysis of regionalism, have also been suggested.

It has become increasingly evident that the men who fill corporate elite positions are predominantly of upper class extraction or have become accepted into the upper class in terms of life-style and social circles. The process by which the upper class is able to maintain itself may be understood as one of co-optation and inherited advantage. Porter has argued, "Class continuity does not mean that there is no mobility. Rather it means that there is sufficient continuity to maintain class institutions" (1965:285n). As long as the upper class remains in control of dominant corporations and is able to keep its social class institutions such as private schools and clubs intact, it will be able to maintain itself in Parkin's terms as a "class of reproduction" and ensure conformity through "class nomination" of those members of the middle class, and occasionally lower class, deemed acceptable and, conversely, excluding those who are not. This means accepting the life-style, attitudes, and values of the upper class. As guardians of institutions of power and avenues of access, they are able to dictate that the system should operate as they see fit, that is, as a system of exclusion and monopoly for their own privileges and prerogatives of power. The economic elite in Canada is that section of the upper class which operates the major economic institutions of Canadian society on behalf of, and in the interests of, the upper class. As long as economic power is allowed to remain in its present concentrated state, there appears to be no hope for equality of opportunity or equality of condition in Canada.

Notes

1. For an excellent summary and discussion of similar positions taken by a variety of sociologists, see Goldthorpe (1966).
2. For a definition of dominant corporations, see Clement (1974:19–20).
3. The relationship between opportunity and condition has been examined elsewhere (see Clement, 1974:4–5).
4. In a recent paper Parkin (1974) has examined two types of "social closure as exclusion." One he calls "class nomination," whereby "ruling groups claim the right to nominate their successors, but not to transmit their statuses to their own lineal descendants... class nomination depends upon the use of exclusion rules which single out specific attributes of individuals, rather than the attributes of a particular social group." On the other hand, "classes of reproduction" are "those exclusion practices which *are* based upon purely group attributes — lineage, race, religion, or whatever." He goes on to say the distinction "is of course a purely notional one; in most modern societies both sets of exclusion practices seem to operate"(4). In the following analysis of inequality of access to the Canadian corporate elite, it is apparent that both

means of exclusion operate. For example, "classes of reproduction" are evident in terms of both class and ethnicity and explain a great deal of the means of access to these elite positions, while for some others university education and particular career patterns based on "class nomination" offer an explanation. Unfortunately, Parkin's paper became available only in the last stage of manuscript preparation and could not be integrated into the analysis, but it obviously offers a useful framework.

5. See Clement (1973:13–50 and forthcoming, chap. I) for a detailed discussion of the issues summarized here.

6. "At or near the top" refers to those who began their careers having previous-generation kin in one of the three elites or having a substantial business with a substantial business possibly dominant in the past but minimally "middle range."

7. The current elite structures have been discussed in detail elsewhere, including the definitions and relationships between comprador, parasite, and indigenous elites (see Clement, 1974:16–18). The reason for using the main corporate affiliation — which was self-identified — as the major criterion for determining indigenous or comprador elites is that this is the main base of power the person has for operating within the elite. For example, when the presidency of a foreign-controlled company (a comprador position) changes hands the outgoing president typically drops his indigenous directorships when he returns home and these are often picked up by his successor. In other words, outside directorships are usually dependent upon one base of power, the main corporate affiliation, from which the elite member operates.

8. It should be noted that these figures refer only to Canadian-born members of the elite and to persons, not positions. The degree of structural compradorization by corporate sector has been examined elsewhere (Clement, 1974:21–3, Table II).

9. A much more extensive analysis of ethnicity and the economic elite, as well as comparisons with the political and bureaucratic elites, is provided in Clement and Olsen (1974).

10. The traditional classical college system was removed in the early 70s in Quebec. The effect of this and whether or not alternative upper class institutions will develop are not known. Of course, this does not affect the current elite, most of whom were educated in the 30s.

References

CLEMENT, WALLACE
  1973   "The Corporate Elite: Economic Power in Canada." MA thesis, Department of Sociology and Anthropology, Carleton University. Ottawa. (Expanded and revised; forthcoming as The Canadian Corporate Elite: An Analysis of Economic Power. Toronto: McClelland and Stewart, Carleton Library).
  1974   "The Changing Structure of the Canadian Economy." The Canadian Review of Sociology and Anthropology. Aspects of Canadian Society: 3–27.
CLEMENT, WALLACE AND DENNIS OLSEN
  1974   "Official Ideology and Ethnic Power: Canadian Elites 1953–1973." Presented at the American Sociological Association meetings, Montreal (29 August).
DEATON, RICK
  1972   "The Fiscal Crisis of the State." Our Generation 8(4):11–51.
GOLDTHORPE, JOHN
  1966   "Social Stratification in Industrial Society." Pp. 648–59 in Bendix and Lipset, eds, Class, Status and Power (2nd ed.). New York: Free Press.
HEIDRICK AND STRUGGLES INC.
  1973   "Profile of a Canadian President." Chicago, Illinois.

JOHNSON, LEO A.

  1973   "Incomes, disparity and impoverishment in Canada since World War II."
  Toronto: New Bytown Press.

KALBACH, W.E. AND W.W. MCVEY

  1971   The Demographic Basis of Canadian Society. Toronto: McGraw-Hill.

MASLOVE, ALLAN M.

  1972   The Pattern of Taxation in Canada. Economic Council of Canada. Ottawa:
  Information Canada.

OLSEN, DENNIS

  1973   "The State Elite in Canadian Society: A Thesis Proposal." PHD proposal,
  Department of Sociology and Anthropology, Carleton University. Ottawa.
  Mimeo.

PARKIN, FRANK

  1972   Class Inequality and Political Order. London: Paladin.

  1974   "Strategies of Social Closure in the Maintenance of Inequality." Presented at
  the Eighth World Congress of Sociology. Toronto (August 24).

PARSONS, TALCOTT

  1970   "Equality and Inequality in Modern Society or Social Stratification Revisited."
  Pp. 13–72 in E.O. Laumann, ed., Social Stratification. New York: Bobbs-
  Merrill. 72.

PORTER, JOHN

  1957   "The economic elite and the social structure in Canada." Canadian Journal of
  Economics and Political Science 23: 376–94.

  1965   The Vertical Mosaic. Toronto: University of Toronto Press.

PRESTHUS, ROBERT

  1973   Elite Accommodation in Canadian Politics. Toronto: Macmillan.

STATISTICS CANADA

  1970   Incomes of Canadians. Ottawa: Information Canada.

ZEITLIN, MAURICE

  1974   "Corporate Ownership and Control: The Large Corporation and the Capitalist
  Class." American Journal of Sociology 79(5): 1073–119.

Status Inconsistency in the Toronto Elite of the 1920s *

Lorne Tepperman

The study of social stratification is the study of enduring, pervasive social inequality. Because the types of inequality that make up stratification are so tightly connected to one another, knowing where to begin an analysis is often difficult. One thing leads to another: the influences of wealth, status, esteem, power and the like on social position, and on one another, form a seamless web. Thus the choice of a starting point is largely arbitrary. Or is it? Is there a rational way to decide whether to begin the analysis by examining wealth first, fame later? First social connections, then life-styles? This paper is an attempt to *unravel* the skein of variables that, together, constitute social position in a stratification system.

We shall look at a group of elite people who stood at the top of Toronto society during the 1920s. They enjoyed material prosperity, held positions of some authority, and had social eminence, even fame. We shall try to understand how they came to attain this consistency or crystallization in amounts of wealth, authority, and prestige; and how some of their statuses (or assets) might have been used to improve or purchase others. In this way, we shall attempt to discover which aspects of stratification are more fundamental and which more superficial to the attainment of a high social position.

STATUS CONSISTENCY BY EXCHANGE

Theorizing about social stratification is made especially difficult by the variation in beliefs about what stratification is. As Ossowski (1963) has shown, sociologists who follow Marx view stratification as a system of binary oppositions, of haves and have-nots defined in relation to capital and the ownership of the means of production. However differentiated a society may become, it is thought to be ultimately reducible to these polarities. This binary thinking fits an expectation of class conflict and change of the system through victory by one of the two combatants.

Other sociologists follow Max Weber, Lloyd Warner and other American scholars in preferring to analyze a tri-partite phenomenon — socio-economic

* Supported by a Canada Council Leave Fellowship.

status—which comprises wealth (or property), authority, and prestige. This view of stratification is explicitly and irreducibly multidimensional. Hence it is less suited to expectations of class conflict than to analyses of horizontal differentiation, intergroup competition and social mobility among statuses. Attention is focused on occupational stratification and mobility, since most people today get their personal property, authority, and prestige mainly through their jobs, and on educational attainment since schooling is for most people the immediate, if not the final, cause of occupational positioning.

These differences in approach not only have sociologists talking about the same things in different terms, but they lead to a division of labor among sociologists. Of the two, the binary sociologists are more likely to study social elites and movement in and out of the elite (if they choose to study mobility at all); the multidimensionalists largely ignore elites and focus upon the common experiences of ordinary, largely powerless people.

Talcott Parsons has been the most eminent in the latter tradition in recent times. His contribution (1953) to the so-called functionalist debate (cf. Bendix and Lipset, 1966) on stratification inadvertently showed, more clearly than others had, the impossibility of holding the functionalist position. The assumption of a tacit value-consensus in society is no more plausible when stated by Parsons than when posited by Rousseau as a "general will." Each such formulation assumes an emergent or voluntarily contrived social contract to accept benign inequality. The most powerful attack upon this position is to ask, Where was I when this social contract was signed? And can it be renegotiated?

But Parsons' subsequent work on stratification was more important than this, for it carried the multidimensional viewpoint of stratification to its logical conclusion in the concept of "generalized media of exchange." Starting with the assumption that social position is founded on a variety of things elsewhere termed power resources, Parsons (1966) noted that these resources were more valuable in exchange than valuable in themselves (cf. Tepperman, 1975: Chap. 2). Like dollar bills, they were generally useful in commanding compliance, in purchasing services, and in obtaining other power resources, though they could not themselves serve as food, shelter, and other necessities of life. Indeed, for Parsons the modernization of societies demanded a *generalization* of media of exchange, a movement away from barter to a money economy and from bald coercion to such sophisticated uses of power as influence.

The very generality of these media — their intrinsically neutral character — permitted and stimulated a development of modern power-broking as exemplified by bankers in respect to money. Thus, Parsons sees the exercise of power as the manipulation, exchange, investment, and recombination of very abstract, primarily symbolic objects. He goes on to marvel at how much modernity depended on this abstractness. The very existence of so abstract a system of exchange implies a popular value consensus, the non-contractual elements of contract, of which Durkheim (1964) has written. And following Weber he stresses the importance of legitimation as a process for creating as well as maintaining these resources (cf. Parsons, 1960).

Parsons states the multidimensional position with force and elegance. More than that, he points out several aspects of power and stratification which must be taken into account by any analyst, whether of the binary or multidimensional persuasion. First, bald coercion is relatively rare in our society, as is barter; the exercise of power has become very subtle. Second, as C. Wright Mills (1956) and others note, movement from one type of elite to another is relatively easy — for example, President Eisenhower changing from army general to college president to politician. This kind of movement can be most easily understood as an *exchange* of positions (or resources), one for another. Many military heroes have cashed in their medals for a position as statesman or politician, while others have become corporate executives. Whether this proves the existence of a unitary elite in which all sectors cooperate with each other at all times, as Clement (1975) tries to argue against Porter (1965), is more difficult to say. Yet, this kind of intersectoral mobility at least suggests a generalization and exchange of some kinds of authority or prestige for other kinds.

Third, Parsons' conception squares with the common observation that if some people experience "status inconsistency" (Lenski, 1954), the majority do not. People with a lot of money generally have a lot of authority and receive a lot of deference as well, while poor people receive little deference and have little authority. Status consistency is the norm, and allows for the formation of social *strata*, levels within society which contain like individuals and differ between themselves in average wealth, authority, and prestige. These strata are the basic units of *stratification*. What explains this homogeneity within strata? Parsons would guess it is the exchange of some power resources for others, in order to bring about a state of social and psychological equilibrium.

These questions are important enough to suggest the utility of the "generalized media" concept; but to go further is to enter the conflict between binary and multidimensional theorists. Leave aside the question which cannot possibly be answered as posed: whether the existence of abstract or generalized media of exchange proves that social cohesion is maintained by value consensus, the so-called non-contractual elements of contract, of which Parsons is so fond. Let us rather pose a question with greater appeal for the binary thinker: Are the generalized media of exchange unequally important, and can we tell, ultimately, what is infrastructure and what superstructure, what is fundamental and what superficial to social positioning? Can we establish a table of equivalences among these various generalized media of exchange to determine which can control the other? If it can be demonstrated that one mega-unit of wealth can command ten mega-units of prestige or five mega-units of authority, then surely (this argument might run) we ought to begin our study of stratification with the study of wealth, not with political authority (cf. Parsons, *op. cit.*; Manzer, 1974) or reputation (cf. Warner, 1960).

If wealth can "buy" authority and prestige, and authority can "buy" prestige but not wealth, and if prestige can "buy" neither wealth nor authority, then stratification is properly measured by a Guttmann scale of generalized media which reveals wealth to be the most important resource of all. But how to construct this scale? The present paper analyzes the relationship between wealth and prestige (or fame) for a Toronto elite of the 1920s. If status consistency is obtained through exchange, we should expect to find a strong linear relationship between these variables. Further, if indeed wealth is infrastructure and fame superstructure, we should expect to discover that famous people lack wealth more often than wealthy people lack fame.

Power resources are not perfectly inheritable, some being lost in every change of hands; but they are inherited often enough to support the notion that power is exercised through media of exchange. But, as before, the power may be unequally inheritable, with parental wealth the most stable, protected, and invulnerable of resources and parental prestige the least so. Like the unequal exchangeability of resources within generations, the unequal inheritability of power resources across generations supports a binary thinker's view that wealth, property control, or relations to the means of production, are primary in the stratification system, and all else is secondary, if not trivial.

Eventually, therefore, a study of the inheritance of elite status, through the inheritance of power resources, will need to be done.

THE STUDY DESIGN

The present study group comprised all males listed in the 1925-26 edition of *Who's Who in Canada* who lived in what is today considered Metropolitan Toronto, and whose names were also found in the 1921-22 and 1928-29 editions of the same publication. This method selected men who had enjoyed some prominence and power for at least a decade. Toronto was chosen as the study location largely for convenience in obtaining data. The few elite women who would otherwise have qualified for inclusion were neglected because they would have unnecessarily complicated the analysis. Many men who became important in Toronto after the 1920s but were not prominent by the beginning of the 1920s were neglected in this study; as were men who were important in the early 1920s (and before) but died before the end of that decade.

The men selected are a relatively homogeneous group of prominent and prosperous men, even if they are not equally important. Further, some important Torontonians of the 1920s are not found here. This method of selecting a study population was arbitrary but at least unbiased in favor of any particular subpopulation. It yielded 277 men (out of about 3,000 entries in the 1925-26 *Who's Who in Canada*, of whom 627 were residents of Toronto).

Information about these men was collected from at least ten biographical sources[1] and the varied amount of data that could be found testifies to the varying importance of these men. Information was found in an average of three sources for each man, although for 16 percent no information was found beyond that in *Who's Who* and for 34 percent only one or two of the sources consulted contained any information. By contrast about 20 percent of these men were written up in five or more of the ten basic sources. Some additional sources were used to locate and verify these demographic data. The annual Toronto *Blue Book* was especially useful. It named the household members of all prominent Toronto families during the period under study and so supplied an independent check of the nuptiality and fertility of these elite men.

The 277 men were born in the late 19th century, 70 percent of them in the 1860s and 1870s. Only one in six was born in Toronto, suggesting a high degree of turnover in the Toronto elite even by the 1920s. The majority (55 percent) were born in other parts of Ontario, chiefly in small towns and cities. About one in eight was born in the United Kingdom, and fewer still were born in the United States; these men had come to Canada in childhood or early adulthood.

Two in every five of these men were financiers or manufacturers, another quarter were scholars (educators), lawyers, and judges. The high proportion educated beyond secondary school is remarkable here. The apprenticeship structure of many professions at that time, especially of law, makes comparing the educational attainment of this group with a contemporary legal elite difficult. Yet about half of all these elite men appear to have gone beyond high school. Even more interesting, and perhaps indicative of their relatively high class origin, the amount of formal education attained by these men does not appear to vary with their year of birth. It does so in the general Canadian population, with higher education becoming more common over the years.

DEFINING ECONOMIC POWER AND FAME

Following Weber, one can distinguish three kinds of power resources: property, authority, and prestige. These resources are described more fully elsewhere (Tepperman, 1975: Chap. 2). We shall now endeavor to define two of these resources, if in a limited fashion, in order to measure their association with each other. We shall limit our definition of property to directorships in major economic organizations, and rename this kind of resource *economic power*. Our present definition of prestige will limit us to measuring the number of times a person has been mentioned in ten major biographical sources; and this latter variable will be called *fame*.

Each such narrowing of terms requires justification. Clement argues (1975: Chap. 1) that the distinction many have struggled to maintain between corporate ownership, directorship, and management is needless. In practice, the same people are often involved in more than one of these capacities in the course of time. By acquiring stocks in the company that employs him, a manager becomes an owner and sometimes a director of it; by making policy and seeing that it is carried out, the director may become a manager; and so on. This being so, Clement argues, identifying the holders of directorships in major economic enterprises is equivalent to identifying the economically powerful. Further, the board of directors is the agency through which property owners must exercise control and by which managers are held to account. So, following Clement, I have used the *Directory of Directors*, published by the Financial Post since the early 1930s, as a source of information on all directorships ever held by the Toronto elite under study and hence as a measure of economic power. Information about the directorships these men held before the first publication of the *Directory of Directors* is found in the ten biographical sources named in note 1.

TABLE I Main Occupations of Men in the Toronto Elite, circa 1925

Occupation	Percentage
Financier[1]	22.4
Manufacturer[2]	20.0
Educator	13.0
Lawyer or Judge	11.6
Artist[3]	5.4
Merchant[4]	5.0
Physician, health researcher	4.7
Public servant[5]	3.6
Applied scientist[6]	2.5
Politician	2.2
Other	9.6
Total	100.0
	N = 277

1. Banker, stock broker, insurance or real estate executive.
2. Owns or manages factory, construction firm.
3. Includes authors, musicians, journalists, painters.
4. Owns or manages store; wholesale or retail seller of goods.
5. Holds appointive public office (e.g. Lieutenant Governor)
6. Consulting engineer or architect.

Prestige is more difficult to measure; it implies celebrity (or repute), popular approval, honor, and the receipt of deference. Outside of a first hand community study one can do little better in studying prestige than to measure how much a man has been written about and hence remembered by his country.

It is unlikely, though possible, that some men may have been celebrated, honored, and deferred to *on a wide scale* without ever having been mentioned in a biographical dictionary. Thus, while the present study does not include everyone who enjoyed such prestige in Toronto in the 1920s, yet everyone in the present sample had accumulated an uncommon amount of prestige. Since our purpose is to measure the association of (relative) prestige and (relative) property among a select group of men, the conclusions we reach are legitimately based on variations within the sample group and not between it and the rest of Canada's population.

Prestige of a particular kind is measured here. Had it been measured differently we might have got a different result. For example, the number of times a person was mentioned approvingly in the newspapers might have served as another measure of prestige about which information could be collected, even analyzed by computer. These data would have been much more expensive to get than the data used here, and their meaning would have been at least as ambiguous. What passes for prestige here is in fact a measure of cultural remembering. To be recorded in any of the biographical sources I examined is to be remembered by posterity, which is a very particular kind of prize but one that anyone might desire. This aspect of prestige — posterity — shapes our whole culture; at the very least it serves to distinguish the upper class from the merely rich. Yet anyone's fortunes might be advanced by a mention in the annual or irregular dictionaries of biography examined in this study.

Since at any given moment the members of the Toronto elite were at different stages in their careers, I have counted all the directorships and biographical mentions they received in their lives. Thus this count sums up the achievement of a lifetime, and not that of any given year.

This paper, therefore, is theoretically about the relationship between two power resources — property and prestige. Concretely, it is about the relationship between the number of directorships held (economic power), and the number of biographical mentions received (fame) by members of the Toronto elite in the 1920s. We shall examine whether this relationship is strongly linear, as the concept of generalized media of exchange would imply. If it is not linear, we shall try to explain why not and decide what this suggests for the debate between binary and multidimensional analysts of stratification.

MEASURING ECONOMIC POWER

In examining the directorships held by this Toronto elite it became clear that these could be differentiated by sector; and their socio-metric centrality, as well as their economic significance, could be measured. Clement *(op. cit.:* 161) has shown variously dense links between different sectors of the economy, with financial establishments having the greatest centrality or inter-sectoral linkage. Thus the directorships held by those in the sample were classified by the sector in which they were found, following Clement's convention.

Also, some boards of directors were found to contain a relatively large number of persons in the sample, while the majority contained only one or two. That any members of the sample were (ever) directors of a particular company did not necessarily prove the importance of the given company (or man); but it did suggest the integration of these men with others in the sample. For example, if Messrs. A and B each held three directorships, but A's directorships were in firms of which no other members of the sample were directors, while B's directorships were in firms in which other members of the sample *were* directors, then B could be considered more integrated into the Toronto business elite than A. A greater degree of such integration probably means more opportunities, more valuable business and social connections: surely an important aspect of power.

Finally, the various organizations in which these men held directorships were classified according to whether they were dominant economic concerns, in the sense Porter and Clement have specified (see Clement, *op. cit.:* Appendix IV). Measuring this dominance was difficult because many firms had amalgamated or otherwise changed their name between the times that these directorships were held and the 1950s, when Porter showed they were in dominant corporations. Other corporations conceivably lost or gained dominance in the economy during that interim period. Despite these hindrances, I applied Porter's (and Clement's) definition of dominance to all of the firms in which these earlier elites held a position, while recognizing that doing so might introduce error into the study. (This error would lie in underestimating the economic importance of the Toronto elite of the 1920s.)

For each person in the sample, these data counted the number of directorships he had ever held (1) overall, and in particular sectors of the economy; (2) in dominant corporations; and (3) in those corporations whose boards contained more than one member of the 1920s Toronto elite. The analysis of these data by computer showed extremely high intercorrelations among the variables, using Pearson's r to measure association.

My aim was to devise a single summary measure of economic power, and the high intercorrelations among indicators suggested this was possible. The data were therefore factor-analyzed in order to reveal this summary economic power factor hidden among the various measurements. This economic power factor was the first factor the analysis yielded, and all the variables were correlated with it in predictable ways: the total number of directorships, the number of directorships in dominant corporations, and the number of directorships in "popular" corporations were highly loaded on this factor. Slightly lower were the loadings for the number of directorships in finance, manufacturing, transportation, and utilities. Just under half of all variance in the directorship data was accounted for by this single factor, making it a very effective summary measure of economic power. Using this factor, economic power scores were assigned to each member of the study population. Sixteen men in the sample had factor scores of two or more standard deviations above the mean. They were almost all financiers rather than manufacturers or merchants, or otherwise. A few are remembered for their public service or philanthropy but the most are not.

THE RELATIONSHIP BETWEEN ECONOMIC POWER AND FAME

On the average, each of the 16 very powerful men received four or five references in the biographical dictionaries, out of a possible ten references. This was more than the average number of references for all men sampled — in fact about one standard deviation above the three references enjoyed by the average man sampled. But this did not prove a strong linear relationship between economic power and fame.

Multiple regression afforded a more direct means of measuring the relationship between economic power and fame. Regressing the number of references in biographical dictionaries[3] on all the directorship measures only accounted for 15 percent of the variance.[4] This suggested that the relationship between economic power and fame was not linear, and hence not well suited to unmodified regression analysis. Tabular analysis supported that conclusion: the average sample member with no directorships had as much prominence as the sample member with many directorships. The men with only a few directorships — that is, intermediate economic power — were the least prominent of all in the sample.

TABLE II   Loadings of Variables on the Economic Power Factor

Variable name	Loading[1]
Number of directorships	.907
Number of directorships in "popular" corporations	.882
Number of directorships in "dominant" corporations	.814
Largest weight*	.806
Number of directorships in finance	.782
Average weight*	.659
Number of directorships in manufacture	.647
Number of directorships in transport, utilities	.640
Number of directorships in real estate, construction	.539
Number of directorships in mining	.423
Number of directorships in retail, wholesale trade	.181
Eigenvalue	5.286

* "Weight" is the number of elite men on the same board of directors.
1. "Loading" is the size of the correlation between the specific variable and the economic power factor.

TABLE III   Mean Number of Biographical References, of Ten Possible,[1] by Directorships Held*

A. Number directorships held	N=	Mean number references
None	107	3.61
Some (1–6)	108	2.76
Many (7 or more)	61	3.66
Total	276	

B. Number dominant directorships held	N=	Mean number references
None	91	2.73
Some	78	3.50
Total	169	

*See Note 1 for a specification of the ten sources used.
1. This total comprises only those men who hold any directorships.

This suggested that regression analysis should be applied separately to those 169 members of the sample who held one or more directorships. This analysis revealed that, among directors, the more and better the directorships, the greater the coverage in biographical dictionaries. Economic power now accounted for 30 percent of the variance in fame, as we have measured it. The number of directorships held in dominant corporations and the number of elite directors in the most "popular" company of which a man was director — a measure of integration into the Toronto business community — were the two variables most influencing fame, as their relatively high beta weights indicated.

To summarize at this point: we have shown that economic power, as measured by directorships in various ways, can reasonably be considered unidimensional. People with a great deal of economic power tend to receive a great deal of prominence or fame; but people with no economic power whatever can receive as much fame. The least famous men in this sample are those who enter business and do only moderately well. This curvilinearity suggests "two solitudes" in the elite class: the famous and very rich. But ignoring this, much of the variation in fame is left to be explained even after we have taken economic power into account. Although the ability of economic power to explain 30 percent of the variance in fame is important, 70 percent of the variance in fame is left unexplained and not all this residue can be random — that is, theoretically trivial — error.

THE UNDERPROMINENT AND OVERPROMINENT MEN

To better understand what contributes to fame or prominence besides economic power, we should eliminate economic power as a factor by explicitly controlling for it, and then analyze the variation in what remains. This can be done by calculating an expected prominence score for everyone in the sample, a score based on the formula that resulted as a by-product from the regression analysis. When the expected number of biographical references is subtracted from the observed number, a residue remains, and where the residue is large, the individual can be considered overprominent, given his economic power. Where the expected number is larger than the observed number of references, the remainder is small or even negative and we can consider that individual less prominent than his economic power would indicate, or underprominent.

Following this method, I selected the 20 most overprominent and the 20 most underprominent men. In each group, ten held no directorships, and in all cases, the men were more than one and a half standard deviations away from their expected level of prominence. By comparing these two sub-groups I hoped to learn which variables besides economic power contributed most to prominence. The 20 overprominent people were mentioned in an average of seven biographical sources each, and the 20 underprominent people were mentioned in only one each, on average.

Five characteristics distinguished overprominent from underprominent men: occupation, family composition, education, period of birth, and national or international connections.

First, the underprominent men tended to be financiers much more often than the overprominent men, who were more likely to be in politics, public service, law, the arts, or manufacturing. It is probably fair to say that the financiers shunned publicity more than others, rather than that the others chased after it more than the financiers. Also, what the financiers did was less comprehensible, and often less interesting to the public, than what politicians, artists, or churchmen did. Finally, what the overprominent men did for a living was more often subject to review and a public mandate — was more often public business — than what financiers did.

Second, the overprominent men tended to have been married younger and have lived in wedlock longer, to have fathered more sons (though not more daughters), and to have seen more sons reach adulthood, than the underprominent men. Conceivably these sons connected their fathers to other important families through marriage, thus enhancing their father's opportunities for fame and fortune. Preliminary evidence suggests that the daughters of these men married "down," accepting poor but talented suitors. Yet rarely were the sons of these overprominent men especially successful or famous; so one can scarcely maintain that sons brought their fathers additional prominence through their own achievement. It is also hard to explain why sons would forge more useful connections with other families than daughters. The most that can be concluded from this quick analysis is that family size and composition probably do affect the attainment and preservation of parental status (cf. Tepperman, 1972); but it is difficult to say exactly why.

Third, though the overprominent men were born slightly earlier than the underprominent men, both groups died at about the same time. In any case, a few extra years of life could not make much difference to the fame of men who were already living 75 years on average. Thus the difference made by an earlier date of birth must have to do with periods of socialization and, perhaps, differences in the conception of elite position. Another paper (Smith and Tepperman, 1973) comparing 19th and 20th century elites reveals a transition from broad-gauge, public spirited patricians to more private (if not more self-seeking) specialists. The present comparison of overprominent and underprominent men reveals a similar contrast.

There is no one among the underprominent men who compares in breadth of interests and activities with the most able of the overprominent men. Take three of these overprominent men as examples: Sir William Mulock, Henry Cody, and Charles Mitchell. The first two were respectively Chancellor and President of the University of Toronto, the third the Dean of Applied Science (Engineering) at the University of Toronto. Mulock had been active in law and politics, and had served as a federal cabinet minister and as the Chief Justice of Ontario, before accepting his position at the University of Toronto. Henry John Cody had been a nationally prominent churchman and provincial Minister of Education before becoming president of the University. Charles Hamilton Mitchell had worked as a consulting engineer, a distinguished military intelligence officer, and a consultant to the national government on various matters before coming to the University of Toronto. None of the underprominent men had a similarly varied history of activities and interests.

But besides showing a greater than average heterogeneity within and across careers, the overprominent men were also more likely to work in national or international organizations, or to have attained international fame in other ways. Six of the 20 overprominent men had been knighted for their activities; by contrast none of the underprominent men had been knighted.[5] The overprominent included Reverend Neil McNeil, the popular Roman Catholic Archbishop of Toronto; Sir Robert Falconer, another president of the University of Toronto; George Herbert Locke, Chief Librarian of the Toronto libraries and, apparently, a famous librarian outside Canada; Henry Sproatt, an internationally celebrated architect; Sir Robert Frederic Stupart, the father of Canadian meteorology; Newton Wesley-Rowell, Chief Justice of Ontario and the co-author of the Rowell-Sirois Report on federal-provincial relations; and several men as renowned for their philanthropy and public service as for their wealth — Sir Joseph Flavelle, Sir Albert Edward Gooderham and Sir Albert Edward Kemp among them. One looks in vain for men of similar attainment among the underprominent. Meritorious service to the public appears to have led to fame, although this influence may not prove greater, when adequately measured, than the impact of wealth upon fame.

Finally, the overprominent men had received more formal education than the underprominent men, as one might expect from their occupational characteristics. In part, higher education led indirectly to the attainment of prominence through the occupational attainment it made possible. But it may also be spuriously related to prominence, simply indicating a high class or origin and a strong correlation between (childhood) class of origin and adult prominence.

This conjecture is hard to verify, due to limitations upon our information about the underprominent and their class origins. Further, although some of the overprominent men came from old and respected Ontario families, by no means did all do so. Yet it must have been more difficult in the early part of this century to have gone through university without parental assistance than today. One must assume that those who graduated from university often, or usually, came from prosperous families. Thus adult prominence may have depended in some part upon high class origins or, more particularly, upon family repute as it often does in a traditional society.

CONCLUSION

This paper has been concerned with status consistency in the elite, and with inferring from the presence or absence of such consistency conclusions about the value of a multidimensional approach to stratification. Viewed from a distance, all the people in *Who's Who* are both prosperous and famous — certainly more famous and prosperous than the majority of Canadians. Viewed from up close, these same men vary widely in fame and wealth. Some are millionaires, others income earners falling below the top decile of the income distribution; for example, some of the artists, educators, and small businessmen. Some are men of international repute, others men who have dropped completely out of sight and memory after their inexplicable appearances in the *Who's Who* during the 1920s.

Viewed at a distance, the men who are wealthiest gain and exercise their wealth through the most important positions of authority in our society — through directorships and often, also, through government positions — and they achieve the greatest fame in doing so. Those who do the least and have the least appear to be the least celebrated. Yet this analysis has shown that the consistency of statuses is not quite so great when viewed from up close; many men are found to have great wealth but little public visibility, while many famous men have little economic power. This suggests at least two pathways to fame: One through economic power attained in business, and the other through a variety of activities that might be construed as public service.

These data suggest that fame can be "bought" with wealth; that is, economic power can make a man famous. Some evidence in the biographies also suggests that fame can make a man wealthy: for example, Billy Bishop, the celebrated flying ace in the First World War later gained access to important directorships apparently unrelated to his flying experience or skills. Perhaps half a dozen men in the sample appear to have been able to use the fame and connections they achieved in some public post as keys to the house of economic power. Yet the impression gained from reading these biographies is that the purchase of fame with wealth is much easier and more common than the purchase of wealth with fame. For wealth allows philanthropy and free time for public service, both of which are almost certain to bring fame as we have measured it.

The purchase of fame with wealth is a choice open to rich men; the purchase of wealth with fame is less often possible. As a consequence of wealth's flexibility, wealthy people can also exercise the option not to be famous; thus many wealthy people are underprominent, given their level of economic power. And underprominence may be a central feature of elite modernization and specialization (Smith and Tepperman, *op. cit.*).

Thus rich people can buy fame, or they can buy an escape from it, retreating into private anonymity. There is little evidence that the famous can acquire wealth unless, as in the kinds of examples C. Wright Mills cited, fame was accompanied by — even attained through — important positions of authority relevant to economic power. If fame signifies important connections (e.g. in business, government, or the military) as well as popular respect and celebrity, then it may be convertible into wealth; otherwise, not.

Two solitudes co-exist in the elite defined by *Who's Who* and the other "elite makers": there are the wealthy people and the famous but not wealthy people. There is no unitary elite because there is no perfect two-way movement between wealth and fame. Stated otherwise, there is imperfect status consistency in the elite, and this because of imperfect convertibility among the generalized media of power: property, authority, prestige. Of these three, wealth seems the most important since it offers the greatest number of choices. Thus of all the power resources, property seems the most fundamental. Even if it is unwise to define an elite as unitary just because wealth holds primacy among the power resources, it would be more foolish still to accept the multidimensional viewpoint simply because of an imperfect convertibility of resources, and status inconsistency, in the elite.

An elite that is defined by its fame or prominence, like the group studied, comprises different types of people. The economic power of these men accounts for a small part, perhaps only 30 percent, of the (statistical) explanation for selection. The largest part of selection into the elite, or more properly of allocation of fame within the elite, results from other factors that are not directly economic and may be cultural. Thus reading dictionaries of biography provides an insight into someone's value-system. (Whether these are the public's values or the elite's values, expressed through a "cultural Mafia," is hard to say.) Surely it would be precipitous to follow Parsons (1953) in supposing that the stratification system and the definition of elites expresses society's hierarchy of valued services. Yet the change in style of dictionaries of biography between the first and second halves of this century is unmistakeable, and marks a change in culture, if only the recognition that you cannot sell soap (or wealthy men) to the public the same way today as you once did.

If anything, today's biographies imply more status consistency than they once did. Not only did the early dictionaries demonstrate a traditional concern with moral worth and family respectability among the rich, they sometimes seemed to be raising the low and lowering the mighty. Hutson (1971) has shown that some peasant communities praise the weak and derogate the powerful simply to equalize status among people jealous for equality. Moral excellence is invoked to compensate for a shortage of cash, for example; such balancing of virtues is a valuable, even necessary means of controlling envy and conflict in a closed community. Perhaps this strategy was once followed by such biographers as Middleton and eventually dropped as the elite lost its insularity and gained greater size. That men such as Middleton and Charlesworth could have made their own careers from this kind of biography suggests a ready constituency for cultural mythologizing and self-glorification among the middle and upper classes.

Can power resources be cashed in for one another, on par, thus vindicating the multidimensional approach to stratification? The evidence here has been negative: Wealth can buy fame (or avoid it), but fame rarely buys wealth. This conclusion is based on a static model of status inconsistency, and on impressions of the sequence by which men in this sample achieved their fame. A historically grounded study of the sequence remains to be done.

Notes

1. Sources of biographical data on the Toronto elite *circa* 1925 (primary sources):
   i) *Canadian Necrology.* A 13-volume collection of obituary notices from the *Globe and Mail*, since 1933; plus index cards on additional eminent people from 1853 to 1930 (Robarts Research Library, Toronto).
   ii) Charlesworth Hector, ed. *A Cycolopedia of Canadian Biography.* Toronto: Hunter-Rose Company Ltd., 1919.
   iii) *Encyclopedia Canadiana.* Toronto: Grolier Society of Canada, 1958.
   iv) Greene, B.M., ed. *Who's Who in Canada*, 1925-26. Toronto: International Press Ltd.
   v) Hamilton, Ross, ed. *Prominent Men of Canada,* 1931-32. Montreal: National Publishing Company.

vi) Middleton, Jesse Edgar et al. *The Municipality of Toronto: A History*, 3 volumes. Toronto: Dominion Publishing Company, 1923.

vii) Middleton, Jesse Edgar and W. Scott Downs, eds. *National Encyclopedia of Canadian Biography*. 2 volumes. Toronto: Dominion Publishing Company, 1935.

viii) Roberts, Sir Charles G. D. and Arthur L. Tunnell, eds. *The Canadian Who's Who*, Volume II. Toronto: Trans-Canada Press, 1936-37.

ix) Roberts, Sir Charles G. D. and Arthur L. Tunnell, eds. *A Standard Dictionary of Canadian Biography*. 2 volumes. (The Canadian "Who was Who.") Toronto: Trans-Canada Press, 1934, 1938.

x) Wallace, W. Stewart. *The Macmillan Dictionary of Canadian Biography*. Third edition, revised. Toronto: The Macmillan Company of Canada, 1963.

(Supplementary sources):

Morgan, Henry James, ed. *The Canadian Men and Women of the Time*. Second edition. Toronto: William Briggs, 1912.

Reference Book. Third edition. Montreal: Canadian Newspaper Service Registered, 1929-30.

2. The men with the most economic power in the Toronto elite, circa 1925, were as follows:

    Alfred Ernest Ames, 1866-1934; Edward Rogers Wood, 1866-1941; Arthur Frank White, 1844-1949; Gordon Foxbar Perry, 1889-1963; Charles Boyd McNaught, 1877-1934; Sir Henry Mill Pellatt, 1860-1939; David Blythe Hanna, 1858-1938; Thomas Alexander Russell, 1877-1940; Sir John Aird, 1855-1938; Alfred James Mitchell, 1879-1948; Samuel John Moore, 1859-1948; Kenric Rudolphus Marshall, 1880-1962; Sir (William) Thomas White, 1866-1955; William Donald Ross, 1869-1947; Wilmot Love Matthews, 1878-1933; Colonel Henry Cockshutt, 1868-1944.

    All had factor scores on the economic power factor 2 or more standard deviations above the mean.

3. Transformed by taking the square root, to compensate for a skewed distribution.

4. Year of death was also included as an independent variable in the regression analysis, since some evidence suggested that the earlier a man died, the fewer biographical sketches were written about him. This is because two of the sources, published in the 1930s, were about living men only. A third source, the Canadian necrology, had poor coverage of men who died in the early 1930s. The effect of controlling for year of death in the regression was to ensure that these peculiarities in the data did not affect our measurement of the relationship between economic power and fame.

5. Those knighted were Sir Robert Alexander Falconer, Sir Joseph Wesley Flavelle, Sir Albert Edward Gooderham, Sir Albert Edward Kemp, Sir William Mulock, and Sir Robert Frederic Stupart.

References

BENDIX, REINHARD AND SEYMOUR MARTIN LIPSET, EDS.
Class, Status and Power. Second edition. New York: Free Press, 1966.

CLEMENT, WALLACE.
The Canadian Corporate Elite. Toronto: McClelland and Stewart, 1975.

DURKHEIM, EMILE.
The Division of Labor in Society. Translated by George Simpson. New York: Free Press, 1964.

HUTSON, SUSAN.
 "Social ranking in a French Alpine community," in F. G. Bailey, ed. *Gifts and Poison: The Politics of Reputation*. Toronto: Copp Clark, 1971.

LENSKI, GERHARD E.
 "Status crystallization: a non-vertical dimension of social status," *American Sociological Review*, 19, 405–413, 1954.

MANZER, RONALD.
 Canada: A Socio-Political Report. Toronto: McGraw-Hill Ryerson, 1974.

MILLS, C. WRIGHT.
 The Power Elite. New York: Oxford, 1956.

OSSOWSKI, STANISLAW.
 Class Structure in the Social Consciousness. Translated by Sheila Patterson. New York: Free Press, 1963.

PARSONS, TALCOTT.
 "A revised analytical approach to the theory of social stratification," *Essays in Sociological Theory*. New York: Free Press, 1953.
 "Authority, legitimation and political process," Chapter V in *Structure and Process in Modern Societies*. New York: Free Press, 1960.
 "On the concept of political power," in Reinhard Bendix and Seymour Martin Lipset, eds., *Class, Status and Power*. Second edition. New York: Free Press, 1966.

PORTER, JOHN.
 The Vertical Mosaic. Toronto: University of Toronto Press, 1965.

SMITH, DAVID AND LORNE TEPPERMAN.
 "Changes in the Canadian business and legal elites, 1870–1970," *Canadian Review of Sociology and Anthropology*, II, 97–109, 1974.

TEPPERMAN, LORNE.
 "The natural disruption of dynasties," *Canadian Review of Sociology and Anthropology*, 9, 111–133, 1972.
 Social Mobility in Canada. Toronto: McGraw-Hill Ryerson, 1975.

WARNER, W. LLOYD ET AL.
 Social Class in America. New York: Harper and Row, 1960.

Income Disparity and the Structure of Earnings in Canada, 1946-74

Leo A. Johnson

After almost a decade of debate, it is now generally acknowledged that Canada's great post-war prosperity has not brought about a narrowing of the income gap between upper and lower income groups in Canada.[1] As one recent federal government study commented:

> Over the entire 1951–1973 period there is a slight tendency towards increasing inequality. This is generally true regardless of the inequality measure or unit of analysis examined. . . . This is certainly surprising in the light of the great expansion of social security programs over the period, most of which are supposed to be redistributive in nature. . . .[2]

The concentration on poverty and the income gap, and on the failure of redistributive welfare plans to redistribute income, has not, however, yet produced any more basic insight into the roots of poverty among the working poor. Generally overlooked has been the growing disparity of income derived from the most important source of personal income in Canada—the labor market. It is not until one examines the pattern of increased disparity among income earners and the employment patterns which lock low income earners into the category of the working poor that the more generally understood phenomena — the failure of redistributive welfare and incomes programs to redistribute—can be understood.

Canadians have enjoyed an enormous increase in wealth and purchasing power since World War II. As Table I[3] shows, between 1946 and 1974 per capita gross national income increased by 549 percent and per capita earned income by 838 percent.

Of course, the Table I figures are distorted by the effects of inflation which has greatly eroded the purchasing power of the Canadian dollar. For example, the consumer price index increased from 60.0 in 1946 (1961 = 100.0) to 166.8 in 1974. The goods that $100.00 would buy in 1946 cost $278.00 in 1974. Table II[4] shows the same data as Table I, but translated into constant (1961) dollars. In real purchasing power the per capita gross national product increased by 126 percent between 1946 and 1974, while the per capita earned income increased by 237 percent. Thus, in spite of inflation, high unemployment, and recessions, the years 1946–1974 have been prosperous indeed.

141

TABLE I   Gross National Product and Earned Income of Canadians: Current Dollars, 1946–1974

	1946	1951	1961	1971	1974
G.N.P. in millions of dollars	11,885	21,060	39,080	93,094	150,880
Personal earned income in millions of dollars	5,316	10,469	21,480	56,016	90,928
Total population in thousands	12,292	14,009	18,238	21,568	22,446
Per capital G.N.P.	967	1,503	2,143	4,316	6,271
Per capita earned income	432	747	1,178	2,597	4,051

TABLE II   Gross National Product and Earned Incomes of Canadians: Constant (1961) Dollars, 1946–1974

	1946	1951	1961	1971	1974
Consumer price index	60.0	88.0	100.0	133.4	166.8
G.N.P. in millions of dollars	20,493	25,004	39,080	69,786	84,460
Personal earned income in millions of dollars	8,860	11,897	21,480	41,990	54,513
Per capita G.N.P.	1,667	1,785	2,143	3,236	3,760
Per capita earned income	721	849	1,178	1,947	2,429

Unfortunately, increases in national average income are meaningless when translated into personal terms. Beyond the averages there emerges a pattern of earned income distribution where not only is the disparity between high and low earners increasing, but the poorest paid workers have experienced an actual decline in purchasing power since 1951. To clarify these data, Tables III and IV break down the incomes of all earners into 10 percent groups (deciles), and show the average per earner earnings of each decile in current and constant (1961) dollars.

Tables III[5] and IV[6] show that average Canadian earners receive very little money for their labor. For example, in 1946 the median income was $1,294, while in 1974 it was $6,625 (in constant 1961 dollars, the figures were $2,332 and $3,972. In 1974, therefore, half of all earners received $6,625 or less. If earners received $2,757 in 1946 or $15,667 in 1974 (or $4,594 and $9,393 in constant 1961 dollars), they were earning at the 90 percentile level. Thus, although incomes have risen strikingly since 1946, they are much below what most Canadians believe them to be.[7]

Examination of the lower deciles, however, shows the most significant aspects of changes in earnings. Earnings at median and higher levels are surprisingly low, yet they are still rising — even when translated into purchasing power relationships. Earnings below median levels reveal a very different picture. As Tables III and IV show, incomes rose marginally for the third, fourth and fifth deciles, and revealed a small decline in the bottom deciles. Were it not for the inclusion of Old Age Pension, Canada Pension Plan, etc., in the earnings calculations (payments from pension sources increased 85.8 percent from $1,825 million in 1971 to $3,374 million in 1974), the declines in purchasing power in the 1951–71 period would have continued to 1974.[8]

Tables V[9] and VI[10] show the reason for the difference in earning patterns between upper and lower deciles. Between 1946 and 1974, the highest paid income earners received a disproportionate amount of the new wealth. As time goes by, the top deciles continue to receive an ever-increasing proportion of Canada's new wealth. By 1974 the top ten percent received 42.0 percent of the new wealth created between 1971 and 1974. As a result, even those in the seventh and eight deciles noticed an increased disparity between themselves and the top deciles.

Table VII shows that increases in disparity over the past two decades have been significant. For example, in 1946 the highest 20 percent of earners received about 8.3 times as much income as did the lowest 20 percent. By 1974 it was 15.1 to one. In 1951, the high point of relative earnings for the lowest two deciles, it was only 7.5 to one. In just over 20 years, the degree of disparity doubled.[11] In 1946 the income received by the best paid ten percent of earners equalled that of the poorest paid 55 percent. In 1951 this ratio had declined so that earnings of the highest decile equalled those of the lowest paid 52 percent. By 1974 the earnings of the best paid decile equalled that of the lowest paid 62 percent.

In Tables V, VI and VII[12] a striking pattern emerges: earnings at the lower levels climb slowly, then level off or decline, first in proportional, then in

TABLE III   Average Income of Income Earners by Decile: Current Dollars, 1946–1974

	1946	1951	1961	1971	1974
No. in decile	316,203	410,217	596,438	953,329	1,160,217
Bottom 10%	$ 247	$ 413	$ 483	$ 381	$ 633
10–20%	649	1,008	1,091	1,413	1,801
20–30%	883	1,299	1,755	2,274	2,895
30–40%	1,094	1,744	2,286	3,275	4,168
40–50%	1,294	2,068	2,805	4,274	5,488
50–60%	1,513	2,375	3,359	5,380	7,020
60–70%	1,730	2,700	3,938	6,634	8,737
70–80%	1,994	3,134	4,606	8,021	10,729
80–90%	2,407	3,586	5,541	9,914	13,326
Top 10%	4,995	7,093	10,148	17,209	23,575
Median	1,294	2,224	3,085	4,085	6,625
Average	1,681	2,552	3,601	5,876	7,837

TABLE IV   Average Income of Income Earners by Decile: Constant (1961) Dollars, 1946-1974

	1946	1951	1961	1971	1974
Bottom 10%	411	469	483	286	379
10-20%	1,082	1,145	1,091	1,059	1,080
20-30%	1,472	1,590	1,755	1,705	1,736
30-40%	1,774	1,982	2,286	2,442	2,499
40-50%	2,157	2,350	2,805	3,204	3,290
50-60%	2,522	2,699	3,359	4,033	4,209
60-70%	2,884	3,068	2,938	4,973	5,238
70-80%	3,324	3,562	4,606	6,017	6,432
80-90%	4,012	4,075	5,541	7,432	7,989
Top 10%	8,325	8,060	10,148	12,900	14,134
Median	2,332	2,527	3,085	3,601	3,972
Average	2,802	2,900	3,601	4,405	4,698

TABLE V   Changes in Purchasing Power (1961 Constant Dollars) Received by Average Earners in Each Decile, 1946-1974

	1946-51	1951-61	1961-71	1971-74	1946-74
Bottom 10%	$+ 58	$+ 14	$- 197	$+ 93	$- 32
10-20%	+ 63	- 54	- 32	+ 21	- 2
20-30%	+ 118	+ 165	- 50	+ 31	+ 264
30-40%	+ 208	+ 304	+ 156	+ 57	+ 725
40-50%	+ 193	+ 455	+ 399	+ 86	+1,133
50-60%	+ 177	+ 660	+ 674	+ 176	+1,687
60-70%	+ 184	+ 870	+1,035	+ 265	+2,354
70-80%	+ 238	+1,044	+1,411	+ 415	+3,108
80-90%	+ 63	+1,466	+1,891	+ 557	+3,977
Top 10%	- 265	+2,088	+2,752	+1,234	+5,809
Average change	+ 104	+ 701	+ 804	+ 804	+1,903

absolute, terms. By 1974 the relative decline in earnings had reached as high as it can go, the ninth decile, while in absolute terms the levelling off pattern had reached the fifth decile. Thus, all those below the median can expect no increase in purchasing power (except from transfer payments) in future, and may experience declines if the 1951-71 pattern for the lowest deciles is repeated. What may be even more dangerous is the likely extension of this pattern of zero or near-zero purchasing power increases to the upper middle deciles earners, who traditionally have high ambitions — particularly when they are confronted with an ever-greater concentration of earnings in the hands of the most-successful.

One argument for the inequality of earnings is that under the Canadian taxation system highly-paid earners pay more taxes than lower-paid earners.

Unfortunately, as several recent studies have shown, such is not the case. Lower-paid earners pay a far greater proportion of their earnings in taxes than those with higher incomes. For example, a study of the Canadian taxation systems done for the Economic Council of Canada by Allan M. Maslove demonstrates the regressive nature of the Canadian taxation system. In his data, families with earnings of less than $2,000 per year had effective tax rates of more than 100 percent of earnings, while families earning more than $15,000 paid only 42 percent. According to Maslove, the regressive municipal property taxes and provincial and federal sales taxes outweighed the progressive aspects of federal income taxes. He concluded:

> By far the most striking conclusion to be drawn from an examination of total tax payments is the extreme regressivity of the systems at the lower end of the income scale and the lack of any significant progressivity over the remainder of the income range ... Indeed, over the lower portion of the income scale, the system tends to contradict the ability to pay principle by taxing the poor at a higher rate than those who are better off.[13]

Thus, even the Canadian taxation system discriminates against the low income earner.

How are incomes allocated? Although no thorough analysis can be undertaken here, a few useful generalizations can be made. In the capitalist labor market, the capacity of an individual to labor — his or her labor time — is a commodity. The market place for labor, however, is not entirely free, nor are the opportunities for success equal. There are economic, social, cultural, geographical and structural factors which inhibit pure wage competition and complete access by all individuals.

One problem in studies dealing with jobs, job allocation, and income distribution is that they concentrate on the individual who works or seeks work without considering the opportunities available. In Canada there are two circumstances in which employment returns income. First, there is self-employment, whereby the individual has the means, skills, and opportunity to sell a commodity or service. Second, there is wage and salary employment, whereby someone else has the means of employment and therefore determines the need, circumstances, and conditions of employment. Under normal conditions, between 80 and 85 percent of all gainful employment in Canada occurs in the second case.

Before a job opportunity is created, an employer has to believe that it is economically profitable. Inefficient employment, except in most unusual circumstances, deprives the employer of the means to employ labor.

What counts for a single employer, generally counts for the national economy.[15] If on a given day ten million Canadians need or want work and there are nine million job opportunities, then one million people will be unemployed. If of the nine million jobs, six million are full-time while three million offer intermittent or reduced-hour employment, then the job-seeker is restricted to what is offered. Those competing for available work do not have the luxury of waiting for the ideal job. From the employee's point of view there exists a zero-sum game. Among those looking for a job (or a promotion), one person's advancement means another's loss, except if an entirely new job is created. In the latter case, the competition is merely distributive.

Competition for jobs is not free of constraint and biases. There exist economic and social barriers. Economic barriers consist of factors such as strength, health, skill, agility, education, intelligence, location, motivation, which may inhibit an individual's performance capabilities. Social barriers are more subtle and diverse and range from biases in the mind of both potential employers and employees (e.g., racism, sexism, age, antagonism to "dirty work") to preconditions in the social structure that prevent the development of the individual's full potential (e.g., poverty, culture, sexual stereotyping, physical, intellectual or psychological neglect or damage, inadequate health care, schooling). Although we can not assess the cumulative effects of these and other barriers on individuals, we know they profoundly affect the earning capacity of Canadians in the competitive labor market.

Table VIII[16] shows how competitive situations within a variety of occupations can affect average incomes. In a period when average earners received a purchasing power increase of $1,896 (in 1961 constant dollars), doctors received $14,625, dentists $12,696 and lawyers $14,316. In contrast, farmers had an increase of $4,098 and pensioners lost $243. No doubt the professions' jealously guarded ability to restrict access to their ranks has contributed to these huge increases in purchasing power.

The situation of farmers is particularly interesting. Between 1946 and 1972 farmers were caught in a situation of international food surpluses and intense price competition. As a result, between 1946 and 1971 purchasing power increases for farmers amounted to an average of only $637 or 35 percent.[17] Then, between 1971 and 1974, two changes occurred: first, disastrous harvests around the world created huge food price increases; and second, the institution of government-backed marketing boards, which create national monopolies of production and prices, greatly reduced competition for many farm commodities in the domestic market. The results were spectacular. Between 1971 and 1974, purchasing power increased by 140 percent, from $2,465 to $5,926. Yet this actual purchasing power increase of $3,461 still fell far short of the increase of $4,290 received by lawyers.[18]

The situation of pensioners tells a different story. Discriminated against in the job market because of age, and without significant political impact which would motivate governments to modify legislation on their behalf, pensioners lost four percent of their purchasing power between 1946 and 1971 and, with rapid inflation eating up their incomes, a further six percent between 1971 and 1974. The current government denunciations of "indexed" pensions clearly indicate that this erosion is likely to continue.

Among the most important causes of disparity in earning power are the high incidences of unemployment in certain regions and age groups. Before examining Tables X to XII it is important to remember that persons referred to as unemployed in government data are not merely those without employment (even one hour a week places one in the "employed" category) but must also have been actively seeking work in the survey period. In effect, the unemployment rate is the proportion of persons active in the labor force who do not have any employment.[19] If a person becomes discouraged and stops looking for work temporarily because no jobs are available, that person is no longer officially unemployed.

As Table IX[20] shows, there are large variations in unemployment rates across Canada. For example, rates in the Atlantic Region are normally double those in Ontario or the Prairies, while those in Quebec and British Columbia fall between the two extremes. If a person resides in a high unemployment incidence region the likelihood of experiencing reduced income because of unemployment is greatly enhanced. Being under 25 years of age has exactly the same effect.

As Table X[21] makes clear, a statement such as "in 1976 the average rate of unemployment in the Atlantic Region was 11 percent" does not indicate the magnitude of potential earnings lost because of unemployment. For example, if in 1976 the rate of unemployment in the Atlantic provinces was 11 percent, and the average duration of unemployment was 20 weeks, then 29 percent of the region's labor force lost an average of 38 percent of its potential earnings. Similarly, if 13.3 percent of males under 25 were unemployed an average of 13 weeks, then 52 percent of males under 25 lost 25 percent of their potential earning power.

The serious effect that unemployment has on individual and family earnings has been demonstrated in a number of recent studies by Statistics Canada. One such study conducted by R. K. Chawla noted that:

> A male earner with no unemployment experience earned an average 89 percent more than one who did experience some unemployment. Put another way, persons experiencing some unemployment were largely concentrated in the lower earnings groups, with over 60 percent of the male and over 90 percent of the female earners experiencing unemployment [in 1971 and 1973], earning less than $5,000.[22]

Table XI[23] provides a useful summary of the impact of unemployment and part-time work on the employment incomes of men and women. Two points must be kept in mind: first, because there is a large surplus of persons in the labor force, even the least desirable job slot must be competed for; second, when potential employees are reluctant to voluntarily compete for part-time or short-term jobs, the threat by government agencies of cutting off unemployment insurance and welfare enforces that competition.[24]

Unemployment insurance and other forms of transfer payments fall far short of making up for incomes lost due to unemployment. One study pointed out that in 1971, when the average family income was $10,368, those families in which the head experienced no period of unemployment received $10,643. In contrast, where the family head was unemployed for any period, family income averaged only $7,558. In reviewing the results of the study one commentator said that the greater the duration of unemployment, the more catastrophic were the costs in family income:

> When those suffering relatively short-term unemployment — that is, less than nine weeks — are excluded, the pattern becomes clear....
>
> In this smaller sample, one quarter of the heads of families were unemployed for 9 to 14 weeks. Average family income was $8,336, of which government transfer payments provided 6.5 percent.
>
> As the duration of unemployment of the family head lengthens, the figures deteriorate steadily. For the one-fifth of the sample in which the family head was unemployed for 33 weeks or more, family income dropped to $4,929, less than half of the national average. Of this amount, transfer payments represented 28.8 percent.[25]

Not only individual incomes fall drastically when workers experience unemployment; family earnings fall as well. While unemployment insurance helps alleviate the effects of unemployment, it is clear that such payments make up for only a very small part of the total personal economic loss.

Not only has the capitalist labor market affected incomes through its continued utilization of part-time workers who are unemployed when not required, but the growing differentiation of capital-labor ratios between different industrial sectors also has an important effect upon wage levels in those industries. As capital increases in an industrial sector, and as monopoly increases generally, certain sectors of organized labor find themselves in a very advantageous position in comparison to other sectors of labor. In industries such as mining, steel, automobiles, and oil and chemicals, where capital-labor ratios are high (there is a large investment of capital per worker), and where it is difficult or impossible to move operations without large loss of capital, labor unions have

TABLE VI　Percentage of New Purchasing Power, Received by Average Earners in Each Decile, 1946–1974

	1946–51	*1951–61*	*1961–71*	*1971–74*	*1946–74*
Bottom 10%	+ 5.6	+ .2	− 2.5	+ 3.2	− .2
10–20%	+ 6.1	− .8	− .4	+ .7	—
20–30%	+ 11.4	+ 2.4	− .6	+ 1.1	+ 1.9
30–40%	+ 10.0	+ 4.3	+ 1.9	+ 1.9	+ 3.8
40–50%	+ 18.6	+ 6.5	+ 5.0	+ 2.9	+ 5.9
50–60%	+ 17.1	+ 9.4	+ 8.4	+ 6.0	+ 8.8
60–70%	+ 17.7	+ 12.4	+ 12.9	+ 9.0	+ 12.3
70–80%	+ 23.0	+ 14.9	+ 17.6	+ 14.1	+ 16.3
80–90%	+ 6.1	+ 20.9	+ 23.5	+ 19.0	+ 20.8
Top 10%	− 25.5	+ 29.8	+ 34.2	+ 42.0	+ 30.4
Bottom 30%	+ 23.1	+ 1.8	− 3.5	+ 5.0	+ 1.7
Middle 40%	+ 73.4	+ 32.6	+ 28.2	19.8	+ 30.8
Top 30%	+ 3.6	+ 65.6	+ 75.3	75.1	+ 67.5

TABLE VII Proportion of Total Earned Income, Income Received by Each Decile, 1946–1974

	1946	1951	1961	1971	1974
Bottom 10%	1.47	1.62	2.34	.65	.81
10–20%	3.86	3.95	3.03	2.41	2.30
20–30%	5.26	5.48	4.87	3.87	3.69
30–40%	6.51	6.83	6.35	5.54	5.32
40–50%	7.70	8.10	7.79	7.27	7.00
50–60%	9.00	9.31	9.33	9.16	8.96
60–70%	10.29	10.58	10.93	11.29	11.15
70–80%	11.88	12.28	12.79	13.65	13.70
80–90%	14.32	14.05	15.39	16.87	17.00
Top 10%	29.71	27.80	28.18	29.29	30.08

TABLE VIII Purchasing Power Changes in Selected Occupations, 1946–1974

	Average income				Purchasing power	
	Current dollars		1961 constant dollars		Percent change	Dollar change
	1946	1974	1946	1974	1946–74	1946–74
Doctors	$7,032	$44,222	$11,887	$26,512	+ 123	$+ 14,625
Dentists	5,044	34,590	8,041	20,737	+ 158	+ 12,696
Lawyers	6,085	40,796	10,142	24,458	+ 141	+ 14,316
Farmers	1,097	9,385	1,828	5,926	+ 224	+ 4,098
Pensioners	1,425	3,556	2,375	2,132	− 10	− 243
All earners:						
— average	1,681	7,837	2,802	4,698	+ 68	1,896
— median	1,294	6,625	2,332	3,972	+ 70	1,640

TABLE IX Unemployment by Region, Sex, and Age Group, 1961–1976

	1961	1966	1971	1976
Canada — average	7.1	3.6	6.4	7.1
Females — under 25	6.0	4.8	9.9	12.1
Males — under 25	11.7	6.3	12.1	13.3
Females — over 25	2.5	2.7	5.0	6.7
Males — over 25	7.2	2.6	4.5	4.2
Atlantic region	11.2	6.4	8.6	11.0
Quebec	11.5	4.7	8.2	8.7
Ontario	5.5	2.5	5.2	6.2
Prairies	4.6	2.1	4.5	4.1
British Columbia	8.5	4.5	7.0	8.6

TABLE X   Proportion of Population Affected at Specified Levels and Average Durations of Unemployment

Average weeks unemployed	Annual average percentage unemployed											
	4%	5%	6%	7%	8%	9%	10%	11%	12%	13%	14%	15%
4	52%	65%	78%	91%	—%	—%	—%	—%	—%	—%	—%	—%
5	42	52	62	73	83	94	—	—	—	—	—	—
6	35	43	52	61	69	78	86	95	—	—	—	—
7	30	37	45	52	59	67	74	82	89	97	—	—
8	26	33	39	46	52	59	65	72	78	85	91	98
9	23	29	35	41	46	52	58	64	69	75	81	87
10	21	26	31	36	42	47	52	57	62	68	73	78
11	19	24	28	33	38	43	47	52	57	62	66	71
12	17	22	26	30	35	39	43	48	52	56	61	65
13	16	20	24	28	32	36	40	44	48	52	56	60

won high wages. These gains are largely achieved because high levels of capitalization create high fixed costs which cause large losses when there is no production. Because of the near-monopoly situation in these industrial sections, the corporations pass on these increased labor costs to the consumer in the form of higher prices. Gilbert Burck reports about one such sector:

> Although many contractors resist union demands, a contractor usually finds it easy and profitable to cooperate with unions. For so long as he cooperates, he simply bases his bids on costs and tacks on a suitable profit. If the costs of building a mile of highway double, so do his revenues and profits.[26]

In contrast to workers employed in capital intensive sectors of the economy, workers in sectors which employ relatively low levels of capital per worker find themselves at a distinct disadvantage. Where manufacturing or service-type industries require low levels of skills and little fixed capital for permanent facilities (such as electronics assembly, textiles, and clothing manufacturing), or where strong competition still exists (for example, in clothing), workers are forced to accept low wages or to see their employer move to a low-wage area (or even go out of business). Since areas which experience high rates of unemployment offer the best opportunities for exploitation of low-wage labor, there is a constant movement of such concerns from metropolitan to hinterland areas.[27] Although such movements help to alleviate the initial problems of unemployment they ultimately create a regional structure of income differentials which promise permanent underdevelopment and poverty wages.

Not only are incomes of workers structured by the demands of the capitalist labor market, but within that structure the personal attributes of individuals and the structural biases of society affect the position of workers. The effects of such factors as education and health need no explanation, but there are subtler factors.

The age and sex of workers has an important effect on incomes. There are obvious reasons for young workers' lower incomes, such as lack of experience, lower levels of education, and low seniority, but reports are not uncommon of overt discrimination in hiring practices against the young because of their reputed unreliability, laziness, and so on. It is the punishment of the individual for alleged characteristics of the group that lies at the heart of discrimination.

The situation of women in the labor market is rendered very difficult by just such discriminatory practices. The Royal Commission on the Status of Women has pointed out that not only do women receive lower average incomes than men, but they receive lower wages when doing jobs that are identical — even though this practice is generally illegal in Canada.[28] Largely as a result of such discrimination, and through the social stereotyping of females into certain low paid occupations, women suffer a huge disparity of income. Unemployment rates for women are increasing more rapidly than for men and such disparities are likely to increase.[29]

Ethnic origin of income earners also has a significant effect on average income. A study done for the Royal Commission on Bilingualism and Biculturalism shows that individuals with identical educations and occupations, but of different ethnic backgrounds, earned differing incomes. Among salaried engineers in the Metropolitan Montreal area, for example, ethnic British engineers earned an average of $1,504 per year more than their ethnic French counterparts — of which $825 could be attributed directly to ethnic bias.[30]

In an elaborate study of incomes for the commission, A. Raynauld, G. Marion and R. Beland concluded that in the Metropolitan Montreal area ethnicity had the effects shown in Table XII.[31] On average, French Canadians earned $1,649 per year less than their ethnic English-Scottish counterparts, of which $873 was due to ethnic bias. For workers having Eastern European or Italian backgrounds it was even more drastic: bias cost them $1,086 and $976 respectively in annual earnings.

Herein lies the heart of the dilemma of poverty in Canada. Because the capitalist labor market requires a large number of low-skilled or periodically employed workers who are structurally destined to receive low annual incomes, and because increases in purchasing power are distributed on a competitive basis, not only between individual workers but between economic sectors, the underlying problem of poverty and the poor worker must exist so long as capitalism and the capitalist labor market exist in the present form.

Within this context workers compete for the better jobs and higher incomes. Factors such as education, age, sex, ethnic and social origin, location of residence, and health all help to determine the position of the individual worker in the over-all incomes scale. Poverty programs aimed at improving the competitive abilities of individual workers do not change the over-all structure of employment and incomes, but only change that individual's position within it.

TABLE XI Persons 15 Years and over, Who Worked Full- and Part-Time in 1970, by Weeks Worked, Showing Average Employment Income, 1971

Weeks		Total	Worked		Worked full-time			Worked part-time		
			Male	Female	Total	Male	Female	Total	Male	Female
Total	No.	9,586,280	6,093,085	3,493,190	7,870,030	5,388,080	2,481,950	1,716,250	705,005	1,011,240
With income	No.	9,272,760	6,023,320	3,249,440	7,675,010	5,346,325	2,328,685	1,597,750	676,995	920,755
Average empl. income	$	5,392	6,574	3,199	6,125	7,111	3,864	1,867	2,341	1,518
1–13 weeks	No.	1,036,620	492,740	543,880	529,015	282,645	246,375	507,600	210,100	297,505
With income	No.	987,195	474,280	512,910	508,460	274,465	234,000	478,730	199,820	278,915
Average empl. income	$	998	1,328	692	1,248	1,591	845	732	967	565
14–26 weeks	No.	993,325	519,485	473,835	629,050	357,645	271,400	364,275	161,840	202,435
With income	No.	956,780	509,350	447,435	611,010	352,280	258,735	345,770	157,070	188,700
Average empl. income	$	2,155	2,650	1,592	2,514	2,973	1,889	1,520	1,925	1,184
27–39 weeks	No.	971,820	572,635	399,185	649,065	446,070	247,995	277,755	126,565	151,190
With income	No.	943,055	566,465	376,590	678,695	442,425	236,265	264,360	124,040	140,325
Average empl. income	$	3,646	4,395	2,521	4,174	4,788	3,026	2,291	2,992	1,672
1–39 weeks	No.	3,001,765	1,584,860	1,416,900	1,852,130	1,086,360	765,770	1,149,630	498,505	651,130
With income	No.	2,887,025	1,550,095	1,336,935	1,798,170	1,069,175	728,995	1,088,860	480,920	607,935

Average empl. income	$	2,246	2,883	1,508	2,783	3,369	1,922	1,361	1,802	1,013
40–48 weeks	No.	1,300,650	818,640	482,015	1,084,575	740,560	344,015	216,080	78,075	138,000
With income	No.	1,259,985	811,810	448,175	1,059,215	736,045	323,165	200,765	75,765	125,010
Average empl. income	$	5,700	6,849	3,619	6,205	7,162	4,026	3,037	3,810	2,568
49–52 weeks	No.	5,283,865	3,689,585	1,594,285	4,933,330	3,561,155	1,372,175	350,540	128,430	222,110
With income	No.	5,125,755	3,661,420	1,464,330	4,817,630	3,541,100	1,276,525	308,125	120,315	187,810
Average empl. income	$	7,087	8,076	4,614	7,356	8,230	4,932	2,892	3,571	2,458
40–52 weeks	No.	6,584,515	4,508,225	2,076,300	6,017,905	4,301,715	1,716,190	566,620	206,505	360,110
With income	No.	6,385,740	4,473,225	1,912,505	5,876,845	4,277,155	1,599,690	508,895	196,080	312,820
Average empl. income	$	6,813	7,853	4,381	7,149	8,046	4,749	2,949	3,663	2,502

TABLE XII   Effects of Ethnic Origin on Average Earnings in Metropolitan Montreal, 1961

	Average income 1961	Deviation from average	Index: English–Scottish = 100	Net contribution due to ethnic origin
English-Scottish	$5,762	$+ 1,319	100	$+ 606
Irish	5,455	1,012	95	+ 468
French	4,113	− 330	71	− 267
Northern European	5,644	+ 1,201	98	+ 303
Italian	3,482	− 961	60	− 370
Jewish	5,321	+ 878	92	+ 9*
Eastern European	4,343	− 100	75	− 480
German	4,830	+ 387	84	+ 65*
Other	4,132	− 311	72	− 334
Average	4,443	−	77	−

*Not statistically significant

What holds the entire structure of income disparity in place? Perhaps Karl Marx had the answer when he argued that such enormous disparities in income and wealth were indispensable for the reproduction and continuance of the capitalist system:

> When a certain stage of development has been reached, a conventional degree of prodigality, which is also an exhibition of wealth, and consequently a source of credit, becomes a business necessity to the "unfortunate" capitalist. Luxury enters into capital's expenses of reproduction. Moreover, the capitalist gets rich, not like the miser, in proportion to his personal labor and restricted consumption, but at the same rate as he squeezes out the labor-power of others, and enforces on the laborer abstinence from all life's enjoyments....[32]

In other words, a rate of income which allows the richest portion of society to live in luxurious style, to meet their class compatriots in expensive surroundings, and to see that their children, and their children's children, have the education, environment, and upbringing to reproduce their parents' social roles, may be indispensable to the perpetuation of the capitalist system. Business leaders and professionals certainly justify their high incomes by supporting this supposition. If there is only so much wealth created each year, and if competition *within* the ranks of the wealthiest earners requires ever-increasing incomes to maintain and enhance their position in life, the weaker competitors in society must necessarily be restricted to the lowest possible income[33] — thereby reproducing *their* position in society as well. While a few born to the lower orders of society rise because of talents or accidents of fate, the general structure remains, continuously reproducing the conditions of income disparity necessary to its existence.

Notes

1. For example, see: The Atlantic Development Council, *Productivity, The Use of Human Resources, and the Income Gap*, Pamphlet No. 11 (Fredericton, N.B.: 1967), pp. 9–15.

   Among extensive treatments of poverty which have appeared in recent years are: Fifth Annual Review of the Economic Council of Canada, *The Challenge of Growth and Change* (Ottawa: 1968); John Harp and John R. Hofley, *Poverty in Canada* (Scarborough: 1971); Report of the Special Senate Committee on Poverty, *Poverty in Canada* (Ottawa: 1971); Ian Adams, et al., *The Real Poverty Report* (Edmonton: 1971).

2. Roger Love and Michael C. Wolfson, *Income Inequality: Statistical Methodology and Canadian Illustrations*, Ministry of Industry Trade and Commerce (Ottawa: Statistics Canada, March, 1976), p. 74.

3. Data are from *Canada Year Book*, appropriate years, *Canada Census*, appropriate years, and Department of National Revenue, *Taxation Statistics*, appropriate years. Data for 1974 earned incomes have been adjusted by deducting items 7, 8, and 25 (Family Allowance, Unemployment Insurance, and Capital Gains) so that the data conform more closely to the 1946–1971 period. For an early version of this data see my *Poverty in Wealth* (New Hogtown Press, Toronto: 1974), pp. 2–12.

4. *Ibid*.

5. Data are from *Taxation Statistics*, *op cit*, appropriate years. Data for 1974 have been modified by the removal of Family Allowances, Unemployment Insurance, and Capital Gains in order to conform more closely to the earlier data. It should be noted that the "earners" referred to include in their earnings those sums received by dependent earners as defined by the Income Tax Act.

6. *Ibid*.

7. For example, a survey in 1971 revealed that more than 25 percent of Canadians in the $8,000–10,000 income range (the 80 to 90 percentile level) believed they were poor. See Walter Stewart, "The Real Poor in Canada — and Why We Don't Know Who They Are," *Maclean's* (January, 1971), p.45.

8. Between 1971 and 1974 pension income of all Canadians increased by 85.8 percent from $1,825 million to $3,374 million (in 1961 constant dollars the increase was 48.6 percent from $1,361 million to $2,023 million). In the same period persons reporting pensions as main source of income increased by 66.2 percent from 486,843 to 808,925; at the same time the average earned income of pensioners increased from $3,042 per annum to $3,556, thus placing the average pensioner in the fourth decile. For the lowest decile, average earnings from wages and salaries rose from $435 per year in 1971 to $500 in 1974 (in 1961 constant dollars, a decline from $326 to $300), while for average earners in the same decile pensions increased from $33 per year to $214 (in 1961 constant dollars, $25 to $128).

9. *Taxation Statistics*, see note 5.

10. *Ibid*.

11. *Ibid*.

12. *Ibid*.

13. Allan M. Maslove, *The Pattern of Taxation in Canada*, Economic Council of Canada (Ottawa: 1972), p. 64.

14. For a more detailed discussion of the approximately five percent of persons who are self-employed, see my "Precapitalist Economic Formations and the Capitalist Labor Market" in this volume.

15. On this issue, Karl Marx would agree with Harry Johnson and other free enterprise economists.

16. *Taxation Statistics*, see note 5. Calculations are my own.

17. *Ibid.*

18. *Ibid.*

19. A minor exception is those people not employed and not seeking work due to temporary illness or holiday. For the official definition of "unemployment" see *Facts about the Unemployed 1960-1971* (Statistics Canada, catalogue no. 71-520 occasional), p. 6.

20. *Ibid.*

21. Calculations are my own.

22. R. K. Chawla, "Earnings and Unemployment Experience of Canadians, 1971-1973," *Canadian Statistical Review* (Ottawa: Statistics Canada, August, 1976), p. 7.

23. *Canada Year Book, 1975*, (Ottawa: 1975), p. 324.

24. Although it is not generally realized, the Unemployment Insurance Commission maintains a special staff just to cut off from aid people who do not appear eager enough in their job search. Personnel managers are encouraged to report back to Manpower Canada on persons referred to jobs; so are welfare workers. See "Job seekers: Be neat or be turned in," *The Globe and Mail*, Toronto (August 12, 1977), p. 1.

25. Ronald Anderson, "Jobs lost cost," *Toronto Star* (December 13, 1973).

26. See Gilbert Burck, "The Building Trades Versus the People," *Fortune*, (October, 1970); Restrictive Trade Practices Commission, *Road Paving in Ontario* (Ottawa: 1970); L. A. Skeoch, *Restrictive Trade Practices in Canada* (Toronto: 1966).

27. Clairtone and General Instrument Company moving to Nova Scotia, Hamilton Cottons to Mount Forest, Ontario, and Sperry-Gyro from Ontario to Quebec are examples of the mobility of low-skilled labor-intensive industries leaving areas with rising wages for low-wage areas.

28. *Report of the Royal Commission on the Status of Women* (Ottawa: 1970), Chapter II, pp. 19–159, especially 154–6. Commission staff studies numbers 1, 3, and 4 contain more detailed studies of women in the capitalist labor market.

29. Proportions of workers by age and sex are changing constantly. Prior to the mid-1960s men under 25 were withdrawing from the labor force; after that they began to return, although not to 1961 levels. Between 1964 and 1974 the proportion of men under 25 of all male earners increased from 17.3 percent to 22.8 percent. In contrast, although females increased from 30.3 percent of all earners to 39.0 percent during this period, there was no significant change in the ratio of female earners under 25 to those over 25. With the decreasing participation rate of men over 25 and the increase in participation rate of women and men under 25, the proportion of male earners over 25 to all earners declined from 57.6 percent in 1964 to 47.0 percent in 1974 *(Taxation Statistics)*. Calculations are my own.

30. *Report of the Royal Commission on Bilingualism and Biculturalism*, Vol. 3A (Ottawa: 1969), pp. 64–5.

31. *Ibid*, pp. 71–8. See especially Table 30, p.77.

32. Karl Marx, *Capital* (New York: International Publishers, 1967), Vol. I, pp. 593–4.

33. By "lowest possible" one refers to the social, political and economic exigencies of the moment. See Francis Fox Pivan and Richard A. Cloward, *Regulating the Poor: The Functions of Public Welfare* (New York: 1971). The arguments of these authors also apply to minimum wages, labor legislation, and other government interventions in the area of earned incomes.

B. Power

Changes in Class and Power Relations in Quebec[*]

Hubert Guindon

POLITICAL STRUCTURES AND LEGITIMATIONS

Political structures in a mass society are fragile things. Since World War II, we have witnessed the collapse of age-old political regimes. The break-up of formal political empires, with the intellectual backing and sympathetic understanding of the majority of liberal intellectuals of the Western world, is now nearly complete. Seldom was the use of force necessary to achieve this. Massive ideological agitation with wide popular support achieved what armed might would not have attained. In most cases, the two structural conditions prerequisite to national liberation were: 1) a newly created native elite, highly educated, politically conscious and through nationalist identification effectively engineering the revolt of expections within 2) an awakened, restless native population whose aspirations were to be fulfilled by political independence. National independence has often been achieved though the heightened expectations usually have yet to be met.

Political structures need legitimations. Formal political empires collapsed because of a bankruptcy in legitimations. Legitimations are created by intellectuals and become sacred values for the other social groups.

Withdrawal of support from political structures by wide segments of the intelligentsia therefore becomes a crucial clue of imminent political instability. When this disenchantment of intellectuals is widely publicized and finds massive support in the lower social strata, the political regime, short of tyranny, is doomed. For a political structure is, in the final analysis, a moral order requiring for its existence consensus.

Confederation is a political structure. For growing numbers of French Canadian intellectuals its legitimations are unconvincing. The Massey-Lévesque brand of national feeling, the mutual-enrichment theory of ethnic co-habitation, seems, in 1964, so quaint, archaic and folklorish, that for many young French Canadian university students it is hard to believe it was formulated as late as 1950.

In the early 60s we have therefore witnessed the collapse of the latest legitimation of Confederation produced for the post-war period of peace. The

* Revised from *Queen's Quarterly* 71 (Summer, 1964), pp. 150–162, by permission of the author and the publisher.

Laurendeau-Dunton Commission, in my opinion, is searching for just that. Whether it will be successful is still very problematical. For the first time in the history of royal commissions concerned with national identity, dissent from many French-speaking Canadians is loud, clear, and emotional. Traditionally, such dissent came from a marginal, vocal group of French Canadian nationalists. Their voice today is still vocal, but no longer marginal, for it stems from official circles with the blessing of academia. Lionel Groulx in the 30s, Michel Brunet in the early 50s could be dismissed as narrow-minded chauvinistic nationalists both within and without French Canadian society. René Lévesque in the 60s cannot be so easily dismissed and he, in fact, is not so dismissed.

In terms of my opening remarks, where does Confederation as a political structure stand within French Canada? Intellectual disenchantment with Confederation is widespread within the French Canadian intelligentsia, including the social scientists. This disenchantment of intellectuals, artists, writers, newspapermen, film directors, etc., has been widely publicized in all forms of mass media. Furthermore, wide segments of French Canada's new middle class are either openly committed to, or sympathetic with, this heightened nationalist feeling if not with separatism itself. This disenchantment, measured by belief in separatism, has not yet found massive support in the rural and lower urban social strata, but rather has met with indifference, apathy, and skepticism, though seldom with outright hostility. Had massive support from these social strata been forthcoming, the separatist idea would have been acted upon. Paradoxical as it may seem, it is the uneducated, unskilled and semi-skilled French Canadian farmer and worker, the "ignorant," "joual"-speaking French Canadian, oft-maligned and spoofed by his ethnic middle class and the perfect fit of the anti-French Canadian stereotype, who is at present quite unconsciously holding Confederation, unsettled as it is, on its shaky legs.

This leads me to raise specifically, the questions I shall attempt to answer in this essay. Why has the lower-class French Canadian been relatively immune to separatist agitation? Why has the new French Canadian middle class become virulently nationalist and, to an important extent, separatist? Why has the emergence of this new middle class heightened ethnic tensions in Confederation? What is the nature of social unrest in the lower social strata?

SOCIAL UNREST AND THE NEW MIDDLE CLASS

The emergence of what is commonly called the new middle class is not something specific to French Canada; quite on the contrary, the growth of such a class was rather belated, in fact, essentially a post-war phenomenon. With the growth and the increased size of large-scale formal organizations of business and government, the middle class was overwhelmingly transformed into a bureaucratically employed white-collar group with professional and semi-professional status, displacing the dominant "entrepreneurial," self-employed character of the middle class in the last century. The new middle class is a product of the bureaucratic expansion of organizations.

The Growth and Characteristics of the New Middle Class in French Canada

Structurally, the French Canadian new middle class is the same as its counterparts in industrially developed societies. But the circumstances of its emergence and some of its characteristics are somewhat at variance with most.

The bureaucratic revolution is, demographically speaking, the result of mass exodus from country to city. The demographic pressure created a need for expansion of the urban institutions serving this influx. In the process of expansion the urban institutions changed character, becoming large-scale organizations, marked by increased specialization. This bureaucratic revolution opened new channels of upward mobility. It required diversified staffs, trained in new skills. The growth of bureaucratic urban institutions became the structural basis of a new social class called the new middle class.

The French Canadian new middle class, I have said, is somewhat different in some of its social-psychological characteristics from other new middle classes. First of all, its emergence was more dramatic and sudden than in many cases. Second, the ethnic cultural traditions from which it came provided no models for the broad spectrum of the new occupational roles. Third, French Canadian bureaucracies are to be found overwhelmingly in the public and semi-public sectors as against the area of private enterprise. Finally, the bureaucratic revolution, in French Canada, has not changed the power elite of French Canadian society; it has not displaced, but rather rejuvenated traditional elites. Much of the unrest, in my opinion, in the French Canadian new middle class can be related to these special characteristics.

The Duplessis Era and the New Middle Class

New middle class unrest dates back to the mid and late 50s. The post-war period saw a massive migration of French Canadians to the cities, mostly the major ones. This massive urbanization altered the existing nature of urban institutions. Urban institutions of welfare, health, and education rapidly had to increase their size, their staffs, and their budgets to meet the new demographic needs. This bureaucratic growth was being stifled by Duplessis's habit of discretionary spending of public funds. In the process, the economic and status interests of this new middle class were not being met. Salaries could not be increased. Why? Because of Duplessis. Staff could not be hired. Why? Because of Duplessis.

Duplessis became a symbol of oppression, of reactionary government. He was depicted as a tyrant corrupting political mores. A persistent theme of Duplessis's political oratory was his opposition to "bureaucracy." Even though ideologically neutral, the theme was becoming increasingly impertinent structurally. The celebrated attack on the political mores of the Union Nationale Party by Fathers Dion and O'Neil paved the way for a new bureaucratic type of political morality. The growth of semi-public bureaucratic institutions required greatly increased and predictable amounts of money from the provincial treasury. Because he refused to meet these class demands, Duplessis was emotionally and unanimously resented by the new middle class. Where Duplessis failed, Sauvé succeeded. By a single declaration of policy, namely, increased grants to universities, hospital insurance and increased salaries to civil servants, he immediately got the emotional endorsement of the new middle class for the very same party. His untimely death was perceived by members of this social class as a tragic personal loss. Duplessis stifled the class interests and the status aspirations of the new middle class. He was resented. Sauvé decided to meet them; he was acclaimed.

The New Middle Class and the Lesage Regime

With the death of Duplessis, the critical importance of the new middle class on politics became unchallenged. Following in Sauvé's footsteps, the Liberal Party under Jean Lesage proceeded to base its political strength on the enthusiastic support of the new middle class, recently become politically aroused and vocal.

The link between the Liberal Party and the new middle class can easily be established. Its existence can be shown in terms of (a) the "nucleus" of its political support, (b) the choice of "competent" administrative personnel in the civil service, and (c) the nature of its legislative reforms. The "volunteer" workers of the Liberal Party in the past elections were urban, more highly educated, younger, new middle class people. The concern for qualified personnel in the expanding provincial civil service spells the end of the "self-made" man or politically appointed party supporter. The party man must also be professionally qualified.

The Liberal legislative reform is a bureaucratic reform. It has sought to expand and strengthen the bureaucratic services of education, health and welfare. The Quebec renaissance or silent revolution, or whatever it is called, is a bureaucratic revolution. The tremendous expenditures in education and health are coupled with a constant concern with increasing the salaries of white-collar occupations in these institutions. Current concern for portable pensions equally reflects the interests of the new middle class.

From anti-Duplessism to Separatism

It is not, in my opinion, by sheer coincidence that separatism became a social force only after the death of Duplessis. By stifling the status aspirations of the new middle class, Duplessis became a scapegoat upon which its frustrations could be vented. Middle class unrest did not die with Duplessis. The middle classes, however, did lose a scapegoat.

The Liberal Party, champion of bureaucratic reform, endeavoring to meet the aspirations of this social class could not easily be indicted. Unrest in new middle class circles took on the form of separatist agitation. The class origins of separatism can be ascertained both in terms of the social location of its supporters and the class nature of its grievances.

Separatist leaders as well as their rank and file are to be found among the better-educated, younger, professional and semi-professional, salaried, white-collar ranks. This class constitutes the core of its support. The nature of separatist grievances also underlines its class bias. Separatist discontent, in the final analysis, boils down to protest against real or imagined restricted occupational mobility. The objects of separatist indictment are the promotion practices of the federally operated bureaucracies, of crown and private corporations. This class bias is also the reason why the separatist appeal has gone largely unheeded by the rural classes and the lower social strata of the cities.

National Unrest, the Liberal Regime, and Confederation

Sheer coincidence cannot alone account for the fact that separatism and disenchantment with Confederation appeared on the political scene, in its massive form, after the Liberal regime came into power and not during the Duplessis era.

Meeting the status aspirations of the new middle class in French Canada, as the Liberals surely know by now, is an expensive proposition. It is more costly than most services since, as I have mentioned, French Canadian bureaucracies tend to be in the public or semi-public sectors that typically rely on public funds for a sizable proportion of their budgets. The income squeeze that resulted from trying to meet new middle class demands created a political crisis in dominion-provincial relations.

Ethnic tensions, unheard of during the Duplessis era, were brought back once again to the forefront of public discussion. Maîtres chez nous, the Liberal Party's slogan in the last election, is actually the official endorsement of a forty-year old slogan first put forward by Lionel Groulx:

"Le seul choix qui nous reste est celui-ci: ou redevenir maîtres chez nous, ou nous résigner à jamais aux destinées d'un peuple de serfs."[1]

Lionel Groulx's was a voice in the desert until the new middle class made it theirs. His historical, economic and social views were academically marginal and politically ineffective until the emergence of the new middle class and its access to political power. His views have become the unifying ideology giving political cohesiveness to this new social class.

Many of the current themes of political concern are to be explicitly found in his writings. Ambivalence toward foreign capitalists and foreign labor unions, indignation at the handing over of natural resources to foreign investors, the lack of an entrepreneurial bourgeoisie, the positive role of the state in economic affairs, the lack of proper academic institutions and training for the world of business, the "bi-national" theory of Confederation, all of these themes are clearly and eloquently pleaded in his writings.

The financial strain of the French Canadian bureaucratic revolution and the nationalist ideology of the French Canadian new middle class, have brought about a reinterpretation of Confederation specifically and of ethnic co-habitation generally. The reinterpretation is not new; its widespread acceptance in the new middle class is.

Confederation is on probation. The French Canadian new middle class does not view it as something valuable in itself. It is to be judged on its merits as a means to achieving national aspirations. It has, for a long time, been viewed as an instrument of British Canadian nationalism.[2] With the rise of ethnic tensions this view is becoming widespread in many circles and a postulate of the political analysis of separatist groups of every tendency.

What, in effect, needs clarification is the history of ethnic co-habitation in Canada. Ethnic accommodation, it seems to me, has been historically constructed, successfully in Quebec, on a basis of mutually desired self-segregated institutions. In the fields of education, religion, welfare, leisure and residence, institutional self-segregation has been total. The only two areas of societal living where inter-ethnic contact has been institutionalized are those of work and politics.

The pattern of ethnic contact in the area of work was established with the introduction of industrialization. Anglo-Saxon industry moved into a society faced with an acute population surplus, a distinctive political and religious elite, a developing set of institutions anchored in the rural parish. This society, politically stable, economically conservative, and technically unskilled, provided ideal conditions for investing Anglo-Saxon capitalists; they could invest their capital, open industries and be supplied with an abundant source of unskilled labor seeking employment. The managerial and technical levels were filled, with no protest, by the incoming group, who also brought along their own set of institutions, servicing their own nationals.

This social setting provided an easy introduction to industry. The French Canadian elite was ideologically co-operative, sensitive only about its continued control over its demographic substructures. This fitted in quite well with the aims of the incoming groups, who could develop their economic pursuits and enterprises with minimum involvement in the local society. There was a minimum of involvement in local politics. The local elite of politicians and the clergy welcomed the transaction of business and the development of business institutions. All this took place with no unrest whatsoever. Industry was relieving the economic burden of the demographic surplus of French Canadian rural society. The local elites' leadership was not being challenged.

This pattern of mutually satisfying, self-segregated institutions worked with no dissent up to and including World War II. This historical pattern is now being challenged. It is being challenged by the recently emerged French Canadian new middle class. Making room for this new social class in the managerial levels of industry and government is the crucial test of Canadian unity. This cannot be achieved without the shedding of old habits that surrounded the traditional ethnic division of labor.

SOCIAL UNREST IN THE RURAL AND LOWER URBAN SOCIAL CLASSES

The Creditiste Episode

"Nous sommes simples, nous autres habitants, et vu notre ignorance, nous sommes contraints de mettre à la tête de nos municipalités et de nos administrations des citoyens instruits mais qui, au fond, nous exploitent..." — Isidore Gauthier, a farmer, 1862.[3]

New middle class unrest, vocal and well publicized, overshadowed another social unrest, that of the lower social class of the country and city, until the unforeseen sweep of rural Quebec by Réal Caouette's Creditiste movement.

Indeed, for the first time in Quebec's political history, the rural lower classes transgressed the political script described by Isidore Gauthier. Instead of sending to the Federal Parliament traditional middle class professionals, they elected class peers to represent them.

Unforeseen, this political development brought about a reaction of bewilderment, astonishment and nervous laughter in middle class circles. The Creditiste surge was viewed with alarm, ridicule and embarrassment. The French Canadian new middle class had the identical reaction as its English Canadian counterpart towards the Creditiste sweep. It focused immediately and exclusively on its unorthodox economics not on the social discontent that gave rise to it.

The Creditiste appeal successfully tapped the unrest of farmers and unskilled workers where the middle class separatist protest failed. The Creditiste criticism of the traditional parties found fertile soil in the economically deprived regions of rural Quebec. "You have nothing to lose" went the slogan. Another major theme was the right to economic security. Economic security to middle class people means decent pension plans. To a sizeable part of the French Canadian population it means something quite different. It means stable employment, a year-round job, the right not to live in the constant fear of unemployment. Caouette, who is no new middle class symbol by any means, but a small entrepreneur, the product of the barren Abitibi region, spoke their language. His charge that the old parties really do not care or cannot change their socio-economic plight, comes dangerously close to regional historic truth, for this state of economic insecurity has been a pattern that dates back close to a century.

The dramatic emergence of the Social Credit Party in rural Quebec can be viewed as a boomerang or latent resentment of the class-oriented Liberal course in Quebec. Duplessis, whatever his shortcomings, based his political machine on the rural and lower-urban social strata. After the ousting of the Union Nationale, these classes felt unrepresented, uncared for, with no significant voice in the political arena. Duplessis had never been viewed as a dictator or tyrant in these strata. The Lesage resolve to dissolve patronage increased the Creditiste supporters because of disenchanted rural Liberals who had expected the continued exercise of patronage by their own group.

The possibly unanticipated effect of the crackdown on patronage was to halt or substantially reduce the flow of provincial funds to the lower social strata. Holding up the new "bureaucratic" political morality was a hidden net reorienting public expenditures to other social classes. In the light of this interpretation, the Creditiste slogan "you have nothing to lose" takes on added meaning. Whatever the dubious ethics of the political organizers of Duplessis may have been, and whatever the size of the cake they kept as their part, they managed, in their own devious ways, to let the rest funnel down in numerous bits into kinship systems. With the Liberal regime, the cake is properly and ceremoniously cut up, but the slices are fewer and the number of guests is greatly reduced.

Whether the Creditiste movement will manage to hold its own politically is uncertain; whether it does or not, is of little interest; the social unrest that gave rise to it is, however, of considerable importance. To make intelligible the social forces behind its success, whether temporary or not, is the legitimate and necessary concern of the social scientist.

Messianic Social Movements and Deprived Social Classes

Messianic social movements tend to take roots in the economically deprived social classes. The utopian dream they hold up may seem unattainable and irrational to middle class logic, but its purpose and function are different. Its function is to present an alternative to the state of things for those who benefit the least from the status quo. In the process, the present state of society is shown to be man-made and therefore amenable to change. The "funny money" policies of the Creditiste movement can be understood in the light of such classical social movement theory. The Creditiste attack on the financial "sharks" and its insistence on monetary reform served this purpose. To set off the printing presses is an alarming idea for those who have money because of its inflationary effect; for those who do not have money, it becomes a pleasant dream, a dream about magical access to middle class status. And when believed in, it becomes a political force.

Eric Kieran's brave foray from the Board of Trade's executive suite to Creditiste territory with an orthodox economic gospel, quite unprecedented as it was, only underlined the establishment's somber assessment of the situation.

The Liberal solution to the economic plight of these deprived regions goes little beyond the faint hope of recruitment over the generations to middle class status through education. This is equally utopian; it has yet to be achieved anywhere in Western Capitalist society. The fact of the matter is that no operational solution to these pockets of poverty has actually been found.

The Conservative Urban Proletariat and the Uprooted New Middle Class

The French Canadian urban lower classes behave improperly in terms of classical theory. They remain Catholic, faithfully go to church, never vote socialist, and in times of family crisis will spontaneously turn for help to their extended kinship group, their priests and their landlords and only as a last resort, and with a loss of self-respect, to social agencies, social workers and union leaders.

The traditionalism of the urban lower class has been the scourge of socialist efforts. It has also stubbornly resisted appeals from the nationalist circles to become an ethnically conscious consumer. It does not share the anti-Americanism of both French Canadian and English Canadian nationalism.

The rural-urban transition, eased by the kinship group, has not been as textbooks usually describe it, as personally unsettling and culturally shocking as earlier massive urbanization may have been in other societies.

Uprootedness is more characteristic of French Canada's new middle class than of its urban proletariat. The traditional pattern of land inheritance, of keeping the farm intact and handing it over to only one heir, coupled with the high rural birth rate, has meant that moving, looking for work, settling elsewhere, is not a dramatic event in the life-cycle of the rural surplus population and it has been provided for in the cultural script.

What have not been provided for by the cultural traditions are the role models for the new middle class occupations. For this reason, the traditional culture is something far from sacred and useful, very often the object of contempt and ridicule within new middle class circles. Part of the anxiety and anguish of the new middle class psyche may be traced to this lack of cultural continuity.

SUMMARY

The emergence of a new middle class in French Canada is a structural change that cannot be wished away. Its status aspirations are challenging the historical pattern of the ethnic division of labor. Whether its heightened national mood will lead to the separatist experiment is dependent upon two things: (a) on how successful the present political and economic structure of the Canadian society will be in coping with its bureaucratic aspirations, and (b) on the future direction of lower class unrest.

The bureaucratic revolution of the last few years in Quebec has brought to the surface latent resentment in French Canadian society. The traditionally conservative substructure of French Canadian society has expressed discontent of its own. Its course has not, until now, been in the same direction. But who can say with absolute confidence that it will never be?

Bold, imaginative and responsible decisions are in order from the power elites of this country, whoever they may be. It is doubtful that the current concept of "co-operative federalism" in its present confused and blurred state will tide us over.

*   *   *

EPILOGUE: THE DEMISE OF THE CHURCH, AND THE CHALLENGE TO CONFEDERATION

Fifteen years later, it becomes clear that the economic and political structures of Canadian society were unable to integrate the growing new middle class of Quebec. Further, lower class social unrest to a considerable extent began to coalesce with the frustrations of the new middle class, thus setting the stage for the crisis in Confederation.

We witnessed in this short space of time, the accelerated growth of the public sector and state-dependent institutions, the massive secularization of Quebec society and the emergence of language as a central political issue.

The Demise of the Church

Many symbolic changes that took place during the 50s and early 60s had great structural impact during the later 60s and 70s. In church-state relations, the Asbestos Strike of 1949 signaled the first formal, public split between members of the church hierarchy and the provincial state. By the end of the decade the unions in Quebec were deconfessionalized. In the area of culture, basic changes in the Censor Board brought about the eclipse of the Catholic church's role as a public custodian of morality. In health, education, and welfare, the state supplanted the church as the purveyor as well as the bursar of these services. The control of hospitals, of educational institutions, and of the organization of welfare was divorced from religious orders of nuns in the case of the first, from nuns, brothers and clergy in the case of the second and from the context of the parish and the diocese in the case of the third. The modernization of Quebec involved a massive growth and professionalization of these services as well as universalization and territorial reorganization.

Only the state had the resources and the constitutional jurisdiction to achieve this swift redistribution of resources. This state-initiated modernization required political centralization and bureaucratic growth previously unparalleled not only in Quebec but in all liberal democratic industrialized states. It involved the transfer to the state of services that traditionally have been provided, financed, staffed, and managed at the level of local communities. This is the structural basis for the eclipse of the community.

These structural changes were welcomed, by and large, by the mushrooming professions and the strengthening trade-unions, and by local community elites including the business elites who could profit from the community growth that the process entailed. The countervailing power to the state became the professional associations for the new middle classes and the trade-unions for organized workers. Professional solidarity was no longer tied to community, just as the expanding services were not designed to fit traditional local communities. These services expanded the communities when they did not actually create them in the process of suburban growth.

The church was no longer the center of influence. The drop in religious practice was followed by the drop-out of the clergy: thousands of clerics left the church in this time. Their re-integration into society, unheard of and unthinkable 20 years earlier, was smooth, and met with sympathetic encouragement.

The demise of the Catholic church in Quebec and the nature of this state-initiated modernization had some unforeseen consequences. They are now visible and have led to the central political issues of the late 70s.

Language as a Political Issue

One unforeseen consequence of the increasing centralization of the provincial state was to cast the anglophones in Quebec into a minority status. So long as institutions were managed, funded, and staffed within community settings, the institutional autonomy was ensured. State-initiated modernization had the consequence of creating a French-speaking bureaucracy on which the English institutional sector became dependent. Anglophones in Quebec became dependent on the majority's definition of the rules of the game. The breaking up of the two solitudes was under way, but in the process the anglophones could not escape a minority status they had never experienced before.

This structural change set off a series of language incidents and created a mood of dissatisfaction that eventually led to the downfall of the Bourassa Liberal government in 1976. Previous to that, however, the Union Nationale who had, under Premier Bertrand, introduced despite stiff opposition, most of it extra-parliamentary, the right of parents to choose the language of instruction in schools in Bill 63, experienced a total collapse as a political force in 1970. The Parti Québecois made its entry in the political arena with 16 percent of the popular vote in the election of 1970. In that election, Montreal's East End workers, who traditionally supported the Union Nationale, crossed over to the P.Q. The P.Q. also had high support in the francophone new middle class. A bridge was emerging between the diverse interests of Quebec. In 1973, the P.Q. made some progress in the rural countryside. Finally, in 1976, the P.Q. had mustered sufficient strength both in the lower urban strata and among the disgruntled farm people to become the government of Quebec. The victory was equally attributable to the first massive defection of the anglophone and allophone vote from the Liberal Party over the passage of Bill 22 by the Bourassa administration. Bourassa, who tried to strike a balance between the anglophone minority and the Québecois majority, failed to impress the latter and reaped the anger of the former, who withdrew their traditional monolithic support from the Liberal Party.

The Crisis in Confederation

The political crisis in Canada that followed the assumption of power by the Parti Québecois is related to the demise of the Catholic church in Quebec. The church was the invisible other party to the Act of Confederation. As such it loyally enforced the "two solitudes" that the novelist Hugh MacLennan observed as characterizing French-English relations in Quebec. The concept of two solitudes, far from being accidental, was deliberately designed as a central feature of the B.N.A. act. This feature of the act met the demands of the church, as a recognized embodiment of the French Canadian nation, as well as the inclination and political philosophy of the anglophone fathers of Confederation who saw Canada as British North America.

The changing power relations within Quebec are also having repercussions in national politics. The official federal language policy, far from being designed to break down unacceptable language frontiers to the Québecois majority in its interaction with the economy of Quebec, was exclusively concerned with shoring up crumbling French communities outside Quebec. These communities are losing viability due to the collapsing traditional economy and traditional institutions. By refusing to commit itself to a bilingual Canada on a territorial basis — Quebec French and the rest of Canada English — the federal government stands to lose more of its eroded popularity with the Québecois majority. That the language regime of Canada be territorially defined in terms of language majorities seems a precondition to a new consensus. It is an unfortunate but a necessary condition. Whether such changes are forthcoming is far from certain at the present time.

Notes

1. Lionel Groulx, *Directives,* les éditions du Zodiaque, 1937, p. 20.
2. See Michel Brunet, *Canadians et Canadiens,* Fides, 1952, pp. 47–49. "Une autre manifestation du nationalisme Canadian, le Rapport Massey."
3. Quoted in Léon Gérin, *Le Type Economique et Social des Canadiens,* éditions de l'A.C.F., 1938, p. 54.

An Alternative Approach to the Study of Power*

Bernd Baldus

Few concepts have exerted as long and unchallenged a dominance as Weber's definitions of power and authority. Weber sees power as "the chance of a person or a number of them to realize their own will in a common action, even against the resistance of others participating in it" (Weber, 1964: 678). Political or "social" power, as a particular form of power institutionalized and directed toward the realization of public goals, is the capacity to influence "a common action irrespective of what its content may be" (Weber, 1964: 688). Authority is defined as "the chance to find obedience among identifiable persons for a command with a specific content" (Weber, 1964: 38). It is a special case of power (Weber, 1964: 691), and is characterized by an absence of resistance and, where a command rests on a legal base, by its "legitimacy." A very brief reference to the motivational processes involved in such "voluntary" compliance — for instance, utility considerations, apathetic accustomation to obedience, or affective ties to those in command — is not pursued. Instead, Weber examines extensively the institutional bases of legitimate authority: rational-legal arrangements, tradition, and charisma.

Weber's concepts of power and authority have been used directly or indirectly in numerous subsequent definitions and have had a profound influence on the direction of research on power. Weber's definition of power contains two essential components: power can appear only *in an interaction* between two or more social units — this is implied in the reference to "common action" — and it requires the presence of "resistance" in some observable form. The word "even" in Weber's definition is redundant — discussing power only in terms of the realization of one's interests leads to subjectivist reductions and to a definition of little empirical use. Research on power has largely concentrated on these two elements. Attempts to develop an operational concept of power have generally tried to refine the definitions of interaction (Riker, 1964; Shapley and Shubik, 1954; Harsanyi, 1962; Cartwright, 1959; March, 1955, 1956, 1957; French and Raven, 1959) or of resistance (Dahl, 1957, 1958; Polsby, 1959a, 1959b, 1960; Wolfinger, 1960; Rossi, 1957; Danzger, 1964). Interest in the resistance criterion has also led to research on the means by which it is overcome. Respect, skill, or wealth (Lasswell and Kaplan, 1950), control over cash, credit, and wealth, or over the sources of information (Dahl, 1961), "utilitarian," "normative," and

* Abridged from the *Canadian Journal of Sociology*, 1 (2) 1975, pp. 170–201. Used with permission.

"coercive" factors (Lehman, 1969), or ecological positioning within an organizational structure (Olson, 1970: 75–77) are often identified as such "resources" with whose help compliance and cooperation are secured.

Research on authority has taken up the dual emphasis on the voluntary and the institutional aspects of authority in Weber's writing. Authority is distinguished from power either on the basis of the resistance-free flow of compliance in a command-obedience relationship (Gerth and Mills, 1953: 195), or on the basis of its institutionalization. In the latter case authority is seen as "the institutional code within which the use of power as a medium is organized and legitimized" (Parsons, 1966: 249; see also Biersted, 1969: 159). As in the case of power, such concepts always assume that authority can be identified only in *interactive* relationships. Work on the subjective processes involved in voluntary compliance has mainly concentrated on the development of group norms and roles which define the use of "legitimate" power (Emerson, 1962: 38), and on the notion of "trust." Social units comply with the demands of an authority holder because they trust that their cooperation will be used within a shared normative framework, or in the pursuit of collective shared goals. Empirical research on trust has concentrated on the development of political support attitudes, especially among children (Easton and Dennis, 1969; Hess and Torney, 1967), and on the resources available to political institutions to create support and manage discontent (Gamson, 1968). Often, however, the concepts of trust and legitimacy are used as residual categories which describe summarily all forms of compliance which do not involve recognizable resistance.

It is the purpose of this paper to show that Weber's concept and subsequent work influenced by it have serious deficiencies. The most important of these is that relations between units which are free of resistance, or which do not involve direct interaction, are excluded from the analysis of power. It will be shown that this results in major distortions in the appraisal of the distribution of power between units, and in social systems as a whole. An alternative interpretation of power will be offered: that it is the capacity to maintain a given pattern of structured social inequality over time. Research on power is consequently directed at the identification of such patterns and of the causal determinants of their maintenance.

SOME CONSEQUENCES OF INTERACTION AND RESISTANCE CRITERIA FOR THE STUDY OF POWER

One of the clearest contributions to a theory of power in the Weber tradition has been made by Dahl (1957, 1958). Dahl specifies three properties which are necessary and sufficient for the existence of a "power" relationship between two units, A and a. First, there must be a time lag — however small — between an action by A and the response of a, the unit over which A has power. Second, there must be a "connection" between A and a, a reformulation of the "common action" element in Weber's definition. The presence of such an interaction is indispensable: "In looking for a flow of influence, control, or power from A to a, one must always find out whether there is a connection, or an opportunity for a connection, and if there is not, then one need proceed no further" (Dahl, 1957: 204). Third, the behavior of *a* after the incidence of power must differ in an observable way from the behavior he would have shown without it; A must get *a* to do "what [he] would not otherwise do" (Dahl, 1957: 203). The modification of *a*'s behavior can be the result of A's overcoming the resistance of *a*, or of his voluntary compliance. Dahl's theory is formulated generally enough to include Weber's concept of power as well as the special case of "authority."

The three conditions set by Dahl specify at the same time those areas of social behavior which are not covered by his concept of power. Specifically, they exempt from the investigation of power all behavior which can not be seen as an "interaction" between two or more units, and of the remaining interactive behavior that part which is not characterized by an initial divergence of interests. The first exclusion replicates in the analysis of power the general emphasis on *interaction* as the sole object of sociological investigation which has governed much recent sociological thinking. (This point is programmatically stressed, for instance, by Parsons [1964a: 3]). It is correct in that at any given time no interaction exists between most units in a social system; a complete interaction matrix of such a system would contain a large number of elements with zero values. It would be wrong, however, to conclude that such elements indicate a social void which is of no interest for sociological research. In addition to direct interaction, the various parts of social systems are linked together by a wide variety of non-interactive links which are essential to the system's functioning. In the most general sense they include cases in which a behavior of one unit becomes a necessary condition for the goal-realization of another even though the two do not interact. Such non-interactive links are of prime importance in maintaining and reproducing system structures, including structured forms of social inequality, and that is, in the definition proposed later, power.

The second sector of social relations not covered by Dahl's concept of power consists of interactions which are not characterized by "differences in initial preferences" (Dahl, 1958: 464). Power and consensual or co-oriented behavior — or, more generally, behavior which is supplied without resistance — are treated as mutually exclusive. Dahl stresses repeatedly that wherever "the consensus is perpetual and unbreakable,... there is no conceivable way of determining who is ruler and who is ruled" (Dahl, 1958: 468). Bierstedt makes a similar point: "Power thus appears both in competition and in conflict and has no incidence in groups which neither compete nor conflict, i.e. between groups which do not share a similar social matrix and have no social relations.... Power thus arises only in social opposition of some kind" (Bierstedt, 1969: 162). The exemption of consensus from the analysis of power is frequently further defended by a vehement rejection of any notion of "false consciousness." To suspect power in co-oriented behavior is seen as an attempt to impose "the values of the analysts ... arbitrarily on groups in the community. ... The presumption that the 'real' interests of a class be assigned to them by an analyst allows the analyst to charge 'false consciousness' when the class in question disagrees with the analyst" (Polsby, 1963: 23, 116).

The restricting effects of a resistance and interaction-based concept of power can be illustrated by some examples. Consider, for instance, the Methodist miner in early capitalist England who believed "that every man carried within him his own fate, and that the sovereign happiness of all, the happiness of faith and resignation, was not the prize of wealth or power or learning or conquest, but of a state of mind and heart that poor could attain as readily as rich; the slave as readily as his master" (Hammond, 1968: 238). Or, more recently, the blue-collar worker who expresses his confidence in the foresight and the wisdom of the rich: "I think anybody that has money—I think their interest is much wider than the regular working man. He has money and he has a much wider view of life — because he is in the knowledge all the time" (Lane and Lerner, 1970: 104), and who believes that "equality...would deprive society, and oneself, of a group of friendly, wise and helpful leaders" (Lane and Lerner, 1970: 104). Such beliefs show the acceptance of and resignation to their situation by people in a dependent position. Their views are such that "differences in preferences" with those in dominant social positions are not likely to appear in the first place. Resistance does not have to be overcome because their behavior has already a desirable form. At the same time, the origins of such acquiescence are often not related to a prior action by a dominant group or class. Unless, however, such behavior can be shown to have been initiated at some earlier time by the groups that benefit from it, it can not be considered in an analysis of power. At most, it can be interpreted as "consensual," a result which is clearly unsatisfactory in view of the structural imbalance which it supports.

The distorting effect of a concept of power that neglects that part of the structural relationship between individuals or groups which is not perceived as problematic and does therefore not become the object of conflicting interests grows with the scope of the analysis. It is most pronounced in the study of power in contemporary capitalist societies by "pluralist" theories. Their focus on divergences of opinions on "issues," and on the outcome of conflicts to which they give rise, leads to substantial distortions in the appraisal of the relative power of each group, and of the total distribution of power in the system. Since structural characteristics of such societies which do not become an "issue" remain outside the scope of the study of power, basic structures of domination in the system may be entirely ignored, while a conflict whose effect on these structures is negligible is interpreted as an important indicator of the "power" of the parties involved. The pluralist concept of power offers no way in which to take into account the degree to which the declared interest of one party covers the structural features of the position of its opponent. As a result, all interests seem alike. They differ only with respect to their intensity and their organizational characteristics. Judged by their manifest conflicts of interests alone, contemporary capitalist societies appear accordingly as "fractured into a congeries of hundreds of small special interest groups, with incompletely overlapping membership, widely different power bases, and a multitude of techniques of exercising influence on decisions salient to them" (Polsby, 1963: 118). Such a view effectively precludes any search for underlying forms of structural domination.

THE TREATMENT OF POWER IN FUNCTIONAL AND CONFLICT THEORIES

The systematic neglect of undisputed structural forms of dependence and domination appears also in major current theories of social systems. Central to Parsons's theory of social systems is the assumption that in a fully integrated society "the interests of the collectivity and the private interests of its constituent members ... approach coincidence" (Parsons, 1964: 42). System interests and unit interests converge, and the consensus which the society's members share with respect to the system's objectives and directions is not merely formal, but expresses a structural flow of benefits from the system's goal-realization process which is equitable and fair. Such an assumption clearly precludes the possibility that consensus can coexist with structural inequity above a "functionally necessary" division of labor and ranks. In particular, it precludes the possibility that consensus legitimates the pursuit of the interests of a ruling group in the system. This condition is, of course, built into the construction of the theory itself: the linear derivation of system objectives from the interests of its members make the appearance of inequity and of objections to it unlikely. Instead, people in Parsons's society interact in a fictitious free space where they arrive at shared value standards under the auspices of individual autonomy and freedom in the rational pursuit of their personal desires.

How uneasy Parsons himself is with the construct of a social system where consensus is pervasive and where, as a result, power of dominant groups disappears and the only power left is that of the government to mobilize system members in order "to get things done in the interest of collective goals" (Parsons, 1960: 181), is evident from the many instances where he feels compelled to defend this idea by giving assurances such as the following:

> For some classes of participants the significance of collectivity membership may be predominantly its usefulness in an instrumental context to their "private" goals. But such an orientation cannot be constitutive of the collectivity itself, and so far as it predominates, tends to disrupt the solidarity of the collectivity (Parsons, 1964: 41).

Elsewhere, Parsons states that,

> A relatively established "politically organized society" is clearly a "moral community" to some degree, its members sharing common norms, values and culture, which is to say that I start with a view that repudiates the idea that any political system that rests entirely on self-interest, force, or a combination of them, can be stable over any considerable period of time" (Parsons, 1964: 34).

"Self-interest" and "common values" are claimed to be incompatible. A social system whose actions are not "in the best interest" of all its members is not viable and will not last.

Parsons encounters the problem of the coincidence of domination and consensus most openly in his discussion of stratification. Here, he uses a concept of power that comes much closer to Weber's original definition than the "systemic" approach to power usually employed in Parsons's writings. Power is seen as "the realistic capacity of a system-unit to actualize its 'interests' (attain goals, prevent undesired interference, command respect, control possessions, etc.) within the context of system-interaction and in this sense to exert influence on processes in the system" (Parsons, 1954: 391). Parsons admits that such interests have considerable independent influence on the inequality pattern in a society and counteract the basic functional process of the development of stratification. However, the possibility that a segment of the system becomes so powerful that it can independently determine system structure and system processes, including shared values, is expressly rejected:

> Empirically, the imperfections of integration of social systems formulated by the...
> non-valuation components of the power of a unit may be extremely important.
> However, the point of view from which we approach an analysis of stratification
> prescribes that analysis should focus on the common value-pattern aspect. Only
> through this we can gain stable points of reference for a technical theoretical
> analysis of the empirical influence of the other components of the system process
> (Parsons, 1954: 393).

No further reason is given. But it is clear that only in this rather forceful way can Parsons maintain his claim that any lasting consensus must be in the "own best interest" of those who share it (Parsons, 1968: 143), and that its presence indicates the absence of structural domination and unilateral power.

The same deficiencies which characterize functionalist approaches to the analysis of power are present in what is commonly called conflict theory, notably in the writings of Dahrendorf. Dahrendorf starts out with what seems to be an emphasis on the structural dimensions of norms and interests. In his article on the nature and types of social inequality he stresses, for instance, that "in the last analysis, established norms are nothing but ruling norms, i.e. norms defended by the sanctioning agencies of society and those who control them.... the established or ruling values of a society may be studied in their purest form by looking at its upper class" (Dahrendorf, 1969b: 38). It becomes soon apparent, however, that he is not interested in making the structural characteristics of rule the object of the study of power. After rejecting any discussion of "objective interests" as "pure speculation" (Dahrendorf, 1969a: 174), he interprets structural forms of rule entirely in terms of their subjectively perceived equivalent. Rule and domination enter Dahrendorf's analysis only through the "role" definitions of the interacting units. Power remains, in close approximation to Weber's term, the capacity of one group to make its interest prevail over an opposed interest of another. Wherever these interests and roles cover only a fraction of the structure of dependence between these units, the uncontested portion is excluded from the investigation of power: in the case of the submissive feudal peasant the constituent distribution of land, in the case of the docile and modest labor union the uncontested distribution of productive property. As a consequence, serious distortions must occur in the estimate of power in the system. The token democratization by the Prussian aristocracy in response to the changing modes of agricultural production and the increasing attraction of peasants to the growing urban industries (Rosenberg, 1969: 23–25), or the establishment of welfare systems as a means to create a loyal and stable labor force and to discourage "dishonest labor agitators" in the American steel industry in 1910–1915 (Brody, 1960: 179) must be interpreted by such a theory as major concessions by dominant groups, and as major gains in "power" by peasants or steel workers. In fact, both measures were intended to and did reinforce the existing structural ties of rule and dependence. Further, the neglect of the structural origins of group interests precludes any study of the complex influences of such structural bases on the appearance of manifest interests in the system: processes of selective learning and conditioning which prevent the appearance of more far-reaching and disruptive role definitions and interests and encourage those which are compatible with the existing structure of rule.

The striking similarities in the conceptualization of power and its resulting shortcomings which characterize the various theories of social power in spite of their self-proclaimed differences point to an underlying political assumption which they all share. It has its roots in the ideology of liberalism where individuals appear as free, autonomous, and politically equal in the pursuit of their own best interest. These attributes of the political individual work as a powerful corrective force in the social system: where structural inequities and injustices arise which are not in the interest of all concerned they will be noticed, opposed, and eliminated. Precisely because such corrective conflict is inevitable, however, structures in a society which are not opposed by a substantial portion of the populace must be fair and equitable. An absence of opposition is thus a reliable indicator of the objective justice of the structure in question. It is for this reason that it is considered "legitimate" and meets the consensual approval of the population involved. Only on the basis of assumptions such as these can power and consensus be treated as mutually exclusive. The absence of conflict effectively terminates the investigation of power.

AN ALTERNATIVE FOR THE STUDY OF POWER

If the stagnation into which the Weber tradition has led research on power is to be overcome, a radical departure from Weber's original concept is required. An empirically useful concept of power must consider the following points:

1. Power must be identified by structural, not by subjective, indicators. The structural characteristics of power must be clearly separated from the cognitive and behavioral processes to which they give rise.

2. Power becomes evident in the *maintenance* of a structure of inequality over time. Correspondingly, power declines or disappears to the extent that such structures disintegrate or disappear.

3. Research on power must consequently be directed at the investigation of the causal processes which determine the maintenance or the change of a pattern of structured social inequality. More particularly, it must investigate the behavior of the units in the structure of reference which contributes to its continuity or its change. Such an analysis treats the maintenance of a referent structure as a dependent, and its behavioral determinants as an independent variable. The latter includes all behavior which can be empirically identified as a causal factor in the continuity of the structure of reference. This comprises, among others, forms of

behavior which are not conflict-oriented or are not part of a direct interaction connecting the units observed.

On this basis, power is defined as the ability of a center unit to maintain, reproduce, or reinforce over time its position with respect to a periphery unit in a structure of social inequality of which both are a part. This definition requires, first, an operational definition of inequality structures and of means of distinguishing between "center" and "periphery" units within them, and second, an identification of those links between center and periphery which contribute causally to the continuity of the center's position.

STRUCTURAL FORMS OF SOCIAL INEQUALITY

Social inequality exists where an individual or a group in a social system is excluded from behavior which is open to others. Similar to Galtung's terminology this means that inequality is seen as a form of "structural violence" (Galtung, 1971: 81), and not as the result of unequal "rewards" for contributions to shared objectives. Structures of social inequality consist of limitations which are differentially imposed on system members and which restrict their actions in comparable behavior parameters to different degrees.

Differential limitations of behavior may originate outside the units under review. In this case they merely regulate the behavior of several units without having been set by one of them. On the other hand, one unit in a structure of reference may have independently imposed such limitations on the behavior of others. Second, differential limitations can be imposed in the form of normative regulations or by the differential distribution of goods or services. While often accompanied by normative rules, the possession of material goods must be considered as a separate and independent determinant of behavior parameters. This is, in particular, the case with differential access to productive, surplus-yielding goods which can become the basis for characteristic forms of dominance and subordination.

On this basis, an analytical distinction can be drawn between four structural types of social inequality:

1. *Simple normative differential limitations* exist where normative regulations which have not been set by one of the units of reference prohibit one unit from carrying out activities which are permitted to another, irrespective of whether they interact or not. Some of the caste regulations in India are an example of this type of inequality. They may regulate the distance up to which members of different castes may approach temples, or may reserve the right to wear certain garments, to use certain building materials, foods, speech patterns, or to enter certain occupations for members of particular castes (Hutton, 1963: 71–90). Caste strictures such as these are regulations whose enforcement often rests with a group or institution other than the individuals from the different castes involved. The distinction between center and periphery is, in this case, a distinction between the less and the more restricted of the units observed.

2. *Normative subordination* arises where one or several units (center) are able to set regulations for the behavior of other units (periphery). As in Weber's concept

of "herrschaft," there is no attention to the basis on which the capacity to set limitations rests; i.e. whether it is the result of a threat of negative sanctions, of "voluntary" obedience, or any other form of compliance.

3. *Simple distributive differential limitations* result from the differential distribution of usable goods between two or more units, irrespective of whether they interact or not. The possession of goods can be converted into property rights by formal rules which reserve their use to the owner and, by the same right, exclude non-owners from them. The possession or the ownership of goods, opens parameters of behavior which are closed to possession- or property-less units. Income differentials in contemporary societies are an example of such simple distributive differences. Center and periphery differ in that the former has more, the latter less of the possession in question.

4. *Distributive subordination* arises in an interaction between units where one side is able, through its possession of goods, to elicit a desired behavior from the other side. Such a relationship of distributive subordination can arise where an exchange between units leads to a creditor-debtor relationship which subjects the debtor to various obligations. Much more important is the development of distributive subordination as a result of the differential distribution of means of production, especially where access to them has been formally restricted by property rights. The accumulation of property of means of production not only excludes property-less units from access to these means. It usually prevents these units from using hitherto available sources of subsistence; as a consequence, property-less units are forced to offer their labor for use with the productive property under conditions set by its owners. These conditions normally concern the distribution of surplus value and designate it as "profit" which accrues to the owner as a part of his property right. Center and periphery are differentiated on the basis of the possession or non-possession of surplus-producing resources.

The distinction between these four types of social inequality merely serves to identify clearly the inequality structure whose maintenance is studied, no matter whether this structure consists of a single type of inequality between two individuals, or of multiple types in a complex and large social system. Empirical structures of inequality are frequently composites of the four types. Where such combinations exist, they reflect a historical and organizational interdependence which can often be traced back to an original core type which gave rise to the subsequent development of more complex forms of social inequality.

SOME DETERMINANTS OF THE MAINTENANCE OF INEQUALITY STRUCTURES

In any inequality structure the behavior of the center *as well as that of the periphery* can contribute to the maintenance of that structure. Determinants originating in the center are most commonly efforts in the area of socialization or coercion, the former frequently used to create behavior in the periphery which supports existing inequality structures and eliminates the desire for alternatives, and the latter primarily directed at the prevention or correction of behavior in the periphery that could weaken the center's position. In a more general sense, center-originating determinants include any direct intervention by the center which intends to modify maintenance-relevant behavior in the periphery.

Contributions from the periphery comprise, in the most general form, all periphery behavior which is a causal factor in the maintenance of the inequality structure of reference, but which is not the result of a prior intentional center intervention. Such behavior will be called complementary. A special part of it consists of adaptive and adjustive reactions by periphery units to the experience of social inequality. The following examples of center and periphery contributions are intended to indicate some of the directions in which empirical research on power may go.

Efforts by a center to maintain an existing inequality structure can be expected to concentrate on creating among its own members as well as those of the periphery cognitive images of social inequality which make it appear acceptable, deserved, or unalterable. Mann (1970) shows some of the processes involved in the "mobilization of bias" in favor of an existing inequality structure. This effort is complemented by attempts to immunize the periphery against alternatives to these structures which endanger the center's position. This is usually achieved through the inculcation of boundaries which designate what is socially tolerable and what is not, and by labelling these alternatives as unacceptable, "utopian," "leading to chaos," and so on. In contemporary capitalist societies such boundaries protect the system primarily against "socialist" or "communist" forms of social organization. Litt (1963) and Zeigler (1967) provide evidence of the establishment of boundaries in schools. Stouffer (1963) shows that they have been internalized on a very large scale, and that they effectively prevent the examination or acceptance of alternatives which would be detrimental to existing inequality structures. Both positive images of inequality and boundary-maintaining negative labels are frequently represented by symbols. (For an excellent study of the manipulative use of political symbols in the maintenance of the status quo of social inequality see Edelman, 1960.) In addition to these two basic themes, center efforts to maintain social inequality can be observed in the creation of motivations such as conformity or obedience, and in modern liberal systems motivations to achieve and to consume which are of particular instrumental importance in the economic reproduction of inequality in such systems (Baldus, 1977).

Empirical research on coercive control as a determinant of power is unproblematic where coercion restricts or eliminates behavior which intentionally opposes a given inequality structure, or where it can be clearly established that the threat of coercion prevents the development of such behavior. Possible areas of research are the histories of coercive intervention in different societies against movements which threaten the status quo of inequality. Another important area covers the legal and institutional provisions for coercive control. Virtually all capitalist societies have, for instance, preventive legal regulations such as the Criminal Syndicalism Act in the United States, Seditious Conspiracy statutes in Canada, or "emergency" legislations designed to control the activities of revolutionary movements. The informal use of coercion, for instance by right-wing murder squads in Latin American countries, would also be included. In addition, research would be needed on the impact of coercive control on periphery behavior, such as the signal effect of coercive measures or the social construction of permissible targets of coercion.

Compared to the relatively well-investigated areas of persuasive or coercive control by the center, contributions to the maintenance of inequality which originate in the periphery have received virtually no attention. The common characteristic of such complementary periphery behavior is that is is *autonomous* in the sense of not being the result of any planned prior center initiative. The most obvious example of this would be the complementary "fit" between a particular condition in the periphery — say disunity between periphery groups which has not been instigated by the center — and the interest of a center in maintaining its dominant position. In a more general form, this means that periphery behavior oriented towards one goal is used by the center for the realization of its own different goal. But periphery behavior may also be complementary to the maintenance of the center's position without the center making conscious use of it. Most important, complementarity does not require interaction: the very absence of action in the periphery, or the ignorance of a particular center behavior, may be essential causal conditions for the continuity of the inequality status quo.

Complementary behavior is of crucial importance for the integration of any complex social system. Since it is judged only by its utility, it makes it possible to organize behavior which serves the diverse personal goals of individual units into directed schemes of collective action whose objectives need not be known to the contributing units. In addition, complementary behavior accrues to its ultimate beneficiary frequently without any costs. Unlike periphery behavior which results from persuasive or coercive control, complementary behavior represents an unsolicited contribution to the center's position. No systematic empirical work has been done in this area. Brody's study of the American steel industry between 1900 and 1929 provides, however, an excellent example of the discovery and the use by industry owners of a complementary condition: the cultural tradition and the personal obligations and fears of immigrant workers from Eastern and Southern Europe. The docility and restraint of workers from peasant cultures, "their habit of silent submission, their amenability to discipline and their willingness to work long hours and overtime without a murmur" (Brody, 1960: 135) were quickly recognized as complementary virtues by the steel industry. They were part of the cultural heritage which the immigrant brought to the United States. Therefore they did not have to be created and accrued to the steel industry as a windfall gain. The continuing ties with his family in Europe, the obligation to send financial support, and the quasi-irrevokable nature of the immigration itself had similar complementary results: they led the worker to accept employment under conditions unacceptable to American workers. The steel industry was well aware of the complementary qualities of immigrant labor.

Its desirable features coincided perfectly with the industry's interests:

> Although claiming natives to be superior workmen, employers understood very well their good fortune. They dealt with the immigrant steelworkers as they did because nothing else was necessary. Developing without any effort on their part, the unskilled labor pattern of mobility fitted perfectly into the scheme of economical steel manufacture. The steelmakers were content. (Brody, 1960: 111)

Complementarity of the kind described above involves a situation where existing periphery behavior contributes in its initial form to the maintenance of the relative positions of center and periphery. But a complementary condition may also develop in an often complex process in which periphery units adjust to the limitations imposed on their behavior. The end result is the same, but because of its characteristics adjustive behavior requires separate attention.

Adjustment occurs where the limitation of the behavior of a periphery unit necessitates a change of existing or the abstention from intended behavior. The experience of such limitations frequently causes stress. Adjustive behavior is designed to alleviate it. The costs of adjustment, both psychological and material, are normally borne by the adjusting unit. Costs for the center, with a few exceptions, do not arise. On the other hand, the reduction of personal stress reduces at the same time the potential of systemic strain in the inequality structure. As in the case of complementary behavior, this effect is normally not intended and not even known to the adjusting unit. Nor is it necessary that a particular adjustive behavior is a part of an interaction between adjusting and beneficiary unit. In terms of the definitions of power discussed earlier, neither "common action" nor "resistance" requirements are met in such a case. The usual result of adjustment is precisely the elimination of any resistance and the conflict-free incorporation of the behavior of the adjusting unit into the process of maintaining and reproducing inequality.

The empirical manifestations of adjustive behavior are as diverse as the subjective experience of inequality itself. His involvement in the reproduction of inequality in dependent industrial work may appear to the individual worker as boring, unattractive, monotonous, and as characterised by high external control and by an absence of chances for occupational advance. Workers may adjust to such stress by developing intricate ways of reducing or breaking up the workload (Walker and Guest, 1952: 76). They may "retaliate" by damaging tools, or through small-scale theft of company property, which in turn may be accepted as complementary by the company because the cost of theft is smaller than the cost of industrial conflict which might otherwise be expected (Zeitlin, 1971). A janitor may adjust to the demeaning aspects of low-paid service work by developing a "craft ego" by conveying an image of being "his own boss" and a "responsible guardian of the building," and by assuming new tasks such as minor plumbing repairs which suggest an artisan status (Nosow and Form, 1962: 132, 133; Berger, 1964). In order to close the gap between ideologically raised ambitions and the reality of permanent factory work "workers may try to maintain the illusion of persisting ambition by defining their jobs in the factory as 'temporary' and by incessantly talking about their out-of-the-shop goals and expectations. As long as workers can sustain this illusion, they can escape from the problems of self-justification created by their inability to rise and their low level of aspiration" (Chinoy, 1965: 123). Similarly, "workers may try to protect themselves from guilt and self-blame by stressing other values as substitutes for success, minimizing the importance of wealth." In a few instances, for example, workers asserted that what mattered was "happiness — and you don't need a lot of money for that," that what counted was "the kind of person you are and not how much money you have" (Chinoy, 1965: 127). Popitz observes similar adjustments to the structural limitations of their position by industrial workers in Germany. He also notes that adjustive behavior provides not only an opportunity for the individual to "let off steam," but reduces the amount of claims, tension and conflict in the system as a whole: "a relatively small chance of a career advance [favors] the growth of a collective consciousness that manifests itself positively as an arrangement with a common fate, and negatively as a resigned passivity and eventually as a devaluation of all subjective desires for advance. The smaller the gate that leads upward, the smaller, as a rule, the crowding in front of it. Our results confirm this experience" (Popitz, 1957: 241).

The distributive limitations imposed by an inequality structure may be experienced as deprivation, and may give rise to adjustive responses which alter or compensate for the need for a valued objective which is, in one's present social position, unattainable. Lockwood's study of clerical workers in Britain identifies the imitation of the "gentleman ideal" as one of the adjustive behaviors of clerical workers in response to their gradual loss of occupational and status privileges. The imitation of gentleman-like behavior became a "dominating feature of the clerical consciousness" in the course of industrialization and helped clerical workers to maintain a perceived distance toward the manual laborer (Lockwood, 1958: in particular, 29, 32). The subjective benefits received from this imitative behavior were strong enough to survive the derision which the "poor sad snob of a clerk" encountered from those he revered as well as those he despised (Lockwood, 1958: 31). Similar forms of self-enhancement are reported in many of the community studies of the 1940s. Members of Elmtown's "class V," mainly workers, describe themselves as "the backbone of the community" (Hollingshead, 1949: 103). People in the "upper-lower class" in Davis's study, who are labeled by the classes above them as "poor whites" or as "no count lot" describe themselves as "poor but honest folk," and the very bottom group identified as social outcasts by everyone else in the community rates itself as "people just as good as anybody" (Davis, Gardner, and Gardner, 1941). In a more recent study Lewis reports that "lower class" persons see fewer social classes than members of "higher class" standing, and explains this as an attempt at self-elevation: individuals near the bottom of a perceived inequality structure can enhance their position by seeing few categories above themselves, while the opposite holds for members of "high class" ranking (Lewis, 1964). Young and Willmott's (1962) study of occupational rankings by workers in East London produced similar findings. Where social inequality leads to feelings of powerlessness or dependence, periphery individuals or groups may look for corresponding surrogates. The institution of voting in liberal systems seems to provide, together with a more general ideological folklore of "grassroots" activities, an important structural opportunity for the experience of surrogate "power" (Trow, 1958; Sokol, 1967). Horton and Thompson find, for instance, a consistent pattern of negative voting on local referenda among "socially and economically deprived" parts of the population and suggest that "voting down local issues does not represent an organized, class-conscious opposition, but a type of mass protest, a convergence of the individual assessment of the powerless who have projected into available symbols the fears and suspicions growing out of their alienated existence" (Horton and Thompson, 1962: 485).

The limitations which inequality imposes on one's life may be experienced as frustrating. Either because of the intensity of the desire for an objective which cannot be reached or because of the lack of perceived alternatives, frustration may result in some form of cathartic behavior such as aggression. Fanon gives a description of aggressive responses to inequality-induced frustration in a dependent population.

> The colonized man will first manifest his aggressiveness which has been deposited in his bones against his own people. This is the period when the niggers beat each other up, and the police and magistrates do not know which way to turn when faced with the astonishing waves of crime in North Africa.... While the settler or the policeman has the right the livelong day to strike the native, to insult him and to make him crawl to them, you will see the native reaching for his knife at the slightest hostile or aggressive glance cast on him by another native; for the last resort of the native is to defend his personality vis-a-vis his brother. (Fanon, 1963: 42, 43; for similar findings see Baldus [1974] and Fals Borda's study of peasants in Columbia [1962: 209])

Whatever its target, adjustive aggression such as this is either neutral to or supportive of the maintenance of existing patterns of social inequality. Only if frustration results in aggression against elements of the inequality structure itself are further control efforts necessary if the structure is to be maintained.

The preceding discussion has made clear that center inputs such as socialization or control are not the only determinants of the center's power. The periphery itself can through complementary and adjustive behavior contribute to the very inequality structure that forms the basis for its dependence. Further, the presence of such periphery inputs has important consequences for the general structure of action in the system. If the periphery inputs are essentially cost-free for the center, and if one assumes that the center acts rationally and tries to minimize the costs required for the maintenance of its position, then the amount of such periphery inputs should determine the presence and the visibility of the center in the system. For the center, socialization and control are costly. Wherever possible, the center can therefore be expected to rely on existing adjustive and complementary behavior in the periphery. In this sense, center and periphery contributions to power are interdependent: as a rule, the center will invest into its own cost-producing input only to the extent that existing periphery inputs are not sufficient to maintain an inequality structure. In the extreme case, a center can entirely rely on such periphery behavior for the stability of existing inequality patterns (for a study of such a case, see Baldus, 1974). The other extreme, of course, can also be found: that the resistance in the periphery is such that the maintenance of an inequality structure has to be based entirely on persuasion and force. The reality of most social systems lies somewhere in between. In any case, the need for the center to intervene to save its position depends ultimately on the presence or absence of adjustive or complementary behavior in the periphery.

SOME IMPLICATIONS OF THE STUDY OF POWER AS THE CAPACITY TO MAINTAIN INEQUALITY

Power has been defined as the capacity to maintain and reproduce a pattern of social inequality. Some advantages of this approach over those discussed earlier become now apparent.

First, even that part of inequality-maintaining behavior which is free of manifest conflict and resistance is much more complex than its residual treatment as "legitimacy," "consensus" or "voluntary compliance" in most social science research suggests. This is particularly the case where behavior responds directly to the experience of social inequality. Marx, in his distinction between a class as such and a class for itself, had already pointed out that individuals could react to structured class environments in a variety of ways. While seemingly obvious, this view contrasts sharply with the mechanistic view of the relationship between inequality structure and responding behavior in much of current sociology. In the functionalist view, social inequality is, except in the case of "imperfections" (Parsons, 1954: 386 et seq.; Barber, 1957: 9), always consciously accepted by the members of a system because they recognize its instrumental role in the pursuit of common interests. This view is perhaps best expressed in Barber's claim that "men have a sense of justice fulfilled and virtue rewarded when they feel that they are fairly ranked as superior and inferior by the value standards of their own moral community. This sense of justice is an important element in the integration of society" (Barber, 1957: 7). Conflict interpretations of societies are equally simplistic. Here, the experience of inequality leads necessarily to opposition to it in the form of "latent" or open conflict (Dahrendorf, 1969b: 42). The distortions which such theories create can be avoided only by returning to the empirical study of behavior which maintains inequality.

Second, it is precisely in the area of resistance-free and non-interactive behavior which remained inaccessible to the Weberian approach that one finds important determinants of power. Periphery units can make unsolicited and often inadvertent contributions to the maintenance of an inequality structure, and they can do so even where they are not directly linked through interaction with the ultimate beneficiary of their behavior. Power, and the integration of systems of inequality in general, are not merely maintained through an unbroken network of consensual or coercive links which encompasses all members of the structure in question. Instead, networks which mobilize and organize periphery contributions to center goals are frequently interspersed with complementary and non-interactive links.

Third, the study of power suggested here avoids the distortions concerning the distribution of power in social systems which was built into resistance- and interaction-based concepts of power. There, structural inequality between system units entered the analysis of power only to the extent that it was perceived and became the basis of conflicting interests. Whatever part of an inequality structure was uncontested received no attention. The analysis suggested here begins with the identification of such a structure and investigates the causal determinants of its continuity. In this way, it avoids both the danger of overlooking a pattern of domination which does not give rise to recognizable resistance, and of misjudging the distribution of power in a system where the gains and losses of units in manifest conflicts of interest leave a basic uncontested pattern of inequality intact.

Social inequality has so far been treated as a variable whose maintenance or change depend on a variety of forms of center and periphery behavior. If one makes the further assumption that in purposive and self-controlling social systems the maintenance of an inequality structure is an important objective of center groups, then it is reasonable to expect that this objective has a powerful independent effect on the institutional and cultural characteristics of that system. In the most general sense, it will tend to ensure that behavior in the system remains compatible with the system's inequality structure. More specifically, it will lead to selective processes by which behavior which is supportive of the maintenance of inequality is identified and reinforced, while behavior which is judged incompatible with this objective is discouraged and suppressed.

This relationship between inequality and behavior has not gone unnoticed. Some 40 years ago Wilhelm Reich wrote that "every societal order «which Reich, writing from a Marxist perspective, saw as an order of exploitation» creates for itself those character types which it needs for its perpetuation" (Reich, 1933: 12). Though he investigated this relationship with inadequate means, Reich correctly saw that behavior which contributed to the maintenance and reproduction of social inequality tended to become a stable part of the personality types as well as of the culture of a society. More recently, Lewis wrote of the "culture of poverty" that it "is both an adaption and a reaction of the poor to their marginal position in a class-stratified, highly individuated, capitalistic society. It represents an effort to cope with feelings of hopelessness and despair which develop from the realization of the improbability of achieving success in terms of the values and goals of the larger society. Indeed, many of the traits of the culture of poverty can be viewed as attempts at local solutions for problems not met by existing institutions and agencies because the people are not eligible for them, cannot afford them or are ignorant or suspicious of them" (Lewis, 1966: XLVI). If this perspective is correct, it could provide an explanation for many processes of institutional and cultural development in societies. Behind the apparent diversity and change of a society's culture one would discover processes which favor over time those cultural elements which are peculiarly suited to maintain and reproduce dominant structures of inequality. This proposition has received considerable support in recent anthropological work (Teray, 1972; Murra, 1960; Godelier, 1973). The idea itself is, of course, not new. It merely restates one of Marx's most seminal thoughts: that particular structural forms of exploitation give rise to the growth of a corresponding ideological superstructure which serves, in part, to maintain the position of the society's ruling class.

References

BALDUS, B.
1974 "Social Structure and Ideology." *Canadian Journal of African Studies* 8 (2).
1977 "Social Control in Capitalist Societies: An Examination of the Problem of Orders in Liberal Democracies." *Canadian Journal of Sociology* 2 (3).

BARBER, B.
1957 *Social Stratification.* New York: Harcourt, Brace and World.

BERGER, P., ed.
1964 *The Human Shape of Work.* New York: Macmillan.

BIERSTEDT, R.
1969 "An Analysis of Social Power." In *Sociological Theory: A Book of Readings,* edited by L.A. Coser and B. Rosenberg. New York: Macmillan.

BLAU, P.
1964 *Exchange and Power in Social Life.* New York: Wiley.

BRODY, D.
1960 *Steelworkers in America: The Non-Union Era.* Cambridge, Mass.: Harvard University Press.

BUCKLEY, W.
1967 *Sociology and Modern Systems Theory.* Englewood Cliffs: Prentice Hall.

CARTWRIGHT, D., ed.
1959 *Studies in Social Power: Research Center for Group Dynamics.* Publication No. 6, Ann Arbor, University of Michigan, Institute for Social Research.

CHINOY, E.
1965 *Automobile Workers and the American Dream.* Boston: Beacon Press.

COLE, S., and R. LEJEUNE
1972 "Illness and the Legitimization of Failure." *American Sociological Review* 37: 347–356.

DAHL, R.A.
1957 "The Concept of Power." *Behavioral Science* 2: 201–215.
1958 "A Critique of the Ruling Elite Model." *American Political Science Review* 52 (June): 463–469.
1961 *Who Governs? Democracy and Power in an American City.* New Haven: Yale University Press.
1967 *Pluralist Democracy in the United States.* Chicago: Rand McNally and Co.

DAHRENDORF, R.
1969a *Class and Class Conflict in Industrial Society.* Stanford: Stanford University Press.
1969b (1968) "On the Origin of Inequality among Men." In *Social Inequality,* edited by A. Betaille. Harmondsworth: Penguin.

DANZGER, M.H.
1964 "Community Power Structure: Problems and Continuities." *American Sociological Review* 29: 707–717.

DAVIS, A., B.B. GARDNER, and M.R. GARDNER
1969 (1941) *Deep South.* Chicago: University of Chicago Press.

DOHRENWEND, B.P., and B.S. DOHRENWEND
1969 *Social Status and Psychological Disorder: A Causal Inquiry.* New York: John Wiley and Sons, Inc.

EASTON, D., and J. DENNIS
  1969 *Children in the Political System.* New York: McGraw-Hill.

EDELMAN, M.
  1960 "Symbols and Political Quiescence." *American Political Science Review* 54: 695-704.

EMERSON, R.
  1962 "Power-Dependence Relations." *American Sociological Review* 27: 31-41.

ETZIONI, A.
  1968 *The Active Society.* New York: Free Press.

FALS-BORDA, O.
  1962 *Peasant Society in the Colombian Andes: A Sociological Study of Saucio.* Gainsville, Florida: University of Florida Press.

FANON, F.
  1963 *The Wretched of the Earth.* New York: Grove Press.

FESHBACH, S.
  1955 "The Drive-Reducing Function of Fantasy Behavior." *Journal of Abnormal and Social Psychology,* 50: 3-11.

FRENCH, J.P.R., and B.H. RAVEN
  1959 "The Bases of Social Power." In *Studies in Social Power,* edited by D. Cartwright. Ann Arbor: University of Michigan Press.

GALBRAITH, J.K.
  1952 *American Capitalism.* Boston: Little, Brown.

GALTUNG, J.
  1971 "A Structural Theory of Imperialism." *Journal of Peace Research* 2: 81-117.

GAMSON, W.A.
  1968 *Power and Discontent.* Homewood: Dorsey Press.

GERTH, H., and C.W. MILLS
  1953 *Character and Social Structure.* New York: Harcourt, Brace and World.

GODELIER, M.
  1973 *Okonomische Anthropologie.* Rowohlt: Reinbeck.

GOLD, M.
  1963 *Status Forces in Delinquent Boys.* Ann Arbor: University of Michigan Press.

HAMMOND, J.L., and B. HAMMOND
  1968 *The Town Labourer.* Garden City: Doubleday.

HARSANYI, J.C.
  1962 "Measurement of Social Power, Opportunity Costs, and the Theory of Two-Person Bargaining Games." *Behavioral Science* 7: 67-80.

HESS, R.D., and J.V. TORNEY
  1967 *The Development of Political Attitudes in Children.* Chicago: Aldine.

HOLLINGSHEAD, A.B.
  1949 *Elmtown's Youth.* New York: Wiley.

HORTON, J.E., and W.E. THOMPSON
  1962 "Powerlessness and Political Negativism: A Study of Defeated Local Referendums." *The American Journal of Sociology* 67 (March): 485-493.

HUTTON, J.H.
  1963 *Caste in India.* 4th edition. London: Oxford University Press.

LANE, R.L., and M. LERNER
  1970 "Why Hard-Hats Hate Hairs." *Psychology Today* 4 (November): 45-48, 104-105.

LASSWELL, H.D., and A. KAPLAN
  1950 *Power and Society.* New Haven: Yale University Press.

LEHMANN, E.W.
1969 "Toward a Macrosociology of Power." *American Sociological Review* 34 (August): 453–465.

LEWIS, L.S.
1964 "Class and the Perception of Class." *Social Forces* 42 (March).

LEWIS, O.
1966 *La Vida*. New York: Random House.

LITT, E.
1963 "Civic Education, Community Norms and Political Indoctrination." *American Sociological Review* 28: 69–75.

LIVINGSTON, S.
1974 "Compulsive Gamblers, a Culture of Losers." *Psychology Today* 7 (March): 51–55.

LOCKWOOD, DAVID
1958 *The Blackcoated Worker*. London: George Allen and Unwin Ltd.

MANN, M.
1970 "The Social Cohesion of Liberal Democracy." *American Sociological Review* 35 (June): 423–439.

MARCH, J.G.
1955 "An Introduction to the Theory and Measurement of Influence." *American Political Science Review* 49: 431–451.
1956 "Influence Measurement in Experimental and Semi-experimental Groups." *Sociometry* 19: 260–271.
1957 "Measurement Concepts in the Theory of Influence." *Journal of Politics* 19: 202–226.

McCLELLAND, D.C.
1971 "The Power of Positive Drinking." *Psychology Today* 4 (January): 40–41, 78–79.

MOORE, W.E.
1963 *Social Change*. Englewood Cliffs: Prentice Hall.

MURRA, J.V.
1960 "Rite and Crop in the Inca State." In *Culture and History,* edited by S. Diamond. New York.

NOSOW, S., and W.H. FORM, eds.
1962 *Man, Work and Society*. New York: Basic Books Publishing Co. Inc.

OLSON, M.E.
1970 *Power in Societies*. New York: Macmillan.

PARSONS, T.
1954 *Essays in Sociological Theory*. Revised Edition. New York: Free Press.
1960 *Structure and Process in Modern Society*. Glencoe: Free Press.
1964 *The Social System*. New York: Free Press.
1966 "On the Concept of Power." In *Class, Status, and Power,* edited by R. Bendix and S.M. Lipset. New York: Free Press, 240–265.
1968 "On the Concept of Value Commitments." *Sociological Inquiry* 38: 135–160.

POLSBY, N.W.
1959a "The Sociology of Community Power: A Reassessment." *Social Forces* 37: 232–236.
1959b "Three Problems in the Analysis of Community Power." *American Sociological Review* 24: 796–803.
1960 "How to Study Community Power: The Pluralist Alternative." *Journal of Politics* 22: 474–484.
1963 *Community Power and Political Theory*. New Haven: Yale University Press.

POPITZ, H., H.P. BAHRDT, E.A. JURES, and H. KESTING
  1971 *Das Gesellschaftsbild des Arbeiters,* JCB, Mohr, Tubingen (translations are mine).
REICH, W.
  1933 *Charakteranalyse.* Selbstverlag des Verfassers.
RIKER, W.H.
  1964 "Some Ambiguities in the Notion of Power." *American Political Science Review* 58: 341–349.
ROSENBERG, H.
  1969 *Probleme der Deutschen Sozialgeschichte.* Frankfurt: Suhrkamp Verlag.
ROSSI, O.I.
  1957 "Community Decision-Making." *Administrative Science Quarterly* 1: 415–443.
SCHNEIDER, D.J.
  1969 "Tactical Self-Presentation After Success and Failure." *Journal of Personality and Social Psychology* 13: 262–268.
SHAPLEY, L.S., and M. SHUBIK
  1954 "A Method for Evaluating the Distribution of Power in a Committee System." *American Political Science Review* 48: 787–792.
SINGER, J.L.
  1966 *Daydreaming, An Introduction to the Experimental Study of Inner Experience.* New York: Random House.
SINGER, J.L., and V.G. McCRAVEN
  1962 "Daydreaming Patterns of American Subcultural Groups." *International Journal of Social Psychiatry* 8: 272–282.
SOKOL, R.
  1967 "Power Orientation and McCarthyism." *American Journal of Sociology* 73 (3): 443–452.
STOUFFER, S.
  1963 *Communism, Conformity, and Civil Liberties.* Gloucester: Peter Smith.
SWARTZ, M.J.
  1968 *Local Level Politics.* Chicago: Aldine.
TERRAY, E.
  1972 *Marxism and "Primitive" Societies.* New York: Monthly Review Press.
THOMPSON, E.P.
  1968 *The Making of the English Working Class.* Harmondsworth: Penguin.
TROW, M.
  1958 "Small Businessmen, Political Tolerance and Support for McCarthy." *American Journal of Sociology* 64: 270–281.
TRUMAN, D.B.
  1951 *The Governmental Process.* New York.
TUMIN, M.M.
  1967 *Social Stratification.* Englewood Cliffs: Prentice Hall.
WALKER, C.R., and H. GUEST
  1952 *The Man on the Assembly Line.* Cambridge: Harvard University Press.
WEBER, M.
  1964 *Wirtschaft und Gesellschaft.* Bd. 1, 2. Kòln: Kiepenheuer un Witsch (all translations are mine).
WOLFINGER, R.
  1960 "Reputation and Reality in the Study of 'Community Power.'" *American Sociological Review* 25: 636– 645.

YOUNG, M., and P. WILLMOTT
  1962 (1957) *Family and Kinship in East London.* Harmondsworth: Penguin.

ZEIGLER, H.
  1967 *The Political Life of American Teachers.* Englewood Cliffs: Prentice Hall.

ZEITLIN, L.R.
  1971 "A Little Larceny Can Do a Lot for Employee Morale." *Psychology Today* 5 (June): 22.

Implications of the Continental Economy for Canadian Society*

Wallace Clement

Is it correct to argue that multinational corporations "transcend the nation-state"? In the sense that capitalism is international and not confined to a particular national territory, it is correct. But this is not all that is implied in this argument. To the extent that it implies that multinationals are without national bases, are without important national ties, and do not need the protection, legitimacy, and resources of the home state, the argument is clearly wrong. At the most basic level, and this is what binds the capitalist class together, nationally or internationally, multinationals must maintain a capitalist society where property rights are ensured. To provide this most basic guarantee, multinationals need nation-states. Yet multinational corporations do not promote an equal sharing among or within nations of the resources they control. On the contrary, they ensure that inequality within and between nations will be maintained and even expanded.

Since Canada is located midway in the world economic system, acting as both a receiver of branch plants from foreign-owned multinationals and a base for Canadian multinationals operating in the rest of the world, its place in this world system of inequality is ambiguous. The two types of multinationals dominate Canadian industry, resources, and trade patterns; the nature of the Canadian labor force and of research and development is shaped by their presence; and they have great leverage in dealing with various branches of the Canadian state. The power contained in these companies is private power, exercised by sets of people in ways they feel to be most beneficial to themselves and their companies, with very limited accountability for their actions to the people directly affected. Those who own and control these enormous operations are not subject to popular elections, nor are they often brought to account publicly for their decisions. They are a self-selecting, self-perpetuating set of people who have wide-ranging control over the lives of Canadians and the shape of Canadian society.

In the world system there are some barriers to capital, or more specifically to capitalists, that limit the activities of multinationals. The most important of these is political, and the half of the world that is not capitalist imposes important

* From *Continental Corporate Power* by W. Clement, pp. 289–302. Reprinted by permission of The Canadian Publishers, McClelland and Stewart Limited, Toronto.

limits on the "free" movement of multinationals (e.g. China or Cuba). Aside from this, some nations regulate the type, amount, and areas of multinational intrusion from the outside (e.g. Japan or Sweden). Besides political barriers, a strong obstacle to multinational expansion is local capitalists already engaged in economic activities who are able to fight for their turf. This opposition has varied with the period of entry and the kind of economic activity (e.g. Canada or Europe). But to stress these constraints is to miss the tremendous freedom giant capitalists have in much of the world to extract economic surplus. This is nowhere more evident than in the relationship between the United States and Canada, the subject of this study.

Since the end of the Second World War, the United States has lost some of its hegemony in the world system, although it remains the most powerful of the capitalist nations. While the absolute GNP of the United States continues to rise, its share of the "gross world product" is on the decline (from about half in 1950 to about a third in 1976). Countering the United States in the post-war era have been the USSR, China, Japan, and the European Economic Community. Nevertheless, Canada's reliance on the United States has steadily increased and its other outside relations have declined dramatically (Canada's exports to the United States have increased from about half of all exports in 1961 to over two thirds in 1971). Canada cannot easily withdraw from the continental economy and shift its trade elsewhere because now, unlike earlier periods, much of its "trade" consists of intracompany transfers to U.S. parents. Canada is, therefore, locked into the continental economy, even if other nations challenge the world hegemony of the United States.

THE NATURE OF THE CANADIAN ELITE: THE QUESTION OF DOMINATION

As has been stressed throughout this study, multinationals alone do not explain the amount of U.S. direct investment in Canada's sphere of production. At least part of the answer lies in the nature of dominant Canadian capitalists and their essentially complementary relationship with U.S. control in production. These elements in turn are related to the nature of the Canadian elite. For example, the explanation of why the Canadian economic elite is more exclusive in 1972 than it was in 1951 (from 50 percent upper-class origin to about 60 percent) is more complex than simply U.S. penetration, because the U.S. comprador elite in Canada is more open to mobility than the indigenous elite. There is, however, a direct relationship. The Canadian indigenous elite is boxed in by its own past, in which most of the productive areas of the economy — manufacturing and resources — were given up to foreign capitalists, and it has meanwhile stayed safely one remove from industrialization and enriched itself on the avails — interest on capital, provision of services such as transportation and utilities, and the buying or selling of existing companies. The narrowness of its recruitment base has been induced by its specialization.

What happened to the powerful Canadian commercial interests at the turn of the twentieth century that saw Canada as the rising center of a new imperial design? Internationally, they declined with the British Empire. Internally, they shared their power in an alliance with U.S. industrial capitalists. They have not faded quietly away. Their legacy remains in an overdeveloped financial and transportation/utilities system in Canada and in the remnants of their commercial activities in the rest of the world, particularly in the West Indies. But just as their earlier prosperity depended on the hegemony of the United Kingdom, so their continued prosperity is now predicated on the ascendancy of the United States.

The power of Canadian capitalists in the circulation sector has shaped Canadian society in many ways. An economy dominated by financial capitalists, particularly ones whose business is mainly in long-term interest-bearing investments (unlike the many equity dealers among U.S. financial capitalists), will not strongly resist state ownership of particular sectors such as transportation or utilities because they can still extract their surplus by investing their capital in those enterprises, regardless of ownership. Moreover, these outlets are much more secure than private outlets, at least private entrepreneurial ventures. The financial capitalists are thus unlikely to fund entrepreneurial capitalists in Canada, but when the state takes charge of wavering capitalist ventures—such as the railways that became the CNR — the owners who are bailed out and the financial capitalists who hold their debts can only be pleased.

Nor are Canadian financial capitalists at a loss for a defence. For example, before a Vancouver Board of Trade gathering in late 1975, Earle McLaughlin, president and chairman of the Royal Bank, proceeded to list the major capital-intensive projects in Canada's future such as the Alberta tar sands, James Bay hydro, and Arctic pipelines, going on to explain that

> consortium financing is becoming an important activity of the major Canadian banks. This is a way in which banks can get together to share the financing and to spread out the risks of these gigantic capital projects.
>
> Can you imagine trying to form a loan syndicate to finance a major gas pipeline with hundreds of little banks? So don't underestimate the advantages of the Canadian system with its very big banks.[1]

Whether the project is owned by a consortium of U.S. and state capital, by state capital alone, or by U.S. capital alone, the banks are equally willing to "share." Their correspondent relationships with one another help secure their dominant place rather than threaten it. McLaughlin's logic is sound, given one assumption, which is that the state needs to go to the "private market" to finance such ventures. In a capitalist society, the logic is certainly sound, since it is the private financial capitalists that control the greatest capital reserves; and they determine to whom they will lend these reserves. But what McLaughlin fails to ask is, what are the disadvantages of a banking system where over 90 percent of all activity is controlled by only five banks?

One disadvantage is well known to small capitalists, who certainly do not need bank consortia to finance them. Because of their orientation to "bigness" (which means security), Canadian financial capitalists were drawn to the industrial corporations controlled from the United States rather than to small Canadian industrialists. At the turn of the century, as Canada began its process of industrialization and as corporate capitalism was taking hold, a major outlet for capital was opened in the sphere of production, and Canadian financial capitalists did not hesitate to enter into this activity, but did so in their own way. If these Canadian financial capitalists were to retain their traditional pattern of stable, long-term, interest-bearing investments, they had to search for appropriate outlets. They would suffer losses if there were no outlets that could generate surplus, but if there were surplus-generating outlets in production, they could maintain their strong and secure position. The need for productive outlets explains the search for them by Canadian financiers, and it did not matter whether they were Canadian or U.S. controlled. Indeed, since the U.S. industrial system was further advanced in technology, management, and marketing, the U.S. companies were often favored as more secure investments. Complementing the finanacial capitalists' search was the willingness of U.S. industrialists to expand as their national market was filled and resources were needed.

In the present age of corporate capitalism, which has witnessed the coalescence of industrial and financial capital, it might have been anticipated that the two would become one, but the Canadian dominant capitalists have found it difficult to abandon their past, a past that they have found profitable and secure even in an industrial age. They have remained with financial and related mediating activities, carried over from their old imperial ties with Britain, and from this stable base of power they have entered into an alliance with U.S. industrial capitalists at home and extended their own base of power abroad under the U.S. sphere of influence. The existence of a developed industrial structure to the south that could be imported to Canada by way of branch plants provided the surrogate for indigenous industrial development. Although they are still active in some industrial fields, particularly in steel, so closely tied to earlier railway expansion, and food and beverages, tied to agriculture, they have abandoned most other manufacturing pursuits and almost all resource-related activities outside the traditional pulp and paper field, historically key staples.

While in class societies the various classes are related to each other by unequal exchanges that form asymmetrical relationships based on surplus extraction, various fractions within the same class need not be so related. That is, various class fractions, such as industrial and financial capitalists, may form symmetrical relationships within a broad economic system, each mutually complementary to the other. If these alliances cross political boundaries, then little matter — capitalism is international. But various fractions within a class may make alliances more readily than others. For example, Canadian financial capitalists at the beginning of this century had to choose an ally in moving Canada into an industrial era. They had the choice of the nascent Canadian industrialists, the counterpart of today's middle-range indigenous capitalists, or their powerful U.S. competitors, the counterpart of today's dominant comprador capitalists. Consistent with their philosophy of stable investments, they chose the latter. In some instances compatible with the movement from entrepreneurial to corporate capitalism, they chose to enter industrial activities themselves, not as entrepreneurs or industrialists but as financiers, by consolidating existing small-scale industries into corporate complexes.

The upshot is that the power of Canadians to make decisions about specific economic activities in Canada has regressed to a state of underdevelopment (although not total underdevelopment of "material" well-being), with control over future development and stability lost because of the lack of an indigenously controlled base in manufacturing and resources. In the overdeveloped finance, transportation, and utilities sectors originally built on U.K. portfolio investment, the dominant indigenous capitalists now in control still remain powerful components of the total class. In other words, the process of compradorization has been sector specific and took place in the presence of traditionally powerful Canadian capitalists rather than displacing them. The effect on weak capitalists in production was, of course, to bring about their downfall.

The resulting fragmentation of the capitalist class in Canada does not mean that the whole class is not still powerful vis-a-vis the working class — indeed, it may have gained power because of its alliance with U.S. capitalists in the continental context. It does mean, however, that the Canadian component must commit itself to the continental contest. The existence of a powerful Canadian commercial elite, based in the Canadian upper class, and a predominantly foreign-controlled elite in production means that Canada remains a "low mobility" society. Concentration and centralization in commercial sectors have been the work of indigenous forces while the same processes in the productive sectors have been imposed from outside (with the aid of Canadian capitalists in circulation). The result is a highly structured economy with few avenues through which the lower class can rise. The process of compradorization has offered a few middle-class Canadians mobility into the elite, but many of the uppermost positions created by this process have been filled by the indigenous elites. In fact, very few Canadians have moved from the branch-plant structure into the real power positions within the parent company. This middle-class comprador elite is largely trapped in the backwater of the U.S. subsidiaries.

Unlike the portfolio investment typical of the British Empire, the direct investment of the U.S. empire does not eventually break off as a result of economic forces alone but deepens its hold. Nor is there any reason to suspect that the indigenous capitalists in circulation are contemplating taking over the U.S. enterprises.

Is the size of the U.S. economy a sufficient explanation for the dominant position of U.S. capitalists in Canada, particularly in production? The Canadian society is clearly of a much smaller scale than that of the United States (with about one-eleventh the population). Size has two strong effects on the nature of their respective elites. First, because of scale, whenever the interpenetration of the two societies occurs, the United States overwhelms Canada. Secondly, because Canada is much smaller than the United States and the turf of Canadian capitalists is more limited, the Canadian elite is a much closer-knit community in terms of interaction and recruitment. But the difference between Canada and the United States is not only one of scale but also one of type, in the sense of the relative concentration of economic activities and the differing strengths by type of activity, as has been stressed so frequently. Would relations between Canada and the United States be very different if there were only the factor of a giant market eleven times the size of the Canadian to the south rather than this factor in combination with U.S. control of over half the entire manufacturing and resource sectors of the Canadian economy? The clear answer is yes. Ownership by Canadian capitalists would allow them to trade outside the United States to a greater degree than branches of U.S. companies are liable to do, thus reducing market dependency. In addition, surplus generated from Canadian operations would remain in the hands of Canadian capitalists for future growth, whereas under current conditions, much surplus is withdrawn to the United States or reinvested in the branch plants. But this discussion is merely an academic exercise. The reality is that the two countries are of radically different size and type. In combination, they have created the present structure of dominance.

As was argued in detail earlier, any attempt to analyze Canada in terms of a simple dominance/subordination dichotomy (as in many of the Latin American models of dependency) necessarily misses the complexity of its internal class and power relations. While *in general* the United States dominates Canada, and the dominant capitalists in Canada hold sway over those of the middle range, there are still important mediations and significant political struggles between each. It is important to look for points of alliance and of tension, points where each gains and where one gains at the expense of the other. While the type of methodology used here can specify *some* of these complexities, the real work in specifying these political struggles remains to be done through detailed case studies (some of which were reviewed earlier). But without some broader context, cases remain simply cases and do not lend themselves to broader trends and developments (such as those outlined here). For example, use of either the automobile or the steel industry in Canada would lead to radically different conclusions if they were not placed in the broader context of the economy as a whole. While one is clearly a dependent industry, the other has enjoyed much more support from and success with indigenous capitalists. To understand how and why they coexist requires a broad understanding of the historical and contemporary development of the entire economic structure in Canada and its complex relationship with the U.S. structure.

EFFECTS OF THE CONTINENTAL ECONOMY ON CANADIAN SOCIETY

The "common sense" of Canadians (and the dominant ideology) would tell them that foreign direct investment means greater investment in their economy, more jobs and better ones, more affluence, and, however vaguely, "progress." On the contrary, the "uncommon" reality is that after a brief period of growth, foreign direct investment means that more capital flows *out* of than into the economy; that there are fewer jobs in the capital-intensive branch plants than in Canadian-controlled firms; that there are few jobs in branch plants requiring highly trained manpower because much of the research and development is done in the country of the parent; and finally, that the "affluence" and "progress" created by these developments are deceptive, favoring the already privileged. Each of these inequalities has been analyzed, but one, regional inequality, merits closer examination.

Canada is a particularly fragmented nation. It is a federation of ten provinces and two territories, each of which has increased its demands for power vis-a-vis the central government since the dismantling of the Ottawa war machine created for the Second World War. But do these political boundaries alone explain regionalism in Canada? Are the real regional splits not based more on economics than on politics? While political fragmentation aggravates regionalism, it is not itself the cause of regionalism. That cause must be found in the uneven development of the country and the branch-plant structure of corporate capitalism, both indigenous and foreign.

"Regionalism" is an unequal sharing of the wealth and benefits a nation has to offer, expressed in geographical terms. But alone this is not a sufficient definition. There is also a relationship involved — a region is a part of something else, and herein lies the key to the *unevenness* of economic development. It is only uneven when more capital and profits are extracted than are put in — otherwise it is *un*developed, not *under*developed. A region can only be underdeveloped if it is tied to an external economy that is doing the underdeveloping. The only way it can be truly developed is if all those on site who participate in the development share equally in the surplus produced. If part of the surplus is shipped outside, underdevelopment is occurring. This principle applies equally to class relations or to regionalism, the latter frequently passing for the former.

Upon examination the issues of class and regionalism become closely intertwined because, at the most basic level, both are rooted in extractive relationships and both, in Canada, are reproduced through the institution of private property. This is not to say that there are no extractive relationships in societies that are not capitalist or that they too do not have a type of regionalism, but they have these problems for different reasons and under different political regimes.

When Canada is referred to as an industrial society, what is really meant is that *part* of it is industrialized — the rest is more aptly characterized as a resource hinterland. Most of Canada's industrial capacity is located below a line beginning at Windsor, encompassing Toronto, and moving on to Montreal. This is industrial Canada; all other areas rely on key resources for their economies. In British Columbia the resources are wood, pulp and paper, with some hydro-electric power; they are gas, petroleum, and potash, along with wheat, in the Prairies; mining and pulp and paper in northern Ontario and Quebec, along with hydro; in the Atlantic region pulp and paper, fish, and some coal along with hydro in Newfoundland. These outliers feed the Ontario-Quebec industrial heartland and the U.S. markets with their resources and, in turn, consume some of the finished products from these regions. In finance the branch structure is represented in the dominant banks, all with headquarters in Toronto and Montreal and branches spread throughout the country to tap capital for the center. The varied economies in these regions produce different types of class structures. At the same time, the regional economies are tied to national economies, and national economies to international economies. Thus, the regional class structures (and, contingent upon these, the varieties of life-styles and opportunities) are to some extent dependent upon the way they fit into the national and international economic order. Regions that have capital and profits extracted from them will have limited access to the means of obtaining goods, services, and opportunities while regions that receive the extracted capital and profits have greater advantage. The overdevelopment of one region depends on the underdevelopment of another; the overdevelopment of one class depends on the underdevelopment of subordinate ones.

Concretely, how does this pattern express itself in the economies of the various regions? The effects of different types of economies can be examined by looking at the tax bases they provide to the provincial governments. This method is significant because taxes are an important means for securing the revenues necessary to pay for various social services. It can be readily demonstrated that the levels of industrial development impinge on the resources provincial governments have; moreover, it can be demonstrated that the effect of the continental economy is to aggravate regionalism in Canada.

While Ontario has 36 percent of the Canadian population, in 1972 it received 46 percent of all provincial corporate taxes paid by non-financial companies, 51 percent of the taxes paid by foreign-controlled companies, and 54 percent of the taxes paid by U.S.-controlled non-financials. In the manufacturing sector 72 percent of Ontario's taxes are from foreign-controlled companies.[2]

Table I illustrates two aspects of regionalism. The first is seen in Ontario's overrepresentation in taxes from industrial corporations compared to the other areas of Canada. The second is evident in the effect of U.S. direct investments in compounding this overrepresentation in Ontario. Consistently, in all regions, the distribution of tax income by Canadian-controlled industrials is much more in line with the population distribution than is the distribution of taxes paid by U.S.-controlled companies. In other words, if it were not for U.S. industrials, the problems of regionalism would not be as serious as they now are for the Atlantic provinces, Quebec, and British Columbia. In the Prairies the situation is somewhat different because of oil revenues. This is evident in Table II, which examines only manufacturing. Here every area except Ontario is underrepresented compared to its population base, although for income from Canadian-controlled manufacturing only, Quebec and British Columbia are actually above their proportions of the population. Mining provided the provinces with $279.7 million in taxable income in 1972, compared to $3,344.5 million from manufacturing, and Alberta alone received half of this income ($138.6 million), with 88 percent of Alberta's share coming from foreign-controlled companies. In this sector all other provinces were well below their proportion of the population, with Ontario's 22 percent the closest to its population base. Thus, it can be argued that foreign investment in manufacturing, because it has been so Ontario-

TABLE I   Distribution of Non-financial, Industrial Tax Income by Region and Control of Company, 1972 (percentages)

Control of companies	Atlantic	Quebec	Ontario	Prairies	British Columbia	Total
United States	3.2	18.1	53.5	17.6	7.3	100
Canada	5.2	26.0	41.8	13.4	13.0	100
All	4.5	22.5	45.7	15.9	11.0	100
Population	9.5	28.0	35.7	16.4	10.1	100

Source: Calculated from CALURA, *Report for 1972*, and *Canada Year Book, 1973*.

TABLE II   Distribution of Taxable Income from Manufacturing, by Region and Control of Company, 1972 (percentages)

Control of companies	Atlantic	Quebec	Ontario	Prairies	British Columbia	Total
United States	2.7	18.9	62.2	9.6	6.7	100
Canada	3.6	28.8	43.2	9.8	14.4	100
All	3.1	23.3	53.7	10.2	9.6	100
Population	9.5	28.0	35.7	16.4	10.1	100

Source: See Table I.

centered, and in petroleum, because it has been so Alberta-centered, has added greatly to regional disparity in Canada. An understanding of regionalism in Canada requires a look outside to see the forces initiating the problems.

Aggravation of regional inequalities is not the only effect of foreign investment on Canadian society, although it is a major one. Many others have already been explored, such as the implications for research and development, the social rigidity caused by a limited base of power, and the fact that the resource sector of the economy is overdeveloped to meet the demands of the United States.

Based on the proposition that social relations follow from the economic and political organization of society, it is evident that there must be a relationship between foreign ownership in Canada and the class structure of *both* Canada and the United States. And further, these class relations will be affected by the nature of Canada's economic and political position in the world capitalist order. It is therefore useful to look beyond Canada to the United States to gain some perspective on internal Canadian developments. Moreover, this larger perspective allows us to make an analysis of class alliances and conflicts, both nationally and continentally. To do so is of necessity to understand a political relationship; nowhere is the politics of economics more apparent than in foreign investment, since the amount, type, location, and encouragement of foreign investment permitted in a nation is a political act. The class dynamics of foreign investment can also provide important insights into the relationships between classes, class fractions, and the state and its branches. While an analysis of the class dynamics of Canadian society in a continental context is beyond the scope of this study, even a limited exploration will illustrate some of the political dimensions of the power relations created by the continental economy.

THE CANADIAN STATE IN THE CONTINENTAL ECONOMY

It would be absurd to suggest that the political boundary has not made a difference — a great difference — in the nature of the continental economic system. It is a system composed of two distinct nation states, one with a much larger population and a much more significant impact on the other. Nevertheless, there are two national political systems. As has already been demonstrated [W. Clement, *Continental Corporate Power* (Toronto: McClelland and Stewart, 1977), pp. 124–131], the fact of a political boundary affects the economic system through tariffs (which encourage particular national bases for economic activities), through state rents on resources, and through taxation policies.

The political boundary between Canada and the U.S. has not, however, been an impediment to the penetration of the sphere of production in Canada by U.S. foreign investment (although circulation, the turf of Canadian capitalists, has been protected). The fact of such extensive U.S. investment reflects political decisions to allow and encourage such a pattern of development. The system has emerged not in spite of politicians but because they have permitted it. Conversely, since they have allowed these events to occur, the national independence has been allowed to shift outside the country to the board rooms of U.S. corporations. But even within a country the state does not control the decisions of corporations, whether national or foreign, although it can certainly influence them.

What does national sovereignty mean? It is the right, reinforced by might, to control and regulate developments within a territory. But at what point is this right abdicated if it is not employed? What level of external control is necessary before the original right becomes *de jure* but not *de facto?* Certainly in the public domain the *de facto* rights of sovereignty are intact. But in liberal democracies, there is a very large area of private control beyond the public domain, and it is in this area that sovereignty has been eroded. It is only because of the public/private split of liberal democracies that foreign dominance can prevail in one domain but only to a lesser extent in the other.

How far can foreign dominance be allowed to go? Is the public domain not influenced by what happens in the private sphere? Most certainly it is, and when levels of foreign ownership become high the result is erosion of the autonomy of the state itself. It is at this point that the various systems of power — state, military, and economic—become contingent upon one another. The political and military decisions of one nation begin to have direct effects on the other because their economies are so tightly intertwined.

For example, as early as 1902, Prime Minister Laurier was moved to say to Lord Dundonald, "You must not take the [Canadian] militia seriously, for though it is useful for suppressing internal disturbances, it will not be required for the defense of the country, as the Monroe Doctrine [of the United States] protects us against enemy aggression."[3] Thus in the world political system Canada was perceived as being under the wing of U.S. military power, except for internal uprisings, and that view continues some seventy years later. John Warnock's contemporary review of Canada's military policy concludes that "there is no doubt that the Cold War has intensified the problem of creating a Canadian nation and organizing a rational development of the economy."[4]

The political constraints of foreign ownership greatly affect internal policies. In his review of the politics of northern development between 1968 and 1975, Edgar Dosman points out that "in most well-established countries, the develop- ment of a peripheral region would be largely a domestic issue. In Canada, however, the development of the North was inextricably linked to the issue of the Canadian relationship with a foreign power, the United States." The reason was that "northern development after 1968 affected Canadian trade relations with the United States, particularly oil and gas exports."[5] Under such pressures, internal development policies are made in light of continuing cordial political and military relations with the U.S.

The capitalists who are actually formulating and benefiting from the politics of development cannot be expected to be guided by the best interests of the nation because they operate for private, not public, interest. As John Porter has written, "Corporations... are governed by human beings who behave in accordance with a set of institutional norms — those of corporate capitalism. To argue that national sentiments and the 'national interest' would supplant the historical and inexorable norms of capitalist enterprise is to reveal an ignorance of the capitalist economy."[6]

On the other hand, state power (whether political, bureaucratic, or judicial) is a very real power in liberal democracies. Ultimately the state does have the power to make decisions about the very existence of private power. Private property is an institution granted by the state. It is thus territorially bounded and sanctioned. In corporate capitalism, the right of private property is embodied in incorporation laws, which sanction the operation of various corporations. Each charter issued by the state (federal or provincial) legitimizes the operation of foreign branches or Canadian companies. Therefore, each and every incorpo- rated company operates in Canada under the wish of the state and only by its consent. Canada is not a puppet state because it is a liberal democracy, a society which maintains a distinction between public and private power. A socialist state, where this dichotomy does not exist, could not have the extent of foreign control that Canada has without in fact being a puppet. But even in liberal democracies, the public/private distinction is frequently transgressed, and the extent to which this occurs in Canada reduces the sovereignty of the Canadian state.

The state's role in foreign investment in Canada is a complex one. In areas where Canadian capitalists have been strong, particularly in banking, life insurance, trust companies, transportation, utilities, and the mass media, the state has provided strong protection. In these areas, legislation prohibits foreign capitalists from owning sufficient stock to control or take over companies. But legislation to protect other areas such as retail trade, manufacturing, and resources, although recommended by many government inquiries, has only recently been enacted. Moreover, the Foreign Investment Review Act simply reviews or examines proposed takeovers of Canadian companies in these sectors by foreign capitalists, and there are no across-the-board prohibitions or any effect on the many companies that already exist. The agency's track record since its inception is to approve 80 percent of these takeovers; it is certainly not a major barrier to foreign capital.

If the state is to carry out its various functions in society, it must gain revenues from the economic sphere. In a capitalist society, this means ensuring that the state creates the conditions necessary for the orderly extraction of economic surplus to go into private hands. The Canadian state, at both the central and the sub-central levels, finds itself in a paradoxical situation regarding foreign investment. On the one hand, the Canadian state elite, aware of the state's capacity to extract a part of the economic surplus bound up with foreign capital and foreign markets, has acted to facilitate foreign investment in productive activities and assist in searching out foreign markets. On the other hand, there has been growing opposition to foreign control and fear that sovereignty is being eroded. An enormous part of both the federal (45 percent) and the provincial (41 percent) corporate tax revenue comes from foreign-controlled corporations. To continue to increase its revenues to meet the growing pressure on its purse, the state is forced to create a favorable investment climate for foreign capital. The common ground between the state and capitalists in a liberal democracy is that both are interested in growth and stability and both see corporate capitalism as *the* way to attain this goal. But inherent in corporate capitalism is division between public and private power, inequality within societies (where some command great economic power and others are excluded), and, as has been seen, inequality between nations, where some gain at the expense of others.

The basic concern over foreign investment is that power is exercised in the board rooms of multinationals, out of the reach of Canadians. Decisions on trade, employment, research and development, promotion of management, and investment are all beyond the control of Canadians. But is this really a consequence of *foreign* investment or of *private* investment? How much more control do the vast majority of Canadians have over the Royal Bank, Sun Life, Stelco, Eaton's, or MacMillan Bloedel than they have over General Motors of Canada, Imperial Oil, Kresge's, Crown Zellerbach, or Canadian General Electric? Is it justifiable to call for decreasing foreign investment in the name of Canada's people? To some extent, yes, the claim is justifiable because Canadian-based companies are *potentially* more susceptible to state regulation. The Canadian state, however, has been very reluctant to tamper with the rights of corporate property, whether foreign- or Canadian-controlled.

The fundamental structure of corporations, based as they are on the claims of capital, invariably leads to a system of extractive power by which those in "command" positions remove degrees of freedom from persons below and increase their own freedom. Private property, the most basic institution in both

Canada and the United States, remains the principle for organizing production and circulation. Besides being the foundation of the corporate form of organization and therefore of multinationals, private property is also transmitted between generations in the form of inheritance and remains important as a means of perpetuating privilege in both Canada and the United States. In terms of recruiting highly skilled people without *highly* privileged backgrounds, however, the U.S. corporate system has proven more open than the Canadian (although the two patterns are related). In a broader sense, private property is the central institution of both societies, as it is of all liberal democracies, for it is private property as an institution that legitimizes and gives shape to the control structure of corporations. The power exercised by the economic elite is power made possible by private property concentrated into giant corporations. As long as the dominant mode of ownership continues to be private, the power of the economic elite will continue to dominate at the expense of the citizenry.

Notes

1. *Financial Post,* 13 December 1975: C5.
2. Calculated from CALURA *Report for 1972*, pp. 21–22, Statements 4 and 5. Data are available only on a provincial basis and do not lend themselves to intraprovincial regionalism.
3. Quoted in J.B. Brebner, *North Atlantic Triangle*, pp. 270–71.
4. J.W. Warnock, *Partner to Behemoth*, p. 17.
5. Edgar Dosman, *The National Interest*, pp. xiv–xv.
6. J. Porter, *The Vertical Mosaic*, p. 269.

C. Other Status and Prestige Dimensions

OCCUPATIONS

EDUCATION

ETHNICITY AND RACE

SEX AND AGE

Occupational Prestige in Canada*

Peter C. Pineo/John Porter

Interest in the public evaluation or social ranking of occupations stems from the theory of social stratification, and from the need for a standardized indicator of social class or measure of socio-economic status. A subsidiary interest has been the need in industrial societies to recruit specialized manpower.

This manpower interest has meant that occupational ranking has often been done by special and restricted populations, such as school children or college students. It has also meant that the occupations to be ranked were over-weighted with high-prestige and professional occupations. These two facts raise questions about the relevance for general stratification analysis of the occupational prestige data so far available.

Exceptions are the few instances where occupations have been ranked by national samples. The first of these was the 1947 ranking of 88 occupations, by the National Opinion Research Centre (NORC), employing old quota sampling techniques and based on a national sample of adults and youths. One of its major findings was that with small variation between the major sub-groupings there was a remarkable consistency in the prestige of occupations, enough to indicate a general ranking consensus for the society. Since 1947 there have been many studies of occupational ranking in both industrialized and developing countries, but only two of these, by Svalastoga[1] in Denmark and Carlsson[2] in Sweden, were truly national studies. Others have been extremely limited. For example, in the Hall-Jones study in the United Kingdom the rankers came mainly from the membership of white-collar trade unions.[3] Thus despite the fact that there have been many studies of occupational prestige only a few can be considered to have measured a national consensus, and very few are really comparable with each other.

* Abridged from *The Canadian Review of Sociology and Anthropology*, 4 (1) 1967, by permission of the authors and the publisher.

    Revision of a paper presented to the Canadian Association of Sociology and Anthropology, Sherbrooke, Quebec, June, 1966. Financial assistance for this project came from Canada Council, Department of Labour, Department of Citizenship and Immigration, McConnell Foundation, Social Science Research Council, and Carleton University. The authors are very much indebted to the National Opinion Research Center for making available the necessary materials to replicate their study in Canada, and for their advice. They should also like to acknowledge the help of Ann Kitchen and Kathleen Kelly, research assistants.

The present study, in addition to being the first national study of occupational prestige for Canada, was also designed to make rigorous U.S.-Canada comparisons. We hope, therefore, it will be a contribution not only to Canadian sociology but also to comparative studies.

We can claim only minimal credit for the complexity and ingenuity of the research design, which we will outline briefly. In 1962 NORC decided to undertake a much more ambitious study of occupational prestige than any so far. Their plan had two stages. One was an exact replication of the NORC 1947 study, using the same questions, occupational titles, and sampling methods, with the object of seeing if the prestige of occupations had changed since that time. The main finding of this replication, published in 1964,[4] was that there was a high degree of stability in occupational prestige over time, represented by a Pearsonian correlation coefficient of .99. For the second stage, NORC designed a study in which a national sample of adults would rank 200 occupations. It is this second stage, with the necessary adaptations in design, which we have replicated in Canada.

The research design which we adapted required all respondents to rank 204 occupational titles. Although occupation is undoubtedly the principal element entering into a person's status there are other elements such as the place or "situs" in which he works, ethnicity, and religion. For this reason sub-samples of respondents were required to rank 72 industries and corporations, 36 ethnicities, and 21 religions. As well as the ranking of occupations the interview elicited social background characteristics of the respondents, their spouses, their parents, and information relating to work experience, mobility, attitudes to education, and inter-ethnic relations.

Because of our interest in a comparative study we sought to minimize changes, but some important ones could not be avoided. There had to be changes in the occupational titles to make them representative of the Canadian labor force. We ended up with 174 titles common to the U.S. and Canadian studies, including 13 U.S. titles which required only slight changes; for example, "state governor" became "provincial premier" and "member of the United States House of Representatives" became "Member of the Canadian House of Commons." We increased the number of primary occupations and also took into consideration the regionality of occupations to discover differences in ranking and differences in knowledge about occupations. ("Whistle punk" and "cod fisherman" are examples.) We also added, at the suggestion of Oswald Hall, two non-existent occupations, "biologer" and "archaeopotrist," to see what proportion would respond "don't know." We felt that if a large proportion of the sample declined to rank non-existent occupations or specifically regional occupations it would indicate that the ranking task was being taken seriously.

The second major adaptation for Canada was to make the study bilingual by ensuring satisfactory translations of the occupational titles so that the stimulus would be nearly the same in English and French. In any language occupations have emotionally charged words to describe them, "soda jerk" and "grease monkey," for example. Moreover, masculine and feminine gender gave some trouble. Since the entire ranking task was an evaluative one, obviously extreme care had to be taken in the translations. Our occupational titles were initially translated by a bilingual social scientist whose mother tongue is French. The translations were then given to two others to rate on a four-point scale of being satisfactory translations, and to suggest improvements; changes were made in the light of their suggestions. As we now try to explore French-English differences, however, we wish we had spent more time on this problem.

Since each respondent would rank from three to four hundred titles some relatively easy method was required. Each title stimulus was printed in English and French on a one-third size I.B.M. stub card, color coded for each ranking task and pre-punched with a case number and a stimulus number. The ranking task required the respondent to sort the cards on a ladder of "social standing." The ladder had nine boxes into which the cards could be sorted, from high social standing at the top to low at the bottom. After sorting, the cards were put in special envelopes corresponding to the place on the ladder into which the cards had been sorted. When they were returned they were fed into a reproducer and the data on them, including the order into which they had been sorted, converted onto full-size cards for subsequent processing.

The ranking question went as follows:

"Now let's talk about jobs. Here is a ladder with nine boxes on it, and a card with the name of an occupation on each. Please put the card in the box at the *top* of the ladder if you think that occupation has the highest possible social standing.

Put it in the box at the *bottom* of the ladder if you think it has the lowest possible social standing.

If it belongs somewhere in between, just put it in the box that matches the social standing of the occupation."

Interviewers were instructed to repeat these instructions if the respondent showed uncertainty. They were told in their instructions that they were not to explain what the words *social standing* meant. Synonyms such as prestige, respect, or regard were specifically disallowed. Rather they were to repeat the words *social standing* in various ways, as in "Well, you probably think some jobs have higher standing than others. If you think this is one of those then place it ... " and so on. The interviewers were also instructed never to explain the nature of any job the respondent did not recognize. Rather respondents were to be allowed to place the card to the side and it eventually ended up in an envelope marked "Don't Know."

After the respondent had sorted the first card given him, he was given the rest of the pile and the interviewer said:

"Here are some more cards with names of occupations. Just put them in the boxes on the ladder which match the social standing they actually have. If you want to you can change your mind about where an occupation belongs and move its card to a different box."

After the sorting was completed the interviewer was instructed to encourage the respondent to make any changes he wanted and also to attempt once again to sort any which he had placed in the "Don't Know" pile.

In French, the crucial words "social standing" became "*position sociale*." Since this ranking question came right at the beginning of the interview it was not contaminated by previous questions, as was the case with the NORC 1947 study.

We, of course, inherited this question from the NORC study. Once again there is some of the ambiguity noted in the 1947 NORC[5] question where the respondent was asked to give his *personal* opinion of the *general standing* that an occupation had. The question still does not make the path completely clear for a respondent who feels his personal judgment of the social standing of a job is at variance with that of the community at large. It may be difficult for any question to do so satisfactorily. Do we want him to report his own opinion of the job's standing, or his opinion of the general community evaluation of the job? Presumably the question is workable because cases of this discontinuity between personal evaluation and perceived community evaluation are rare. In a later ranking task, the specifications to interviewers make it clear that the respondent should ignore his own opinion if it is at variance with that of the community at large. We suspect that the inclusion of this new rule for the later ranking, which is the ranking of ethnicities, may have influenced the sort of advice given by our interviewers to respondents who found difficulty in any of the ranking tasks.

We can now present some initial findings: the occupational prestige scores for the national sample and for its English and French components; some differences between English and French; and the occupational prestige of the major census classifications.

The appendix table arranges the occupations in alphabetical order within socio-economic groupings. The eight-level classification plus one other for farmers is much like those used in studies of social mobility. The scores are a transformation of the mean which makes it adopt a range from 0 to 100 for rough comparison with earlier, published prestige scores. We point out a few results that struck us as interesting.

The highest score given (89.9) was to Provincial Premier. The French gave this occupation an extraordinarily high score (93.6). As can be seen, federal political occupations ranked highly also. We may question, therefore, the view that what has been described as a decline of political skill in Canada can be attributed to "a relative loss in the attractiveness and prestige of politics as compared to other vocations."[6]

Professional occupations ranked highly, particularly physician, university professor, county court judge, and lawyer. Moreover, these occupations relative to others are homogeneously judged to be high as measured by the standard deviation. Artistic occupations are not ranked particularly highly, for example, ballet dancer, jazz musician, musician in a symphony orchestra, sculptor, and T.V. star. In spite of the stereotype of French Canadians as placing greater value on artistic pursuits than on others, the French ranked all of the artistic occupations, except jazz musician, lower than did the the English. The lowest ranked occupations were newspaper peddler and garbage collector. For Canada we introduced several farming titles which ranked fairly close to each other, except for farm laborer and hog farmer, the latter probably affected by the word "hog." Attention is drawn to eight titles at the end of the table which are not labor force titles. Our non-existent occupations ranked reasonably well, but the "don't know" response was high, that is 44 percent for "archaeopotrist" and 30 percent for "biologer." The only other occupations which equalled these two in "don't know" responses were those which we had included for their regionality, for example "whistle punk" and "troller." It is interesting that "Occupation of my family's main wage earner" was right in the middle of the range. Someone who lives on relief has no prestige at all.

Earlier Canadian information suggests, as do Inkeles and Rossi's cross-national comparisons,[7] that there would be a high correlation between the ranking of occupations in Canada and in the U.S. The original Tuckman data [8] (1947), based on the ranking of 25 occupations by 379 college students and 40 job applicants at a Jewish vocational service, produced correlations with U.S. rankings (NORC, 1963) of .96 over 19 occupations. Blishen's scale developed from the 1951 Canadian Census, using a combination of education and income as the measure of occupational rank, correlated with U.S. prestige scores, from the 1947 study, at a similarly high level (r = .94). Blishen also reports that, over 18 occupations, his scale correlated .91 with the Tuckman scores.[9]

A major question answered by our survey is whether, with a substantial improvement in the quality of the data, the correlation between the rankings in the U.S. and Canada increases or decreases from the .96 which Tuckman's scores produced. Our study is an improvement on Tuckman's in many respects: it ranks a longer and more representative list of occupations, it is based on a proper sample of the whole country, it uses a ranking question which is more acceptably worded. Had the correlation between the rankings produced in our study and that of the recent NORC study been smaller than any previous ones some questioning of the hypothesis of identical rankings in all industrialized nations would be appropriate. In fact, the correlation was higher: it went up from .96 to .98.[10]

So far, findings are limited to an initial search for basic differences in ratings. We have been concerned with two kinds of differences. There is the traditional problem of describing the prestige hierarchy. We can compare the ranking of occupations in other countries with Canada, and of sub-groups within Canada, such as French with English Canada. The second problem is the study of the total amount of prestige given the occupational system as a whole. In this case we look for tendencies in a country or a sub-group to rate all jobs systematically higher, suggesting that, within that group, work itself has a greater prestige. Additional differences in the level of ranking may also be found for sub-classes of occupations.

Our vague hypothesizing went something like this: cross-national comparisons led us to expect high correlations between the U.S. and Canada and between English and French Canada in the rating of occupations. However, in respect to differences in the level of ranking we expected the U.S. to be higher than Canada. That is the total amount of prestige put into the system or more correctly into the 174 matching occupations would be greater. Theoretically it could be anticipated that as the process of industrialization advances the prestige of work and occupations associated with a high level of industrialization would increase. This condition would seem functionally appropriate to provide a fit between the value system, the motivation of actors and socialization to occupational roles in a more complex economy. This is the central manpower problem for industrial societies at present.

One of the interesting findings in comparing the NORC 1963 rankings with NORC 1947 (it will be recalled the latter was a replication of the former) was that in the U.S. there was a slight increase in the average prestige given jobs between the two points in time.[11] Since Canada is less industrialized than the U.S., and has a labor force with a much lower level of education, we anticipated Canada would put much less prestige into the occupational structure than did the U.S. and that similarly French Canada would put even less than English Canada. We were therefore surprised to discover that the Canadian rankings on the average were two points higher on the 100 point scale than those in the U.S.

It is clear we must do a great deal of thinking and tabulating before we can interpret this Canadian-U.S. difference. It could be something as trivial as the fact that our study had a higher refusal rate than the U.S. study, although we doubt this is the explanation.

There may be more than one reason for differing amounts of prestige in the occupational world. It occurs to us there may be a deferential element in the Canadian rankings derived from the elitist value pattern suggested by Lipset[12] as being important in Canadian society. The tendency in Canada to rate jobs higher is greatest for the professional and semi-professional categories of jobs where on the average, the jobs are ranked about four points higher than the U.S. Elitist values do not account for all the difference. The tendency for Canadian ratings to be higher is found to some degree throughout the whole list of occupations; they average 2.4 points higher for the white-collar jobs and 1.4 points higher for the blue-collar jobs.

The differences between our occupational rankings and others in Canada are much as we expected. In over 20 occupations in common with Tuckman's study our scores correlated .93 with his. In a study by Robson a sample of Canadian undergraduates ranked some of the original NORC titles. These ratings and ours over 31 matching titles produced a correlation of .96. With Blishen's scale based on the 1951 census our ratings correlate .93 when the comparison is restricted to 57 very closely matching titles and .88 when the comparison includes another 73 titles which are relatively poor matches. These correlations may be compared to the multiple correlation of income and education on prestige of .91 found by Duncan in the U.S.[13]

Some French-English differences in the ranking of jobs were pointed out in the discussion of the table of occupational rankings where scores for the two groups are given separately. Calculations based on these scores suggest some distinctiveness in ratings of French-speaking respondents. Overall, the prestige hierarchy in French Canada differs slightly from that in English Canada and in the U.S.: the French rankings correlated with the English Canadian rankings .95.

TABLE I   English–French Differences in Evaluation of Occupations

Occupational category	Number of occupational titles with higher prestige score given by:	
	English	French
Professional	12	9
Proprietors, managers and officials, large	12	3
Semi-professional	22	7
Proprietors, managers and officials, small	10	13
Clerical and sales	6	17
Skilled	9	18
Semi-skilled	11	23
Unskilled	4	14
Farmer	2	4

TABLE II   Twenty Occupational Titles with Greatest Differences in Ranking by Respondents Interviewed in English and in French

English title	English score	French score	French title
Apprentice to a master craftsman	38.9	18.0	Apprenti
Protestant minister	71.7	53.7	Pasteur protestant
Timber cruiser	36.1	53.1	Estimateur forestier
Whistle punk	14.3	29.4	Siffleur (forestage)
Department head in city government	74.5	60.4	Chef de départment dans l'administration municipale
Advertising executive	59.4	46.5	Membre de la direction d'un agence de publicité
Bill collector	·26.8	38.4	Agent de collection
Ballet dancer	51.6	40.7	Danseur ou danseuse de ballet
Lunchroom operator	29.2	39.9	Propriétaire d'un casse-croute
Physicist	79.9	69.3	Physicien
Social worker	57.4	47.4	Travailleur social
Typesetter	40.0	49.9	Typographe
Quarry worker	24.4	34.0	Ouvrier dans une carrière
Construction laborer	24.4	33.8	Manoeuvre dans l'industrie de la construction
Troller	26.3	16.9	Pêcheur à la cuiller
T.V. star	67.7	58.7	Vedette de la télévision
Musician in a symphony orchestra	58.0	49.3	Musicien dans un orchestre symphonique
Paper-making machine tender	29.5	38.2	Préposé à une machine à faire le papier
Locomotive engineer	50.9	42.2	Conducteur de locomotive
Farm laborer	19.6	27.9	Ouvrier agricole

The tendency for jobs to be rated higher in Canada than in the U.S. is true of both French and English Canada, but the French show an additional tendency in their rankings not to sort the jobs into the very highest and the very lowest categories to the extent that the English Canadians and U.S. respondents do. Table I shows this tendency. For blue-collar jobs and for clerical, sales, and small managerial jobs the French rankings tend to be higher and for the superior white-collar jobs they tend to be lower. This pattern is similar to that found for lower income groups by Hall and Jones in Great Britain, and Reiss, et al., in the U.S.[14] and might be interpreted as a self-enhancing manner of ranking the occupations; jobs to which blue-collar workers can reasonably aspire are slightly upgraded and those which are unattainable are slightly downgraded. We would not have been surprised to have found the overall Canadian ranking showing such a pattern.

A major problem in our analysis will be to determine the extent to which the French-English differences or French-U.S. differences are because of translations. Table II contains the occupational titles for which the French-English differences are greatest. Some of the differences are probably due to translation and we are having all our translations rated for adequacy by several bilingual judges. "Whistle punk," for example, is rated lower by the English; the word "punk" may have too negative a connotation which is absent in the French version "siffleur."

One of the important products of a public ranking of occupations is the basic material to construct a scale of socio-economic status. The NORC 1947 rankings have been widely used in this way in the U.S. and to some extent in Canada. The theoretical support for the use of rankings of occupations made by a representative cross-section of the society is that class is a subjective phenomenon experienced by actors in a social system. Class is also analyzed by objective criteria such as income, property, and so forth, selected by investigators and considered as independent of the evaluations of actors. As we have seen there is a high correlation between occupations ranked subjectively and objectively on such criteria as income and education. We feel these two approaches are complementary and necessary to the understanding of the structure of stratification.

One of our aims would be to establish prestige levels for a much greater proportion of the labor force than has been previously possible. We are, of course, faced with the problem of matching our titles with census titles, but we feel that we can do that sufficiently well to relate our rankings to a wide range of objective attributes of occupations derived from census data. Sociologists have long been critical of the way in which occupations have been treated in the Canadian census, particularly of the major categories, sociologically meaningless, into which they are arranged: now we feel we have some empirical justification for this criticism.

Table III shows the mean occupational rank on those occupations falling into each of the major census codes. Table IV similarly arranged these occupations into sociologically common-sense socio-economic status categories which are

TABLE III   Occupational Prestige Scores by Major Census Classifications

Census major occupation group	Number of titles	Mean score	Standard deviation
Owners and managers	27	60.38	15.71
Professional occupations	46	64.11	10.95
Clerical occupations	14	37.46	7.23
Sales occupations	11	36.99	12.91
Service and recreation occupations	23	37.17	15.92
Transport and communications	13	41.72	12.83
Farmers and farm workers	6	34.98	10.01
Loggers and related workers	3	27.87	11.25
Fishermen, trappers, and hunters	2	23.50	0.32
Miners, quarrymen, and related workers	5	33.12	7.22
Craftsmen, production process workers	43	36.55	8.00
Laborers n.e.s.*	3	21.47	6.02

*Not elsewhere specified.

TABLE IV   Occupational Prestige Scores by Socio-Economic Categories

Occupational title	Number of titles	Mean score	Standard deviation
Professional	21	72.04	8.16
Proprietors, managers, and officials, large	15	70.42	12.99
Semi-professional	29	57.73	8.29
Proprietors, managers, and officials, small	23	48.79	8.91
Clerical and sales	23	38.57	8.90
Skilled	27	38.76	6.98
Semi-skilled	34	32.91	7.71
Unskilled	18	23.46	6.23
Farmer	6	34.98	10.01

also the classifications of the Appendix table. A good coding system produces homogeneous categories. In each table the standard deviation of the prestige scores for the occupations within each category is given as a test of homogeneity. If we restrict the analysis to categories with at least five occupations in them and arbitrarily define homogeneity by a standard deviation of less than ten, only three of the nine possible census categories are homogeneous while seven of the nine socio-economic status categories are.

A good coding system must also differentiate, as it will do if the categories are homogeneous. The socio-economic status classification shows almost a clear gradient from professional to unskilled in the means for each category. The exception is the almost identical score of "clerical and sales" occupations and "skilled" occupations. Many have doubted the justification of the non-manual/ manual dichotomy so frequently used in sociological research. In a highly industrialized society at least, there are many white-collar occupations which have less prestige than many skilled blue-collar occupations. The census shows a much less satisfactory pattern. If the analysis is confined to those categories with at least five occupations the socio-economic status classifications cover a much wider range of occupational prestige than do the census categories, that is 23.46 to 72.04 for the SES classifications, compared to 33.1 to 64.1 for the census categories. The SES classifications separate "skilled," "semi-skilled," and "unskilled" whereas the census lumps them all together under "craftsmen, production process workers." The differences in the prestige levels of manual workers justifies their being sub-divided. Quite meaningless from the point of view of stratification theory is the census category "owners and managers." Its occupations range in their scores from 31.6 to 89.9 or 60 percent of the entire theoretical prestige hierarchy and 80 percent of the actual. The use of such a category for the tabulation of census data is sociologically absurd; it is extraordinarily difficult to find any defensible reason for it. Only slightly less absurd are the "service and recreation" and the "transport and communications" categories. In some respects these last two constitute families of occupations, but they have little relevance to stratification. Sociologists have sought in vain for a relationship between census occupational categories and the structural categories of sociology, and it is all the more distressing because it is sociology more than the other social sciences which could make the most use of the mass of census and other macro data.

APPENDIX I   Occupational Prestige Scores by Occupational Classes

Occupational title	National N = 793		National English N = 607		National French N = 186	
	Score	S.D.	Score	S.D.	Score	S.D.
Professional						
Accountant	63.4	19.2	62.9	19.4	65.4	18.4
Architect	78.1	18.3	77.6	18.4	79.6	17.9
Biologist	72.6	20.9	73.4	20.2	69.7	23.0
Catholic priest	72.8	25.5	71.5	25.0	77.2	26.6
Chemist	73.5	19.3	73.3	18.8	73.9	21.1
Civil engineer	73.1	19.0	72.6	18.8	75.1	19.3
Country court judge	82.5	18.6	81.0	18.6	87.4	17.7
Druggist	69.3	20.0	68.5	19.8	72.0	20.5
Economist	62.2	22.3	63.0	21.6	59.5	24.2
High school teacher	66.1	20.7	67.8	20.0	60.4	22.2
Lawyer	82.3	16.7	81.6	17.0	84.4	15.5
Mathematician	72.7	20.1	73.7	20.1	69.5	19.9
Mine safety analyst	57.1	20.5	57.2	20.5	56.6	20.8
Mining engineer	68.8	20.5	68.6	20.1	69.3	21.6
Physician	87.2	15.9	87.5	16.1	86.1	15.2
Physicist	77.6	21.4	79.9	20.0	69.3	24.1
Protestant minister	67.8	26.3	71.7	23.0	53.7	32.1
Psychologist	74.9	20.3	76.0	19.6	71.3	22.2

Public grade school teacher	59.6	20.5	59.8	20.8	58.8	19.2
University professor	84.6	17.3	86.1	16.9	79.9	17.7
Veterinarian	66.7	21.3	66.7	20.9	66.6	22.5

Semi professional

Airline pilot	66.1	20.5	67.4	19.9	61.6	21.8
Author	64.8	21.7	65.8	21.7	61.4	21.6
Ballet dancer	49.1	26.2	51.6	25.2	40.7	27.6
Chiropractor	68.4	22.0	67.2	21.6	72.2	22.9
Commercial artist	57.2	20.5	58.1	20.4	54.1	20.6
Computer programmer	53.8	21.6	53.6	21.2	54.8	22.9
Disc jockey	38.0	23.1	38.2	23.0	37.3	23.6
Draughtsman	60.0	20.6	59.9	20.4	60.0	21.1
Funeral director	54.9	23.7	55.2	22.8	53.7	26.5
Jazz musician	40.9	24.5	40.9	24.3	41.2	25.2
Journalist	60.9	20.0	62.3	19.5	56.4	21.0
Medical or dental technician	67.5	21.7	66.7	21.8	70.0	21.4
Musician	52.1	22.9	53.7	22.5	46.6	23.2
Musician in a symphony orchestra	56.0	23.0	58.0	22.1	49.3	25.0
Physiotherapist	72.1	19.4	72.3	19.0	71.3	20.6
Playground director	42.8	22.3	43.1	21.7	41.8	24.1
Professional athlete	54.1	24.2	54.5	24.3	52.9	23.9
Professionally trained forester	60.0	20.6	60.4	19.9	58.9	22.8
Professionally trained librarian	58.1	21.7	58.5	21.2	56.7	23.1
Registered nurse	64.7	21.4	66.1	20.8	59.9	22.5
Research technician	66.9	19.1	67.1	19.1	66.1	19.2
Sculptor	56.9	23.6	58.0	23.5	53.5	23.9
Social worker	55.1	24.0	57.4	23.2	47.4	25.2
Surveyor	62.0	20.4	60.6	20.1	66.9	20.7
T.V. announcer	57.6	21.6	57.9	21.4	56.5	22.4
T.V. cameraman	48.3	21.4	47.8	21.0	49.9	22.6
T.V. director	62.1	21.5	63.1	21.4	58.9	21.7
T.V. star	65.6	26.8	67.7	25.9	58.7	28.6
YMCA director	58.2	21.8	59.2	21.0	54.5	24.4

Proprietors, managers and officials, large

Administrative officer in Federal Civil Service	68.8	20.1	69.9	19.6	64.9	21.6
Advertising executive	56.5	21.8	59.4	21.2	46.5	20.9
Bank manager	70.9	19.3	72.1	19.4	67.1	18.5
Building contractor	56.5	19.3	56.4	18.9	56.7	20.7
Colonel in the army	70.8	22.0	71.6	21.3	68.4	24.2
Department head in City Government	71.3	21.3	74.5	19.5	60.4	23.7
General manager of a manufacturing plant	69.1	19.2	70.4	18.5	64.9	20.8
Mayor of a large city	79.9	20.4	80.6	20.2	77.5	20.7

APPENDIX I (Continued)

Occupational title	National N = 793 Score	S.D.	National English N = 607 Score	S.D.	National French N = 186 Score	S.D.
Member of Canadian Cabinet	83.3	19.9	84.2	18.8	80.4	22.9
Member of Canadian House of Commons	84.8	18.8	84.9	18.4	84.5	20.2
Member of Canadian Senate	86.1	21.1	86.0	20.8	86.1	22.3
Merchandise buyer for a department store	51.1	19.3	52.7	19.0	45.5	19.3
Owner of a manufacturing plant	69.4	21.3	69.8	20.6	67.9	23.4
Provincial Premier	89.9	18.1	88.7	19.1	93.6	13.3
Wholesale distributor	47.9	20.5	49.1	19.9	43.6	22.0

Proprietors, managers and officials, small

Advertising copy writer	48.9	20.6	48.3	19.8	50.9	22.8
Beauty operator	35.2	20.9	34.4	20.3	37.9	22.6
Construction foreman	51.1	20.0	50.4	19.7	53.3	20.8
Driving instructor	41.6	21.6	40.0	20.9	46.9	23.2
Foreman in a factory	50.9	19.3	49.2	18.6	56.8	20.4
Government purchasing agent	56.8	21.6	56.9	21.0	56.2	23.4
Insurance claims investigator	51.1	20.1	50.8	20.1	52.0	20.2
Job counsellor	58.3	20.7	58.7	20.0	56.8	23.0
Livestock buyer	39.6	21.5	40.6	20.6	36.1	24.2
Lunchroom operator	31.6	21.4	29.2	20.3	39.9	23.2
Manager of a real estate office	58.3	20.9	58.8	20.7	56.8	21.8
Manager of a supermarket	52.5	20.2	52.7	20.0	51.9	20.6
Member of a city council	62.9	21.4	64.7	20.3	57.1	24.0
Motel owner	51.6	23.5	50.9	21.7	53.8	28.0
Owner of a food store	47.8	21.3	49.7	20.8	41.7	21.9
Public relations man	60.5	19.4	60.3	19.2	61.4	20.2
Railroad ticket agent	35.7	21.1	36.5	20.6	33.0	22.5
Sawmill operator	37.0	21.7	36.4	21.4	38.9	22.5
Service station manager	41.5	20.4	42.5	18.9	38.1	24.5
Ship's pilot	59.6	22.7	59.6	22.4	59.7	23.5
Superintendent of a construction job	53.9	20.4	55.3	20.4	49.0	19.5
Trade union business agent	49.2	21.0	48.6	20.9	51.1	21.3
Travel agent	46.6	20.7	45.0	19.5	52.0	23.5

Clerical and Sales

Air hostess	57.0	21.1	55.7	21.0	61.0	20.7
Bank teller	42.3	21.0	42.4	20.1	41.9	24.0
Bill collector	29.4	21.5	26.8	21.1	38.4	20.4
Bookkeeper	49.4	20.2	50.0	20.1	47.3	20.7

Cashier in a supermarket	31.1	21.4	30.5	21.1	33.0	22.1
Clerk in an office	35.6	20.3	35.0	19.8	37.8	22.1
File clerk	32.7	21.2	31.5	20.4	36.7	23.1
IBM keypunch operator	47.7	21.5	46.5	21.0	51.9	22.8
Insurance agent	47.3	19.7	46.6	19.1	49.7	21.5
Manufacturer's representative	52.1	19.1	51.7	19.0	53.5	19.1
Post office clerk	37.2	21.9	37.2	21.6	36.9	22.8
Real estate agent	47.1	21.1	46.2	20.1	49.8	23.9
Receptionist	38.7	20.9	39.7	20.4	35.5	22.1
Sales clerk in a store	26.5	19.7	26.6	19.4	25.9	20.7
Shipping clerk	30.9	20.1	30.7	19.3	31.7	22.7
Stenographer	46.0	20.2	44.6	19.6	50.6	21.5
Stockroom attendant	25.8	19.2	24.9	18.8	29.0	20.1
Telephone operator	38.1	22.0	37.6	21.7	39.9	23.0
Telephone solicitor	26.7	23.0	28.3	23.2	21.7	21.6
Travelling salesman	40.2	21.1	38.8	21.0	45.1	20.6
Truck dispatcher	32.2	20.4	32.1	20.1	32.7	21.2
Typist	41.9	20.7	41.1	20.1	44.7	22.4
Used car salesman	31.2	21.0	30.4	20.0	34.0	24.0

Skilled

Airplane mechanic	50.3	22.4	49.3	22.1	53.4	23.1
Baker	38.9	20.5	38.8	20.1	39.4	22.1
Bricklayer	36.2	21.6	36.0	21.3	36.9	22.6
Butcher in a store	34.8	20.2	34.7	19.7	35.0	21.6
Coal miner	27.6	22.1	26.2	21.9	32.3	22.4
Cook in a restaurant	29.7	21.0	28.9	21.3	32.3	19.8
Custom seamstress	33.4	20.3	33.7	19.3	32.5	23.3
Diamond driller	44.5	21.7	44.8	21.4	43.2	22.5
Electrician	50.2	20.5	49.5	20.5	52.3	20.4
House carpenter	38.9	20.7	38.7	20.3	39.4	22.1
House painter	29.9	19.4	29.0	19.0	33.0	20.4
Locomotive engineer	48.9	22.2	50.9	21.7	42.2	22.7
Machinist	44.2	21.9	44.0	21.9	45.0	22.0
Machine set-up man in a factory	42.1	21.4	41.9	21.5	42.6	21.4
Mucking machine operator	31.5	20.5	30.3	20.3	35.1	20.5
Plumber	42.6	20.8	42.7	20.7	42.4	21.5
Power crane operator	40.2	20.7	39.8	20.7	41.4	21.0
Power lineman	40.9	21.2	41.8	20.3	37.5	24.3
Pumphouse engineer	38.9	21.8	40.6	21.6	33.3	21.7
Railroad brakeman	37.1	20.9	37.5	20.8	35.9	21.2
Railroad conductor	45.3	21.8	44.5	21.2	48.2	23.5
Saw sharpener	20.7	20.1	19.6	19.1	24.6	22.9
Sheet metal worker	35.9	20.5	36.8	19.9	32.5	22.6
T.V. repairman	37.2	20.4	36.5	20.2	39.3	20.9
Tool and die maker	42.5	22.2	44.1	21.8	36.7	22.6
Typesetter	42.2	20.5	40.0	19.6	49.9	21.4

APPENDIX I (Continued)

Occupational title	National N = 793 Score	S.D.	National English N = 607 Score	S.D.	National French N = 186 Score	S.D.
Welder	41.8	21.5	41.4	21.3	43.2	22.2
Semi-skilled						
Aircraft worker	43.7	21.6	43.6	21.6	43.9	21.8
Apprentice to a master craftsman	33.9	23.1	38.9	21.9	18.0	19.5
Assembly line worker	28.2	20.4	27.6	20.3	30.4	20.8
Automobile repairman	38.1	20.8	36.9	20.2	41.9	22.2
Automobile worker	35.9	21.2	34.4	20.6	41.3	22.2
Barber	39.3	20.2	38.9	19.6	40.4	22.2
Bartender	20.2	19.5	19.4	19.5	22.8	19.2
Book binder	35.2	20.1	33.5	19.6	41.0	20.8
Bus driver	35.9	21.3	35.8	21.9	36.1	19.2
Cod fisherman	23.4	21.0	24.8	21.0	18.6	20.5
Firefighter	43.5	24.4	44.2	24.5	41.4	23.8
Fruit packer in a cannery	23.2	20.7	22.0	20.3	27.6	21.4
Logger	24.9	21.3	25.4	20.9	23.2	22.5
Longshoreman	26.1	21.1	26.5	21.0	24.9	21.5
Loom operator	33.3	19.7	32.3	19.3	36.4	20.7
Machine operator in a factory	34.9	22.2	33.1	21.7	41.1	23.0
Newspaper pressman	43.0	20.6	44.3	20.2	38.4	21.2
Oil field worker	35.3	21.9	34.6	21.6	37.5	22.7
Oiler in a ship	27.6	21.2	26.3	20.2	31.7	23.7
Paper making machine tender	31.6	20.4	29.5	19.8	38.2	20.8
Policeman	51.6	23.0	52.1	23.0	49.9	22.9
Private in the army	28.4	22.9	29.6	23.5	24.4	20.4
Production worker in the electronics industry	50.8	23.0	50.4	22.7	52.2	23.7
Professional babysitter	25.9	22.5	25.2	22.3	28.5	23.1
Quarry worker	26.7	22.3	24.4	21.3	34.0	23.8
Sewing machine operator	28.2	19.9	26.7	19.2	33.1	21.3
Steam boiler fireman	32.8	21.1	33.9	21.0	29.0	21.0
Steam roller operator	32.2	20.7	32.0	20.2	32.7	22.3
Steel mill worker	34.3	20.6	35.2	20.9	31.2	19.1
Textile mill worker	28.8	19.5	28.6	19.5	29.7	19.6
Timber cruiser	40.3	22.6	36.1	21.5	53.1	21.3
Trailer truck driver	32.8	22.0	31.8	21.7	36.5	22.4
Troller	23.6	20.7	26.3	20.9	16.9	18.8
Worker in a meat packing plant	25.2	20.3	24.3	19.7	28.3	22.1

Unskilled

Carpenter's helper	23.1	20.0	22.5	20.0	24.9	19.8
Construction laborer	26.5	22.7	24.4	22.1	33.8	23.1
Elevator operator in a building	20.1	20.7	21.8	20.9	14.4	18.8
Filling station attendant	23.3	20.3	22.2	19.7	27.7	22.1
Garbage collector	14.8	20.0	15.0	20.3	13.8	18.9
Hospital attendant	34.9	24.9	34.2	24.2	37.6	26.8
Housekeeper in a private home	28.8	23.5	28.5	24.1	30.0	21.2
Janitor	17.3	19.1	16.3	18.5	20.8	21.0
Laundress	19.3	20.1	19.3	19.8	19.6	21.3
Mailman	36.1	23.0	36.2	23.0	35.8	23.3
Museum attendant	30.4	21.8	31.5	21.2	26.9	23.1
Newspaper peddler	14.8	19.0	14.3	18.7	16.5	20.1
Railroad sectionhand	27.3	21.8	25.7	21.7	32.6	21.5
Taxicab driver	25.1	20.3	24.3	19.8	27.8	21.7
Waitress in a restaurant	19.9	19.4	19.1	19.0	22.6	20.3
Warehouse hand	21.3	18.3	20.2	18.1	25.1	18.7
Whistle punk	18.4	21.2	14.3	18.7	29.4	23.4
Worker in a dry cleaning or laundry plant	20.8	19.6	20.3	19.4	22.4	19.9

Farmer

Commercial farmer	42.0	22.3	41.7	22.0	42.9	23.3
Dairy farmer	44.2	22.9	43.3	22.4	47.3	24.5
Farm laborer	21.5	22.0	19.6	21.7	27.9	22.0
Farm owner and operator	44.1	23.7	44.8	23.2	41.7	25.5
Hog farmer	33.0	23.6	31.3	23.5	38.8	23.1
Part-time farmer	25.1	22.4	26.6	22.3	20.1	21.9

Not in labor force

Archaeopotrist	63.7	23.9	64.7	22.5	59.7	28.4
Biologer	64.2	24.1	66.0	22.8	57.8	27.4
Occupation of my family's main wage earner	50.9	25.1	50.3	24.5	53.0	27.0
Occupation of my father when I was 16	42.5	25.6	42.6	25.2	42.2	26.8
Someone who lives off inherited wealth	45.8	31.5	45.8	31.9	46.0	30.2
Someone who lives off property holdings	48.7	25.9	46.9	25.4	54.4	26.7
Someone who lives off stocks and bonds	56.9	27.9	56.7	28.0	57.5	27.8
Someone who lives on relief	7.3	15.9	7.2	15.5	7.8	17.4

Notes

1. K. Svalastoga, *Prestige, Class and Mobility* (Copenhagen: 1959).

2. C. Carlsson, *Social Mobility and Class Structure* (Gleerup/Lund, 1958).

3. John Hall and D. Caradog Jones, "The Social Grading of Occupations." *British Journal of Sociology*, I (March, 1950).

4. R. W. Hodge, P. M. Siegel, and P. H. Rossi, "Occupational Prestige in the United States, 1925-1963," *American Journal of Sociology* (November, 1964), 286-302.

5. "Jobs and Occupations: A Popular Evaluation," *Opinion News* IX (September, 1947).

6. John Meisel, "The Stalled Omnibus: Canadian Parties in the 1960's," *Social Research*, XXX (Autumn, 1963), 386.

7. A. Inkeles and P. H. Rossi, "National Comparisons of Occupational Prestige," *American Journal of Sociology,* LXI (January, 1956).

8. J. Tuckman, "Social Status of Occupations in Canada," *Canadian Journal of Psychology*, I (June, 1947).

9. B. R. Blishen, "The Construction and Use of an Occupational Class Scale," in B. R. Blishen, et al., eds., *Canadian Society* (Toronto: 1964).

10. The N.O.R.C. rankings were supplied to us on a confidential basis and we are not, therefore, in a position to comment extensively, at this time, on Canadian-U.S. differences.

11. "Occupational Prestige in the United States, 1925-1963."

12. S. M. Lipset, *The First New Nation* (New York: 1963), Chap. 7.

13. Otis Dudley Duncan, "A Socio-Economic Index for All Occupations" in Albert J. Reiss, Jr., *Occupations and Social Status* (New York, 1961), 124.

14. "The Social Grading of Occupations," 42-43, and Reiss, *Occupations and Social Status*, 183.

Occupational Mobility over Four Generations[*]

John C. Goyder/James E. Curtis

CUMULATIVE EFFECTS IN FAMILY ASCRIPTION[1]

In analyses of mobility over two generations, the socio-economic characteristics of the father are usually taken as indicators of ascribed family status even though these may not capture the full implications of family background. Extensions of mobility models beyond these basic status variables have sometimes used attitudinal predictors (e.g., Duncan, Featherman, and Duncan, 1972), but seldom have they involved variables pertaining to other family members. However, the status of grandparents and great-grandparents might be expected to have some independent effect upon the status of respondents. If such effects were of any magnitude the impact of family status could be said to be cumulative over generations and the conventional .40 father-son correlation found in previous two-generational studies would understate the full degree of "family ascription" in the process of occupational attainment.[2] Thus, one way in which the addition of information on the statuses of grandfathers and great-grandfathers might lend perspective to interpretations of ascription is by clarifying the contemporary ascriptive importance of past generations. Another way in which such variables might be of value is in assessing the long run permeability of the social structure. This is something that can usually only be estimated using techniques such as Markoff chains and these may involve unrealistic assumptions.

The most direct manner in which grandparents may influence their grandchildren's occupational attainment is probably by direct adoption or guardianship. More subtle forms of influence might take the form of trust accounts and inheritances that bypass the father's generation. Along with the transmission of

---

[*] Abridged from the *Canadian Review of Sociology and Anthropology* 14 (3) 1977, pp. 308–19. Used with permission.

The authors thank Professors H. Clarke, J. Jenson, L. LeDuc, and J. Pamment for including detailed social background questions in interviews for a male subsample of their National Federal Election Survey. The above bear no responsibility for the authors' analyses and interpretations of the data here, however. The authors thank Sue Dier, Chantal Locatelli and Reza Nakhaie for work on coding and computing. They also gratefully acknowledge that their project was supported by a small grant from the Canada Council's general research grants program support to the University of Waterloo and that James Curtis received leave fellowship support from the Council in 1975-6. They are also grateful to Carl Cuneo, Stephen Hawkins, Frank Jones, Peter Pineo, and anonymous readers for the *Review* for helpful comments on a draft of this paper.

such resources, grandparents may have some role in socializing grandchildren if contact between them is frequent. Even lacking contact, the influence might persist posthumously as in the case where a grandfather is venerated and held up as a role model to the new generation.[3] The possible influence of great-grandparents, which could not be supposed to be of any great strength, would seem likely to be exerted almost entirely through the form of reputation and role model. No doubt, individual cases can readily be found where grandparents or even great-grandparents could be seen to be influences affecting the socio-economic attainment of their progeny. This is certainly a theme which occurs in literature. Whether the transmission of resources, values, and role models over non-adjacent generations is of sufficient frequency and importance to be detectable in a general population is a question that only a survey analysis is likely to answer.

Some survey analyses of mobility over three generations, in general populations, have appeared in foreign studies (e.g., Svalastoga, 1959; Hodge, 1966; Ridge, 1973), though not in Canada. The nearest Canadian equivalents have been studies of such specialized groups as elites (e.g., Tepperman, 1972; Clement, 1975) and the very poor (e.g., Gonick, 1970; Puxley, 1971). The poverty studies have emphasized that there is perpetuation of low status over several generations. Tepperman's study (1972), by far the most systematic attempt to generate data on elite mobility over several generations, found reasonably high rates of downward mobility from "prominence" after three generations (cf. Clement, 1975). Findings from such specialized populations cannot be assumed to apply to the general Canadian population though. The principal innovation in our own research was to address questions of cumulative ascription in Canada using national level data representative of the entire population.

DATA SOURCE

Our data come from a set of mobility questions included in a political opinion survey conducted following the 1974 federal election. The survey used a national sample of Canadian voters (for fieldwork details, see LeDuc et al., 1974). The mobility questions were asked of males only (N = 1191, 1143 when weighted). Several previous three generational mobility studies (cf. NORC, 1953; Davidson and Anderson, 1937; Svalastoga, 1959; Zelan, et al., 1968) have asked respondents to report the occupations of their fathers and paternal grandfathers, as well as their own. An alternative method of linking three generations, used in the Glass study (1954), is to ask respondent's father's and respondent's son's occupations. Judging from two recent reports on re-analyses of the Glass and NORC data sets (Ridge, 1973; Hodge, 1966 respectively) the two methods of constructing a comparison of mobility over three generations yield somewhat different results. Findings from the two reports are difficult to compare because of the different analytical tools (and societies) involved in each, but Ridge (1973) appears to have found stronger direct grandfather effects than Hodge (1966) did. In the election study the two approaches were combined. Respondents were asked to report the "main" occupation of their paternal grandfathers, fathers, and eldest sons, as well as their own current occupation.[4] Responses were coded into 1971 Blishen scores (Blishen and McRoberts, 1976) and into a scale suitable for matrix analysis (Pineo and Porter, 1967:61).

FINDINGS

Correlational Results

The intercorrelations among the statuses of grandfathers (G), fathers (F), respondents (R), and eldest sons (S) are shown in Table I. Farmers are a difficult group to code into an occupational SES scale because of their great heterogeneity; since they constitute a large proportion of occupations in Canada, the correlations are given first with farmers included (above the diagonal in Table I) and then excluding farmers in each generation (below the diagonal). Including farmers, the correlation of respondent's and father's occupation, with a value of $r = .38$, follows closely the "western european model" (r of about .40) found in a number of such countries and in the U.S. (Svalastoga, 1965).[5] With farmers excluded, this figure drops to $r = .33$. Among grandfathers and fathers the effect of excluding farmers is to raise the intercorrelation of their occupations by .01 points.

Of principal interest for our purposes is the relationship grandfather's occupation has with those of the succeeding generations. Over the generations the intuitively obvious pattern holds; the strength of association between grandfather's occupation and those of the following generations steadily declines. The results reported in Table II show that grandfather's occupational status retains a moderately large zero-order association with the occupational status of the third generation (respondents). A less obvious finding is that by the fourth generation (sons of respondents) family ascription due to the status of grandfathers disappears almost entirely. The correlation of grandfather's with respondent's son's occupational scores ($r = .05$ with farmers, .03 without) fails the test for statistical significance and is so small that any possibility of cumulative ascription extending to the fourth generation is ruled out. The correlations involving eldest sons fluctuate somewhat according to whether all working sons are used or only those aged 25 or over. The coefficients reported in Table II include all sons. It may be more reasonable to analyse data only for older sons because they are relatively settled in their careers, but this dissipates the case base. Restricting the calculations to sons aged 25 or over, the association between grandfather's and respondent's son's occupation scores declines to $r = .02$ with farmers included. This figure actually takes a negative value ($r = -.07$) with farmers excluded.

We have seen that there is some first order association between respondent's and grandfather's occupation. This, however, does not necessarily demonstrate that family status ascription is cumulative. Some degree of correlation between the occupations in these two generations is inevitable because both share a strong association with the intervening generation (Table I). In fact, when the combined contribution made by grandfather's father's occupations in explaining variance in respondent's occupation is examined, the resulting multiple correlation is found

TABLE I   Intercorrelations of Occupational Status Scores among Grand-fathers, Fathers, Respondents, and Sons

Generation	G	F	R	S
Grandfather (G)	1.00*	.49	.22	.05
Father (F)	.50	1.00	.38	.13
Respondent (R)	.27	.33	1.00	.26
Sons (S)	.03†	.09†	.22	1.00

* Figures above the diagonal are for the total sample; those below the diagonal are for farmers excluded in each generation.
† $p. > .05$

TABLE II   Simple Frequencies: Respondent's Occupation by Father's Occupation by Grandfather's Occupation

Grandfather's occupation	Respondent's occupation	Father's occupation		
		White col.	Blue col.	Farm
White collar	White collar	67	19	3
White collar	Blue collar	11	19	2
White collar	Farm	0	1	6
Blue collar	White collar	45	55	5
Blue collar	Blue collar	18	80	8
Blue collar	Farm	1	2	1
Farm	White collar	37	56	54
Farm	Blue collar	18	47	89
Farm	Farm	3	4	46

to be little larger than the conventional two generation (father-respondent) correlation. Indeed, the correlation of $r = .38$ seen in Table I for fathers and respondents is raised only in the third decimal place. In the non-farm population the cumulative effect is larger but still not important (the zero-order $r = .33$ becomes a multiple $R = .35$). In sum, correlational analysis reveals an extremely low association between occupations over four generations, and over three generations a moderate association is found to possess only a minor cumulative component.

Matrix Results

So far, we have described only the over-all degree of congruency between occupational status over four generations. This does not reveal the details of the interchange between occupational categories. A matrix analysis is required for this, where the actual contingency between occupation levels for different generations is compared This could reveal important cumulative ascriptive patterns between certain occupation categories, hidden within the summary results presented above.

Both the correlational and matrix methods yield the conclusion that mobility between grandfathers and respondents' sons is high. A simple cross-tabulation of the two occupations, without resorting to controls for structural causes of mobility, exhibits no statistically significant association ($p = .80$). In this matrix, occupation was coded into seven broad groupings, and there are large proportions of great-grandsons in the blue-collar categories whose great-grandfathers were professionals or business owners. And, of course, there is a great deal of upward mobility by great-grandsons of manual workers. Only 20 percent of great-grandsons of unskilled manual workers are also unskilled, while the rest are scattered throughout the other categories; 24 percent are in the professional category. So, this analysis corroborates what the correlational analysis suggested, that occupational status ascription all but disappears after an interval of four generations down the male side of a family.

There is a contingency between the occupation categories held by grandfathers and respondents ($X^2 = 79.95$, DF = 25, $p < .001$). Table II shows the simple frequencies of respondents classified simultaneously according to their own occupation group and those of their grandfathers and fathers. To prevent having too large a number of cells, occupations were recoded here into the traditional white-collar, blue-collar, and farm scale. This grouping is only a crude categorization and for contemporary generations may over-simplify because of the overlap in incomes between lower white- and upper blue-collar occupations. However, it may also capture more reality for occupations in past generations, from a time when the blue-collar/white-collar boundary was more distinct. In examining the frequencies in Table II, no separation is made between structural mobility (that attributed to changes in occupation distributions in each generation) and the underlying patterns often referred to as 'net mobility.' However, the over-all incidence of different status combinations seems to us to have intrinsic importance. It allows an understanding of what the occupational backgrounds of Canadians have typically been over the past three generations.

The single most frequent status combination observed in Table II is that of the blue-collar respondent whose grandfather and father were both farmers (N = 89). Indeed, as one would expect, over half of all respondents in the sample have farming backgrounds either in the father's or paternal grandfather's generation. The opposite pattern, that of migration back to farming by respondents having grandfathers in the industrial sector is, of course, infrequent. For example, only one respondent had a white-collar grandfather, a blue-collar father, and was himself a farmer. It can be observed that the incidence of consistency in occupational groups over three generations is, in terms of simple frequency, rather large. Sixty-seven respondents reported white-collar occupations in 1974 and said that their fathers and grandfathers also did white-collar work as their main occupations. The combination of blue-collar occupations over three generations is even more frequent (N = 80). And, the inheritance of farms over generations (N = 46) is by far the most common means by which respondents entered into farming. These consistent patterns, particularly those for the industrial sector, are of theoretical interest because they reflect cases in which the social structure has been impermeable. There are two other patterns of mobility over three generations that hold particular theoretical interest. One of these is the progression from blue-collar grandfather to white-collar father and back to blue-collar respondent. The other is the opposite; white-collar grandfather, blue-collar father, and white-collar respondent. These patterns are odd because, if all respondents fitted into them, father's occupation would correlate -1 with both the grandfather's and respondent's occupations, while respondent's and grandfather's occupations would hold a perfect positive correlation. The pattern of blue-collar grandfather, white-collar father, and blue-collar respondent is expressed in folklore by the saying "clogs to clogs is only three generation" (Apperson, 1929: 102).[6] This proverb seems to imply that mobility is likely to be sustained only over two generations and that somehow the class structure will reassert itself by the third generation. If this was true, then the opposite pattern, which we would term "reverse clogs," might also hold. Some incidence of these two patterns is to be expected merely by chance and according to the principle of regression towards the mean over generations (Allingham, 1967; Blau and Duncan, 1967: 199). That is, if occupational status was determined randomly, having no connection with the levels held in previous generations, sons of both high and low status fathers would generally be found to have occupations closer to the mean level than would their fathers. In fact, the frequency of the "clogs to clogs" and "reverse clogs" patterns does seem small (N = 18 and 19 respectively). Both are minor patterns in the over-all table and we will give below an assessment of whether they occur any more frequently than simple chance would predict.

A summary statistic representing the over-all direct association between grandfather's and respondent's occupation, net of father's occupation, can be generated within the matrix approach by making use of Goodman's (1972) "log-linear modelling." An advantage of log-linear analysis is that it permits one to take explicit account of the importance of the marginal distributions in each generation. The technique involves assembling an expected set of values for a contingency table, using different pieces of information about the constituent variables (e.g., the marginal distribution of each one). Then, conventional procedures for comparing the statistical significance are followed. If the test is significant, one concludes that fresh information is needed in the construction of the expected cell values. A non-significant result tells one that the model used to predict the cell values is adequate. (Hauser et al., 1975, provide a fuller explanation of the technique together with further references.)

Summary results for a log-linear analysis of the three-way mobility matrix respondent's occupation by father's occupation by grandfather's occupation are shown in Table III. Parallel results for the father-respondent-son matrix are omitted because of the small number of cases in some cells. (We became particularly uncomfortable, in working with the Goodman procedure, with the distorting effects that differing constants inserted in zero cells seemed to have on the effect parameters.) As in Table II, occupation is coded into the white-collar, blue-collar, and farming groups. The first column of Table III shows the likelihood ratio chi-square, the second the degrees of freedom, and the third the result of the significance test. Three different models were tested. The first takes account of

TABLE III   Log-Linear Analysis of Three-Generational Mobility Matrices

	Likelihood ratio (X^2)	DF	p
Grandfathers, fathers, and respondents:			
Model			
1 (G) (F) (R)	404.55	20	.0001
2 (G) (F) (R) (GF) (FR)	27.07	12	.008
3 (G) (F) (R) (GF) (GR) (FR)	15.02	8	.06

Note: G, grandfather's occupation; F, father's occupation; R, respondent's occupation

changes in the occupational distributions for the three generations, but enters no information about rates of inflow and outflow for any combination of generations. In other words, the model makes the unlikely assumption that no relationship exists between any of the three pairs of occupations. From Table III we see that such a simple model is far from adequate for the purpose of predicting the cell values in the three-way contingency table for these occupations. The next model adds the 'two-way interactions' for grandfathers and fathers and for fathers and respondents. However, the interaction between grandfathers and respondents is left out. If grandfather's occupation had no relationship with respondent's except that which they held mutually with father's occupation, this model should adequately predict the cell values in the table and there consequently should be no statistically significant differences between the expected and observed values. The significance test reported in Table III demonstrates that this does not happen. The refinement considerably decreases the chi-square observed in the previous model but the model still does not adequately fit the actual cell values. Adding the interaction between grandfather's occupation and respondent's occupation further reduces the chi-square, showing that this third model has an even closer fit with the actual cell values. In fact, the difference between the actual cell values and those predicted fitting this model do not exceed those attributable to chance alone, at the .05 level of significance, and so further additions to the model are unnecessary.

The Goodman technique also generates "effect parameters" (λ) which describe the effect of each category of a variable or cluster of variables in predicting any cell frequency in a contingency table. The "main effects" of each variable merely reflect the marginal distributions of, in our case, the occupations held by each generation. The next level of effect involves the joint distributions of variables. In our analysis, these are analogous to zero-order correlations between occupations. The highest order of effect, in an analysis of mobility over three generations, is the three-variable effect parameter (GFR). This takes a different value for each cell in the three way classification of grandfather's, father's, and respondent's occupation. The values of λ express in logarithmic form the odds of a case falling into a given cell, after having already taken into account the effect of all the lower order lambdas (see Goodman, 1972:1042–6 and his other articles for a fuller interpretation). These three-variable λ's are shown in the upper portion of Table IV. Comparable either down columns or along rows, they sum to zero along each dimension (except for possible rounding error). It can be seen that a white-collar consistency effect does hold net of the additive consequences of father's and grandfather's occupations. The λ of .45 for this combination is the highest in the row for white-collar respondents. This means that, even after taking account of the two-variable (or additive) effects, the odds of a person being in white-collar work are stronger if both his grandfather and father were also in white-collar work than for any other combination of background statuses. The corresponding consistency effect for blue-collar respondents does not appear. Blue-collar background in the father's and grandfather's generation produces a mild probability that the respondent will be in farming and almost identical probabilities that he will be blue collar vs white collar. The statistics in Table IV also permit a reading of the importance of the "clogs to clogs" type of pattern mentioned earlier. Clogs to clogs predicts a tendency for respondents having blue-collar grandfathers and white-collar fathers to be downwardly mobile to the blue-collar sector themselves. From Table IV it can be observed that the rank order of probabilities for the occupational destination of such respondents is first farming, secondly white collar, and last blue collar. Thus, if anything, the "clogs to clogs" pattern occurs slightly less frequently than one would expect from the additive effects of the two previous generations. Similarly, the "reverse clogs" pattern finds no support; those with white-collar grandfathers and blue-collar fathers are most likely to remain blue collar themselves. We would not want to over-emphasize these findings and the others shown in this part of Table VI. It should be remembered that in total these three-way effects are too weak to meet the conventional .05 level of significance (Table III).

CONCLUSION

The three-generation data bear on the interpretation of the degree of ascription in Canadian society by revealing the amount of mobility taking place between non-adjacent generations and by allowing tests of whether the degree of family ascription represented by the effects of father's occupation should be adjusted upward to take account of cumulative ascription effects over another generation. To recapitulate the main findings: (1) mobility between grandfather's and grandson's occupation is, not unexpectedly, a good deal greater than that over the two generations represented by fathers and sons; (2) when a fourth generation is included in the analysis, the mobility between great-grandfathers and great-grandsons is so great that there is no statistically significant association between the two sets of scores; and (3) cumulative effects in family ascription over three generations do exist, but they are not large in terms of increased variance explained. We were able to add only slightly to the .38 correlation between father's and respondent's occupation scores by including as a predictor grandfather's occupation. Several alternative approaches to the data were taken, including the use of alternative three generation designs, sub-group analyses, and different types of analysis techniques, to see if greater evidence of cumulative ascription could be found, but none of the results indicated that such effects are very strong.[7]

TABLE IV   Two Tests of Cumulative Ascriptive Effects for Pairs of Background Statuses

1/ Lambda values from log-linear model (saturated)

Grandfather's occupation	White	Blue	White	Blue	Farm	Farm	White	Blue	Farm
Father's occupation	White	White	Blue	Blue	White	Blue	Farm	Farm	Farm
Respondent's occupation									
White	.45	−.15	−.14	−.08	−.30	.22	−.31	.23	.08
Blue	.23	−.19	.23	−.05	−.04	−.19	−.46	.24	.23
Farm	−.68	.34	−.09	.13	.34	−.04	.77	−.47	−.31

A substantial upward revision in the interpretation of ascription in Canadian society does not seem in order in light of the results. In addition, the high level of mobility between non-adjacent generations seems a consideration which should enter into assessments of the degree of ascription in the Canadian social structure. To us, the patterns of findings suggest the "achievement" interpretation of Canadian social structure, although it is achievement in a limited sense. If the correlation between father's and son's occupations is .4 it is, of course, not diminished by our finding of a low correlation among more distant generations. In addition, it is probably small consolation to those dissatisfied with their occupational status to know that, if previous trends continue, their great-grandsons or grandsons are likely to end up at any occupational level. Nevertheless, from the point of view of describing social structure, the impermanence of family status over non-adjacent generations does suggest an achievement society rather than an ascriptive one.[8]

For the general public, the long-term perpetuation of family status seems to be much less than that found at the very upper end of Canadian society by writers such as Clement (1975:72–269) or at the very bottom of the social order by studies of poverty (Gonick, 1970: Puxley, 1971: cf. Croll, 1971). Our findings do not contradict those from these other studies, of course. The two types of processes may well occur together: high over-all three-generation mobility in the general population along with low three-generation mobility in poverty and elite groups.

One of our colleagues asked, concerning our analyses: "Why do powerful families fall and, conversely, how do lowly families rise?" Our main impression from the three and four generation findings is that over several generations the randomizing process is very pervasive in the general population. What we called the "clogs to clogs" and "reverse clogs" hypotheses, our main attempts at a theory of upward and downward mobility over three generations, were not substantiated. We would conceptualize the problem the other way around, arguing that the fundamental principle is that status regresses towards the mean over generations in the general population, and that efforts in theory construction should be directed to accounting for the exceptions to this rule. Some leads towards understanding how status is perpetuated over generations are suggested by the results described herein. For instance, the white-collar sector was found the group most likely to perpetuate status over at least three generations.

Notes

1. In this paper we understand "ascription of social status" to refer to the linkage between a person's status and different components of his family background statuses. We acknowledge that there are alternative definitions in the literature. The term "mobility" is a well-known but somewhat vague label and we employ it here because it conveys more to many readers than more technically precise but awkward phrases such as "achievement-oriented." Mobility encompasses two components: 1/ the degree to which parental status is found to be unrelated to son's status and: 2/ the distance moved by sons, upwards or downwards, from father's status. Our own conception of a highly mobile society is one having comparatively high levels on both characteristics. In the following analysis the issue of achievement vs. ascription is principally addressed in the correlational analysis, while the distances moved are seen more in the matrix analysis.

2. International comparisons have shown that the correlation of father's and son's occupation seems to cluster around $r = .40$ among the western european countries and the U.S. (Svalastoga, 1965:176). Some interesting variations in mobility rates across a broader range of countries have been reported, but their importance has also been given rival interpretations (e.g., see Jones, 1969).

3. A form of mediated influence of grandfathers on grandsons would be where the grandfather trains the father to believe that high (or low) values ought to be placed on occupational success, high educational attainment, having authority and power, etc., and these values are then passed on to the grandson by the father.

4. The occupation questions were: Q76a "What is your occupation?" (Probe, "What exactly do you do?"); Q80a "Is your father living?"; Q80b "What is (was) his main occupation?" (Probe, "What kind of work does [did] he actually do? In what industry is [was] that?"); Q81a — same sequence for paternal grandfathers; Q82d — same for eldest son. The research design would have been enriched had questions been asked of female respondents as well as of males and for female family lines. We were offered the opportunity to ask mobility questions of a half-sample of males and females or of all males in the sample. We selected the latter because a half-sample would have given us too small a number of respondents of each gender (especially working females) for proper analysis. Our findings here, and some reported elsewhere (e.g., Cuneo and Curtis, 1975, on the effects of mother's education), suggest that further work including information on the mother's side should give a very modest increase in variance explained.

5. The relationship between respondent's education and his occupation ($r = .61$) also follows closely the American figure ($r = .60$, reported in Blau and Duncan, 1967:169).

6. Lipset and Bendix (1966:74) note that the American version of this saying is: "Three generations from shirt-sleeves to shirt-sleeves."

7. Results discussed more fully in the *Canadian Review of Sociology and Anthropology*, 14 (3) 1977.

8. If there is a sense in which some of the findings might be taken as lending additional serious support to the ascription interpretation of Canadian society it would be where one was, above all, impressed with the social distance (e.g., limited contacts) and temporal separation between grandfather's and grandson's statuses. One could argue that any statistical association, however weak, between the two statuses is theoreti-

cally important because with such great social distances between variables it is remarkable if the background status has any opportunity at all to affect the dependent variable. We are still left, though, with the fact of high levels of mobility from grandfather's to grandson's occupation.

References

ALLINGHAM, J.D.
1967 "Class regression: an aspect of the social stratification process." *American Sociological Review* 32 (3):442–9

APPERSON, G.L.
1929 *English Proverbs and Proverbial Phrases*. London: J.M. Dent & Sons

BLALOCK, H.M.
1967 "Causal inferences, closed populations, and measures of association." *American Political Science Review* 61:130–6

BLAU, P.M., and O.D. DUNCAN
1967 *The American Occupational Structure*. New York: Wiley

BLISHEN, B., and H. McROBERTS
1976 "A revised socioeconomic index for occupation in Canada." *Canadian Review of Sociology and Anthropology* 13 (1):71–9

BOWLES, S.C.
1972 "Schooling and equality from generation to generation." *Journal of Political Economy* 80 (3), Part II (May, June):5219–51

BROOM, L. et al.
1974 "Two perspectives on social mobility." Mimeograph, Research School of Social Sciences, Australian National University

CLEMENT, W.
1975 *The Canadian Corporate Elite*. Toronto: McClelland & Stewart

CROLL, D.A.
1971 *Poverty in Canada: Report of the Special Senate Committee on Poverty*. Ottawa: Queen's Printer

CUNEO, C.J., and J.E. CURTIS
1975 "Social ascription in the educational and occupational attainment of urban Canadians." *Canadian Review of Sociology and Anthropology* 12 (1):6–24

CURTIS, J.E., and W.G. SCOTT, eds.
1973 *Social Stratification: Canada*. Scarborough, Ontario: Prentice-Hall

DAVIDSON, P.E., and H. ANDERSON
1973 *Occupational Mobility in an American Community*. Stanford, California: Stanford University Press

DE JOCAS, Y., and G. ROCHER
1958 "Inter-generation occupational mobility in the province of Quebec." *Canadian Journal of Economics and Political Science* 23(1):57–68

DOFNY, J., and M. GARON-AUDY
1969 "Mobilitiés professionnelles au Québec." *Sociologie et Sociétés* 1 (2):277–301

DUNCAN, B., and O.D. DUNCAN
1968 "Minorities and the process of stratification." *American Sociological Review* 33 (June):356–64

DUNCAN, O.D., D. FEATHERMAN, and B. DUNCAN
1972 *Socioeconomic Background and Achievement*, New York: Seminar

FORCESE, D.
1975 *The Canadian Class Structure*, Toronto: McGraw-Hill Ryerson

GILBERT, S., and H.A. McROBERTS
 1975 "Differentiation and stratification: the issue of inequality." Pp. 91–136 in D. Forcese and S. Richer, eds., *Issues in Canadian Society: An Introduction to Sociology.* Scarborough, Ontario: Prentice-Hall

GLASS, D.V., ed.
 1954 *Social Mobility in Britain.* London: Routledge and Kegan Paul

GONICK, C.W.
 1970 "Poverty and capitalism." Pp. 66–81 in W.E. Mann, ed., *Poverty and Social Policy in Canada.* Vancouver: Copp Clark

GOODMAN, L.A.
 1972 "A general model for the analysis of surveys." *American Journal of Sociology* 77 (6):1035–86

HAUSER, R.M. et al.
 1975 "Temporal change in occupational mobility: evidence for men in the United States." *American Sociological Review* 40 (3):279–97

HODGE, R.W.
 1966 "Occupational mobility as a probability process." *Demography* 3 (1):19–34

HODGE, R.W., P.M. SIEGEL, and P.H. ROSSI
 1966 "Occupational prestige in the United States: 1925–1963." Pp. 322–34 in R. Bendix and S.M. Lipset, eds., *Class Status and Power.* New York: Free Press

HUNTER, A.A.
 1976 "On status and class in Canada." Pp. 111–54 in S.D. Johnson and G.N. Ramu, eds., *Introduction to Canadian Society.* Toronto: Macmillan

JENCKS, C.
 1972 *Inequality: A Reassessment of the Effect of Family and Schooling in America.* New York: Basic Books

JONES, F.L.
 1969 "Social mobility and industrial society: a thesis re-examined." *Sociological Quarterly* 10 (Summer):292–305.

KUBAT, D., and D. THORNTON
 1974 *A Statistical Profile of Canadian Society.* Toronto: McGraw-Hill Ryerson, 1974

LEDUC, L., H. CLARKE, J. JENSON, J. PAMMETT
 1974 "A national sample design." *Canadian Journal of Political Science* 7 (4):701–5

LIPSET, S.M., and R. BENDIX
 1966 *Social Mobility in Industrial Society.* Berkeley: University of California Press

NATIONAL OPINION RESEARCH CENTER
 1953 "Jobs and occupations: a popular evaluation." Pp. 411–26 in R. Bendix and S.M. Lipset, eds., *Class, Status and Power.* Glencoe, Illinois: Free Press

PETTIGREW, T.F.
 1973 "Review symposium." *American Journal of Sociology* 78 (May):1523–44

PINEO, P.C.
 1976 "Social mobility in Canada: the current picture." *Sociological Focus* 9 (April): 109–23

PINEO, P.C., and J. PORTER
 1967 "Occupational prestige in Canada." *Canadian Review of Sociology and Anthropology* 4(2):24–40

PORTER, J.
 1965 *The Vertical Mosaic.* Toronto: University of Toronto Press

PUXLEY, E.
 1971 *Poverty in Montreal.* Montreal: Dawson College Press

RIDGE, J.M.
1973 "Three generations." Pp. 47–71 in J.M. Ridge, ed., *Oxford Studies in Social Mobility: Working Papers*. London: Oxford University Press

SVALASTOGA, K.
1959 *Prestige Class and Mobility*. Copenhagen: Gyldendal.
1965 "Social mobility: the western european model." *Acta Sociologica* 9:175–82

TEPPERMAN, L.
1972 "The natural disruption of dynasties." *Canadian Review of Sociology and Anthropology* 9 (2):111–23
1975 *Social Mobility in Canada*. Toronto: McGraw-Hill Ryerson

TURITTIN, A.H.
1974 "Social mobility in Canada: a comparison of three provincial studies and some methodological questions." *Canadian Review of Sociology and Anthropology*: (A special publication on the occasion of the Eighth World Congress of Sociology): 163–86

WALKER, H.M., and J. LEV
1953 *Statistical Inference*. New York: Holt, Rinehart and Winston

ZELAN, J.H., E. FREEMAN, and A.H. RICHARDSON
1968 "Occupational mobility of Spanish-American war veterans and their sons." *Sociology and Social Research* 52 (3):211–23

Educational Opportunity and Reform*

Guy Rocher

INTRODUCTION

A complex and diversified system of education constitutes one of the peculiar traits of modern industrial society. The industrial, technological, and scientific revolution of the nineteenth century has created a growing number of new jobs and new occupations which require various types of general or specific training. Modern industry calls for a great variety of skilled and semi-skilled workers, various levels of technicians and clerks, as well as research people in its laboratories. Similarly, public services have grown tremendously, requiring specialized public servants in all kinds of areas — from public administration, engineering, natural and physical sciences to the more modern social sciences like economics, sociology, political science, demography, and anthropology. The development of health and welfare services, both public and private, which has accompanied urbanization, has also created new positions in hospitals, welfare services, public and private clinics, and convalescent homes.

One of the consequences of the creation of these new occupations has been the development of a more and more complex educational system. Primary education has become progressively generalized; the traditional rural one-classroom school has been replaced by central schools, and bussing children from home to school and back home has become the rule; after the last world war, secondary education became more and more generalized as well as more diversified; vocational and technical schools multiplied to meet the requirements of the labor force in various areas; higher education grew as it had never done in the past. The idea that children needed to be educated as thoroughly as possible so that they could earn a living in the new industrial society became plain common sense in the Western world.

At the same time, requirements for entering old as well as new occupations rapidly increased. Jobs which required only an elementary school education a few years ago are now open only to people who have completed high school and sometimes even college. Competence is judged foremost by a diploma.

In this context, the relationship between education and society has changed and become extremely complex. In the pre-literate or traditional society, educa-

---

* Abridged from D. Forcese and S. Richer, eds., *Issues in Canadian Society*, Prentice-Hall of Canada, Ltd. (1973), Chap. 5.

tion was part of daily life within the structures of family and kinship. In modern industrial society, new types of institutions (nurseries, kindergartens, schools, colleges, universities of various sorts) have replaced the family and kinship in at least part of their socializing function.

It is impossible to deal here with all the problems linked to the new relationship between education and society. We will focus on one of them, which is particularly important and which has been the subject of many discussions and much research: economic and social inequalities with regard to the educational system.

EQUALITARIAN AND DEMOCRATIC IDEOLOGY

Because it has become so vital to the industrial society as well as its members, the educational system comes necessarily to be related to a great variety of values, value judgments, aspirations and expectations. As a matter of fact, the educational system is built on values and value judgments, of which it is a reflection. Each society has its own image of what its educational system should be or, one might more precisely say, there are several such images in each society, more or less conflicting and more or less contradictory. These images are the expression of judgments on the society as a whole, of wishes and hopes for oneself and for the society to which one belongs, of frustrations that one suffers for oneself or for those one loves. It is in that sense that one can say that the educational system becomes part of various ideologies.

This is particularly clear in modern society. Thus, since the beginning of this century and still more *since the end of the Second World War, the ideology of a democratic and equalitarian educational system has become dominant in the Western world*. This ideology has been expressed in various arguments, such as reports by royal commissions, official programs for curricula proposed or imposed by departments of education, speeches by politicians, and writings of experts on education. Summarizing the content of this ideology is not easy. But we can at least introduce it here by proceeding to underline three of its main traits.

First, *democratizing the system of education means making education not the privilege of the few, but bringing it to every citizen as his right, a right which is guaranteed by official public declarations and documents, such as a constitution or a law*. This means simply that the educational system is open to any citizen without discrimination of race, religion, sex, age, or income.

This right of every citizen to formal education has been expressed still more firmly as an obligation: in practically every country in the world, and especially those of the Western world, the state has taken upon itself the authority to enforce compulsory education for all children up to a certain age, generally fourteen or fifteen years old. The ideological basis of compulsory education is that the state must protect the right of each child to receive an education, even against the will or the authority of the parents.

Secondly, because of his right to an education, *each citizen is now called upon to share in the public financial support of the educational system*. Education is not secured solely or mainly by private institutions any more as was the case for a long time when the churches directly assumed the responsibility of educating the people. Today, in nearly all countries of the world, the state has taken the responsibility of supporting or financing a public network of schools, as well as sometimes a parallel network of private institutions, and each citizen is called upon to contribute to this financing, through a system of taxation.

In some countries, the state has refused to subsidize private institutions, in the name of educational democracy. This is the case in the United States, and was the case for a long time in France. However, generally speaking, most states have reached some kind of agreement with private institutions or with some groups of private citizens, and have agreed to assume a part or even sometimes the whole of their expenses.

Thirdly, *the most important trait of the democratization of education is probably the equality of opportunities for all.* Theoretically speaking, one of the main objectives of the modern democratic society is to eliminate the various factors of inequality which still exist and which inhibit groups or categories of citizens who have fewer chances than others of benefiting from the educational system. At least, this is the official ideology of the democratic society. It is the image it wants to create of itself and it is the objective it aims to realize. But, precisely because it is an ambitious and difficult objective, it is clearly far from being realized. The questions that are being raised more and more strongly are: "Is the democratic modern society fair to all its groups of citizens?" and "Are all groups or classes or categories of citizens treated on an equal footing, especially in terms of educational accessibility?" These questions are becoming increasingly the focus of much research and discussion among social scientists.

THE THESIS OF SOCIAL REPRODUCTION

In North American society, it has generally been taken for granted, for quite a long time, that the school was the normal channel of mobility open to all citizens who were willing to use it, since it was available to all without any kind of discrimination. Thanks to its educational system, North American society was regarded as having no closed class sytem, but as being, on the contrary, a society where social stratification was largely open and where more social mobility was possible. With a general system of education, what Vilfredo Pareto has called the "circulation of elites" was possible and, in fact, partly realized. One did not need to be born within the ruling class in order to accede to a position of power, influence or wealth.

More recently, this view of an open society, which was shared by most American sociologists for many years, has come to be more and more seriously questioned. *Many sociologists, both American and European, have recently supported the thesis that the educational system is not a channel of social mobility, but rather a factor of stagnation of the stratification system.* This point of view had already been expressed by Robert and Helen Lynd in their pioneering study of Muncie, Indiana, published in 1929. They described the ways in which the school served to inhibit the educational aspirations of children from the lower social classes. Since then, the sorting process of the educational system, which plays against the lower class children who are more or less forced either to drop out or to go into the vocational and technical classes or schools, has been described by some other sociologists, like Warner, Havighurst and Loeb (1944), as well as August B. Hollingshead (1949). This view of the educational system has been expressed still more strongly by critical philosophers and sociologists, like Paul Goodman (1962) and E.Z. Friedenberg (1959).

In France, the thesis of social reproduction was developed by two sociologists, Bourdieu and Passeron (1970). According to these authors, the educational system is not an agent of social change. In industrial society, its action has been rather to the advantage of the middle classes and the social groups which are already privileged and which have always been so. *On account of the cultural as well as the economic obstacles with which it opposes the mobility of the lower classes, the system of education reproduces indefinitely existing social inequalities, and can even create wider discrepancies and more inequalities.* Bourdieu and Passeron founded their thesis on an empirical study of the social origins of French students at the Faculté des Lettres of the University of Paris (1964).

The thesis of social reproduction brings up the problem of the relationship between the educational system and society, not in a static but in a dynamic way. The fundamental question that it raises is the following: Is the system of education a factor of social change, as has long been thought, or does it simply reflect or even amplify the actual system of social stratification?

This is precisely the topic that will be dealt with in this chapter. In the first part, we will bring to light the main inequalities that contradict the official equalitarian democratic ideology and that are related to the role of the school in modern society: social class inequalities, regional differences, racial and ethnic discrimination, cultural disparities. In the second part, we will try to assess the role of education with regard to social change in the modern industrial society.

SOCIAL INEQUALITIES

Socio-Economic Inequalities

A few years ago, having access to high school was far from being as general as it is now. Table I shows the rapid and drastic change which has taken place over the last decade throughout Canada. While 66 percent of Canadian 14- to 17-year-olds (male and female) were enrolled in grade nine in 1960–61, 98 percent (male) and 97 percent (female) were to be found in grade nine in 1970–71. The percentage increase has been marked for each province, and for girls as well as boys.

Table II provides similar information, still more refined. It gives us the "retention rate" (adjusted for interprovincial and international movement of population), that has been calculated for 1960, 1965, and 1970. This rate compares the enrollment in grade 11 to the enrollment of the same age group in grade two, nine years earlier. For Canada as a whole, the retention rate has jumped from 50 to 80 percent over a period of ten years, a most remarkable increase indeed.

On account of this increase, starting in the 1950s and still more in the 1960s, inequalities of educational opportunity have been measured more and more in terms of unequal access to higher education. In this respect, a great many studies

TABLE I   Grade 9 Enrolment for Canada and Provinces, Selected Years*

Province	1960–1961		1965–1966		1970–1971	
	M	F	M	F	M	F
	%		%		%	
Newfoundland	50.8	52.9	55.0	55.1	62.5	66.1
Prince Edward Island	50.3	68.6	68.8	78.1	76.9	94.8
Nova Scotia	53.9	68.7	66.5	71.6	76.8	85.8
New Brunswick	55.8	63.6	65.2	72.4	81.6	85.7
Atlantic Provinces	53.6	60.0	63.2	67.8	74.4	80.8
Quebec	43.9	43.9	75.3	72.7	98.7	98.1
Ontario	83.1	82.9	98.9	93.1	107.5	103.2
Manitoba	70.2	69.9	83.5	80.9	93.5	91.8
Saskatchewan	74.9	78.8	85.5	86.1	90.2	93.2
Alberta	85.2	84.5	92.0	88.8	99.0	96.6
British Columbia	83.2	84.6	93.0	89.7	99.0	96.4
Western Provinces	79.4	80.6	89.4	87.0	96.5	95.1
Canada	66.1	66.8	85.4	82.4	98.5	97.1

* Source: *Education in Canada, 1973* (Ottawa: Statistics Canada, 1973), p. 338. Reproduced by permission of Information Canada.

TABLE II   Retention Rate for Canada and Provinces, Selected Years*

Province	1960–1961 %	1965–1966 %	1970–1971 %
Newfoundland	38.1	46.3	65.6
Prince Edward Island	33.5	55.4	64.2
Nova Scotia	47.4	62.3	69.7
New Brunswick	44.0	55.0	68.2
Atlantic Provinces	43.1	55.2	67.8
Quebec	34.2	61.3	81.1
Ontario	57.0	69.9	81.7
Manitoba	61.4	75.4	81.2
Saskatchewan	56.3	70.7	78.4
Alberta	67.1	74.1	84.2
British Columbia	71.2	75.8	84.0
Western Provinces	64.5	74.2	82.7
Canada	49.8	66.6	80.0

* Source: *Education in Canada, 1973* (Ottawa: Statistics Canada, 1973), p. 358. Reproduced by permission of Information Canada.

undertaken in different countries all converge towards the same conclusion: upper class children have more chances of completing high school and entering college than lower class children. This conclusion is valid for Canada as well, as far as can be judged from the available data.

For instance, the Canadian sociologist John Porter analyzed class differences with regard to the educational system (1965). Tables III, IV, and V, reproduced from his book, illustrate class inequalities in Canada. We see from Table III that the father's occupation has a strong influence on the children's chances of getting access to higher education. In Table IV, it is the influence of the father's level of education that is shown, and in Table V, the influence of the family income.

These three variables (the father's occupation, the parents' level of education, the family income) are generally regarded as the three main factors that determine the socio-economic status of the family and its members. It is clear from the three tables that these three variables all have the same influence, always playing against the underprivileged and in favor of the children who belong to upper class families.

These class differences are both reflected in and reinforced by regional or geographic inequalities. For instance, important differences exist in the large industrial cities between the schools that are to be found in the underprivileged areas and the schools of the middle class suburbs. These differences have already been brought to light in the United States, especially by Patricia Sexton (1961; 1967) and James B. Conant (1959). In Canada, a study undertaken a few years ago in Montreal by the Catholic School Board[1] shows that the proportion of first-grade children who fail differs greatly from one district to another in the same city. In the districts of Montreal defined as "underprivileged," the number of children who failed their first year of primary school was much higher than both in Rosemont, a relatively middle class district, and in the total population of children attending the schools of the Catholic School Board.

The same differences can be observed from one city to another. The rate of school retention is much higher in residential cities and towns than in working class cities and towns. For example, in the city of Outremont, which constitutes a middle class enclave within the metropolitan area of Montreal, the proportion of 20- to 24-year-old men and women who still go to school is much higher than in working class cities like Oshawa and Hull, where the proportion of young men and women of the same age who are still in school is very low.

Why the Socio-Economic Inequalities?

All the inequalities that have just been described call for an explanation. Where do they come from? How are they maintained? Why are they transmitted from one generation to another?

In order to answer these questions, it will be useful to start from another disparity which is related to those we have just described. All the studies in Europe as well as in North America have proven the existence of a high correlation between the socio-economic status and the I.Q. of children. Children who grow up in underprivileged urban districts or in rural areas far away from the urban centers have a lower mean I.Q. than other children. For instance, a broad survey made in France in 1944 by a group of psychologists and social scientists clearly demonstrated these disparities (Institut national d'études démographiques, 1950; 1954). Many studies have come to the same conclusion in the United States.[2] In Canada, the same correlation has been observed in Montreal. The research undertaken by the Catholic School Board, mentioned earlier, brought to light the difference between the I.Q. of lower class children and upper class children, shown in Table VI. Moreover, this relation between I.Q. and socio-economic status is to be found again in the relationship between school achievement and socio-economic status. Lower class children have lower grades, less academic motivation and are more likely to fail, even in their first years in school, than upper class or middle class children.

This question has recently been the object of passionate debate among American social scientists, following an article by Jensen (1969), who supported

TABLE III   Percentage Distribution of University Students' Parents by Occupational Level, 1956*

Occupational level	Students' parents	Total labor force
Proprietors and managers	25.7	8.3
Professionals	24.9	7.1
Clericals and sales	12.3	16.5
Skilled and semi-skilled	21.1	30.6
Agriculture	10.9	15.7
Laborers	5.1	20.5
Total	100.0	100.0

* Source: John Porter, *The Vertical Mosaic*, Chapter VI, Table XXII. © University of Toronto Press 1965.

TABLE IV   Distribution of Grade 7 Students according to I.Q., in Selected Districts of Montreal, 1963–1964*

District	Higher third %	Middle third %	Lower third %
St. Henri/Pointe St–Charles	24.0	30.0	46.0
Centre–Ville	19.0	36.0	45.0
Mile–End	21.0	33.0	46.0
Centre–Sud	24.0	32.0	44.0
Hochelaga	29.0	32.0	39.0
Rosemont	38.0	35.5	26.5
Montreal Catholic School Board	34.2	33.3	32.5

* Source: Pierre Bélanger and Guy Rocher (eds.), *Ecole et Société au Québec* (Montreal: HMH, 1970), p. 340

TABLE V   Percentage Distribution of University Student Families and All Canadian Families, by Family Income Groups, 1956*

Family income ($)	Student families	All Canadian families
10,000 and over	15.2	3.3
7,000–9,999	12.2	8.4
5,000–6,999	21.3	18.7
4,000–4,999	14.8	15.7
3,000–3,999	17.5	22.9
2,000–2,999	11.6	17.0
Under 2,000	7.4	14.0
Total	100.0	100.0

* Source: John Porter, *The Vertical Mosaic*, Chapter VI, Table XXI. © University of Toronto Press, 1965.

the view that I.Q. is heritable and therefore largely stable. I.Q. cannot be increased, according to Jensen, by a change of environment or by special educational programs. Jensen applied his conclusions to the black population. But his reasoning also applied to lower class white children. As opposed to Jensen's, the viewpoint most generally held by social scientists is that intelligence is a product of both heredity and environment, and that a change of environment or special educational programs can upgrade the I.Q. of children (Senna, 1973).

For our purposes, three main conclusions have come out of that debate. First, it is clear that *I.Q. is not intelligence as such, but rather a measurement by specific tests of a type of mental or intellectual activity*. Second, the mental ability measured by I.Q. tests is *less familiar and less natural to lower class children* than it is to upper class or middle class children. Third, it is precisely this very type of intellectual activity that is *valued at school and that is assessed in the classroom*.

The type of intellectual activity that is favored by the school is very largely verbal. It is based on the manipulation of abstract and general concepts which call for a certain capacity to use language and symbolic communication. It is more and more generally believed that there lies probably one of the main advantages that upper and middle class children have in school. They have been better initiated in their families to the manipulation and use of abstract thought, to the type of language that is most valued in the classroom, and to the patterns of reasoning that are generally used by educators. A study made in Halifax, N.S. by Barbara Clark (1971) among the population of underprivileged black children showed that a pre-school program helped these children to develop the intellectual capacities and aptitudes that lead to school achievement and to better grades.

Some sociologists, psychologists, and linguists have supported the view that language deficiencies, or what some have rather called language differences, are responsible for the fact that working class children have less success in school, drop out in greater numbers and are so weakly represented in higher education (Williams, 1970).

Still more broadly, it has been pointed out that the school is a reflection of the spirit, the culture, the aspirations of the middle class. Therefore, working or lower class children have more difficulty in adapting to the school climate than middle class children. To most of the lower class children, the school climate always remains foreign, to the point where they feel almost marginal and more or less unwelcome in the schools. This viewpoint has been expressed in the United States by sociologists like Cohen (1955), Friedenberg (1959), Conant (1961) and Riessman (1962); it has also been presented by British sociologists like Halsey, Floud and Martin (1956), and by French sociologists like Bourdieu and Passeron (1964), and Baudelot and Establet (1971).

For people living in underprivileged districts of the cities, or for lower working class people, as well as for those living in rural areas, especially in remote areas, sending their children to a college seems practically impossible. There is a kind of *socio-cultural distance* between themselves and higher education. The economic obstacles or the geographic distance appears to be still more serious because of the socio-cultural distance from which they are perceived. Therefore, the educational and professional aspirations of the parents for their children are still weaker and lower, because they do not think it possible for their children to have access to higher education. Because of the attitude of their parents, the children themselves are not motivated to enter higher education. They rather feel that this is something for "the others," i.e., those who are both economically and intellectually fit for advanced studies. Lower class children do not enter higher education because they do not aspire to do so; they do not aspire to enter higher education because they do not think they are fit for advanced studies; they do not think they are fit for higher education because they have never been told that they can have access to higher education.

This is the vicious circle that is sometimes called a "self-fulfilling prophecy." The self-fulfilling prophecy is quite a common phenomenon in social life: things happen because people think they will happen the way they do and because people expect or want them to happen the way they do. The difference between the educational and vocational aspirations of middle or lower class children is a nice case in point.

One could add that the teachers also contribute to the self-fulfilling prophecy. In many subtle and more or less conscious ways, they tend to discourage the lower class children from aspiring to higher education. They operate a discreet but efficient selection: they push to higher education only the lower class children who have a very high I.Q., who are totally motivated and whose parents support the children. Consequently, fewer lower class children than middle class children will be supported by their teachers in their aspirations to higher education.

Whether or not the teachers themselves come from middle class families is immaterial. The significant fact is that the middle class becomes their class of reference with regard to the values they possess, the norms they follow, and the aspirations they have for their students. More broadly, the image of the society and of the conditions for one to succeed in that society comes directly from the ideology of the middle class.

Racial and Ethnic Inequalities

The racial inequalities in the access to education have been amply illustrated in research in the United States. James Conant (1961), Patricia Sexton (1961), and many others have shown how the American blacks and the Puerto Ricans have never benefited from the same educational services as the white population. The buildings, the quality of the equipment, the teachers, the curricula have long been of lower quality for the blacks. Therefore, only very few black children could compete with white children at college entrance examinations and tests. More recently, the same kind of discrimination has been brought to light with regard to the Chicanos, the Mexican Americans.

Racism of one kind or another has not been completely absent from the Canadian educational scene. One case has been reported by Hobart and Brant, a sociologist and an anthropologist, with regard to the Eskimos of the Western Canadian Arctic. After several months of field work in 1963, 1964, and 1965, they drew a comparison between the treatment of the Eskimos in Greenland by the Danish Government and the Eskimos of the Canadian Arctic. Here is how they summarize the situation of the Canadian Eskimos:

> The Canadian Government has almost completely ignored the Arctic during most of the twentieth century ... There was no systematic provision of education for Eskimos until 1959... The educational system which has come into existence in the Western Arctic, at first under mission auspices and, since 1952, increasingly under Federal auspices, contrasts as sharply with the Greenland system as have the Danish and the Canadian Arctic administrative philosophies. The educational system in the Western Arctic is characterized by these features: continuous use of non-native teachers, in the past predominantly clergy, changing to lay teachers today; throughout its history, instruction given wholly in English; establishment and heavy utilization, from the beginning, of residential schools, with latter-day emphasis upon large units; curriculum almost entirely oriented to the southern Canadian culture and value system; and minimal attempts to produce text materials appropriate to the Arctic... Obviously, much of contemporary Eskimo education in the Western Canadian Arctic is inappropriate, and perhaps even dis-educative from the standpoint of preparation for the life children will lead as adults.[3]

Similar conclusions have been reached by several other anthropologists who have worked among the Eskimos.[4]

Moreover, in a young and complex country like Canada, which is bicultural in its origins and which has become multicultural as a result of successive waves of immigration, one can also expect to find ethnic inequalities. The greatest disparity is to be found between the French Canadians and the British-born Canadians. This disparity was investigated at the end of the nineteenth century by the first Canadian sociologist, Léon Gérin.[5] Using the census data up to 1891, Léon Gérin showed that the educational level of French Canadians was much lower than that of British-born Canadians. A remarkable difference could be observed within Quebec, where the districts with an Anglophone majority had a much higher average educational level than the districts with a Francophone majority. Outside of Quebec, in Ontario and New Brunswick, the districts where a significant proportion of Francophones were to be found had a lower level of education than the others.

Léon Gérin explained this phenomenon by the manner in which children were trained and educated in their families. According to him, the Anglophone families helped develop initiative, craftsmanship, respect for knowledge, a love of work, and competitive individualism. In the French Canadian families, togetherness and belongingness were more developed, at the expense of personal ambition and competitiveness.

Seventy years later, a similar analysis was undertaken, using the data of the 1961 Census (Rocher, 1965). It appears from this study that *in the 1950s, the French Canadians still had a much lower level of education than the British-born Canadians, that they were ill-equipped, intellectually and professionally, for the industrial society in which they lived*. There appears therefore to have been a continuity in time, both in the disparity between French- and English-speaking Canadians, and in their attitudes towards education. But an important change has taken place since 1961. The so-called "quiet revolution" which started about that time brought with it a drastic change in the educational and professional aspirations of the French Canadian population.

However, if it is less acute, the problem of ethnic disparities has not been solved. It is still there and needs to be understood. The explanation of the phenomenon which was given by Léon Gérin (1964) was "culturalist" in the sense that he was explaining the lack of interest in education among French Canadians through the cultural climate in the family and kinship, and the types of inter-personal links that it developed and maintained. More recently, another explanation was provided by the sociologists Jacques Dofny and Marcel Rioux (1964). They present the hypothesis that the French Canadians can be regarded as what they have called an "ethnic social class." According to them, it is not enough to define the French Canadians as an ethnic group, because it does not provide us with the right concept to analyze and understand their behavior and attitudes. The social class concept, they say, applies very well to the French Canadian group, and what we already know of class behavior and attitudes may help us understand the French Canadians. As a matter of fact, this type of analysis was made more or less explicitly by American sociologists speaking of the black population. Like the American blacks, the French Canadians constitute an underprivileged economic group whose labor force serves mainly economic interests which are linguistically and culturally foreign to them. The long-standing lack of interest of the French Canadians in education, their slow integration into the industrial society, their refusal to accept modern culture, show a behavior typical of an underprivileged social class, which feels alienated from the economic advantages and benefits of the industrial capitalistic society.

This line of analysis does not necessarily contradict Léon Gérin's. On the contrary, the two can be fused together. The familistic behavior described by

Léon Gérin can be regarded as one aspect of the general attitudes of the French Canadians when defined as an ethnic social class.

French Canadians outside Quebec

The foregoing explanation is probably valid for the Quebec French Canadians, but the situation of the French Canadians outside Quebec is different enough to call for other elements of explanation. What has just been said is probably not untrue of the French Canadians living in Ontario or New Brunswick, and Léon Gérin as well as Dofny and Rioux do not seem to question the validity of their explanation, both for the French Canadians outside Quebec and for those living in Quebec.

On the other hand, the context within which the French Canadians in Quebec and those living outside Quebec have to function is so different that it is hard to believe that other elements of explanation should not be added in order fully to understand the behavior of the French Canadians outside Quebec. As a matter of fact, a study recently made in Ontario shows that the lower level of education of the French Canadians living in that province is closely related to the meaning that the public school has for them and the threat they think it represents for themselves and their culture.[6] As is well illustrated by this research, *no other ethnic group in Ontario finds itself in a situation as conflicting as the French Canadians*. For the latter, the public school is in open contradiction with both their national identity and their fundamental values. This is why the French Canadians in Ontario have a lower level of education, not only than the British-born Canadians, but also than practically all the other ethnic groups in Ontario.

Indeed, some ethnic or religious groups in Canada voluntarily restrict the formal education of their children. This has been the case with the Mennonites, a religious group which has a strong internal cohesion and tends at the same time to isolate itself from the rest of society. The Mennonites, at least the traditional groups, do not allow education beyond the age of 14, that is, only up to the age of compulsory education. They believe that after the age of 14, their children must be withdrawn from school in order to avoid being submitted to a pernicious influence and being cut off from their religious community (Kurokawa, 1971). One could also mention the case of other anabaptist sects, like the Hutterites and Amish, who cut themselves off still more drastically from the rest of society, to a point where they may refuse to send their children to public school.

These attitudes differ greatly from those of the French Canadians, in that they reflect an explicit rejection of school and what it represents in modern society. As to the French Canadian group of Ontario, the research reported above has underlined an ambivalence towards public school: the French Canadians would like to see their children get more education, as they value education; but at the same time, they want to resist the cultural influence of the school on their children.

THE EDUCATIONAL SYSTEM AND SOCIAL CHANGE

School as a Channel of Social Mobility

It is true, as we have illustrated above, that the culturally, socially or economically privileged social classes are disproportionately represented in the educational system as we approach higher education; but it is also true that *a certain proportion of lower class children have access to colleges and universities*. This is clear from Tables III, IV, and V. The parents of about half the students registered in Canadian colleges and universities in 1956 were clericals, skilled and semi-skilled workers, farmers, laborers, i.e., below the occupational level which most of these students could expect to achieve (Table III). Seventy percent of the students registered in the Arts and Science faculties of Canadian universities in 1961 had achieved a higher level of education than their parents (Table IV). The family income of 35 percent of Canadian university students in 1956 was under $4,000 per annum.

Of course, these figures are not proportionate to the distribution of the total labor force or to the distribution of income among Canadian families. Had the general population been "normally" represented in higher education, 54 percent of the university students would have come from families with an income of less than $4,000, instead of 35 percent, and only 15 percent would have had parents in the two upper educational levels (proprietors and managers, professionals) instead of 50 percent. But this fact, which reflects the process of social reproduction discussed earlier, must not hide the other fact that there is a certain amount of social mobility through education which brings some fluidity to the system of social stratification.

On the whole, the obstacle of social class to higher education is therefore not absolute. Some other factors must also be taken into account, which can help a certain proportion of lower or working class children enter higher education. Three main factors may break the social class barrier: *a high I.Q., strong motivation on the part of the student, high educational and professional aspirations on the part of the parents and the student*. When these three factors meet, lower and working class children have a chance of staying in school as long as they can or as they wish.

Indeed, in many cases more intelligence, work, and energy may be necessary for lower and working class children to achieve the same educational level as middle class boys and girls. They have to break more resistance and overcome more obstacles. But the fact remains that for these children, the school really is a *channel of upward mobility* in terms of educational achievement, occupational level, and income. And the number of lower and working class children who have benefited from this type of mobility has increased enormously over the last three or four decades, and again since the figures just quoted were calculated. This can be interpreted as a contribution of the educational system to the greater fluidity of the class system in modern industrial societies, especially North American societies.

On the other hand, a very important distinction must be made here between the individual level and the societal level. It can be said that the educational system plays the role of the channel of individual mobility for a certain proportion of young men and women, but the *overall system of social class and social stratification is not modified at all*. For instance, Spady (1967) has shown that in the United States, the absolute number of undergraduates and graduates from the working class has increased steadily over the last few years, but that the same trend can also be observed at the same tempo for middle class children. Therefore, there are more working class children at the college and university level, but the representation of the working class compared with the middle class remains the same. This means that more individuals have been mobile, but that the system has not changed. Although no specific study has been made of the same phenomenon in Canada, it is most probable that the same conclusions can be reached for this country.

Social mobility at the individual level may therefore conceal the stability or the stagnation of the social structure, as well as the process of social reproduction that still goes on. Because it brings some satisfaction to a certain proportion of the lower and working class, this type of mobility can also serve to justify a policy that favors the status quo of the society and that blocks the social, economic or political changes that the state should undertake or at least support or encourage. In that sense, the greater fluidity of the social stratification system for individuals can at the same time be an obstacle to change for the society as a whole.

The Spirit of Educational Reforms

A second aspect of the dynamic role of the educational system in society needs to be underlined. On the one hand, it is generally said that the school is essentially conservative and that the educational system is an agent of social reproduction. On the other hand and at the same time, it is precisely in the educational institutions, especially at the level of higher education, that one finds the most radical questioning of current values, present social structures, and established ideologies. Thus, the educational institution appears as the main place where some cultural changes take place in modern society.

Particularly since the last world war, education in industrial societies as well as in developing societies has been the object of many studies, inquiries, seminars, and symposiums, all of which were aimed at operating more or less drastic changes in the content as well as in the pedagogy of teaching at all levels, and adapting the educational system to the needs and the spirit of modern society. A systematic analysis of all these works has not yet been made, but it is most certain that one could extract out of them an ideology of change which, if fully realized, would modify not only the system of education but the system of modern society as well.

This ideology of educational reform has been characterized mainly by two basic principles which have served as the main guidelines of thought. The first was the *democratization of education*. All the reforms which were proposed were inspired by the principle that secondary education must be open to all, and that post-secondary education must be open to all those who are able to enter it. Put in different terms, this principle might be expressed in the following way: *each student should have the opportunity to benefit by an education which corresponds to his capacities, his tastes, and his interests, and he should be able to pursue his studies in the field or fields in which he is interested as far as he can or will go.* This principle was based on the ideology of "equal opportunities for all" and on the confidence that this principle could be implemented. In practice, this meant the organization of a public system of education at all levels, free education for all and at all levels, and a system of scholarships for those who need more help than just free education. Moreover, the democratization of education called for reforms of the school itself, in order to make the educational structures more flexible, to modify the pedagogy and to organize the counselling of students.

The second basic principle was probably less explicit and less generalized than the first, but it was probably more important than the first. Put in simple terms, it was a proposal to *develop to their utmost all the capacities and aptitudes of each student*. The traditional system of education in Western societies aimed at the exclusive development of intelligence, and only a certain type of intelligence. The proposed reforms tried to broaden this concept of intelligence and to put forward a more general and more global training with the view that the traditional concept of intelligence was too limited and that it needed to be much more diversified. For instance, the general trends of the educational reforms of the last few years have all been focused on a greater freedom of expression, more spontaneity and creativity on the part of the student, more imagination in his work. Following this line of thought, all the reforms proposed have aimed at the liberation of resources which have not been exploited enough in the human being up to now.

Of course, these principles for educational reform could not be implemented completely or perfectly. It is not easy to persuade a large body of teachers and professors to modify the teaching and training methods to which they themselves were submitted and which they have been practising for several years. It is not easy to change the mentality or the expectations of parents with regard to the school, nor to convince the administrators of the educational system to undertake difficult transformations of the same system. One can say, therefore, that educational reform has met with serious resistance on the part of various groups: teachers, parents, students, administrators, as well as public opinion in general.

And yet, in spite of this resistance, one must recognize that the proposed reforms have been partly implemented. And where they have been implemented, they have sometimes clearly contributed to significant changes, not only in the educational system, but in society as a whole. For instance, Stephen Richer (1974) measured the consequences of some pedagogical changes. He spent several hours in a primary school in urban Canada, observing the interactions between the children and their teachers in teacher-centered classrooms and in student-centered classrooms. He concludes:

> The open classes (student-centered) are relatively successful in elevating working-class interaction primarily by virtue of this capacity to elicit greater *student* initiation of relationships with the teacher. Such an atmosphere appears much more

compatible with their life style than does the traditional closed classroom (teacher-centered).

In sum, the study documents lower than chance teacher interactions for working class children in closed classrooms, and higher than chance interactions in open settings. In the educational literature open classes have typically been advocated on philosophical and/or pedagogical grounds. This paper suggests that such learning environments may have an additional unanticipated consequence; namely, enhancing the probability of success of working-class children in our schools.

More generally speaking, one can say that educational reforms and the spirit they reflected have had some impact on public opinion and sometimes social policies. They have become the object of public discussions, which is at least a way of not denying the need for them. And, as often happens, even those who were opposed to the reforms were progressively influenced by the new spirit and the new mentality which inspired them. Even though it is a far cry from what might have taken place, one can say that an important educational reform has begun, that the spirit of the schools as well as of the colleges has changed, that the objectives of education have been questioned and re-evaluated, that the role and the function of teachers and professors have changed and that, on the whole, many new ideas have circulated in the educational milieu.

Marcel Fournier (1973) has analyzed the changes that the introduction of the teaching of the social sciences has brought about in the political climate and social policies of Quebec. He traces part of the so-called "quiet revolution" which took place in Quebec in the 50s and still more in the 60s to the role played by the Faculty of Social Sciences at Laval University in the 30s and 40s.

On the whole, it is hard to find another sector of modern society where more drastic reforms have been proposed, and where the established structures and the current ideology have been questioned to the same extent. Compared to education, the rest of society has changed rather slowly and very little in the last two or three decades. Thus, one can say that the educational system has served as a kind of laboratory where current social values and social attitudes have changed most rapidly and to the largest extent. In this manner, the system of education has served as an indirect agent of social change and has played the role of a dynamic element in modern society.

CONCLUSION

One general conclusion which comes out of all that has been said here is surely that the relations between education and society are far more complex than is generally assumed. It is surely not true to say that society is what education makes it. But one cannot say either that education simply reflects what society is. There is between the two a network of interactions that is exceedingly complex. The educational system is the mirror of a society, its social stratification, its culture, its dominant ideologies, its political structure. But it is also the main place where society and culture are discussed and questioned, and where the roots of social criticism are generally to be found. It is therefore true to say at the same time that the educational system is conservative and that it is the seedbed of the social changes to come.

Notes

1. Quoted in *Ecole et Société au Québec*, edited by Pierre W. Bélanger and Guy Rocher (Montreal: HMH, 1970), pp.341–342.
2. See especially A.L. Baldwin, Urie Bronfenbrenner, D.C. McClelland, J.L. Strodlick, *Talent and Society* (Princeton, N.J., Van Nostrand, 1958); J.S. Coleman *et al.*, *Equality of Educational Opportunity* (U.S. Dept. HEW, 1966); C. Jencks, *Inequality* (New York, Basic Books, Inc., 1972); G.S. Lesser, G. Fifer, D.H. Clark, "Mental abilities of children from different social-class and cultural groups," *Monog. Soc. Res. Child Develop.*, 1965.
3. C.W. Hobart and C.S. Brant, "Eskimo Education, Danish and Canadian: A Comparison." Reprinted from *The Canadian Review of Sociology and Anthropology*, 3:2 (1966), by permission of the authors and the publisher.
4. See especially the chapters by J. Ferguson, G.J. Uranos and Margaret Stephens, John and Irma Honigman, and Frank J. Vallee, in *Native Peoples*, edited by Jean Leonard Elliott (Scarborough, Ontario: Prentice-Hall of Canada, 1971).
5. Léon Gérin's analysis has been summarized and discussed by Guy Rocher, "La sociologie de l'éducation dans l'oeuvre de Léon Gérin" in *Ecole et Société au Québec*, edited by Pierre W. Bélanger and Guy Rocher (Montreal: HMH, 1970).
6. *Report of the Royal Commission on Bilingualism and Biculturalism*, Vol. II (1968), pp. 80–94.

References

BAUDELOT, CHRISTIAN, AND ROGER ESTABLET,
L'École Capitaliste en France. Paris: Franois Marpero, 1971.

BÉLANGER, PIERRE W., AND GUY ROCHER, EDS.,
Ecole et Société au Québec. Montreal: HMH, 1970.

BOURDIEU, PIERRE, AND JEAN-CLAUDE PASSERON,
Les Héritiers. Paris: Editions de Minuit, 1964.
_____ *La Reproduction*. Paris: Editions de Minuit, 1970.

CLARK, BARBARA S.,
"Pre-school Programs and Black Children," in Jean Leonard Elliott (ed.), *Immigrant Groups*. Scarborough: Prentice-Hall of Canada, 1971, ch. 8.

COHEN, ALBERT K.,
Delinquent Boys. Glencoe, Ill.: The Free Press, 1955.

CONANT, JAMES B.,
The American High School. New York: McGraw-Hill, 1959.
_____ *Slums and Suburbs*. New York: McGraw-Hill, 1961.

DOFNY, JACQUES, AND MARCEL RIOUX,
"Social Class in French Canada," in Marcel Rioux and Yves Martin (eds.), *French-Canadian Society*. Toronto: McClelland and Stewart (The Carleton Library), 1964, pp. 307–318.

FELDMAN, KENNETH A., AND THEODORE M. NEWCOMB,
The Impact of College on Students. San Francisco: Jossey-Bass Inc., 1970.

FLOUD, J., A.H. HALSEY, AND F.M. MARTIN,
Social Class and Educational Opportunity. London: Heinemann, 1956.

FOURNIER, MARCEL,
"L'institutionnalisation des sciences sociales au Québec," *Sociologie et sociétés*, 1 (May, 1973), pp. 27–57.

FRIEDENBERG, E.Z.,
Coming of Age in America. New York: Random House, 1965.
———— *The Vanishing Adolescent*, Boston: Beacon Press, 1959.

GÉRIN, LÉON,
"The French-Canadian Family: Its Strengths and Weaknesses," in Marcel Rioux and Yves Martin (eds.), *French-Canadian Society*. Toronto: McClelland and Stewart, 1964, pp. 32–57.

GOODMAN, PAUL,
Compulsory Mis-education. New York: Knopf, 1962.

HOBART, C.W., AND C.S. BRANT,
"Eskimo Education, Danish and Canadian: A Comparison," *Canadian Review of Sociology and Anthropology*, III, 2 (May, 1966), pp. 57 and 64.

HOLLINGSHEAD, AUGUST B.,
Elmstown's Youth. New York: John Wiley and Sons, 1949.

INSTITUT NATIONAL D'ÉTUDES DÉMOGRAPHIQUES,
Le niveau intellectuel des enfants d'âge scolaire, 2 vols. Paris: Presses Universitaires de France, 1950 and 1954.

JENSEN, A.R.,
"How much can we boost I.Q. and scholastic achievement?" *Harvard Educational Review*, XXXIV, 1, Winter-Spring, 1969.

KENISTON, KENNETH,
Young Radicals, Notes on Committed Youth. New York: Harcourt, Brace and World, 1968.
———— *Youth and Dissent: The Rise of a New Opposition*. New York: Harcourt, Brace, Jovanovich, 1960.

KUROKAWA, MINAKO,
"Mennonite Children in Waterloo County," in Jean Leonard Elliott (ed.), *Immigrant Groups*. Scarborough: Prentice-Hall of Canada, 1971.

LIPSET, S.M.,
"Youth and Politics," in R.K. Merton and R. Nisbet (eds.), *Contemporary Social Problems*, 3rd edition. New York: Harcourt, Brace, Jovanovich, 1971, pp. 743–791.

LYND, ROBERT S., AND HELEN LYND,
Middletown: A Study in American Culture. New York: Harcourt, Brace and World, 1929.

PORTER, JOHN,
The Vertical Mosaic. Toronto: University of Toronto Press, 1965, especially Chapter VI.

REPORT OF THE ROYAL COMMISSION ON BILINGUALISM AND BICULTURALISM,
Vol. II. Ottawa: Queen's Printer, 1968.

RICHER, STEPHEN,
"Middle Class Bias of Schools: Fact or Fancy?" *Sociology of Education*, Fall, 1974.

RIESSMAN, FRANK,
The Culturally Deprived Child. New York: Harper and Row, 1962.

ROCHER, GUY,
"Carences de nos ressources humaines et évolution des besoins," in *L'utilisation des ressources humaines: un défi à relever*, 1965 Conference of L'Institut Canadien des Affaires Publiques. Montreal: Les Editions du Jour, 1965, pp. 69–80.

SENNA, CARL, ED.,
The Fallacy of I.Q. New York: The Third Press, 1973.

SEXTON, PATRICIA CAYO,
   Education and Income: Inequality of Opportunity in the Public Schools. New York:
   Viking Press, 1961.
   _____ *The American School, A Sociological Analysis*. Englewood Cliffs: Prentice-
   Hall Inc., 1967.

SPADY, WILLIAM,
   "Educational Mobility and Access: Growth and Paradoxes," *American Journal of
   Sociology*, LXXIII, No. 3 (November, 1967), pp. 273–286.

WARNER, W. LLOYD, ROBERT G. HAVIGHURST, AND M.D. LOEB,
   Who Shall be Educated? New York: Harper and Row, 1944.

WILLIAMS, FREDERICK, ED.,
   Language and Poverty. Chicago: Markham Publishing Co., 1970.

Academic Stratification in Secondary Schools and Educational Plans of Students[*]

Raymond Breton

When adolescents are asked about their aspirations and expectations for the future, they are asked primarily about the position they would like and expect to occupy in the society's stratification system. Or, to use Turner's (1964:210-213) terms, students are asked about their "class of destination." The basic postulate underlying the analysis in this paper is that an adolescent's views about his class of destination can be explained as much, if not more, by the position he occupies, during his formative years, in the school stratification system as by his class of origin. The argument is that an important dimension of the school as a formal organization is its stratification system and that a student's position in that system has important implications for his life chances.

It has been frequently pointed out that one of the principal roles of the school in relation to society is to serve as an agency of allocation of people among the various positions in the social system.[1] The fact that this role is performed primarily through the stratification system that develops within the school itself has less frequently been recognized. To a certain extent, it is by finding their position in the school stratification that adolescents find their position in the socio-economic system of the society.

The sources of stratification in a school are social, cultural, and academic. Some of these sources exist outside the school itself, as for example the stratification in the community from which the school recruits its students. To a degree, the shape of the stratification within the school is a carry-over of the social status of the families of the students (Hollingshead, 1949). But to a large extent, the stratification that develops within a school stems from processes occurring within its own boundaries. There are several features of the school culture, of its formal structure and of its activities which bring about a ranking of the students with respect to each other. These features of the school as a formal

[*] Reprinted from *The Canadian Review of Sociology and Anthropology*, 7:1 (1970), by permission of the author and the publisher.

   This paper was based on the results of a larger study initiated under the co-operative auspices of the Canadian Department of Labour and the Provincial Departments of Education, and carried forward by the Department of Manpower and Immigration. The author wishes to thank Professor Joseph Lennards for his valuable suggestions in the revision of an earlier draft of the paper.

organization contribute to determine the criteria of stratification, the mechanisms whereby students are allocated among the strata, and the over-all shape of the stratification. For example, the character of the stratification system and the position of given *types* of students in it are likely to vary among schools in which academic achievement is unequally emphasized in the student sub-culture. Coleman has shown that the system of values affects the character of the competition among students and consequently the ranking of different kinds of students with respect to each other.[2]

The present paper deals with some of the academic sources of the internal stratification of the school and their effect on the educational plans of the students.[3] Several academic factors could be examined as relevant to the stratification system: the structure of the curriculum as articulated in the set of programs of study, the particular combination of programs in the school, the rules and procedures for the evaluation of the student's performance, the marks he receives for his performance and the resultant class standing, the grouping of students on the basis of their ability. Less formal factors could also be considered as, for instance, the expectations of teachers and principals concerning the academic performance of certain categories of students. Three of these have been selected for discussion in this paper: the set of programs of study and two factors related to the evaluation of performance, namely the experience of failure on the part of the individual student and the rate of failure in the school.[4]

The approach adopted for the present analysis has three distinguishing characteristics. First, in contrast to much of the literature on aspirations (and achievement), it does not focus primarily on what the adolescent brings with him from his community, social class, and family into the school situation but rather on what the school itself contributes to his behavior and career orientations. In other words, the present approach attempts to explain the output of the school in terms of the structure and processes internal to the school as well as in terms of the character of its input.

Second, the system of stratification in the school is seen as one of its crucial organizational features. Several studies have been carried out on the effect of the school on the student's achievement or aspirations, but most studies have conceptualized the school as a different kind of system. For example, the school has been seen as a system of technical expertise and pedagogical facilities (e.g. qualification of teachers; size of library); it has been examined as a system of procedures and techniques for the transmission of knowledge; as a cultural system defined primarily in terms of the value orientations prevailing among students; and as a system of interpersonal influences and pressures (teacher-student and peer relationships). But in spite of the stress on stratification in the theoretical literature on formal organizations in general and on schools in particular, few empirical studies can be found dealing with this aspect of the school.[5]

Finally, the stratification system in the school is seen as resulting primarily from formally organized structures and patterns of activities within the school and the educational system to which it belongs, rather than mainly from informal processes or processes occurring outside the school.

SOURCE OF DATA

The data utilized derive from a national survey of public secondary schools which was carried out in the fall and spring of 1965–1966. The sample was designed as a stratified probability sample, and includes academic schools, composite schools, vocational and technical schools, and academic and commercial schools. In Quebec, provincially operated trade schools and privately operated classical colleges were added to constitute a coverage of schools equivalent to that in the other provinces. Further, French Roman Catholic, English Roman Catholic, and Protestant schools are represented. Ontario special vocational and commercial schools and Newfoundland district vocational schools were also included.

A sample of 373 schools was randomly selected (8.3 percent of the total number of secondary schools in Canada); 360 of these schools, comprising an enrolment of 151,252 students (13.3 percent of all Canadian secondary school students), participated in the study.

By design, the sample is not self-weighting. Some types of schools in some provinces were purposely over-sampled. Each questionnaire was therefore assigned a weight in order that the estimates for a province as a whole or for Canada as a whole would be unbiased. Moreover, the weights were such that the tabulations would yield estimated frequencies for the whole secondary school population rather than simply for the sample. Therefore, the marginal totals for the tables of this paper, when added together, yield estimates for the total number of secondary school principals, teachers and counsellors in Canada. The estimate for principals is 4235, that for teachers and counsellors is 65,674. Because each question has a number of no answers, however, these totals are only approximated in the ensuing tables. The actual sample size, however, is 360 principals and 7884 teachers.

In the case of students, the results are based on three sub-samples: a weighted sample of 144,960, a weighted sub-sample of 72,480 and a self-weighting sub-sample of 12,160. Because the cases in the first two sub-samples are assigned weights, the marginal totals in some of the tables represent an estimate of the total and half of the total secondary school population respectively. The justification for using different sub-samples was to reduce data processing costs while keeping marginal totals sufficiently large.

Measurement of Educational Intentions

To assess the student's educational plans, the following questions were asked: (1) Do you think you will leave school soon, leave later, or stay until finishing? (2) Do you think you will continue your education after high school on a full-time basis, on a part-time basis, or not at all?

For the analysis, it was decided to treat secondary and post-secondary plans separately, that is, to treat them as distinct decisions on the part of the student. In one case, the analysis bears on the students who have decided to finish high school over all students; in the other instance, it bears on those who plan to attend a post-secondary school on a full-time basis as a proportion of the students who plan to finish high school only. The separate analyses were done because preliminary analysis revealed that several independent variables were not related in the same way to both types of educational plans. Some variables affected, for example, the decision to finish high school but not the one to continue beyond high school. The shape of the relationship would be different for each of the two types of educational intentions.

SCHOOL CURRICULUM

One of the important bases of stratification in secondary schools is the system of programs of study. In fact, the various programs are, by design, stratified with respect to each other: the programs are intended to be more or less difficult and to sort out students according to their ability which, in practice, frequently means their past performance. In certain school systems, the curriculum includes some programs for which recruitment is based on a student's interest (e.g. a technical specialty) as well as on his ability or past performance, but such a differentiation in the curriculum is relatively infrequent.[7]

The ranking of the various programs of study is made explicit in several different ways. The labelling of some programs frequently points to the terminal or non-terminal character of the program (e.g. "college or university preparatory"; "terminal"). The publications of the provincial departments of education pertaining to the programs of study are usually quite clear in their description of the kind of student each program is designed for and of what the program prepares the student for.[8]

The stratification built into the set of programs is also made explicit by the way in which students are allocated into the various programs. The allocation is usually based on some indicator of the student's ability. In the present study, the principals of the schools included in the sample were asked to indicate the importance of different criteria "in assigning students to each of the programs of

TABLE I   Importance of Different Criteria in Assigning Students to Programs of Study

	Very important (per cent)	N^*
Intelligence or achievement test	27	(2361)
School marks or grades	63	(2372)
Judgment of teachers or principal	52	(2394)
Judgment of guidance counsellor	36	(2070)
Parents' wishes	9	(2354)
Interest test	11	(2016)
Student's expressed interest in certain subjects or career	31	(2263)

* The schools with only one program of study are not included in the calculation of these percentages. The "no answers" are also excluded.

TABLE II   School Principals' Judgments Concerning the Required Level of Ability for Admission to the Various Programs of Study

	Percent	N*
Academic: non-terminal	91	(1218)
Academic: terminal	21	(709)
Commercial: non-terminal	87	(368)
Commercial: terminal	41	(805)
Technical: non-terminal	94	(456)
Technical: terminal	30	(1002)
Occupational	1	(551)

* Schools with only one program are not included here. The reason why the Ns vary so much from program to program is that there are types of programs that are not offered in certain schools. Moreover, the rate of non-response to this question was relatively high, particularly with respect to the academic-terminal program.

courses of study." The proportion indicating each criterion as very important in this respect is shown in Table I.

Although the student's interest is not neglected in the process of allocation, it is seen as having much less importance than the student's past academic performance. It is also interesting to note that the judgment of the teachers, principal, or guidance counsellor is the next most important criterion used in placing students in the various programs of study. Whether this factor operates to accentuate or to reduce the importance of academic performance in the allocation process cannot be ascertained with the data available. However, given its importance in the eyes of the school principals, its effect on the academic stratification in the school would warrant further examination.[9]

It was mentioned above that the ranking of the various programs of study is frequently indicated in publications of provincial departments of education. That this ranking does not exist only in the books but also in the minds of those who are running the schools is clearly shown by the principals' response to the following question: "In your school, what level of ability is required for admission to each of the programs or courses of study?" The proportion who responded "high" and "moderately high" level of ability for each type of program[10] is shown in Table II.

Given such considerations, it is not surprising to find a correlation between a student's program of study in high school and his educational plans, particularly with respect to post-secondary training (Table III).[11] Boys and girls in non-terminal programs are more likely to plan to continue beyond high school than those in the terminal ones. Among boys the difference between the proportion of students in non-terminal and terminal programs who plan to have post-secondary schooling is 20.9, 21.6 and 34.6 percent in the case of the academic, commercial, and technical programs respectively.

Among girls, the corresponding differences are 21.1, 27.9, and 24.7 percent[12] (Table III).

But, being in a terminal program not only lowers the probability of wanting to continue beyond high school; it is also associated with a higher probability of wanting to drop out of high school. Among boys, this is the case in the academic, commercial and technical programs where the difference in the proportion of students planning to finish high school between non-terminal and terminal programs is 13.0, 16.6 and 11.8 percent. Among girls, the difference between non-terminal and terminal students is substantial only in the case of the academic programs (14.4 percent); it is small in the case of the commercial programs (4.4 percent) and negligible in the case of the technical ones (1.8 percent). It is worthwhile noting that the type of program of study in high school is more strongly associated with post-secondary plans than it is with the intention to finish high school.

The intention to continue beyond high school is also more frequent in the programs which prepare for a wider range of occupational possibilities (academic) than in the more restrictive ones (technical and commercial). This can be observed among students in terminal as well as among those in the non-terminal programs; it can be observed among girls as well as among boys. In the case of secondary plans, the difference between academic and non-academic programs occurs only among girls in non-terminal programs.

It is important to control for the socio-economic origin of the student and for his mental ability rank.[13] This is required not only by the previous discussion but also by the fact that these two variables are correlated with program of study.

TABLE III   Educational Plans by Program of Study*

Program of study	Percent planning to finish high school		Percent planning post-secondary school†	
	Boys	Girls	Boys	:irls
Academic				
Non-terminal	84.4	85.8	78.2	75.8
	(171,277)	(157,764)	(144,641)	(135,428)
Terminal	71.4	71.4	57.3	54.6
	(49,747)	(26,928)	(35,531)	(19,220)
Commercial				
Non-terminal	83.1	75.0	54.2	47.2
	(1,863)	(6,314)	(1,547)	(4,734)
Terminal	66.4	70.6	32.6	19.3
	(11,638)	(41,636)	(7,729)	(29,384)
Technical				
Non-terminal	80.7	74.9	67.9	57.1
	(8,248)	(699)	(6,654)	(524)
Terminal	68.9	73.1	33.3	32.4
	(28,784)	(3,806	(19,831)	(2,783)
Occupational	49.8	56.8	26.7	30.8
	(6,452)	(4,089)	(3,213)	(2,322)

* Based on weighted sub-sample of 144,960, and excludes non-responses.
† Based on those who plan to finish high school, applies to this and all subsequent tables.

TABLE IV   Percent Planning Post-Secondary School by Program of Study, Controlling for Father's Occupation

	Occupational status of father			
Program of study	I	II	III	IV*
Boys				
Academic				
Non-terminal	86.1	80.7	78.9	69.3
	(27,911)	(15,129)	(53,103)	(27,003)
Terminal	67.1	46.3	59.4	52.6
	(4,455)	(2,687)	(13,973)	(6,326)
Commercial and technical				
Non-terminal	76.7	63.2	64.0	66.3
	(1,293)	(838)	(3,660)	(1,090)
Terminal	39.5	29.2	32.1	30.3
	(2,633)	(2,203)	(11,257)	(5,266)
Girls				
Academic				
Non-terminal	82.7	77.6	76.9	70.6
	(23,132)	(12,081)	(48,726)	(31,476)
Terminal	57.5	50.9	47.8	56.1
	(2,054)	(1,222)	(6,776)	(4,194).
Commercial and technical				
Non-terminal	58.7	61.8	43.8	44.8
	(693)	(539)	(2,380)	(1,043)
Terminal	27.2	24.6	17.9	23.3
	(3,616)	(2,857)	(14,356)	(6,059)

* The occupational status categories are: I managerial and professional; II other white collar; III skilled and semi-skilled manual; IV unskilled and farming.

Indeed, 73 percent of the boys from managerial and professional families are in the academic non-terminal program as compared with 59.3 percent of the sons of skilled workers and 63.9 percent of the sons of unskilled workers. Among girls, the corresponding percentages are 73.6, 62.2 and 69.4 percent. The association between mental ability rank and programs of study is much stronger: among boys, 82.6 percent of those who rank high as compared with 40.9 percent of those who rank low in mental ability are in the academic non-terminal program; among girls, the corresponding percentages are 85.0 and 48.6 percent.

Tables IV and V present the association between program of study and post-secondary plans controlling for occupational status of fathers and for mental ability rank, respectively. Although the space available does not allow the presentation of the data for secondary plans, the results are similar to those for post-secondary plans. The data show not only that the effect of the program of study on educational plans remains when father's occupational status[14] and mental ability rank are controlled but that its effect is substantially larger than either of these variables. The relevant effect parameters,[15] based on Tables IV and V, are shown in Table VI. The parameters for secondary plans are based on comparable tables, with the difference that they include the occupational program which is left out for post-secondary plans because of the small number of cases.

It is clear that students who occupy different positions in the academic stratification system are considerably affected in the planning for their future, whether they be high, medium, or low in mental ability; or whether they come from high, middle, or low status families.

TABLE V   Percent Planning Post-Secondary School by Program of Study, Controlling for Mental Ability Rank

	Mental ability (percentile) rank		
Program of study	70th or higher	30th or 69th	29th or lower
Boys			
Academic			
Non-terminal	84.9	75.9	65.3
	(63,413)	(58,318)	(22,909)
Terminal	61.0	58.0	55.5
	(4,278)	(15,911)	(15,341)
Commercial and technical			
Non-terminal	71.8	63.5	57.2
	(2,966)	(3,738)	(1,497)
Terminal	35.6	34.2	31.0
	(3,606)	(12,614)	(11,340)
Girls			
Academic			
Non-terminal	84.2	72.7	67.0
	(50,118)	(56,904)	(28,405)
Terminal	65.2	51.9	54.5
	(2,084)	(7,609)	(9,526)
Commercial and technical			
Non-terminal	49.9	50.6	39.3
	(1,831)	(2,410)	(1,018)
Terminal	22.4	20.5	19.8
	(3,429)	(13,986)	(14,752)

TABLE VI   Comparison of Effects of Program of Study and Father's Occupation on Educational Plans

	Secondary plans		Post-secondary plans	
	Boys	Girls	Boys	Girls
A Program of study	34.4	30.7	44.1	53.7
Father's occupation	12.7	14.7	17.1	7.1
B Program of study	25.5	19.5	41.7	53.8
Mental ability rank	12.9	14.8	14.4	11.3

A crucial issue in the light of these results concerns the allocation of students among the various programs. How are students assigned to the various programs? On what basis? What procedures are used for this purpose? The operation of the mechanisms of allocation do not figure very prominently in studies dealing with the effects of the school on the performance and plans of students.

It was mentioned above that mental ability rank and class of origin are important factors in this allocation process. However, even though the observed correlations are significant, they are far from perfect. There are obviously other factors in operation in the allocation of students among programs, and these factors are likely to be found within the school itself. For instance, there is the fact that 52 percent of the school principals said that the judgments of the teachers and principal are very important in assigning students to the various programs, and that 36 percent said that the judgment of the guidance counsellor is very important in this respect. These are diffuse criteria whose role requires further study. Second, the examination policies and practices, discussed below in relation to the rate of failure, are also important with respect to the allocation mechanisms through their implications for grades as a measure of past performance.

Moreover, several teachers and students seem to have serious doubts about the assignment of students to the various programs. For instance, students were asked about the program of study they were in and about the one they thought they were most suited for. While the majority are in the non-terminal academic program, the proportion who think this is the program they are the most suited for is at least 15 percent lower and can be as much as 40 percent lower, depending on the province.[16] In response to the related question, "Among your students, about how many would you say are in a program of study for which they are not suited?", almost half of the teachers and counsellors (47 percent) stated that at least one-fourth of their students are in a program for which they are not suited.

Finally, students, teachers, and principals were asked about the point in the student's high school career at which a judgment can be made about the program of study into which he should be assigned.[17] The proportion who feel that it is only after at least two years in high school, or never, that enough is known about the student's interest and abilities to assist him in choosing his program of study or for him to choose his own program varies between 45 and 67 percent depending on the person to whom the question is addressed (Table VII). If we add those who declare that they simply don't know, the proportions vary between 55 and 82 percent.

When these data are examined, remembering that in most schools the decision about the program of study is taken after one year in high school if not upon entering high school,[18] serious questions can be raised about the allocation mechanism. At least, it would seem that there are serious doubts about the efficiency of the existing mechanisms and procedures in the minds of many of those who have the job of administering the system. The data of Table VII and those concerning the suitability of the program are consistent with each other. Further analysis of the allocation process within schools and of its efficiency in terms of the distribution of talent is necessary. The above results suggest that this would be a profitable avenue for the analysis of school effects on student behavior.

ACADEMIC FAILURE

Another important feature of the school's stratification is the evaluation made of the student's performance. As we have seen above, this is related to the ranking brought about by the structure of the curriculum, since assignment to the various programs is based on marks obtained. But a further ranking of the students occurs within each of the programs of study based on performance during each academic year. The effect of the evaluation made is not only that a student is assigned a given rank, but also that a certain level of performance is defined as having failed.

The experience of low grades and particularly of failure is important in at least two respects: first, admission to post-secondary school (and, as seen above, to programs preparing for post-secondary school) is dependent on "satisfactory marks"; second, it is psychologically important for the student in that it provides him with a clue as to what he can realistically aim for in his career. In this situation most students react like economic entrepreneurs: they plan to invest where the relative yield will be the highest. In other words, a student is not likely to work very hard or plan to study for long if he thinks that his chances of success are poor. He is likely to adjust his investment of time and effort to what he expects to reap from the investment. This is shown by the data on the relationship between the student's estimate of his chances of success in post-secondary school, given his ability[19] and his educational intentions. The boys who feel that their chances are above-average are 38 percent more likely to plan to finish high school than those who feel that their chances are below-average. In the case of post-secondary plans, the difference is 44 percent. Among girls, the corresponding differences are 28 and 39 percent.

For these reasons, we can expect to find that students who have experienced failure in at least one subject[20] will have lower educational plans than those who have not had such an experience. We can also expect failure to have a greater impact on post-secondary than on secondary plans. Indeed, a student who experiences failure in high school may well decide that he still has a good chance of completing his secondary education but that further education is really beyond his reach. He may reach this conclusion, for example, as a result of having been placed in a terminal program.

Among boys, there are 11 percent less of the students who have failed than of those who have not who are planning to finish high school (84 and 73 percent respectively) and 16 percent less who plan to continue beyond high school (73 and 57 percent respectively). Among girls, the corresponding differences are ten and 17 percent respectively (85 and 75 percent; 68 and 51 percent).

The experience of failure may be related to the program of study in which the student is registered. This is partly because students are allocated among programs largely on the basis of marks or grades. Controlling for the program of study reduces the relationship between failure and post-secondary plans but not its relationship with secondary plans. In the case of post-secondary plans, the reduction is from 16 to eight percent among boys and from 17 to nine percent among girls. The effect of failure remains significant. Moreover, it is worthwhile to note that the effect or program of study remains about the same when the experience of failure is controlled. Finally, the effect of failure is about the same when mental ability rank and father's occupation are simultaneously controlled as when program of study is controlled.

TABLE VII   Opinion as to the Time at which a Decision Can Be Made Concerning the Program of Study in High School

	When counsellor knows enough according to		When teacher knows enough according to	When student knows enough according to	
	Principal (percent)	Counsellors (percent)	Teachers (percent)	Teachers (percent)	Students* (percent)
1. When a student enters high school	8	7	3	2	16
2. When the student has completed: one year of high school	26	28	24	15	29
two or more years of high school	41	45	48	56	35
3. Never know enough no matter what grade the student is in	15	9	11	11	10
4. Don't know	10	11	14	15	10
N	(4,068)	(690)	(65,674)	(65,674)	(1,231,029)

* Based on weighted sub-sample of 76,390, and excludes non-responses.

TABLE VIII   Failure Rates

Rate of subject failure in school (percent)	Percentage	
	Boys	Girls
Less than 20	9.6	15.2
20–29	16.3	15.5
30–39	37.7	31.6
40–49	27.7	26.6
50 or higher	8.7	11.0
N	(306,173)	(266,645)

Rate of Academic Failure

It has been shown that the experience of failure in school has negative effects on the educational plans of students. This makes sense and would perhaps fall in the category of "obvious" findings. But, presumably, students are not only affected by their own experience of success or failure but also by the success and failure of their fellow students. Does it affect the planning of students to be in a school where there is a lot of failure? Does it affect bright and less intelligent students in the same way? What if a student has failed himself? In such a case, does it make a difference if there are only a few other students who have also failed or if there are many of them?

We have found no empirical studies dealing with the effect of the rate of failure in a school on the educational intentions of students.[21] This is somewhat surprising in view of the close connection between marks or grades and admission to post-secondary school. When the occurrence of low marks (which

TABLE IX   Educational Plans by Rate of Failure, Controlling for Individual Failure*

Rate of failure (percent)	Percent planning to finish high school Failed a subject		Percent planning post-secondary school Failed a subject	
	No	Yes	No	Yes
Boys				
Less than 20	78.1	55.7	78.6	69.0
	(20,316)	(4,494)	(15,863)	(2,504)
20–29	81.9	76.6	76.8	69.3
	(30,070)	(13,750)	(24,638)	(10,536)
30–39	84.9	76.0	73.1	60.6
	(62,021)	(41,977)	(52,662)	(31,895)
40–49	86.0	72.2	68.5	54.1
	(42,509)	(38,271)	(36,559)	(27,647)
50 or more	82.8	65.7	62.5	48.9
	(10,053)	(15,019)	(8,327)	(9,866)
Girls				
Less than 20	70.8	57.1	69.0	63.4
	(28,040)	(3,650)	(19,860)	(2,083)
20–29	85.3	79.0	72.8	59.9
	(28,067)	(9,738)	(23,952)	(7,689)
30–39	89.4	76.6	67.6	53.5
	(50,914)	(29,165)	(45,514)	(22,353)
40–49	86.5	73.5	65.8	52.5
	(37,993)	(30,826)	(32,863)	(22,662)
50 or more	85.0	66.0	62.4	45.1
	(14,088)	(14,542)	(11,972)	(9,604)

* Based on weighted sub-sample of 72,480, and excludes non-responses.

TABLE X   Measure of Effect of Rate of Failure on Post-Secondary Plans

	Boys	*Girls*
Control variable		
Individual failure	18.0	12.4
In addition to individual failure:		
Mental ability	17.5	13.8
Father's occupation	16.7	11.4
Program of study	12.2	4.6

is reflected in the rate of failure) is frequent in a school, many students may think: "If things are that rough in high school, I wonder what it's going to be in post-secondary school, and especially at the university." This kind of anxiety can easily lead to the decision that one can save himself a lot of hardship, disappointment and loss of self-esteem by staying away from the whole thing or at least by not entering another phase of it once the present one is over.

The experience of failure is partly a matter of ability on the part of the student and partly a matter of policy on the part of educational officials or of decisions and practices on the part of the teachers. As is well known, questions in exams can be more or less difficult. Moreover, teachers, schools, or school systems use different procedures for the marking of exams. For instance, some informants interviewed in the present study have indicated that a number of teachers, schools, and school systems use the normal curve or some bell-shaped distribution as a basis for their grading. Such a procedure involves the *a priori* decision that so many will have As, so many will have Bs, and so on. It also means that so many will be failed. Obviously, such a procedure can involve a considerable degree of arbitrariness on the part of the examination system.

In a survey of the provincial policies concerning central examinations, Bruns, Jasper, and MacDonell obtained results supporting our informants. They reported that in a certain province, the "practice with respect to all provincial examinations is to scale the raw scores so that approximately fifteen percent of the papers will be in the range 0–48, 30 percent in the range 50–59..." (1964:85). Their report shows that in most provinces, the adjustment of marks involves a scaling procedure which "makes provision for a certain percentage of firsts, seconds, thirds, credits and failures in each paper" (p. 84).

There is also an element of chance involved. Bruns and his colleagues, for example, write that "with respect to marking, there has been little or nothing done in Canada to adjust marks to compensate for the easy or tough marker. To the extent that a given student may have had his paper, or a section of it, marked by a light or a heavy hand, his fate may be determined not by merit but by chance" (p.83).

The Bruns survey concerns central examinations in each province. It is probable that similar policies and practices exist at the level of the individual school or teacher. However, no direct data are available to support this, except the actual rate of failure in the schools. The percentage of students failing a subject was computed for each school included in the sample. The range of variation from school to school is considerable as can be seen (Table VIII) from the percentage of students in schools with different rates of failure.

Given the data available, it is not possible to decide whether this distribution is the result of the IQ composition of the student body in each school, or the examination policies and practices prevalent in each school, or of some other set of factors. However, it is likely that the policies for central examinations are also in effect, at least to a degree, with respect to local examinations.

The rate of failure in a school has a considerable effect on the educational plans of students. In the case of high school plans the effect is curvilinear: the percentage who plan to finish high school is relatively small when the rate of failure is either high or low and it is relatively high when the rate of failure is in between. In the case of post-secondary plans, the relationship is linear: the proportion who plan to continue beyond high school decreases steadily as the rate of failure increases. These correlations are stronger among boys than they are among girls: among boys, the percentage difference for post-secondary plans is 21.1 percent while it is only 12.5 percent among girls. Moreover, as Table IX shows, the rate of failure has an effect on the educational plans of both students who have not themselves failed and those who have failed. As far as secondary plans are concerned, however, the curvilinear pattern seems to be more pronounced among the boys and girls who have experienced failure than among those who have not. In the case of post-secondary plans, the effect is larger if the student has failed himself than if he has not, particularly among girls (the effect of the rate of failure on the post-secondary plans of boys is 20.1 and 16.1 percent in the case of those who have and of those who have not failed respectively; the corresponding measures for girls are 18.3 and 6.6 percent).

Furthermore, the effect of the rate of failure — curvilinear on high school plans and linear on post-secondary plans — does not disappear when we control for the level of mental ability, socio-economic origin, and program of study. This is the case for the students who have themselves experienced failure as well as for those who have not. Generally, the rate of failure has a stronger effect on the plans of boys than on those of girls. It also tends to have a stronger effect on those who have experienced failure than on those who have not. A measure of the over-all effect on the rate of failure on the post-secondary plans of boys and girls is shown in Table X (the measures were computed with mental ability rank, socio-economic background, and program of study as successive control variables; in each case, individual failure is also controlled).

These results show that the effect of the rate of failure on post-secondary plans is reduced significantly among girls when program of study is controlled. But, the effect is not completely eliminated. Among boys, the effect of the rate of failure remains strong when each of the control variables is introduced, although it is somewhat reduced when program of study is controlled.

SUMMARY

This paper analyzed the effect of two processes related to the stratification system within the school: the organization of the curriculum into programs of study and the evaluation of students. The latter was examined from the point of view of the experience of failure by the student and of the rate of failure in the school. It was found that, of these three factors, the program of study has the strongest impact on the educational intentions of students. The effect of the other two factors, however, is far from negligible.

The results presented emphasize the importance of examining the internal stratification of a school when attempting to assess the effect of the school on the behavior and attitudes of students. They also support the notion that an adolescent's class of destination is very much a function of the position he occupies in the school stratification system. Indeed, it seems to depend more on such a position than on the social class position of his family. Finally, these results underline the necessity of examining the formal organization of the school rather than limiting the analysis of school effects to "informal" factors such as the student sub-culture and peer relationships.

Notes.

1. See papers by Parsons, Becker, and Turner in A. H. Halsey *et al.* (eds.) (1961).
2. One of the processes involved has been described by Coleman. He argues that in activities highly rewarded in a social system "the persons who achieve most should be those with most potential ability... « while » in unrewarded activities... the persons who achieve most will be persons of lesser ability" (1960:340). Applying this proposition to the school context, he formulates and supports with data the following hypotheses: "In a school where «academic» achievement brings few social rewards, those who 'go out' for scholarly achievement will be few." The high performers, those who receive "good grades, will not be the boys whose ability is greatest but a more mediocre few; those with intellectual ability will be off cultivating other fields which bring social rewards" (1960:341).
3. See below for a discussion of the measurement of educational plans.
4. For an analysis of the effect of other aspects of the school on the career decisions of students, see Raymond Breton (1972).
5. This is fairly evident from Boocock's (1966) excellent review of the literature of the effects of several features of the school.
6. Although the first of these questions appeared clear and straightforward when put in the questionnaire, it turned out to present problems of interpretation. The cross-tabulation of the two questions revealed that a number of students were planning to attend a post-secondary school but did not intend to complete high school. There were cases like this in each of the ten provincial samples, although the magnitude of their relative frequency varied from one province to another and in all cases was quite small. These "inconsistent" cases were not rejected on the assumption that a student who intends to continue full-time beyond high school will be completing as much high school education as he will need to be admitted to a post-secondary institution. For additional details, see Breton (1972).

7. Only three provincial educational systems differentiate non-academic programs into terminal and non-terminal: Ontario, Alberta, and British Columbia.

8. For example, an Ontario Department of Education publication states that the five-year program in the Arts and Science Branch "makes provision for pupils of good general ability who desire to proceed to Grade 13 ... to qualify for admission to a university course ... " (1966:13). About the four-year program in the same branch it indicates that it is designed for those who "do not plan to proceed to university or other studies that require standing in Grade 13 subjects ... " (p. 29).

9. On the role of guidance in secondary schools, see Cicourel and Kitsuse (1963).

10. Using the documentation from the provincial departments of education, the programs offered in each province were classified as to "area of training" and in terms of their terminal and non-terminal character. For more details, see Breton (1972).

11. For the relation between program of study and occupational plans, see Breton and McDonald (1968:284ff.).

12. With the sample size on which the results of this paper are based, the problem of statistical significance is not an issue. All the percentage differences and measures of effect presented, even the small ones, are statistically significant. What is important to consider is their magnitude, especially their relative magnitude.

13. The test administered was the *Otis-Lennon Mental Ability Test* (advanced Form Ac.), New York: Harcourt, Brace and World, 1965. Students were assigned a percentile rank by grade level. The categories used here are: the first three deciles, the next four, and the last three.

14. Very similar results are obtained if the father's education is used as a measure of the student's socio-economic background.

15. The technique for estimating the effect of the independent variables used here has been developed by Coleman (1964:chap. 6).

16. For more details, see Breton and McDonald (1967:24 and Table 22).

17. Students were asked the following question: "When do you feel a student knows enough about his interests and abilities to choose his program or course of study in high school: (a) when entering high school; (b) after one year in high school; (c) after two or more years in high school; (d) never knows enough, no matter what grade he is in; (e) don't know?" The questions asked to principals, teachers and counsellors were identical, except for the opening sentence which would be adapted to each type of respondent (e.g., when do you feel a teacher knows ...).

18. All students were asked to indicate the program of study they were in. A response category provided for the possibility that he had not chosen his program yet. The percentage of the first year students who had not chosen their program is less than five percent in three of the provinces; it is less than or equal to ten percent in four other provinces; it is about 15 percent in one province; and it reaches about 25 percent in only two provinces.

19. The question asked is as follows: "Suppose you continued your education after high school. Thinking of your ability, how good do you think your chances would be of being successful in getting a degree or diploma: (a) much better than average; (b) above average; (c) average; (d) below average; (e) much worse than average?"

20. The question asked is as follows: "Did you fail any subject last year?"

21. An interesting study of failure and rates of failure has been carried out by W. D. Hall and his associates (1962).

References

BOOCOCK, S. S.
1966 "Toward a sociology of learning: a selective review of existing research." *Sociology of Education* 39:1–45.

BRETON, R. AND J. C. MCDONALD
1967 *Career Decisions of Canadian Youth: A Compilation of Basic Data*. Ottawa: Department of Manpower and Immigration.
1968 "Occupational preferences of Canadian high school students." Pp. 269–294 in B. Blishen et al., eds., *Canadian Society*. Toronto: Macmillan of Canada.

BRETON, R.
1972 *Social and Academic Factors in Career Decision-making: A Study of Canadian Secondary School Students*. Ottawa: Department of Manpower and Immigration.

BRUNS, J., ET AL.
1964 "Standards in secondary schools." In *The Canadian Superintendent: Secondary Educatio in Canada*, Toronto: Ryerson Press.

CICOUREL, A. V. AND JOHN I. KITSUSE
1963 *The Educational Decision-Makers*, New York: Bobbs-Merrill

COLEMAN, J S
1960 "The Adolescent subculture and academic achievement." *American Journal of Sociology* 65:337–347.
1964 *Introduction to Mathematical Sociology*, New York: The Free Press of Glencoe.
1961 *The Adolescent Society*. New York: The Free Press of Glencoe.

HALL, W. D. ET AL.
1962 *Failure in School*. Hamburg: Unesco Institute for Education.

HALSEY, A. H. ET AL., EDS.
1961 *Education, Economy and Society*. New York: The Free Press.

HOLLINGSHEAD, A. B.
1949 *Elmtown's Youth*. New York: John Wiley.

ONTARIO DEPARTMENT OF EDUCATION
1966 *Requirements for Diplomas and Statements of Standing*, 1966–1967. Toronto.

TURNER, R.
1964 *The Social Context of Ambition*. San Francisco: Chandler Publishing Company.

Ethnic Stratification Viewed from Three Theoretical Perspectives[*]

Raymond Breton

An examination of the literature reveals that studies of ethnic stratification are carried out within the orientation of a particular theoretical perspective whether this is explicitly acknowledged or not. Moreover, three perspectives organize most of the existing research in the area of ethnic stratification: the individual competition approach, the class approach, and the conflict or social closure approach. These perspectives have oriented much of the study of stratification generally and of ethnic stratification in particular.[1] The first has received the most attention in the empirical literature, but the other two have been at the origin of models and hypotheses and some empirical research as well.

This paper attempts to describe the three perspectives and to examine their implications for ethnic stratification. Three dimensions of ethnic stratification and the ways they are dealt with in each approach are examined. First, the analysis considers the sources of ethnic inequality and the hypotheses to which each approach leads. Second, whether and to what extent each approach views ethnicity as an asset or a liability for various categories of social actors in the socio-economic system is examined. This question is dealt with in relation to the orientations and strategies that people are likely to adopt with regard to their ethnic identity and background. Finally, what each approach identifies as the main occasions of interethnic conflict is considered briefly.

The analysis is limited to ethnic stratification in its socio-economic or instrumental aspects. Status or symbolic stratification among ethnic groups will not be considered. Though the three aspects of ethnic stratification selected for analysis are interrelated, their inter-connections will not be analyzed systematically.

First, applying the three perspectives to the analysis of ethnic stratification, an attempt is made to show that each approach focuses on different features of the organization of work and of the related institutions — different structural conditions within which people work and pursue careers. Second, given differ-

* The author is indebted to Daiva Stasiulus, Jeffrey Reitz, Réjean Lachapelle and Gail Grant Akian for their willingness to read an earlier draft of this paper under pressures of time and for their useful comments and suggestions.

ences in structural conditions, each points to different social organizational mechanisms by means of which people cope with these conditions. Third, the actors or decision-making units seen as critical in the stratification system differ from one perspective to the other. Finally, the processes that the actors must set in motion, the factors they must activate or manipulate in order to reach their career goals and certain income levels, are also different according to the approach adopted.

The next three sections of the essay take up each of the approaches consecutively. The fourth section deals briefly with changes in the structural conditions of work and how such changes can interact with particular configurations of ethnic diversity and affect the shape of ethnic stratification.[2]

Each approach captures different aspects of the social structure and different social processes.[3] The approaches should be seen as complementing rather than opposing each other: each has something significant to reveal about social reality.

It is important to emphasize that the analysis is not meant to apply to all types of ethnic diversity. The pertinent type of situation is that of "ethnic heterogeneity" as distinct from "ethnic segmentation."[4] The concern is with structures and processes in situations where the different ethnic groups participate in a common institutional system, especially those that have to do, directly or indirectly, with the organization of work. In plural situations where ethnic groups function in parallel institutional systems, and to the extent that they do so (since institutional parallelism is a matter of degree), somewhat different structures and processes are involved. It would be inappropriate to use the models and propositions presented here under each of the three approaches for an analysis of stratification in ethnically segmented societies.

INDIVIDUAL COMPETITION APPROACH

In this approach,[5] the organization of work is seen as consisting of a collection of interrelated occupations involving complex tasks and thus requiring different kinds and levels of skills. The result is an organization that is hierarchically shaped, largely as a result of technological and administrative requirements. Another basic premise of this approach is that those who are to occupy the positions in that structure differ in motivation and/or ability to perform the tasks associated with the different positions. The motivation and ability are determined by such factors in the individual's biography as family influences, educational background, and experience.

The processes whereby the supply of individuals with different kinds and levels of skills are allocated among the positions in the occupational structure are embedded in labor market institutions. The main components of these institutions are, of course, employers and potential employees, and the mechanisms through which they relate to one another. The critical function of these mechanisms is to permit the flow of information between the two categories of individuals; information for potential employees as to what jobs are available and what conditions are offered by various employers; information that would reveal to employers what is likely to be the true productivity of different individuals.[6] This flow of information is the essential ingredient of the bargaining process; and it allows the necessary comparisons among employers or among potential employees.

In this perspective, the distribution of earnings results from the interplay among these three phenomena: an occupational structure, a supply of individuals with characteristics relevant for the performance of occupational tasks and institutionalized mechanisms that allocate the supply of workers throughout the structure. A basic proposition in such a system is that individuals are rewarded according to their productivity. This proposition is based on the assumption of a perfectly competitive labor market. But it is also held to be applicable under conditions of imperfect competition due to factors such as incomplete information, the existence of monopolies, or an individual's social attachments and loyalties. The propositions are still considered applicable, but the processes of allocation operate inadequately and take much longer to have their effect than they would if conditions of perfect competition prevailed.

The actor considered critical in this approach is the person acting as an individual, autonomous agent. As someone selling his labor, the actor is faced with the opportunities offered by the occupational structure and what he has to take advantage of are the processes leading to information about it. This actor operates within a labor market in which employers buy labor services: information about employers and the conditions they offer is also important. Finally, the actor must engage in the more or less explicit bargaining with possible employers. Once the actor is employed, the factors that count are those related to job performance (with given technology, materials and organization).

The individual actor, then, faces an occupational structure, a labor market, and a technological/organizational system. His eventual productivity within those parameters is a function of three sets of factors. First, there are those related to finding the best possible niche in the occupational structure. They include access to information, opportunities to discover one's potential, and the resources for the geographical mobility that may be required. Second, there are factors related to the ability for "impression management," since one is involved in "judgmental competition."[7] Finally, there are those affecting one's proficiency in the performance of an occupational task. At the actor's disposal are personal resources: motivation, talent, physical energy, training, material resources, contacts[8] and whatever other personal characteristics may be relevant.[9]

How is this approach applied to situations of ethnic heterogeneity? What sorts of hypotheses does it allow to be formulated concerning ethnic stratification? These questions will be examined in relation to three issues indicated earlier: the source of ethnic inequality; whether ethnicity is an asset or a liability and the related orientations that individuals are likely to adopt with regard to their ethnic origin; and the occasions of ethnic conflict.

Sources of Ethnic Inequality

If one observes occupational and income differences among people of different ethnic origins, it is due, according to this model, to the distribution of relevant personal attributes across ethnic groups—attributes which affect the processes of allocation in the occupational structure and performance on the job. Two kinds of attributes have been given considerable attention in studies, and could be classified under this approach: personal resources and inter-ethnic attitudes and the accompanying discrimination. These attributes are in turn seen as the result of factors such as child rearing practices, religious values, achievement and present/future orientations and education.

Personal resources are important for three kinds of processes: gaining access to information, bargaining with employers and performing on the job. While some resources may be relevant to all three processes (e.g. motivation, education), some are more pertinent for some of these processes than for others. Networks of contacts appear as particularly relevant for access to information about jobs (Granovetter, 1974). A network confined to an ethnic community will affect access to pertinent labor market information. Abilities for impression management and persuasive communication are important in the bargaining process. If cultural and linguistic differences exist between employer and potential employee, the latter's ethnic origin may be a liability compared to a competitor who shares the employer's cultural background and language. Finally, there are resources more directly related to the performance of occupational tasks such as specialized skills and experience, and achievement motivation.

The central point is that because of their cultural background and community attachments, members of different ethnic groups acquire and maintain personal attributes which affect their ability to function in the labor market, to find a niche in the occupational structure such that they can reach their optimal level of output. Thus in a perfectly competitive system, if different ethnic groups are allocated differently, it is in part because they are unequal in their competitive ability either in terms of taking advantage of existing opportunities or in terms of performance on the job.

It is recognized, however, that there are imperfections in the labor market— imperfections stemming from such factors as the difficulties of moving people around, the costs of making information widely available, or the difficulties of making systematic comparisons either among employers or among potential recruits for a job. Insofar as there are such imperfections, ethnic inequalities can be the result of the interaction between them and certain ethnic characteristics. For example, social attachments increase the difficulties of moving people around; thus, differences among ethnic groups in the proportion of their members with strong ethnic ties would explain part of the variations in ethnic differences in income. Ethnicity accentuates certain rigidities in the functioning of labor markets or brings rigidities of its own.

Discrimination is also recognized as generating ethnic inequalities in this perspective. Discrimination derives from prejudice and stereotypes which, it must be underlined, are seen as characteristics of individuals. Whether they behave discriminatorily depends on their circumstances. As will be seen later, discrimination is approached differently in the other perspectives.

One effect of prejudice and stereotypes in this approach is to prevent individuals from either recognizing the right cues as to the true productivity of potential employees (if one is an employer) or from recognizing the best opportunities (if one is looking for a job). Another effect is to lead individuals to prefer certain types of people either as employers or as employees. Thus, the distribution of members of different ethnic groups in the occupational structure is affected by ethnic differences, blinding either employers or employees to what would be in their economic interests; or by ethnic identity being associated with patterns of positive and negative inter-ethnic attitudes.

In this approach, discrimination is considered possible only because there are imperfections in the market; that is, rigidities which make it impossible for the market to effect rapid adjustments by eliminating the factors that decrease productivity. For example, according to the purely competitive model, discriminating employers would eventually lose out to the non-discriminating ones who hire the best workers at the lowest price, irrespective of ethnic origin. But because there are imperfections in the market, discriminating employers can frequently remain in the market.

Ethnicity as Asset or Liability, and Orientation toward One's Ethnic Identity

In the individual competition approach, then, ethnicity is either a determinant of personal resources or attitudes associated with job placement processes and productivity or a factor bringing about or accentuating imperfections in the labor market. In this approach, the relevance of ethnicity stems from the fact that it determines individual characteristics. It provides the individual, whether buyer or seller of labor, with a package of traits and attitudes that may be useful or detrimental in relation to labor market processes.

The occupational structure and the labor market are ethnically neutral: in their ideal form, they are free of ethnicity or of any other phenomena such as sex or religious affiliation. In other words, the occupational structure and the labor market are seen as dissociated from other elements of the social organization of society. When factors such as ethnicity enter into the situation, it is as attributes of individuals who function in an ethnicity-free structure.

With this approach, and assuming no prejudice at all, we would hypothesize that individuals would adopt a personal strategy of selective acculturation: people would tend to retain those elements of their ethnic background and affiliation that help in acquiring information, in bargaining with employers, or in performing the job. A variation of this hypothesis is that members of some ethnic groups have a greater adaptive capacity,[10] possess cultural elements that are more suited to the requirements of a particular type of socio-economic system than others and therefore would tend to retain those elements. The proposition that ethnic cultures are slowly disappearing, giving way to a technological culture, is another variation of the selective acculturation hypothesis. Indeed, if each group retains from its culture only those elements that are useful in a particular technological/economic environment, a cultural homogenization is inevitable.

Under conditions of prejudice and discrimination, the model predicts individuals will tend to adopt a personal strategy of complete assimilation, that is removal of all elements that serve as cues to one's ethnic origin; this would be one of the rational strategies to adopt. Underlying this hypothesis, however, is the assumption that ethnic traits are under one's control. To a considerable extent, this is the case. But what happens when a trait, such as color, cannot be removed or kept in the private sphere of the person's life or, where it can be done, only with great difficulty, as with language?[11] In such instances, since individual strategies are not useful, there would be a tendency toward collective action.[12] To the extent that acculturation and individual integration is difficult or impossible, people will tend to revert to collective action in order to reduce or eliminate the discriminatory behavior of employers or the institutional circumstances that lead the employers to discrimination. On the other hand, the more control individuals have over their ethnic traits, the more they will tend to adopt individual strategies of either selective or complete assimilation. This does not mean, of course, that they will not support actions aimed at reducing discrimination in the labor market. It is a matter of direction of the main propensity.

However, even in completely benign conditions, sheer ethnic differences may be a liability as well as an asset, depending on whether one belongs to a dominant or a subordinate group. This is particularly evident in the case of linguistic differences. For instance, linguistic and other cultural differences between employer and employee may reduce the latter's ability for impression management or for the manipulation of social networks to reach certain career goals. If the employee belongs to the same ethnic group as the employer, he will generally be in a position of relative advantage compared to one who is not. The model then leads to the hypothesis that members of the dominant ethnic group (the one to which most employers belong) would tend to make the most of that, while others would tend toward acculturation and structural assimilation — the adoption of the dominant culture and integration into networks connected with the dominant group. Such processes, however, would especially occur under conditions of prejudice and discrimination.

This approach leads to the proposition that ethnicity can be a liability in the labor market. Therefore, individuals who are not members of the dominant ethnic group tend to adopt a personal strategy of acculturation and integration. In some instances, certain elements of the ethnic background may be useful, leading to personal strategies of selective acculturation and integration. In either case, the result is a tendency toward cultural homogenization and the dissolution of ethnic boundaries.[13] However, if the ethnic characteristics are beyond the individual's control, there will be a tendency for collective strategies aimed at controlling the behavior of employers. For members of the dominant ethnic group, however, ethnic identity and background tend to be an asset. They do not have to incur the social and psychic costs of acculturation for the pursuit of their careers.

Occasions of Inter-Ethnic Conflict

In this approach, intolerance is a matter of individual attitudes and behavior that originate in early socialization or in the psychological stress experienced in life situations. Accordingly, tolerance is increased through education, favorable intergroup contacts, and legal constraints. Whether practised by employers or employees, prejudice is a phenomenon that prevents the labor market from functioning well; it introduces imperfections such as individuals not being allocated in the occupational structure according to potential or not being rewarded according to productivity. It is the failure (because of individual intolerance) to apply appropriate labor market or job performance criteria that occasions conflict. Typically, the issues involved fall under the category of "equality of opportunity for all." Discontent occurs when the actual operation of the labor market fails to approximate the ideal model; when facing an occupational structure and labor market mechanisms, some individuals, because of their ethnicity, are not able to operate as effectively as others.

CLASS APPROACH

The class approach[14] captures different features of the organization of work. The structural conditions that are considered important are those that derive from the social organization of production. The basic social phenomena are those of contract and property. In a class society these phenomena become defined and institutionalized in certain ways. A contractual system defines the mutual obligations, prerogatives, and restrictions in specific types of social relations. Property, on the other hand, is a system of rights in relation to objects. The essential property rights "may be classified as those of use, of control (specifying who shall use and for what purposes) and of disposal" (Parsons, 1960: 146). The content of contracts as well as the "legitimate and illegitimate means of securing the assent of the other party to a contract" (145) are usually defined within the perimeters of socially established rights.

In a class society, the crucial social relationships are those that pertain to the organization of production, and the definitions of property rights that are embedded in the institutionalized contract define the relationships of the groupings to the means of production. As stated by Giddens, the character of the property relations that constitute the basis of the class system is: "a minority of 'non-producers,' who control the means of production, are able to use this position of control to extract from the majority of 'producers' the surplus product which is the source of their livelihood" (1973: 28).

The basic social relations in a class system are those of conflict and mutual dependence. In the basic dichotomous system classes are "placed in a situation of reciprocity such that neither class can escape from the relationship without thereby losing its identity as a distinct 'class.'" On the other hand, the interests of the classes are "at the same time mutually exclusive, and form the basis for the potential outbreak of open struggles" (Giddens, 1973: 29). Classes are conflict groups who need each other, but whose interests are fundamentally opposed.

This opposition does not necessarily involve class consciousness and mobilization; it is based on contradictory interests, a contradiction rooted in particular institutional forms of property and contract.

A class system usually involves more than the basic class dichotomy. There is considerable debate among class analysts as to the criteria that should be used to identify other classes accompanying the basic dichotomy and for defining their boundaries. This debate will not be reviewed here.[15] There are two critical points regarding the emergence of a more complex class system. First, classes or quasi-class groupings[16] emerge as a result of a further differentiation of the *social* organizations of production. Poulantzas, for instance, analyzes the differentiation that has emerged historically between "ownership" which refers to the "real economic control of the means of production to given uses... to dispose of the products obtained" and "possession" which refers to "the actual control over the physical operation of production" (1975: 18). The relations of possession can become further differentiated between those having to do with the control of the physical means of production and those pertaining to the control over labor power (supervisory relations). In addition to the basic dichotomy, there may exist other classes such as the petite bourgeoisie or "contradictory class positions" such as with managers or semi-autonomous wage-earners (Wright, 1976: 29-31). The role of such additional classes or quasi-class groupings cannot be understood outside the context of the basic class relations that provides the fundamental structure of the social organization of economic production in a society.

Classes themselves can be internally differentiated as well. Here, the distinction between the social and the technical division of labor is important. The class structure pertains to the social relations that surround the organization of economic production. But there is also a division of labor based on the differentiation of activities in relation to such factors as the nature of the task and the technology available for its performance. The technical division of labor exists both within and between classes. As a result the occupational structure tells a poor and perhaps misleading tale about the class structure, that is, the social relations of production. But it is relevant for the analysis of differentiations within classes, because these relate to mobilization for concerted action in the pursuit of class interests.

In an organization of production, the significant social relationships are not those between individuals or between coalitions of individuals whose interest in a particular segment of the occupational structure happen to coincide. Rather, the critical social units are classes which are groupings whose interests are defined in relation to the basic social organization of production. The distribution of income is determined by the character of the relationships between classes. The critical factor in that relationship is the relative power of the classes. The conflict may take the form of bargaining or of a struggle in which the parties attempt to inflict losses on each other, to weaken or destroy their organizational apparatus. The conflict can be geared to two basic types of outcomes: obtaining as large a share as possible of the benefits of production — an outcome occurring within an existing class structure; or bringing about extensive structural modification of the class system itself.

The source of power that appears to be of greatest interest is the organization for collective action that exists within each class, and perhaps especially among those who sell labor. A critical area of concern, then, pertains to the conditions of class mobilization and of effective collective action.[17]

Sources of Ethnic Inequality

Since the critical social groupings are classes and since these are defined in terms of their relationship to the modes of production, there appears to be little room for ethnicity as a factor in the social organization of the system of work and of the critical relationships that it entails. In other words, ethnicity is not seen as a dynamic element of the social organization of a community that could impinge on the structuring of the class system. Rather, it is the system of production and the particular institutionalization of property relationships which are the determinant factors.

The ethnic differentiation of a community, however, may play a role in the historical formation of classes. Because of circumstances, individuals who are the active agents in the formation of a class, such as the bourgeoisie, may be of an ethnic origin different from those who end up in the class selling their labor. Through some sort of historical "accident," class cleavages would thus coincide with ethnic cleavages — a coincidence which would account for observed ethnic inequalities. The same argument could be true for the composition of other classes (petty bourgeoisie) or of "contradictory class locations"[18] (managers, small employers).

As long as the boundaries of social classes coincide with those of ethnic groupings, the class model is quite applicable to ethnic differentials in economic benefits. But in its classical form the model has little to say about ethnic differentials occurring within classes. Ethnic cleavages are seen as having an impact on the dynamics of class relations (as will be seen later), but the approach did not go far in identifying processes through which ethnic stratification would emerge within classes.

To class analysts, ethnicity is an epiphenomenon: even if ethnic cleavages coincide with class cleavages, the true dynamic of the relationship stems from the class interests involved, not the ethnic differences. Generally, one could argue that pure class analysts see ethnicity as bringing about imperfections in class relations somewhat in the way that the individual competition analysts see ethnicity as bringing imperfections in the labor market.

Ethnicity *can be* a basis of social solidarity and social organization. Because of this, it can be seen as "competing" with class — not a very fruitful way of looking at the phenomenon because it will tend to be seen as a source of embarrassment, of distraction from, or contamination of, the "true" social processes. Rather, ethnicity should be seen as interacting with class in the structuring of societal institutions and in generating inequality. This is the approach adopted by Bonacich (1972, 1976) in her split labor market theory.

According to Bonacich, "a split labor market refers to a difference in the price of labor between two or more groups of workers, holding constant their efficiency and productivity" (1976: 36). The labor market may be split along such lines as ethnicity, sex, and religion. Moreover, ethnic diversity in the labor force does not necessarily yield a split labor market. For a split condition to occur, the ethnic groups in the economic system must have such unequal resources and/or goals that their prices to employers are different. For instance, recruits from a poorer economy may offer their labor at a cheaper price; or they may sell it more cheaply out of ignorance of the unfamiliar economy; or they may be badly organized or without external protection and therefore more likely to strike a poor bargain (Bonacich, 1972: 549–550).

Ethnic groups who compose the labor force may have such a different socio-economic history and/or may exhibit such differences in their socio-political organization that on the aggregate the experience of their members as sellers of labor differs in some significant way. Bonacich's model recognizes a significant role to ethnicity (or other so-called ascriptive factors) in the social organization of the labor market. In class analysis terms, this means that ethnicity can be the basis for the formation of groups (sub-classes?) that have a different position in the basic social relation of production. The result of an ethnic differentiation of labor in terms of price to employers is a "conflict between three key classes: business, higher paid labor, and cheaper labor" (1972: 553), the last two corresponding to an ethnic cleavage.

These three classes have divergent interests which are at the basis of the dynamics of their conflict. For instance, employers have an interest in as cheap a labor price as possible and, because of this, they are always on the lookout for cheaper labor than that which they presently employ. The higher paid labor, on the other hand, is threatened by the possibility of, or the actual introduction of, cheaper labor, a phenomenon that would undermine its position. The class of cheaper labor wants to sell its labor but, because it is relatively weak (because of ignorance, poor organization, different goals), it is used by employers to undermine the position of the more expensive labor. Thus, as a result of the operation of another basis of social organization — ethnicity — the basic class dichotomy of the classical model is differentiated into a trichotomy involving more complex processes of conflict and interdependence.

At the beginning of this section, mention was made of the debate among class analysts over the delimitation of class boundaries. Wright's argument is that the class system can become differentiated as a result of the imperatives of "three central processes underlying the basic capital-labor relationship: control over the physical means of production; control over labor power; control over investments and resource allocation" (1976: 30). A possible result of this differentiation of the social organization of production is the emergence of "contradictory locations within class relations." The contradiction is due to an inconsistent position with respect to the three control processes. For example, some locations may involve control over labor power but none over the two other factors.[19]

In the classic class approach, economic relations of property determine class positions. Poulantzas, however, argues that political and ideological relations are also important in determining position within class relations (1975: 226–50). Wright attempts to specify Poulantzas' argument by suggesting that political and ideological factors are important in regard to contradictory class positions. For instance, many technicians are close to the working class because they have no control over labor power and over investments and resource allocation, but they are in a contradictory location because they have some control over their immediate labor process. This control not being very extensive, they remain close to the boundary of the working class as far as the organization of production is concerned. For them, however, the status division between mental and manual labor — an ideological factor — could be important and, if used, would tend to push them away from the working class (Wright, 1976: 39–40).

Although Wright does not mention it, it is easy to hypothesize that a social factor such as ethnicity could also influence position in a system of class relations. If the incumbents of a particular contradictory location happen to be of the same ethnic origin as that of the members of the bourgeoisie, it may in certain circumstances bring them closer to the bourgeoisie through a process of social identification. Wright's argument about contradictory locations and the role of non-economic factors in determining their position in class relations appears to provide an interesting avenue for exploring ethnicity in class relations. If this were the case, class analysis could integrate ethnicity as a significant agent in the structuring of the class system and in the dynamics of class relations rather than treating it at best as a marginal phenomenon or at worst as an epiphenomenon. Indeed, the dynamics that are proper to ethnicity and its role in social organization would be seen as a factor in the determination of the position of some classes in the system of class relations.

Ethnicity as Asset or Liability, and Orientation toward One's Ethnic Identity

For the class of sellers of labor, this approach sees ethnicity as a definite liability. It is a factor of social differentiation that detracts from the critical conflict relevant for social stratification, namely class conflicts. Moreover, as a basis of social solidarity, ethnicity can weaken or prevent class solidarity, a fact that is detrimental to the pursuit of class interests. If the employers/sellers of labor cleavage correspond to an ethnic one, the ethnic difference tends to facilitate the exploitative process because the dominance of the class of employers can be buttressed by ideologies of racial, cultural or social superiority. In the split labor market situation, the ethnic differentiation is a source of antagonisms within the class of sellers of labor (as well as between the sub-classes of sellers and the class of buyers of labor) and thus plays against the interests of the class as a whole. So, under this perspective, the rational strategy to adopt is acculturation and assimilation as rapidly as possible.

For the class of employers, however, ethnic difference in the supply of labor can be an asset either because it can be used to undermine the position of that segment of the labor force that has acquired a certain level of benefits from employers or because, being a source of antagonism within the labor force, it can prevent or weaken employee organization, a fact that is in the interest of employers.

Occasions of Inter-Ethnic Conflict

In the class approach, there is little ethnic conflict in that it has virtually no dynamism of its own independent of class conflicts. The antagonisms of class interests may be accentuated by ethnic differences, but the basic source of the conflict is found in class relations, not ethnic differences. There are no ethnic interests, only class interests. This is so in Bonacich's theory as well: "Ethnic antagonism is specifically produced by the competition that arises from a price differential" (1972: 554).

To the extent that there are "truly" ethnic conflicts, they are seen as vestiges of the past which will eventually disappear from the class-based social structure.[20] Or they are seen as artificially fomented by employers to weaken the capacity for concerted action by the sellers of labor.[21]

THE GROUP COMPETITION OR "SOCIAL CLOSURE" APPROACH

A third approach[22] focuses on different aspects of the labor market and of the occupational structure and on different occupational attainment behaviors as relevant in determining the allocation of workers in the structure and the distribution of earnings. To a large extent, this approach focuses on what the two previous approaches consider as imperfections. These imperfections, it will be recalled, stem primarily from the fact that non-economic factors, which are seen as exogenous to the organization of economic activity, distort either market or power conflict processes. Both approaches view non-economic factors as preventing complete actualization of the true interests of the actors involved. While the first two approaches dissociate the economic and non-economic basis of social organization, the third approach sees them as inevitably intermeshed. The third approach systematizes, incorporates as an integral part of its framework what the other two consider as imperfections. This is reflected in the conceptualization of the organization of work, of the social unit that is seen as the critical actor, and of the dynamics through which the system functions.

To begin with, not all jobs are seen as disconnected from each other: some jobs are conditions for other jobs in a more or less rigid step-by-step system of advancement; other jobs are in relationships of functional interdependence with each other; others are not interdependent but are located in the same physical and social space. As a result of such interconnections, the labor market can be described as being organized into a series of occupational domains[23] with more or less clearly defined boundaries. These domains or sets of jobs are not purely physical or statistical groupings; rather, they become established through social and technical processes and constitute the structure of opportunities and constraints within which workers build careers.[24]

Moreover, the labor market institutions that link individuals to the occupational structure exhibit a corresponding pattern of segmentation. Certain channels of information and influence lead to certain sets of jobs or domains and not to others. These networks of job channels are also seen as socially organized and not simply as mechanisms for the diffusion of information.

Several features of these domains and labor market channels are seen as problematic: criteria for jobs to be included in a domain; criteria of eligibility to the various domains and jobs within the domains; rules through which mobility from one job to another is regulated; stratification among jobs within a domain; linkages among points in channels of information; and so on. These aspects of the organization of work or of particular domains are not taken as given, but as modifiable. They are not seen as emerging from purely technical imperatives, as if technology had a logic of its own, independent of the actors who have an interest in the organization of the work-setting. Rather, within certain technical and economic parameters, the organization of work itself, as well as the factors that determine one's place in that organization, are objects of individual and social action. In other words, the importance of the various aspects of the structure stems not from the fact that one's place in it and in the corresponding distribution of earnings is the result of "finding the best possible job," but of processes whereby the boundaries of occupational domains, their internal organization, and the rules governing behavior within them are defined.

In a system of occupations and jobs organized into domains, taking advantage of opportunities takes a meaning quite different from the one it has in a system conceived as an array of individual positions. Rather than being a question of finding out about available positions and of bargaining over the conditions of employment, it is a matter of establishing control over a domain or a segment of it. Such control may be more or less extensive; but extending control over a domain, over its definition and internal organization, is an important mechanism for increasing one's access to economic rewards. And since to an occupational structure organized in domains there corresponds a segmented system of channels of access, taking advantage of opportunities also means controlling access to the channels of information and influence.

A critical issue, then, concerns the kind of social organization that will tend to emerge, especially among workers, in response to or in order to deal with conditions characterizing a system of work structured into domains. What will tend to be the distinguishing features of that social organization? Since the critical social process is the extension of control over a domain, the problem is to identify the features of the social organization stemming from the imperatives of control.

The Weberian notion of social closure is basic in this connection: "The relationship will be known as 'closed' to those on the outside, so far as and to the extent that... the participation of certain persons is excluded, limited, or subject to conditions" (1962: 97).[25] Weber identifies three main categories of motivations for restrictive social relationships: "the maintenance of quality and eventually that of prestige and the opportunity deriving from it to enjoy honor and possibly even profit"; "the scarcity of opportunities in relation to the needs of consumption"; and "the scarcity of opportunities for gaining a livelihood" (101-2). Because of this scarcity, an interest arises for restricting numbers relative to opportunities. This involves establishing monopoly over a set of given opportunities, a process which in turn entails social exclusion or regulated entry.[26]

Different elements of social organization can emerge for carrying out social closure; for instance, there is "gatekeeping." The gatekeeper is one who has access to information about jobs (and therefore controls who will obtain that information) and who may also have influence on the selection of persons to occupy various positions.[27] A related phenomenon is sponsorship. Defining the content of rules is another important mechanism for regulating participation. Of course, the rules defining the conditions of entry are critical here. But other kinds of rules can also be important. Language requirements affect the distribution of control of occupational domains: a given specification will be to the advantage of some and to the disadvantage of others. Because competence in the language used in an organization is necessary for job performance and success, the existing linguistic rules have an impact on career contours, access to jobs, and information about opportunities. These are matters of serious contention in the competition for ethnic control over domains.[28]

Seniority rules constitute another example. Sayles observed that "the rank and file find in the seniority provisions of the contract a fruitful means of obtaining new vested interests, not at the expense of management but rather at the expense of groups and individuals within the plant... Within the plant, the purposeful use of seniority as a means of gaining individual and group advantage is a recognized and tacitly accepted phenomenon" (1952: 56).

The social actors in this approach are not persons acting individually, but as members of a mobilized collectivity — mobilized for the pursuit of certain advantages. Becoming employed is not just a question of getting a job; it is also a matter of joining a group that has certain interests in a particular department, a particular organization, occupation, or an otherwise defined domain and that expects its members to at least protect if not actively pursue these interests. One's competitors for scarce opportunities are not simply other individuals; they are "outsiders," members of another collectivity.[29]

What counts in "taking advantage of opportunities" is not so much individual skills (either to obtain job information, for impression management, or for job performance)[30] as the effectiveness of the social organization for the control of domains and of access to them developed by the group with which one is affiliated. This effectiveness depends on gatekeeping and sponsorship mechanisms, on the applications of rules having a direct or indirect impact on access to the opportunities in the domain, and on the group's ability to pressure its own members to stay in line.

What is the pertinence of this approach for ethnic stratification? Does it lead to similar or different hypotheses as the previous ones? Its implications for ethnic stratification will be reviewed under the same three major headings.

Sources of Ethnic Inequality

In the first approach, observed income and occupational differentials between ethnic groups were thought to be the result of differences in personal resources of relevance for productivity or of imperfections in the labor market. With the present approach, such differentials are thought to be caused by differences in the group's ability to organize so as to either take or maintain control of a particular work domain. This involves as indicated above, ethnic control of gatekeeping positions, ethnic sponsorship, and struggles over rules and processes of selection that may directly or indirectly affect the ethnic distribution of advantages.

The resources that are critical in this regard are group resources such as leadership, cohesive social networks,[31] mutual trust, means of communication. Personal resources are not irrelevant, but the important point is that the social organization of the group (cohesion, trust) must be such as to allow the sharing of these resources (information, techniques of job performance, etc.) (Coleman, 1969). The critical factors in this approach are those that affect the group's capacity to organize for common occupational goals and to control certain domains and the channels leading to them.

A key question is why the social organization that emerges for the control of occupational domains (either within departments, firms, industries or occupational specializations) is based on ethnicity rather than on some other social factor? The social closure model predicts group formation for the monopolization of certain advantages. But on what basis will groups get formed? Theoretically, almost any factor of social differentiation can provide such a basis: age, sex, ethnicity, religion, political or social ideology, language, and so on. In fact, a systematic survey of work settings in a society like Canada would show that the basis of group formation varies considerably from one type of work setting to another. For instance, in organizations dealing with ideas, such as university departments and churches, school of thought and social ideology would be more likely to be the basis of group formation for occupational control than in organizations producing commodities.

But how can the issue of variations in the basis of group formation be approached? Mayhew, in his discussion of the continuing importance of ascription in modern societies, argues that "the staying power and functional capacity of ascription can be summed up in three words: it is cheap. Ascription involves using an existent, pre-established structure as a resource rather than creating a new specialized structure for the same purpose" (1968: 110). This principle can be applied to the formation of an organization for social closure: it will tend to occur on the basis of existent, pre-established structures of social relationships. Thus, if for historical, ecological, or other reasons, a community is structured along ethnic lines, that existing structure will tend to be reproduced in the organization of work and of labor market processes.

As was mentioned earlier, occupational domains are not purely physical or statistical groupings. Rather, they are socially organized in that their boundaries and their internal organization are socially, and not purely technically, determined. Mayhew's argument suggests that the social organization of occupational domains will reflect the social organization of the community in which they are located simply because it is cheaper and more expedient to use existing structures than to build new ones. Because of this, it can be said that the social closure approach does not assume the occupational structure and the labor market institutions to be necessarily free of ethnicity or ethnically neutral; it is so only if the community is ethnically homogeneous or if ethnicity plays virtually no part in shaping its social structure.

Ethnicity as Asset or Liability and Orientation toward One's Ethnic Identity

While in the first approach ethnicity was seen as an individual attribute, in this approach it is seen primarily as a basis of social organization, as a basis for social mobilization and concerted action.[32] In such a perspective, it is an asset to the extent that the ethnic collectivity has the resources to get organized for the control of occupational domains and to the extent that its organization will be strong enough to obtain results. If there is a chance of success, a rational strategy is needed to mobilize the existing loyalty, cohesion and other social assets in the ethnic group for increasing one's advantages in the labor market and/or to compete with other groups attempting to do so.

What is critical, then, is the distribution across ethnic collectivities of the resources and conditions necessary or useful for organization. Generally, there are two interrelated sets of factors that are relevant: those pertaining to the conditions internal to the ethnic collectivities and those associated with the position that each collectivity occupies in the social, economic and political structure of the society. A number of characteristics of ethnic collectivities were already mentioned: level of resources, social cohesion and trust, channels of communication, leadership, and so on. Features of the social organization of an ethnic collectivity emerge in part from its own internal attributes and social dynamics, but they are also determined by the circumstances of its position in the social structure.

By looking at the position of the dominant ethnic collectivity, one can say that the institutional system of the society, in its overall dimension, constitutes the "domain" of the dominant ethnic collectivity. This is reflected in the fact that the cultural values of that collectivity are those that are embedded in the institutions of the society: the political, educational, religious, recreational, economic and legal institutions incorporate features such as definitions of roles, rules for language use, knowledge considered valuable,[33] criteria of evaluation and success, and mechanisms for occupying various positions, especially those of authority, that reflect the cultural system of the dominant group.

As mentioned earlier, in this approach the institutional system is not ethnicity-free; the dominant ethnic collectivity is the one that has historically succeeded in imposing its own ethnicity on the structure and functioning of the institutions of the society. Needless to say, members of the dominant ethnic group (and those who become integrated into it) have, as a result of this situation, a tremendous advantage in the control of occupational domains.

The point illustrated by the case of the dominant ethnic collectivity and to which this third approach draws our attention is that a collectivity's capacity to organize for gaining occupational control is not only a function of its internal characteristics but also of the factors that are associated with its position in the social structure, a position that has political, legal, and symbolic as well as economic components.

Thus, when a collectivity is strong in its capacity to organize, its members will tend to perceive their ethnicity as an asset; when it is weak, however, they will tend to perceive it as a liability. They will tend to show strong assimilationist tendencies, acculturating as rapidly as possible and doing their utmost to gain acceptance by one or another of the existing ethnically controlled segments of the structure. Generally, the collectivity selected will tend to be the one that controls most, or the most interesting, segments of the occupational structure.

Occasions of Inter-Ethnic Conflict

The social closure approach points to three types of factors that may occasion conflict. Insofar as the organization of work is the result of technological and administrative factors, changes in these areas may well modify the boundaries and/or internal organization of work domains. If this occurs, it is likely to upset the existing distribution of ethnic control over the domains, a situation which can cause conflict.

The experience of discrimination is also an occasion of inter-ethnic conflict. However, the present approach does not see discrimination as an individual phenomenon, but as an institutional and a social one. Institutional discrimination stems directly from the fact that an ethnic collectivity has control over an area of institutional activity and has thus established structures, procedures and rules of behavior that are in accordance with its own cultural imperatives and interests. Since institutions are not ethnicity-free, discrimination is the result of the very functioning of those institutions. The unequal treatment that results may become an occasion of conflict between members of the collectivity that is victimized by the institutional practices and those that benefit by them. Whether such processes and their consequences are intentional or not, on the part of individuals, the effect is equally real and may lead the institutionally disadvantaged to challenge the group they see as responsible for the institutions and their functioning.

Social discrimination, on the other hand, occurs when the competition for the control of occupational domains takes place under norms considered illegitimate. If one of the parties in the competition engages in practices considered unacceptable (e.g. undercutting, strikebreaking, parachuting), it will be an occasion of inter-ethnic conflict. The dynamics of such discriminatory practices are those of intense group competition rather than those of individual prejudice.

Conflict may also be occasioned when the strength and/or aspiration of an ethnic collectivity changes. This can result from immigration or internal migrations, changes in the level of personal resources within the collectivity as a consequence of a general increase in the standard of living, appearance of a new class of leaders in the community, the "demonstration effect" of the activities of other groups, and so on. An increase in the relative strength and/or aspiration of a collectivity could lead it to attempt to expand the size or number of occupational domains under its control — attempts which are likely to occasion conflict. Or, it could lead it to attempt to change its social, legal, or political status, such as changing the legal status of its language. By affecting its relative position in the social structure, such changes could improve the collectivity's advantage in the competition over occupational (and other) domains. The changes are thus likely to be resisted by other collectivities who feel they would become relatively disadvantaged — another occasion of conflict.

VARIATIONS IN OCCUPATIONAL OR CLASS STRUCTURE AND ETHNIC DIVERSITY

Up to now, the occupational structure, the labor market institutions, and the class structure have been taken as given. But these structures and institutions can differ from one community or region to another or change with time — variations which can be associated with certain patterns of ethnic stratification. The three approaches draw attention to different components of the structure that is important to consider.

With the individual competition approach, the focus is on changes in the number of positions in the various occupational categories, on introduction of new occupations or elimination of existing ones. A secondary focus is on the labor market mechanisms such as those for the distribution of occupational information. The group competition or social closure approach is concerned with variations in the pattern of segmentation or discontinuities in occupational structure and in networks of labor market channels and mechanisms. New patterns may emerge at the level of the economy as a whole, in particular industries, firms or occupations. Organizational changes or differentiation can be at the origin of new domain boundaries. The emergence of specializations or sub-specializations may signal the appearance of new domains. Finally, what is important in the class model is the social organization of production and the particular structuring of property relationships that it entails. Important changes are those that pertain to the internal differentiation of classes, to differentiation of the class system through emergence of new classes, of contradictory class positions, or through the progressive disappearance of a class and to the conditions of class conflict and its outcome.

Variations in the structural components can occur as a result of a multiplicity of factors. For instance, the functioning of the system itself can be at the origin of structural changes as in the case of differentiation of control over the physical means of production from the control over labor power that came with expansion of the system. Technological changes, such as automation, and the implementation of new theories of management or of the organization of the work process can redefine work domains, create new positions and eliminate some. Legislation concerning labor-management relationships, work practices, labor market processes and so on can also have an impact.

The interaction of a particular social and technical division of labor with the characteristics of different ethnic categories of participants in the economy may have an impact on the patterns of ethnic stratification. For instance, in their review of the literature on occupational concentration of immigrants, Yancey et al. point out that "to understand the occupational concentrations of immigrants, it is necessary to consider both the diverse educational and occupational skills which immigrants brought, as well as the specific work opportunities which were available at the time of their arrival" (1976: 392–3).

The interaction of the character of the economic structure with the characteristics of an ethnically differentiated labor force is also clear in Willhelm's argument that automation is eliminating jobs for which blacks are the primary suppliers of labor and, as a result, blacks will progressively become more and more marginal to the economy: the black worker is becoming "not so much economically exploited as he is irrelevant" (1970: 162). A number of years ago, Rayack presented evidence which "indicated that the relative rise in the position of the Negro was a product of the acute labor shortages which persisted throughout the war and post war period of 1940-48, shortages which opened up a wider range of job opportunities for Negroes" (1961: 214). In a similar vein, Tobin argues that "by far the most powerful factor determining the economic status (both absolute and relative) of Negroes is the overall state of the U.S. economy" (1965: 895). Katzman (1969) points out that ethnic groups are exposed to different sets of economic opportunities as a result of their differences in regional location. He is referring to variations in factors such as the demand for labor at each skill level, the pattern of wages in different jobs and the level of unemployment. He shows that the economic performance of an ethnic group is "highly sensitive to the economic opportunities of the metropolitan region in which it lives."

The structural conditions in particular occupations may be of relevance as well. In some occupations, individual skills and talents may be more important than in others; or performance may be more easily measured and evaluated. Further, in some occupations there is no hierarchy of positions; or the job tenure is inherently insecure.[34] The number and distribution of such occupations in relation to the distribution of ethnic groups at certain times and places may affect the pattern of ethnic stratification.

The basic point that the few studies cited are meant to illustrate is that ethnic stratification may be the result not only of the characteristics and behavior of members of various ethnic groups and of inter-ethnic relationships, but of characteristics of the occupational and class structures as well and of their interaction with given ethnic configurations and patterns of migration and settlement.

CONCLUSION

Three perspectives for approaching the study of stratification have been described and applied to the question of ethnic stratification. The conception of ethnicity underlying the perspectives differs. One takes ethnicity as an individual attribute, a set of characteristics — identity, cultural traits — a person inherits at birth and through early socialization. The others see ethnicity as a basis of group formation and social mobilization for action that is cultivated whenever conditions are propitious. Moreover, ethnicity is seen sometimes as an asset and sometimes as a liability for the individuals involved. This varies with the different sets of circumstances identified by each of the approaches. Under the individual competition approach, it tends to be a liability and, to the extent that they have a choice, individuals will tend toward acculturation or selective acculturation retaining the traits that fit well in the prevailing system. In the class approach, it is an asset for a class that is ethnically homogeneous and is in conflict with another class of a different ethnic background. Ethnicity in such a case simply reinforces class solidarity. Otherwise, it is a liability because it weakens class solidarity and thus acts against the fundamental interests of those involved. Finally, in the social closure approach, ethnicity is an asset if the group has sufficient mobilization potential and if groups can successfully assume control of an occupational domain. It is a liability for those who cannot do so.

If we assume that the different perspectives do capture different aspects of social reality, then whether ethnicity is an asset or a liability is a highly circumstantial phenomenon that depends on the social process selected for attention and the location of people with regard to those processes. It is not surprising, then, that we find considerable ambivalence in our society with regard to the desirability of ethnic retention. This ambivalence may exist within individuals, especially those with young children. It may exist within ethnic groups, some segments of it favoring retention, others favoring acculturation. Or it may exist in the society at large. The analysis presented here suggests that the issue cannot be resolved in a general way: it depends on the aspects of the social structure upon which one focuses.

Notes

1. In his analysis, Westhues (1976) argues that three major approaches have shaped not only the study of stratification but sociological thinking and research generally, the approaches being differentiated in terms of which is regarded as the most critical decision-making unit in a society: the individual, a class or an organization. The three approaches discussed in this paper parallel closely the three identified by Westhues. See also Collins' (1971) discussion of the functional and conflict approaches to the study of educational stratification.

2. In a way, the essay is a sort of review of the literature. However, it does not pretend to present a comprehensive analysis of the existing research. No attempt is made to fit most of the existing studies in the analysis. References to studies are presented primarily for purposes of illustration.

3. It could be shown that they also lead to different policy orientations and decisions. But such an analysis is beyond the scope of this paper.

4. On plural or segmented societies see, for example, Smith (1969), Van den Berghe (1969).

5. In sociology, functionalism is another label for this approach; in economics, it is the approach underlying the marginal productivity of labor theory. The "human capital theory" also falls under this perspective.

6. See, for example, Stigler (1961, 1962), Thurow (1972), McCall (1973), Spence (1973), on the role of information in the labor market.

7. The expression is from Bernard. In judgmental competition, someone decides who the winner is. By contrast, in autonomous competition — a race for example — the process itself selects the winner (1949: 64).

8. Note that social networks are treated as an individual resource. Social networks and contacts can be manipulated to achieve certain personal goals. Networks are egocentric (Boissevain, 1968; Kapferer, 1969).

9. A similar description could be drawn, *mutatis mutandis*, from the vantage of an employer.

10. On the social and cultural characteristics defining the adaptive capacity of any ethnic group, see Wagley and Harris (1958: 264–273).

11. There is an ambiguity that runs through much of the sociological literature regarding ethnicity. On the one hand, ethnicity is frequently given as a prime example of ascription: it is determined by one's birth and early socialization and therefore is something beyond one's control. It is not something that one achieves, or shapes, through experience or deliberate action. On the other hand, the literature on acculturation, assimilation, absorption or integration or on ethnic retention, maintenance, and especially resurgence definitely considers ethnicity as being to some degree under individual control. Perhaps the critical distinction is between ethnic origin which is ascriptive and ethnicity which is achieved, in the sense that it is modifiable through life experiences. But the issue is more complex. There are some ethnic traits which are not modifiable (skin color), others which are modifiable, but with difficulty (language) and still others which are easily modifiable (cultural customs). Treating ethnicity as an ascriptive phenomenon is ambiguous, not to say misleading.

12. Of course, collective action may not necessarily occur. Other conditions are required.

13. These tendencies may take a long time to manifest themselves. Their visibility would also be affected by factors such as the rate of arrival of new immigrants.

14. The dual labor market theory and other segmented labor market theories build on this approach. See Stolzenberg (1975) and Cain (1976).

15. E.C. Hughes was one of the first to introduce this concept in the sociology of work (see Hughes and Hughes, 1952).

16. The size of the domains can vary considerably. Moreover, domains can be defined in terms of a small set of jobs in a department, of an entire department, of an organizational level (e.g. management), of an occupation, a firm, a set of firms within an industry, or an entire industry.

17. See also Neuwirth (1969), Cohen (1974).

18. It should be noted that Weber does not exclude the possibility of competition among workers. But it occurs within the social enclosure or domain and is regulated more or less severely by the members of the domain.

19. On "gatekeeping," see Anderson (1974: ch. 6).

20. See Brazeau (1958) for further discussion.

21. Such a collectivity can be either a group or a quasi-group. Quasi-groups are "aggregates ... which have no recognizable structure, but whose members have certain interests or modes of behavior in common, which may at any time lead them to form themselves into definite groups" (Ginsberg, 1953: 40). See also Dahrendorf (1959: 179–189).

22. Individual skills may be a necessary condition, but in this approach they are definitely not sufficient.

23. Social networks are seen as a factor in the social organization for purposive group action. In the first approach, social networks were seen as a set of channels that

individuals could manipulate or activate in the pursuit of their individual goals. Here social networks are instruments of concerted action.

24. Weber (1962, 1946), Cohen (1974), Barnet (1974).

25. The argument is not that the dominant group can impose its cultural character in some total way on the society and its institutions. There are other determinants of the characteristics of institutions both from within and from outside the society. The argument is that the dominant group has considerably more impact in shaping institutions than the other ethnic groups.

26. This is the Marxist approach which is at the base of a number of Marxist or neo-Marxist models.

27. See, for example, Giddens (1973), Poulantzas (1975), Wright (1976, 1977).

28. Wright provides an analysis of positions which occupy "objectively contradictory locations within class relations." These positions are in a double contradiction: as classes they are in an antagonistic, contradictory relation with other classes; but since they share interests with other classes, they "are torn between the basic contradictory class relation" (Wright, 1976: 26). Giddens refers to the same phenomenon when he writes of "quasi-class groupings" that "share certain common economic interests, but, for different reasons, stand on the margin of the dominant set of class relationships . . . " (1973: 31).

29. See Dahrendorf (1959: 182-9), Tilly (1964), Clark (1975), Brym (1977).

30. The expression is from Wright (1976: 26).

31. Wright identifies three sets of "contradictory locations": managers, small employers and semi-autonomous wage earners (1976: 26-38).

32. Blumer's critique (1965) of the functionalist argument that with industrialization and the rationalization of socio-economic processes, ethnicity could eventually disappear as a factor in social organization seems to be applicable, *mutatis mutandis*, to the argument of the class analysts. Both appear to make the dubious assumption of the dominance of technical and economic factors in shaping a society rather than examining the interaction that is taking place between those factors and other dynamic forces in social organizations, such as ethnicity.

33. Bonacich's theory throws doubt on the proposition of the deliberate fomenting of ethnic antagonisms for the sheer purpose of weakening the class of sellers of labor. Her theory states that such ethnic antagonisms as do emerge within that class are the result of employers' pursuit of cheap labor. But the proposition that employers have an interest in dividing the other class is certainly consistent with the approach. The question is partly an empirical one: to what extent have employers done so and by what means? It is also partly theoretical: it would seem relatively easy to formulate a theory of conflict in which the attempts of one of the parties to divide its opponents would only serve to strengthen the latter's solidarity.

34. These features of occupations as well as others are discussed by Blalock in his discussion of professional sports and of the blacks' position in athletic occupations (1967: 92-100).

References

ANDERSON, G.M.
Networks of Contact: The Portuguese and Toronto. Waterloo, Ontario: Wilfrid Laurier University Press, 1974.

BARNETT, M.R.
"Creating Political Identity," *Ethnicity* 1 (1974), 237–265.

BEATTIE, C., ET AL.
Bureaucratic Careers: Anglophones and Francophones in the Canadian Public

Service. Ottawa: Information Canada, 1972.

BERNARD, J.
American Community Behavior (Revised Edition) New York: Holt, Rinehart & Winston, 1962.

BLALOCK, H.M., JR.
Toward a Theory of Minority-Group Relations. New York: John Wiley & Sons, 1967.

BLUMER, H.
"Industrialization and Race Relations," in G. Hunter (ed.): *Industrialization and Race Relations*. London: Oxford University Press, 1965.

BOISSEVAIN, J.
"The Place of Non-groups in the Social Sciences," *Man* 3 (1968), 542–56.

BONACICH, E.
"A Theory of Ethnic Antagonism: The Split Labor Market," *American Sociological Review* 37 (1972), 547–59.

BONACICH, E.
"A Theory of Middleman Minorities," *A.S.R.* 38 (1973), 583–94.

BONACICH, E.
"Advanced Capitalism and Black/White Relations in the United States: A Split Labor Market Interpretation," *A.S.R.* 41 (1976), 34–51.

BRAZEAU, J.
"Language Differences and Occupational Experience," *Canadian Journal of Economics and Political Science* 24 (1958), 532–540.

BRYM, R.J.
"Explaining Variations in Canadian Populist Movements," paper presented at Canada/Poland Seminar, Warsaw: 1977.

CAIN, GLEN G.
"The Challenge of Segmented Labor Market Theories to Orthodox Theory," *Journal of Economic Literature*, Dec. 1976, 1215–57.

CLARK, S.
"The Political Mobilization of Irish Farmers," *Canadian Review of Sociology and Anthropology* 12 (1975), 483–499.

COHEN, A. (ED.).
Urban Ethnicity. London: Tavistock Publications, 1974.

COLEMAN, J.S.
"Race Relations and Social Change," in I. Katz & Gurin (eds.), *Race and the Social Sciences*, New York: Basic Books, 1969.

COLLINS, O.
"Ethnic Behavior in Industry: Sponsorship and Rejection in a New England Factory," *American Journal of Sociology* 51 (1946), 293–98.

COLLINS, R.
"Functional and Conflict Theories of Educational Stratification," *American Sociological Review*, 36 (1971), 1002–19.

DAHRENDORF, R.
Class and Class Conflict in Industrial Society. Stanford, Calif.: Stanford University Press, 1959.

GERTH, H.H. AND MILLS, C.W. (EDS.).
From Max Weber: Essays in Sociology. New York: Oxford University Press, 1958.

GIDDENS, A.
The Class Structure of the Advanced Societies. London: Hutchinson, 1973.

GINSBERG, M.
Sociology. London, 1953.

GRANOVETTER, M.S.
Getting a Job: A Study of Contacts and Careers. Cambridge, Mass.: Harvard University Press, 1974.

HUGHES, E.C. AND HUGHES, H.M.
Where People Meet: Race and Ethnic Frontiers. Glencoe, Ill.: The Free Press, 1952.

KAPFERER, B.
"Norms and the Manipulation of Relationships in a Work Context," in J.C. Mitchell, (ed.), *Social Networks in Urban Situations.* Manchester: Manchester University Press, 1969.

KATZMAN, M.T.
"Opportunity, Subculture and the Economic Performance of Urban Ethnic Groups," *A.J.E.S.* 28 (1969), 351–66.

MAYHEW, L.
"Ascription in Modern Societies," *Sociology Inquiry* 38 (1968).

McCALL, J.J.
Income Mobility, Racial Discrimination and Economic Growth. Lexington, Mass.: Lexington Books, 1973.

NEUWIRTH, G.
"A Weberian Outline of a Theory of Community: Its Application to the 'Dark Ghetto,'" *B.J.S.* 20 (1969), 148–63.

PARSONS, T.
Structure and Process in Modern Societies. New York: The Free Press, 1960.

POULANTZAS, N.
Classes in Contemporary Capitalism. Atlantic Highlands, N.J.: Humanities Press, 1975.

RAYACK, E.
"Discrimination and the Occupational Progress of Negroes," *Review of Economics and Statistics*, May 1961, 209–14.

SAYLES, L.R.
"Seniority: An Internal Union Problem," *Harvard Business Review* 30 (1952), 55–61.

SMITH, M.G.
"Some Developments in the Analytic Framework of Pluralism," In L. Kuper and M.G. Smith, (eds.), *Pluralism in Africa*, Berkeley, Calif.: University of California Press, 1969.

SPENCE, A.M.
"Job Market Signaling," *Quarterly Journal of Economics* 83 (1973), 355–74.

STIGLER, G.J.
"The Economics of Information," *Journal of Political Economics* 69 (1961), 213–225.

STIGLER, G.J.
"Information in the Labor Market," *Journal of Political Economy (Supplement)* 70 (1962), 94–105.

STINCHCOMBE, A.
"A Structural Analysis of Sociology," *A.S.R.* 10 (1975), 57–64.

STOLZENBERG, R.M.
"Occupations, Labor Markets and The Process of Wage Attainment," *A.S.R.* 40 (1975), 645–665.

THUROW, L.C.
Generating Inequality. New York: Basic Books, 1975.

TILLY, C.
The Vendée. Cambridge, Mass.: Harvard University Press, 1964.

TOBIN, J.
"On Improving the Economic Status of the Negro," *Daedalus* 94 (1965), 78–98.

VAN DEN BERGHE, P.L.
"Pluralism and the Polity: A Theoretical Exploration," in L. Kuper and M.G. Smith (eds.), *Pluralism in Africa*. Berkeley, Calif.: University of California Press, 1969.

WAGLEY, C., AND M. HARRIS
Minorities in the New World. New York: Columbia University Press, 1958.

WEBER, M.
Basic Concepts in Sociology. New York: The Citadel Press, 1969.

WESTHUES, K.
"Class and Organization as Paradigms in Social Science," *American Sociologist* 11 (1976), 38–49.

WILEY, N.F.
"America's Unique Class Politics: The Interplay of the Labor, Credit and Commodity Markets," *A.S.R.* 32 (1967), 529–40.

WILLHELM, S.M.
Who Needs the Negro? Cambridge, Mass.: Schenkman, 1970.

WRIGHT, E.O.
"Class Boundaries in Advanced Capitalist Societies," *New Left Review* 98 (1976), 3–41.

WRIGHT, E.O., AND L. PERRONE.
"Marxist Class Categories and Income Inequality," *A.S.R.* 42 (1977), 32–55.

YANCEY, W.L. ET AL.
"Emergent Ethnicity: A Review and Reformulation," *A.S.R.* 41 (1976), 391–403.

Languages in Conflict: Canada, 1976[*]

Richard J. Joy

THE EIGHT REGIONS OF CANADA

Canadian census data are customarily published by provincial totals. Although this is convenient for most other purposes, such a breakdown is less than satisfactory for the study of language characteristics: since three of the provinces are non-homogeneous, clarity of interpretation makes it desirable that New Brunswick, Quebec and Ontario each be split into two distinct parts. Elsewhere, however, similarity permits several provinces to be grouped. Accordingly, the major tables in this paper present figures on the basis of eight regions, rather than of ten provinces.

Each region has its own distinctive characteristics, with regard to language usage and other factors. Of the eight regions, one is overwhelmingly French, two have French majorities, one has a strong French minority and the other four have virtually insignificant francophone populations. Table I presents 1971 census data for the language most often spoken at home (French, English and Other). Table II shows the extent to which the two official languages are spoken in each of the eight regions. Three of these regions constitute a zone of transition between the French heartland and the English-speaking continent. Although this "Bilingual Belt" contains less than one quarter of Canada's population, over 60 percent of all those Canadians who claim to speak both English and French were found to be living in northern New Brunswick, southern and western Quebec and eastern and northern Ontario.

In the four regions of what might best be called "English Canada," barely 800,000 persons were capable of speaking French, in 1971. As there were over 400,000 persons of French mother tongue included in this total, it can be seen that, among the 14 million of mother tongues other than French, not more than three percent claimed to be bilingual (in the "official" sense; there were several million people in these regions who could speak English plus some non-official language). The conclusion to be drawn from these figures is that the French language is of very little interest to most Canadians living outside a line drawn from Sault Ste. Marie to Moncton.

[*] Abridged from the *American Review of Canadian Studies*, Autumn, 61 (2) 1976, pp. 7–22. Used with permission.

TABLE I   Language Most Frequently Used in the Home, 1971, for Each of the Eight Regions of Canada

| Region | Language used in the home | | |
| | French | English | Other |
	(thousands of persons)		
Atlantic	41	1,657	13
Northern N.B.	192	151	3
N. & E. Quebec	2,264	69	17
S. & W. Quebec	2,606	818	252
N. & E. Ontario	281	887	60
S. & W. Ontario	72	5,671	732
Prairies	78	3,127	337
B.C.	12	2,027	146
Canada	5,546	14,446	1,576
	(% of total population in each region)		
Atlantic	2.4%	96.8%	0.8%
Northern N.B.	55.4	43.7	0.9
N. & E. Quebec	96.3	3.0	0.7
S. & W. Quebec	70.9	22.2	6.9
N. & E. Ontario	22.9	72.2	4.9
S. & W. Ontario	1.1	87.6	11.3
Prairies	2.2	88.3	9.5
B.C.	0.5	92.7	6.8
Canada	25.7	67.0	7.3

At the other extreme is that part of Quebec Province situated east of Montreal and north of Sherbrooke, where over 98 percent of the total population could speak French and where five persons out of six could speak only that language. The predominance of the French language is so strong that this is the only region of Canada in which persons of English mother tongue are less numerous than those of British origin.

LANGUAGE RETENTION

Table III presents, by region, the number and percentage of persons classed as "French" according to each of the three criteria of the 1971 census. Ethnic Origin is traced back through the male line to the first ancestor arriving in North America. Mother Tongue is defined as "That language first learned and still understood," even if no longer spoken. The third criterion, that of the language most often used in the home, was introduced in 1971, after the Laurendeau-Dunton Commission had criticized the Mother Tongue question as giving results that were "a generation behind the facts." In 1971, all Canadians were asked the Mother Tongue question but only a one-third sample received the other two questions. The wording of the questions and certain editing procedures have

TABLE II   Number of Persons speaking "French Only," "French and English," and "English Only," for Each of the Eight Regions of Canada, 1971 Census

Region	French only	French and English	English only
		(thousands of persons)	
Atlantic	7	91	1,611
Northern N.B.	100	116	130
N. & E. Quebec	1,943	365	36
S. & W. Quebec	1,725	1,298	597
N. & E. Ontario	79	345	794
S. & W. Ontario	14	372	5,930
Prairies	10	208	3,275
B.C.	2	101	2,055
Canada	3,879	2,900	14,470
	(% of total population in each region)		
Atlantic	0.4	5.3	94.2
Northern N.B.	28.8	33.6	37.5
N. & E. Quebec	82.7	15.5	1.5
S. & W. Quebec	46.9	35.3	16.2
N. & E. Ontario	6.4	28.1	64.7
S. & W. Ontario	0.2	5.7	91.6
Prairies	0.3	5.9	92.4
B.C.	0.1	4.6	94.1
Canada	18.0	13.4	67.1

provoked considerable criticism but the published census results are probably sufficiently accurate for the purposes of this paper and will be used without further comment.

The table suggests that the French language is strong in Quebec, is probably viable within the border regions of New Brunswick and Ontario but has virtually no expectation of survival outside the Soo-Moncton Line. The four regions of English Canada which lie outside this line are notable, not only for the small number of francophones living in each but, more particularly, for the fact that the population of French mother tongue is much less numerous than that of French ethnic origin and those using French in the home are far fewer than those of French mother tongue; it is evident that assimilation and language transfer are rampant in these regions.

SOME EFFECTS OF MIGRATION

Immigration has played a major role in determining the characteristics of Canada's population and has had a two-fold effect in reducing the importance of the French language. Within Quebec, a constant flow of immigrants has maintained the vitality and the relative strength of the anglophone minority. More important, however, is the fact that 83 percent of Canada's foreign-born are to be found in the five provinces west of Quebec; they and their children have made major contributions to the growth and progress of their regions and have greatly increased the relative political and economic power of Ontario and the western provinces. If Quebec continues to repel immigrants, it could well slide toward political impotence.

TABLE III   Number of Persons Reporting French as Ethnic Origin, as Mother Tongue and as Home Language, for Each of the Eight Regions of Canada, 1971 Census.

Region	Total population	French ethnic origin	French mother tongue	French home language
		(thousands of persons)		
Atlantic	1,711	137	65	41
Northern N.B.	346	208	201	192
N. & E. Quebec	2,350	2,213	2,257	2,264
S. & W. Quebec	3,677	2,546	2,611	2,607
N. & E. Ontario	1,228	398	330	281
S. & W. Ontario	6,475	339	152	72
Prairies	3,542	237	139	78
B.C.	2,185	97	38	12
Canada	21,568	6,180	5,794	5,546
		(% of total population in each region)		
Atlantic	100	8.0	3.8	2.4
Northern N.B.	100	60.3	58.0	55.4
N. & E. Quebec	100	94.2	96.0	96.3
S. & W. Quebec	100	69.2	71.0	70.9
N. & E. Ontario	100	32.4	26.9	22.9
S. & W. Ontario	100	5.2	2.3	1.1
Prairies	100	6.7	3.9	2.2
B.C.	100	4.4	1.7	0.5
Canada	100	28.7	26.9	25.7

TABLE IV   Official Languages Spoken by Postwar Immigrants, 1971

	Living in Quebec		Living elsewhere	
English only	135,405	(36%)	1,682,255	(85%)
English and French	129,540	(35%)	128,255	(6.5%)
French only	70,915	(19%)	6,185	(0.5%)
Neither	35,675	(10%)	157,710	(8.0%)
Total	371,545		1,970,395	

The 1971 census reported 3,295,530 foreign-born living in Canada, including 2,341,940 who had immigrated since 1941. Table IV shows the official language spoken by the latter.

Table IV shows that immigrants settling outside Quebec have tended to learn only the English language but that those enumerated within Quebec seem undecided, as to whether they should assimilate to Quebec's majority or to Canada's majority. There are valid reasons for this indecision: census figures show that a high percentage of the immigrants initially locating in Quebec will leave that province within a few years. During the five-year period 1956–60, Quebec received 163,502 immigrants but only 82,720 of this group were to be found in the province by 1971; of the 166,000 who arrived in 1951–55, only 72,000 remained in 1971.

Departure of those who cannot or will not learn French is only one of several factors contributing to an increase in the use of French among foreign-born residents of Quebec. There has been an increase in the percentage of new immigrants who are of French mother tongue (this includes a substantial number of Haitians) and these made up 19 percent of the foreign-born in 1971, as against only 13 percent in 1961. Meanwhile, those of other mother tongues, including English, have been learning to speak French as a second or third language.

The 1961 census showed that, among the 128,000 male postwar immigrants living in Quebec, only 46 percent claimed to be able to speak French, hardly more than the 45 percent who reported that they spoke "English Only." By 1971, however, when there were 192,000 male postwar immigrants in Quebec, 59 percent could speak French and the English Only had dropped to just under 35 percent (the remaining 6 ½ percent spoke neither official language).

The departure, from Quebec, of those who prefer to speak English is a significant factor in maintaining the language balance in that province. As noted on the previous page, fewer than half the immigrants who come to Quebec are prepared to settle there permanently. This impermanence of the foreign-born population has been overlooked by many of those attempting to forecast the possible language composition of Quebec's population in future decades; any forecast based on the gross number of expected immigrants will give results that are far too high, with regard to the percentage of non-francophones in Quebec at any future date.

Native-born anglophones also leave Quebec and their departure is only partially balanced by the movement of anglophones from other provinces into Quebec. In 1971, there were 194,000 persons of English mother tongue who had been born in Quebec but who were living elsewhere in Canada, as against 140,000 born elsewhere and living in Quebec. Any discouragement of migration into Quebec will result in a reduction of the anglophone population, even if there is no increase in the rate of outward migration; a post-Olympics slump in employment opportunities could be as effective as Bill 22 in this regard.

In contrast to the outward migration of the anglophones, today's Quebec-born francophones tend to remain within their own province. Their predecessors spread the French language from coast to coast but the 1971 census showed that, of the 4,808,000 Quebec-born persons of French mother tongue, only 144,160 were living elsewhere in Canada and 97 percent were still to be found within Quebec. To some extent, in fact, the disappearance of francophone minorities in other provinces is being accelerated by a movement back to Quebec of those who have the strongest desire to retain the language of their parents: 111,000 persons of French mother tongue, born elsewhere in Canada, were living in Quebec in 1971 and over 90 percent of those reported French as the language used most often at home; among their cousins who remained outside Quebec, only 71 percent were still using French in their homes.

BIRTH RATES AND SCHOOL-AGE MINORITIES

For many decades, the French-speaking population of Canada was able to maintain its relative importance through a high birth rate which compensated for the influx of anglophone immigrants. In 1931, francophones made up only 24 percent of the adult population of Canada but 34 percent of the children and "La Revanche des Berceaux" seemed on the way to success. The recent drop in French births has been very painful to French-Canadian nationalists and they find it difficult to believe that today's potential mothers are more interested in amassing material wealth than in winning the battle of the cradle (some credit for this drop is due to the federal government, which subsidizes the operation of French-language television stations throughout Quebec and in all other areas of Canada where there may be substantial concentrations of francophones).

In 1961, among the French-speaking population of Quebec, there were 563,600 children aged 0–4 and 716,800 women aged 20–44; by 1971, the number of children had dropped to 390,600 although the number of women had risen to 860,000. More recent figures suggest that barely 70,000 francophone children are being born annually in Quebec; this indicates a birth rate per 1000 women that is less than half that noted 20 years ago.

Although school-aged populations are now declining rapidly, the drop in birth rates will take a few more years to fully work its way up the school system and its effects were only beginning to be felt, at the time of the 1971 census. At the five to 14 age group, there were 157,125 children outside Quebec who reported French as the language most often used at home. The great majority of these were to be found in Ontario and New Brunswick, 81,850 in the former and 50,540 in the latter. Both these provinces have complete French-language tax-supported school systems, including universities at Ottawa and Moncton. Elsewhere, however, the situation of the French language is desperate: in the seven provinces west of Ontario and east of New Brunswick, there were fewer than 25,000 francophones among the 1.5 million total population in the 5 to 14 age group. Although most of the laws against French schools have been repealed, there will soon be no clientele for such schools: with francophones outnumbered sixty-to-one, there can be very little expectation of survival for the French language among the younger generation and the drop in birth rates is merely one more negative factor.

Although anglophones represent 15.8 percent of the adult population of Quebec, the 172,800 children from English-speaking homes were only 13 percent of the total five to 14 population of that province in 1971. However, this exceeds the total number of French-speaking children outside Quebec and is more than adequate to support a complete school system, including universities. In fact, almost 16 percent of Quebec's total school enrolment is in English-language schools, as these attract many children from homes in which "Other" languages are spoken.

DISAPPEARING MINORITIES

One hundred and fifty years ago, English was the language most commonly spoken in the Eastern Townships of Quebec, on both sides of the Ottawa Valley and even in the foothills of the Laurentians, north of Quebec City (in many of these areas, Gaelic was the second language and French ran a poor third). At the census immediately preceding Confederation, persons of French origin were a minority at Montreal and made up barely 20 percent of what is now the metropolitan area of Hull; even Quebec City was 40 percent British at that time.

By the early 1900s, excess population spilling out of the old French parishes along the St. Lawrence had filled up most of Quebec Province and expanded into eastern and northern Ontario, while smaller groups had migrated to St. Boniface and further west. Now, however, Canada is in a period of consolidation and we arc witnessing the final assimilation of those French Canadians whose fathers or grandfathers ventured too far afield from their homeland.

To permit an evaluation of what has happened over the past 30 years, Table V compares 1941 and 1971 census figures, for each region, according to the two key criteria of origin and language. Changes in the number of persons of French origin within a region reflect the natural increase and net migration of the intercensal period; when an increase in the French-origin population of a region is not matched by a corresponding increase in the French-speaking population, we can infer that there has been anglicization of the minority.

From the table, it can be seen that, for Canada as a whole, the increase in the francophone population was substantially less than that of the French-origin population: 2,190,000 against 2,690,000. During this period of 30 years, assimilation and language transfer must have reduced the French-speaking population by half-a-million persons.

At first glance, such a loss may appear moderate, since it represents only eight percent of the total French-origin population. However, the geographical distribution of the losses gives them an importance far greater than would be suggested by the figures for the country as a whole. In the two regions of Quebec, net language transfer actually augmented the number of francophones, so the losses elsewhere were staggering. While the French-origin population outside Quebec was increasing by 625,000 persons, the francophone population increased by only 35,000.

In the seven provinces west of Ontario and east of New Brunswick, there was an actual decline in the francophone population, from almost 200,000 in 1941 to

TABLE V   Distribution of the French Population of Canada, According to the Two Criteria of Origin and Language, by Region, 1941 and 1971 Censuses

| | French by origin | | French by language | |
| | 1941 | 1971 | 1941 | 1971 |
Region	(in thousands of persons)			
Atlantic*	100	137	61	41
Northern N.B.	153	208	151	192
N. & E. Quebec	1,475	2,213	1,504	2,264
S. & W. Quebec	1,220	2,546	1,213	2,607
N. & E. Ontario	238	398	218	281
S. & W. Ontario	136	339	71	72
Prairies	147	237	127	78
B.C.	22	97	11	12
Canada*	3,491	6,180	3,357	5,546
	(as percentage of total for Canada)			
Atlantic	2.9	2.2	1.8	0.7
Northern N.B.	4.4	3.4	4.5	.
N. & E. Quebec	42.2	35.8	44.8	40.8
S. & W. Quebec	35.0	41.2	36.1	47.0
N. & E. Ontario	6.8	6.4	6.5	5.1
S. & W. Ontario	3.9	5.5	2.1	1.3
Prairies	4.2	3.8	3.8	1.4
B.C.	0.6	1.6	0.3	0.2

*Atlantic and Canada 1941 figures increased to reflect estimated French population of Newfoundland. "Language" is mother tongue in 1941, home language in 1971.

under 125,000 in 1971, although the number of persons of French origin had risen to 445,000. A continuing downtrend is almost certain, in these provinces, as the age distribution of francophones shows that the number of French-speaking children is below the level required for replacement of the older generation.

ONTARIO

The largest francophone population outside Quebec is to be found in Ontario, where 352,460 persons reported French as the language most often used at home. In any other province, a group of this size would have enormous political power; the misfortune of the Franco-Ontarians is that they represent only 4.5 percent of the total population of Ontario and live chiefly in peripheral areas where they do not greatly impinge on the consciousness of administrators at Toronto.

Table V showed a considerable migration of persons of French origin toward the cities of southern Ontario: from 136,000 in 1941, the French-origin population of this region grew to 339,000 in 1971. However, the urban milieu has been fatal to the French language and the 1971 census found that four out of five of the

French-origin population were speaking English even when in their own homes; those still speaking French represented only 1.1 percent of the total population of southern Ontario.

French does not have the status of a major language in most of the cities of southern Ontario. At Toronto, the 20,580 persons who spoke French at home were only a small fraction of the 190,000 who spoke Italian and the francophones were also outnumbered by several other language groups, including those who spoke Greek, German, and Ukrainian. At Hamilton, the picture was similar, with less than one percent of the total population reporting French as the language of the home. Even at St. Catharines, francophones were only 3 ½% of the total population of the metropolitan area, although their local concentration within the city of Welland has enabled them to obtain French-language schools and other facilities and to resist anglicization somewhat more successfully than elsewhere.

In the Windsor area, where one third of the population was French-speaking at the time of Confederation, assimilation has virtually wiped out the language, except in a few rural pockets, and even these are disappearing as the expansion of the metropolitan area destroys the former isolation of fringe areas. Although there were 59,000 persons of French origin in Essex county in 1971, only 11,900 reported French as the language used most often at home.

The situation is quite different in the north and the east of Ontario, areas which show up on a map as the westward extension of Quebec. Here francophones make up one-quarter of the total population and are actually in the majority in some counties. Although many live in rural areas and small towns, the survival of their language has been greatly helped by the fact that the federal government, with its policy of employment for francophones, is the major employer in the only large city located within this region. Despite declining birth rates, net outward migration and some assimilation, it is probable that the French-speaking minority will persist almost indefinitely in this region.

NEW BRUNSWICK

During my school days, it was considered virtually certain that the high Acadian birth rate would, perhaps well before the end of the century, result in New Brunswick becoming the second province with a francophone majority. However, demographic forecasts were, as usual, confounded by the actual behavior of the population: after peaking at 36 percent in 1951, the French-speaking minority had dropped back to only 31 percent in 1971.

Heavy outward migration from the economically-depressed northern counties of New Brunswick removed many of the younger generation and those who remained have followed the example of Quebec, toward lower birth rates. The result has been a relatively low rate of increase of the French-origin population (19 percent between 1951 and 1971, as against 43 percent in Quebec during the same 20 years). Assimilation, although minimal in northern New Brunswick, has been high among the French-origin residents of Saint John and significant even at Moncton. Future trends will depend largely on the extent to which government programs can hold the population within the Acadian area as the old labor-intensive occupations have disappeared.

UNE PROVINCE QUI N'EST PAS COMME LES AUTRES

From the preceding pages, it can be seen that the French language has virtually no expectation of survival outside the Soo-Moncton line and is in some difficulty even within northern New Brunswick and the east and north of Ontario.

Within Quebec, however, the use of French has been increasing during the past four decades, as the author of this paper can attest from personal observation. Census figures support the aural evidence and a continuing rise in French unilingualism among the active male population shows quite conclusively that it is the English language which is losing ground in this province.

Over 90 percent of the adult males claimed to be able to speak French in 1971, as against only 55 percent claiming the ability to speak English. This is a sure indication that a majority of the province's population was working in French, long before the introduction of Bill 22.

From other census figures, it can be seen that the French-origin residents of Quebec have been able not only to retain the language of their forefathers but even to absorb a significant percentage of their British-origin neighbors. A table presenting the cross-classification of mother tongue versus ethnic origin would show that, even in 1971, 98 percent of the French-origin residents of Quebec were also of French mother tongue. Equally noteworthy, of the 438,000 persons of British origin born in Quebec and living in Quebec at the time of the 1971 census, just over 22 percent were of French mother tongue and an even greater number reported French as the language most often used at home.

Despite these losses, the English-speaking minority in Quebec has remained reasonably constant, at about one sixth of the total population, for reasons discussed in the earlier section on migration. Between 1941 and 1971, the number of anglophones in Quebec rose to 888,000 from about 500,000, although the population of British origin grew at only half that rate, to 640,000 from 453,000; this shows the importance of the anglophone population of non-British origins. Care must be taken, however, to differentiate between "foreign-born" and "of other origins"; the two terms are not interchangeable: of the 245,000 anglophones of other origins, living in Quebec, only 83,000 had been born outside Canada, a number exceeded by the 86,000 foreign-born anglophones who were of British origin.

CONCLUSIONS

Languages in Conflict[1] was written in 1966 and traced the historical development of Canada's two major language groups up to 1961. The census of 1971, with its new question on the language of the home, confirmed the picture of a French heartland separated from English-speaking North America by a bilingual belt which includes Ottawa, Montreal and Moncton. A line drawn from Sault Ste. Marie to Moncton marks the limits of the area within which the French language is in common use; among the 14 million Canadians living outside this Soo-Moncton line, barely 800,000 claimed to be able to speak French, including only 200,000 who reported French as the language they spoke most often at home.

Although the French language has been declining elsewhere, it is the English language which is falling into disuse within Quebec. If this trend continues, as seems probable, there will be no valid grounds for concern, on the part of the francophone majority, as to the future of their language within that province, although the continuing fall in French birth rates does have serious implications, with regard to the relative strength of Quebec within Canada.

Canada is, therefore, showing a trend toward a linguistic polarization similar to that now found in Belgium, with the two official languages co-existing only in northern New Brunswick and within a narrow belt along both sides of the Quebec-Ontario border; linguistically, Montreal and Ottawa are the Canadian equivalents of Brussels.

Note

1. Richard J. Joy, *Languages in Conflict* (Toronto: McClelland and Stewart, 1972).

Ascription by Race and Nationality in Professional Football*

Donald W. Ball

One of the emergent characteristics of the sociology of the sixties was the development of a substantive focus on sport. Among the major reasons for this development were the increasingly large number of persons and volume of resources involved in sport and the recognition of the pre-eminently social nature of sport as a form of conduct.

Sport as a social activity is particularly amenable to general sociological scrutiny because sports *qua* games may be heuristically treated as closed systems, with explicit and codified normative regulations, for example, rulebooks, and precise and public measures of outcomes, performances, efficiency, and the like. Such an approach is basically one of a "sociology *through* sport," using sport data to address more general sociological questions.

Although sport may be treated "as if" it is a bounded system, empirically it is embedded in the larger society — acting and reacting and mirroring that broader societal context. Sport is neither trivial nor merely a laboratory for the sociologist, but an important dimension of human experience and concern. This perspective is one that focuses on "sport and society" or the "sociology *of* sport," viewing sport as a social reality *sui generis*.

The following discussion will be concerned with patterns of differential treatment of professional football players in Canada and the United States. Such differences will be considered with regard to the variables of race and national origins; that is, a sociology *of* sport.

* Abridged from the *Canadian Review of Sociology and Anthropology*, 10 (2) 1973, pp. 97–113. Used with permission.

Cameron Ball, Neil Ball, and Philip Pollard helped in procuring some of the data on players in the Canadian Football League used in this article. This project was partly supported by a University of Victoria Faculty Research Grant (08 518). Helpful comments were received from colleagues when earlier versions of this material were presented in seminars at the University of Alberta and the University of Calgary; from Brian Currie of the University of Victoria, and John Loy of the University of Massachusetts. A more extensive formulation was presented to the symposium on Man, Sport, and Contemporary Society, Queen's College of the City University of New York, March 1972.

I

In considering the differential treatment of professional athletes on the basis of race, there are two broad approaches. One, "the Jackie Robinson story" basically says (regarding blacks), "you never had it so good" (Boyle, 1963; Olsen, 1968). This view emphasizes the opportunities for mobility made available to minority group members by professional sport. Thus, professional sport is seen as an accessible "legitimate opportunity structure" (Cloward and Ohlin, 1960).

The other view might be called "the Harry Edwards corrective" (Edwards, 1969). This perspective acknowledges the availability of entrance into sport for minority members, but points to continued discriminatory practices within the context of the structure of sport. Of special attention by this school have been their allegations of "stacking."

Stacking, the practice of positioning athletes in team sports on the basis of particularistic rather than universalistic characteristics has been alleged and described by Edwards (1969), Meggysey (1970), and Olsen (1968); and empirically demonstrated by Loy and McElvogue (1970), along with confirmatory research by Brower (1972). Essentially, *stacking in sports involves assignment to a playing position, an achieved status, on the basis of an ascribed status* (Davis, 1949:96–117). A focal concern by sociologists of sport has been the stacking of team members on the ascriptive basis of race, (for example, Loy and McElvogue, 1970; Brower, 1972; and Edwards, 1969). As is the case with much material of a sociological perspective, the works cited above are primarily or exclusively referring to situations in the United States.

In the following discussion, the theoretical formulation and empirical investigation begun on U.S. professional football by Loy and McElvogue (1970) will be applied to Canadian sport, replicated on race (also see Smith and Grindstaff, 1970; Barnes, 1971), and *extended to national origins* with comparative data drawn from professional football in the U.S. and in Canada from the Canadian Football League (CFL).

II

The Centrality Theory

Drawing upon Grusky's theory of organization structure (1963) and Blalock's propositions regarding occupational discrimination (1962), Loy and McElvogue (1970:5–7) have formulated a theory to explain the disproportionate presence — stacking — of blacks in some positions, and their practical absence from others in professional football and baseball. In doing so, they conceive of teams as work organizations, and the positions within them as analogous to occupations.

Employing baseball teams *qua* formal organizations for his empirical examples, Grusky has asserted that the formal structure of an organization systematically patterns the behaviors associated with its constituent positions along three interdependent dimensions: spatial location, nature of organizational tasks, and frequency of interaction. The major theoretical thrust of Grusky's organizational model is contained in the statement that "all else being equal, the more central one's spatial location: (1) the greater the likelihood dependent or coordinative tasks will be performed and (2) the greater the rate of interaction with occupants of other positions. Also, the performance of dependent tasks is positively related to frequency of interaction" (1963:346).

Centrality, then refers to (i) spatial location and (ii) the attendant kinds of tasks and interaction rates. From a structural standpoint it is best operationalized, at least in the case of fixed-position team sports taken-as-formal-organizations (for example, football or baseball), by spatial location.

Like Grusky, Blalock's consideration of interaction, task dependency, and occupational discrimination turned to baseball for empirical examples to bolster the theoretical propositions. Blalock's propositions can be readily synthesized with Brusky's model. As Loy and McElvogue put it, "since the dimensions of interaction and task dependency treated by Blalock are included in the concept of centrality, we integrated his propositions under a more general one, stating that *discrimination is positively related to centrality*" (1970:7; emphasis added).

Centrality and Professional Team Sports

In professional team sports a specific variant of occupational discrimination is *stacking*: the arbitrary inclusion or exclusion of persons vis-a-vis a playing position on the basis of ascriptive status, for example, race. Thus, Loy and McElvogue predicted as their specific theoretical proposition that stacking, a form of "racial segregation in professional team sports is positively related to centrality" (1970:7).

The Original Test of the Proposition

For their first test of the prediction, Loy and McElvogue turned to major league baseball in the United States. Using 1967 data and treating catchers and infield positions as central, the outfield as non-central (and excluding pitchers as unique and neither), they found that seven out of ten white players (N = 132) occupied central positions, while only one out of three blacks (N = 55) were so located (1970:8–10; also see 15–24). Statistically significant beyond the .0005 level, the baseball data were strongly supportive of their model and the stacking prediction it generated. They next turned their attention to U.S. professional football.

III

The Case of Professional Football

Although there are differences between the rules and positions regarding professional football in Canada and the United States, these are increasingly more historical than actually differentiating (on the convergence between the two games, see Cosentino, 1969). Table I indicates the central and non-central positions which characterize both offensive defensive formations, and subsumes

TABLE I   Central and Non-Central Positions on Offence and Defence*

	Offence	Defence
Central:	center quarterback guards	linebackers
Non-central:	tackles ends flankers, wide receivers running backs	tackles ends backs, safeties

* Adapted from Loy and McElvogue (1970:10–12).

the minor differences between the two sets of procedures in force on each side of the border.

Data

Loy and McElvogue's American football data (1970:11–13) were drawn from yearbooks for the 1968 seasons of the American Football League and the National Football League and classified all starting players (except specialty teams) by offensive or defensive position, along with race, black or white. All data on American professional football employed in the following is taken from their study.

The data on the Canadian Football League personnel presented here is for the 1971 season. It is drawn from the *Canadian Football League Player Photos, Official 1971 Collection*, a widely distributed promotional device, and checked where possible against other and similar sources (on the rationale for using such mass-circulation-based data see Ball, 1967:452–453). These materials provide a 75 percent sample of the 32-man roster allowed each of the nine teams in the league, and like the Loy and McElvogue data, are based upon pre-season, but accurate, forecasts. For each player information is available on position, on race (from a photograph), and usually on national origin and on prior education and playing experience. Although a 75 percent sample should yield an N = 216, due to missing information it is reduced slightly here to N = 209. On the whole, visual inspection suggests the sample is representative. However, it is slightly biased toward imports in terms of national origins.

Although this attribute, national origin, is an important independent variable, its bias is neutralized by percentaging against the unbalanced marginal totals. However, because of the limitations of the sample, the following is claimed to be no more than a "demonstration" (Garfinkel, 1964), rather than a more rigorous "investigation." (On the methodological problems of using rosters, for example the lack of stability within seasons, see Smith and Grindstaff, 1970:60–62.) Finally, though the data cover only one season in each case, other research has shown aggregate sport data to be quite stable over time (on international figure skating, see Ball, 1971; on baseball, see Loy and McElvogue, 1970:15–22).

Centrality, Stacking, and Race: A Comparison

According to the Loy-McElvogue hypothesis, blacks in professional football will be stacked at non-central positions and excluded from central ones. Comparing their data on the American NFL (columns B and D of Table II) with data on the CFL (columns A and C) indicates a similar pattern in each case: blacks are virtually excluded from central positions in professional football on either side of the border. The similarity of the patterns is as striking as the moral implications are obvious; neither virtues nor vices are respecters of national borders (also see Smith and Grindstaff, 1970:47–66; and more generally, Cosentino, 1969, on the "Americanization" of Canadian football).

IV

Centrality, National Origins, and Stacking

Unlike professional football in the United States, Canadian football has been historically cross-cut by another ascriptive status of its players; national origin, Canadians and imports (for the latter, read Americans). Americans have been playing football in Canada at least since 1912, in the forerunners of the CFL, the rugby unions (Cosentino, 1969:48–49).

It should be understood that the categorization of national origins to be used here, Canadians and imports, is not the same as that used by the CFL itself. The League's definition emphasizes prior experience as well as citizenship and nativity, the criterion herein employed. Thus, an American player without U.S. high school or college experience becomes a non-import under League definitions. Put another way, national origins are ascriptive, while League definitions may be achieved. Consistency suggests the utility of opting for the former as an analytical variable.

Canadians and Imports: The Data

When nativity is considered, the null form of the stacking hypothesis predicts no differences between the proportion of centrally located Canadians and imports. In other words, the relationship should be one of parity.

Following Loy and McElvogue (1970), Table III presents the distribution of imports (Americans) and Canadians in the CFL in terms of the centrality model. It is clear that whether one looks at overall patterns, or at offensive or defensive alignments separately, imports predominate over Canadian players in terms of the proportion of central positions they occupy. The difference on offence is particularly interesting, since almost half of the central Canadians are at one position only ($N = 8$), that of centre. Smith and Grindstaff (1970:36) have described the centre as a position usually manned by Canadians and "generally acknowledged to require less skill." Thus, if central positions are assumed to be in some ways more "difficult" as well as more "desirable," Canadians predominate at only the least of these. Additionally, because of the restrictive quota on imports (maximum of 14 out of 32 players *per* team in 1971), quantitative differences are actually more extreme than their apparent magnitude.[1]

To demonstrate that Canadians and imports are differentially distributed is not to demonstrate "stacking" *per se*, however. It is frequently alleged that imports are the more skilled players by virtue of their superior training rather than their ability; especially in terms of their college and university football experience (see former import Hardimon Curetan, quoted in Barnes, 1971:43–54). At the same time, although perhaps not widely recognized, the fact is that approximately half

TABLE II   Race of Players by Centrality of Position for Canadian and U.S. Professional Leagues (Adjusted Percentages)

Position	Percentage of whites		Percentage of blacks	
	(A) Cdn.	*(B) U.S.†*	*(C) Cdn.*	*(D) U.S.†*
Offence				
Central	47	45	06	02
Non-central	53	55	94	98
Total percentage	100	100	100	100
N	97*	220	19*	66
Defence				
Central	28	37	—	06
Non-central	72	63	100	94
Total percentage	100	100	100	100
N	83*	192	12	94

* Percentage adjusted to compensate for the additional position in Canadian football. This position is non-central; thus the non-central raw number is multiplied by .875 (7/8) to equalize with U.S. formations. Adjusted base numbers, upon which percentages are calculated are: $97 \approx 90$; $83 \approx 75$; and $19 \approx 17$. This procedure is not necessary in subsequent tables where comparisons are limited to CFL players only.

† U.S. data for 1968 from Loy and McElvogue (1970:10–12).

TABLE III   National Origins of CFL Players and Centrality of Position

Position	Percentage of Canadians	Percentage of imports
Central, all	27	35
Non-central	73	65
Total	100	100
N	94	110
Offence		
Central	34	41
Non-central	66	59
Total	100	100
N	50	64
Defence		
Central	18	26
Non-central	82	74
Total	100	100
N	44	46

of the Canadians in the Canadian Football League played football while attending college or university in the United States. Such "crash courses" have often been the instigation of CFL teams themselves (Barnes, 1971).

Thus, examining Canadian players in terms of prior playing experience would allow for an assessment of a *training* versus *stacking* hypothesis. Table IV presents data on Canadian players in terms of centrality and whether or not they played collegiate football in the United States or had some other form of prior experience, for example, Canadian university, junior football, or high school participation.

TABLE IV   Background of C.F.L. Players and Centrality of Position

Position	Percentage U.S. college	Percentage other
Central, all	31	20
Non-central, all	69	80
Total	100	100
N	45	44
Offence		
Central	37	21
Non-central	62	79
Total	100	100
N	32	14
Defence		
Central	15	20
Non-central	85	80
Total	100	100
N	13	30
Central positions		
Offence	86	33
Defence	14	67
Total	100	100
N	14	9

[1] Unfortunately, sample data do not allow for this factor to be weighted or otherwise controlled. Its effect is to minimize actual differences, and to make apparent differences more conservative.

TABLE V   Offensive and Defensive Players in the C.F.L. by National Origin and Background

Position	Percentage by national origin		Percentage by background, Canadians only	
	Imports	Canadians	U.S. college	Others
Offence	58	53	71	26
Defence	42	47	29	74
Total	100	100	100	100
N	110	94	45	44

If training accounts for the differential positioning of imports and Canadians, it should virtually disappear in the cases of Canadians with U.S. collegiate experience. From these data can be seen: (i) over-all, American collegiate experience is associated with centrality; (ii) that this association is especially marked on offence; but (iii) slightly reversed for the defensive unit. However, recalling Table III, neither the over-all nor the offensive proportions of U.S. trained Canadians at central positions reaches the percentage of such positions occupied by imports. Although these data do not compel the acceptance of a stacking hypothesis, they do argue the rejection of one based upon training alone.

The reversal of the association between U.S. training and centrality when the defence is considered is somewhat anomalous. However, upon closer examination it appears to be at least partly artificial. Few U.S.-trained Canadians play defence: less than half as many as the "others" without such experience (13 to 20). Further, most Canadians *cum* American collegians in central positions are on offensive units, while the reverse is true for those without such experience.

This last is part of a more general pattern. "Most teams play more of their imports on offense rather than defense because coaches feel that normally it takes more talent and experience to play offense, and that it is possible to train Canadian players with less experience to do an adequate job of defense" (Smith and Grindstaff, 1970:60). The data in Table V substantiate this statement. Imports predominate over Canadians on offense, but U.S.-trained Canadians do so especially compared to those without such experience.

Centrality: An Overview

In general, the ascriptive statuses of Canadians and imports do appear to be differentially positioned in terms of the centrality model. Assuming, for whatever reasons, that central positions are more desirable or more rewarding, the ascribed status of imports is associated with such location, and that of Canadian with the alternative of non-centrality. When Canadians are categorized as those with U.S. collegiate football experience, or those without it, the deficit position is explained and reduced, but not removed.

Still, the differences are not of sufficient magnitude to warrant an exclusive employment of the centrality model as an explanatory tool in the case of differential positioning by national origins in the CFL. In sum, centrality shows more power as regards stacking and the ascriptive criterion of race than it does regarding nativity.

References

BALL, DONALD W.
    1967 "Toward a sociology of toys: inanimate objects, socialization and the demography of the doll world." *Sociological Quarterly* 8:447–458.
    1971 "The cold war on ice: the politics of international figure skating." Paper presented to the third Canadian Symposium on Sport Psychology, Vancouver.
BARNES, LAVERNE
    1971 *The Plastic Orgasm.* Toronto: McClelland and Stewart.

BLALOCK, HUBERT M., JR.
1962 "Occupational discrimination: some theoretical propositions." *Social Problems* 9:240–247.

BOYLE, ROBERT H.
1963 *Sport — Mirror of American Life*. Boston: Little, Brown.

BROWER, JONATHON J.
1972 "The racial basis of the division of labor among players in the National Football League as a function of racial stereotypes." Presented to the Pacific Sociological Association, Portland, April 13–15.

CLOWARD, RICHARD A., AND LLOYD E. OHLIN
1960 *Delinquency and Opportunity*. Glencoe: The Free Press.

COSENTINO, FRANK
1969 *Canadian Football: The Grey Cup Years*. Toronto: Musson.

DAVIS, KINGSLEY
1949 *Human Society*. New York: Macmillan.

EDWARDS, HARRY
1969 *The Revolt of the Black Athlete*. New York: The Free Press.

EDWARDS, HARRY, AND BILL RUSSELL
1971 "Racism: a prime factor in the determination of black athletic superiority." Presented to the American Sociological Association, Denver, September.

ETZIONI, AMITAI
1961 *A Comparative Analysis of Complex Organizations*. Glencoe: The Free Press.

GARFINKEL, HAROLD
1964 "Studies of the routine grounds of everyday activities." *Social Problems* 11:225–250.

GRUSKY, OSCAR
1963 "The effects of formal structure on managerial recruitment: a study of baseball organization." *Sociometry* 26:345–353.

HOMANS, GEORGE C.
1950 *The Human Group*. New York: Harcourt, Brace and World.

LOY, JOHN W., AND JOSEPH F. McELVOGUE
1970 "Racial segregation in American sport." *International Review of Sport Sociology* 5:5–24.

MEGGYSEY, DAVE
1970 *Out of Their League*. Berkeley: Ramparts Press.

OATES, BOB
1972 Column on the 1971 National Football League all-star team. *The Sporting News* 173 (January 15):17.

OLSEN, JACK
1968 *The Black Athlete — A Shameful Story*. New York, Time.

ROSENBLATT, AARON
1967 "The failure of success." *Trans-action* 4:51–53.

SMITH, GARY, AND CARL F. GRINDSTAFF
1970 "Race and sport in Canada." London: University of Western Ontario (mimeo).

VALLIÈRES, PIERRE
1971 *White Niggers of America* (trans. by Joan Pinkham). New York and London: Monthly Review Press.

Theoretical Issues in Sex and Age Stratification*

Sharon Abu-Laban/Baha Abu-Laban

The definition most commonly cited by both proponents and opponents of the extension of the minority group concept is that developed by Louis Wirth. He defines a minority as "a group of people who, because of their physical or cultural characteristics, are singled out from others in the society in which they live for differential and unequal treatment and who therefore regard themselves as objects of collective discrimination" (1945:347).

The purpose of this paper is to examine critically major arguments concerning the propriety of applying the minority label to two subgroups — women and the aged — which currently are on the periphery of the traditional minority perspective. Both of these subgroups have at times been labeled as minorities. Of all the new categories to which the concept of minority group has recently been applied, those based on sex and age merit special attention, for these criteria have universal applicability for the assignment of roles and statuses in society.

WOMEN AND MINORITY STATUS

Gunnar Myrdal's analogy (1944: appendix 5) between the social situation of women and that of Negroes is often cited as the first reference to women as a minority group (Streib, 1965:36n; Barron, 1953:477). However, although Myrdal indeed comments at some length on women's disadvantaged position in American society and forcefully draws the parallel between that and the Negroes' subordinate position, he states elsewhere in his discussion (67n) that women do *not* constitute a minority group. He apparently reserves the use of the minority concept for "color castes" (e.g. Japanese, Chinese, and Mexicans) and immigrant groups (e.g. Czechs, Italians, and Poles) (Myrdal, 1944: 1237). In recent years, Myrdal's analogy between women and Negroes has acquired a high degree of popularity among social critics and sociologists alike. In particular, supporters of women's liberation have frequently drawn analogies between racism and sexism and at times have been accused of "cashing in" on the black movement and diverting its purposes.[2]

---

* Abridged from the *Canadian Review of Sociology and Anthropology*, 14 (1) 1977, pp. 103–116. Used with permission.

In a widely cited article, Helen Hacker (1951) applies the minority group perspective to the analysis of women's disadvantaged position in society.[3] Although this article is frequently cited to support the assertion that women constitute a minority group, Hacker in fact concludes that the minority group concept cannot be applied to women for two main reasons: first, many women are not aware of being discriminated against as a group; second, many women do not regard differential treatment based on sex as objectionable. Hacker sees these two conditions as widespread and suggests that the thorough sex-role socialization of most women precludes the application of the minority group label.

Hacker recognizes, however, the utility of studying women as possessors of "minority group *status*." To support the attribution of this status to women (and as a partial listing of the characteristics of a minority group) Hacker suggests the existence of the following characteristics of the female experience: (1) a distinctive subculture; (2) group self-hatred, (3) job and wage discrimination, (4) legal discrimination; (5) discrimination relating to social conduct, and (6) discriminatory socialization practices within the family. In Hacker's view, studying women from the perspective of minority group status would sensitize the researcher to the potential utility of reformulating techniques and developing research areas common to traditional studies of minority groups. In particular, she suggests parallel studies of the marginal woman, female socialization as an aspect of minority group socialization, male-female social distance, caste and social class differences, the "sex relations cycle," subcultural differences, and group identification.

In referring to the minority-group-like characteristics of women, Milton Barron (1953) similarly describes women as constituting a partial or quasi-minority group. He acknowledges that women occupy a subordinate position and are debarred from full and equal participation in society. However, salient to his counter-argument is the fact that women are encompassed within the families of the supposed majority and are thus, in his view, unable to function as a separate subgroup in society. For this reason, Barron sees women as appropriately qualifying for quasi-minority status.

The belief that women do not constitute a minority group is supported by Streib (1965), who bases his position on Simone de Beauvoir's (1953) early notion that women are not bound together by a distinctive subculture since they have no group past or history, no religion of their own, and no collective consciousness. Further, women are dispersed in society and, in Streib's view, are more inclined to identify with their social class position than with their sex.

Newman (1973) also argues against the propriety of the minority label for women. His position is based upon his definition of minority groups, which represents one of the most recent attempts to redefine the concept of minority group and broaden the range of collectivities that may be subsumed under it. Using Schermerhorn's (1970) insights as a basis, Newman defines minority groups as those that "vary from the social norms or archetypes in some manner, are subordinate with regard to the distribution of social power and rarely constitute more than one-half of the population of the society in which they are found."

TABLE I   Women: Arguments for and against Minority Status

For	*Against*
Physical characteristics	
None	None
Sociocultural characteristics	
1. Subordinate social status (Barron; Newman)	1. Dispersed; encompassed within the family system; not functioning as an independent subgroup (Barron; Streib)
2. Tendency toward separate subculture (Hacker)	2. Lack of distinctive subculture (Streib)
	3. Lack of distinctive belief system; behavior does not vary from social norms or archetypes (Newman)
	4. Constitute more than one half of the population (Newman)
Differential treatment	
1. Objects of prejudice and stereotyping (Hacker)	1. Lack of awareness of being discriminated against on a group basis (Hacker)
2. Discriminatory socialization practices (Hacker)	2. Acceptance of the property of differential treatment (Hacker)
3. Restrictions on behavior and full participation in society (Barron; Hacker)	
4. Discriminatory treatment in employment practices, education, and the legal system (Hacker)	
Group consciousness/awareness	
1. Group self-hatred (Hacker)	1. Lack of group identification (Hacker; Newman; Streib); stronger identification with social class position than with sex (Streib)

Although Newman sees women in general as having a subordinate status in society, in his view this is not equivalent to minority status. In Newman's terms, women do not qualify as a minority group, because they constitute more than one-half of the population and, more importantly, because they do not vary from the social norms and archetypes. Interestingly, although Newman rejects minority status for women, he regards women who support and identify with the "Women's Liberation Movement" as a minority group because they (1) possess a distinctive ideological trait which separates them from the social norm and (2) have group consciousness (175-6). He feels this "minority movement" has been on the scene for over a century.[4]

Table I summarizes the arguments discussed above and distinguishes between characteristics invoked as qualifying women for status as a minority group and others which are cited as eliminating women from eligibility for minority status.

The table reveals two broad patterns: the existence of substantive discrepancies regarding the characteristics of women and the existence of disagreements concerning the essential defining characteristics of a minority group per se.

For example, there is disagreement concerning the existence of a female subculture. Whereas Hacker (1951) sees a tendency toward a separate female subculture, Streib (1965) and Newman (1973) deny the existence of one. In part, this disagreement revolves around the definition of a subculture. Hacker argues that although group identification among women is missing, there are language differences and distinctive subgroup interests which define "women's world" (e.g. interest in people, family, and what may be generally summarized as the expressive domain). On the other hand, Streib supports his negative position by emphasizing women's lack of group past or history and their lack of collective consciousness or a distinct religion. Similarly, Newman argues that women lack a distinctive belief system and, in addition, that their behavior does not vary from social norms or archetypes because there are roles for women that are considered "very desirable."

Barron and Streib emphasize that because women are dispersed among the families of the supposed majority, they do not (and cannot) function as an independent subgroup in society. The implication here is that a major distinguishing feature of a minority group is that it should constitute a relatively closed system and not be merely a status category (Francis, 1951:229). Although not explicitly stated by Wirth (1945), this distinctive element of minority status is probably implicit in much of this discussion, as evidenced by his illustrations and typology of minority groups.

None of the writers examined, in discussing the applicability of the minority group concept, questions the subordinate social status of women in society or the existence of discriminatory treatment. Rather than emphasizing this, several writers seem to assign little or no import to differential treatment.

It is interesting to note that none of these authors singles out the distinguishing physical characteristics of women as significant aspects of possible minority status. Sex, along with age, is one of the most basic classifications made in human societies. Yet secondary sexual characteristics are not regarded by these writers as important for consideration.

THE AGED AND MINORITY STATUS

Milton Barron (1953) is generally acknowledged as one of the first to study the aged from the minority group perspective. Barron concludes that the aged possess the following minority group characteristics: (1) they are viewed by some as a menace and a group to fear; (2) they experience prejudice and stereotyping in employment; (3) they possess feelings of self-consciousness and defensiveness; and (4) they increasingly benefit from antidiscrimination legislation paralleling that for ethnic minorities. In Barron's view, these characteristics qualify the aged for status as a *quasi*-minority group. Barron's position is that neither the aged nor women constitute genuine minority groups and for the same reason: both are found within the families of the supposed majority and hence are not unique subgroups functioning independently in society.

In opposition to Barron's above-noted conclusions, Breen (1960:157) argues that "in many parts of our society [the aged] constitute a functioning subgroup." In addition, Breen sees the following characteristics as contributing to the development of minority status among the aged: their relatively high visibility and negative self-concept, and the fact that they are treated as stereotypes, discriminated against in the labor market, and segregated in institutions and special housing. In combination, these characteristics underline the minority status which, in Breen's view, the aged are progressively acquiring.

Taking a somewhat more definitive position, Palmore (1969) contends that the aged *are* a minority group. They qualify, he maintains, because they are the objects of negative stereotypy and discrimination and, in addition, they manifest self-hatred and increasing group consciousness. Palmore raises the issue of *quantity* of characteristics in arguing the legitimacy of the concept as applied to the aged. He maintains that while some may feel "the aged are no more like minority groups than are women [and] children," there is an important difference. In Palmore's view, "while these other groups may have some minority group characteristics, we believe that there is more prejudice, segregation, and discrimination directed toward the aged than toward women and children" (57).

In a similar vein, Jarvis (1972) also views the aged as a minority group. To support this contention, he cites the physical visibility of the aged, the exclusion of those over sixty-five from many occupations, lower pay for those over sixty-five, social and physical isolation of the elderly, the expectation that older people will "pursue passive, acquiescent roles," negative self-definitions among older persons, and the increasing numbers of groups concerned with the interests of the aged.

Newman (1973) also regards the aged as a minority group, primarily on the basis of their physical distinctiveness and subordinate power position in society. In contrast to his elaborate examination of the minority status of women (which, as noted in the previous section, he rejects), his examination of the status-role of the aged is much less searching. This appears to be the case because in his judgment the aged qualify as a physical minority group, whereas women do not.

Gubrium (1973), distinguishing between a minority group and an interest group, maintains that the aged constitute the former because of their age awareness (negative self-image). If and when this develops into group consciousness, the aged may be viewed as an interest group. In sharp contrast to previous authors, Gubrium argues that it is not necessary that a collectivity have group consciousness or be an active interest group to qualify for minority group status. "It is only when the delineation of a particular collection of persons is devalued that it is acted toward, and itself acts, like a minority group" (157). The aged are a minority group, Gubrium maintains, because they meet these conditions.

Streib (1965), in a widely quoted article, takes the position that the aged are not a minority group. He argues that because the aged do not have distinctive cultural traits and do not have "consciousness of kind," they are more of an aggregate or social category than a distinct group. Streib outlines what he regards to be important elements of minority group status according to his understanding of Wirth's definition. He concludes that the aged do not qualify as a minority group for the following reasons. First, the status-role expectations associated with age are variable throughout the life cycle. Thus the characteristic of "agedness" occupies only a fraction of a person's life span. Second, self-image evidence indicates that many chronologically "old" people do not regard themselves as "old" but rather as "middle-aged." This renders the criterion of "old age" problematic. Third, stereotypes regarding the aged are refuted in two important areas: work performance and appropriate activities. Research indicates that younger people not only favorably evaluate older people's work performance but also regard as appropriate for older people many activities which are even more vigorous than those which older people regard as appropriate for themselves. Fourth, there is a lack of readiness on the part of the aged to organize as an identifiable pressure group. Fifth, older people do not face restricted access to power, privilege, and civil rights. On the contrary, older people are disproportionately represented in elite and superordinate positions in society. Finally, the deprivation of the aged in several areas may be questioned. For example, although a large proportion of the aged may be classified as underprivileged, many of them, in Streib's view, were also underprivileged prior to retirement. In addition, unequal access to work is a characteristic not solely of the aged but also of the middle-aged. Streib further notes that the amount of involuntary residential segregation of the aged is minimal and finally questions the extent of social isolation of the aged, suggesting that it may be related to social class. Regardless, Streib asserts, "a deprived group is not synonymous with a 'minority group'" (1965:43).

Atchley (1972) also argues against the applicability of the minority concept to the aged. To begin with, he agrees that age discrimination is similar to racial discrimination in that it is dependent on the "visibility" of the stigmatizing characteristic(s). (According to him, "Old people who 'do not look their age' escape the effects of age discrimination."[5]) He also agrees that many older people, like members of racial minorities, have an inadequate income, feelings of self-hatred, a low-status, and inequality of opportunity. The major reason Atchley gives for the inappropriateness of the minority group concept for older people is that there is variability in discriminatory treatment. Older people, for example, do not face discrimination in the holding of political office. Like Streib, Atchley observes that the aged are disproportionately represented in this area.

Table II summarizes the arguments for and against minority group status for the aged. Like Table I, it reveals definitional as well as substantive disagreements. For example, while Atchley (1972), Breen (1960), Jarvis (1972), and Newman (1973) point to the visibility of the aged as an aspect of minority status, Streib (1965) questions this, noting that there is no agreement among observers on the parameters of agedness.

Although several writers agree that there is a general pattern of disadvantage, Streib questions whether this is sufficient for the attribution of minority group status. Some writers argue that the old have subordinate social status and power positions, whereas others (Streib and Atchley) argue that older people are overrepresented in some power positions (basically political). There is disagreement concerning whether the aged constitute a subgroup. Writers disagree on the issue of older people's readiness to organize. As in the case of women, the group consciousness of the aged is also questioned, with Gubrium taking the position that group consciousness is, in fact, not necessary for minority status.

DISCUSSION

It is apparent from the above that supporters and opponents of the extension of the minority label to women and the aged share some common understandings. For example, it is agreed that women and the aged tend to occupy subordinate positions in society and that both groups are subjected to discriminatory treatment in many institutional areas. However, the disagreements between the two sides in the controversy overshadow the agreements. In the remainder of this paper we will discuss certain factors related to these disagreements.

Ideological Utility of the Minority Group Concept

Ideological considerations appear to have played an important part in encouraging the extension of the minority group concept or perspective to the study of women, the aged, and other subordinate groups. The central focus of these considerations has been on discrimination and its personal and social consequences. Hence, to label a subgroup as a minority serves to announce some humanitarian inclinations regarding that group. It implies recognition of differential treatment which is at odds with the society's or the researcher's manifest value system. The increased outspokenness of disadvantaged people is a related factor prompting the wider use of the minority concept and continued emphasis on discriminatory treatment.

The contrasting arguments under examination illustrate both commonalities and differences between women and the aged and such traditional minority groups as Blacks. These features have been differentially emphasized, and some of the disagreements seem to reflect an element of territoriality regarding the concept itself. To the extent that one moves to broaden the minority concept to include more and more disadvantaged categories of humankind, one runs the risk of muting the humanitarian message regarding the racial groups to whom the concept was first applied. Since the more common tendency is to work toward the resolution of social problems by piecemeal techniques, as opposed to radically and totally restructuring society, one must be aware that the minority concept, as an ideological weapon, may be Janus-faced: while it may sensitize different categories of people to commonalities of disadvantage, it may at the same time divert attention from the "original" minority groups. Part of the disagreement regarding the potential broadening of the concept may reflect an awareness of this. Additionally, the minority concept, when used as a form of ideological shorthand to communicate concern regarding women or the aged (see

Blau, 1973; Hochschild, 1973; Kirkpatrick, 1955; Blalock, 1967), may cloud some important structural considerations. In fact, for those wishing to translate humanitarian inclinations into social action, the structural uniqueness of women and the aged in contrast to "traditional" minorities may have important implications both for the nature of the experiential component and also for potential militancy.

Experiential versus Structural Components

The sociological fruitfulness of identifying experiential commonalities among groups which otherwise are recognized as being articulated differently into the social structure has been demonstrated by Myrdal's (1944: appendix 5) aforementioned analogy between the social situation of women and that of Negroes and, more recently, by Blauner (1969) in his use of the colonial analogy for the analysis of racial conflict in America. Blauner's argument rests on a simple, but necessary, distinction between colonialism as a socioeconomic and political system and colonization as a process. Though Afro-American and colonized peoples are part of different social systems, Blauner successfully argues that they commonly share the *experience* of colonization. Likewise, in the process of subordination, women and the aged, among others, may have experiences similar to those of racial and cultural minorities as well as colonized peoples. As a consequence, the experience of minority status may be characteristic of many people who are in some way stigmatized. This experiential component is particularly worthy of note in social psychological studies that take into consideration the attributes of relationships between those with a surfeit of power and those with power deficiencies. However, the component of experiential commonality has been emphasized by some writers (Hacker, 1974; Breen, 1960) at the expense of delineating structural differences. And, inevitably, to be Black is not the same as to be old or to be female.[6] Nevertheless, other writers have called attention to structural differences. Baron (1953) and Streib (1965) were among the first to argue that women and the aged do not qualify for minority status, because both groups are encompassed within the family system of the "majority" and hence do not function independently in society. But both of these writers stopped short of detailing the implications of family membership and of considering still other structural differences.

For women and the aged, being part of the family system has some of the following consequences: (1) it tends to conceal their oppression, both from themselves and from the "majority"; (2) identification with the family limits their subgroup identification, hence dampening their militancy potential; (3) they are provided with vicarious achievement/mobility opportunities, for example the pleasure of "having" a "successful" adult child or a "successful" husband to compensate for lower personal status. Researchers attempting to understand the tepid consciousness of women or the aged might do well to look at the family as a desensitizing agent.

An additional aspect concerning the role of the family relates to traditional sex-role socialization. In the traditional family system members of the "majori-

TABLE II   The Aged: Arguments for and against Minority Status

For	Against
Physical characteristics	
1. Visibility (Atchley; Breen; Jarvis; Newman)	1. Not constant through life cycle (Streib)
	2. No agreement on parameters of agedness (Streib)
Sociocultural characteristics	
1. Subordinate social status (Atchley; Barron; Gubrium; Jarvis; Newman)	1. Overrepresented in some power positions (Atchley; Streib)
2. Functioning subgroup in many parts of society (Breen)	2. Dispersed; encompassed within the family system; not functioning as an independent subgroup (Barron; Streib)
	3. Lack of distinctive cultural traits (Streib)
Differential treatment	
1. Objects of prejudice and stereotyping (Breen; Palmore)	1. Refutation of stereotyping in the vital areas of "work performance" and "appropriate activities" (Streib)
2. Economic deprivation (Atchley; Jarvis); discriminatory treatment in general (Palmore); discriminatory treatment in employment practices (Barron; Breen; Jarvis); restrictions on full participation in society (Barron); social and/or physical segregation (Breen; Jarvis)	2. Deprivation (poverty, unemployment) does not characterize only the old; no restricted access to power, privilege, and rights; minimal involuntary residential segregation; social isolation may be class-related (Streib)
3. Anti-discrimination legislation paralleling that for ethnic groups; arouse fear, seen as a threat (Barron)	3. Discrimination is situational (Atchley)
Group consciousness/awareness	
1. Negative self-concept (Atchley; Breen; Gubrium; Jarvis; Palmore)	1. Variability in self-definition of agedness (Streib)
2. Group identification, increasing group consciousness, increasingly likely to organize (Breen; Jarvis; Palmore)	2. Lack of group identification, no consciousness of kind, lack of readiness to organize (Streib)
3. Group consciousness not necessary, organization not a requirement (Gubrium)	

ty" (fathers) socialize a portion of their offspring (daughters) to "minority" status (or at least acquiesce while others do). A situation in which members of the so-called majority group replenish the ranks of the minority group with some of their own offspring underlines a unique aspect of women's subordinate status in society.

The roles of women and the aged within the institutional structure and their patterned relationships with their respective superordinate counterparts are qualitatively and quantitatively different from those roles and relationships characterizing ethnic or racial minorities. In a society stratified along ethnic, sex, and age lines, as Lieberson (1970:173) notes, "ethnic groups are the only strata that have the inherent potential to carve their own autonomous and permanent society from the existing nation without, in effect, re-creating its earlier form of stratification all over again." Neither disadvantaged age groups nor disadvantaged sex groups possess a similar potential for the creation of an autonomous, viable society. The only practical course of action available to these groups is to direct their efforts to changing the existing system (Lieberson, 1970:173–4). One important implication of the aforementioned structural differences is that Wirth's (1945) well-known typology of minority groups, involving the policy alternatives of assimilation, pluralism, militancy, and secessionism, is not altogether realistic in relation to women and the aged.

Conceptual Ambiguities

Even allowing for variations in the quality of researchers' interpretive insights or methodological techniques, Tables I and II reveal differences in the characteristics attributed to women and the aged, as well as differences in the characteristics attributed to minority status, suggesting major conceptual difficulties at both the nominal and the operational levels. The differences tend to cluster around two issues: those regarding subculture and subsystems and those regarding group consciousness. Not unexpectedly, these are the qualities in most definitions of minority group which are probably the most difficult to measure.

Subculture and/or Subsystem

With reference to both women and the aged, some writers claim the existence of a distinctive subculture while others deny its existence. Some writers view the aged as possessors of an incipient subculture (Rose, 1962) or as a "functioning subgroup" aware of their identity and of restrictions on their full and equal participation in society; others sharply disagree. The qualities invoked to substantiate or disavow the existence of a subculture differ. For example, while some maintain that there is no women's subculture because women lack a distinct religion or history, others argue that there is a distinct subculture because of a characteristic language style and unique interest patterns. While one may be tempted to suggest that androcentric bias has contributed to the inability to perceive a female subculture, a stronger case may be made for definitional ambiguities.[7] Debates regarding the existence or lack of existence of subcultures are familiar (as illustrated, for example, by the long-running adolescent subculture exchanges of a few years past).

A related disagreement concerns the ability of a particular group to function as a subsystem or as a separate subgroup in society. Assuming that the condition of "functioning as a subsystem" is an important characteristic of a minority group, the following observations become important. First, the literature reflects little, if any, concern with empirical operationalization of this element or with transformations of a given segment of the population either away from or in the direction of separate group existence (minority status). Second, since the openness or closure of a "subsystem" is a matter of degree, the question concerning the point at which a collectivity is transformed into a "subsystem" becomes important to answer. Third, there are several considerations relating to the social situation of women in present day North American society which merit serious attention within this context. For example, in 1972, 33.9 percent of the Canadian labor force consisted of women, and 41.3 percent of the female labor force were unmarried (four out of five were single) (see White, 1973:216); these figures suggest that a large proportion of Canadian households are headed by women. All of these observations point to the need for empirical investigation of how and to what degree women are functioning as a separate subgroup in society, research that will take into account various household arrangements and new family forms.[8]

Apart from substantive disagreements concerning whether or not women and the aged function as separate groups in society, there is no agreement on the importance of this characteristic relative to other characteristics, or on the minimum degree of "separateness" necessary for minority status. The previously noted arguments by Barron (1953) and Streib (1965) on the one hand and Breen (1960) on the other are a case in point.

Group Consciousness

The extent and nature of group consciousness has also occupied those debating the minority group characteristics of women and the aged. The importance placed on this aspect is exemplified by Hacker. In 1951 she did not regard women as a minority group, mainly because in her judgment they lacked group consciousness (but none of the other defining characteristics of a minority group). In 1951 Hacker viewed women not as a minority group, but as possessors of "minority group *status*." Twenty-three years later, Hacker (1974) has asserted that women are now a minority group because, in her estimation, a sufficient degree of group consciousness has developed among them. "With the flowering of feminism today, the concept of women as a minority group has become banal ... Today women, as much as traditional minority groups, can qualify for full-fledged membership" (Hacker, 1974:124–5). Regardless of whether Hacker's 1951 and 1974 conclusions were accurate or inaccurate, they were not based on methodologically reproducible procedures. The criterion of reproducibility is particularly important in view of the fact that other writers (e.g. Eichler, 1973:44) continue to assert that the element of group consciousness is missing among women.

Another variation on the complexities of measuring group consciousness or group identification is found with the aged. To the extent that it is agreed that "old" people must age-identify to qualify as a minority group, there are problems involved in measuring "agedness." These raise the classic issue of "objective," as opposed to "subjective," definitions of personal characteristics. With reference to the objective determination of agedness, researchers have found, for example, that gross categories such as "over-fifty," or "pre-retirement" versus "post-retirement" are insensitive to many important subtleties (Cumming and

Henry, 1961; Thompson and Streib, 1958). Also problematic is the use of inconsistent age categories, for example utilizing data derived from the "over-forty" age-group to support assertions about the aged (see Breen, 1960). Self-image also presents problems. Researchers have found that when people are asked to indicate how old they regard themselves, there is a consistent tendency to view themselves as younger (Tuckman and Lavell, 1957; Zola, 1962). For example, Streib and Schneider (1971) found that about one-third of their respondents saw themselves as "middle-aged" at 70. Other research indicates that personal attribution of agedness is related to social status (Rosow, 1967), sex (Leake, 1962), and ethnicity (Crouch, 1972). For older people, as Streib (1965) pointed out, agedness is not constant through the life cycle. There is a *process* whereby one moves or is pushed to a realization of advanced age and its societal implications. The aging individual must come to terms with changing personal conditions, a gradual "minoritization" unlike that any other subordinate group may experience. These observations suggest that the problems in measuring the group identification of the aged are of a different type than those found with women.

As an example, it is easier for one to reject the attribution of "old age" than it is for women to reject the gender label. Perhaps because of this women have thus far been more vocal and active than the aged. In addition to this, however, the group mobilization of women has attracted and will probably continue to attract more out-group hostility than the mobilization of the aged. A unique factor contributing to the difference between the situation of women and that of the aged is that all people will acquire the status of old age with sufficient longevity. For this reason, it is probably easier for non-aged males ("majority") to identify with the aged and tolerate their mobilization than to identify with women and readily accept their mobilization.[9]

To the extent that group consciousness is agreed upon as a crucial defining element of minority group status (but remembering that Gubrium, for one, claims it is unnecessary), there needs to be allowance made for its relativity. Towards this end: (1) process needs to be acknowledged and reintegrated into the minority group perspective; (2) it must be agreed what constitutes a sufficient degree of consciousness; (3) it should be noted that the extent of group awareness and identification varies even within the "traditional" minorities. In the absence of a clear and precise conceptual apparatus, and given the condition of on-going change in society, substantive disagreements, such as we have examined, would seem inevitable.

Attempts at Redefinition

Existing conceptual deficiencies have led several writers to redefine the field of majority-minority relations (see, for example, Gordon, 1964; Shibutani and Kwan, 1965; van den Berghe, 1967; Schermerhorn, 1970; Sagarin, 1971; Newman, 1973; Kinloch, 1974). Most pertinent to the present discussion are the works of Sagarin, Newman, and Kinloch, which have considerably expanded the range of collectivities under the minority group concept. However, the attempts to reconceptualize the field to encompass such subordinate groups as women and the aged, among others, have not been satisfactory. The new definitions and classifications of minority groups have masked important differences in the institutional roles of traditional and "new" minority groups, and have also failed to address standing issues in the current controversy.

For example, Sagarin (1971) has taken Goffman's concept of stigma as the unifying thread for the analysis of minority groups, including deviant people and other disadvantaged groups traditionally excluded from the field. Kinloch (1974:50) has redefined a minority group as "any group that views itself and/or is defined by a dominant power elite as unique on the basis of perceived physical (race, sex, age), cultural (religion, ethnicity), economic (social class), and/or behavioral (deviation) characteristics and is treated accordingly in a negative manner." Apart from other deficiencies in their perspectives, neither of these writers provides a sufficiently convincing rationale for the definitions, nor do they address standing issues in the current debate.

In comparison with the works of Sagarin and Kinloch, Newman's (1973) reconceptualization of the field, which draws heavily on Schermerhorn's (1970) work, is more elaborate and sophisticated. It readily admits the aged, along with several other "new" collectivities, into the arena of majority-minority relations. But it has serious drawbacks. According to Newman, minority groups are distinguished on the basis of difference from social norms or archetypes. These differences may be physical (Blacks, the aged, the handicapped), cognitive (Jews, religious sects, social communes), or behavioral (homosexuals). As noted earlier, Newman's conceptual scheme does not recognize women as a minority group, with the exception of those who support and identify with the Women's Liberation Movement. To quote Newman: "There are highly desirable normative social roles for both men and women in society ... [and] being female is not a form of variance from society's sexual norms" (Newman, 1973:176).

It should be noted that Newman's definition of minority groups refers to social norms and archetypes, whereas his discussion of women as a minority group refers to *sexual* norms. That this is problematic can be shown by substituting racial norms for sexual norms and arguing that there are desirable roles for Negroes (e.g., being subservient, hard-working, appreciative of paternalism, etc.) and that being Black is not at variance with society's racial norms. The "highly desirable normative social roles" for women do not, in fact, compare favorably with those for men. Studies indicate that both men and women evaluate the male role and traits more favorably than the female (Fernberger, 1948; McKee and Sherriffs, 1956). Broverman et al.'s (1972) study indicates that stereotyped female traits which mental health therapists regard as healthy for women are not regarded as healthy for males or "people." Newman's suggestion (1973), then, that there may be dual archetypes in society, would only seem valid if in the area of role allocation these archetypes were regarded as equally desirable for males or females. Also, to regard certain women but not others as members of a minority group is as problematic as regarding some Blacks as members of a minority group and others as members of the majority group.

There is no agreement on the necessary and sufficient conditions which define minority status. At the same time there has been a tendency to treat minority status as an all-or-none attribute, albeit relative, rather than as a variable capable of assuming different magnitudes. Thus the minority label has been applied equally to all traditional minority groups even though they may differentially possess the elements that define minority status. To be sure, writers have compared minority groups on certain variables, such as discriminatory treatment, but on the whole there has been no concern about viewing minority groups as higher or lower on an over-all index of minority status. This tendency has been carried over into the debate concerning the minority status of women and the aged. The nearest that writers have come to regarding minority status as a variable has been to view women and the aged as quasi-minority groups. But this may be judged as a phase in the process of finding a yes or no answer to the question. The tendency to view minority status as an attribute rather than a variable has been an important factor in concealing important structural differences among minority groups, both "new" and traditional, and thus has contributed to disagreements in the field of study.

To alleviate some of the conceptual problems noted above, researchers need to agree upon the necessary and sufficient conditions of minority status and also to determine the importance of these conditions relative to each other, as well as to different types of subordinate groups. Also, there is a need to explore the implications of the multi-dimensional nature of the minority concept and to explicate different elements both in terms of the requisite levels minimally necessary for minority status and in terms of more generally acceptable measurement techniques and procedures.[10] Unless some degree of consensus on criteria and measurement techniques is established, different researchers will continue to invoke and emphasize different elements and criteria selectively and will thus continue to arrive at different conclusions concerning the same group. Conceptual and methodological advances made along these and similar lines will facilitate the development of a common universe of discourse and will render research findings more comparable.

Notes

1. This definition, focusing on both social structural and social psychological attributes, encompasses at least four important elements. The first and perhaps most basic element in the definition is that minority status may be a product of racial (or physical) and/or cultural traits (e.g. language, religion, or national origin). The second important element in the definition is its intra-societal focus, thereby emphasizing the relativity of minority status. The third major element in Wirth's definition is its emphasis on discriminatory and unequal treatment of minority groups thus focusing attention on majority-minority *relationships*. Finally, the definition contains the element of group consciousness as a major defining characteristic of minority status.

2. A historical parallel can be drawn here with the abolitionist movement of the 1800s (see Myrdal, 1944).

3. As an interesting sign of our times, Hacker (1974) recently noted that when her article

was first written it was rejected on the grounds that it was too journalistic; some 20 years later it was critically described as impersonal and professional.

4. One is faced with questions here regarding the various subgroupings under the umbrella of women's liberation. Does each subgroup constitute a separate minority group? At what point in time is any organized group or movement large (or mature) enough to warrant being labeled as a minority group? Does any social or political movement qualify for the minority group label?

5. It should be noted, however, that even if one does not "look" her/his age, there are many situations in Western society (e.g. completing employment application forms) which require age information and in which only direct misrepresentation will protect the individual from age discrimination. "Acceptable" appearance is not enough. Chronological age is a barrier to full participation in Canadian society (see Baum, 1974).

6. Note, for example, various studies of those who experience a so-called double negative, e.g. old women, Black women. The double burden faced by aged women is also suggested cross-culturally by Simmon's (1945) study of the aged in pre-literate societies. Simmons (81) concludes that "wherever aged women have been respected, old men have rarely been without honor; but prestige for aged men has offered no assurance of the same status for women. If either sex has lost respect in old age, it has been more likely to be the women than the men." For a collection of recent articles examining the problems of being old and female, see Institute of Gerontology (1974;1975).

7. One is also tempted to ask: Whose *sub*culture? If population numbers are considered a pivotal consideration, then perhaps it is misleading to refer to a female *subculture*.

8. Similar figures for the United States have led Watson and Barth (1964) and Acker (1973), among others, to question certain assumptions in stratification theory involving the appropriateness of using the family as a unit of equivalent evaluation and of father's or husband's occupation as a basis for stratificational placement of women.

9. This is not to deny that women researchers have been more active in research on the aged than in many other areas (see Hochschild, 1973b:144). For several reasons, women may identify with and/or be interested in the aged. However, if males were forced to choose between the two, the "cause" of the old might seem more reasonable than the "cause" of women.

10. The degree to which the different elements of this multidimensional concept must coexist has not been made clear. As a recent example of this, Stoll (1974:44–5) singles out *one* component of Wirth's definition (i.e. "different and unequal treatment") to conclude that, using this definition, men, because "they are singled out as being inappropriate for child rearing and housekeeping," may also be viewed as unidimensional but also very questionable indicators of women's minority group status.

References

ACKER, JOAN
    1973 "Women and social stratification: a case of intellectual sexism." *American Journal of Sociology* 78:936–45

ATCHLEY, ROBERT C.
    1972 *The Social Forces in Later Life*. Belmont, Calif: Wadsworth

BARRON, MILTON L.
    1953 "Minority group characteristics of the aged in American society." *Journal of Gerontology* 8:477–82

BAUM, DANIEL
   1974 *The Final Plateau: The Betrayal of Our Older Citizens.* Toronto: Burns and
       MacEachern

BLALOCK, HUBERT M.
   1967 *Toward a Theory of Minority-Group Relations.* New York: John Wiley and Sons

BLAU, ZENA SMITH
   1973 *Old Age in a Changing Society.* New York: New Viewpoints

BLAUNER, ROBERT
   1969 "Internal colonialism and ghetto revolt." *Social Problems* 16:393–408

BREEN, LEONARD Z.
   1960 "The aging individual." In Clark Tibbits, ed., *Handbook of Social Gerontology.*
       Chicago: University of Chicago Press.

BROVERMAN, INGE K. ET AL.
   1972 "Sex-role stereotypes: a current appraisal." *Journal of Social Issues* 28:59–78

CROUCH, B.M.
   1972 "Age and institutional support: perceptions of older Mexican Americans."
       Journal of Gerontology 27:524–9

CUMMING, ELAINE, AND WILLIAM H. HENRY
   1961 *Growing Old: The Process of Disengagement.* New York: Basic Books

DAVIS, ANN E.
   1969 "Women as a minority group in higher education." *American Sociologist* 4:95–9

DE BEAUVOIR, SIMONE
   1953 *The Second Sex.* New York: Alfred Knopf

EICHLER, MARGRIT
   1973 "Women as personal dependents." Pp. 36–55 in Marylee Stephenson, ed.,
       Women in Canada. Toronto: New Press

FERNBERGER, SAMUEL W.
   1948 "Persistence of stereotypes concerning sex differences." *Journal of Abnormal
       and Social Psychology* 43:97–101

FRANCIS, E.K.
   1951 "Minority groups — a revision of concepts." *British Journal of Sociology*
       2:219–29, 254

GORDON, MILTON M.
   1964 *Assimilation in American Life.* New York: Oxford University Press

GUBRIUM, JABER F.
   1973 *The Myth of the Golden Years: A Socio-Environmental Theory of Aging.*
       Springfield: Charles C. Thomas

HACKER, HELEN MAYER
   1951 "Women as a minority group." *Social Forces* 30:60–9
   1974 "Women as a minority group: twenty years later." Pp. 124–34 in Florence
       Denmark (ed.), *Who Discriminates against Women?* Beverly Hills: Sage

HOCHSCHILD, ARLIE RUSSELL
   1973a "A review of sex role research," *American Journal of Sociology* 78:1011–29
   1973b *The Unexpected Community.* Englewood Cliffs, NJ: Prentice-Hall

INSTITUTE OF GERONTOLOGY
   1974 *No Longer Young, The Older Woman in America: Work Group Reports.* Ann
       Arbor: Institute of Gerontology, University of Michigan-Wayne State University

INSTITUTE OF GERONTOLOGY
   1975 *No Longer Young, The Older Woman in America*: Proceedings of the 26th
       Annual Conference on Aging. Ann Arbor: Institute of Gerontology, University
       of Michigan-Wayne State University

JARVIS, GEORGE K.
1972 "Canadian old people as a deviant minority." Pp. 605–27 in Craig L. Boydell, Carl F. Grindstaff, and Paul C. Whitehead (eds.), *Deviant Behavior and Societal Reactions*. Toronto: Holt, Rinehart and Winston of Canada

KINLOCH, GRAHAM C.
1974 *The Dynamics of Race Relations*. New York: McGraw-Hill

KIRKPATRICK, CLIFFORD
1955 *The Family*. New York: Ronald

LEAKE, C.D.
1962 "Social status and aging." *Geriatrics* 17:785

LIEBERSON, STANLEY
1970 "Stratification and ethnic groups." *Sociological Inquiry* 40:172–81

McKEE, JOHN P. AND ALEX C. SHERRIFFS
1956 "The differential evaluation of males and females." *Journal of Personality* 25:356–71

MYRDAL, GUNNAR
1944 *An American Dilemma*. 2 vols. New York: Harper

NEWMAN, WILLIAM M.
1973 *American Pluralism: A Study of Minority Groups and Social Theory*. New York: Harper and Row

PALMORE, ERDMAN
1969 "Sociological aspects of aging." In Ewald W. Busse and Eric Pfeiffer (eds.), *Behavior and Adaptation in Late Life*. Boston: Little, Brown

ROSE, ARNOLD M.
1962 "The subculture of the aging: a topic for sociological research." *The Gerontologist* 2:123–7
1968 Also in Bernice L. Neugarten (ed.), *Middle Age and Aging*. Chicago: University of Chicago Press

ROSOW, IRVING
1967 *Social Integration of the Aged*. New York: Free Press

SAGARIN, EDWARD (ED.)
1971 *The Other Minorities*. Waltham, Mass.: Xerox College Publishing

SCHERMERHORN, R.A.
1970 *Comparative Ethnic Relations*. New York: Random House

SHIBUTANI, TAMOTSU, AND K.M. KWAN
1965 *Ethnic Stratification*. New York: Macmillan

SIMMONS, LEO W.
1945 *The Role of the Aged in Primitive Society*. London: Oxford University Press

STOLL, CLARICE STASZ
1974 *Female and Male*. Dubuque, Iowa: Wm. C. Brown

STREIB, GORDON F.
1965 "Are the aged a minority group?" Chap. 24 in Alvin W. Gouldner and S.M. Miller (eds.), *Applied Sociology*. New York: Free Press of Glencoe

STREIB, GORDON F., AND CLEMENT J. SCHNEIDER
1971 *Retirement in American Society*. Ithaca, NY: Cornell University Press

THOMPSON, WAYNE E., AND G.F. STREIB
1958 "Situational determinants: health and economic deprivation in retirement." *Journal of Social Issues* 14:18–34

TUCKMAN, JACOB, AND MARTHA LAVELL
1957 "Self classification as old or not old." *Geriatrics* 12:666–71

UNGER, RHODA K., BETH J. RAYMOND, AND STEPHEN M. LEVINE

1974 "Are women a 'minority' group? Sometimes!" Pp. 73–83 in Florence Denmark (ed.), *Who Discriminates Against Women?* Beverly Hills: Sage

VAN DEN BERGHE, PIERRE
1967 *Race and Racism.* New York: John Wiley and Sons

WATSON, WALTER B., AND E.A.T. BARTH
1964 "Questionable assumptions in the theory of social stratification." *Pacific Sociological Review* 7:10–16

WHITE, TERRENCE H.
1973 "Autonomy in work: are women any different?" Pp. 213–24 in Marylee Stephenson (ed.), *Women in Canada.* Toronto: New Press

WIRTH, LOUIS
1945 "The problem of minority groups." Pp. 347–72 in Ralph Linton (ed.), *The Science of Man in the World Crisis.* New York: Columbia University Press

ZOLA, IRVING
1962 "Feelings about age among older people." *Journal of Gerontology* 17:65–8

Some Evidence of Sexual, Ethnic, and Racial Antagonism*

Sanford Labovitz

The major purposes of this paper are to present a technique for studying discrimination and prejudice and to give information on these topics for two samples composed predominantly of English Canadians. Methods of measurement in the areas of prejudice, discrimination, racism, sexism, oppression, and antagonism are in an unsettled state. Although some scales and measurement instruments have been developed and used (see, for example, Larimer, 1970; Dutta, et al., 1969; Gardner, 1970; Adorno, 1950; and Allport, 1954), there are potentially severe biases in any one technique. To illustrate, the various questionnaire items, adjective lists, and experimental manipulations may sensitize subjects to the negative nature of prejudice and discrimination so that they respond in ways quite different from their true feelings. One way to handle this problem is to develop and use techniques with different biases. The technique described below is of this nature.

Two inquiries on the nature of discrimination and prejudice in a Canadian setting were carried out in 1972 and 1973. Observational data were obtained on these particular manifestations of intergroup antagonism — in general, discrimination and prejudice and, in particular, ethnic antagonism, racism, and sexism. Antagonism[1] was explored by analyzing responses to hypothetical names representing Canadian Indians, French Canadians, English-Canadian females, and English-Canadian males. The positive or negative evaluation of each name type serves as an indicator of discriminatory behavioral practices and prejudicial attitudes.

Both inquiries were carried out with the participation of students in introductory sociological classes at the University of Calgary in spring 1972 and again in spring 1973. In each instance, the class members were the interviewers; each selected four subjects on the average (there was much broader participation and enthusiasm among the students in the 1973 class).

---

* Abridged from the *Canadian Review of Sociology and Anthropology*, 11 (3) 1974. Reprinted with the permission of the publisher, Fitzhenry and Whiteside Limited.

The selection processes were not random and, consequently, did not result in statistically precise samples of well-designated populations. In the 1972 study, students were asked to select four other students in the university who were not class members; in the 1973 study students were asked to select at least two subjects under 30 and two over 30. It was suggested that those under 30 could be other university students, while those over 30 could be the class members' parents or other relatives whenever possible. The students were given detailed instructions on how to carry out the interview with a minimum of bias. The number of usable interviews for 1972 was 126 and for 1973 it was 209. The nature of the selection process suggests at least one possible sampling bias — some of the students chose to interview friends, acquaintances, and students in their other classes. Since the interviewers are introductory students, they probably selected a somewhat younger set of subjects than the average for the university.

To determine how subjects evaluated the different name types, a study carried out by Miyamoto and Dornbusch (1956) was summarized into three short paragraphs for each respondent to read. Instead of citing these sociologists as the authors of the study, the summary included either one of the following four names as authors: Edward Blake (English-Canadian male), Edith Blake (English-Canadian female), Joseph Walking Bear (Canadian Indian), and Marcel Fournier (French Canadian). To illustrate the procedure, about 25 percent of the subjects were given the following to read and evaluate:

> It has been assumed that an individual's self-awareness (whether he conceives of himself as popular or unpopular, good or bad, bright or dull, pretty or plain) depends on his perception of how others think of him and treat him.
>
> To test this notion, Edith Blake conducted an experimental study of self-awareness. She divided subjects into several small groups and after a period of interaction asked each subject (with regard to four characteristics) to (1) rate himself, (2) rate the others in the group, and (3) rate himself as he perceives others in the group would rate him. The characteristics to be rated were intelligence, self-confidence, physical attractiveness, and likableness.
>
> Subjects in general rated themselves as others rated them and as they perceived others would rate them. The results support the thesis that a person's conception of himself is based on how others perceive and treat him in everyday interaction.

For the other subjects, the name of Edith Blake was replaced by the other three name types (and the "she" in the next sentence was changed to "he"). Except for the name (and the change from "she" to "he"), the summary was exactly the same for each subject.[2]

Since subjects read only one of the names, they did not know that the study was concerned with discrimination and prejudice as manifested in differential responses to the four social groups in question. The two possible sources of bias of (1) variation in the summary of the study and (2) subjects' knowledge of the purpose of the investigation were controlled by this design. No individual, furthermore, could be identified as being a racist or a sexist — a subject may negatively evaluate the summary because he or she truly thinks it is a poor study.

Group responses, however, that show large differences in name-type evaluation indicate the presence of racism and sexism.

Immediately after reading the summary, a short interview schedule was administered to the subjects. To determine responses to the name types, the subjects were asked to evaluate the study by checking one of the following: highly favorable, somewhat favorable, neither favorable nor unfavorable, somewhat unfavorable, and highly unfavorable. The rest of the schedule contained a series of background questions concerning ethnicity, age, sex, race, religion, occupation, income, and year and major in college if relevant.

A few observations are necessary on the reliability and validity of this technique. No reliability test was administered in the sense of questioning respondents twice and checking for similarity of response. The indirect indicator of reliability is the similarity in ranks for the 1972 and 1973 classes. On the nature of validity, only the type generally labeled "soft validity" or "face validity" was used. The results of the study are consistent with the prevalent view that the French and Indians in Canada are rated low by the English, and females are generally rated lower than males.

The name-type technique may be compared with the matched-guise technique used by Larimer (1970) in which bilingual speakers (speaking in one language and then in another) are evaluated by subjects according to personality traits reflected in their voice. The rather complex and diverse results of Larimer's study are consistent with the low comparative evaluations of the French name for the two studies reported here. The attitude scale developed by Dutta et al. (1969) and the semantic differential used by Gardner et al. (1970) also yielded results largely consistent with those reported here. It should be noted that each of the studies used different measuring techniques on a variety of "ethnic types" and employed diverse samples (in terms of ethnicity, age, and sex). Nonetheless, where they overlap in purpose, they tend to yield consistent results which adds a degree of validity to the different techniques.

The mean evaluational response (based on assigning the numbers one through five to the five evaluational categories of highly favorable to highly unfavorable), the percentage responding highly favorable, and the percentage responding highly or somewhat favorable are presented in Table I. The results clearly suggest some degree of antagonism (or racism, sexism, and ethnic prejudice) as indicated by the differential response to the four name types. Edward Blake, the English-Canadian male, received the most favorable evaluations in both the 1972 and the 1973 studies. This top ranking is clearly indicated by both the mean responses and the percentage responding highly favorable. A somewhat surprising result is the close second ranking of Edith Blake, the English-Canadian female. The 1973 mean response is only .06 higher than that for Edward Blake; and on those responding highly or somewhat favorable in 1973, Edith Blake has the highest percentage of all four name types. On most comparisons, however, Edith Blake is ranked second to her male counterpart.

Joseph Walking Bear (Canadian Indian) is generally ranked third and Marcel Fournier (French Canadian) is consistently ranked last. The gap between Joseph

TABLE I   Responses to Four Hypothetical Names by Two Canadian Samples, 1972 and 1973*

Name	Mean response		Percentage responding "highly favorable"		Percentage responding "highly or somewhat favorable"	
	1973	1972	1973	1972	1973	1972
Edward Blake	2.11	2.09	27.7	24.2	72.4	81.8
Edith Blake	2.17	2.29	24.1	12.9	76.0	67.7
Joseph Walking Bear	2.32	2.53	19.6	23.3	69.6	60.0
Marcel Fournier	2.46	2.56	11.5	12.5	69.2	53.1

* See text for description of the study and for the theoretical representation of each name type. Sample sizes are 126 for 1972 and 209 for 1973. The samples are not random or clearly representative of any particular Canadian population.

† Based on the following measurement scheme: 1 = highly favorable; 2 = somewhat favorable; 3 = neither favorable nor unfavorable; 4 = somewhat unfavorable; 5 = highly unfavorable.

Walking Bear and Edith Blake is usually the largest compared to the other adjacent name pairs. That is, the amount of the differences between Edward Blake and Edith Blake and between Joseph Walking Bear and Marcel Fournier are less than those between Edith Blake and Joseph Walking Bear. The two representative names of English Canadians, therefore, receive substantially more favorable evaluations than the two Canadian minorities of Indians and the French. The comparatively lower evaluation scores for the French name reflect the frequent displays of animosity between the English and the French in Canada. There is general agreement, furthermore, on the comparatively low evaluations of the French name. As measured by the coefficient of relative variation $[V = (\sigma/X) (100)]$, there is less variation in subjects' responses to the French name than to any of the other name types. That this is true for both the 1972 and the 1973 studies increases the confidence in the conclusion that there is comparatively high agreement on the comparatively low evaluation of the French name. These results are consistent with the interpretation that ethnic discrimination and prejudice (including racism) are directed towards these Canadian minority groups. Because of the comparatively low status of Indians and the French in Canadian society, these results may be inferred, with caution, to include most of the country (primarily the English-Canadian population).

In Table II, the mean responses and the percentage responding highly favorable are presented for the four name types by six variables: sex, age, occupation (of father if the subject is a student), income (of father if the subject is a student), religion, and year in university. Only the 1973 study cases are analysed by these variables, because a fairly large N is necessary for this type of analysis. Interviews from the two studies were not combined (to achieve a larger N), because of the differences in instructions in carrying out the studies and the

TABLE II Mean Response* and Percentage Responding "Highly Favorable" to Four Name Types by Sex, Age, Occupation, Income, Religion, and Year in College†

	Edward Blake		Edith Blake		Joseph Walking Bear		Marcel Fournier	
	Mean	Percentage	Mean	Percentage	Mean	Percentage	Mean	Percentage
Sex								
Male	2.18	27.3 (22)	2.13	25.8 (31)	2.12	21.2 (33)	2.81	0.0 (21)
Female	2.22	28.0 (25)	2.22	21.7 (23)	2.61	15.6 (23)	2.23	19.4 (31)
Age								
15–29	2.16	25.8 (31)	2.03	32.2 (31)	2.46	9.1 (33)	2.32	14.3 (28)
30–74	2.00	31.2 (16)	2.38	14.3 (21)	2.13	34.8 (23)	2.56	8.7 (23)
Occupation								
Professionals	1.92	30.8 (13)	2.21	21.7 (23)	2.27	13.6 (22)	2.30	15.0 (20)
Proprietors and managers	1.86	28.6 (7)	2.08	33.3 (12)	1.91	27.3 (11)	3.00	10.0 (10)
Sales, clerical, crafts, operatives, laborers	2.21	21.4 (14)	1.89	44.4 (9)	2.82	16.7 (12)	2.47	7.2 (14)
Income								
$15,000 and over	2.38	36.4 (11)	2.38	27.8 (18)	2.68	5.9 (17)	2.93	0.0 (16)
Below $15,000	1.91	37.5 (16)	1.99	41.2 (17)	1.99	26.3 (19)	2.28	14.3 (21)
Religion								
Protestant	2.03	30.0 (30)	2.16	24.3 (37)	2.28	22.2 (36)	2.21	11.8 (34)
Non-Protestant	2.24	23.5 (17)	2.18	23.5 (17)	2.40	15.0 (20)	2.94	11.1 (18)
Year in University								
First	2.24	17.6 (17)	1.79	35.7 (14)	2.67	13.3 (15)	2.19	25.0 (16)
Second, third, fourth, grad	1.82	36.4 (11)	2.21	21.0 (19)	2.25	8.3 (12)	2.75	0.0 (8)

* See text or Table I for a description of the measurement scheme on which the mean is based.
† Based on 209 cases for the 1973 study only. Number of cases are in parentheses.

differences in response rates between members of the two classes. It should be noted that five of the six variables in Table II are treated as dichotomies because of the small cell frequencies that resulted when more categories were used. To illustrate, when 209 cases are spread out over 16 cells (four name types by four, say, age categories), some means and percentages are based on less than five cases. Even dichotomizing and trichotomizing as the variables are presented in the table resulted in a small number of cases for a few of the cells. The results in Table II, consequently, are somewhat unstable, and should be interpreted as suggestive only.

With regard to sex, two results stand out: (1) males much more negatively evaluated the French name (mean = 2.81) than did females (mean = 2.23); and (2) females much more negatively evaluated the Indian name (mean = 2.61) than did males (mean = 2.12). On age, the most striking difference is in the evaluation of the Indian name. Older people (aged 30–74) give a much more favorable evaluation (mean = 2.13) than do younger people (aged 15–29) (mean = 2.46). On the female name, the younger group responded much more favorably (mean = 2.03) than did the older group (mean = 2.38). In occupations, the lowest occupational prestige grouping (sales, clerical, crafts, operatives, and laborers) have the lowest favorable response to the Indian name (mean = 2.82) and the highest favorable response to the female name (mean = 1.89). In contrast to occupations, on the income variable the lower income group (below $15,000) evaluates each of the four names more highly than the higher income group (above $15,000). A rather surprising finding occurs in the religious categories where protestants respond to the French name more favorably (mean = 2.21) than do non-protestants (mean = 2.94). Finally, for the variable designated as year in university, first-year students evaluated the female name (mean = 1.79) and the French name (mean = 2.19) more favorably than did the more advanced students (mean = 2.21 and 2.75, respectively); and they evaluated the English male name (mean = 2.24) and the Indian name (mean = 2.67) less favorably (as compared to 1.82 and 2.25, respectively).

CONCLUDING COMMENTS

The results of this study should be interpreted with caution as indicators of intergroup antagonism. Responses to names may be far removed from the way people interact with those from other social groups. The results, however, clearly warrant further study, which should be carried out on different races and ethnic groups and in different sections of the country.

Notes

1. Antagonism, discrimination, prejudice, racism, sexism, and ethnicity are defined and used in the following way. The more general and neutral term of antagonism is used to refer to all types of discriminatory behavior or prejudicial attitudes from one group to another. Discrimination is overt antagonism and refers to behavior of members of a group in preventing or restricting access to scarce resources to members of other groups. Prejudice is covert antagonism and refers to negative evaluation of members

of a group, because he or she is a member of that group. Racism is antagonistic behavior or attitudes of members of one group towards members of another on the basis of certain physical characteristics. Sexism is subsumed under racism and refers specifically to the differences between males and females. Ethnicity is used as the most encompassing category referring to any social, cultural, or physical differences between groups.

2. For a similar type of study using a female name only, see Goldberg (1968).

References

ADORNO, T.W., E. FRENKEL-BRUNSWIK, D.J. LEVINSON, AND R.N. SANFORD
  1950 *The Authoritarian Personality*. New York: Harper & Row.

ALLPORT, G.W.
  1954 *The Nature of Prejudice*. Cambridge, Mass.: Addison-Wesley.

DUTTA, SATRAJIT, LEONARD NORMAN, AND RABINDRA N. KANUNGO
  1969 "A scale for the measurement of attitudes toward French Canadians," *Canadian Journal of Behavioral Science* 1, 3:156–161.

GARDNER, R.C., D.M. TAYLOR, AND H.J. FEENSTRA
  1970 "Ethnic stereotypes: attitudes or beliefs?" *Canadian Journal of Psychology* 24, 5:321–324

GOLDBERG, PHILIP
  1968 "Are women prejudiced against women." *Trans-action* 5(April):28–30.

LARIMER, GEORGE S.
  1970 "Indirect assessment of intercultural prejudices." *International Journal of Psychology* 5, 3:189–195.

MIYAMOTO, S. FRANK, AND SANFORD DORNBUSCH
  1956 "A test of interactionist hypotheses of self-conception." *American Journal of Sociology* 61(March):399–403.

The Gap between Women and Men in the Wages of Work*

Lynn McDonald

The women's movement in Canada has already become something of a force to be reckoned with, and shows every sign of growing strength and importance. Nearly every week some new breakthrough is registered, so much so that women and men both may be lulled into thinking the situation is much rosier than it is. For, when such crucial matters as employment opportunities, wages and salaries are concerned, the trends are very gloomy indeed.

The problem is not just that women are paid less than men for doing the same job. Or, that the better the job, the less likely it is that women will be doing it at all. Less obvious is the fact that the gap in wages and salaries between women and men is *increasing* — in all the provinces, and any way you look at it. For Canada as a whole the gap in average income increased from $2,694 in 1965 to $4,719 in 1973, and the *gap* is greater than the average income for women. These figures, however, include part-time workers, who are disproportionately women, so do not give the most reliable indication of the problem. But, where average *hourly* earnings in manufacturing are reported clearly the gap is still substantial, and growing. It actually doubled between 1955 and 1969. Women's wages increased throughout this period, of course, but men's increased at a much greater rate.

Women who work full-time in Canada earn on average about 60 percent as much as male full-time workers.[1] Roughly half the difference is due to women being paid less than men for the same work which is what current "equal pay" legislation is supposed to forbid. The other half is due to women being relegated to badly paying jobs, the concern of "equal opportunity" legislation. (But this kind of discrimination is still legal in federally regulated industries, notably banks and airline companies.)

Inequities in pensions, insurance, and other fringe benefits are still legal for most of Canada. With fringe benefits equal to about 10 percent of earnings, the issue is of some consequence, and hence the expression "equal remuneration," not simply "equal pay," ought to be applied. It seems that governments are ready

* Reprinted from the *Canadian Forum*, 55 (650) April–May 1975, pp. 4–7. Used with permission.

to concede the point, but the question is when. Ontario, for example, included fringe benefits in its equal pay legislation in 1972, but didn't proclaim the section. Nevertheless, the *main* reason women have poor pensions is because they have had poor earnings while working, which gets us back to the central problem.

Conceptually, it's easy to distinguish between unequal pay and unequal opportunity, but in real life the two go together. Wherever studies have uncovered discrimination of the one type the other turns up, too. Yet there are separate acts for the two types of problem in five provinces: Nova Scotia, New Brunswick, Ontario, Manitoba and Saskatchewan, and no equal opportunity legislation, so far, for federally regulated industries. With separate acts there are separate enforcement agencies, and endless possibilities for officials to lose cases in the red tape in between. A woman, for example, may be paid less than a man because she was promoted later — and neither agency will deal with the matter.

If the current equal pay legislation worked, women full-time workers would earn on average roughly 80 percent of their male counterparts. There should be differences also by province. Ontario, with relatively good legislation, should have a lesser gap than Quebec, which has only a vague clause about "conditions of employment." But the gap does not vary markedly from province to province. We would also expect to see the gap diminish when provinces brought in their legislation, or after making changes to strengthen enforcement. This has not happened either. Detailed studies in Ontario notably have shown no diminution in the gap, even when careful comparisons of "similarly described occupations" are made.

The Ontario government commissioned studies on the effectiveness of its legislation before drafting its new bill. The studies showed persuasively that the legislation was not working, whereupon precisely the same approach was repeated in the new bill. The drafting of the bill was itself a well-kept secret. The government consulted no women's groups, not even the Advisory Council it had itself appointed. The bill was rushed through the House in November and December, 1974. As early as January, 1975, a spokesman for the Ministry of Labour admitted that there was not much that could be done about enforcement with the present legislation!

The failure of current equal pay laws is due both to defects in legislation and lack of enforcement. The wording is effectively the same in all the provinces, equal pay for "the same or substantially the same," or "similar or substantially similar" work. For a woman to have a case she must have the same or similar work as a male worker, either "in the same establishment," or "employed by the same employer," depending on the province. "Establishment" may itself be imaginatively interpreted, so that a woman selling blouses may not be in the same "establishment" as a man around the pillar selling shirts.

The main catch is that women are trained, from the cradle, to aspire to *different* jobs from men and, in fact, women and men tend to do different jobs. Rough estimates for Ontario indicate that some 500,000 women of the 1,200,000 in the paid labor force are excluded from the protection of current equal pay legislation. Examples are secretaries, typists, receptionists, lab technicians, waitresses, chambermaids, many sales clerks, and industrial workers such as packers, sewing machine operators and electrical assemblers.

While "equal pay" legislation has proved to be a sorry failure there is nothing to suggest "equal opportunity" has done any better. The increase in the gap is one tell-tale sign for, if women were getting into the better jobs, their average earnings would be increasing — and the gap narrowing. More to the point, the concentration of women in the low paying service and clerical sectors is *growing*. Women held 45.2 percent of the service jobs in 1971, and 51.4 percent in 1974. In clerical work they moved from 68.4 percent to 72.9 percent in the same period. Nor has there been any compensating movement of women into managerial-administrative positions. The proportion of these jobs held by women was 15.7 percent in 1971, and still only 16.0 percent in 1974.

Enforcement procedures for both equal pay and equal opportunity laws are extremely cumbersome. Decisions are made far up the line, away from the complainant. The minister, director, commission or whoever *may* call for an

TABLE I   Hourly Earnings in Manufacturing

	1955			1969		
	Average for men	Average for women	Diff-erence	Average for men	Average for women	Diff-erence
Newfoundland	$1.46	0.55	0.91	2.68	1.22	1.46
Nova Scotia	1.34	0.62	0.72	2.46	1.35	1.11
New Brunswick	1.34	0.73	0.61	2.58	1.39	1.19
Quebec	1.43	0.89	0.54	2.80	1.83	0.97
Ontario	1.64	1.02	0.64	3.28	2.00	1.28
Manitoba	1.50	0.87	0.63	2.81	1.71	1.10
Saskatchewan	1.51	0.99	0.52	3.09	1.88	1.21
Alberta	1.56	1.04	0.52	3.15	1.98	1.17
B.C.	1.81	1.12	0.69	3.71	2.26	1.45

Source: *Canada Year Book; Earnings and Hours of Work in Manufacturing.*

TABLE II   Income Differences by Sex

	1965			1973		
	Average income men	Average income women	Diff-erence	Average income men	Average income women	Diff-erence
Atlantic	$3,497	1,397	2,100	6,306	2,936	3,380
Quebec	4,347	1,881	2,466	7,755	3,682	4,073
Ontario	5,094	1,952	3,142	9,093	3,834	5,259
Prairies	4,210	1,802	2,408	7,778	3,197	4,581
B.C.	4,749	2,019	2,730	9,448	3,604	5,844
Canada	4,551	1,857	2,694	8,310	3,591	4,719

Source: *Income Distribution by Size in Canada.*

investigation, *may* establish a Board of Inquiry, *may* order compensation paid — or not, as he sees fit. The complainant has no right to information about her case, reasons for refusal to investigate or the like. Employers are well protected from unfavorable publicity. In none of the acts is disclosure of offending employers obligatory. Most permit disclosure but, in practice, "confidentiality" is the rule.

Penalties are low. In several provinces (Manitoba, PEI, Newfoundland, and the Northwest Territories) the maximum fine is $100 for an individual, $500 for a corporation or trade union. Ontario's new act specifices a maximum of $10,000 — but Ontario does not prosecute employers anyway. The written consent of the Minister is a requirement for prosecution in a number of acts and, throughout the country, prosecutions are extremely rare.

Just how feeble enforcement measures really are becomes even more obvious when they are compared with enforcement for criminal matters. The police routinely handle complaints involving trivial thefts and property damage. The average loss in break-ins is less than $150, while women lose thousands of dollars every year by being paid less than men. The major cities have thousands of police officers, while for whole provinces there are only handfuls of investigating officers for job discrimination cases, and these typically with responsibilities also for other kinds of investigation. "Quotas" for job discrimination cases are unheard of. Nor do ministries of labor aspire to "rising discrimination rates" the way ministries of justice work on "rising crime." It requires only a Justice of the Peace to lay a criminal charge, and the decision to prosecute is normally made in the local prosecutor's office. The names of criminal offenders are public information, unless they are children, but employers are protected whether juvenile delinquents or adult.

So far, equal pay legislation has been a useful tool for nurses' aides, but few other categories of workers. In Ontario, 409 women were successful in claims in 1973, obtaining altogether nearly half a million dollars in settlements. This represents, however, only 17¢ for every $1000 lost by the female work force that year through unequal pay. B.C. seems to be the only province to date to have achieved any really impressive settlement. The Human Rights Commission there managed to obtain some five million dollars for women hospital workers, including those in jobs different from men's, using a job evaluation scheme to compare jobs.

The defects of equal pay legislation were well known by the time of the Report of the Royal Commission on the Status of Women, in 1970. Accordingly, its recommendation was for "equal remuneration for work of equal value," with enforcement through a system of job evaluation. This approach the Commission took from the International Labour Organization, Convention 100, and it is the approach supported by women's groups in Canada ever since. The idea is that people should be paid according to the skill, effort, responsibility and working conditions associated with the job they do, whether it is a job done by men, women, or both. Comparisons of jobs would be made on the basis of *objective* criteria — difficulty of task, job training required, responsibility for other workers, equipment and so forth. Practically speaking, enforcement would mean

TABLE III   Estimated Discrimination Bill

	Number women employed	Average actual f. income	Average est. "equal pay" income	Average difference due to "unequal pay"	Total est. discrimination bill
Canada	3,152,000	$3,591	$5,817	$2,226	$7,016,352,000
Nfld.	54,000	2,813	4,157	1,344	72,576,000
P.E.I.	14,000	2,426	3,507	1,081	15,134,000
N.S.	92,000	3,172	4,660	1,488	136,896,000
N.B.	80,000	2,789	4,486	1,697	135,760,000
Que.	841,000	3,682	5,428	1,746	1,468,386,000
Ont.	1,238,000	3,834	6,365	2,531	3,133,378,000
Man.	145,000	3,154	5,121	1,967	285,215,000
Sask.	111,000	3,068	5,132	2,064	229,104,000
Alta.	244,000	3,286	5,800	2,514	613,416,000
B.C.	333,000	3,604	6,614	3,010	1,002,330,000

Note: The average estimated "equal pay" income is estimated as 70 percent of average income for male earners. This can be thought of as the average income women would earn if paid at the same rate as men for doing the same job, which is what equal pay legislation is supposed to ensure. The difference (30 percent) is largely due to women being relegated disproportionately to badly paying jobs, and to the higher proportion of women part-time workers.

Source: Col. 1, *The Labour Force*, May, 1974, pp. 80, 81. Col. 2, *Income Distributions by size in Canada*, preliminary estimates, pp. 14, 15. Col 3, 70 percent male average income, taken from same source as Col. 2. Col 4, Col. 3–Col. 2. Col. 5, Col. 1 x Col. 4.

applying the same criteria that are now used to determine men's wages and salaries to women's. This is not an argument for job evaluation *as such*, but for machinery to challenge unfair evaluation schemes in use.

The Royal Commission also recommended formal ratification of the ILO equal remuneration convention, which was done in 1972. This required approval of all the provinces, which the federal government duly sought and obtained. Yet none of the provinces, nor the federal government, has actually incorporated the principle into legislation. In Ontario, the Liberal and New Democratic Parties are on record as advocating it, and in B.C. there has been some use of job evaluation, short of complete acceptance of the principle.

Otto Lang, as Minister of Justice, has promised "landmark legislation" for women this spring, but there is little reason to expect it will follow the Royal Commission recommendation. It seems that no women have been involved in drafting the bill, though the Associate Deputy Minister assured me that the men who were working on it were "sympathetic to women." Lang himself cancelled an appearance at the recent Women and the Law Conference in Winnipeg, where the equal value approach was strongly supported.

The very timing of the bill raises some questions. Why is the federal government going for human rights legislation *now*, when it's been found not to work in *any* of the provinces in which it has been tried?

The cynic must entertain some such explanation as a predilection for window-dressing; "we have to do *something* for International Women's Year, and how can these women object to human rights?" If the federal government had a reasonable record on implementation of Royal Commission recommendations one might be more optimistic, but it has been notoriously slack, especially on the recommendations that involve money.

The explanation for the failure of the human rights approach ultimately gets down to the simple ingredient of money. It is one thing to ask a white landlord to rent to a non-white tenant at the going rate. It is quite another to ask an employer to pay his women employees the same as men when he is used to paying them less. There just is no basis for a "meeting of minds," and "educational approach" or the "spirit of conciliation" human rights commissioners love to talk about. Nor, we must remember, did human rights legislation work on race discrimination when landlords thought they would lose money by taking non-white tenants.

The amount by which women are underpaid in Canada is staggering. Using even the most conservative estimates assuming women should be earning 70 percent of men, the discrimination bill comes to over seven billion dollars for the country as a whole. And this does not begin to include the deployment problem, but only lesser pay for the same work, as understood in existing equal pay legislation. Obviously if we were to take a broader view, the bill would be higher still.

The reasonableness of equal pay for women is no longer at dispute; virtually everyone agrees with the principle. Indeed we have to depend on the highly committed miser to have any argument at all. That equal pay is not a reality reflects no disagreement about *values*, but *cost*. It would be expensive to pay women what they are worth.

Realistically, equal remuneration for work of equal value can only be implemented gradually. This women are prepared to accept, so long as there is a genuine start on it. Instead, governments proclaim "equality for all" — on paper — and then fail to enforce their own laws. Much more realistic approaches are being taken in European countries, which Canada would do well to consider. Equal pay legislation in Britain specifies a gradual approach, with a modified job evaluation scheme. In Sweden, women workers in industry are getting better wage increases than men, so that the gap is actually decreasing.

Expensive as genuinely equal pay would be, there are costs to be considered as well in perpetuating present inequities. Cheap labor is too often unproductive labor. The use of women for enhancing a male boss's status, as in rug ranking, is an especially foolish practice. The concentration of women in dead-end jobs means a loss of talent where it is needed, and who would argue any excess of talent in high places in Canada? Women increasingly bear the responsibility for raising families alone, so that large numbers of children suffer, too. (The proportion of female-headed households below the poverty line is increasing, while for male-headed it is decreasing.)

Clearly this whole issue is not just one of women's interests versus men's, but of short-term expedience versus long-run productivity and prosperity. Of course we can appreciate employers not wanting to cough up, but we all suffer the consequences insofar as we let them have their way.

Note

1. Sylvia Ostry's *The Female Worker in Canada* shows women full-time workers earning 59 percent as much as male full-time workers, with 1961 Census data. Numerous subsequent studies, of particular industries and occupational groups have consistently shown similar proportions. The 60 percent figure turns up routinely as well in studies of western European countries and the United States. (See Evelyne Sullerot, *Woman, Society and Change*.) The extent to which the discrepancy is due to rational criteria like education or years of service varies somewhat by industry. Ostry's study showed from 15 to 22 percentage points of the difference left unexplained by rational criteria. Studies of particular occupation and industries I have reviewed have tended to show half the discrepancy unexplained. See, for example, Robson and Lapointe, "A Comparison of Men's and Women's Salaries and Employment Fringe Benefits in the Academic Profession," Royal Commission study No. 1.

PART THREE

Selected Correlates of Class, Power, and Status Differences

A. Differences in Life Chances

Social Status Differentials in Infant Survival*

Ursula M. Anderson

The fact that social, political and cultural factors affect the health status of individuals and greatly modify their utilization of available facilities has not, until recently, been taken into account in the delivery of health services.[1] The present health care system has, for the most part, grown in response to the advancements of science and technology, becoming ever more complicated and expensive but being hardly ever adapted to the social, cultural and other differences existing between individuals and groups of individuals. In this context, primary care defined as being the *actual* availability of a physician to an individual, on either an episodic or continuous basis, is of particular interest. Economic as well as cultural factors in the West brought about the development of two systems of primary care, namely, private for those who knew where to find it and could afford it and public for those who couldn't afford to pay for it or didn't know where and how to find it.

INSURANCE SCHEMES

This discrepancy has led most Western countries in recent years to provide money to people through private and government insurance schemes so that, in effect, everyone could contract the services of his own doctor. Recently, this concept took effect in Ontario, through the Ontario Health Services Insurance Plan of the Ontario Provincial Government.

The availability of money immediately brings into focus the availability of manpower. In Canada this means in particular the family practitioner who is regarded as the primary care physician for all members of the family. Reports such as the one made in April, 1970, by the Committee on the Healing Arts to the Ontario Minister of Health, leave no doubt that there is concern that there are too few family practitioners available to provide primary care to all residents of the province. This is evidenced by many of the Committee's recommendations, particulary the following: that a sixth medical school be opened in Ontario; that financial inducements be made to prospective entrants to personal and family practice; that community health centers be developed to permit more free time to

* Anderson, U.M.: "Infant Survival Differentials in the City of Toronto: A Challenge to Health Planning and Research." *Canadian Family Physician*, 16:45-50, September 1970. Reprinted by permission of the publisher.

the individual practitioner and that new programs of health technology and nursing be introduced to provide more allied health personnel. Availability of service is only one aspect of sound health planning. It brings into focus utilization by the consumer, namely, the patient. Studies show that real barriers to the utilization of health facilities, as presently structured, do exist and that provision of money and of health services does not ensure utilization.[2]

PEOPLE'S HEALTH NEEDS

Availability and utilization of health services means catering to the health needs of the people and taking the necessary steps to maintain health and prevent and cure sickness. Health needs may be defined either subjectively or objectively. Although subjective health needs are of prime importance they will not be considered here. Objective definition of health needs cannot be made without reference to health status. Health status is the sum of the interplay of biological, social and cultural factors on the one hand and the type, delivery, availability and utilization of health services on the other. Measurement of the effects of the interplay can be made if health data pertaining both to defined indices and defined populations are obtainable, and then available for analysis. Because socio-economic and other information is already plentifully available on small city sub-divisions, namely, census tracts because of census taking, etc., it is logical to assume that health data available on a similar basis could provide not only an objective measurement, immediately referable to demographic data, but would provide also a means for comparing the health status of one group of individuals with another. In terms of what has been said about availability of manpower and utilization of services, collection of proper data is essential in terms of health planning and determination of community health priorities. The value of this approach has been clearly shown.[3]

A decision to initiate Community Health programs from The Hospital for Sick Children in Toronto lead to a search for ways to define the health status of children in the city, in order that sound recommendations could be made for hospital involvement. This was approached in a variety of ways; what follows is an illustration of the use of health data to describe differences in health status.

METHOD

Some of the more sensitive yet still crude indices of child health are the mortality rates surrounding birth and infancy. To know that in 1968, the infant mortality rate in the City of Toronto was 19.1 per 1,000 live births is really to know little, because it is an average reflecting tremendous diversity in socio-economic status, life experience, life style, and infant mortality itself. It was therefore felt necessary to obtain data concerning the pregnancy, birth and infancy experience of the population, by small geographic breakdown in order to find out what differences exist.

The indices sought were as follows:

1. Infant Mortality Rate for Infants, 1-11 Months.
2. Stillbirth Rates.
3. Perinatal Death Rate.
4. Prematurity Rate.
5. Obstetrical Complications of Pregnancy.
6. Birth Rate.
7. Average Number of Previous Births to Mothers Delivering Within the Stated Year.
8. Amount of Prenatal Care Received.
9. Out-Of-Wedlock Care Received.
10. Utilization of Hospitals by Demographic Characteristics.
11. Types of Delivery by Hospital.

This information by census tract breakdown was sought from several different places but was not available. However, the Toronto City Health Department agreed to run, on a special basis, the only indices it had available, which were:

Birthrate	/ 1,000 1966 population.
Infant Mortality Rate	/ 1,000 live births.
Stillbirth Rate	/ 1,000 live births.
Perinatal Mortality Rate	/ 1,000 live births.

Numbers and rates for the years 1966, 1967 and 1968, were given by the Health Department, for each of the 135 census tracts in Toronto. The Division of Community Health then arranged these figures as follows:

1. An average was made for each census tract for the three-year period for each index. This was to obviate chance occurrences of high or low indices in one year or two year figures and to render comparison valid.
2. The census tracts were then ranked from highest to lowest for each index and ranged for each index thus obtained. These ranged were then sorted and grouped into census tracts which had four high indices, three high indices, two, one, and none. Cut-off points between high and low indices or rates were taken as follows and approximate to the average value for each index for the city as a whole. Cut-off points are not meant to indicate acceptability of the measurements involved; they are merely tools for making two broad categories for comparison.

Birthrate	20/1,000 1966 population.
Infant Mortality Rate	20/1,000 live births.
Stillbirth Rate	15/1,000 live births.
Perinatal Mortality Rate	25/1,000 live births.

3. Having defined differences in health experience, validation of differences was sought in regard to the 16 census tracts with high indices. Certain data taken from the Bureau of the Census were compared to the same data averaged for the

remainder of Toronto so that comparisons could be made and demographic differences demonstrated. The factors chosen for comparison are as follows:

1. *Population Characteristics.*
Size.
Age.
Birth Place.
Ethnic Group.
Migration Movers 1956-61.
2. *Housing Characteristics.*
Period of Construction —
    Before 1920. Since 1945.
Owner Occupied.
Crowded Dwellings.
Occupied less than one Year.
In Need of Major Repair.
3. *Occupation, Salary, Education.*
Labor Force.
Women in Labor Force.
Family Wage and Salary Income.
Male Wage and Salary Income.
    under $2,000.
    6,000 and over.
4. *Family Characteristics.*
Number of Families.
Children per Family.
Juvenile Offenders.

RESULTS

The ranges for each index are as follows:

Birthrate	from 49.06 to 8.1 / 1,000 1966 population.
Infant Mortality Rate	from 57.68 to 3.79 / 1,000 live births.
Stillbirth Rate	from 4.204 to 2.86 / 1,000 live births.
Perinatal Mortality Rate	from 81.61 to 5.05 / 1,000 live births.

There are 16 census tracts in the City of Toronto that have four high indices and there are 25 census tracts in the City that have no high rates. The 16 census tracts with four high rates are: 5, 16, 24, 26, 27, 32, 40, 44, 59, 97, 98, 99, 106, 114, 115, 119.

The average rates for these 16 census tracts are:

Birthrate	26.5 / 1,000 1966 population.
Infant Mortality Rate	29.2 / 1,000 live births.
Stillbirth Rate	22.3 / 1,000 live births.
Perinatal Mortality Rate	37.9 / 1,000 live births.

TABLE I Comparison of Infant Births and Deaths in High Risk and Low Risk Areas of Toronto*

Characteristics	High Risk Area	Low Risk Area	Statistical Significance
Birthrate	26.5	15.2	p < .001
Infant mortality rate	29.2	11.8	p < .001
Stillbirth rate	22.3	10.3	p < .001
Perinatal mortality rate	37.9	16.1	p < .001

* High Risk Area is defined as 16 census tracts with High Indices, Low Risk Areas as 12 census tracts with no High Indices

TABLE II Population Characteristics of Risk Area Compared to the Remainder of the City of Toronto

Characteristics	Risk area[a]	Remainder of Toronto	Statistical significance[b]
Population size total	91023	648009	p < .001
Age[c]			
0–14 Years	254.9	236.8	p < .001
65 Years and Over	93.8	112.4	p < .001
Schooling[d]			
Elementary	577.2	477.2	p < .001
High school	388.3	443.8	p < .001
University	34.4	78.7	p < .001
Birth place[e]			
Canada	584.1	580.3	p < .05
Outside	416.1	419.7	p < .05
Immigrated to Canada, 1946–61	295.8	290.5	p < .01
Ethnic Group[e]			
British Isles	465.7	525.6	p < .001
Italian	99.3	393.4	p < .001
German	48.1	45.4	p < .001
Other	386.8	310.5	0 < .001
Migration (movers 1956–61)	605.7	550.3	p < .001

a. Risk Area is defined as the 16 census tracts with 4 high indices (see text).
b. Statistical significance has been determined by use of the Z Test. Three levels of probability have been used where p = < .05, p = < .01, and p = < .001.
c. Per 1,000 1966 population.
d. Per 1,000 population five years and over.
e. Per 1,000 1961 population.

TABLE III   Housing Characteristics of Risk Area Compared to the Remainder of the City of Toronto

Characteristics[b]	Risk area[a]	Remainder of Toronto	Statistical significance
Construction			
Before 1920	801.8	526.7	p < .001
Since 1945	286.6	265.1	—
Occupied dwellings			
Owner occupied	68.7	87.3	p < .001
Crowded	170.4	158.9	p < .001
Less than 1 year	208.9	171.0	0 < .001
In need of major repairs	105.4	105.9	—

a. Risk area is defined as the 16 census tracts with 4 high indices (see text).
b. /1,000 total households.

TABLE IV   Occupation, Salary, and Education Characteristics of Risk Area Compared to the Remainder of the City of Toronto

Characteristics	Risk area[a]	Remainder of Toronto	Statistical significance
Labor Force			
Male/1,000			
1961 population	300.9	297.0	p < .05
Female/1,000			
1961 population	163	181	p < .001
Total/1,000			
1961 population	463	479.2	p < .001
Women/1,000 of total			
labor force	351.4	379.2	p < .001
Occupations			
Managerial, professional,			
and technical	114.8	180.8	p < .001
Primary, craftmen, and			
laborers	487.8	413.8	p < .001
Male wage and salary income[b]			
Under $2,000	186.9	149.8	p < .001
$6,000 and over	34.1	89.1	p < .001
Average family wage and			
salary income	$4281	$5156	p < .001

a. Risk area is defined as the 16 census tracts with 4 high indices (see text).
b. /1,000 male labor force.

TABLE V   Family Characteristics of Risk Area Compared to the Remainder of the City of Toronto

Characteristics	Risk area[a]	Remainder of Toronto	Statistical significance
Number of families /1,000 population	236.9	244.2	p < .001
Children per family	1.3	1.2	—
Juvenile offenders, 1963–65 per 1,000 5–14 population	60.8	39.5	p < .001

a. Risk area is defined as the 16 census tracts with 4 high indices (see text).

Approximately 14 per cent of the population of the City of Toronto lives in these 16 census tracts (from 1966 census data). These 16 census tracts can be grouped together as a Risk Area, risk being defined here as pertaining to pregnancy outcome and infant life.

The 25 census tracts with no high rates are as follows: 4, 19, 21, 33, 34, 48, 58, 63, 66, 67, 68, 70, 71, 77, 78, 79, 81, 86, 89, 90, 93, 95, 104, 130, 134.

Because census tracts 19, 33, 34, 48, 58, 67, 68, 70, 77, 90, 95, 104 and 134 had data for two or less of the indices only, they were eliminated from the totals and not included in the averages. Among the reasons for unavailable data was the fact that some of these census tracts are totally occupied by industries of various sorts and institutions, etc. This left 12 census tracts with no high indices. Approximately 11 per cent of the population of the City of Toronto lives in these 12 census tracts. Comparison of the rates with the Risk Area is shown on Table I.

The average rates for these 12 census tracts are:

Birthrate	15.2 / 1,000 1966 population.
Infant Mortality Rate	11.8 / 1,000 live births.
Stillbirth Rate	10.3 / 1,000 live births.
Perinatal Mortality Rate	16.1 / 1,000 live births.

The results of comparing census and other data relating to the 16 census tracts with four high indices with the average for the remainder of the City of Toronto are shown in Tables II-V.

Table VI shows a comparison of Infant Births and Deaths in the 16 census tracts with the remainder of the City of Toronto. Significance levels are included in these tables. Significant differences exist in the birth and mortality rates of infants from the Risk Area compared to the remainder of Toronto (Table VI). The infant mortality rate is 29.2 in the Risk Area compared to 18.8 for the remainder of Toronto; the stillbirth rate is 22.3 compared to 14.7; the perinatal mortality rate is 37.9 compared to 26.1 and the birthrate is 26.5 compared to 23.4. The disadvantage of survival of these infants is reinforced by analysis of demographic data (Tables II-V). The level of education of people in the Risk Area is lower than in the rest of Toronto: the number of recent migrants, the number of old houses and the degree of overcrowding is higher. The average family income is $4,281 in the Risk Area compared to $5,156 for the remainder of Toronto and the number of families with incomes under $2,000 is higher and the number with incomes over $6,000 much lower. Juvenile offences are recorded nearly twice as frequently in the Risk Area.

TABLE VI   Infant Birth and Death Characteristics of Risk Area Compared to the Remainder of the City of Toronto

Characteristics	Risk area[a]	Remainder of Toronto	Statistical significance
Birth rate[b]	26.5	23.4	p < .001
Infant mortality rate[c]	29.2	18.8	p < .001
Stillbirth rate[c]	22.3	14.7	p < .01
Perinatal mortality rate[c]	37.9	26.1	p < .01

a. Risk area is defined as the 16 census tracts with 4 high indices (see text).
b. Per 1,000 total 1966 population.
c. Per 1,000 live births.

COMMENTS

It is clear that in the City of Toronto there are well-defined areas where the health of infants, as measured by their chances of survival within the first year of life, is definitely at a lower level than in the remaining areas of the city. This indicates a need to concentrate child health services in these areas and to research the reasons for these high levels of pregnancy wastage and infant deaths.

The extremely high perinatal death rate in these areas indicates the need for more information concerning the amount of prenatal care of mothers and the types of care they received during delivery. In-depth study of the causes of perinatal deaths of infants born to women living in these areas as compared to perinatal deaths of infants born to women living in the remainder of the city is needed to clarify the interplay of biological and environmental factors. The high infant mortality rates would indicate a need for in-depth study of utilization of health facilities and the types of health services that are needed in these areas. High infant mortality after the first month of life indicates a major environmental role: this needs to be studied, and gaps in service located. For this reason, major breakdown of infant mortality rates into neonatal mortality and mortality of infants, 1-11 months is needed on an ongoing basis. The census tracts with high birth rates would indicate the need for educational and service programs in regard to family planning.

The picture obtained from these four mortality indices is meaningful in terms of implications for health services but it is still incomplete. This is due to lack of information about the pregnancy and delivery experience of the mothers of these infants. It points to a need for record linkage and for collection of data by the Ontario Health Services Insurance Plan and the Ontario Hospital Services Commission on a census tract basis which would then give more information about utilization of existing facilities by these women and its relation, quantitatively if not qualitatively, to the occurrence of infant mortality whether pre-, para-, or post-natally. More information would enable one to determine more accurately the point at which the link between patient and care is weakest and where efforts should be applied. The general lack of vital statistical data on a census tract basis and the divided responsibility for its collection demonstrates a real need for legislation to change the items of data collection as well as the method of collection. The fact that 11 percent of the population living in the 12 best census tracts enjoys infant survival rates two to two-and-a-half times as good as 14 percent of the population living in the worst 16 census tracts (Table I), is not only a measure of what can be achieved but stands as a challenge to health services and points to the need for systematic research on health care systems tailored to these entities.

Notes

1. HAGGERTY, R.J.
   Community Pediatrics, *New Eng J Med* 278:15, 1968.

   RICHMOND, J.B.
   Gaps in Nation's Service for Children, *Bull NY Acad Med* 41:1237, 1965.
   Report of National Advisory Commission on Health Manpower, Vol. 1, Wash., D.C., Supt. of Documents, U.S. Govt. Printing Office, 1967.

   LOWE, C.U.
   Science and Public Policy, Child Care, *Med Opinion Review* 4:21, 1968.

   WISHIK, S.M.
   More Children and More Responsibilities for Pediatricians, *Pediatrics* 37:1 1966.

   TINKER, K.II.
   American Journal Orthopsychiatry, Vol. 24:165, 1959.

2. PAGE, M.D.
   Children, 8:63, 1961.

   HILL, E.M.
   Children, 19:132, 1963.

   PARSONS, M.II.
   Children, 7:181, 1960.

   BANKS, J.G.
   Children, 6:208, 1959.

   CORNELY, P.B., AND BIGMAN, S.K.
   Children, 10:23.

   ANDERSON, U.M., ET AL.
   High Risk Groups — Definition and Identification, *New Eng J of Med*, 273:308-313 (August 5), 1965.

3. GABRIELSON, I., ET AL.
Relating Health and Census Information for Health Planning, *Am J of Pub Health*, Vol. 59, No. 7, July, 1969.

SCHLESINGER, E.R., AND ALLAWAY, N.C.
Use of Child Loss Data in Evolving Priorities in Maternal Health Services, *Am J of Pub Health*, Vol. 47, p. 573, 1957.

WALLACE, HELEN M.: EISNER, VICTOR; AND DOOLEY, S.
Availability and Usefulness of Selected Health and S/E Data for Community Planning, *Am J of Pub Health*, Vol. 57, No. 5, May, 1967.

WOOLSEY, T.D., AND LAWRENCE, P.S.
Moving ahead in Health Statistics, *Am J of Pub Health*, Vol. 59, No. 10, October, 1969.

MATTISON, BERWYN
The Administrative Value of Statistics to a Local Health Officer, *Public Health Reports*, Vol. 67, No. 8, pp. 747–754, August, 1952.

Race and Plea Negotiation*

Derek F. Wynne/Timothy F. Hartnagel

Sociologists have long been interested in the possible effects of extra-legal attributes of offenders on the administration of the criminal law (Sellin, 1928). One such attribute — race — has been the subject of a number of empirical investigations. With respect to police disposition of juvenile suspects, Piliavin and Briar (1964), on the basis of their observational data, reported that Negro youth were more frequently stopped and interrogated by patrolmen and usually were given more severe dispositions for the same violations compared to white youth. However, McEachern and Bauzer (1964) found that even when legal variables were ignored, ethnicity did not affect police disposition decisions for juveniles. Terry (1967) found that when the number of previous offences and seriousness of offence were controlled, the weak zero-order relationship between race and severity of disposition of juvenile offenders vanished. Black and Reiss (1970), from field observations of police-delinquent interaction, concluded that in addition to the larger number of legally more serious crimes in which Negro juveniles were involved, the higher arrest rate of Negro juveniles was largely the consequence of the tendency for the policy to comply with Negro complainant preferences for more severe dispositions. When no complainant was involved the racial difference in arrest rates was negligible. Recently, Thornberry (1973) reported that when the legal variables of number of previous offences and seriousness of offence were controlled, black juveniles were still more likely than whites to receive more severe dispositions.

The sentencing literature has also examined the effect of race on judicial dispositions. Green (1960), on the basis of his study of factors affecting severity of sentence, concluded that when other variables were controlled there was no evidence of racial discrimination in sentencing. Bullock (1961) investigated the effect of legal and extra-legal characteristics on length of prison sentence from data obtained through a survey of prisoners. He concluded that Negro prisoners received sentences significantly different from those given white prisoners when certain other factors such as type of offence and plea were controlled. However, since his Table 4 was percentaged in the wrong direction and his other tables are difficult to interpret, little confidence can be placed in this conclusion. Hagan (1974a) has recently faulted previous investigations of the effect of extra-legal

---

* Reprinted from the *Canadian Journal of Sociology*, 1 (2) 1975, pp. 147–56. Revised version of a paper presented at the annual meeting of the Western Association of Sociology, Banff, Alberta, December 1973.

attributes on sentencing for the uncritical use of tests of significance, for overlooking the size of the relationships reported, and for frequently failing to consider the effect of legal variables. Based upon his review of this literature Hagan concluded that knowledge of the extra-legal attributes of the offender contributes relatively little to our ability to predict judicial dispositions.

Closer to the concern of the present investigation, Hagan (1974b), using path analytic techniques, discovered that there was no direct link between race (native versus white) and charge alteration in a Canadian province. Similarly, no direct link was obtained between race and retaining of defence counsel or between race and initial plea. Race had direct effects only upon prior arrests and socio-economic status. Hagan concluded that these data suggest that Indian and Metis defendants, no less than their white counterparts, benefit from the procedural maneuvers of the prosecutory process. However, since Hagan's focus was on explaining the relative contribution of extra-legal, legal, and procedural (one of which was charge alteration) variables to the final disposition of a case, he measured charge alteration by ranking the particular charge being altered in terms of its seriousness rather than simply focusing upon whether charge alteration had occurred or not.

Recent theoretical work, applying a conflict approach to the examination of criminal justice administration, may help to place the empirical work reviewed above in a somewhat larger perspective. Chambliss (1969) has argued that a consequence of the unequal ability of members of different social classes to reward the legal system is that at every step of the legal process the lower class person is more likely to feel the sting of the law enforcement process. Of particular relevance here is his statement that the lower class person is, among other things, more likely to come to trial. Chambliss also stated that there are undoubtedly systematic biases against lower class and minority group members built into the prosecutory system.

Chambliss and Seidman (1971) have argued that since a guilty plea is obtained by a bargain between the defendant and the court, the benefit to the defendant depends upon the strength of his bargaining position. How favorable a bargain a defendant can strike with the prosecutor in pre-trial confrontations is a direct function of the defendant's political and economic power. They conclude that the lower class, indigent, minority group defendant is more likely to be prosecuted for his offences and to receive the brunt of the disadvantageous possibilities of bargain justice.

The present paper represents a continuation of the type of research outlined above with a focus upon one component of the administration of the criminal law, namely plea negotiation. Specifically, this research explores the effect of the extra-legal defendant characteristic of race on the occurrence of plea negotiation. The research literature on plea negotiation (Newman, 1956; Vetri, 1964; Hartnagel and Wynne, 1975) is rather limited and has not examined the effect of race on negotiation. In addition to this extra-legal attribute, the legally relevant factors of previous arrest record, type of offence charged, the presence of repetitious counts and/or multiple charges in the indictment, and representation by defence counsel will be introduced as controls.

The data were collected from the files of the crown prosecutor's office in one metropolitan area in the Prairie Provinces in Canada. The population from which the sample was drawn consisted of all those defendants formally charged with offences contrary to the Canadian Criminal Code from March 1972 through January 1973. In order to obtain a representative number of cases a stratified random sample was drawn. The decision to stratify was made because all cases were initially referred to a magistrate's court and therefore were included in the prosecutor's files. Therefore, it was necessary to employ stratified sampling in order to ensure that the sample did not contain a large number of petty offences which experience relatively little negotiation. Given our desire to obtain a sample size of approximately 2,000 and having estimated the number of working days per year as 225, approximately 9 cases per day had to be selected. A sampling fraction of four, four, one was used: for each working day four indictable offence cases, four alcohol related driving offence cases, and one summary conviction offence case were selected.

A criticism of previous research on plea negotiation is the failure, in our view, to measure adequately the dependent variable (Hartnagel and Wynne, 1975). Plea negotiation or bargaining requires evidence of interaction or communication between prosecution and defence in addition to an indication that the original charge has been reduced and a guilty plea entered. Therefore, evidence of plea negotiation for this research was indicated by the presence of all of the following in a case file: a change in the original charge; a change in plea from either "not guilty" or "reserved" to "guilty"; letters of correspondence between defence and prosecution and/or comments written by the prosecutor indicating a reduction in charge in exchange for the assurance of a guilty plea.[1] The extra-legal attributes of the defendants and the legally relevant characteristics were obtained from information contained in each file.

The data in Table I represent the zero-order relationship between defendants' race and plea negotiation. Native defendants are less likely to experience plea negotiation than are white defendants (12 percent compared to 31 percent respectively). Race therefore appears to have a moderate effect upon plea negotiation.[2] However, as indicated above, a number of legally relevant variables must be introduced as controls in order to interpret the meaning of this initial two-variable relationship. Thus while it appears from the data in Table I that native defendants are discriminated against with respect to obtaining negotiated pleas, alternative explanations must be considered before any confidence can be placed in this conclusion.

One obvious possibility that should be considered is that the variable of previous arrest record intervenes in the causal sequence between race and negotiation such that race has an effect on negotiation through its effect on previous arrest record. More native than white defendants may have a previous arrest record and defendants with a previous record are somewhat less likely to experience negotiation. Alternatively, race may be related to negotiation only under certain conditions. In this instance, race may be related to negotiation only under the condition of the defendant having no previous arrest record. The data in Table II permit an evaluation of these possibilities. First, comparing natives and

TABLE I   Plea Negotiation by Race

	Race	
Negotiation	Native	White
Yes	12 percent (28)	31 percent (494)
No	88 percent (198)	69 percent (1113)
$X^2 = 31.9$ Phi = .13		
p < .001		

TABLE II   Plea Negotiation by Race by Previous Arrest Record

Previous arrest record	Race	
Negotiation	Native	White
Yes	11 percent (20)	28 percent (177)
No	89 percent (158)	72 percent (452)
$X^2 = 20.6$ Phi = .16		
p < .001		
No previous arrest record		
Negotiation	Native	White
Yes	23 percent (8)	34 percent (294)
No	77 percent (27)	66 percent (584)
$X^2 = 1.27$ Phi = .04		
N.S.		

whites with previous arrest records, we find that natives still experience less negotiation and the magnitude of the difference between the natives and whites in negotiation is approximately the same as originally observed in Table I. When those defendants with no previous arrest record are considered, the percentage of natives experiencing negotiation is increased (23 percent) and the magnitude of the difference between natives and whites is reduced somewhat from 19 percent in Table I to 11 percent in this instance. However, the small number of cases involved — there are only eight natives with no previous record experiencing negotiation — necessitates caution in interpreting these results since the percentages may be unstable. Based upon the data in Table II however, we would tentatively conclude that previous arrest record does affect the relationship between race and plea negotiation since there is some indication that the defendant's race has less effect on negotiation when the defendant has no previous arrest record.

A second control variable that should be considered is the presence of repetitious counts and/or multiple charges in the indictment. When such counts/ charges are present negotiation is more likely and the presence of such counts and/or charges may be related to the defendant's race. Race may therefore have an effect upon negotiation through its effect on repetitious counts and/or multiple charges. Another possibility is that race and repetitious counts and/or multiple charges may interact to affect negotiation. Table III presents the data for considering the possible impact of such counts/charges. When defendants are charged with repetitious counts and/or multiple charges, the natives experience substantially less negotiation than do whites (16 percent compared to 38 percent). However, the racial difference in negotiation is reduced considerably when no repetitious counts and/or multiple charges are present in the indictment (10 percent for natives; 19 percent for whites). The data in Table III indicate, then, that the effect of race on negotiation depends upon the presence of repetitious counts and/or multiple charges; when such counts/charges are absent from the indictment natives experience only slightly less negotiation than whites.

The type of offence the defendant has been charged with is another factor that could affect the relationship between race and negotiation. Plea negotiation is more likely in the case of alcohol-related driving offences and indictable offences than with summary conviction offences and it is possible that a relationship exists between race and type of offence charged. Thus race may have its effect on negotiation through its effect on the type of offence charged. On the other hand, race and type of offence may interact to affect plea negotiation such that natives experience less negotiation than whites only under the condition of a summary conviction offence being charged. The data in Table IV are presented to evaluate these possibilities. Table IV demonstrates that race and offence charged interact to affect negotiation. With the more serious, indictable offences natives obtain fewer negotiated pleas than whites (16 percent compared to 29 percent). This racial difference in negotiation is a slight reduction from the zero-order relationship presented in Table I. Similarly, natives experience fewer negotiated pleas than whites in the case of alcohol related driving offences (12 percent compared to 39 percent) which can be prosecuted as either summary conviction or as

TABLE III Plea Negotiation by Race by Repetitious Counts and/or Multiple Charges

Repetitious counts and/or multiple charges

	Race	
Negotiation	*Native*	*White*
Yes	16 percent (14)	38 percent (375)
No	84 percent (74)	62 percent (610)
$X^2 = 16.2$ Phi = .13		
$p < .001$		

No repetitious counts and/or multiple charges		
Negotiation	*Native*	*White*
Yes	10 percent (14)	19 percent (119)
No	90 percent (124)	81 percent (503)
$X^2 = 5.7$ Phi = .09		
$p < .02$		

indictable offences. However, under the condition of summary conviction offences no racial difference in negotiation occurs: neither whites nor natives experience much negotiation when charged with summary conviction offences. The data in Table IV lead us to conclude that the effect of race on negotiaion depends upon the type of offence charged.

TABLE IV   Plea Negotiation by Race by Offence

Indictable		Race	
Negotiation		Native	White
Yes		16 percent (23)	29 percent (190)
No		84 percent (125)	71 percent (460)
X^2 = 10.9	Phi = .12		
p < .001			

Alcohol-related driving			
Negotiation		Native	White
Yes		12 percent (4)	39 percent (296)
No		88 percent (30)	61 percent (469)
X^2 = 8.55	Phi = .11		
p < .002			

Summary			
Negotiation		Native	White
Yes		2 percent (1)	4 percent (8)
No		98 percent (43)	96 percent (184)
X^2 = .02	Phi = .04		
N.S.			

TABLE V   Plea Negotiation by Race by Defence Counsel

Defence counsel		Race	
Negotiation		Native	White
Yes		29 percent (24)	63 percent (466)
No		71 percent (59)	37 percent (269)
X^2 = 35.5	Phi = .21		
p < .001			

No defence counsel			
Negotiation		Native	White
Yes		3 percent (4)	3 percent (27)
No		97 percent (138)	97 percent (814)
X^2 = .0001	Phi = .008		
N.S.			

The final factor to be considered in clarifying our interpretation of the relationship between race and negotiation is representation by defence counsel. Plea negotiation is strongly related to representation by counsel and native defendants may be less likely to be represented. In this way race may exert its effect on negotiation through the variable of representation by defence counsel. Alternatively, race may be related to negotiation only under the condition of representation by counsel and thus race and representation may interact to affect negotiation. The data in Table V allow us to consider these possibilities. Among defendants represented by counsel, natives are even less likely than whites to obtain a negotiated plea (29 percent compared to 63 percent). This represents a difference of 34 percentage points compared to the 19 percentage point difference observed in Table I. However, those defendants not represented by counsel experience virtually no negotiation and there is no racial difference present. It appears, then, that the effect of race on negotiation varies with or depends upon representation by defence counsel: when represented by counsel, natives are less likely to obtain a negotiated plea.

To summarize our findings from this elaboration of the relation between race and negotiation, we have observed several conditional relationships or interactions. Natives are less likely than whites to obtain a negotiated plea. However, this effect of race on plea negotiation appears to depend upon previous arrest record, the presence of repetitious counts and/or multiple charges in the indictment, being charged with an indictable or alcohol related driving offence, and representation by counsel. Under these conditions natives are not as likely as whites to experience plea negotiation.

The results reported above appear to offer some support for the position of Chambliss (1969) and Chambliss and Seidman (1971) that the minority group defendant is disadvantaged in the process of criminal justice administration, at least with respect to that aspect of this process examined here. However, we have been able to go beyond this general conclusion to specify certain of the conditions under which these disadvantageous consequences occur.

While examining the relationship between race and plea negotiation, it would have been desirable to control simultaneously for the effects of previous arrest record, type of offence charged, the presence of repetitious counts and/or multiple charges, and representation by counsel. Such an analysis would permit us to explore the combined effects of these variables and the possibility of higher order interactions among them. Unfortunately, such a procedure is not feasible in the present study due to the severe attenuation of cases that would occur.

Before concluding this discussion of the effect of race on negotiation, some additional factors which could affect this relationship should be noted. First of all, it is possible that controls for specific offence categories could modify the results reported above. It is possible that race is related to the commission of certain specific offences and that specific offences are in turn, related to the probability of plea negotiation. Controlling for offence in terms of the distinction between indictable versus alcohol related driving versus summary conviction offences, as in the present research, may not be adequate. It may be necessary to group offences into categories such as: violent personal crime, crime against property with violence, crime against property without violence, public nuisance crimes, etc. in order to more adequately examine the effect of type of offence committed on the relationship between race and plea negotiation.

The quality of representation by counsel is another factor which could be affecting the relationship between race and negotiation. This study has examined the effect of the simple presence or absence of representation by counsel. However, such factors as the competence and motivation of counsel may be of at least equal importance. Natives who obtain counsel may be less able to exercise a choice with respect to who represents them because of factors such as their financial status. It is possible that they receive less competent and/or less motivated counsel, factors which may in turn affect their chances for obtaining a negotiated plea. In this regard, it may be useful to examine the possible effects of representation by counsel provided through legal aid services.

A slightly higher percentage of natives than whites are not represented by counsel. In the absence of representation these native defendants may be unaware of the possibilities for plea negotiation and plead guilty without any bargaining. Furthermore, this lack of representation may make it more difficult with a previous arrest record and/or with repetitious counts/multiple charges in the indictment for these unrepresented natives to be able to negotiate a plea.

In any event, it is possible that a rather complex series of interrelationships exist among the several legally relevant variables and the extra-legal attribute of race as far as effect on plea negotiation is concerned. Subsequent research, with a larger sample for simultaneous control, should investigate these possibilities.

Notes

1. It should be pointed out that there are other forms of negotiation — such as bargaining between the police and a suspect and bargaining for a light sentence or concurrent sentences — not covered by the present research. Furthermore, we are only dealing here with successful plea negotiation — where a charge is reduced in exchange for a guilty plea — not with attempts to plea bargain.

2. These results are not directly comparable to Hagan's findings (1974) due to differences in the dependent variable and in the operational definitions used. Hagan measured charge alteration by ranking the particular charge being altered in terms of its seriousness whereas in the present research charge alteration — one of the criteria for measuring plea negotiation — was recorded as either having occurred or not.

References

BLACK, D. J., AND A. J. REISS, JR.
   1970 "Police Control of Juveniles." *American Sociological Review 35: 63–77.*

BULLOCK, H. A.
   1961 "Significance of the Racial Factor in the Length of Prison Sentences." *Journal of Criminal Law, Criminology and Police Science* 52: 411–417.

CHAMBLISS, W. J.
   1969 *Crime and the Legal Process.* New York: McGraw-Hill Book Company.

CHAMBLISS, W. J., AND R. B. SEIDMAN
   1971 *Law, Order and Power*. Reading, Mass.: Addison-Wesley Publishing Company.
GREEN, E.
   1960 "Sentencing Practices of Criminal Court Judges." *The American Journal of Corrections* July-August: 32–35.
HAGAN, J.
   1974a "Extra-Legal Attributes and Criminal Sentencing." *Law and Society Review* 8: 357–383.
   1974b *Criminal Justice in a Canadian Province*. Unpublished PhD Dissertation, University of Alberta.
HARTNAGEL, T. F., AND D. F. WYNNE
   1975 "Plea Negotiation in Canada." *Canadian Journal of Criminology and Corrections* 17: 45–56.
McEACHERN, A. W., AND R. BAUZER
   1967 "Factors Related to Disposition in Juvenile Police Contacts" in M. W. Klein and B. G. Meyerhoff (eds.) *Juvenile Gangs in Context*. Englewood Cliffs: Prentice-Hall.
NEWMAN, D. J.
   1956 "Pleading Guilty for Consideration." *Journal of Criminal Law, Criminology and Police Science* 46: 780–790.
PILIAVIN, I., AND S. BRIAR
   1964 "Police Encounters with Juveniles." *American Journal of Sociology* 70: 206–214.
SELLIN, THORSTEN
   1928 "The Negro Criminal: A Statistical Note." *The Annals of the American Academy of Political and Social Science* 140: 52.
TERRY, R. M.
   1967 "Discrimination in the Handling of Juvenile Offenders by Social Control Agencies." *Journal of Research in Crime and Delinquency* 4: 218–30.
THORNBERRY, T. P.
   1973 "Race, Socio-economic Status and Sentencing in the Juvenile Justice System." *Journal of Criminal Law and Criminology* 64: 90–98.
VETRI, D. R.
   1964 "Guilty Plea Bargaining" *University of Pennsylvania Law Review* 112: 865–908.

B. Differences in Political Behavior

Party Class Images and the Class Vote*

Rick Ogmundson

INTRODUCTION

In the spectrum formed by industrialized Western democracies, Canada stands out sharply as a country in which the relationship of social class to electoral politics appears to be almost non-existent (Alford, 1963a). Lenski and Lenski (1974:356) found, in a survey of nine countries, that the association of social class with the vote, as measured by Alford's Index of Class Voting (See Alford, 1963a), varied from a high of +58 in Norway to a low of +7 in Canada. In a survey of seventeen countries, Rose and Urwin (1971:220) found only three without a nation-wide class party — the United States, Ireland and Canada. Furthermore, experts who compare the United States with Canada argue that political parties in the United States are much more clearly associated with class than those in Canada (e.g., Scarrow, 1965).

Canadian politics thus provide an outstanding exception to the usual generalizations about the role of social class in the politics of industrialized democracies. The dominant explanation of the Canadian case has reflected the widespread assumption that the politics of a democracy are strongly influenced by the wishes of its citizens and has emphasized the nature of class sentiment within the general population. Generally speaking, it has been assumed that, for whatever reasons, Canadian voters do not care about class issues. Alford (1963a:257), noting the classless image of Canadian political parties, assumes that this fact faithfully reflects the opinions of the electorate. "Neither class nor national identities are well developed, and the major diffuse loyalties or attachments of people are to regional and religious loyalties." Englemann and Schwartz (1967:58), in another authoritative work, agree with this interpretation:

> His interpretation, compatible with our own view of Canadian society, is that regional-ethnic and regional-economic interests and loyalties are so strong, that

* Reprinted from the *American Sociological Review*, 40 (4) August 1975, pp. 506–12. Used with permission.

The author is indebted to the Canada Council and the H.H. Rackham School of Graduate Studies at the University of Michigan for financial support during the time when this research was done as part of his doctoral dissertation. He is also indebted to P. Converse, W. Gamson, D. Segal, R. Pierce, M. Heirich, M. Schwartz, M. Pinard, L. McDonald and R. Hamilton for reactions to various aspects of the research of which this is a part. Dan Ayres provided invaluable help with the computer. None of the above bears any responsibility for the opinions expressed here.

even in the case of economic interests, they work against the emergence of national class-oriented behavior.

Similar points of view are expressed by a number of other authorities (Beck, 1968:420; McLeod, 1966:335; Smith, 1967:192; Fox, 1966:337; Meisel, 1972:60).

More recently however, Alford (1967) has revised his earlier view and has argued that explanation of the low class vote in Canada has more to do with the Canadian party system than with the motivations of the Canadians themselves. Similarly, Schwartz (1974:589) has argued that: "... class-based voting exists; it is consistent class-based parties that are missing."

This paper outlines a measure of the class vote which can take the nature of voter perceptions of electoral options into account. This measure permits inferences as to the nature of voter motivation which are more plausible than those drawn from conventional measures. The results of this measure will, in turn, allow us to make comments on these contrary interpretations of the Canadian case.

DATA

The data used in this paper came from John Meisel's national survey of the 1965 Canadian federal election.[1] It contains a battery of semantic differential questions on party images which run on a scale from 1 to 7. One of these items provides a measure of the class images of the Canadian political parties. It asks respondents to rate parties on a scale from 1 "for the working class" to 7 "for the middle class." This provides a measure of voter perception of the class positions of the political parties.[2]

Measurement of Class Voting with the Actual Party Image Variable

The standard method of estimating the rate of voting on the basis of social class has been to cross-tabulate the social class position of the respondents with the social class position of the political parties. Class of respondent is usually measured by occupation or respondent class self-image. The class position of the parties is assigned by academic opinion. Partisanship is measured by the vote or by partisan identification. The rate itself is calculated either with tau beta (as is done in the paper), or with Alford's Index of Class Voting which is based on the index of dissimilarity (see Alford, 1963a). The two methods yield essentially the same figure when the marginals of the fourfold table are not extremely skewed — the usual case for estimates of the class vote.

Little attention is usually paid to the placement of the political parties. To begin with, it tends to be assumed that the political elites of a polity will present a meaningful choice on issues of importance to the population. This is not necessarily the case. For example, Butler and Stokes (1969) found that the two major political parties did not present a choice on the issue most salient to the British population at the time — colored immigration. Similarly, Hamilton (1972) found that majority desires on class issues in the United States have been largely ignored by the major parties. As Campbell et al. (1960:364) point out, it is difficult to vote on the basis of an issue if the political parties do not differ on that issue. This may not prevent people from casting votes on the basis of a perceived difference which does not exist. However, it would seem likely to reduce the proportion of the people who attempt to do so. Additionally, the less pronounced the choices provided on the issue, the greater is the likelihood of dissensus among the general population as to the positions which the parties take. This can easily lead to a situation in which two voters with identical motivations vote for two different parties because their perception of the positions of the parties differ. Conventional measurements do not take this into account. Consequently, they may easily underestimate the degree of voter interest in a given issue in political units where a clear choice on an issue is not provided by the parties.

A second, and related assumption, is that the expert assessment of the scholar as to the position of parties will be shared by the general population. Again, this is not necessarily the case. Even in a highly class polarized society, such as the United Kingdom, there are some people who do not share expert evaluations. Butler and Stokes (1969:89) report that: "Fully 90 percent of our respondents placed the Conservatives toward the middle class end of the scale and 83 percent put Labour toward the working class end." In societies such as the United States, there is considerable dissensus between academic authorities and portions of the general population on the class positioning of the political parties. For example, it would appear that from twenty-five to thirty-three percent of the American population see little difference between their major political parties (Alford, 1967:79), and hence would not agree with the designation — conventional in calculations of the class vote — of the Democrats as "working class" and the Republicans as "middle class."

This means that many people attempting to cast a class consistent vote may not vote for the party which the social scientist thinks they should vote for. For example, a working class Canadian might remember that former Prime Minister John Diefenbaker raised the old age pension and decide to vote Conservative. This class-motivated vote lowers the level of the class vote as it is conventionally measured. Consequently, it will usually be interpreted as a sign that the voters are not motivated to vote on the class issue. In sum, the greater the dissensus on party positions in any given society, either between academics and voters or within the voting population itself, the greater the degree to which conventional measures will underestimate the degree of mass sentiment on that issue.

Such dissensus does exist to an unusual degree in Canada. The standard classification of Canadian political parties for purposes of measurement of the class vote has been that of Alford (1963a:13-4) who bases his classification on the opinion of a leading Canadian authority, Dawson (1954:501). For purposes of the calculation of class voting, he usually lumped the Liberals and New Democratic Party together as "Left" and the Progressive Conservative and Social Credit Parties together as "Right."

However, the conventional wisdom of academics as to the class positions of the parties is very definitely not shared by the general population. (See Table I.) In distinct contrast to the Alford/Dawson classification, the aggregate view of the

TABLE I   The Class Images of Canadian Political Parties, 1965

	NDP	Creditistes	Social Credit	Conservatives	Liberals
Canada	2.7	3.2	3.4	4.4	4.4

The numbers presented are mean scores. The higher the score, the more "for the middle class" the image on a scale from 1 to 7. The midpoint on the scale is, of course, 4.

TABLE II   The Canadian National Class Vote in 1965 As Measured by Tau Beta with Different Measures of Respondent's Social Class and Different Classifications of the Political Parties

Measure of social class	Classification of political parties			
	ALFORD ($)	NATIONAL (b)	IND'L-I (c)	IND'L-II (d)
Income	− .09 (2106)	.03 (2106)	.11 (1996)	.125 (1212)
Occupation	− .03 (1863)	.08 (1863)	.11 (1786)	.13 (1093)
Education	− .01 (2171)	.07 (2171)	.12 (2055)	.18 (1246)
Subjective class	− .06 (2088)	.10 (2088)	.18 (1992)	.21 (1213)

(a) ALFORD Classification — The Liberals and New Democratic Party are classified as "working class" or Left and the Progressive Conservative Party, Social Credit Party and Creditiste Party are classified as "middle class" or Right.

(b) NATIONAL Perceptions Classification — Parties are classified on the basis of national means of perception of the Canadian population. The Liberal and Progressive Conservative Parties are seen as "middle class" while the others are seen as "working class."

(c) INDIVIDUAL Perceptions Classification I — A vote for a party viewed by respondent as being from 1 to 3 on scale from "for the working class" at 1 to "for the middle class" at 7 is classified as being a working class vote and vice versa.

(d) INDIVIDUAL Perceptions Classification II — Same as the previous category except that votes for parties viewed as "4" are removed

citizens places the two major parties, the Liberals and the Progressive Conservatives, together as "middle class" and the minor third parties together as "working class."[3]

Similar dissensus exists within the population itself. For example, a full forty-one percent of the citizenry with an opinion views the two major parties as taking the same position on the class issue. Another twenty-nine percent sees the Conservatives as being more middle class than the Liberals, while yet another twenty-nine percent sees the Conservatives as being more working class than the Liberals.

In sum, dissensus on party class positions exists between the academics and the voters, and within the voting population itself. Furthermore, it appears that the two major parties do not, in fact, present a meaningful choice on class issues to the population (Ogmundson, 1975a). If the arguments previously outlined have been correct, conventional measures have likely underestimated the degree of intended class voting by the Canadian citizenry. Consequently, they have likely also led to an underestimation of the degree of interest in the class issue.

One gets a better idea what the voter thinks he is voting for it one allows the voters to assign the class position of the parties. This allows a more plausible inference as to their motivation. To begin with, the effects of dissensus between academics and the general population on the positioning of the parties can be removed by assigning the party position in accordance with the aggregate means provided by voter perceptions. The effects of dissensus within the population can be removed by allowing the individual voter to assign the class position of the party he votes for. This is fairly simple in those cases where individuals rated a party as "for the working class" at 1 to 3 on the scale of 7, or as "for the middle class" at 5 to 7 on the scale of 7. A problem arises with the classification of a response of "4" on the scale. One might argue that a "4" response is one which favors no change, which is consequently for the *status quo* and continuation of the relatively privileged position of the middle classes, and call the "4" a middle class response. Indeed, the aggregate preference of the middle classes is for an ideal party with a position of 4. On the other hand, one might throw out the "4s" leaving only those who voted for a party perceived as 1 to 3 as voting for a working class party, and leaving those who voted for a party perceived as 5 to 7 as voting for a middle class party. This method loses some data while making no assumptions about the 4s. Both classifications are used. The results are similar in either case.[4]

FINDINGS AND DISCUSSION

The results are presented in Table II. Four measures of social class are used so as to increase confidence in the findings.[5] The four classifications of the political parties are those discussed in the previous section. The first classification is the conventional Alford/Dawson one which considers the Social Credit, Creditiste and Progressive Conservative parties as "middle class" and the Liberal and New Democratic parties as "working class." When this classification is used, an unusual pattern of negative rates of class voting appears. The second classification assigns political party class position according to the aggregate perceptions of the population — the Liberals and Progressive Conservatives are both viewed as "middle class" while the other parties are viewed as "working class." This classification removes the effects of disagreement between the perceptions of academics and the general citizenry. In this case, very moderate, but positive rates of class voting appear. Finally, the third and fourth classifications allow the individual voters to classify the party they voted for according to their own perceptions. This removes the effects of the substantial within-population dissensus concerning the positioning of the parties and allows us to classify similarly motivated votes for different parties as being class consistent. When this is done, the class vote increases again.[6]

Before proceeding to a discussion of the findings, it may be wise to outline the uses and limitations of this new approach. The measure allows us to ascertain what the voters thought they were voting for. Consequently, it provides an improved measure of voter motivation. However, it does not provide a complete indication of voter sentiment on the issue. On the one hand, it cannot tap that portion of the population which, while motivated to cast a class consistent vote, fails to try to do so because of the lack of a perceived or realistic choice. It also cannot ascertain the degree of class interest which would emerge if Canadians were exposed to elite mobilization on this issue comparable to that found in ᴄ~untries like Norway.[7] Furthermore the measure does not provide a measure of wʜat we might term an objectively defined class vote. If a laborer votes Conservative and believes that this is a class consistent vote, this is important information if one is concerned about voter motivation. However, this does not mean that the social scientist must accept the voter's view that he is acting in such a way as to further his class interests. Indeed, from this point of view of the realities of power and the policy outputs of government, the intended class voting revealed by this measure is insignificant.

From the point of view of an interest in voter motivation however, this new measure can tell us something. In the case of Canada, the findings clearly show that voter interest in the class issue is substantially greater than conventional measures indicate. This supplements research reported elsewhere (Ogmundson, forthcoming) which indicates that class-related economic issues are the most important ones at the mass level in Canada, and that, consequently, the classless nature of Canadian politics cannot be attributed to a lack of voter interest in class issues. All this tends to focus attention on the important roles played by political elites[8] and suggests that explanation of the anomalous Canadian pattern may lie with the nature of elite activities. In particular, it would appear that minimization of the issue by the two major political parties is crucial to a full explanation of the classless nature of Canadian politics and of the considerable dissensus on the positioning of the political parties. In short, the findings of this paper support the revised view of Alford (1967) and Schwartz (1974) that explanation of the classless nature of Canadian electoral politics has more to do with the Canadian political parties than with the Canadian voters.

These findings also indicate, perhaps not surprisingly, that voter behavior is influenced by what the voters think they are doing. More particularly, these findings indicate that conventional measures, which do not take into account what the voters think they are voting for, would seem likely to be inadequate as a measure of mass sentiment. This would be especially true concerning issues which are minimized by the major parties. More particularly still, these findings indicate that voter perception of their electoral options, and indeed the actual nature of those options, is likely to influence voter behavior and hence should be taken into systematic consideration in studies of the vote. Consequently, they also suggest that regional and international variations in voting patterns may often best be attributed in the main to the nature of electoral options, and not, as is so often assumed, to the nature of mass social structure and public opinion (e.g., Ogmundson, 1975b). The measures used in this paper provide a means by which differences in electoral options, on a variety of dimensions, may be partially taken into account.

The finding that the classless nature of Canadian politics apparently has more to do with the Canadian political parties than with the Canadian citizenry is very similar to that of Hamilton (1972) in the United States. Findings such as these lead to the more general suggestion that one cannot reasonably assume, as is so often done, that the politics of a democracy faithfully reflect the salient concerns of its citizens. This, in turn, points to the importance of elite variables and the need for integrated conceptual frameworks which simultaneously consider both mass and elite variables. In distinct contrast to conventional approaches which assume that political explanation somehow resides in the nature of mass social structure and the consequent public will, a simultaneous emphasis on the explanatory power of elite variables suggests that present realities may be an outcome of elite interests rather than mass desires, and that the *status quo* may be illegitimate in terms of democratic values. (For further discussion of these points, see Ogmundson [1976].)

Notes

1. Data were gathered from a modified cluster sample of 2113 Canadian voters selected randomly from voting lists. The data were subsequently weighted to the point where the weighted N is 2718. The response rate was only 62.8 percent. For further information, see Meisel and Van Loon (1966).

2. If a consensus methodology for the class positioning of political parties is developing, it would appear to be in the nature of voter perceptions. Barnes and Pierce (1971:646) argue that: "This method of ordering the parties transfers the subjectivity involved in the measurement process from the researchers to the population involved. And that measurement technique permits us to report statistics at the ordinal level . . . ."

   This consensus has been encouraged by the fact that voter perceptions have tended to correspond reasonably well with the opinions of expert observers. (For the United Kingdom, see Butler and Stokes, 1969; Norway, Converse and Valen, 1971; France, Converse and Pierce, 1970; Italy, Barnes and Pierce, 1971.)

3. This perception of similarity of major party class positions by the Canadian citizenry is not typical of mass populations. Citizens in other countries perceive clear differences in the class positions of the major political parties. (For example, on the United Kingdom, see Butler and Stokes, 1969; on Norway, see Converse and Valen, 1971.)

4. Very similar findings also emerge when different measures of partisanship (1963 vote, partisan identification) are used. (See Ogmundson, 1972: Ch. 6.)

5. Since the main purpose of this research was to explore the political party variable, the measures of social class were dichotomized in the manner customary to studies of the class vote. Professional, executive, sales, clerical and other white collar occupations were classified as middle class. Those with twelve or more years of education were considered middle class. Those with an income of more than $6,000 were classified as middle class. (The median income in 1965 was approximately $5,200.) Those who identified themselves as upper class, upper middle class or middle class were also considered middle class.

6. It has been pointed out that these increases could be partially attributed to cognitive consistency factors. I believe the role of cognitive consistency to be minimal and the criticism unimportant. To begin with, one can point out that cognitive consistency on this topic would be an indication of the class consciousness we are attempting to measure. However, the construction of the questionnaire is such that only the most alert and class conscious respondent could be expected to match the variables of party class image, the vote and class background. The party class image questions are part of a complicated battery of semantic differential questions in the first half of a long questionnaire. They elicit opinion of six different parties — Liberal, Conservative, NDP, Social Credit, Creditiste and Ideal— on no less than 12 different dimensions —

out of date to modern, competent and incompetent, powerful to weak, foolish to wise, for the middle class or working class, united to split, good to bad, left wing to right wing, strong to weak, honest to dishonest, dull to exciting, young to old, and slow to fast. Forty more questions pass before the respondent is asked for whom he voted in 1965. About another forty questions pass before the respondent is asked his subjective social class. It would take a very alert and class conscious voter indeed to be sufficiently aware of his party image response 40 or 80 questions ago in such a way that he would vary his report of his vote or class position to maintain his own cognitive consistency. In order to give deliberately consistent responses to the party class image questions initially, he would have to be very aware of the class issue.

Furthermore, the increase of the class vote using this new measure varies dramatically from region to region. This variation would be unlikely if the increases were a simple artifact of a new measure which allowed people to express their bent toward cognitive consistency. If cognitive consistency factors were significant, one would expect them to be most important in class-conscious, urbanized, industrialized, highly-educated in Ontario and British Columbia. The increase is almost non-existent in Ontario and there is actually a drop in British Columbia. (See Ogmundson, 1972:Ch. 6.) This is exactly the opposite of what one would expect if cognitive consistency factors were playing an important role.

7. There is reason to believe that the effects of such mobilization may be considerable. For example, the level of the class vote in the United States jumped from its average .16 level to .41 in 1948 (Alford, 1963b:103) when the Truman-Dewey confrontation made class issues salient to the population. (See Berelson et al., 1954.)

8. The term "elite" is used in the sense that Porter (1965) uses the term. It refers to the relatively small groups of people in the important positions at the head of our major institutions, i.e., generals, bishops, deputy ministers, cabinet ministers, corporation directors and so forth. More specifically, the phrase "political elites" refers, of course, mainly to political party leadership. However the broader rubric is used in order to keep the general picture in mind. Political elites may be strongly influenced by other elites. For example, it would seem unwise to assume that the fact that the business elite finances the two major political parties in Canada has no influence on their minimization of the class issue.

References

ALFORD, ROBERT
1963a *Party and Society*. Chicago: Rand McNally.
1963b "The role of social class in American voting behaviour." *Western Political Quarterly* 16:180–94.
1967 "Class voting in the Anglo-American political systems." In Seymour M. Lipset and Stein Rokkan (eds.), *Party Systems and Voter Alignments*. New York: Free Press.

BARNES, SAMUEL AND ROY PIERCE
1971 "Public opinion and political preferences in France and Italy." *Midwest Journal of Political Science* 15:643–60.

BECK, J. MURRAY
1968 *Pendulum of Power*. Scarborough, Ontario: Prentice-Hall.

BERELSON, BERNARD R., PAUL F. LAZARSFELD AND WILLIAM N. McPHEE
1954 *Voting*. Chicago: University of Chicago Press.

BUTLER, DAVID AND DONALD STOKES
1969 *Political Change in Britain*. New York: St. Martin's Press.

CAMPBELL, ANGUS, PHILIP CONVERSE, WARREN MILLER AND DONALD STOKES
1960 *The American Voter*. New York: Wiley.

CONVERSE, PHILIP AND ROY PIERCE
"Basic cleavages in French politics and the disorders of May and June, 1968."

Paper presented at the 7th World Congress of Sociology.

CONVERSE, PHILIP AND HENRY VALEN

1971 "Cleavage and perceived party distances in Norwegian voting." *Scandinavian Political Studies* 6:107–52.

DAWSON, R. McGREGOR

1954 *The Government of Canada.* Second edition. Toronto: University of Toronto Press.

ENGELMANN, FREDERICK AND MILDRED SCHWARTZ

1967 *Political Parties and the Canadian Social Structure.* Scarborough, Ontario: Prentice-Hall.

FOX, PAUL

1966 "Politics and parties in Canada." Pp. 337–43 in Paul Fox (ed.), *Politics: Canada.* Second edition. Toronto: McGraw Hill.

HAMILTON, RICHARD F.

1972 *Class and Politics in ths United States.* New York: Wiley.

LENSKI, GERHARD AND JEAN LENSKI

1974 *Human Societies.* Second edition. New York: McGraw Hill.

McLEOD, JOHN T.

1966 "Explanations of our party system." In Paul Fox (ed.), *Politics: Canada.* Second edition. Toronto: McGraw Hill.

MEISEL, JOHN

1972 *Working Papers on Canadian Politics.* Montreal: McGill-Queen's University Press.

MEISEL, JOHN AND RICK VAN LOON

1966 "Canadian attitudes to election expenses, 1965–66." In *Report of the Committee on Election Expenses: Studies in Canadian Party Finance.* Ottawa: Queen's Printer.

OGMUNDSON, RICK

1972 "Social Class and Canadian Politics: A Re-interpretation." Unpublished doctoral dissertation. University of Michigan.

1975a "On the measurement of party class positions: the case of Canadian political parties at the federal level." *Canadian Review of Sociology and Anthropology* 12:565–76.

1975b "On the use of party image variables to measure the political distinctiveness of a class vote: the Canadian case." *Canadian Journal of Sociology* 1:169–77.

1976 "Mass-elite linkages and class issues in Canada." *Canadian Review of Sociology and Anthropology* 13:1–12.

PORTER, JOHN

1965 *The Vertical Mosaic.* Toronto: University of Toronto Press.

ROSE, RICHARD AND DEREK URWIN

1971 "Social cohesion, political parties, and strains in regimes." Pp. 217–36 in Mattei Dogan and Richard Rose (eds.), *European Politics: A Reader.* Boston: Little, Brown.

SCARROW, HOWARD A.

1965 "Distinguishing between political parties — the case of Canada." *Midwest Journal of Political Science* 9:61–76.

SCHWARTZ, MILDRED

1974 "Canadian voting behaviour." Pp. 543–618 in Richard Rose (ed.), *Electoral Behaviour: A Comparative Handbook.* New York: Macmillan.

SMITH, DENIS

1967 "Prairie revolt, federalism and the party system." Pp. 189–200 in H. G. Thorburn (ed.), *Party Politics in Canada.* Second edition. Scarborough, Ontario: Prentice-Hall.

Status Inconsistency and Party Choice[*]

David R. Segal

The notion that a relationship exists between social stratification and politics is axiomatic in political sociology. In Canada, as in other western industrial nations, we know that such elements of the stratification system as economic class, race, and religion are associated with political party choice (Reid, 1967; Meisel, 1967).

In traditional societies there tends to be a high correlation among the various dimensions of the stratification system. That is, a person who is of high status on one dimension will tend to be of high status on others, and vice versa. Since traditional societies also tend to be characterized by ascriptive stratification systems, individuals pass their relative advantages or disadvantages on to their children, and the class structure remains more or less stationary.

With the rationalization of economic systems through the process of developing industrial organization, achievement-oriented bases of social status become differentiated from traditional ascriptive bases, and assume increased importance. Thus, capable people from low status backgrounds may through education or skill enter high status occupations, that is, social mobility occurs.

Such social mobility confounds the relationship between stratification and politics, because the correlation between dimensions of social stratification becomes more imperfect. Some members of society who have little claim to status on the basis of ascriptive criteria find themselves in high status positions through their own achievements. At the same time, others from high status backgrounds find themselves earning through their own achievements lower status positions than their parents occupied.

Lenski (1954) has postulated that in such a situation, a model that deals merely with the additive effects of status dimensions is inadequate for describing the relationship between social stratification and politics. Rather, specific forms of statistical interaction must be taken into account.

* Reprinted from *The Canadian Journal of Political Science*, 3 (September 1970), by permission of the author and publisher.

    This report, and the larger study of which it is a part, were supported by a grant from the Horace H. Rackham School of Graduate Studies, University of Michigan. The author is grateful to David Knoke and John Fox for research assistance, and to Daniel Ayres for technical advice. Professor Fred Schindeler of the Institute for Behavioural Research, York University, generously made these data available.

Briefly stated, the theory of status inconsistency argues that if an individual is of low status on one prestige dimension, and of high status on another, he will experience stress (Jackson, 1962). It is assumed by Lenski (1966:26) that a person in such a situation will tend to define himself in terms of his higher status, and will expect deference on that basis. Other people, however, are likely to define him in terms of his lower status, frustrating his deference expectations and thereby producing the hypothesized stress. While recent research has thrown this assumed dynamic into question (Segal, Segal, and Knoke, 1970), an impressive body of literature suggests that certain traits are indeed characteristic of individuals in status inconsistent situations. Among these characteristics is support of left-of-centre political parties.

While most research on the political consequences of status inconsistency has been carried out using data from the United States, Lenski (1967) has explored the cross-national applicability of the hypothesized relationship between status inconsistency and party choice. A secondary analysis of Alford's (1963) data on party choice in Australia, Britain, Canada, and the United States indicated that among people experiencing inconsistencies between social class and religious status, there was a tendency to support liberal political parties. In the Canadian case, this tendency was manifest in eight out of the nine surveys analysed.

STATUS INCONSISTENCY MODEL

Lenski's method was to construct a 2X2 table by dichotomizing each status variable. He then compared the sum of the percentage of liberal party supporters in the two consistent cells with the percentage of liberal supporters in the two inconsistent cells. A surplus of liberals in the inconsistent cells was taken as support for the inconsistency hypothesis (cf. Lenski, 1964). Such a measure does not specify what the main effects of the status variables are. It merely indicates whether there is an interaction effect between status variables that has a predicted effect on some hypothesized consequence of status inconsistency.

In the present analysis, we operated explicitly with the model:[1]

$$y = \sum_{i=1}^{2} f_i(x_i) + \sum_{i=1}^{2} g_i(z_i) + \sum_{i=1}^{4} h_i(x_i, z_i)$$

where y is the hypothesized effect of status inconsistency, viz., support of liberal political parties; x_i is a dimension of achieved status, that is, occupation or education; z_i is a dimension of ascriptive status, that is, ethnicity or religion, and $h_i(x_i z_i)$ is the effect of inconsistencies between x_i and z_i. Previous research has demonstrated that the most stressful status inconsistencies are those that arise from differences between an achieved and an ascribed status (Segal and Knoke, 1968).

Our dependent variable was defined in terms of support for the Liberal party. Lenski (1967), in his analysis of Canadian partisanship, had combined support for the Liberal party and the New Democratic party. We have excluded the latter party from this analysis for two reasons. First, Canada is not only a multi-party system, but has a multi-dimensional party system (Engelmann and Schwartz, 1967). That is, the Canadian parties cannot be placed on a single liberal-conservative continuum. To group together the Liberal party and the NDP would be to disregard this complexity. Indeed, were one to include the NDP in this analysis, it would make at least as much sense to combine the two major parties, that is, Liberal and Conservative, as to combine the Liberals with the NDP.

Secondly, previous research has shown that social structural factors can differentiate the support base of the Conservative party from that of the Liberal party, which has been innovative with regard to status group politics. Considerably less variance has been explained in NDP support, and here regional considerations are primary (Segal, forthcoming).

DATA AND METHOD

Our analysis was based upon six combined surveys conducted by the Canadian Institute for Public Opinion (CIPO) between 1965 and 1967. Previous analyses have indicated that in the Canadian case, the benefits of cumulating samples to achieve a large N far outweigh the costs of adding variance due to temporal differences (Segal, forthcoming). Through the cumulation of samples, a total case base of 6,286 was achieved. Of these cases, 3,937 expressed support for the Liberals or Conservatives and are included in this analysis.

The mode of analysis used was Multiple Classification Analysis (MCA). MCA is a linear analysis model capable of handling missing data, non-linear data, and nominal independent variables with the accuracy of least squares methods. It can be conceived of as a form of dummy variable multiple regression (see Suits, 1957). The coefficients obtained through MCA are analogous to those obtained through dummy variable regression, and indeed the coefficients derived by either of these techniques may easily be converted to the other by the addition or subtraction of a constant for each predictor. MCA has the advantage of requiring no conversion of basic data. All variables are automatically dealt with as dummy variables (Andrews et al., 1967).

In the present analysis, status inconsistency terms were defined by the pair relationships of status variables. The status inconsistency variables and the status dimensions themselves were then used as predictors of political party choice.

RESULTS

The MCA equation included two ascriptive variables (religion and ethnicity), two achieved variables (education and occupation), and four inconsistency terms, based on the combination of each ascriptive with each achieved variable. The zero-order and the partial relationships of all eight terms to party choice are presented in Table I.

While all coefficients are significant at at least the 0.01 level due to the large case base, it is apparent in terms of both gross and net effects that the primary

TABLE I Relationships of Status Variables and Inconsistency Terms to Political Party Choice

	eta	beta
Ascriptive statuses		
Religion	.28	.28
Ethnicity	.18	.09
Achieved statuses		
Education	.06	.05
Occupation	.12	.09
Inconsistency effects		
Religion–education	.13	.04
Religion–occupation	.14	.04
Ethnicity–education	.14	.09
Ethnicity–occupation	.14	.07

Multiple r = .31.
Eta measures zero-order relationships; beta measures partial relationships.

TABLE II Main Effects of Religion and Occupation, and Effects of Inconsistencies between Religion and Occupation, and Party Choice

Effect	eta	beta
Religion	.28	.26
Occupation	.12	.11
Religion–occupation	.14	.07

Multiple r = .30.

source of differentiation of Liberal and Conservative supporters is the main effect of religion. The magnitudes of the zero-order relationships of ethnicity, occupation, and the four inconsistency terms, all of which are appreciable, are greatly diminished when all factors are considered. Beta cannot in the present analysis be strictly interpreted as the square root of the percent of variance explained, because of the problem of multi-collinearity. However, beta does indicate the relative importance of the predictors included in the analysis.

We considered the possibility that the impact of each inconsistency term was being reduced not by the main effect of the status variables, but rather by the other inconsistency terms. We therefore performed a separate analysis for each inconsistency term plus the main effects of its component statuses. These analyses yielded minor changes in the magnitude of some effects, but no significant change in the overall pattern. Table II presents an example of this type of analysis.

In anticipation of identifying regional effects in these findings, the provinces in which the interviews were taken were subjected to analysis. Our experience with data on the electorate in the United States has been that when states are used as input data, the states within a given region prove to be statistically similar, thus providing a test for the assumption of political regionalism as well as a means of measuring variance attributable to regionalism. In the present case, we found variation among provinces, but the provinces were not grouped according to any meaningful definition of regions in Canada. Indeed, variation among provinces did not seem to follow any particular pattern at all. Because of the apparent complexity of the issue of provincialism versus regionalism, these data are not presented here but will receive extensive treatment in a subsequent report.

CONCLUSION

We have replicated Lenski's findings to the extent that we have demonstrated statistically significant results due to status inconsistency independent of the main effects of status variables themselves. In carrying out this analysis, we have heeded the admonitions of Blalock (1967) and others regarding the specification both of additive and interaction effects, and the precise nature of the expected interaction effect.

While our inconsistency results are statistically significant, it is clear that the main effect of religion is by far the most important determinant of party choice, and that in general, main status effects are more powerfully related to party choice than are status inconsistency effects.

We have identified provincial effects in these data, but these effects do not suggest political regionalism.

Note

1. This notation, admittedly strange, was adopted as a convenient shorthand for the longer multiple regression equation that the analysis approximated, viz.,

$$
\begin{aligned}
y_{12345678} = a_{y.12345678} &+ b_{y1.2345678}x_1 \\
&+ b_{y2.1345678}x_2 + b_{y3.1245678}x_3 \\
&+ b_{y4.1235678}x_4 + b_{y5.1234678}x_5 \\
&+ b_{y6.1234578}x_6 + b_{y7.1234568}x_7 \\
&+ b_{y8.1234567}x_8 + e_y
\end{aligned}
$$

References

ROBERT ALFORD,
  Party and Society (Chicago, 1963).

FRANK ANDREWS, JAMES MORGAN, AND JOHN SONQUIST,
  Multiple Classification Analysis (Ann Arbor, Mich., 1967).

HUBERT M. BLALOCK, JR.,
  "Status Inconsistency, Social Mobility, Status Integration and Structural Effects," *American Sociological Review*, 32 (Oct. 1967), 790–801.

FREDERICK C. ENGELMANN AND MILDRED A. SCHWARTZ,
  Political Parties and the Canadian Social Structure (Scarborough, 1967).

ELTON F. JACKSON,
  "Status Inconsistency and Symptoms of Stress," *American Sociological Review*, 27 (Aug. 1962), 469–80.

GERHARD LENSKI,
  "Status Crystallization: A Non-vertical Dimension of Social Status," *American Sociological Review*, 19 (1954), 405–13; "Comment," *Public Opinion Quarterly*, 28 (Summer 1964), 326–30; *Power and Privilege* (New York, 1966); "Status Inconsis-

tency and the Vote," *American Sociological Review*, 32 (April 1967), 298–301.

JOHN MEISEL,
"Religious Affiliation and Electoral Behaviour: A Case Study," in John C. Courtney, ed., *Voting in Canada* (Scarborough, 1967), 144–61.

ESCOTT M. REID,
"A Study of the Economic and Racial Bases of Conservatism and Liberalism," in *Ibid.*, 72–81.

DAVID R. SEGAL,
"Social Structural Bases of Political Partisanship in the United States and Canada," forthcoming.

DAVID R. SEGAL AND DAVID KNOKE,
"Social Mobility, Status Inconsistency and Partisan Realignment in the United States," *Social Forces*, 47 (Dec. 1968), 154–7.

DAVID R. SEGAL, MADY W. SEGAL, AND DAVID KNOKE,
"Status Inconsistency and Self-evaluation," *Sociometry*, Sept. 1970.

JOHN A. SONQUIST,
"Finding Variables That Work," *Public Opinion Quarterly*, 33 (Spring 1969), 83–95.

DANIEL B. SUITS,
"Use of Dummy Variables in Regression Equations," *Journal of American Statistical Association*, 52 (1957), 548–51.

C. Differences in Lifestyles and Beliefs

The Alienating Effects of Class and Status on Social Interaction[*]

W. Peter Archibald

Sociologists have long been concerned with the ways in which social class impinges upon such characteristics of interpersonal interaction as the amount of interaction which occurs and the symmetry or asymmetry of familiarity and influence patterns. A number of theories have been offered to identify and explain such patterns. The "exchange" theories of Homans (1974) and Blau (1964) represent one such attempt; another is the "expectation states" theory of the Stanford group (Berger, Cohen and Zelditch, 1972); the work of Goffman (1967; 1959; 1961), an eclectic blending of elements of exchange, functionalism and conflict, is yet another.

The present paper is an attempt to develop and substantiate a Marxian-oriented theory of micro-stratification phenomena as an alternative to the above-mentioned approaches. I begin by presenting and substantiating four empirical generalizations extrapolated from Marx's theory of alienation, and then develop a micro-conflict theory consistent with the latter theory to explain these generalizations as well as a number of exceptions to these same generalizations.

THE EMPIRICAL GENERALIZATIONS

For the immediate purposes of this paper, only a few features of Marx's theory of alienation (Archibald, 1974) need to be noted. First, other people constitute one of four objects from which individuals are alienated. Second, an alienated relationship between an individual and an object of orientation is characterized by four features: (1) the individual is detached from, or indifferent to, the object; (2) when he does approach the object, it is for very narrowly defined, egoistic purposes; (3) when he confronts the object, he does not control it but is instead controlled by it; (4) his orientation toward the object is characterized by certain feelings, among which are (often vague) feelings of dissatisfaction and hostility. The latter feelings need not be conscious, and the crucial indicators of alienation are not consciously expressed attitudes, but overt behavioral orientations. For Marx, the sources of alienation from others centered around class as defined by

[*] Abridged from the *American Sociological Review*, 41 (October 1976) pp. 819–837. The author thanks especially John Gartrell for comments on earlier versions of this manuscript.

position in the productive process, and particularly in the distinction between capitalists and workers. The former earn their livelihood parasitically by hiring workers for a wage and appropriating surplus value, and private ownership of the means of production and conscious control of the work process permit them to do so. However, in the empirical generalizations which follow, class differences often entail simply the middle class/working class or nonmanual/manual distinction. Moreover, the present treatment further extends the scope of the theory by adding Max Weber's concepts of "status" (prestige or honor) and "power" (the ability to control others) as potentially independent sources of alienation from others. Empirically, of course, the three tend to go together.

The Detachment Generalization: Persons of Different Classes, Status and Powers Tend to Avoid Each Other

The empirical validity of this generalization is perhaps so obvious that it is forgotten when theories of cross-class interaction are constructed.

In the first place, those of different class, status and power tend to be physically separated. In work organizations, management tends to have separate maintenance facilities, such as entrances, elevators, washrooms and cafeterias (Goffman, 1967:110), their offices tend to be separate from the production area; and they make extensive use of "go-betweens," such as supervisors and foremen, as buffers between themselves and the production staff (Goffman, 1959:149). Similarly, in the wider community one finds a great deal of "residential segregation," a phenomenon that has been statistically documented for Britain (Wilmott and Young, 1960), France (Rhodes, 1969), the United States (Duncan and Duncan, 1955; Feldman and Tilly, 1960; Uyeki, 1964; Laumann, 1966) and Canada (Balakrishnan and Jarvis, 1968; Adler, 1970).[1]

Second, there tends to be a great deal of "social distance" between those of different classes, statuses and power. Thus even in mixed neighborhoods, voluntary associations and pubs tend to be frequented by those of the same class (e.g., Wilmott and Young, 1960:97; Lorimer and Phillips, 1971:6). On a more intimate level, high school cliques tend to follow class lines (Hollingshead, 1949), working-class students tend to be isolated on college campuses (Ellis and Lane, 1967) and the friends and marriage partners of adults tend to be from the same class and status level (Kahl and Davis, 1955; Curtis, 1963; Laumann, 1966; Lorimer and Phillips, 1971:28; Grayson, 1973).

The Means-Ends Generalization: When Persons of Different Class, Status or Power Do Interact, It Tends To Be on a Narrow, Role-Specific Rather than a Personal Basis. In Short, They "Use" Each Other

That cross-class interaction follows these utilitarian lines has been noted for some time. Of capitalists and workers, for example, Marx (Capital I:195) said there is "'No admittance except on business.' ... The only force that brings them together and puts them in relation with each other, is the selfishness, the gain and private interest of each." Many of the apparent exceptions to the Detachment

Generalization seem to follow this pattern. Thus Goffman (1959:199) notes that British upper-class reserve "has been known to give way momentarily when a particular favor must be asked of ... subordinates," and that North American managers often affect superficial shows of familiarity in order to avert strikes and other incidences of rebellion.[2]

Utilitarian tendencies outside the work place are evident in the fact that psychiatrists express less desire for leisure time than for professional contact with psychologists and social workers in the mental health field (Zander et al., 1959). Even interaction of the (presumably) most intimate kind seems to follow this pattern, in that older, upper-class men who do not fit the advertising image of handsomeness and marry "down," tend to marry women who do fit the advertising image of female beauty (see Rubin, 1973:67-8). Apparently upper-class women in the same position sometimes do the same, although more often they remain unmarried (Martin, 1970).

The Control-Purposiveness Generalization: Persons of High Class, Status or Power Tend to (a) Initiate Activity, (b) Make Attempts to Influence Others, (c) Actually Influence Others More Than Do Persons in Lower Positions

Much of the comparative quantitative evidence for this generalization in relatively less formalized settings has been referred to by Berger et al. (1972). A great deal of support can also be found in the literature on formal organizations.[3] Finally, to this body of evidence one can add Goffman's observation (1961:129-31; 1967:64-5, 74-9) that the pattern for expressions of familiarity is also asymmetrical.

The Feelings Generalization: An Element of Hostility Underlies Much and Perhaps Most Interaction between "Unequals" and Occasionally Rebellion Occurs.

Perhaps the most common expression of hostility on the part of Low persons are such work group activities as "restriction of output" (Mathewson, 1969) or simply "make-work" when the boss comes by (Goffman, 1959:109). However, during lunch breaks and the like in "back regions," hostility is more openly evident, and perhaps even more evident in actual face-to-face confrontations during strikes (e.g., Doyle, 1974:3; Israel, 1971:225-6). Similarly, in the wider community this conflict is evident in snobbishness and lower status persons' reactions to it. While such expressions of hostility tend to be more subtle in North America (e.g., Dobriner, 1963:107-8; Lorimer and Phillips, 1971:27-8) than in Europe (e.g., Wilmott and Young, 1960:5-6, 97-8, 119-22), they are nevertheless present.

EXPLAINING THE GENERALIZATION:
A THEORY OF INTERPERSONAL THREAT

Let us examine the following set of explanatory principles implied in my review of the literature.

Class, Status, and Power Differences Are Threatening

That those of high position would be *threatened*[4] by those lower than themselves is, perhaps, obvious: while the former's privileges depend upon the continued deference or acquiescence of Lows, such deference and acquiescence is not always assured, as was noted in the feelings generalization. Many and probably most of the "underprivileged" realize that greater equality is in their best interest, as is indicated by the greater importance working-class people place upon equality and government intervention to achieve it (Form and Rytina, 1969; Mann, 1970). Similarly, lower status professionals covet the greater income, status and decision-making power of those higher than themselves (Zander et al., 1959). It would be surprising indeed if the privileged were unaware of this and, in fact, as the latter study indicates (Zander et al., 1959:26–30), they *do* seem to be aware of it. In specific encounters with the less privileged these outcomes could be realized in at least two ways: either directly by rebellion on the part of the less privileged—or at least the refusal to acquiesce—or indirectly by a poor "performance" which would discredit one's image as a superior person and hence lessen one's future power over the less privileged.[5]

That those of low position would be threatened by those higher than themselves is also obvious: "stepping out of line" can be and often is sanctioned by the privileged. Some of the sanctions are obvious, for example, the possibility of being fired from one's job or the consequences of the privileged's greater access to institutional support, particularly governmental and legal, for their interests. But again, the coercive element can be more indirect, as with the anticipation of embarrassment if one "messes up" in front of the privileged.[6] One suspects that their low status makes working-class people particularly self-conscious and prone to embarrassment. While they by no means totally accept the social evaluation of personal worth implicit in their status, this evaluation is difficult to ignore, given its institutionalized support. Therefore, particularly in North America where the predominant ideology has stressed individual achievement and mobility, many working people seem to have an ambivalent evaluation of their personal worth (Kaplan, 1971; Sennett and Cobb, 1972).

It is important to note that this *need not* mean that this ambivalence is accompanied by a high evaluation of the abilities of those higher in status. A worker or other low status person may feel that his ideas are as good as others', but he may simply lack confidence in his ability to express them because he is self-conscious about his vocabulary or lack of education. Rather than acceptance of status differences, his covert orientation may be resentment.

Ways of Dealing with the Threat

As Goffman (1967:15) suggests with regard to the threat of embarrassment (and this can be generalized to most threats), "The surest way for a person to prevent threats to his face is to avoid contacts in which these threats are likely to occur." *Avoidance as a self-protective strategy* is, thus, a very plausible explanation for the Detachment Generalization. Several astute observers of cross-class interaction have used such a coercion explanation (e.g., Goffman, 1967:70; Adams, 1970:50–1), and "harder" evidence for its validity will be presented below.

Obviously those of different classes, statuses and powers cannot avoid each other totally for, in a perverse sort of way, they "need" each other; that is, those of high position can maintain their positions only be exploiting those lower than themselves, those of low position must obtain employment from enterprises controlled by the privileged and those who are unemployed are, of course, extremely dependent upon those in higher positions for various forms of welfare. However, given that one must interact with threatening others to some extent, the next best thing is to try to ensure that the interaction is *predictable* (e.g., Goffman, 1961:128; Sampson, 1963). There are several ways of doing this.

First, *one can try to restrict the scope of cross-position activity to highly circumscribed roles*, such as those of boss-worker, and so forth. What Goffman (1961:30) refers to as "rules of irrelevance" are also likely to be invoked; that is, feelings and other personal characteristics of the "back regions" are not focused upon, officially at least. Literally and figuratively, neither side wants to be "caught with its pants down" (Goffman, 1967:83). The desire for predictability would seem to be a plausible explanation for the Means-Ends Generalization; that is, restricting the number of roles and the scope of activities associated with each role permits one to get some of what one wants from the person in a different class, status or power position while at the same time minimizing threat.

Second, *adhering closely to the prerogatives these roles give to the privileged* would seem to have the same advantages, for those in low as well as those in high positions. Goffman (1961:128) states this well:

> Adherence to formalities seems to guarantee the *status quo* of authority and social distance; under the guidance of this style, one can be assured that the others will not be able to move in on one. Reversing the role point of view, we can see that adherence to the formalities one owes to others can be a relatively protective matter, guaranteeing that one's conduct will be accepted by the others ...

These processes, of course, entail *some* degree of agreement between Highs and Lows, but note that even this modicum of agreement is in the service of self-protection; that is, Lows are *coerced* into upholding the prerogatives of the privileged. This is not to say that there are no secondary satisfactions resulting from conformity. One may, of course, be "patted on the head" for one's performance and, as Goffman also suggests (1961:128), playing strictly by the rules permits one to justify his overt behavior to others and himself as demanded by the situation, while at the same time denying covert personal involvement in potentially demeaning conduct. Or, to put it another way, "role distance" is only possible if one plays the role in the first place. However, these various secondary satisfactions should be seen for what they are — secondary. They may rationalize one's adherence to the formalities, but one feels little choice about adhering to them. Threat and the desire for predictability thus constitute a plausible explanation for the Control-Purposiveness Generalization.

Finally, one may react to threat, not by overtly conforming to protocol and simply covertly decreasing one's involvement, but by *expressing hostility and, perhaps, rebelling* in an effort to circumvent or change the effects of the class, status or power structure. However, one would expect this strategy to occur less frequently than the other three in most circumstances, for this is the only reaction of Lows which is against the interest of Highs, and it is therefore *the only one that is subject to punishment.*

While the above theory obviously over-simplifies the processes occurring in cross-position, face-to-face interaction, it receives a fair degree of independent empirical support in the literature.

Thus, for example, having to perform in front of a group of high status persons has been found to be more anxiety arousing (as measured by physiological arousal and response latency) than having to perform in front of lower status persons (Cohen and Davis, 1973). Furthermore, in this particular study, the anxiety produced by the presence of high status persons is lower when it is made explicit that observers will evaluate the subject than when the role of the observers is not defined and, presumably, less predictable. Similarly, it has long been observed that persons of low status do not feel free to express hostility toward those of higher status. Worchel (1957) found this to be the case after college students had been provoked by a professor (to cite a case where these results are completely common-sensical), but more recent experiments indicate that similar things occur even in seemingly trivial encounters. Thus, after having experimenters drive either a flashy new Chrysler or a beat-up old Ford to a stop light and remain there after the light had turned green, Doob and Gross (1968) found that 84 percent of the drivers behind the Ford honked their horns while only 50 percent of those behind the Chrysler did so, and that two of the former actually hit the experimental car. Similarly, after having a group of sidewalk discussants who appeared to be either older and middle-class or younger and of lower status block the sidewalk, Knowles (1973) found that passers-by were much more likely to walk through the latter than through the former group. In the latter case, age rather than class may have been the more important factor, but age, like class, often gives one coercive power over others.

Variations in Immediate Threat and the Strategies Used

The present treatment is meant to be more illustrative than definitive, but one can already point with a reasonable degree of confidence to many conditions which appear to increase or modify the aforementioned processes. Two categories of conditions are discussed here: (A) those having to do with features of the class, status or power structure *external* to the encounter or potential encounter in question and (B) those having to do with the *internal* structure of the encounter.

The External Structure

Aside from the degree of inequality and/or mobility in the class, status, or power structure itself, one might expect that *the more the structure is supported by other structures* in a society, whether or not the supporting structure is an institutionalized government, the *less* will be the threat. Hence, there will be fewer reactions to it in *Highs*, but *more* threat and reactions to it in *Lows*.

While it is difficult to make cross-societal comparisons, the interpenetration of Canada's economy and polity has been said to be greater than that of the United States (e.g., Myers, 1972). Similarly, the greater insecurity this might produce in

TABLE I   Sources of Political Advice Named by Canadians and Americans

Advisor	Advisee							
	Broadview Riding (Toronto)				Elmira, Ill.			
	P/M	W.C.	SK.	S&U	P/M	W.C.	SK.	S&U
Professional/managerial	38%	35%	25%	13%	68%	54%	34%	26%
White-collar	21%	31%	25%	11%	14%	31%	14%	22%
Skilled	9%	3%	10%	17%	8%	4%	47%	25%
Semi- and unskilled	32%	31%	40%	59%	10%	11%	5%	27%

Source: Grayson, 1973.

Canadian workers presumably would be increased further by the fact that, since World War II, Canada has had one of the highest rates of unemployment among western nations (OECD, cited in Adams et al., 1972:86). Given these considerations, it is interesting to examine Grayson's findings (1973) concerning the occupations of those approached by Canadians and Americans for political advice. Table I shows that upper-class Canadians are *more* likely than upper-class Americans to say that they consult working-class people, while working-class Canadians are *less* likely to say that they consult middle- or upper-class people. These results are at least consistent with the above proposition; that is, if upper-class Canadians receive more support than their American counterparts from institutions external to encounters with working-class people, they should be less threatened by working-class people and hence avoid them less. Working-class Canadians on the other hand, should be more threatened by upper-class people and hence avoid them more than their American counterparts do. While there are many problems in interpreting these results, they are intriguing and warrant further research.[7]

Fortunately, the effects of external support for a class or status structure can be examined more carefully in a number of experiments. In a series of games with teams of working-class boys, Thibaut (1950) simulated certain features of class differences by giving some teams (High Class) and not others (Low Class) the exclusive right to do such things as jump on members of the other team. Similarly, in his experiment with college students Kelley (1960) led some teams to think that they had the better job, the differences between the two jobs described being very similar to the non-manual/manual distinction. The findings that (1) the average number of inter-team communications when there were class/status distinctions was almost identical to those in a control condition and (2) that Lows communicated to Highs more than Highs communicated to Lows appear to contradict the Detachment and Control-Purposiveness Generalizations, indicate that the class/status structure in these experiments is unique indeed. That is, all subjects come from the same class outside the laboratory and the experimenter's support for the class/status structure is its *only* basis. It is therefore understandable that Highs, like the *nouveau riche* more generally (Mills, 1956), would be particularly insecure in this situation, and that Lows would be somewhat bolder than usual, although restrained in their expression of hostility because of the experimenter's control. Thibaut (1950:268–70) and Kelley (1960:787–94) both report that this appears to have been what happened, and this conclusion is supported by the additional findings of Kelley that Highs expressed considerable embarrassment and less criticism of their own jobs to Lows than Lows expressed to Highs. Nor should it be concluded from the latter finding that Lows were necessarily in fundamental agreement with the status structure. While they were more likely than Highs to express confusion about their jobs, they nevertheless tended to "defend its importance and rarely say that it was too easy."

There is some evidence that similar apparent reversals of the Control-Purposiveness Generalization in real life settings occur under conditions analogous to those of the above experiments. Thus Brewer (1971) attributes the fact that management in an insurance company permitted underwriters to communicate upwards to two other conditions, among others. Since the underwriters work with little supervision, monitoring their own reports of their work was simply an efficient means of managing. Second, being more highly educated than their immediate supervisors, the underwriters would more openly resent top-down communication. Similarly, Brewer suggests that the equalization of downward and upward communication in an electrical construction company can in good part be explained by peculiar conditions. Thus because crew leaders were legally required to be union members and were in extremely close, continuous contact with workers, they were particularly susceptible to being "corrupted" by workers. Management therefore not only permitted upward communication from the crew leaders, but also funnelled all downward communication through them in order to co-opt them into the company bureaucracy. Finally, Rosenberg (1962) reports the absence of class differences in participation in a patients' council in a mental hospital; this, however, can be attributed to the fact that this was the explicit intention of the doctors, who had new elections to the council conducted "on a monthly basis" and emphasized that "affiliative skills" rather than "literacy, verbal fluency and problem-solving ability" were prerequisites for participation. The latter would be expected to lessen the threat of embarrassment for Lows.[8] Reports of relatively low worker participation in workers' councils (e.g., see Mulder, 1971) suggests that such explicit restructuring of encounters may be a general prerequisite for more equal participation rates.

The Internal Structure of the Encounter

If it is true that predictability is a major concern for the participants of cross-class interaction, then *the less structured or more ambiguous participants' roles or tasks are in the encounter, the greater should be the threat and use of the strategic reactions to it.*

Cohen's (1959) work confirms this. He told female employees of a public utility company that their partner in the experiment was a supervisor from their own company and that the purpose of the experiment was to see whether or not the subject was capable of working with the company's supervisors. The subject and the supposed supervisor performed a word-symbol matching test, but in

TABLE II   Percentages of Subjects in the Gerard Experiment Sending Directive Notes

Role	Highs		Lows	
	Goal		Goal	
	Clarity	Unclarity	Clarity	Unclarity
Clarity	58%	71%	58%	46%
Unclarity	50%	70%	25%	8%

Source: Gerard, 1957.

some cases the supervisor's interpretations and instructions were clear and familiar (Structured), while in others they were vague and unfamiliar (Ambiguous). As one would predict given the above proposition, threat as measured by anxiety, time to complete the task and perceived agreement with, and approval from, the supervisor was greater in the Ambiguous than the Structured condition. The same was the case when hostility was measured by liking for, and projected anger toward, the supervisor.

Similarly, in an experiment by Gerard (1957), subjects working on a jigsaw puzzle had the job of recording the content of notes which subjects presumably had sent one another. Half thought they were the "boss" with the power to give orders to the others (Highs), while the other half thought they were clerks whose job simply was to record the notes (Lows). Ambiguity was manipulated by (1) whether or not the experimenter described to the subject what his instructions to the rest of the group would be (Role Clarity versus Unclarity) and (2) whether or not the subject was given an alleged record of past groups' performances (Goal Clarity versus Unclarity). Aside from the usual findings that Highs communicated more than Lows, Gerard found other differences in the number of directive notes sent, as shown in Table II. These results indicate that except for one set of comparisons (Role Clarity versus Unclarity for Highs), ambiguity increased the number of influence attempts by Highs and decreased those by Lows.[9]

A second important condition affecting threat and the strategies used against it is *the degree to which an individual is supported by other members of his own class or interest group*. Specifically, one might expect that when the threat from other sources is low, the greater the *number* of persons from one's own class present, the *less* will be the threat. When the threat from other sources is high (e.g., management is attempting to institute a speed-up), one might expect the presence of other members of the lower class to *increase* the likelihood of Lows expressing hostility and rebelling. Also, one would expect that the greater the (observable) *degree of consensus* within one's own class or interest group, the greater the likelihood of reacting to threat by rebelling.

Evidence for these propositions is not definitive, but it is persuasive. Thus, in a partial replication of Kelley's experiment, Cohen (1958:46) found that the number of messages critical of Highs sent by Lows to Highs increased when subjects "felt that they had support from others in their own ... group for their opinions and ideas." Similarly, after having been provoked by a professor-experimenter, subjects who thought their group was composed of others similar to themselves were more likely to initiate physical activity and express hostility than were subjects who thought their own group was heterogeneous (Pepitone and Reichling, 1960). Certainly there is much evidence that the presence of dissenting models increases dissent (e.g., Gerard, 1953; Asch, 1960; Milgram, 1965; Allen and Levine, 1969; Moscovici et al., 1969), and interest groups themselves appear to take this into account by appointing a few articulate spokesmen and sanctioning expressions of disagreement in front of opposing groups (e.g., Goffman, 1959:89–94). Evidence suggests these practices are warranted, because Lows do seem to "move in on" Highs if the latter appear to be in disagreement (e.g., Goffman, 1959:201).

There is less evidence for the effects of these conditions on Highs, but what evidence there is suggests that the effects are similar. Thus, for example, in their study of supervisors in five different light manufacturing companies, Kipnis and Cosentino (1969:465) found that "as the number of men supervised increased, the use of official warnings increased," and the use of "powers that required spending long periods of time with subordinates" decreased (Goodstadt and Kipnis, 1970). Similarly, in a subsequent experiment with college students (Goodstadt and Kipnis, 1970) "supervisors" spent less time talking with a deviant stooge when the subordinate group had eight rather than three people, and threatened to fire him sooner in the former condition. Interestingly, however, supervisors were *less* likely to correct non-problem workers in the eight-man than the three-man group. Could it be that under these circumstances (i.e., one against eight) the pressure against expressing hostility is greater for Highs than Lows, and that hostility is only expressed when Lows' behavior actually threatens Highs' control?

COMPARING THEORIES

In very general terms, the interpersonal threat theory of micro-stratification phenomena advanced here can be summarized as follows.

(1) Class, status and power divisions entail conflicts of interest which engender interpersonal threat.

(2) The engendered threat is a *sufficient*, although in some cases not a necessary condition for avoidance (Detachment), using (Means-Ends), deference and conformity (Control-Purposiveness), hostility and, under certain conditions, rebellion (Feelings).

(3) Threat and/or the reactions to it vary with the degree of external and internal support for oneself and/or one's interest group and the predictability of interaction.

How, then, does the interpersonal threat theory compare with other theories which have been advanced for some of the same phenomena?

Since those who have proposed alternative theories seldom deny that the processes postulated here occur,[10] the real issue appears to be the *extent* to which "coercive power" processes (French and Raven, 1959) such as those postulated by inter-personal threat theory are associated with dimensions of stratification in liberal democracies. As with macro-theories of stratification, one might distinguish two sets of issues. One concerns the relative utility of a *Pluralist* as opposed to a *Marxist* model of stratified conflict. Specifically, whereas a Marxist model is said to give primacy to class over occupational, racial-ethnic or sexual conflict, a Pluralist model gives most of these dimensions roughly equal weight in either or both of two ways. (1) In any given encounter, class is usually assumed to be no more important as a source of conflict than occupation, ethnicity or other dimensions and/or (2) to the extent that class conflict is more important than others, it is assumed to be so only at the work place; in other spheres there may be equality, or working-class people may actually make up for their disadvantaged economic position, through effective political organization, for example. The second set of issues concerns the extent to which relations between people of different classes or strata are better characterized by *consensus and exchange* than *conflict and coercion*. Here, proponents of consensus and exchange theories assume that Highs and Lows have more complementary than conflicting interests and that, for example, Lows exchange deference for the superior ability of Highs to solve mutual problems. Each of these sets of issues will be discussed in turn.

Class versus Pluralistic Conflict

The Pluralist claim that class is no more important than other dimensions of stratification is implied in most previous sociological treatments of micro-stratification phenomena, sometimes directly (e.g., Goffman, 1961:80) and sometimes indirectly through the absence of distinctions among various "external status characteristics" in terms of their relative effectiveness (e.g., Berger et al., 1972).

Actually, however, the predictions to be made from Marxist theory are by no means as clearcut as is usually implied. Thus, the claim that class takes precedence was for Marx a long term prediction, rather than a short term description for bourgeois society. In the meantime, the working class would be divided along occupational and racial-ethnic lines (Marx and Engels, 1968:42, 60, 104; 1961:xiv, 280–1; 1971:293–4). The time element is therefore crucial, and some Marxists (e.g., Johnson, 1972) have suggested that in North America in particular class formation is still at a relatively undeveloped stage. While it is doubtful that Marx expected the process to take this long, the relative weight to be given different stratification dimensions at this time is unclear.[11]

Matching this theoretical ambiguity are only a few pieces of largely inconclusive empirical evidence. Jackman and Jackman (1973), for example, found that whether or not respondents in a national U.S. survey owned stocks and bonds or real estate affected the status of their neighbors and friends more than race, but less than occupation, income and education; self-employment had no effect. Earlier Strodtbeck et al. (1958) also had found that proprietorship had only a slightly greater effect upon participation rates in a mock jury experiment than did sex.

Such studies clearly question the validity of this aspect of the Marxist model, at least if it is interpreted as predicting that class should now overshadow other dimensions of stratification. Yet several facts in the general stratification literature suggest that the issue is worth pursuing further. In the first place, occupation and income are good and reliable predictors of a host of phenomena, including occupational prestige and social class identification (e.g., Blau and Duncan, 1967; Inkeles, 1960; Jackman and Jackman, 1973). Second, these two criteria are closely related logically and empirically to large scale capital ownership (Jackman and Jackman, 1973; Johnson, 1972; Zeitlin, 1974). As with capital ownership and self-employment, occupation and income are not consistently better predictors of such characteristics of interaction as avoidance patterns than are racial, ethnic or religious status (e.g., Laumann, 1973:108); nevertheless, they often are (e.g., Artz et al., 1971:988).[12]

The second pluralist claim, that class-based coercive power does not usually generalize from the formal settings where it arises, is implied by both Berger et al. (1972:243) and Goffman (1961:32), with the latter suggesting that the inequalities of one sphere are often reversed in another.

Earlier in this paper, work organizations were purposely distinguished from other settings in order to demonstrate that class effects *do* generalize, but only a few of the studies cited (e.g., Doob and Gross, 1968) clearly indicate that stratified coercive power itself generalizes. However, a re-examination of two studies whose results Berger et al. (1972) claim argue against the generalization of coercion actually supports the Marxist model.

One of these studies is Torrance's (1965), where bomber crews, some permanent and some constructed for the experiment, worked on a number of group tasks, some clearly related to the formal authority structure (e.g., how to survive if their plane crashed), and some clearly not related (e.g., solving a horse-trading puzzle or counting dots). While Berger et al. (1972:243) imply that coercion would not and did not operate in the latter encounters, Torrance (1965:604–7) reports that the opposite was the case — gunners did not feel free to disagree with pilots and navigators and evidenced considerable tension and hostility. That gunners in temporary crews should have had 25 percent more influence on the group decision regarding at least two of the seemingly irrelevant tasks (the horse-trading and "group story" tasks) also is consistent with a coercion interpretation, since the likelihood of Highs later exacting revenge for Lows' breach of protocol presumably would have been lower in the former.

That militarily-based coercive power generalizes is, of course, hardly startling, but we also find what appears to be a generalization effect in the second study which Berger et al. cite. In this study, Hurwitz et al. (1960) experimentally constructed discussion groups using professionals in the mental health field, ensuring that each had a mixture of High and Low status professions (e.g., psychiatrists and high school teachers, respectively). Although participants need not have come from the same work organizations, they were all from the same city and many presumably knew of each other. Thus the risk for Lows of later meeting Highs, or of at least gaining a "bad reputation" for "stepping out of line," presumably would have carried over to these discussions. Supporting such a coercion interpretation of the researchers' standard participation and deference results are two additional findings: (1) Lows did not like Highs better than Lows at the end of the discussions, but (2) they did tend to overestimate the extent to which Highs liked Lows, which the authors explain as a defensive "need, realistic in these discussion groups, to feel that relations with *highs* are satisfactory and pleasant. ..." (Hurwitz et al., 1960:304–5).

Clearly, much more research is required before these Marxist versus Pluralist issues can be resolved. It should be stressed that a *relative decrease* in class effects as one proceeds from formal work organizations to relatively informal settings is perfectly consistent with the present theory, providing that certain conditions are met. First, external support for the formal stratification structure must remain unchanged; should external pressure actually work against it, as in Rosenberg's study (1962), there may even be *equality* in the informal setting. Second, internal support for Lows (in numbers and consensus) must remain constant. In fact, in many relatively informal settings such as political parties and other voluntary organizations, workers may well be in a small and unorganized minority, such that class effects could *increase* from those in more formal settings, where workers have much more support. Third, the predictability of interaction must remain constant; to the extent that it decreases in informal settings and workers become even more threatened with embarrassment and loss of self-esteem than they would in the formal work setting, as may often be the case, class effects should again actually increase rather than decrease.

The fact that class-based conflicts of interest and coercion-induced threat generalize beyond the work setting supports a Marxist and argues against a Pluralist model, since the latter predicts that to the extent that class inequalities exist at all, they should be restricted to only a few spheres of activity. However, at the present time there is little evidence that class takes precedence over such other dimensions of stratification as occupation, race/ethnicity or sex, and some evidence that suggests that the opposite is sometimes the case. Future research might focus upon additional conditions which could determine when one or another dimension of stratification takes precedence and upon longitudinal designs which might permit one to test Marx's prediction that class is becoming increasingly important relative to the other dimensions.

Notes

1. Some will question using residential segregation and label it an example of the "ecological fallacy." Nevertheless, there is evidence that the residential movements of the middle class can be partially explained as attempts to move away from working-class people (e.g., Wilmott and Young, 1960:5).
2. In a recent case (Snarky Operator and Lippy Representative, 1972:15), Canadian Bell Telephone employees have actually complained that management is eating with them, but the explanation for this anomaly is clear: information operators have a very high workload (120 calls an hour!) and want to organize against it, but management's constant surveillance hinders them.
3. See, for example, Guetzkow (1965:548) and Hage et al. (1972).

4. "Threat" is defined here as a general, aversive psychological state incorporating such tension states as "fear," "anxiety" and "embarrassment." As such, it is conceptually independent of both the stratification conditions which are presumed to produce it and the behavioral strategies which are presumed to defend one against it. While in most of what follows threat has the status of a hypothetical construct, it nevertheless has been measured directly in some studies by such things as physiological arousal and verbally expressed feelings (e.g., Cohen and Davis, 1973: Cohen, 1959).

5. Under some circumstances, workers may also be capable of damaging the interests of their immediate employers by quitting. However, such circumstances — an acute shortage of labor for the employer and attractive alternatives for the employee — have been rare, especially with regard to blue-collar workers. Nevertheless, analysts as divergent as Smith and Marx have noted that generally there has been a greater scarcity of labor, particularly skilled labor, in North America than in Europe, and this may help explain the less rigid class structure of the former.

6. The inclusion of status and power in the domain of the theory thus would seem to be justified not simply by the fact that the above-mentioned generalizations seem to hold for them as well as for class, but by the fact that they, too, appear to be threatening. In fact, I shall argue later that under some circumstances status-derived threat may be greater than class- and/or direct, coercive power-derived threat.

7. Thus since the Broadview Riding has relatively few middle-class residents, the latter may resort to working-class advisors because there are fewer middle-class advisors from whom to choose. Also, the Berelson et al. (1954) data are from the early 1950s and the Toronto data are from the 1970s. Aside from these difficulties, respondents' descriptions of their own behavior may have been biased. For example, if Canada's class structure is more rigid than that of the United States, there may be more pressure on upper-class Canadians than Americans to deny that it exists. The formers' claim that they engage in less discrimination by class may result more from this greater defensiveness than from true differences in actual behavior.

8. Resentment from middle-class persons was not eradicated, however (Rosenberg, 1962:372).

9. Gerard himself (1957:481) makes much the same interpretation of his results as I have made.

10. For example, while clearly preferring exchange theory, Homans (1974) and Blau (1964) extensively discuss "coercive power" in stratified structures and, at one point or another, both touch upon most of the reactions to threat. Similarly, while coercive power plays no part in expectation theory, its adherents nonetheless concede that it occurs (Berger et al., 1972:243).

11. The same ambiguity exists for Weber, who Pluralists often claim assigned occupational, racial-ethnic and religious status an importance equal to, or even greater than class. Thus, his reference to status being "favored" (see Gerth and Mills, 1958:193–4) includes the qualification that this is the case only in times of economic and technological stability; otherwise, he implied, class takes precedence. Similarly, in the same passage he noted that during his time, class was the major determinant of status (Gerth and Mills, 1958:190).

12. It has been suggested that the "status consistency" literature is relevant here and that the apparent consensus that status characteristics combine additively rather than interactively (see Hodge and Siegel, 1970; Jackson and Curtis, 1972) refutes the Marxist claim that class has primacy. However, this appears not to be the case; (1) the phenomena studied are different from those studied here, in terms of the dependent variables (e.g., whereas avoidance is sometimes the dependent variable, it does not pertain to avoidance of those of a different occupational status) as well as the independent variables; (2) that additive effects predominate need not contradict a Marxist model, since the latter predicts only that class will have to be weighted more heavily than status factors.

References

ADAMS, IAN
1970 *The Poverty Wall*. Toronto: McClelland and Stewart.

ADAMS, IAN
1972 *The Real Poverty Report*. Edmonton: Mel Hurtig Ltd.

ADLER, SANDRA
1970 "Residential segregation in 23 Canadian cities." Unpublished M.A. research paper, University of Western Ontario.

ALLEN, VERNON L. AND JOHN M. LEVINE
1969 "Consensus and conformity." *Journal of Experimental Social Psychology* 5:389-99.

ARCHIBALD, W. PETER
1974 "The empirical relevance of Marx's theory of alienation." Paper presented to the Ad Hoc Group for Alienation Theory and Research, International Sociological Association Meetings, Toronto.

ARTZ, RETA D., ET AL.
1971 "Community rank stratification: a factor analysis." *American Sociological Review* 36:985-1002.

ASCH, SOLOMON E.
1960 "Effects of group pressure upon the modification and distortion of judgements." Pp. 189-200 in Dorwin Cartwright and Alvin Zander, eds., *Group Dynamics*. New York: Harper and Row.

BALAKRISHNAN, T. R. AND GEORGE K. JARVIS
1968 "Socio-economic differentiation in the metropolitan areas of Canada." Paper presented at the Annual Meeting of the Canadian Sociology and Anthropology Association, Calgary.

BALES, ROBERT F.
1965 "The equilibrium problem in small groups." Pp. 444-76 in A. Paul Hare, Edgar F. Borgatta, and Robert F. Bales (eds.), *Small Groups: Studies in Social Interaction*. New York: Knopf.

BERELSON, BERNARD R. ET AL.
1954 *Voting: A Study of Opinion Formation in a Presidential Campaign*. Chicago: University of Chicago Press.

BERGER, JOSEPH ET AL.
1972 "Status characteristics and social interaction." *American Sociological Review* 37:241-55.

BERGER, JOSEPH ET AL.
1974 *Expectation States Theory: A Theoretical Research Program*. Cambridge, Mass.: Winthrop.

BERGER, JOSEPH AND M. HAMIT FISEK
1970 "Consistent and inconsistent status characteristics and the determination of power and prestige orders." *Sociometry* 33:287-304.

BLAU, PETER M.
1964 *Exchange and Power in Social Life*. New York: Wiley.

BLAU, PETER M. AND O. D. DUNCAN
1967 *The American Occupational Structure*. New York: Wiley.

BREWER, JOHN
1971 "Flow of communications, expert qualifications and organizational authority structures." *American Sociological Review* 36:475-84.

COHEN, ARTHUR R.
1958 "Upward communication in experimentally created hierarchies." *Human Relations* 11:41-53.

1959 "Situational structure, self-esteem, and threat-oriented reactions to power." Pp. 35–52 in Dorwin Cartwright (ed.), *Studies in Social Power*. Ann Arbor, Mich.: Institute for Social Research.

COHEN, JERRY L. AND JAMES H. DAVIS
1973 "Effects of audience status, evaluation, and time of action on performance with hidden-word problems." *Journal of Personality and Social Psychology* 27:74–85.

CURTIS, RICHARD F.
1963 "Differential association and the stratification of the urban community." *Social Forces* 42:68–77.

DAVIS, KINGSLEY AND WILBERT E. MOORE
1945 "Some principles of stratification." *American Sociological Review* 10:242–9.

DOBRINER, WILLIAM
1963 *Class in Suburbia*. Englewood Cliffs, N.J.: Prentice-Hall.

DOOB, ANTHONY N. AND ALAN E. GROSS
1968 "Status of frustrator as an inhibitor of horn-honking responses." *Journal of Social Psychology* 76:213–8.

DOYLE, KEVIN
1974 "It's dirty, dangerous." *London Free Press* (January 30):p.3.

DUNCAN, OTIS DUDLEY AND BEVERLY DUNCAN
1955 "Residential distribution and occupational stratification." *American Journal of Sociology* 60:493–503.

ELLIS, ROBERT A. AND W. CLAYTON LANE
1967 "Social mobility and social isolation: a test of Sorokin's dissociative hypothesis." *American Sociological Review* 32:237–53.

FELDMAN, ARNOLD S. AND CHARLES TILLY
1960 "The interaction of social and physical space." *American Sociological Review* 25:877–84.

FORM, WILLIAM H. AND JOAN RYTINA
1969 "Ideological beliefs in the distribution of power in the United States." *American Sociological Review* 34:19–31.

FRENCH, JOHN R. P. AND BERTRAM RAVEN
1959 "The bases of social power." Pp. 150–67 in Dorwin Cartwright (ed.), *Studies in Social Power*. Ann Arbor, Mich.: Institute for Social Research.

GERARD, HAROLD B.
1953 "The effect of different dimensions of disagreement on the communication process in small groups." *Human Relations* 6:249–71.
1957 "Some effects of status, role clarity, and group goal clarity upon the individual's relations to group process." *Journal of Personality* 25:475–88.

GERTH, HANS AND C. WRIGHT MILLS
1958 *From Max Weber: Essays in Sociology*. New York: Oxford University Press.

GOFFMAN, ERVING
1959 *The Presentation of Self in Everyday Life*. Garden City, N.Y.: Doubleday-Anchor.
1961 *Encounters*. Indianapolis: Bobbs-Merrill.
1967 *Interaction Ritual*. Garden City, N.Y.: Doubleday-Anchor.

GOODSTADT, BARRY AND DAVID KIPNIS
1970 "Situational influences on the use of power." *Journal of Applied Psychology* 54:201–7.

GRAYSON, PAUL
1973 "Comparative political networks." Unpublished paper, Atkinson College, York University.

GUETZKOW, HAROLD
1965 "Communications in organizations." Pp. 534–73 in James G. March (ed.), *Handbook of Organizations.* Chicago: Rand McNally.

HAGE JERALD, ET AL.
1972 "Organization structure and communications." *American Sociological Review* 36:860–71.

HODGE, ROBERT W. AND PAUL M. SIEGEL
1970 "Nonvertical dimensions of social stratifications." Pp. 512–20 in Edward O. Laumann, Paul M. Siegel, and Robert W. Hodge (eds.), *The Logic of Social Hierarchies.* Chicago: Markham.

HOLLINGSHEAD, A. B.
1949 *Elmtown's Youth.* New York: Wiley.

HOMANS, GEORGE C.
1974 *Social Behavior: Its Elementary Forms.* Revised Edition. New York: Harcourt Brace Jovanovich.

HURWITZ, JACOB I., ET AL.
1960 "Some effects of power on the relations among group members." Pp. 800–9 in Dorwin Cartwright and Alvin Zander (eds.), *Group Dynamics: Research and Theory.* New York: Harper and Row.

INKELES, ALEX
1960 "Industrialized man: The relation of status to experience, perception and value." *American Journal of Sociology* 56:20–1.

ISRAEL, JOACHIM
1971 *Alienation: From Marx to Modern Sociology.* Boston: Allyn and Bacon.

JACKMAN, MARY R. AND ROBERT W. JACKMAN
1973 "An interpretation of the relation between objective and subjective social status." *American Sociological Review* 38:569–82.

JACKSON, ELTON F. AND RICHARD F. CURTIS
1972 "Effects of vertical mobility and status inconsistency: a body of negative evidence." *American Sociological Review* 37:701–13.

JOHNSON, LEO
1972 "The development of class in Canada in the twentieth century." Pp. 141–83 in Gary Teeple (ed.), *Capitalism and the National Question in Canada.* Toronto: University of Toronto Press.

KAHL, JOSEPH A. AND JAMES A. DAVIS
1955 "A comparison of indexes of socio-economic status." *American Sociological Review* 20:317–25.

KAPLAN, HOWARD B.
1971 "Social class and self-derogation: a conditional relationship." *Sociometry* 34:41–64.

KELLEY, HAROLD H.
1960 "Communication in experimentally created hierarchies." Reprinted on pp. 781–99 in Dorwin Cartwright and Alvin Zander (eds.), *Group Dynamics.* New York: Harper and Row.

KIPNIS, DAVID AND JOSEPH COSENTINO
1969 "Uses of leadership powers in industry." *Journal of Applied Psychology* 53:460–6.

KNOWLES, ERIC S.
1973 "Boundaries around group interaction: the effect of group size and member status on boundary permeability." *Journal of Personality and Social Psychology* 26:327–31.

LAUMANN, EDWARD O.
1966 *Prestige and Association in an Urban Community*. Indianapolis: Bobbs-Merrill.
1973 *Bonds of Pluralism: The Form and Substance of Urban Social Networks*. New York: Wiley.

LORIMER, JAMES AND MYFANWY PHILLIPS
1971 *Working People*. Toronto: James, Lewis and Samuel.

MANN, MICHAEL
1970 "The social cohesion of liberal democracy." *American Sociological Review* 35:423–39.

MARTIN, J. DAVID
1970 "A comment on whether American women do marry up." *American Sociological Review* 35:327–8.

MARX, KARL
n.d. *Capital*. Volumes I and III. Moscow: Progress Publishers.

MARX, KARL AND FRIEDRICH ENGELS
1961 *The Civil War in the United States*. New York: International Publishers.
1968 *Selected Works*. Moscow: Progress Publishers.
1971 *Ireland and the Irish Question*. Moscow: Progress Publishers.

MATHEWSON, STANLEY B.
1969 *Restriction of Output among Unorganized Workers*. Carbondale, Ill.: Southern Illinois University Press.

MILGRAM, STANLEY
1965 "Liberating effects of group pressure." *Journal of Personality and Social Psychology* 1:127–34.

MILLS, C. WRIGHT
1956 *The Power Elite*. New York: Oxford University Press.

MOSCOVICI, S., E. LAGE AND M. NAFFRECHOUX
1969 "Influence of a consistent minority on the responses of a majority in a color perception task." *Sociometry* 32:365–80.

MULDER, MAUK
1971 "Power equalization through participation?" *Administration Science Quarterly* 16:31–8.

MULDER, MAUK AND HENK WILKE
1970 "Participation and power equalization." *Organizational Behavior and Human Performance* 5:430–48.

MYERS, GUSTAVUS
1972 *A History of Canadian Wealth*. Toronto: James, Lewis and Samuel.

OPERATOR, SNARKY AND LIPPY REPRESENTATIVE
1972 "Working for Ma Bell." *Canadian Dimension* 8:11–5.

PEPITONE, ALBERT AND GEORGE REICHLING
1960 "Group cohesiveness and the expression of hostility." Reprinted on pp. 141–51 in Dorwin Cartwright and Alvin Zander (eds.), *Group Dynamics*. New York: Harper & Row.

RHODES, A. LEWIS
1969 "Residential distribution and occupational stratification in Paris and Chicago." *Sociological Quarterly* 10:106–12.

RIECKEN, HENRY W.
1958 "The effect of talkativeness on ability to influence group solutions to problems." *Sociometry* 21:309–21.

ROSENBERG, LARRY
  1962 "Social status and participation among a group of chronic schizophrenics." *Human Relations* 15:365-77.

RUBIN, ZICK
  1973 *Liking and Loving: An Invitation to Social Psychology.* New York: Holt, Rinehart and Winston.

SAMPSON, EDWARD E.
  1963 "Status congruence and cognitive consistency." *Sociometry* 26:146-66.

SENNETT, RICHARD AND JONATHAN COBB
  1972 *The Hidden Injuries of Class.* New York: Knopf.

STRODTBECK, FRED L., ET AL.
  1958 "Social status in jury deliberations." Pp. 379-88 in Eleanor E. Maccoby, Theodore M. Newcomb, and Eugene L. Hartley (eds.), *Readings in Social Psychology.* New York: Holt, Rinehart, and Winston.

THIBAUT, JOHN
  1950 "An experimental study of the cohesiveness of underprivileged groups." *Human Relations* 3:251-78.

TORRANCE, E. PAUL
  1965 "Some consequences of power differences on decision making in permanent and temporary three-man groups." Pp. 600-9 in A. Paul Hare, Edgar F. Borgatta, and Robert F. Bales (eds.), *Small Groups: Studies in Social Interaction.* New York: Knopf.

UYEKI, EUGENE S.
  1964 "Residential distribution and stratification." *American Journal of Sociology* 69:491-8.

WILMOTT, PETER AND MICHAEL YOUNG
  1960 *Family and Class in a London Suburb.* London: Routledge and Kegan Paul.

WORCHEL, PHILIP
  1957 "Catharsis and the relief of hostility." *Journal of Abnormal and Social Psychology* 55:238-43.

ZANDER, ALVIN, ET AL.
  1959 "Power and the relations among professions." Pp. 15-34 in Dorwin Cartwright (ed.), *Studies in Social Power.* Ann Arbor, Michigan: Institute for Social Research.

ZEITLIN, MAURICE
  1974 "Corporate ownership and control: the large corporation and the capitalist class." *American Journal of Sociology* 79:1073-119.

Social Class and Bar Behavior during an Urban Festival*

Richard J. Ossenberg

Very little seems to be known about who actually participates in "community" festivals. Social scientists as well as laymen apparently assume that people generally, regardless of status in the community, more or less participate in and benefit from such festivals. In discussing crowds in general, for example, Davis states: "The individuals who constitute any particular crowd ... are together by accident ... Having no organization and being ephemeral, the crowd does not select its participants ... Necessarily, the members ... are drawn *from all walks of life* and are present in the situation only because, in pursuing their private ends, they have to make use of common conveniences ..." (italics added).[1] And in their view of "conventional crowds" (including institutionalized festivals), Killian and Turner state that these " ... function in facilitating the resolution of cultural conflict,"[2] thereby implying that community solidarity is temporarily restored.

It must be obvious from daily observations, however, that such views, while democratic, are anything but accurate. Every community has its distinctive geographical and social boundary lines between rich and poor and between majority and minority ethnic groups. Certainly these lines are not absolute; but there is bound to be disproportionate representation of the various status groups in the crowds that gather for different community activities, whether for nocturnal recreation or Saturday shopping or something else. The "red-light district" thus attracts a rather different clientele than more exclusive entertainment areas, and "hock-shops" and second-hand stores are not frequented by the same persons who patronize exclusive specialty and department stores.

Certain social groups also are known to be more likely than others to participate in relatively uncontrolled forms of collective behavior such as lynchings, race riots, and political separatist movements.[3] On the other hand, it is argued that community festivals (such as the Calgary Stampede discussed here) function specifically to enhance community solidarity through generalized participation in tension-release behavior.[4] An historical example was the "King-of-Fools" festival of the Middle Ages which was subsidized by the aristocracy who actively participated in the fun and games, but which featured a temporary

* Reproduced by permission of the Society for Applied Anthropology, from *Human Organization* 28 (1) 1969, pp. 29–34.

inversion of the class structure. The annual Japanese village festivals also appear to have the same purpose and consist of extremely unorthodox behavior as well as inversion of the class structure and other releases from everyday constrictions.[5] Similar ceremonies in urbanized societies have not received, to my knowledge, as much attention from social scientists. As a result, we lack adequate studies of the Oktoberfest of Germany, the Mardi Gras of New Orleans, the Winter Carnival of Quebec, and the Calgary Stampede of Alberta, not to mention thousands of other community festivals in the United States, Canada, and Western Europe.

Both the paucity of analyzed cases and the implicit acceptance by many sociologists and anthropologists of a functionalist view of the integrating effect of community ritual suggested the present study of selective participation. It is based on observations made during a systematic "pub-crawl" on two evenings of the week-long Stampede which is held every July in Calgary, Alberta, the fastest-growing city of Canada. The study was prompted by curiosity about the role of social stratification in encouraging or discouraging participation in this type of collective behavior, which would be designated by Davis as a "planned expressive group" and by Turner and Killian as a "conventional crowd."[6] From a theoretical point of view, it was assumed that variations in the social class structure of communities largely determine differentiated participation in planned community festivals. In *Gemeinschaft* communities where "mechanical solidarity" within a small and homogeneous population prevails, generalized participation in festival occasions is probably usual. In urban *Gesellechaft* communities, however, social class structure seems too complex to expect the same general response.

In Canada and the United States we have considerable evidence pertaining to the "life-styles" of the different socio-economic classes. In general, for example, it can be said that middle-class attitudes abound with inhibitions and taboos against aggressive and deviant behavior, while people in lower socio-economic class positions are more concerned with immediate gratifications that sometimes explode into temporary violence. On the other hand, members of the middle class are more sensitive to legal and other restrictive norms and consequently may be more responsive to the relaxation of social controls represented by the relatively lax enforcement of those norms during community festivals like the Stampede.

It is therefore hypothesized that participation in the Calgary Stampede (as measured by bar behavior) will be high among middle-class people and low among lower-class people. More specifically, patrons of middle-class drinking establishments during the Calgary Stampede will exhibit more festival-related aggressive/expressive behavior than patrons of lower-class drinking establishments.

BACKGROUND AND METHODS

The annual Calgary Stampede features a rodeo and related "cowboy" themes as central attractions. There is also the usual carnival midway (larger than most), and street dancing is common. In addition, there is a general relaxation of formal social controls, with fewer arrests than usual of ambitious tipplers, "car-cowboys," women of ill repute, and the like ....

In order to study one important aspect of the festival behavior, nine beer parlors and cocktail lounges[7] — representing a cross-section of social-class-related drinking establishments in Calgary — were visited on two separate evenings during Stampede Week. The research team consisted of the author and a graduate student. I had gained some knowledge previously of the social class characteristics and behavioral patterns of customers usually found in these establishments through periodic visits in the year prior to the Stampede festival. During this year I had casually observed behavior in all of these bars in the process of searching for a "shorthand" method of discovering social class structure in Calgary. That is, as other researchers have suggested, bars are an effective informal index of the social structure in which they exist.[8] In this connection, each of the drinking establishments was visited on at least three different occasions, including both weekdays and Saturdays.

The establishments selected for study are located in the central business district, as well as the surrounding fringe area, or "Zone-in-transition," which contains the cheaper hotels and the entertainment areas found in most medium-to-large cities in North America. This fringe area, which includes Calgary's priority urban renewal project, is populated by economically-deprived people. Unlike many older industrial cities, Calgary's ecological pattern also includes deprived areas in what would normally be "affluent" sectors of other cities. Thus, in areas equidistant from the city center can be found *nouveau riche* suburbs as well as deprived and ramshackle neighborhoods. The two types are of course separated, and the annexation by the city of Calgary of formerly rural and presently deprived communities largely accounts for this ecological anomaly.

The bars that were visited were chosen both because of my knowledge of their usual social composition and activites and because of their proximity to the Stampede Grounds, thus assuring a maximum sample of celebrants. The sample was then divided into "class" groups as follows: two upper-class; three middle-class; and four lower-class. The definition of the social class identity of the bars is admittedly subjective and informal but, I believe, valid.

The upper-class establishments are usually patronized by the elite oil and ranching group as well as the *nouveau riche* and the occasional white-collar couple celebrating an anniversary. The middle-class bars are patronized by clerical workers, small businessmen, and generally middle-range employees of the larger local firms, with occasional laborers drifting in. The lower-class bars are the clearest in definition. They are patronized by service personnel, laborers, winos and deprived Indians as well as by members of newly-arrived immigrant groups. The class distribution of bars in the sample was "biased" toward the lower-status groups. Calgary has a higher proportion of white-collar and profes-sional workers than most cities and if the choice of bars had been based on this consideration, only two or three lower-class bars would have been included. My knowledge of composition and activities of the lower-class bars, however, was greater than that of the middle and upper-class bars and the choice was made accordingly.

Being rather conservative with respect to confirming our hypothesis, we selected two evenings in which cross-class interaction could reasonably be expected to be maximized: namely, the first night of Stampede week, and the night before the final day of festivities. We reasoned that these evenings, unlike the "in-between" nights, would reveal the most frantic collective search for gratifications and, if only accidentally, result in cross-class contacts. The anticipation of festivities is so great in Calgary during the few days prior to the Stampede that the first "green light" day witnesses the greatest crowds, both at the rodeo grounds and in the bars. The last day is perceived as the "last chance"; it was assumed that celebrants would then attempt to "let loose" one last time.

We chose drinking establishments rather than other sites of festival activity for the following reasons:

(1) We felt that participant observation would be more easily facilitated in bars than "on the streets" or at the Stampede Rodeo grounds;

(2) It was reasonable to assume that inhibitions concerning cross-class interaction are more easily dissolved with the aid of alcoholic beverages;

(3) We theorized that excessive drinking represents a form of deviant behavior which becomes "normal" and even goal-directed during many community festivals; and

(4) We enjoy beer.

Within the bars, we concentrated on:

(1) The apparent social class composition of patrons;

(2) The wearing of costumes suitable to the "Western cowboy theme" of the Calgary Stampede;

(3) The noise level (including the spontaneity and intent of expressive vocalization); and

(4) Physical and social interaction, including evidences of aggression and general themes of conversation.

FINDINGS

Lower-Class Establishments

In three of the four beer parlors visited, activities could be described as "business as usual." Beer parlors in general are lower-class, and the patrons appeared to be the same as those who frequent these establishments throughout the year. Most of the customers were dressed in their normal work clothes or service-trade uniforms. If anything, there were fewer patrons than usual.

Beer parlors normally abound in service personnel, laborers, marginal drifters, and members of economically-depressed minority groups, most of whom live within walking distance. Conversations generally consist of work problems, family problems, sex exploits, cars, dialogue with self (the drifters), and general backslapping and spontaneous camaraderie. Sex distinctions are maintained by segregating the men's parlor from "ladies and escorts," and fights between patrons erupt about once an hour. Police patrols outside of these bars are conspicuous at most times of the year.

During the evenings of observation only about one out of ten of the tipplers wore Western cowboy costume, and most of those who did were completely ignored by other patrons. The noise level was lower than usual. There were virtually no "yippees" or "yahoos" or other shouts of the sort commonly associated with rodeos. Social interaction was quite normal, and there were fewer than the usual number of fights between patrons. None of the conversation overheard dealt even remotely with the Calgary Stampede. Two patrons whom we questioned specifically about the Stampede indicated that they "couldn't care less," and that the Stampede was "a big fraud." One of these, a loner wearing the service-personnel uniform of a local firm, suggested that if he had his way, he would abolish the Stampede because it interfered with his usual drinking activities by "draining" the number of friends he usually found at the bar. When questioned specifically about this, he responded that during Stampede, "they just stay home." The other patron, a travelling resident of a neighboring province, exclaimed that all he wanted was peace and quiet and he just wished he "had all the money that is spent on the phony Stampede."

The most interesting pattern was the maintenance of sex segregation. In Calgary, as in some other Canadian cities, beer parlors are divided by license into rooms for "men" and for "ladies and escorts." During the Stampede the legal ban against an "open" drinking establishment was lifted. However, patrons of three of the four lower-class establishments sampled continued their usual segregated drinking. In fact, several of us were specifically barred from entering the "ladies and escorts'" sections of these bars; and we observed that at least eight of every ten males were in the "men's" section, leaving a more than usual surplus of females in the "ladies and escorts'" section.

The only evidence of unusual behavior was the greater than usual number of "streetwalker" prostitutes in all four of the beer parlors. During a usual evening about one in ten females in these pubs is a prostitute, whereas one in five appeared to be a prostitute during the evenings under study. We concluded that these girls were present for two reasons: (1) some may have anticipated that there would be more "tricks" in the lower-class pubs on the assumption that "slumming" parties would gravitate toward lower-class areas; and (2) some may have been excluded from middle-class establishments by bouncers hired for the occasion, or may have been discouraged by the general confusion of such places at Stampede time.

In the fourth beer parlor, patterns of behavior deviated more from the usual daily routine. About half of the customers were in the Stampede "spirit." This included appropriate costumes, spontaneous "yippees" and "yahoos," physical interstimulation (e.g., backslapping), cross-sex interaction in the form of indiscriminate necking, and conversations characterized by expressive pleasure-seeking themes such as "sex in the office," "I'll get that bastard [boss]," "let's really rip tonight," "how's about a gang-bang," and the like. The other half of the customers behaved like the patrons of the other three lower-class establishments, but there was very little evidence of any cross-class interaction between them and patrons of different status backgrounds. Apparently the fourth beer parlor differed from the others because of its proximity to the central "high-class" entertainment core of Calgary and to the Rodeo Grounds. Accidental "drifting" seemed to account for the disruption of normal business. Certainly, this conclusion is reasonable in the light of the following observations of middle-class drinking places.

Middle-Class Establishments

Two of the three middle-class drinking establishments were cocktail lounges and the other was a beer parlor in a relatively plush hotel. Since the legal requirements for a lounge generally distinguish the "haves" from the "have nots" in Canada, it is not surprising that the majority of customers at Stampede time were apparently middle-class. Nevertheless, the middle-class constituted a higher percentage than usual at these places. Many of the patrons were frequent and accepted visitors. But some were out-of-towners whose class identification depended on affluent costuming and the spontaneity with which they related to and were accepted by the "regulars." Absent was the usual smattering of blue-collar workers who tend to drift into these bars and are tolerated so long as they "behave themselves."

At least ninety percent of the patrons in these establishments wore cowboy and Western costumes. It is interesting to note that we were consistently ridiculed for not being dressed in similar costumes (hopefully, this will increase our research sophistication in the future although we still may not be able to afford cowboy outfits). The noise level in these middle-class establishments was almost intolerable. There were dozens of spontaneous "yippees" and "yahoos" competing with each other; and verbal and physical stimulation such as males clapping each other on shoulders and couples necking indiscriminately was virtually universal. From the conversations we overheard, we gathered that the collective search for sensate gratifications was extensive. Most of the customers were obviously well along the continuum from sobriety to inebriation. The majority of the table groupings seemed to consist of people who worked in the same office, with executive types freely interacting with secretaries and sundry female assistants. In spite of this clustering, however, there was considerable table-hopping; and tourists were quickly assimilated by locals who seemed ebullient about showing them a good time. For example, a rather lost looking "out-of-towner" who wandered into one of the bars wearing expensive cowboy garb was invited by one of the local celebrants to "come join us, pardner." He was immediately introduced to a newly-acquired "harem" of girls sitting at the table. In another case, a jubilant couple from a neighboring province invited themselves to a table and were immediately accepted as friends. In this latter case, all of the celebrants, including the visitors, whipped off to a party together. Even in the one middle-class beer parlor there was absolutely no sex segregation, and customers took full advantage of the temporary freedom of cross-sex interaction in contrast to the more highly segregated patterns observed in the lower-class establishments.

The prostitutes at the middle-class bars were of the more sophisticated call-girl type. Streetwalkers and lower-class revellers generally were barred from entering these establishments by guards and bouncers stationed at all entrances.

The few streetwalkers who wandered in seemed confused by the chaos and shortly departed without seriously attempting to solicit "tricks." We concluded that even during community festivals middle-class people tend to be endogamous in their deviant behavior.

Upper-Middle-Class Establishments

The two cocktail lounges visited are located in two of Calgary's most plush and reputable hotels. We had not formulated hypotheses about expected behavior patterns of patrons in these lounges but did expect that emotional expressive release encouraged during Stampede week would not so directly affect relatively elite members of the community. Actually, the two cocktail lounges throughout the year cater to both upper-middle-class customers and upper-class customers who for various reasons are not drinking in their private clubs. Our expectation was based on the premise that upper-class people, similar in some ways to members of the lower class in terms of assured status and spontaneity, manage to minimize inhibitions against deviant behavior in everyday life, and consequently generally engage more in tension-release behavior.

Our speculation was largely confirmed. Although there was a higher proportion of costumed patrons than in the lower-class beer parlors (about 25 percent), there was very little noise or celebration. Again, it was generally a picture of "business as usual." The costumed customers who were attempting to stimulate behavior more in keeping with the festival soon became discouraged by the lack of spontaneous emotional contagion and wandered out to seek more gratifying places. We overheard one member of such a group exclaim (with disappointment and disgust), "Let's blow this joint—it's like a graveyard." He was a member of a group of three, all of whom were elaborately costumed and obviously disappointed by the lack of conviviality. He specifically pointed to me as I was jotting down notes and exclaimed, "Jesus, he's working at a time like this!"

CONCLUSION

Observations of behavior in drinking establishments during the Calgary Stampede confirmed our initial hypothesis. Middle-class customers were obviously engaging in more spontaneous expressive behavior than either lower- or upper-class patrons. The Stampede week therefore seems more "functional" for people who tend to be inhibited in their daily lives and look forward to the "green light" of tolerated deviance during a community festival.

We cannot of course conclude that our findings suggest similar selective factors relating to participation in all community festivals. As we suggested earlier, the appeal of a festival probably depends on variations in the nature of social class structure of various communities. More specifically, festival participation may depend on the rigidity of the class structure and the extent to which ventilation of frustrations is inhibited and punished through formal social control. For example, we would expect that members of a lower social class group or a minority group who are systematically exploited and punished for deviant behavior, would participate in "legitimate" community festivals to a much greater extent than found in the present study. We suggest that such situations might include the separate Negro parade and festivities during the Mardi Gras of New Orleans and the widespread "peasant" participation in Rio de Janeiro's "Carnival."

The findings suggest that community festivals held in cities such as Calgary reflect social class structure but do not "function" to reinforce social solidarity of members of different social class status groups. The Calgary Stampede, according to our observations, is a middle-class "binge," suggesting that even socially-approved deviant behavior is endogamous. In a sense, the Calgary Stampede does serve to partially invert social class structure by allowing middle-class celebrants to indulge in the spontaneous and aggressive behavior permitted to members of the lower class throughout the year. Members of the lower class, if our sample is any indication, view the contrived Stampede as frivolous and phony and apparently attempt to avoid being contaminated by the festivities.

Notes

1. Kingsley Davis, *Human Society*, The Macmillan Company, New York, 1949, p. 350.
2. Ralph H. Turner and Lewis Killian, *Collective Behavior*, Prentice-Hall, Englewood Cliffs, New Jersey, 1957, p. 155.
3. See, for example, Durward Pruden, "A Sociological Study of a Texas Lynching," *Studies in Sociology*, Vol. I, No. i, 1963, pp. 3–9; Howard Odum, *Folk, Region and Society: Selected Papers of Howard W. Odum* (Catherine Jocher, *et al.*, editors and arrangers), The University of North Carolina Press, Chapel Hill, 1964, pp. 37–38; E. V. Essien-Udom, *Black Nationalism*, University of Chicago Press, Chicago, 1962; and R. J. Ossenberg, "The Conquest Revisited: Another Look at Canadian Dualism," *The Canadian Review of Sociology and Anthropology*, Vol. 4, No. 4, Nov., 1967, pp. 201–218.
4. Turner and Killian, *op. cit.*, pp. 153–154.
5. William Caudill, "Observations on the Cultural Context of Japanese Psychiatry," in Marvin K. Opler ed., *Culture and Mental Health*, The Macmillan Company, New York, 1959, pp. 218–219.
6. Davis, *op. cit.*, p. 355; Turner and Killian, *op. cit.*, p. 153.
7. Distinctions are made in Calgary between "beer parlors," which may only serve beer, and "licensed lounges," which may serve any alcoholic beverage, including beer. In general, beer parlors tend to serve a lower-class clientele while licensed lounges tend to attract the middle class.
8. See, for example, John Dollard, "Drinking Mores of the Social Classes," in *Alcohol Studies and Society*, Yale University, Center of Alcohol Studies, 1954, esp. p. 96; and Marshall B. Clinard, *Sociology of Deviant Behavior*, Holt, Rinehart and Winston, Inc., New York, 1963, pp. 331–332.

Educational Status and Subscription to Dominant Ideology[*]

Ronald D. Lambert/James E. Curtis

Mechanisms accounting for the dissemination and distribution of dominant ideology are not yet clearly understood in their specifics, but a number of theoretical discussions have singled out the educational system for special attention (see, e.g., Gerth and Mills, 1953:251ff; Porter, 1965; Geschwender, 1967; Alford and Scoble, 1968; Stephens and Long, 1969; Sexton, 1969; Mann, 1970; Rosenberg, Verba and Converse, 1970; Zeigler and Peak, 1970; Collins, 1971; Merelman, 1972; Carnoy, 1974; Bowles and Gintis, 1976; Curtis and Lambert, 1976). Some theorists, such as Mann (1970:437), go so far as to suggest that indoctrination may even be a deliberate goal on the part of educators. Among studies supporting the view that there is perspectivistic teaching in the education system is Porter's (1965). He says that Canadian higher education operates to mute demands for major social change and to legitimize existing power arrangements. Conservative values are said to infuse the analyses and interpretations of the past, present and future which are disseminated in the schools. McDiarmid and Pratt (1971; Pratt, 1975) drew very similar conclusions from their content analyses of civics and history textbooks used in Ontario public schools. They found that a form of "dogmatic liberalism" pervaded the school materials. This view was shown in a consistently negative portrayal of any kind of political extremism in the texts and an apparent effort to teach readers that a middle-of-the-road political posture was rational and right.

What lasting effects the schools have on political attitudes into adult life is unclear from previous research, though. Nor is there any clear indication how education may interact with experiences encountered after schooling has been terminated. There are some studies which have looked at adult differences in political attitude as a function of educational status. These studies have often lacked detailed controls on social status backgrounds, however, leaving open the question of sources of any apparent educational differences. The results have

* Used with permission of the *Canadian Review of Sociology and Anthropology*.

The data analyzed in this paper were collected by the Canadian Institute of Public Opinion and were supplied to us by the Canadian Consortium for Social Research. As usual, neither agency bears responsibility for our secondary analyses and interpretations. Thanks are extended to Neil Guppy, University of Waterloo, and two anonymous reviewers for the *CRSA* for their help with an earlier draft, and to the Canada Council for leave fellowship and grant support to J. Curtis.

generally shown that the higher the educational status the more likely the subscription to dominant attitudes, the latter variously defined. Among studies employing selected controls is our own paper (Curtis and Lambert, 1976) where we presented national survey findings for French Catholics, English Catholics and English Protestants. Our results showed that after appropriate controls for socio-economic and other background characteristics in each of our subsamples, antipathies toward such agents of change as left-wingers, right-wingers and labor unions increased with higher levels of education. The opposite type of relationship occurred for negative reactions toward other social categories such as big business and religious, ethnic, and racial outgroups. In a later study we replicated these results for a U.S. national sample (Curtis, Kuhn and Lambert, 1977; cf. related U.S. findings reported by Rosenberg *et al.*, 1970:64–65 and Knoke and Isaac, 1976).

Research findings such as the above favor the general hypothesis that, other things held equal, exposure to successive levels of education operates to standardize persons' psychologies in the direction of greater acceptance of dominant ideology and dominant institutions. Working simply from this interpretation we would predict that the higher the level of education, after appropriate controls, the more support for major social institutions should be manifested. One would expect that this should apply to institutions such as the government, economic organizations, the courts, the educational system, newspapers, and churches. However, if it is dominant ideology which is being taught, then we might expect the opposite findings for reactions to institutions suspected of promoting economic and political change, such as labor unions.

We wish to test a variant of this perspective, one which permits a significant specification of the relationship. We assume that one of the messages conveyed by the educational system, at least until recently, is the idea that higher education should and probably will lead to greater financial success. Granting this assumption prompts us to look at the explanatory import of the *relationship* between levels of education and economic satisfaction/dissatisfaction. We believe this variant on the indoctrination hypothesis has special merit in explaining subscription or opposition to dominant attitudes when there are large groups of dissatisfied persons at each education level, such as in the current period of economic recession. We predict a *reversal* of the usual education-dominant attitude relationship among persons who are dissatisfied with their economic fortunes. We expect, in other words, that the positive relationship is limited to those persons who feel that the economic system has delivered on what the educational system "promised," so to speak.

Geschwender's (1967) theoretical work on the effects of status inconsistencies defined by educational status and income levels suggests this approach. His discussion assumes that people view years spent in the educational system, and levels of certification successfully completed therein, as investments in the interest of future economic rewards. Following from this, he hypothesized that if an appropriate (or higher) level of economic payoff is perceived as forthcoming from the world of work given one's educational investments, one should be relatively supportive of existing institutions. The reasoning would be that the system has worked as promised. However, if economic rewards are not seen to be satisfactory in relation to investments, anger at unfulfilled promises should result with several possible outcomes, including withdrawal of support for political agents of the status quo.

There is some evidence of an "objective" decline in the relative income and occupational value of higher education since 1960. Harvey (1974), for example, has found evidence of this on a number of indicators (such as prestige of first jobs and reasons for leaving jobs) in his survey of persons who had graduated in 1960, 1964, and 1968 from selected Ontario universities. Zsigmond et al. (1977) have also reported on the current comparatively high oversupply of post-secondary educated persons for jobs formally requiring that level of education and a consequent high level of "underemployment" of persons with post-secondary education. Their projections for Ontario and for Canada, in general, through 1986, are for continuations of both trends. They also speculate that the gap between expectations and achievements will become more prevalent in the future unless there is a change in popular views about what education can deliver. Such trends provide the backdrop for the "investments" hypothesis, and some objective basis for growing disillusionment with society among those higher in education.

Persons who feel under-rewarded would be expected to have greater doubts about existing institutional arrangements than would persons who are economically satisfied vis-à-vis investments. In addition, holding levels of dissatisfaction constant, we would expect higher levels of negative reactions to the institutions with increases in educational status. That is to say, when payoffs are seen as unsatisfactory, the higher the investments in the system the greater the disaffection (cf. Wilson, 1975, for similar theoretical arguments).

METHODS AND DATA SOURCES

Our findings are taken from a survey of 1,050 adult Canadians conducted by the Canadian Institute of Public Opinion (CIPO) in June, 1974.[1] The analyses are restricted to respondents who reported that their mother tongue was English (N=622) or French (N=291).[2] Omitted from the analysis are 128 respondents who gave an "other" language. This group was omitted because the N was small and because there was no additional information on what their languages were, whether they were born in Canada, or how long they had lived in Canada. These issues were judged important because we wished to maximize on respondents' experiences with the institutions in question and the culture in which these institutions are embedded. We also wanted, in part of our analyses, to check on the generality of our basic findings to each of the major language sub-groups.

The overall question tapping *non-confidence in institutions* was as follows: "I'm going to read off a list of institutions in Canadian society. Would you tell me how much respect and confidence you, yourself, have in each one — a great deal, quite a lot, some, or very little?" The institutions, in order, were (1) "churches or organized religion," (2) "public schools," (3) "labor unions," (4) "the Supreme Court," (5) "large corporations," (6) "House of Commons," and

(7) "newspapers." The response options were "great deal," "quite a lot," "some," "very little," and "no opinion." We have dichotomized these variables so that replies of "very little" were scored as 1 and all other responses were scored as 0.[3] In addition, an overall "index of non-confidence in institutions" was constructed by summing across each respondent's responses on the seven items. This index had a range of 0 to 7.

Education level completed, the principal independent variable, had the following categories: (1) some or all of elementary school plus some of high or technical school, (2) all of high or technical school, and (3) some or all of university. Respondents who did not complete high or technical school were grouped in the lower category rather than in the secondary school category because we were mindful both of persons' years of education and of their specific failure to obtain a secondary school certificate. There were, unfortunately, too few cases of university-educated respondents to allow separate analyses for those who had obtained a degree and for those who had not.

Our contingency control, *economic dissatisfaction*, was measured by the following two questions: "On the whole, would you say that you are satisfied or dissatisfied with (a) the future facing you and your family? and (b) your family's income?" Responses to each question were coded so that "No, not satisfied" was scored as 1 vs. "Yes, satisfied," no answer and "can't say" scored as 0. An additive index with a range from 0 to 2 was also developed by combining these two items. Our analyses were done within the dissatisfied and less-dissatisfied subgroups defined by each of the two questions and within each of the two extreme subgroups defined by the index. In other words, a total of six parallel subgroups analyses were done. In addition, we used all three levels of the cumulative index when it was entered as a factor in the analysis of variance checking for its interaction with education.

The literature suggests that several social background characteristics should have effects on attitudes of confidence in institutions and, thus, should be introduced as controls. The statistical controls available to us and on which we focused (and their categories in parentheses), were as follows: *language* (English; French); *age* (18–29; 30–39; 40–49; 50–59; 60+); *income* (under $6,000; $6,000-9,999; $10,000+; refused); and *occupation of head of household* (professional and business executive, manager and owner; sales people and clerical workers; skilled labor; farmer; unskilled labor; pensioned or retired; housewife; miscellaneous). We do not take the space here that would be required to give details on the effects of these control variables on our dependent variables. Let it suffice to say that our preliminary analyses showed that in the case of one or more of our dependent variables each of the control variables had an effect, and they were each correlated with educational status or economic dissatisfaction to some extent. Therefore, the controls were required if we wished to identify precisely the relationships among educational status, economic dissatisfaction and the dependent variables.

The data analysis procedures were analysis of variance (ANOVA) and Multiple Classification Analysis (MCA) (Andrews, Morgan, Sonquist and Klem, 1973). The latter is a multivariate technique for examining the relationship between a single predictor (independent) variable and a dependent variable, or the relationship between each variable in a set of predictor variables and a dependent variable holding constant the remaining predictors.

The uncontrolled relationship between an independent and a dependent variable is given as the gross mean value of the dependent variable for the respondents in each category of the independent variable. To take account of other predictors, MCA yields an adjusted net score which is equivalent to the mean value of the dependent variable for each category of the principal predictor after the effects of the remaining predictors have been partialled out. In the present analysis we were interested in the net effects of education on our dependent variables after the effects of our five control variables had been statistically removed. When categories of the dependent variable are coded as 1 and 0, so that the attribute to be explained (e.g., non-confidence in an institution) is set equal to 1 and those who do not share this attribute are scored as 0, MCA shows what *proportion* within each level of a predictor variable exhibits the attribute after the effects of control variables have been statistically removed. The figures in our tables for all dependent variables except for the "index of non-confidence" (which has several categories) should be interpreted in these terms.

We also report MCA *beta* coefficients for education. These coefficients estimate the proportion of the total variance in the dependent variable accounted for by a given predictor when the effects of other predictors are partialled out. The tests of significance for main effects and for two-way interactions, however, are taken from the ANOVA routine which yields the MCA statistics.

FINDINGS

The effects of educational level and language group membership on attitudes toward the seven institutions, with and without MCA controls, are summarized in Table I. After controls were introduced there was no evidence of a relationship between education and the seven attitudes or the additive index based on them. A number of significant language differences appeared, however. French Canadians were more negative toward schools, the Supreme Court, the House of Commons, newspapers and on the cumulative index of nonconfidence. The paucity of university-educated French Canadians (n=6) means that we were unable to test the full range of education effects for this sub-sample. Analyses of the education relationships among English Canadians only showed the same patterns as reported in Table I for the overall sample. Given that there was not a single education-by-language interaction effect which even approached statistical significance (there was none at the .05 level or better), we decided to merge these two mother tongue groups for the remainder of our analyses and to treat language as a statistical control.

It is also interesting to note, from Table I, that the least trusted institutions overall were labor unions, followed by large corporations and newspapers. The levels of nonconfidence for these three institutions in the overall sample were 36,

31, 27 percent, respectively. The other four institutions elicited considerably less mistrust, with the Supreme Court and schools least mistrusted (10 and 12 percent, respectively). Respondents indicated nonconfidence in a mean of only 1.46 institutions (standard deviation=1.40).

TABLE I   Attitudes of Nonconfidence in Canadian Institutions by Education Level and Language Group, with and without Controls (MCA), 1974 National Sample of Adults[a]

Institution	Education level[b]				Language group[c]			Total working sample
N =	El (539)	Hi (248)	Un (112)	beta /r² (%)	Eng (611)	Fr (288)	beta /	(899)
Churches	.13[d]	.15	.18	.05/	.15	.13	.02	
	(.12)	(.16)	(.21)	6.3	(.15)	(.12)		(.144)
Schools	.12	.11	.14	.02/	.10	.17	.11*	
	(.13)	(.10)	(.12)	3.4	(.10)	(.15)		(.122)
Unions	.34	.39	.38	.05/	.34	.40	.05	
	(.34)	(.39)	(.40)	4.0	(.35)	(.38)		(3.65)
Corporations	.30	.32	.34	.03/	.33	.27	.06	
	(.29)	(.33)	(.35)	2.4	(.33)	(.26)		(.313)
Supreme Court	.09	.11	.11	.03/	.08	.13	.10*	
	(.10)	(.10)	(.11)	3.8	(.08)	(.15)		(.101)
House of Commons	.17	.12	.13	.06/	.12	.21	.11**	
	(.17)	(.12)	(.12)	2.6	(.12)	(.21)		(.146)
Newspapers	.26	.27	.29	.02/	.22	.38	.16**	
	(.28)	(.27)	(.25)	4.3	(.22)	(.38)		(.267)
Index of overall non-confidence[e]	1.46	1.50	1.57	.04/	1.34	1.70	.12**	
	(1.42)	(1.48)	(1.57)	3.3	(1.36)	(1.67)		(1.46)

a. As indicated in more detail above, the controls are for age, income, and occupation of head of household. Language is also included as a control in the first panel of this table showing differences by education level, and education is included as a control in the second panel showing differences by language.
b. El = elementary school or some secondary school; Hi = secondary school completed; Un = some university or more.
c. Eng = mother tongue English; Fr = mother tongue French.
d. The figures without parentheses are the adjusted means, after controls; the figures in parentheses are the means before controls.
e. This index is constructed from attitudes expressed toward the seven institutions. Since a score of 1 is given for expressed non-confidence in each institution, individuals scores could range from 0 to 7.
*   = significance at the .01 level; ** = significant at the .001 level. The level of significance is from the analysis of variance procedure. Beta is from MCA; when squared, beta gives an estimate of the proportion of the variance explained in the dependent variable by the single predictor, with statistical controls. r² refers to the total variance explained by education, language, and the other control variables.

TABLE II Nonconfidence in Canadian Institutions by Education Level within Levels of Economic Dissatisfaction, with and without Controls (MCA)[a]

	Dissatisfied respondents[b]														
	Dissatisfaction with current situation					Dissatisfaction with future chances					Dissatisfaction index				
Institution	El[c]	Hi	Un	beta	/r2 (%)	El	Hi	Un	beta	/r2 (%)	El	Hi	Un	beta	/r2 (%)
	(230)	(77)	(32)			(226)	(93)	(36)			(142)	(49)	(21)		
Churches	.15[d] (.14)	.12 (.15)	.29 (.03)	.12**/	10.5	.15 (.15)	.19 (.19)	.24 (.28)	.07/	11.4	.15 (.14)	.10 (.10)	.27 (.33)	.13/	15.3
Schools	.11 (.12)	.14 (.12)	.33 (.32)	.18/	8.0	.12 (.13)	.16 (.15)	.29 (.27)	.14*/	9.2	.11 (.12)	.15 (.12)	.44 (.43)	.27***/	13.7
Unions	.32 (.32)	.30 (.29)	.48 (.50)	.11/	6.9	.37 (.38)	.40 (.38)	.47 (.45)	.06/	8.8	.30 (.31)	.33 (.33)	.51 (.48)	.13/	11.2
Corporations	.35 (.35)	.45 (.44)	.46 (.47)	.10/	5.6	.32 (.32)	.53 (.54)	.44 (.47)	.18**/	8.4	.34 (.35)	.60 (.57)	.51 (.52)	.22**/	11.7
Supreme Court	.12 (.13)	.15 (.14)	.25 (.22)	.10/	5.7	.13 (.14)	.17 (.16)	.24 (.20)	.10/	6.3	.13 (.15)	.14 (.12)	.28 (.24)	.12/	8.8
House of Commons	.20 (.20)	.12 (.13)	.31 (.28)	.13/	5.7	.20 (.20)	.16 (.16)	.20 (.20)	.05/	2.5	.21 (.22)	.13 (.12)	.38 (.34)	.16/	6.8
Newspapers	.27 (.29)	.31 (.28)	.50 (.41)	.14*/	7.4	.28 (.30)	.37 (.35)	.43 (.36)	.12/	4.9	.29 (.31)	.37 (.35)	.62 (.52)	.21*/	8.1
Index of overall nonconfidence[e]	1.51 (1.53)	1.58 (1.54)	2.60 (2.53)	.21***/	9.9	1.67 (1.61)	1.98 (1.92)	2.30 (2.22)	.17*/	7.3	1.54 (1.60)	1.82 (1.71)	3.02 (2.85)	.28***/	14.8

a. MCA controls are for age, income, occupation, and language.
b. The three measures of dissatisfaction are as described in the text.
c. El = elementary school and some secondary school; Hi = secondary school completed; Un = some university or more.
d. Means with controls; means without controls are in parentheses.
e. Non-confidence index constructed from attitudes expressed toward the seven institutions.
* = significant at the .05 level; ** = significant at the .01 level; *** = significant at the .001 level.

The MCA findings for dissatisfied respondents taken separately appear in Table II. Here we find quite a different pattern than that suggested in Table I. Considering respondents who were dissatisfied on both items, first, the most educated respondents generally expressed more nonconfidence, after controls, than did the less educated across the various dependent variables. This effect was most pronounced and achieved statistical significance in the cases of schools (p= 001) and newspapers (p=.02) and on the cumulative index of nonconfidence (p=.001). High-school-educated respondents were most critical of large corporations, followed by the university-educated (p=.01). The adjusted means on the nonconfidence index for respondents who were dissatisfied on both dissatisfaction items were 1.54 for the least educated, 1.82 for secondary school graduates, and 3.02 for those who had attended at least some university. More-or-less the same trends appeared among respondents who were dissatisfied in terms of either of the two dissatisfaction items (see the first two panels of Table II).

The findings for the less-dissatisfied respondents are another matter. In no case did any education effect reach the .05 level of significance, regardless of the dissatisfaction measure. Nor was there clear evidence of a trend in the pattern of mean effects across levels of education. By small margins, the university-educated were least pessimistic about schools, unions, the Supreme Court, and the House of Commons. The means, after controls, for nonconfidence in unions were .33, .44 and .31 respectively, for elementary, secondary, and university-educated persons (p=.08). We have chosen not to summarize these findings in tabular form.

The Ns in Table II show that the economically dissatisfied were a substantial proportion of the overall working sample. The percentages dissatisfied on the current, future, and composite measures of dissatisfaction were 35, 38, and 39 percent, respectively. These dissatisfied persons, for whom greater education predicts a greater nonconfidence in institutions, also constitute a sizeable proportion at each education level. For example, the percentages dissatisfied on the index were 42, 38, and 32, for the elementary, secondary and university levels of education, in that order. Thus, the education-dissatisfaction interaction shown here does not rest on a small minority, or on an insignificant number of "deviant cases" in the sample. At the same time, we note that the mean score on the nonconfidence index for doubly dissatisfied respondents was only 1.75. We are not dealing, then, with chronic malcontents who simply reject a host of institutions out of hand.

DISCUSSION AND CONCLUSION

The pattern of findings in our analyses generally favored the "investment" hypothesis. As far as findings consistent with the "general indoctrination" view are concerned, all that can be said is that among satisfied respondents there were some instances of lower levels of nonconfidence with increased education level, but the patterns were inconsistent and not statistically significant. In addition, as we indicated earlier, these findings have alternative reward and distributive justice interpretations. Among the satisfied we found no clear pattern of greater disrespect for unions with higher levels of education, after controls, as would be expected from the indoctrination view and contradicting our own earlier findings (Curtis and Lambert 1976:196-7).[4]

When we speak of the "investment" hypothesis, we mean to imply more by the concept than simply rewards. What we have in mind speaks to the role of education in the establishment of perceived *entitlements* to rewards against which the distribution of rewards is assessed (cf., Nozick, 1974:150-82). The concept of unfulfilled promises helps to make sense of the apparent association between nonconfidence in social institutions and levels of education among economically dissatisfied respondents. Anxiety about status, especially among the more and most educated, may undermine people's faith in the dominant social institutions which have "let them down." This interpretation is premised on the assumption that individuals acquire something more than skills and knowledge as they progress through the school system. They learn, among other things, to think of themselves in terms of standards of self-importance and selected reference groups so that they are especially vulnerable to disillusionment with their later earning power and status in the job market. It is, of course, these reference groups to which the Anti-Inflation Board alluded in recent years when it judged contract settlements in terms of what the AIB called "historical relationships" among groups of workers. This precious allusion to social stratification appeals to the special vanities that education inculcates. The peculiar dilemma of the educated worker is that he or she is particularly exposed to a broader range of educationally "inferior" workers who threaten his/her position symbolically and financially. Having acquired a set of beliefs which ties income to individual merit rather than collective muscle, and having also invested heavily in themselves as human capital by virtue of their education, the more highly educated may be resentful of groups of workers whose relative success seems to depart from these fundamental principles. Thus a form of incipient delegitimation may be set in motion among more educated workers whose economic returns fall short of their supposed entitlement. Conversely, however, the instrumental legitimacy of social institutions remains intact to the extent that educated workers feel themselves to be well and properly rewarded. This line of argument takes us well beyond the data currently available, of course. Further research should attempt to incorporate measures of the kinds of intervening variables that we have just noted.

Notes

1. This was one of the CIPO regular monthly polls. Each is based on "a national probability sample in all centres over 1000 in population" and "a quote sample...in rural farm and rural non-farm centres" (The Canadian Gallup Poll, no date).

2. The question asked about "the language you first spoke in childhood and still understand."

3. We ran parallel analyses where we declared answers of "no opinion" as missing values to see if our inclusion of these respondents' responses appeared to be affecting our results in any way. For each of our analyses the results were substantially the same whether or not the responses of "no opinion" were included. In addition, we also conducted parallel analyses in which the dependent variables were treated as

continuous measures and "no opinion" and "no answer" were declared as missing values. We were reluctant in this case to assign some scale value to "no opinion" on the grounds that this would be purely arbitrary. In any event, these analyses yielded essentially the same results as those using the dichotomous measures.

We report here only on the analyses with the category of "no opinion" included and the variables dichotomized to save space. Our preferred procedure maximizes Ns, allows us to compare the dissatisfied with all others, and allows us to report findings on the same subsamples across dependent variables (the levels of no opinion responses and the individuals giving them differed across the items for the different institutions). This procedure probably gives less sensitivity in measurement for each attitude, and in some instances it meant that our variance explained was slightly lower than it would have been with the procedures using the continuous measures.

4. Further to our earlier paper (1976), we replicated as closely as possible our analyses on the 1968 national election survey data used for that paper. The paucity of dissatisfied and university-educated respondents, however, seriously limited the scope of these analyses especially for French Canadians. The proportions of economically dissatisfied English Canadians were 10 and 17 percent, respectively, on similar items measuring current and anticipated economic dissatisfaction. These figures compare with 35 and 38 percent in the 1974 data. The direction of the relationship between education and reactions to left-wingers and unions was specified by whether respondents were currently dissatisfied or satisfied. Higher education and opposition to these agents of change were positively associated among economically satisfied persons. But among dissatisfied persons there was less opposition to agents of social change with higher education. These findings are suggestive, but caution should be exercised in interpreting them. The differences in our findings across the 1968 and 1974 studies, especially considering the greatly different levels of economic dissatisfaction, suggest that whatever dynamics adduced here are probably time-bound. This is apart from differences in the dependent variables available in the two surveys. A table summarizing the results of this analysis is available from the authors on request.

References
BETTELHEIM, B., AND M. JANOWITZ
  1964 *Social Change and Prejudice*. N.Y.: Free Press of Glencoe.
BOWLES, S., and H. GINTIS
  1976 *Schooling in Capitalist America*. New York: Basic Books.
THE CANADIAN GALLUP POLL
  n.d.   The design of the sample. Toronto.
CARLTON, R.A.
  1977 "Popular images of the school." Pp. 36–53 in R.S. Carlton, L.A. Colley and N.J. MacKinnon (eds.), *Education, Change, and Society: A Sociology of Canadian Education*. Toronto: Gage.
CARNOY, M.
  1974 *Education as Cultural Imperialism*. N.Y.: David McKay Co.
CHRISTIAN, W., and C. CAMPBELL
  1974 *Political Parties and Ideologies in Canada*. Toronto: McGraw-Hill Ryerson.
COLLINS, R.
  1971 "Functional and conflict theories of educational stratification." *American Sociological Review*, 36:1002–1014.
CURTIS, J.E., M. KUHN and R.D. LAMBERT
  1976 "Education and the pluralist perspective." Pp. 123–39 in R.A. Carlton, L.A. Colley and N.J. MacKinnon (eds.), *Education, Change, and Society: A Sociology of Canadian Education*. Toronto: Gage.

CURTIS, J.E. and R.D. LAMBERT
   1975 "Status dissatisfaction and out-group rejection: cross-cultural comparisons within Canada." *Canadian Review of Sociology and Anthropology* 12:178:192.
   1976 "Educational status and reactions to social and political heterogeneity." *Canadian Review of Sociology and Anthropology* 13:189–203.

GERTH, H., and C.W. MILLS
   1953 *Character and Social Structure.* N.Y.: Harcourt.

GESCHWENDER, J.A.
   1967 "Continuities in theories of status consistency and cognitive dissonance." *Social Forces* 46:160–71.

GLENN, N.C.
   1966 "The trend in differences in attitudes and behaviour by educational level." *Sociology of Education* 39:255–75.

HAMILTON, R.
   1975 *Restraining Myths: Critical Studies of U.S. Social Structure and Politics.* N.Y.: Halsted-Wiley.

HARVEY, E.
   1974 *Educational Systems and the Labour Market.* Toronto: Longman.

HUBER, J. and W.H. FORM
   1973 *Income and Ideology.* N.Y.: Free Press.

KNOKE, D. and L. ISAAC
   1976 "Quality of higher education and sociopolitical attitudes." *Social Forces* 54:524–29.

LEFCOURT, H.
   1976 *Focus of Control: Current Trends in Theory and Research.* Hillsdale, N.J.: Lawrence Erlbaum Wiley.

MANN, M.
   1970 "The social cohesion of liberal democracy." *American Sociological Review* 35:423–30.

McDIARMID, G., and D. PRATT
   1971 *Teaching Prejudice.* Toronto: Ontario Institute for Studies in Education.

MERELMAN, R.M.
   1972 "The adolescence of political socialization." *Sociology of Education* 45:134–66.

NOZICK, R.
   1974 *Anarchy, State, and Utopia.* N.Y.: Basic Books.

PARKIN, F.
   1967 "Working class conservatives: a theory of political deviance." *British Journal of Sociology* 18:278–90.
   1971 *Class, Inequality and Political Order.* London: McGibbon and Kee.

PORTER, J.
   1965 *The Vertical Mosaic.* Toronto: University of Toronto Press.

PRATT, D.
   1975 "The social role of school textbooks in Canada." Pp. 100–26 in E. Zureik and R.M. Pike (eds.) *Socialization and Values in Canadian Society.* Vol. I, *Political Socialization.* Toronto: McClelland and Stewart.

ROSENBERG, M.J.
   1956 "Cognitive structure and attitudinal affect." *Journal of Abnormal and Social Psychology* 53:367–72.

ROSENBERG, M.J., S. VERBA and P. CONVERSE.
   1970 *Vietnam and the Silent Majority: The Dove's Guide.* N.Y.: Harper and Row.

SEARS, D.O.
1969 "Political behavior." Ch. 41 in G. Lindzey and E. Aronson (eds.). *The Handbook of Social Psychology* (2nd edition), Vol. 5. Reading, Mass.: Addison-Wesley.

SENNETT, R., and J. COBB.
1972 *The Hidden Injuries of Class.* N.Y.: Random House.

SEXTON, P.
1969 *The Feminine Male: Classrooms, White Collars and the Decline of Manliness.* N.Y.: Random House.

SHIBUTANI, T., and K.M. KWAN
1965 *Ethnic Stratification: A Comparative Approach.* N.Y.: Macmillan.

STEPHENS, W.N., and C.S. LONG
1969 "Education and political behavior." Pp. 3-25 in J.A. Robinson (ed.) *Political Science Annual*, Vol. 2. Indianapolis: Bobbs-Merrill.

WILSON, J.Q.
1975 "The riddle of the middle class." *Public Interest* 39:125-9.

ZSIGMOND, A., G. PICOT, M.S. DEVEREAUX and W. CLARK
1977 *Future Trends in Enrolment and Manpower Supply in Ontario.* Ottawa: Statistics Canada, Education, Science and Cultural Division.

Ethnicity and the Perception of Heroes and Historical Symbols[*]

Jean Pierre Richert

The United States is often referred to in the popular literature as a melting pot, a term which implies, presumably, a society in which diverse cultures amalgamate to form a new, dominant culture. Canada, on the other hand, has been likened to a mosaic (Porter, 1965), that is to say, a society in which diverse cultures presumably co-exist and develop separately. However, recent events raise some questions about the co-existence and development of the English- and French-Canadian cultures, the dominant cultures in Canada.

The Royal Commission on Bilingualism and Biculturalism, which has devoted considerable attention to the interaction of cultures in Canada, attributes some of the present tensions to the Canadian historical duality (1968:269).[1] The Commission is not alarmed by the historical duality in itself, but, rather, by the fact that the two traditions of the major cultural groups, anglophones and francophones, appear to be *mutually exclusive* (Royal Commission, 1968:281).

The Royal Commission's observations are based on a study by M. Trudel and G. Jain of Canadian history textbooks. The Commission does not offer any empirical evidence suggesting that the two traditions are reflected in the attitudes of Canadian pupils, though it strongly hints this is so (Royal Commission, 1968:274). The purpose of this paper is to verify empirically the suggestion of the Royal Commission by examining young people's identification with historical figures in Quebec. The data for the study were gathered between October 1970 and March 1971 in Quebec, and are based on nearly 1000 questionnaires, 330 essays, and over 50 in-depth, personal interviews of elementary school children in Montreal, Sherbrooke, and Stanshead.[2]

THE CANADIAN HISTORICAL DUALITY

Trudel and Jain arrive at two major conclusions in their survey of Canadian historical textbooks. The first is that English- and French-Canadian history textbooks focus on different eras of Canadian history (Royal Commission,

* Reprinted from the *Canadian Review of Sociology and Anthropology*, 11 (2) 1974, pp. 156–163, with the permission of the publisher, Fitzhenry and Whiteside Limited.

The author would like to thank Brown University for financial support, and Professors Hargrove, Cornwell, and Feldstein, all from Brown, for critical advice.

1968:275). French-Canadian books tend to focus on the past, while English-Canadian textbooks dwell more on recent events. The second conclusion these writers arrive at is that historical events frequently have different meanings for the two language groups (Royal Commission, 1968:281). Another conclusion arrived at by Trudel and Jain is that the two versions of Canadian history are often irreconcilable. One striking example of this, but not an isolated one, deals with the interpretation of the British conquest in 1760. Trudel and Jain describe how this event is presented in two versions of the *same* textbook. The English version of the book presents the story of the fall of New France accompanied by a picture of "a British redcoat welcoming the arrival of the British fleet at Quebec in the spring of 1760." The French version of the same book includes the same event accompanied by a picture "showing General Murray setting fire to a peaceful French-Canadian village" (Royal Commission, 1968:280). Clearly, the two versions are mutually exclusive.

The Royal Commission suggests that two major consequences result from the duality of Canadian history. The first is that the two groups emerge as threats to each other; the second is that groups other than those of English- and French-Canadian origin are often ignored (Royal Commission, 1968:281–282).

HISTORY AND HEROES: EMPIRICAL ANALYSIS

The most prominent historical symbols are people, events, and dates. Pilot work revealed that most children except those in the higher grades were unable to describe historical events or discuss the meaning of dates. As a result, this study focused primarily on historical figures. However, despite this apparent limitation, it is possible to discuss historical events since many figures are associated with specific events. The following instruction was given: "Write the name of an important person in your country's history whom you admire." An analysis of children's answers revealed two salient features. In the first place, the data confirmed the hypothesis that children identified primarily with symbols of their own culture. Second, the data also supported the hypothesis that pupils identified with different eras of Canadian history.

Cultural Identification with Historical Figures

Historical figures referred to by children were classified into four categories shown in part A of Table I. The first category, Canadians, includes both French- and English-Canadian figures. In addition, it includes figures who are nationals of other countries but who played an important and direct role in Canadian history. The second category, foreigners, includes figures who are not Canadian and did not play a direct role in Canadian history. The third category includes Columbus. It was decided to put Columbus in a special category because of his ambiguity as an historical symbol in Canada. The fourth category includes personages such as religious figures who could not meaningfully be classified in terms of nationality.

Table IA reveals that a majority of children of both groups referred to Canadian heroes.[3] However, of those children who picked Canadian figures

TABLE I   Anglophone and Francophone Children's Identification with Historical Symbols and Eras (in Percentages)

	Francophone	Anglophone
A. *Nationality of the heroes*		
Canadians	60.6	63.3
Foreigners	11.9	11.0
Columbus	14.9	11.6
Other	8.9	9.6
Not sure	3.7	4.5
Total percentage	100.0	100.0
Total *N*	473	335
B. *Cultural membership of the Canadian heroes referred to*		
French-Canadian heroes	98.1	49.5
English-Canadian heroes	1.9	50.5
Total percentage	100.0	100.0
Total *N*	267	190
C. *Historical eras referred to*		
Before 1760	80.5	49.5
After 1760	19.5	50.5
Total percentage	100.0	100.0
Total *N*	267	190

TABLE II   Ten Most Cited Historical Figures by Each Group

	French Canadians		English Canadians	
	Percentage	N	Percentage	N
Bourassa (R)	2.3	11	—	—
Cabot	—	—	5.7	19
Cartier*	31.9	151	6.0	20
Champlain*	7.6	36	10.4	35
Columbus*	14.8	70	11.6	39
De Gaulle	1.3	6	—	—
Hudson	—	—	3.3	11
Iberville	1.5	7	—	—
Laporte	3.2	15	—	—
Maisonneuve	1.7	8	—	—
Macdonald	—	—	6.0	20
Mackenzie (W.)	—	—	3.3	11
Napoleon	4.2	20	—	—
Radisson	—	—	4.8	16
Trudeau*	2.1	10	3.9	13
Wolfe	—	—	5.1	17
Total	70.6	334	60.1	201

* Reconciliation symbols.

(Table IB), 98.1 percent of the francophone children referred to French-Canadian heroes while only 1.9 percent referred to English-Canadian symbols. A majority of anglophone children also referred to heroes of their own group, (50.5 percent) but the pattern was a much more balanced one. However, it may be pointed out that included among the French-Canadian figures referred to by English-Canadian children were such personalities as Pierre Trudeau (3.9 percent) and Pierre Laporte (4.8 percent) who, one may argue, transcend cultural boundaries, the first because he is the prime minister of Canada, the second because he may be viewed as a martyr of Canadian federalism.[4]

Another interesting finding is that age reinforced the ethnocentric perception of historical symbols. While the data revealed only minor changes among francophone children over age, anglophone children increasingly referred to heroes of their own culture: their references to English figures ranged from 41.2 percent at grade level 4, to 68.3 percent at grade level 7, a difference of 27.1 percent. This finding is somewhat surprising since one might have expected to find that older children would be less ethnocentrically oriented than younger ones because of the process of decentration outlined by Piaget and Weill (1951:562).

The analysis may be carried one step further by examining who the specific heroes referred to by children were. This will also highlight the non-reconciliatory aspect of the two versions of Canadian history. Children referred to over 100 different historical figures. Table II shows the 10 most-frequently cited heroes by children of each language group. An examination of this table reveals that only 4 symbols appeared on both lists: Cartier, Champlain, Columbus, and Trudeau. These figures may be called reconciliatory symbols since they are referred to by both groups. Trudeau and Columbus may transcend cultural boundaries, the first because he is both francophone and the prime minister, the second because he is usually depicted as the discoverer of America rather than of a specific province. The relative salience of Cartier and Champlain, two French symbols, among anglophone children may be an indication of the relative openness of the English-Canadian political culture.

The idea that the two versions of history are mutually exclusive can be illustrated by focusing on three specific events and heroes referred to by children: the discovery of Canada, the conquest, and the case of Pierre Radisson. Two men in particular played a prominent role in the discovery of Quebec: Jacques Cartier and John Cabot (Bovey, 1940; Jenkins, 1966). Cartier was a Frenchman in the service of the king of France who discovered the St. Lawrence in 1534 and claimed the territory of Quebec for France in 1535. John Cabot was a Genovese in the service of Henry VII of England who first sailed along the coast of Newfoundland and Labrador, and possibly Cape Breton, as early as 1497. In order to confirm the hypothesis that French Canadians identify with French cultural symbols, while English-Canadian children are most likely to identify with symbols of their own culture, one should expect to find that the former will refer to Cartier, while the latter will be more likely to cite Cabot. The data clearly bear this out since, as Table II shows, 31.9 percent of French-Canadian children referred to Cartier, while only 6 percent of English-Canadian children did. The proportion is reversed when we examine children's references to Cabot to whom 19 anglophones but only one francophone referred.[5]

One way to focus on children's perceptions of the conquest is to study their attitudes toward the two generals, Montcalm and Wolfe, who were the opponents in the battle of the Plains of Abraham in 1759 which marked the fall of New France and the beginning of the English domination of Quebec. Four francophone pupils referred to Montcalm and 17 anglophone children cited Wolfe. While few children overall referred to these figures, the pattern of responses is striking since not one French-Canadian child referred to the English victor, Wolfe, and not a single English-Canadian pupil cited the French hero, Montcalm.

A third example which suggests that anglophone and francophone children's perceptions of history are, in some cases, exclusive, is illustrated by pupils' attitudes toward Pierre Radisson. Radisson was a Frenchman, and as Mason Wade (1967:19) puts it, a renegade, having helped John Kirke establish the Company of Adventurers of England Trading into Hudson's Bay. The company was opposed by Talon, a French administrator of Quebec. Here again, the pattern of children's responses was striking: 16 English-Canadian children referred to Radisson, while only one French-Canadian child mentioned his name.

Identification with Historical Eras

The data also showed that children in Quebec identified with different periods of Canadian history, which was classified into two periods: the first covers the period of the discovery and settlement of New France to 1760 and the second from 1760 to the present.[6] It may be recalled that 1760 marked the fall of French Canada and the subsequent domination of Quebec by England. Table IC indicates the contrast in children's responses. It shows that of the children who referred to Canadian figures, an overwhelming majority of French-Canadian children (80.5 percent) referred to symbols of the pre-1760 era, while a slight majority of English-Canadian children referred to the post-1760 era. Furthermore, most of the later symbols to whom French-Canadian children referred were contemporary political figures such as Trudeau, the federal prime minister, or Robert Bourassa, the former prime minister of the province of Quebec. With the exception of Laurier (3 references), H. Bourassa (1), Curé Labelle (2), and Sir John A. Macdonald (1), no francophone child referred to any prominent figures of the nineteenth century which may be viewed, especially after 1867 (the beginning of the Confederation), as the era *par excellence* of British North America.

English-Canadian children, on the other hand, were almost equally divided in their responses, with a slight majority referring to the post-1760 era. Unlike francophones, anglophone children referred rather frequently to nineteenth-century figures such as Sir John A. Macdonald (20), William Lyon Mackenzie (11), Queen Victoria (4), etc. Almost half of the figures referred to are "English" symbols, for example, John Cabot or Henry Hudson. The data furthermore showed that the pattern of children's identification with historical symbols differed. The difference between the two groups was greatest at grade level seven at which 88.3 percent of French-Canadian, compared to only 38.5 percent of English-Canadian children, referred to pre-conquest historical symbols. The data suggest, therefore, a certain "closure" and inward-looking dimension of the symbolic universe, and ultimately of the political culture, of francophone children included in the sample.

CONCLUSION

The data presented in this note support the Royal Commission's suggestion of a historical duality in Canada, and in some cases, its mutually exclusive characteristic. This conclusion is further highlighted when the Quebec data are compared to similar data from France and the United States, which do not reveal any dualities or incompatibilities in children's identification with historical figures. The French sample ($N = 81$) was selected in Alsace-Lorraine on the assumption that children might identify with German heroes as a result of the geographic proximity of Germany and the past associations between this province and Germany. Yet not a single French child picked a German hero. The American sample ($N = 121$) showed that children identified with the same national heroes (Washington, Lincoln, etc.) irrespective of cultural or racial membership.

While the data on which this note is based are limited in the sense that they are derived primarily from one projective question, the findings nonetheless raise the question of the function of history as an integrative device in Canada. Social scientists have long been aware of the integrative role of history in social and political development. Erikson (1950:244) and Lipset (1963), for example, argue that history shapes national identity. Doob (1964:35) writes that a "nation must have ... a rich heritage if people are to acquire the pride associated ... with their own country." The integrative function of history has not been overlooked by the Royal Commission on Bilingualism and Biculturalism (Royal Commission, 1968:282) which states, in the concluding pages of a chapter dealing with the teaching of history, that "the primary purpose of teaching history is not always the training of historians ... students are taught history because societies believe that it provides a desirable and necessary training for future citizens."

History, then, is frequently viewed as a binding force, at least when historical symbols are perceived in the same manner by all members of the society. But this may not always be the case, as the Canadian data suggest. Rather, it appears that history in Canada may well be a divisive factor, one which may retard social and cultural integration. But considering the limitations of the data, additional research focusing on other variables affecting integration is desirable.

Notes

1. Several authors conceive of Canadian history in terms of a duality; for example, Mason Wade (1953:145) and Erwin C. Hargrove (1967).
2. Children were enrolled in grade 4 through 7 in 11 elementary schools. I wish to thank the many school officials who permitted me to enter their schools.
3. Table IA also shows that about 11 percent of children of each group referred to foreign

heroes, a probable indication of the weakness of the Canadian national identity.

4. Pierre Laporte was a member of the Liberal party and a provincial minister of labor and immigration when he was kidnapped and murdered by members of the *Front de Libération du Québec*, in October 1970.

5. The major reason which accounted for the relatively few references, overall, to the figures discussed here, is that the questionnaire item dealing with historical symbols was an open-ended one, thus allowing references to any historical figure.

6. Dates are, of course, arbitrary and therefore of limited value as criteria of classification. As a result, the period "1760 to the present" includes some events which, in fact, occurred a year or two before 1760, but which are related to the conquest.

References

BOVEY, WILFRED
    1940 *Les Canadiens-Français d'Aujourd'hui*. Montreal: Editions ACF.

DOOB, LEONARD
    1964 *Patriotism and Nationalism*. New Haven: Yale University Press.

ERIKSON, ERIK H.
    1950 *Childhood and Society*. New York: W.W. Norton.

HARGROVE, ERWIN C.
    1967 "Popular Leadership in Anglo-American Democracies." In Lewis J. Edinger (ed.), *Political Leadership in Industrialized Societies*. New York: John Wiley.

JENKINS, KATHLEEN
    1966 *Montreal: Island City of the St. Lawrence*. Montreal. New York: Doubleday.

LIPSET, SEYMOUR M.
    1963 *First New Nation*. New York: Basic Books.

PIAGET, JEAN, and ANNE-MARIE WEILL
    1951 "The Development in Children of the Idea of the Homeland and Relations with Other Countries." *International Social Science Bulletin* 3:561–578.

PORTER, JOHN
    1965 *The Vertical Mosaic*. Toronto: University of Toronto Press.

ROYAL COMMISSION ON BILINGUALISM AND BICULTURALISM
    1968 *Education*, Book II. Ottawa: The Queen's Printer.

WADE, MASON
    1953 "Political Trends." In Jean C. Falardeau (ed.), *Essais sur le Québec Contemporain*. Laval: Presses universitaires de Laval.
    1967 *The French-Canadians*. 2 vols. Toronto: Macmillan of Canada.

Social Class Self-Identification*

John C. Goyder/Peter C. Pineo

Over the past ten years survey data about Canadian society have been accumulating rapidly. Periodic surveys are now used to monitor demographic and attitudinal characteristics that are considered important social indicators but which cannot be included in the decennial census. For instance, three of the federal elections during the past decade — those in 1965, 1968 and 1974 — have been studied by Canadian political scientists using relatively large, national-level interview surveys. These have gone well beyond the scope of simply accounting for voting habits; witness to this is given by the large number of secondary analyses that have used the two "Meisel" studies (collected in 1966 and 1968).[1] These analyses have covered such topics as Canadian nationalism, ethnic attitudes, regionalism, associational activities, and the decline of the middle class (e.g., Cuneo, 1976; Curtis and Lambert, 1975; Schwartz, 1974; Curtis, 1971; Grabb, 1975).

Social class self-identification has been one of the questions routinely asked in election surveys as well as in other interview and questionnaire studies. Respondents might be asked, "In which social class do you feel you belong?" or some variation thereof, and usually a list of class labels to choose from is offered. The question attempts to tap the subjective aspect of social class. It has often been felt that bare statistical groupings, devised by researchers, do not authentically gauge how people perceive their own social class (Schumpeter, 1955) and subjective class identification questions are designed to fill this need. Considerable diversities in opinion seem to exist, however, regarding the adequacy of the conventional class identification question as a measure of social class. It has been included in surveys virtually since the beginning of survey research itself (e.g., *Fortune Magazine*, 1940; Cantril, 1943; Centers, 1949) and the fact that researchers continue to include it could indicate a consensus about its usefulness. However, criticisms have also been made regarding its validity. Whatever else it

* This article is intended to update the paper that appeared in the first edition of *Social Stratification: Canada*. Wording effects have been emphasized here because the greater number of data sets now available allow comparisons of class identification questions that could not be made earlier. We are greatly indebted to Professors David Coburn, John Meisel, Peter Regenstreif, and James Rinehart for supplying copies of questionnaires or information about their surveys. We would like to acknowledge the assistance of Lynda Hayward in checking computations. The checking was funded by a small grant, awarded to Peter Pineo, from the Arts Research Board of McMaster University.

may do, it has been felt that such a simple interview-administered stimulus cannot fully indicate people's perceptions of their own social class. One criticism from American researchers in the 1950s was that responses tended to vary according to changes in the wording of the question (Gross, 1953; Kahl and Davis, 1955). So, the danger in interpreting results from class-identification questions is that there may be more information in the responses about question design artifacts than about how people evaluate their own social class. It is hard, studying the apparent meaning of the different wordings in currency, to conclude that one version of the question has greater validity than the others.

Class identification, however, continues to be asked in surveys. As an independent variable, intended to be used to explain other things, class identification seems to be capable of enriching analyses of class-related phenomena. For example, in several countries research into the relationship between social class and voting has demonstrated that class identification has a relationship with vote independent of other measures of class such as occupation (e.g., Runciman, 1972; Wilson, 1968; Campbell, et al., 1960). Thus, seemingly deviant cases such as "working class Tories" often fall into line with voting theory when allowance is made for how the voters perceive their own class. In such research a flawed subjective measure of social class seems to be regarded as preferable to none at all. It at least provides a rough scale of self-assessed status that can be analyzed in tandem with other socio-economic scales.

As a dependent variable, the instability of class-identification responses according to wording variations becomes more troublesome. The responses should indicate the proportion of people that identify with the middle class, with the working class, and so forth. Data of this kind are intrinsically valuable in answering a question such as whether Canadians really hold an "image of middle class uniformity" (Porter, 1965:4). But the wording effects may dominate results and there are dangers of misinterpretations. The classic demonstration of this is Richard Centers' (1949) work. During the 1940s, *Fortune Magazine* published an article with public opinion poll data showing that most Americans identified with the middle class. Centers insisted that this finding was an artifact of question design; *Fortune* had not offered the choice "working class" in their class identification question and Centers' own survey, with this choice included, showed 51 percent working class identification (Centers, 1949:77). Later studies continue to show that responses to the question vary with question wording (e.g., Schreiber and Nygreen, 1970).

Another interesting aspect of class identification is the proportion that refuses to answer the question or that checks some choice such as "don't know" or "there is no such things as class." This proportion seems to give a rudimentary reading of the percentage who feel no "class consciousness," and the approach is so simple that it might be expected to lend itself well to international comparisons. Again, wording effects render such interpretations risky. The American sociologist Neal Gross (1953) showed that when the question was left open-ended rather than supplied with a checklist of class labels, the proportions declining to categorize themselves into a class rose sharply.

Despite the dangers of misinterpretation, the desire among Canadian social scientists to know the distribution of class-identification responses seems strong. Class-identification results have been cited to support arguments about the nature of social stratification in Canada. A recent introductory sociology text concluded from class identification data in a 1965 survey: "Yet, there is a pervasive feeling among Canadians that they are middle class and that Canadian society is essentially middle class. This is confirmed by a national survey ... in which a sample of adults were asked to identify the social class to which they be-longed..." (Crysdale and Beattie, 1973:165). Rinehart and Okraku (1974:201-2) examined class-identification data from two other samples and reached a different view: "Our results, and those reported in two out of three Canadian studies stand in sharp contrast to allegations that Canadians either are unaware of classes or preponderately regard themselves as middle class...." The temptation to attribute meaning at face value to class identification data seems irresistible, but at least the range of the distortions attributable to wording variations should be known. Our purpose here is to make use of the accumulation of recent Canadian survey data asking class-identification questions in order to establish the patterns of responses that different types of questions typically show and to assess whether these distributions are sufficiently stable to support substantive interpretations.

A second matter addressed in the paper is the comparison of patterns of class identification between Canadians and Americans. The comparison replicates and extends work done using a relatively small Canadian data set collected in 1965 and reported in Pineo and Goyder (1973).

In building on this earlier paper we have employed four national level surveys conducted in Canada; the original Pineo-Porter 1965 sample, plus the Meisel national election studies conducted in 1965 and 1968, and a recent survey of the 1974 election done by a group from Windsor and Carleton (for fieldwork details see, respectively, Pineo and Porter, 1967; Meisel and Van Loon, 1966; Meisel, 1972; LeDuc et al., 1974). A number of Canadian samples collected at the provincial or local level were also used for part of the analysis. A complete listing of the Canadian data sources appears in Table III. In replicating the Canadian-American comparison of class-identification patterns we used pub-lished results given by Schreiber and Nygreen (1970) as well as the data sets for a recent (1974) national American election study by the Survey Research Centre of the University of Michigan, and the occupational prestige study conducted in 1964 by NORC (for details see Inter-University Consortium for Political Re-search, 1975; Hodge and Treiman, 1968, respectively).

VARIATIONS IN RESPONSES TO CLASS-IDENTIFICATION QUESTIONS

The typical pattern of responses to open and closed format class-identification questions is shown in Table I. The first set of results is from the national interview survey collected by Pineo and Porter (1967) in 1965, the second from a

TABLE I   Distributions of Responses to Class Identification Questions

Sample	Open-ended question: What social class do you consider yourself a member of?					
	Upper	Upper-Middle	Middle	Working	Lower	N/A
1965	1.1%	3.9	63.3	10.5	4.4	16.8
1971	0.8%	5.9	53.7	16.4	1.2	22.0

Closed Questions: If you had to pick one, which of the following five social classes would you say you were in — upper class, upper-middle class, middle class, working class, or lower class?					
Upper	Upper-Middle	Middle	Working	Lower	N/A
2.0%	12.9	48.9	30.4	2.1	3.7
1.0%	13.4	46.9	27.4	0.3	11.0

mailed questionnaire survey of four cities in Ontario and Quebec. The questionnaire sample was gathered in 1971 and used identical class-identification wordings to those in the 1965 interview. The open question, shown on the left side of Table I, asked respondents to categorize themselves into a class but did not offer choices to select. Instead, the write-in responses were coded into categories by researchers. The two approaches give quite dissimilar results, and in this way the Canadian findings resemble those found in the United States since the 1950s. In the 1965 sample the open-ended question "What social class do you consider yourself a member of?" yielded 63 percent middle class identification and the relatively high non-response of 17 percent. Only one person in ten chose the working class. The closed question immediately followed in the interview. It asked: "If you had to pick one, which of the following five social classes would you say you were in ... ?" A checklist of five class labels was offered this time, and working class identification tripled while refusals dropped to under 4 percent. Identification with the upper-middle class increased by nine percentage points in the closed version. Much the same patterns occurred in the 1971 questionnaire survey of four cities. Refusals, on both class questions, were higher in the 1971 sample. This might have been because of the data collection by mailed questionnaire; and when a number of interview and questionnaire samples were compared (Table III) we found that this was a consistent pattern. [2]

A cross-tabulation of the open and closed questions in each sample shows, as one would expect, that those not answering the open question often did respond to the checklist in the closed question. Roughly four fifths of the non-respondents to the open question answered the closed. The greatest proportion of these selected the working class (26 percent of all non-respondents on the open question in the 1965 sample, and 29 percent in the 1971 sample). Most respondents (76 percent in 1965; 82 percent in 1971) selecting the working class in the open question also chose it from the checklist in the closed question. A somewhat smaller proportion of those selecting the middle class on the open question did likewise in the closed question (63 percent in 1965; 73 percent in 1971). Among this group, the most frequent shift, proportionately, was from the middle class to the upper-middle class.

The response format, then, has been found in both American and Canadian studies to affect class identification and constitutes one "wording effect." Most analysts seem to favor the closed version but even if one adheres to this there is no guarantee that results from one sample will be reproduced in another. A second major wording effect occurs because a closed question which omits the "working-class" label will, as noted earlier, typically discover greater middle-class identification than one which offers the working class as one of the choices. Even when questions have been standardized by always offering this label, difficulties in finding stable class-identification results from sample to sample have been encountered. Recently-published Canadian data have demonstrated this. Rinehart and Okraku (1974) note that results from their London, Ontario, sample, and from two earlier samples, gave considerably higher working-class identification than that given by the 1965 Pineo-Porter sample (reported in Table I and in Pineo and Goyder, 1973). On the other hand, data published by Coburn and Edwards (1976), from a Victoria sample, showed predominately middle-class identification similar to that observed in the 1965 national sample. Samples from urban areas might not be expected to always reproduce the marginal distributions on subjective class found in national level surveys, but one of the samples Rinehart and Okraku drew attention to was another national level interview survey (the Meisel study of the 1965 election) which was collected in early 1966 — within a year of the completion of fieldwork for the Pineo-Porter survey. The wording of the class question was identical in each study, and both offered a closed response format (although, as noted above, the Pineo-Porter interview first asked an open-ended question). Yet, the proportions in each sample selecting the working class differed by a full 15 percentage points. Such a difference in proportions is well beyond the limits to be expected because of sampling fluctuations. To further compound the mystery, fieldwork for both surveys was conducted by the same commercial agency (Canadian Facts), and the completion rates on the attempted interviews were all but identical (64.3 percent in the Pineo-Porter and 62.8 percent on the Meisel samples). Checks against census data revealed that, overall, there was little to choose between the two samples in terms of their representativeness of the Canadian population. One obvious possibility was that the Pineo-Porter sample carried an upper SES bias or that the Meisel sample over-represented lower SES levels, but the mean occupational and educational level in the Pineo-Porter sample was only slightly higher than that in Meisel's. The difference was too minor to account for anything more than a trivial proportion of the difference in working-class identification. In endeavouring to account for such a marked failure of class-identification distributions to reproduce, even under seemingly well-controlled conditions, we speculated about the possible impact of other factors. Do election surveys politicize respondents, causing a reactive effect of the kind proposed by Phillips (1971), and thereby generate high levels of working-class identification? Are there key

TABLE II   Prediction of the Proportion in a Survey Selecting the Working Class

	r	Beta	F
Used in final model:			
% Blue collar (B)	.64	.45	5.612
Question version (V)	.58	.40	4.593
Appearance of term (W)	.50	.33	3.280
"working class"			
*Not used in final model:**			
Interview or questionnaire (I)	−.11	−.01	0.004
Type of survey (T)	.31	.15	0.570
(election or other)			
Financial dissatisfaction (D)	.10	.24	0.099
question asked			

Final model in unstandardized form:
Y = .521 (B) + 8.950 (V) + 7.471 (W) + 8.760 R^2 = .68   N = 14.
* Added successively as fourth predictor in the model.
Notes on scoring: B — percentage of male heads in total sample falling into the blue collar category (including farm owners in the denominator, but excluding no answers). Some studies use "main earner." V — scored as dummy variable; 1 = version not offering choice "upper-middle class," 0 = upper-middle version. W — scored as dummy variable; 0 = term "working class" does not appear in any questions preceding the class identification question, 1 = one or more appearances of the term working class. I — 0 = interview, 1 = self-administered questionnaire. T — 1 = primarily an election survey, 0 = other types of surveys. D — 1 = question about financial satisfaction/dissatisfaction was asked before class identification; 0 = not asked.

questions, such as those tapping dissatisfaction with various aspects of life, which enhance working-class identification? Or, did the fact that the Pineo-Porter study first asked an open-ended question in some way cause a contamination of the closed version which followed immediately afterwards? Clearly, such tentative speculations required additional comparative data. We located 14 Canadian samples from which class-identification results had been published or from which we could compute results from the data set. These data sources are listed in Table III.

We wanted to establish the main factors influencing class-identification results, and to represent their effects quantitatively. This would allow the prediction of the class distributions under various circumstances, and permit adjustments to offset the factors that prevent a direct comparison between samples. Only samples using a closed format checklist and including the working class in the list were examined; as we have seen above, the consequences of omitting the working-class label, or of offering no checklist at all, are well known.

Using samples as units of analysis, we constructed a regression equation capable of predicting with reasonably high precision (68 percent of the variance) the proportion in a sample selecting the working-class label. We concentrated upon working-class identification because (as noted earlier) this category has

TABLE III Actual and Predicted Working Class Identification

Samples:				Actual		
Year	Prin. Investigators	N	Population	Working (%)	Predicted	Difference
1965	Pineo and Porter	793	National	30	34.3	−4.3
1965	Gagne and Regenstreif	939	Toronto, Hamilton, Sault Ste. Marie	49	50.0	−1.0
1965	Meisel, et al.	2125 (unweighted)	National	45	42.8	2.2
1968	Meisel, et al.	2767	National	41	43.9	−2.9
1970	Richmond	3218	Toronto	54	53.3	0.7
1970	Coburn and Edwards	1037	Victoria	36	29.6	6.4
1971	Jones, Pineo	1104	Hamilton, Ottawa, Sudbury, Hull	27	32.2	−5.2
1971	Pineo	516	Owen Sound, St. Catherines, Guelph	41	40.6	0.4
1971	Rinehart, Okraku	558	London	39	30.1	8.9
1972	Kenyon and McPherson	1022	Montreal, Toronto	15	27.5	−12.5
1973	Wilson, Surich	657[b]	Manitoba	37	34.8	2.2
1974	LeDuc, et al.	2562 (unweighted)	National	35	32.2	2.8
1974	Pineo, Looker	336	Hamilton	41	43.2	−2.2
1974	Surich	1501	Ontario	40	35.3	4.7

Sources: From personal data holdings — 1965 Pineo-Porter; 1971 Hamilton, Ottawa, Sudbury, Hull; 1971 Owen Sound, St. Catherines, Guelph; 1974 Hamilton. From data and codebooks acquired by University of Waterloo through the data bank of the Institute for Behavioural Research (York University) — 1965 and 1968 national; 1970 Toronto. From published sources — 1965 cities (Gagne and Regenstreif, 1967), 1970 Victoria (Coburn and Edwards, 1976), 1971 London (Rinehart and Okraku, 1974). The 1974 national data set was supplied through the kind co-operation of Harold Clarke, Jane Jenson, Lawrence LeDuc, and Jon Pammett, the 1973 Manitoba and 1974 Ontario data through the kind co-operation of Jo Surich (Manitoba and Ontario) and John Wilson (Manitoba).

a. Case base for class identification question.

b. Urban sub-sample.

been crucial to interpretations of class structure. An obvious predictor was the overall socio-economic composition of a sample. To arrive at a common coding scheme of socio-economic status throughout the mixture of samples, the simple proportion of male heads of households employed in blue collar occupations was used to indicate the mean SES level within a sample. This proportion varied from 36 percent blue collar in the 1972 sample of residents of Montreal and Toronto to 66 percent in the 1974 sample collected in Hamilton.[3] By incorporating an objective index of mean sample SES into the formula it was possible to handle results from different types of sample (e.g., urban vs. national). If a sample has a skewed occupation distribution, due to design or to simple sampling bias, this is entered into the formula and its contribution to the percentage giving working-class identification in the sample can be estimated. The complete model of working-class identification is shown in Table II. It can be seen that the proportion blue collar was, not unexpectedly, the strongest (b=.45) of the predictors.

It was evident, from simple inspection of the subjective class distributions in the 14 samples, that a variation in the choices offered in the checklists affected the proportion selecting the working class. Working-class identification tended to be high on questions in which the choice of "upper-middle class" was not offered. This version (using the choices upper, middle, working, and lower) is the form of checklist that Richard Centers (1949) used in the 1940s. Later studies have usually added the choice upper-middle class, and the two versions evidently cannot be considered comparable. The version of the response list, when coded as a dummy variable, has a partial regression weight of b= .40 (Table II) with the percentage working-class identification on surveys. Including the choice upper-middle diminishes working-class identification by an average of some nine points.[4] In attempting to further enrich the model, we experimented with ways of performing a content analysis of questions preceding the class-identification question so that questions might be coded according to their likelihood of stimulating working-class consciousness. This proved difficult to do, and we settled for a simpler approach. We found that surveys in which the term "working class" had appeared in an earlier question gave an enhanced proportion of working-class choices (average 7.5 points) on the class-identification question (b= .33).[5] The rationale for this "content variable" is, of course, that the appearance of the term working class in other questions in a survey draws the respondent's attention to the term and establishes its legitimacy.

The beta weight representing this "content effect" is probably only a rough average of several kinds of bias. A more refined analysis, with many more samples, might show that the augmentation in working-class identification was greatest when the term appeared close to the class-identification question. Our impression is that the form of class-identification question in which the term "working class" appears in a preamble (see section on Canada-U.S. comparisons) is particularly prone to give high working-class identification. Indeed, we were initially surprised to find that our results using the Canadian samples showed the content effect even when the term working class occurred in

questions appearing well before the class-identification question. After developing the formula shown in Table II we subjected the content finding to a further
test. A class project done by a group of research methods students at McMaster,
in the winter of 1977, mailed out a small number (N=241) of questionnaires to
residents of Hamilton. Two versions were sent. The only difference between
them was that one version, A, proposed that: "Most immigrants in this country
hold working-class jobs." Choices ranging from "strongly agree" to "strongly
disagree" were offered. The question appeared some 30 questions before
class-identification. Version B omitted this question. Our formula would predict
greater working-class identification on version A and the results confirmed, by a
small margin, the prediction. Working-class identification reached 31 percent on
version A, but only 28 percent on version B.[6]

The lower section of Table II shows variables which did not prove to have any
important explanatory power in accounting for the strength of working-class
identification. It would appear that results from interview surveys and from
questionnaires can safely be compared; we had imagined that respondents might
be more likely to enhance their status when filling out a self-enumerated class
question. There is a zero-order tendency for election surveys to yield greater
working-class identification than other types of surveys, but this diminishes
following controls for the other factors included in the model. Finally, it seemed
plausible that questions about dissatisfaction with personal economic standing
(asked in four of the surveys) might generate working-class consciousness.
Judged by the size of beta coefficient, this is the next most important predictor
after those used in the final model.

The three-variable model that we eventually decided on helped to account for
the failure of class-identification distributions to replicate in the two 1965
national samples. Table III shows the proportions in all 14 samples selecting the
working-class option, the proportion predicted from the model, and the difference between the two. The model predicts 34.3 percent working-class identification in the Pineo-Porter sample compared to 42.8 percent in the 1965 Meisel
sample. We would expect, from the information entered into the formula, that a
difference of 8.5 percentage points in working-class identification would exist
between the two samples. The model could be said to account for just over half of
the actual 15 points discrepancy found. Of this predicted difference of 8.5
percentage points, only one point is attributable to the greater proportion of
respondents in the Meisel sample holding blue collar occupations. The other 7.5
points reflect the fact that "working class" appeared in a question, in the Meisel
survey, having to do with attitudes about which political parties help the middle
class and the working class. No questions using the term working class appeared,
prior to the class-identification question, in the Pineo-Porter interview.

Part of the remaining difference might fall into the domain of sampling
fluctuations.[7] The Pineo-Porter study could still be said to give somewhat lower
(4.3 points) working-class identification than might be expected, and the 1965
Meisel sample slightly higher (2.2 points). However, the average residual over
the 14 samples tabulated in Table III is 4.0 points and so the residuals for both the

1965 national samples are not out of line with this norm. The largest residuals are found in the 1972 sample from Montreal and Toronto and from the Rinehart and Okraku 1971 London sample. The Montreal-Toronto survey sampled only people aged between 25 and 34. Those in this age bracket may be particularly strong middle-class identifiers. The London survey asked a number of questions about images of stratification (Rinehart and Okraku, 1974) and these may have stimulated working-class identification even though we cannot capture the bias as a general variable and represent it in our regression model.

Because the results reported in Tables II and III are based on only 14 cases they may lack the stability that an individual level analysis based on hundreds of cases would possess. Additional observations on the working-class identification produced under different survey conditions would likely alter somewhat the values in the model presented in Table II.[8] On the other hand, the model's three predictors all achieve statistical significance at the .05 level, even though a case base of N=14 sets stringent conditions for such a test. At the least, the results given by the model suggest the danger of attributing any strong substantive interpretations to subjective class-identification results. The technique is simply too dominated by a variety of design effects to settle any debates on whether Canadians predominately identify with the middle class or the working class.

Subjective class-identification would seem best adapted to comparisons between groups or societies where the design effects can be held constant, or to use as an independent variable in analyses in which it is one of several indices of social status. We turn now to replications of some earlier work done on comparisons.[9]

A COMPARISON OF CANADA AND THE UNITED STATES

We showed in earlier publication (Pineo and Goyder, 1973) that when two well-matched studies were compared Canadians and Americans were found to give almost identical answers to the subjective social class question. In the United States, for example, 34 percent chose the working-class label while in Canada it was chosen by 31 percent (1973:188). Chance alone could have produced this similarity; with only two relatively small samples being compared it is wise to replicate the analysis by using other samples before concluding that Canadians view the stratification system in the same way Americans do. There are, however, no other precisely comparable surveys from the two countries. The class-identification question wordings in other pairs of Canadian and American surveys vary and so this must be taken into account. To further test how closely the two societies resemble one another we wondered if the formula we developed to correct for wording effects in the Canadian samples (see Table II) could be applied to U.S. studies. If, using our formula, we could reconcile any inconsistencies between various U.S. studies in the proportion opting for the working-class label, this would be indirect and perhaps quite persuasive evidence that the two nations are similar in social class identification.

The U.S. studies, like Canadian ones, have often failed to reproduce class-identification distributions from one survey to another; there is, in fact, a controversy in the U.S. literature on this. Evidence presented by Tucker (1966; 1968) showed a decline (between 1945 and 1963) from some 50 percent to around 30 percent identifying with the working class in the U.S. This evidence was reassessed and compared to studies by the Survey Research Center of the University of Michigan (SRC studies) by Schreiber and Nygreen (1970). Concluding that the Tucker study was "unique, and hence suspect," Schreiber and Nygreen suggested, as Hamilton had earlier (1966a, 1966b), that wording effects may have created the differences.

In fact, differences between the Tucker results and those of the SRC are almost precisely what the Canadian formula would lead one to expect. The typical SRC study produces an estimate of 50 percent or more identifying with the working class; the Tucker study only some 30 percent. The evidence as assembled by Schreiber and Nygreen (plus two additional samples) is repeated in Table IV. This difference, of some 20 points, can largely be explained by two factors:

1. Tucker provided the option "upper-middle class." While the tabulations of the SRC studies show such an option as well, it is offered in the questionnaire only as part of a follow-up question. This difference would account according to our formula for some nine percentages points.

2. The preamble to the SRC question includes the term "working class." It occurs in such a strong form as to constitute almost a loaded question.[10] The Tucker study contains no prior mention of the term. This factor would account for another 7.5 points difference.

The actual proportion holding blue collar jobs does not differ sufficiently between the Tucker and the SRC studies to be a major factor. But the two wording effects suggest that a difference in working-class identification of around 16 percentage points should be expected.

The first column of Table IV shows the percentage that would be expected to opt for the working-class label, based on use of the Canadian formula. Following this the actual percentage selecting this label is given and then, in brackets, the case base involved in the computation. Finally, the magnitude of the difference between the expected and actual result is shown. Thus, in the SRC study of 1956, 56 percent (not shown in Table IV) of the employed males 21 or older who reported an occupation held blue collar jobs. The choice upper-middle class was not offered in the main class-identification question. The term "working class" appearing in a preamble, precedes the class question, and so altogether the formula predicts that 54.4 percent of the men would select the working-class label. In fact some 60 percent did so. The difference is 5.6, meaning that 5.6 percent more than the formula would suggest actually chose the working class label.

The differences, or discrepancies, shown in Table IV generally exceed those found when the Canadian formula was applied to the Canadian studies (see Table III). The largest differences occur for the SRC surveys done before 1964. The formula may be less applicable to earlier studies; all the Canadian studies

TABLE IV   Accuracy of Canadian Predictive Equation when Applied to U.S. Data

| Study and date | Percentage "working class" | | |
	Estimated	Actual	Difference
SRC 1956	54.4	60 (695)	+5.6
SRC 1958	53.3	63 (698)	+9.7
SRC 1960	55.4	68 (734)	+12.6
SRC 1964	51.8	56 (598)	+4.2
SRC 1966	51.2	59 (443)	+7.8
SRC 1968	50.7	54 (536)	+3.3
SRC 1974	50.2	55 (743)	+4.8
Tucker 1963	35.9	31 (525)	−4.9
NORC 1964	37.4	36 (388)	−1.4

Sources: For NORC, 1964, from a data set provided by NORC library; for SRC studies, percent blue collar in sample, Schreiber and Nygreen, 1970: Table 3; actual percent working class, Schreiber and Nygreen, 1970: note 6, p. 351; Tucker data, Tables 1 and 2 of Tucker, 1968; SRC 1974, from a data set provided by the ICPR.

Populations: NORC, males aged 21 and older; other studies, male labor force 21 years of age and older.

analyzed were conducted since 1964. Also, Schreiber and Nygreen analyzed only employed males aged 21 or over and reporting an occupation. The formula is designed to apply to all respondents (including females), and when we analyze the full U.S. samples the formula does perform with slightly enhanced accuracy.

Including the NORC 1964 data (not available at the time Schreiber and Nygreen wrote) in the table adds the information that the Tucker study was not "unique." The NORC wording was the same as Tucker's in the ways the Canadian formula suggests are important. The wording also produces a much lower percentage calling themselves "working class" than in the other U.S. studies. The estimate based on the Canadian formula is only 1.4 points higher than the actual percentage for this study.

What we are arguing is not simply that wording can affect the answers to the subjective social class question. That is precisely the conclusion reached by Hamilton, and by Schreiber and Nygreen in reaction to the Tucker results, and they correctly suspected that one source of the difference was in the offering of such options as "upper middle class." What is new is that we have identified the two crucial elements in wording that do affect the results — the use of the upper-middle-class option and the provision of a prior appearance of the term "working class" in the interview or questionnaire. And we can also estimate the magnitude of the effect. The Canadian results suggest that the two wording changes will produce a total effect of 16 percentage points in the percentages claiming identification with the working class. Much of the discrepancy between the Tucker study and the other U.S. studies investigated by Schreiber and Nygreen can be explained in this manner. The whole discrepancy, which is in excess of 20 percentage points, cannot be explained in this way. If it is assumed, however, that the American respondents are more influenced by the wording effects than are the Canadians the whole effect can be explained. So also can be explained the apparent discrepancies between the typical SRC study and the NORC 1964 study.

We have found it possible, using a formula developed from Canadian data, to make fairly accurate estimates of the proportion identifying with the working class in several U.S. surveys. The Canadian formula, in fact, largely clears up a controversy on this matter which is found in the U.S. literature. These results argue again that the two systems of class identification are highly similar. The results reported from the earlier analysis of only two surveys appear further confirmed by this more extended analysis.

DISCUSSION

A variety of factors related to question design have an influence on the results typically found in studies of class identification. Accurate comparisons of class identification in different societies require a degree of controlled test conditions much higher than previously thought necessary. Internal comparisons of groups within a single survey should present fewer difficulties. Unless groups react to biasing factors in different ways, the consequences of wording should be constant. Here, the main concern should be with ensuring that results based on small sub-samples can be reproduced in replications. It is in the interpretation of overall class identification distributions from samples that we foresee the greatest problems. Knowing that wording partially determines the responses, it may be asked which version of the class identification question is the "best." One kind of evidence for answering this question would be measures of the strength of the relationship between objective indices of social status and the subjective question.

Such a standard does not, however, provide an escape from having finally to rely on judgment. This can be shown in the case of the American studies on class identification where some distinct traditions in question form have developed. It was seen earlier that the Michigan Survey Research Center has adopted a preamble to their class identification question in which respondents are told that "most people say they belong either to the middle class or to the working class." This version of question, we find, exhibits a markedly stronger multiple correlation with the three principal objective indicators of SES (occupation, income, education) than do any of the other versions used in U.S. studies. By this criterion, the SRC version is clearly the superior wording.

Alternatively, one can argue that this is not the proper criterion. It is possible that the form of the SRC question is so strong as to be virtually a loaded question. A voting question with the words in the preamble "Most Canadians identify either with the Liberals or the Conservatives..." would hardly be considered an acceptable survey question. Thus the relationship with the objective indices produced by the SRC wording may be spuriously high as respondents are pressured into identifying with one class or another and fall back upon their objective situation to find some grounds for making the decision. Our own inclination would be to avoid such a strong preamble, and also, whenever the term "working class" or its equivalent must be used in the study to endeavour to place the subjective social class question before rather than after its appearance. So also we would tend to use the "upper-middle-class" option. The evidence is that it is useful; providing the option "lower middle class," for example, does not have the equivalent effect upon the resulting distribution.

We are suggesting as a personal opinion that 30 percent, rather than 50 percent, is a rather more realistic estimate of the number in both Canada and the U.S. who would spontaneously identify with the working class when questioned in a nationally representative survey. It seems unlikely, however, that a question form acceptable to all researchers can be arrived at. A report by the Consultative Group on Survey Research (Canada Council, 1976), concerned with standardizing the wording of questions commonly asked in Canadian surveys, has recommended a version of class identification that uses a preamble similar to the American SRC form.[11] Such a wording is probably defensible in the view of many social scientists, but we would point out that it will be prone to finding higher working-class identification than will other wordings.

Notes

1. The Meisel survey of attitudes towards the 1965 election was evidently collected in early 1966 (Van Loon, 1970:383). This survey is commonly known as the "1965 Meisel Study."

2. Over the 14 samples listed in Table III, there is a correlation of .12 between non-response and whether the sample was an interview (scored 0) or a self-administered questionnaire (scored 1). Thus, there is a small tendency for questionnaires to have the higher non-response on class identification.

3. Most of the surveys included both males and females. Males only were sampled in the Coburn and Edwards 1970 survey of Victoria, the 1971 questionnaire survey of Ottawa, Hull, Sudbury, and Hamilton, the 1971 London survey, and the 1974 Hamilton sample. In these studies we used, of course, respondent's occupation.

4. Two of the samples (London 1971, Victoria 1970) offered the "lower middle class," along with the upper middle class, as an additional label. This refinement does not appear to cause any further diminution in working class identification.

5. This variable too was scored as a dichotomy. Any study in which the term working class appeared somewhere before the class-identification question was scored 1, others received a score of 0. The 1970 Toronto sample collected by Richmond used the term working class as part of a preamble preceding the class-identification question, and we counted this as "1" on our content variable.

6. The diminished working class self-identification in version B is offset by a higher no answer rate (6 percent on version B, 1 percent on version A). Thus, it might be said that the main consequence of including working class content in a questionnaire is to transfer some potential non-respondents into the working class category. The difference between versions A and B in the proportion working class does not meet a one-tailed test of significance (.05 level) but the difference in no answer rates does ($Z = 2.2$).

7. If the two national 1965 samples had actually produced the levels of working class identification we have predicted from the formula the difference in proportions would still easily achieve statistical significance ($Z = 4.2$). If a scoring for election surveys

versus other types is added into the prediction formula, the difference in working class identification sinks to 4.5 points. We would conjecture also that the open question, asked in the Pineo-Porter survey immediately prior to the closed question, caused some extra middle-class identification on the closed question.

8. Indeed, we would welcome communications from readers who can offer us additional information against which to test the model.

9. It has proved necessary, because of space limitations, to delete a section of the paper in which we reported on a replication of an analysis, based on the 1965 Pineo-Porter sample, that appeared in the first edition of this book. In the earlier publication (Pineo and Goyder, 1973), we presented tables showing the relationship between class identification and indices of objective SES, for religious and language sub-groups in Canada. A detailed tabulation of class by occupation and by religion was shown and this revealed a tendency for Catholic respondents to identify with social class in a seemingly idiosyncratic manner. Compared to English-speaking Protestants, there was in this group more working (including lower) class identification among those in the upper occupation categories, and higher middle (including upper middle, upper) class identification among manual workers. A breakdown of the Catholic respondents, into the French and English-speaking groups, revealed the self-depreciation among upper white collar workers to be most prominent among the English-speaking Catholics and the self-enhancement among manual workers to be seen more distinctly among French-speaking Catholics. The replication drew on three additional data sets, the national surveys from 1965 (Meisel), 1968, and 1974, and the results suggested that some revisions in our earlier conclusions were in order. The tendency for self-depreciation by English-speaking Catholics of high objective status was reproduced in two of the three new samples. The pattern of self-enhancement among French-speaking Catholics, however, was not reproduced in any of the new data sets. In sum, the replication suggested that there may be some interesting variations, among the sub-groups examined, in the inter-relationship between objective SES and class identification, but these are not as distinct, and hence important, as they appeared to be when working only with the 1965 Pineo-Porter survey. The principal difference, in the replication, appeared to lie between English-speaking Protestants and Catholics whereas in the original study the most striking pattern was the low overall congruence between occupation and class among French-speaking Catholics.

10. The SRC question is phrased: "There's been some talk these days about different social classes. Most people say they belong either to the *middle class* or to the *working class*. Do you ever think of yourself as belonging in one of these classes?" (ICPR,1973:539; 1975:650).

11. The Consultative Group's question reads: "People often think of themselves as belonging to one social class or another. Most people say they belong to the upper-middle class, the middle class, or the working class. Do you ever think of yourself as belonging to a social class? (choices: yes, no, don't know). If you had to make a choice, would you call yourself upper-middle class, middle class, working class, or what? In what class do you think most other people would place you?"

References

CAMPBELL, A., P.E. CONVERSE, W.E. MILLER AND D.E. STOKES
   1960 *The American Voter*, New York: Wiley.

CANADA COUNCIL
   1976 *Survey Research: Report of the Consultative Group*, Ottawa: Canada Council.

CANTRIL, H.
   1943 "Identification with social and economic class," *Journal of Abnormal and Social Psychology* 38 (January):74–80.

CENTERS, R.
1949 *The Psychology of Social Classes*, Princeton: Princeton University Press.

COBURN, D. AND V.L. EDWARDS
1976 "Objective and subjective socioeconomic status," *Canadian Review of Sociology and Anthropology* 13 (May):178–188.

CRYSDALE AND BEATTIE
1973 *Sociology Canada*, Toronto: Butterworth.

CUNEO, C.J.
1976 "The social basis of political continentalism in Canada," *The Canadian Review of Sociology and Anthropology* 13 (February):55–70.

CURTIS, J.E.
1971 "Voluntary associations joining: a cross-national comparative note," *American Sociological Review* 36 (October):872–880.

CURTIS, J.E. AND R.D. LAMBERT
1975 "Status dissatisfaction and out-group rejection: cross-cultural comparisons within Canada," *Canadian Review of Sociology and Anthropology* 12 (May):178–192.

FORTUNE MAGAZINE
1940 "The people of the United States — a self-portrait" (February).

GAGNE, W. AND P. REGENSTREIF
1967 "Some aspects of New Democratic Party urban support in 1965," *The Canadian Journal of Economics and Political Science* 33 (4):529–550.

GRABB, E.G.
1975 "Canada's lower middle class," *The Canadian Journal of Sociology* 1 (Fall):295–312.

GROSS, N.
1953 "Social class identification in an urban community," *American Sociological Review* 18 (August):398–404.

HAMILTON, RICHARD F.
1966a "The marginal middle-class: a reconsideration," *American Sociological Review* 31 (2):192–199.
1966b "Reply to Tucker," *American Sociological Review* 31 (6):856.

HODGE, R. AND D.J. TREIMAN
1968 "Class identification in the United States," *American Journal of Sociology* 73 (March):535–547.

INTER-UNIVERSITY CONSORTIUM FOR POLITICAL RESEARCH (ICPR)
1973 *Survey Research Center 1968 American National Study*, University of Michigan: mimeo.

ICPR
1975 *The CPS 1974 American National Election Study*, University of Michigan: mimeo.

KAHL, J.A., AND J.A. DAVIS
1955 "A comparison of indexes of socioeconomic status," *American Sociological Review* 20 (June):317–325.

LEDUC, L., H. CLARKE, J. JENSON, AND J. PAMMETT
1974 "A national sample design," *Canadian Journal of Political Science* 7 (4):701–705.

MEISEL, J., AND R. VAN LOON
1966 "Canadian attitudes to election expenses," *Studies in Canadian Party Finance*, Ottawa: Queen's Printer.

MEISEL, J.
1972 "Party images in Canada: a report on work in progress," Pp. 63–126 in J. Meisel (ed.) *Working Papers on Canadian Politics*, Montreal: McGill-Queen's University Press.

PHILLIPS, D.
1971 *Knowledge From What?*, Chicago: Rand McNally.

PINEO, P.C., AND J. PORTER
1967 "Occupational prestige in Canada," *The Canadian Review of Sociology and Anthropology* 4 (February):24–40.

PINEO, P.C., AND J.C. GOYDER
1973 "Social class identification of national sub-groups," Pp. 187–196 in J.E. Curtis and W.G. Scott (eds.) *Social Stratification: Canada*, Scarborough: Prentice-Hall.

PORTER, J.
1965 *The Vertical Mosaic*, Toronto: University of Toronto Press.

RINEHART, J.W., AND I.O. OKRAKU
1974 "A study of class consciousness," *Canadian Review of Sociology and Anthropology*, 11 (August):197–213.

RUNCIMAN, W.G.
1972 *Relative Deprivation and Social Justice*, London: Cox and Wyman.

SCHREIBER, E.M., AND G.T. NYGREEN
1970 "Subjective social class in America: 1945–68," *Social Forces* 48 (3):348–356.

SCHUMPETER, J.
1955 *Imperialism and Social Classes*, New York: Kelley.

SCHWARTZ, M.A.
1974 *Politics and Territory: the Sociology of Regional Persistence in Canada*, Montreal: McGill-Queen's Press, 1974.

TUCKER, CHARLES W.
1966 "On working class identification," *American Sociological Review* 31 (6):855–856.
1968 "A comparative analysis of subjective social class: 1945–1963," *Social Forces* 46 (4):508–514.

VAN LOON, R.
1970 "Participation in Canada: the 1965 election," *Canadian Journal of Political Science*, 3 (September):376–399.

WILSON, J.
1968 "Politics and social class in Canada: the case of Waterloo South," *Canadian Journal of Political Science*, 1 (3):288–309.

Further Readings

Space limitations and the availability of rather detailed bibliographies elsewhere argue against an extensive listing of stratification studies here. An especially valuable general bibliography is N.D. Glenn et al., *Social Stratification: A Research Bibliography* (Berkeley: Glendessary Press, 1970). This is an over 400-page classified listing of theoretical and research material published in English since 1940. Part I of the collection has a listing of other general and specialized bibliographies for various countries. For Canada, A.D. Steeves, *A Complete Bibliography in Sociology of Theses and Dissertations Completed at Canadian Universities up to 1970* (Ottawa: Carleton University, Department of Sociology, 1971) is a useful supplemental listing of limited circulation, Canadian sources on social stratification and other sociological topics. M. Kuhn's forthcoming bibliography of "Sociology Dissertations and Theses Completed at Canadian Universities through 1974" (to be published by the *Canadian Journal of Sociology*) will update this list of Canadian M.A. and Ph.D. theses in Sociology. The following give annotated lists of studies of ethnic stratification and class stratification in Quebec, including numerous French language publications: R.D. Lambert, "Sociology of Quebec Nationalism" and cognate titles in the *Canadian Review of Studies in Nationalism: Bibliography*, 2 (1975), pp. 136–171; 1976, 3, pp. 62–113;1977, 4, pp. 153–207; 1978, 5, in press. See also A. Gregorovich, *Canadian Ethnic Groups Bibliography* (Toronto: Ontario Department of the Provincial Secretary and Citizenship, 1972).

The footnotes and references throughout this volume provide a good introductory bibliography of further readings in theory and in Canadian and non-Canadian substantive research. To these we would add the following as highly recommended on selected topics.

INTRODUCTIONS AND OVERVIEWS

J. Porter's *The Vertical Mosaic* (Toronto: University of Toronto Press, 1965). This is the most comprehensive single volume available on macro-level stratification processes in this country, a detailed national level study of the relations between ethnicity and occupational, educational, income and power attainments and of the manner in which elites are formed; companion readings are his "Research Biography of a Macrosociological Study: The Vertical Mosaic" in J.S. Coleman et al., *Macrosociology: Research and Theory* (Boston: Allyn and Bacon, 1970) and *Canadian Social Structure: A Statistical Profile* (Toronto: McClelland and Stewart, 1969). The latter is a compilation of tabular data from census and other sources (e.g., on demographic bases of stratification) with brief commentaries on the tables. Other tabular materials with discussions of the data are provided in W.E. Kalbach and W.W. McVey, *The Demographic Bases of Canadian Society* (Toronto: McGraw-Hill, 1971); Information Canada, *Perspectives Canada: A Compendium of Social Statistics* (Ottawa: 1974); and D. Kubat and D. Thornton, *A Statistical Profile of Canadian Society* (Toronto: McGraw-Hill Ryerson, 1974).

The following studies give partial updates of Porter's *Vertical Mosaic* Study: W. Clement, *The Canadian Corporate Elite* (Toronto: McClelland and Stewart, 1975) and D.

Olsen, "The State Elite in Canadian Society" (unpublished Ph.D. dissertation, Carleton University, 1978) and "The State Elite" in L. Panitch, ed., *The Canadian State: Political Economy and Political Power* (Toronto: University of Toronto Press, 1977), pp. 199–224.

These pieces contain critiques of Porter's study: J.L. Heap, ed., *Everybody's Canada: The Vertical Mosaic Reviewed and Re-examined* (Toronto: Burns and MacEachern, 1974) and H. Rich, "The Vertical Mosaic Revisited: Toward a Macro-Sociology of Canada," *Journal of Canadian Studies* (*JCS*),* 11 (1976).

Introductory discussions of the phenomenon of social stratification in the Canadian context are contained in these introductory sociology books: F. Jones, *An Introduction to Sociology: Six Talks for CBC Radio* (Toronto: Canadian Broadcasting Corporation, 1961); D.W. Rossides, *Society as a Functional Process* (Toronto: McGraw-Hill, 1968); J. Gallagher and R. Lambert, *Social Process and Institution* (Toronto: Holt, Rinehart and Winston, 1971); M. Rioux and Y. Martin, eds., *French-Canadian Society*, Vol. 1 (Toronto: McClelland and Stewart, 1964); G.N. Ramu and S.D. Johnson, *Introduction to Canadian Sociology* (Toronto: Macmillan, 1976); S. Crysdale and C. Beattie, *Sociology Canada: An Introductory Text* (Toronto: Butterworth, 1977); D. Forcese and S. Richer, *Issues in Canadian Sociology* (Scarborough: Prentice-Hall, 1975); H.H. Hiller, *Canadian Society: A Sociological Analysis* (Scarborough: Prentice-Hall, 1976); G.F.N. Fearn, *Canadian Social Organization* (Toronto: Holt, Rinehart and Winston, 1973).

These textbooks focus on overviews, for Canada, of these topics: social stratification, social mobility, social psychological aspects of social stratification, and problems in selected socio-economic inequalities: D. Forcese, *The Canadian Class Structure* (Toronto: McGraw-Hill Ryerson, 1975); L. Tepperman, *Social Mobility in Canada* (Toronto: McGraw-Hill Ryerson, 1975); W.P. Archibald, *Social Psychology as Political Economy* (Toronto: McGraw-Hill Ryerson, 1978); and R. Manzer, *Canada: A Socio-Political Report* (Toronto: McGraw-Hill Ryerson, 1974).

These articles are also interesting from the point of view of the development of studies of social stratification in this country: A. Dubuc, "Problems in the Study of the Stratification of the Canadian Society from 1760 to 1840," *Canadian Historical Association: Report* (1965), pp. 13–29; J. Dofny and M. Rioux, "Social Class in French Canada" (pp. 307–18) and G. Rocher, "Research on Occupations and Social Stratification" (pp. 328–342) in M. Rioux and Y. Martin, eds., *French Canadian Society*, Vol. 1 (Toronto: McClelland and Stewart, 1964); and D.R. Pullman and D.J. Loree, "Conceptions of Class and the Canadian Setting," *International Journal of Comparative Sociology*, 17(1978), pp.164–82.

For presentations on theory and research issues in stratification and mobility studies form the international literature see these textbooks: B. Barber, *Social Stratification: A Comparative Analysis of Structure and Process* (New York: Harcourt, Brace and World, 1957); J.A. Kahl, *The American Class Structure* (New York: Holt, Rinehart and Winston, 1957); L. Reissman, *Class in American Society* (New York: Free Press, 1959); E.E. Bergel, *Social Stratification* (New York: McGraw-Hill, 1962); H. Hodgesn *Social Stratification* (Cambridge, Mass.: Schenkman, 1964); T.E. Lasswell, *Class and Stratum*

---

* These abbreviations are used here for frequently cited periodicals: *CD —Canadian Dimension*; *CJEPS —Canadian Journal of Economics and Political Science*; *CJPS —Canadian Journal of Political Science*; *CJPH —Canadian Journal of Public Health*; *CJS —Canadian Journal of Sociology*; *CRSA —Canadian Review of Sociology and Anthropology*; *JCS —Journal of Canadian Studies*; *RS —Recherches Sociographiques*; *SS – Sociologie et Sociétés*; *AJS —American Journal of Sociology*; *ASR —American Sociological Review*.

(Boston: Houghton Mifflin, 1965); T. Shibutani and K.M. Kwan, *Ethnic Stratification* (New York: Macmillan, 1965); K. Svalastoga, *Social Differentiation* (New York: McKay, 1965); T.B. Bottomore, *Classes in Modern Society* (New York: Pantheon, 1966); G. Lenski, *Power and Privilege* (New York: McGraw-Hill, 1966zg M. Tumin, *Social Stratification* (Englewood Cliffs, N.J.: Prentice-Hall, 1967); K. Mayer and W. Buckley, *Class and Society* (New York: Random House, 1970); S.N. Eisenstadt, *Sociel Differentiation and Social Stratification* (Glenview, Ill.: Scott Foresmann 1971); R.L. Blumberg, *Stratification: Socio-economic and Sexual Inequalities* (Dubuque, Iowa,: Wm. C. Brown, 1978); L. Duberman, *Social Inequality: Class and Caste in America* (New York: J.B. Lippincott, 1976); A. Giddens, *The Class Structure of the Advanced Societies* (London: Hutchinson & Co., 1973); R. Kelsall and H. Kelsall, *Stratification* (London: Longman, 1974); J. Littlejohn, *Social Stratification* (London: George Allen and Unwin, 1972); J. Lopreato and L.E. Hezelrigg, *Class, Conflict and Mobility: Theories and Studies of Class Structure* (San Franisco: Chandellar, 1972); W. McCord and A. McCord, *Power and Equity: An Introduction to Social Stratification* (New York: Praeger, 1977); F. Parkin, *Class Inequality and the Political Order* (London: Paladin Publishing, 1972); L. Reissman, *Inequality in American Society* (Glenview, Ill.: Scott Foresman, 1973); R.A. Rothman, *Inequality and Stratification in the U.S.* (Englewood Cliffs, N.J.: Prentice-Hall, 1978); and H. Stub, *Status Communities in Modern Society* (Hinsdale, Ill.: The Dryden Press, 1972). Also very informative are review and "state of the field" articles by R.W. Hodge and P.M. Siegel ("The Measurement of Social Class"), A.L. Stinchcombe ("The Structure of Stratification Systems") and H. Rodman ("Class Culture") in the *International Encyclopedia of the Social Sciences* (New York: Macmillan and Free Press, 1968), Vol. 15, pp. 288 ff. and Vol. 14, pp. 460 ff.

Useful substantive readings covering aspects of social stratification and social mobility in other societies are included in these edited collections: B. Barber and E.F. Barber, *European Social Class: Stability and Change* (New York: Macmillan, 1965); R. Bendix and S.M. Lipset, *Class, Status and Power: Social Stratification in Comparative Perspective* (New York: Free Press, 1953 and 1966); A. Beteille, *Readings in Social Inequality* (Baltimore, Penguin Books, 1969); P. Blumberg, *The Impact of Social Class* (New York: Crowell, 1972); D.V. Glass, *Social Mobility in Britainu92 (London: Routledge and Kegan Paul, 1954); C.S. Heller, *Structured Social Inequality: A Reader in Comparative Social Stratification* (New York: Macmillan, 1969); J.A. Jackson, *Social Stratification* (Cambridge: Cambridge University Press, 1968); J. Kahl, *Comparative Perspectives on Stratification* (Boston: Little, Brown, 1968); W.E. Lane, *Permanence and Change in Social Class* (Cambridge, Mass.: Schenkman, 1968); E.O. Laumann et al., *The Logic of Social Hierarchies* (Chicago: Markham, 1970); E.O. Laumann, *Social Stratification: Research and Theory for the 1970's* (New York: Bobbs-Merrill Co., 1970); J. Roach et al., *Social Stratification in the United States* (Englewood Cliffs, N.J.: Prentice-Hall, 1969); N.J. Smelser and S.M. Lipset, *Social Structure and Mobility in Economic Development* (Chicago, Aldine, 1966); *Transactions of the Second World Congress of Sociology*, Vol. 2 (1964) and *Transactions of the Third World Congress*, Vols. 3 and 4 (1959); M.M. Tumin, *Readings on Social Stratification* (Englewood Cliffs, N.J.: Prentice-Hall, 1967); A. Coxon and C. Jones, eds., *Social Mobility* (Middlesex: Penguin, 1975); S. Feldman and G. Thielbar, eds., *Life Style Diversity in American Society* (Boston: Little, Brown, 1972); K. Hope, ed., *The Analysis of Social Mobility: Methods and Approaches* (Oxford: Clarendon Press, 1972); R. Lejeune, ed., *Class and Conflict in American Society* (Chicago: Markham, 1972); J. Lopreato and L.S. Lewis, eds., *Social Stratification: A Reader* (New

York: Harper and Row, 1974); F. Parkin, ed., *The Social Analysis of Class Structure* (London: Tavistock Publications, 1974); and P. Stanworth and A. Giddens, eds., *Elites and Power in British Society* (London: Cambridge University Press, 1974). The volumes by Barber and Barber, Bendix and Lipset, Beteille, Heller, Kahl, and the World Congress of Sociology especially provide comparative analyses and juxtaposed studies from several countries.

ON THEORETICAL PERSPECTIVES

On different theoretical perspectives on social stratification discussed in this volume we would call attention to these pieces, from among many useful ones:

Marxian Approaches

W.P. Archibald, *Social Psychology as Political Economy* (Toronto: McGraw-Hill Ryerson, 1978); H. Braverman, *Labor and Monopoly Capital* (New York: Monthly Review Press, 1976); G. Lukacs, *History and Class Consciousness* (Cambridge, Mass.: MIT Press, 1971); M. Mann, *Consciousness and Action among the Western Working Class* (London: Macmillan, 1973); K. Marx, *Capital*, Vol. 1 (New York: New World Paperbacks, 1967); K. Marx, *Selected Writings in Sociology and Social Philosophy*, T. Bottomore and M. Rubel, eds., (New York: McGraw-Hill, 1964); K. Marx and F. Engels, *Manifesto of the Communist Party* (New York: International Publishers, 1932); R. Miliband, *The State in Capitalist Society* (London: Weidenfeld and Nicholson, 1969); C.W. Mills, *The Marxists* (New York: Harcourt Brace, 1948); G. Petrovic, *Marx in the Mid-20th Century* (New York: Anchor, 1967); N. Poulantzas, *Classes in Contemporary Capitalism* (London: New Left Books, 1975); E.O. Wright, "Class Boundaries in Advanced Capitalist Societies," *New Left Review*, 98 (1976), pp. 3–41; and E.O. Wright and L. Perrone, "Marxist Class Categories and Income Equality," *ASR*, 42 (1977), pp. 32–55.

Other Conflict Approaches

W. Clement, "Macro-sociological Approaches toward a 'Canadian Sociology,'" *Alternative Routes*, 1 (1977), pp. 1–37; R. Collins, *Conflict Sociology* (New York: Academic Press, 1975); L.A. Coser, *Continuities in the Study of Social Conflict* (New York: Free Press, 1967); L.A. Coser, *The Functions of Social Conflict* (New York: Free Press, 1956); R. Dahrendorf, *Class and Class Conflict in Industrial Society* (Stanford, Calif.: Stanford University Press, 1959); C.F. Fink, "Some Conceptual Difficulties in the Theory of Social Conflict," *Journal of Conflict Resolution*, 12 (1968), pp. 412–60; W. Gamson, *The Strategy of Social Protest* (Homewood, Ill.: Dorsey Press, 1975); I.L. Horowitz, *The New Sociology: Essays in Social Science and Social Theory* (New York: Oxford University Press, 1964); G. Lenski, *Power and Privilege: A Theory of Stratification* (New York: McGraw-Hill, 1966); C.W. Mills, *The Power Elite* (New York: Oxford Press, 1956); F. Parkin, *Class Inequality and Political Order* (London: Paladin Publishing, 1972); J. Porter, *The Vertical Mosaic* (Toronto: University of Toronto Press, 1965); J.H. Turner, "From Utopia to Where: A Strategy for Reformulating the Dahrendorf Conflict Model," *Social Forces*, 52 (1973), pp. 236–44; J.H. Turner, "Marx and Simmel Revisited: Reassessing the Foundations of Conflict Theory," *Social Forces*, 53 (1975), pp. 618–27; G. Simmel, *Conflict*, trans. K.H. Wolff (Glencoe, Ill.: Free Press, 1955).

Functionalist Approaches

M. Abrahamson, "Functionalism and the Functional Theory of Stratification," *AJS*, 78 (1973), pp. 1239–46; B. Barber, *Social Stratification* (New York: Harcourt, Brace and World, 1957); W. Buckley, "Social Stratification and the Functional Theory of Social Differentiation," *ASR*, 23 (1958), pp. 369–75; K. Davis and W.E. Moore, "Some Principles of Stratification," *ASR*, 10 (1945), pp. 242–47; F.D. Brown and B.D. Grandjean, "The Davis-Moore Theory and Perceptions of Stratification," *Social Forces*, 54 (1975), pp. 166–80; G.A. Huaco, "The Functional Theory of Stratification: Two Decades of Controversy," *Inquiry*, 9 (1966), pp. 215–40; J. Lopreato and L.S. Lewis, "An Analysis of Variables in the Functional Theory of Stratification," *Sociological Quarterly*, 4 (1963), pp. 301–10; S. Ossowski, *Class Structure in the Social Consciousness* (London: Routledge and Kegan Paul, 1963); T. Parsons, "A Revised Analytic Approach to the Theory of Social Stratification" in R. Bendix and S.M. Lipset, eds., *Class, Status and Power* (Glencoe, Ill.: Free Press, 1953), pp. 92–128; A. Stinchcombe, "Some Empirical Consequences of the Davis-Moore Theory of Stratification," *ASR*, 28 (1963), pp. 805–8; A.L. Stinchcombe and T.R. Harris, "Interdependence and Inequality: A Specification of the Davis-Moore Theory," *Sociometry*, 32 (1969), pp. 13–23; M.M. Tumin, "Some Principles of Stratification: A Critical Analysis," *ASR*, 18 (1953), pp. 387–94; D.H. Wrong, "The Functional Theory of Stratification: Some Neglected Considerations," *ASR*, 24 (1959), pp. 772–82; W. Wesolowski, "Some Notes on the Functional Theory of Stratification," *Polish Sociological Bulletin*, 3–4 (1962), pp. 28–38.

SELECTED CANADIAN STUDIES OF STRATIFICATION DIMENSIONS

The following works, selected from among many interesting publications over the past several years, are on dimensions and correlates of stratification and social mobility in this country. These studies are generally listed under headings here in terms of their primary "dependent variable," i.e. the phenomena or issues to be explained. However, many of the studies are wide-ranging in their concerns, often touching on more than one of the topics listed here. In these cases, the studies' titles are generally not repeated under other headings, so some browsing across the readings in different sections of the list would be in order.

Classes

W.P. Archibald, *Social Psychology as Political Economy* (Toronto: McGraw-Hill Ryerson, 1978); W. Clement, *The Canadian Corporate Elite* (Toronto: McClelland and Stewart, 1975); W. Clement, *Continental Corporate Power: Economic Linkages Between Canada and the United States* (Toronto: McClelland and Stewart, 1977); W. Clement, "The Changing Structure of the Canadian Economy," *CRSA* (Special Issue: "Aspects of Canadian Society," 1974), pp. 3–27; C.J. Cuneo, "A Class Perspective on Regionalism" in D. Glenday, H. Guindon and A. Turowitz, eds., *Modernization and the Canadian State* (Toronto: Macmillan, 1978), pp. 133–36; D. Drache, "Rediscovering Canadian Political Economy," *JCS*, 11 (1976), pp. 3–17; P. Fournier, *The Quebec Establishment: The Ruling Class and the State* (Montreal: Black Rose Books, 1976); G.S. Kealy and P. Warrian, eds., *Essays in Canadian Working Class History* (Toronto: McClelland and Stewart, 1976); L.A. Johnson, "The Development of Class in Canada in the Twentieth Century" (pp. 141–83), C. Lipton, "Canadian Unionism" (pp. 101–20), G. Teeple, "Land, Labour and Capital in Pre-Confederation Canada" (pp. 43–66), and several other pieces in G. Teeple, ed., *Capitalism and the National Question* (Toronto: University of Toronto Press, 1972); L. Panitch, ed., *The Canadian State* (Toronto: University of Toronto Press, 1977); R.M. Laxer, ed., *The Political Economy of Dependency* (Toronto: McClelland and Stewart, 1973); Robert Laxer, *Canada's Unions* (Toronto: James Lorimer and Company, 1976); S.H. Milner and H. Milner, *The Decolonization of Quebec* (Toronto: McClelland and Stewart, 1973); R.T. Naylor, "Dominion of Capital: Canada and International Investment" in A. Kontos, ed., *Domination* (Toronto: University of Toronto Press, 1975), pp. 33-88; T. Naylor, *The History of Canadian Business, 1867-1914*, Vol. 1, *The Banks and Finance Capital* and Vol. 2, *Industrial Development* (Toronto: James Lorimer and Company, 1975); J. Rinehart, *The Tyranny of Work* (Toronto: Longmans, 1975). See also frequent articles in these regularly appearing periodicals: *Canadian Dimension* (Winnipeg, Manitoba), *The Last Post* (Toronto, Ontario), *Our Generation* (Montreal, Quebec), and *This Magazine is about Schools* (Toronto, Ontario).

Income and Wealth

I. Adams *et al.*, *The Real Poverty Report* (Edmonton: M.C. Hurtig, 1971); R.C. Baetz, "Causes of Poverty," *Canadian Labour*, 14 (1969), pp. 18-23; G. Belanger, "Housing Policy and the Poor" in D. Glenday, H. Guindon and A. Turowitz, eds., *Modernization and the Canadian State* (Toronto: Macmillan, 1978), pp. 383-95; S.D. Clark, *The New Urban Poor* (Toronto: McGraw-Hill Ryerson, 1978); W. Clement, *The Canadian Corporate Elite* (Toronto: McClelland and Stewart, 1975); W. Clement, *Continental Corporate Power: Economic Linkages Between Canada and the United States* (Toronto: McClelland and Stewart, 1977); T. Copp, *The Anatomy of Poverty: The Conditions of the Working Class in Montreal, 1897-1929* (Toronto: McClelland and Stewart, 1974); R. Hamilton and M. Pinard, "Poverty in Canada: Illusion and Reality," *CRSA* (1977), pp. 247-52; J. Harp and J. Hofley, eds., *Poverty in Canada* (Scarborough: Prentice-Hall, 1971); L.A. Johnson, "Illusions or Realities: Hamilton and Pinard's Approach to Poverty," *CRSA*, 14 (1977), pp. 341-46; L. Johnson, *Poverty in Wealth: The Capitalist Labour Market and Income Distribution in Canada* (Toronto: New Hogtown Press, 1974); C.M. Lanphier and R.N. Morris, "Structural Aspects of Differences in Income between Anglophones and Francophones," *CRSA*, 11 (1974), pp. 53-66; N.H. Lithwick, "Poverty in Canada: Some Recent Empirical Findings," *JCS*, 6 (1971), pp. 27-41; K. Levitt, *Silent Surrender: The Multinational Corporation in Canada* (Toronto: Macmillan, 1971); W.E. Mann, ed., *Poverty and Social Policy in Canada* (Toronto: Copp Clark, 1970); R. Manzer, *Canada: A Socio-Political Report* (Toronto: McGraw-Hill Ryerson, 1974); A.M. Maslove, *The Pattern of Taxation in Canada* (Ottawa: Economic Council of Canada, 1973); J.R. Podoluk, *Incomes of Canadians* (Ottawa: Dominion Bureau of Statistics, 1968); A. Raynauld *et al.*, "Structural Aspects of Differences in Income between Anglophones and Francophones: A Reply," *CRSA*, 12 (1975), pp. 221-28; A.H. Richmond, "The Standard of Living of Post-War Immigrants in Canada," *CRSA*, 2 (1965), pp. 41-51; T.J. Ryan, *Poverty and the Child: A Canadian Study* (Toronto: McGraw-Hill Ryerson, 1972); M.A. Tremblay and G. Fortin, *Les Comportiments Economiques de la Famille Salariée du Québec* (Montreal: Les Presses Universitaires de l'Université Laval, 1964).

Power and Authority

B. Baldus, "Social Control in Capitalist Societies: An Examination of 'the Problem of Order' in Liberal Democracies," *CJS*, 2 (1977), pp. 247-62; E. Baldwin, "The Mass Media and the Corporate Elite: A Reanalysis of the Overlap between the Media Economic Elites," *CJS*, 2 (1977), pp. 1-25; E. Baldwin, "On Methodological and Theoretical

'Muddles' in Clement's Media Study," *CJS*, 2 (1977), pp. 215–22; G. Bourassa, "The Political Elite of Montreal: From Aristocracy to Democracy" in C.D. Feldman and M.E. Goldrick, eds., *Politics and Government of Urban Canada* (Toronto: Methuen, 1969); P. Clarke, "Leadership Succession Among the Hutterites," *CRSA*, 14 (1977), pp. 294–302; S.D. Clark, "The Attack on the Authority Structure of the Canadian Society," *Transactions of the Royal Society of Canada, Series IV*, Vol. 14 (1978), pp. 3–15; S.D. Clark, "The Position of the French-Speaking Population in Northern Industrial Communities" in R. Ossenberg, ed., *Canadian Society: Pluralism, Change and Conflict* (Scarborough: Prentice-Hall, 1971), pp. 62–85; W. Clement, "Overlap of the Media and Economic Elites," *CJS*, 2 (1977), pp. 205–14; R. Collison, "War of the Elites: Two Factions Duel for Power in the New Quebec," *Saturday Night* (May, 1978), pp. 19–25; B.H. Erickson and P.R. Kringas, "The Small World of Politics or Seeking Elites from the Bottom Up," *CRSA*, 12 (1975), pp. 585–93; J.C. Falardeau, "Des elites traditionelles aux elites nouvelles," *RS*, 7 (1966), pp. 131–45; H. Guindon, "Quebec Notes," *This Magazine is About Schools*, 11, 5 (1977), pp. 28–31; C.W.M. Hart, "Industrial Relations Research and Social Theory," *CJEPS*, 15 (1949), pp. 53–75, a study of unions and other powerful groups in Windsor, Ontario; G. Horowitz, *Canadian Labour in Politics* (Toronto: University of Toronto Press, 1968); J. Jackson, "A Study of French-English Relations in an Ontario Community," *CRSA* 4 (1966), pp. 117–31; C.J. Jansen, "Leadership in the Toronto Italian Ethnic Community," *International Migration Review*, 4 (1969); H. Kaplan, *Urban Political Systems* (Columbia University Press, 1967); M. Kelner, "Changes in Toronto's Elite Structure" in W.E. Mann, ed., *The Underside of Toronto* (Toronto: McClelland and Stewart, 1970), pp. 197–204; M. Kelner, "Ethnic Penetration into Toronto's Elite Structure," *CRSA*, 7 (1970), pp. 128–37; A. Kontos, ed., *Domination* (Toronto: University of Toronto Press, 1975); R. Laskin, *Leadership of Voluntary Organizations in a Saskatchewan Town* (Saskatoon: University of Saskatchewan, Saskatchewan Center for Community Studies, 1962); R. Laskin and S. Phillett, "An Integrative Analysis of Voluntary Association Leadership and Reputational Influence," *Sociological Inquiry*, 35 (1965), pp. 176–85; J. Lorimer, *The Real World of City Politics* (Toronto: James Lewis and Samuel, 1970); T.H. Marshall, "Class and Power in Canada," *CRSA*, 2 (1965), pp. 215–21 (critical comments on how power is studied in *The Vertical Mosaic*); N.O. Matthews, "Small Town Power and Politics" in L.D. Feldman and M.D. Goldrick, eds., *Politics and Government of Urban Canada* (Toronto: Methuen, 1959), pp. 134–52; K. McRae, ed., *Consociational Democracy: Political Accommodation in Segmented Societies* (Toronto: McClelland and Stewart, 1974); H. Milner, *Politics in the New Quebec* (Toronto: McClelland and Stewart, 1978); P. Montiminy, "Les grand thèmes de l'étude du pouvoir au Québec," *RSJ*, 7 (1966), pp. 245–50; H.B. Neatlay, *The Politics of Chaos: Canada in the Thirties* (Toronto: Macmillan, 1972); R. Ogmundson, "The Sociology of Power and Politics: An Introduction to the Canadian Polity" in G.N. Ramu and S.D. Johnson, eds., *Introduction to Canadian Society: Sociological Analysis* (Toronto: Macmillan, 1976), pp. 157–211; L. Panitch, *The Canadian State: Political Economy and Political Power* (Toronto: University of Toronto Press, 1977); Robert L. Perry, *Galt, U.S.A.: The 'American Presence' in a Canadian City* (Toronto: Maclean-Hunter Limited, 1971); D. Posgate and K. McRoberts, *Quebec: Social Change and Political Crisis* (Toronto: McClelland and Stewart, 1976); G. Rocher, "Multiplication des elites et changement social au Canada Francais," *Revue de l'Institut de Sociologie*, 1 (1968), pp. 79–94; A.D. Ross, "The Social Control of Philanthropy," *AJS*, 58 (1953), pp. 451–60; C. Taylor, *The Pattern of Power* (Toronto: McClelland and Stewart, 1970); P. Usher, "Hinterland Culture Shock," *CD*, 7,8 (1972), pp. 26–31.

Other Status Dimensions

Occupations and Occupational Prestige

T.R. Balakrishnan and G.T. Jarvis, "Socioeconomic Differentiation in Urban Canada," *CRSA*, 13 (1976), pp. 204–16; E.H. Baxter, "Children's and Adolescents' Perceptions of Occupational Prestige," *CRSA*, 13 (1976), pp. 229–38; B.R. Blishen, "Social Class and Opportunity in Canada," *CRSA*, 7 (1970), pp. 110–27, B.R. Blishen, "A Socio-economic Index for Occupations in Canada," *CRSA*, 4 (1967), pp. 41–53; B.R. Blishen and H.A. McRoberts, "A Revised Socio-economic Index for Occupations in Canada," *CRSA*, 13 (1976), pp. 71–9; J. Brazeau, "Language Differences and Occupation Experience," *CJEPS*, 24 (1958), pp. 532–40; H. Burshtyn, "A Factor Analytic Study of Occupational Prestige Ratings," *CRSA*, 5 (1968), pp. 156–80; L. D'Arcy, "Occupational Specialization vs. Homogeneity: A Canadian Profile," *Urban Affairs Quarterly*, 3 (1967–68), pp. 21–36; G. Fortin and E. Gosselin, "La professionalisation du travail en forêt," *RS*, 1 (1960), pp. 33–60; L.N. Guppy and J.L. Siltanen, "A Comparison of the Allocation of Male and Female Occupational Prestige," *CRSA*, 14 (1977), pp. 320–30; O. Hall, "The Canadian Division of Labour Revisited" in J. Curtis and W. Scott, eds., *Social Stratification: Canada* (first edition) (Scarborough: Prentice-Hall, 1973), pp. 46–54; O. Hall and B. McFarlane, *Transition From School to Work* (Ottawa: Queen's Printer, 1963); A.A. Hunter, "A Comparative Analysis of Anglophone–Francophone Occupational Prestige Structures in Canada," *CJS*, 2 (1977), pp. 179–94; W. Johnson, *Working in Canada* (Montreal: Black Rose Books, 1975); W.E. Kalbach and W.W. McVey, "Occupational Characteristics," Ch. 10 in their *The Demographic Bases of Canadian Society* (Toronto: McGraw-Hill, 1971); M.B. Katz, "Social Structure in Hamilton, Ontario" in S. Thernstrom and R. Sennett, eds., *Nineteenth Century Cities* (New Haven, Yale University Press, 1969), pp. 209–44; J.N. McCrorie, "Discussion on the Farmer as a Social Class" in M.A. Tremblay and W.J. Anderson, eds., *Rural Canada in Transition* (Ottawa: Agricultural Economics Research Council of Canada, 1966); N. Meltz, *Changes in the Occupational Composition of the Canadian Labour Force* (Ottawa: Department of Labour Occasional Paper, No. 2, Queen's Printer, 1965); R.N. Morris and C.M. Lanphier, *Three Scales of Inequality; Perspectives on French-English Relations* (Don Mills: Longman Canada, 1977); *Occupational Trends in Canada, 1931–61* (Ottawa: Canadian Department of Labour, Research Program on Training of Skilled Manpower, No. 11, 1963); P. Pineo *et al.*, "The 1971 Census and the Socioeconomic Classification of Occupations," *CRSA*, 14 (1977), pp. 91–102; Report of the Royal Commission on Bilingualism and Biculturalism, Book 3, *The World of Work* (Ottawa: Queen's Printer, 1969); J.W. Rinehart, "Contradictions of Work-related Attitudes and Behaviour: An Interpretation," *CRSA*, 15 (1978), pp. 1–15; J.W. Rinehart, *The Tyranny of Work* (Toronto: Longman Canada, 1975); G. Rocher, "Les recherches sur les occupations et la stratification sociale," *RS*, 3 (1962), pp. 173–88, also in Rioux and Martin, *ibid*; J. Tuckman, "Social Status of Occupations in Canada," *Canadian Journal of Psychology*, 1 (1947), pp. 71–74; T.R. Warburton and B.R. Blishen, "Canadians, Immigrants and Occupational Status: A Comment (and a Rejoinder)," *CRSA*, 10 (1973), pp. 366–72.

Occupational Mobility and Mobility Aspirations

Department of Educational Research, *Atkinson Study Reports* (Toronto: 1957–1963), a series of ten reports on occupational and educational aspirations and achievements of Grade 13 students in 1955–56; C. Beattie, *Minority Men in a Majority Setting* (Toronto:

McClelland and Stewart, 1975); C. Beattie and B.G. Spenser, "Career Attainment in Canadian Bureaucracies: Unscrambling the Effects of Age, Seniority, Education, and Ethnolinguistic Factors on Salary," *AJS*, 77 (1971), pp. 472–90; R. Breton, *Social and Academic Factors in the Career Decision of Canadian Youth* (Ottawa: Queen's Printer, 1972); R. Breton and J.C. McDonald, "Occupational Preferences of Canadian High School Students" in B.R. Blishen et al., *Canadian Society* (Toronto: Macmillan, 1968); C.J. Cuneo and J.E. Curtis, "Social Ascription in the Educational and Occupational Status Attainment of Urban Canadians," *CRSA*, 10 (1975), pp. 6–24; J. Dofny and M. Garon-Audy, "Mobilites Professionelles au Quebec, 1954 et 1964," *SS*, 1 (1969), pp. 277–301 or "Occupational Mobility in Quebec, 1954 and 1964" in C. Beattie and S. Crysdale, eds., *Sociology Canada: Readings* (second edition) (Toronto: Butterworths, 1977), pp. 241–63; E. Harvey and C.R. Harvey, "Adolescence, Social Class and Occupational Expectations," *CRSA*, 7 (1970), pp. 138–47; J.D. House, "Entrepreneurial Career Patterns of Residential Real Estate Agents in Montreal," *CRSA*, 11 (1974), pp. 110–24; Y. De Jocas and G. Rocher, "Inter-Generation Occupational Mobility in the Province of Quebec," *CJEPS*, 23 (1967), pp. 58–66; F.E. Jones, "The Social Origins of High School Teachers in a Canadian City," *CJEPS*, 29 (1963), pp. 529–35; J.F. Myles and A.B. Sorensen, "Elite and Status Attainment Models of Inequality of Opportunity," *CJS*, 1 (1975), pp. 75–90; R. Pavalko and D. Bishop, "Peer Influence on the College Plans of Canadian High School Students," *CRSA*, 3 (1966), pp. 191–200; P.C. Pineo, "Social Mobility in Canada: The Current Picture," *Sociological Focus*, 9 (1976), pp. 109–23; J. Porter, "The Future of Upward Social Mobility," *ASR*, 33 (1968), pp. 5–19; D. Smith and L. Tepperman, "Changes in the Canadian Business and Legal Elites, 1870–1970," *CRSA*, 11 (1974), pp. 97–109; M.D. Smith and F. Diamond, "Career Mobility in Professional Hockey" in R.S. Gruneau and J.G. Albinson, eds., *Canadian Sport: Sociological Perspectives* (Don Mills, Ontario: Addison-Wesley, 1976z, pp. 275–94; L. Tepperman, "Demographic Aspects of Career Mobility," *CRSA*, 12 (1975), pp. 163–76; L. Tepperman, "The Natural Disruptions of Dynasties," *CRSA*, 9 (1972), pp. 111–134 (intergenerational mobility in 61 originally prominent families of Ontario over five generations); L. Tepperman, "A Simulation of Social Mobility in Industrial Society," *CRSA*, 13 (1976), pp. 26–42; A.H. Turrittin, "Social Mobility in Canada: A Comparison of Three Provincial Studies," *CRSA* (special issue, "Aspects of Canadian Society") (1974), pp. 163–86; five monographs on factors related to occupational and educational aspirations of Manitoba high school students and dropouts: L.B. Siemens, *The Influence of Selected Family Factors on the Educational and Occupational Aspiration Levels of High School Boys and Girls*; D. Forcese and L.B. Siemens, *School-Related Factors and Aspiration Levels of Manitoba Senior High School Students*; L.B. Siemens and J.E.W. Jackson, *Educational Plans and Their Fulfilment*; L.B. Siemens and L. Driedger, *Some Rural-Urban Differences between Manitoba High School Students*, published by the Faculty of Agriculture and Home Economics (Winnipeg: University of Manitoba, 1965); and E.F. Sharp and G. Kristjanson, *Manitoba High School Students and Dropouts* (Winnipeg: Manitoba Department of Agriculture); the entire issue of *Sociologie et Sociétés*, 8, 2 (1976).

Educational Status

R. Breton, *Social and Academic Factors in the Career Decisions of Canadian Youth* (Ottawa: Queen's Printer, 1972); R.A. Carlton et al., eds., *Education, Change, and Society: A Sociology of Canadian Education* (Toronto: Gage, 1977); S. Crysdale, "Workers' Families and Education in a Downtown Community" in K. Ishwaran, ed., *The Canadian Family*, rev. ed. (Toronto: Holt, Rinehart and Winston, 1976), pp. 324–340;

Educational Attainment in Canada: Some Regional and Social Aspects, Special Labour Force Study #7 (Ottawa: Dominion Bureau of Statistics, 1968); S. Gilbert and H. McRoberts, "Academic Stratification and Education Plans: A Re-Assessment," *CRSA*, 14 (1977), pp. 34–47; O. Hall and R. Carleton, *Basic Skills at School and Work: The Study of Albertown* (Toronto: Ontario Economic Council, 1977); E. Harvey, "Accessibility to Post-Secondary Education," *University Affairs* (1977), pp. 10–11; E. Harvey, *Education and Employment of Arts and Science Graduates: The Last Decade in Toronto* (Toronto: Queen's Printer, 1972); E. Harvey, *Educational Systems and the Labour Market* (Don Mills: Longman, 1974); E.B. Harvey and I. Charmer, "Social Mobility and Occupational Attainments of University Graduates," *CRSA*, 12 (1975), pp. 134–49; W.E. Kalbach and W.W. McVey, "Education Attainment," Chap. 8 in *The Demographic Bases of Canadian Society* (Toronto: McGraw-Hill, 1971); A.J. King, "Ethnicity and School Adjustment," *CRSA*, 5 (1968), pp. 81–84; W.B.W. Martin and A.J. Macdonell, *Canadian Education: A Sociological Analysis* (Scarborough: Prentice-Hall, 1978); D. Myers, ed., *The Failure of Educational Reform in Canada* (Toronto: McClelland and Stewart, 1973); R. Pavalko, "Socio-economic Background, Ability and the Allocation of Students," *CRSA* 4 (1967), pp. 250–57; R.M. Pike, *Who Gets to University and Why* (Ottawa: Association of Universities and Colleges of Canada, 1970); M.R. Porter et al., *Does Money Matter? Prospects for Higher Education* (Toronto: Institute for Behavioural Research, York University, 1973); J. Porter, "Post-industrialism, Post-nationalism and Post-secondary Education," *Canadian Public Administration* 104 (1971), pp. 32–50; J. Porter et al., *Toward 2000: The Future of Post-Secondary Education in Ontario* (Toronto: McClelland and Stewart, 1970); Report of the Royal Commission on Bilingualism and Biculturalism, Book II, *Education* (Ottawa: Queen's Printer, 1968); C.J. Richardson, "Education and Social Mobility: Changing Conceptions of the Role of the Educational Systems," *CJS*, 4 (1977), pp. 417–34; J.C.R. Rowley and N. Leckie, "A Further Look at Determinants of Educational Achievement," *CJS*, 4 (1977), pp. 339–54; E. Smallett, "Schools and the Illusion of Choice: The Middle Class and the 'Open' Classroom" in G. Martell, ed., *The Politics of the Canadian Public School* (Toronto: James Lewis and Samuel, 1974); J. Synge, "The Sociology of Canadian Education" in G.N. Ramu and S. Johnson, eds., *Introduction to Canadian Society: Sociological Analysis* (Toronto: Macmillan, 1976), pp. 401–57; Z. Zsigmund et al., *Future Trends in Enrolment and Manpower Supply in Ontario* (Ottawa: Statistics Canada, Education, Science and Culture Division, April, 1977).

Ethnicity and Race, French-English

R. Breton and H. Roseborough, "Ethnic Differences in Status" in B.R. Blishen et al., eds., *Canadian Society* (Toronto: Macmillan, 1968); R.M. Burns, ed., *One Country or Two?* (Montreal: McGill-Queen's University Press, 1971); R. Cook, *The Maple Leaf Forever* (Toronto: Macmillan, 1971); J.E. Curtis and J.W. Loy, "Race/Ethnicity and Relative Centrality of Playing Positions in Team Sports," *Exercise and Sport Sciences Reviews*, 6, forthcoming; R. Drummond, "Nationalism and Ethnic Demands: Some Speculations on a Congenial Note," *CJPS*, 10 (1977), pp. 375–90; F. Elkin, "Ethnic Revolutions and Occupational Dilemmas," *International Journal of Comparative Sociology*, 13 (1972), pp. 48–54; F. Elkin, *Rebels and Colleagues: Advertising and Social Change in French Canada* (Montreal: McGill-Queen's University Press, 1973); J.L. Elliot, ed., *Minority Canadians*, Vol. 2 (Scarborough: Prentice-Hall, 1971); P. Garigue, "French Canada: A Case Study in Sociological Analysis," *CRSA*, 1 (1964), pp. 186–91; G.L. Gold and M.A. Tremblay, *Communities and Culture in French Canada* (Toronto:

Holt, Rinehart and Winston, 1973); H. Guindon, "The Modernization of Quebec and the Legitimacy of the Canadian State" in D. Glenday, H. Guindon, and A. Turowitz, eds., *Modernization and the Canadian State* (Toronto: Macmillan, 1978), pp. 280-96; J. Harp and J. Curtisn "Linguistic Communities and Sociology" in J.E. Gallagher and R.D. Lambert, eds., *Social Process and Institutions: The Canadian Case* (Toronto: Holt, Rinehart and Winston, 1971), pp. 57-70; E.C. Hughes, *French Canada in Transition* (Chicago: University of Chicago Press, 1943); J.D. Jackson, *Community and Conflict: A Study of French-English Relations in Ontario* (Toronto: Holt, Rinehart and Winston, 1975); R.J. Joy, *Languages in Conflict* (Toronto: McClelland and Stewart, 1972); N. Keyfitz, "Canadians and Canadiens," *Queen's Quarterly*, 70 (1969), pp. 163-82; L. Laczko, "Feelings of Threat among English-Speaking Quebeckers" in D. Glenday, H. Guindon, and A. Turowitz, eds., *Modernization and the Canadian State* (Toronto: Macmillan, 1978), pp. 280-96; R.D. Lambert and J.E. Curtis, "Nationality and Professional Activity Correlates among Social Scientists," *CRSA*, 10 (1973), pp. 62-80; W.E. Lambert, "What are They Like, These Canadians," *The Canadian Psychologist*, 11 (1970), pp. 303-33; P. Lamy, "Bilingualism and Identity" in J. Haas and W. Shaffir, eds., *Shaping Identity in Canadian Society* (Scarborough, Ontario: Prentice-Hall, 1978); S. Lieberson, *Language and Ethnic Relations in Canada* (Toronto: John Wiley, 1970); R.N. Morris and C.M. Lanphier, *Three Scales of Inequality: Perspectives on French-English Relations* (Toronto: Longman, 1977); R.J. Ossenberg, "The Conquest Revisited: Another Look at Canadian Dualism," *CRSA*, 4 (1967), pp. 201-18; E. Paris, "The Bilingual Problem: How Do You Identify Yourself to Yourself?" *Saturday Night* (February, 1970), pp. 24-26; M. Rioux, *Quebec in Question* (Toronto: James Lewis and Samuel, 1971); M. Rioux and Y. Martin, eds., *French-Canadian Society*, Vol. 1 (Toronto: McClelland and Stewart, 1964); Royal Commission on Bilingualism and Biculturalism, *Preliminary Report* (1965) and Volume I of *Final Report* (Ottawa: Queen's Printer, 1967); N.W. Taylor, "French Canadians as Industrial Entrepreneurs," *CJPS*, 68 (1960), pp. 37-52. See also the *Journal of Canadian Studies*, 12 (1977) for a number of articles on Quebec separatism.

Ethnicity and Race, Other Immigrant Groups

G. Anderson and D. Higgs, *A Future to Inherit: The Portuguese Communites of Canada* (Toronto: McClelland and Stewart, 1976); E. Baar, "Issei, Nisei, and Sansei" in D. Glenday, H. Guindon, and A. Turowitz, eds., *Modernization and the Canadian State* (Toronto: Macmillan, 1978), pp. 335-55; J.W. Berry et al., *Multi-culturalism and Ethnic Attitudes in Canada* (Ottawa: Minister of Supply and Services, 1977); R.M. Bienvenue, "Intergroup Relations: Ethnicity in Canada" in GMN. Ramu and S.D. Johnson, eds., *Introduction to Canadian Society: Sociological Analysis* (Toronto: Macmillan, 1976), pp. 212-51; P. Cappon, "The Green Paper: Immigration is a Tool of Profit," *Canadian Ethnic Studies*, 7 (1975), pp. 50-54; D.H. Clairmont and D.W. Magill, *Africville: Life and Death of a Canadian Black Community* (Toronto: McClelland and Stewart, 1974); A.G. Darroch and W. Marston, "The Social Class Bases of Ethnic Residential Segregation: The Canadian Case," *AJS*, 78 (1971), pp. 491-510; L. Driedger, ed., *The Canadian Ethnic Mosaic: A Quest for Identity* (Toronto: McClelland and Stewart, 1978); L. Driedger, "Toward a Perspective on Canadian Pluralism: Ethnic Idsntity in Winnipeg," *CJS*, 2 (1977), pp. 77-96; K. Duncan, "Irish Famine Immigration and the Social Structure of the Canadian West," *CRSA*, 2 (1965), pp. 19-40; J. Elliott, ed., *Minority Canadians*, Vol. 2 (Scarborough: Prentice-Hall, 1970); F. Henry, *Forgotten Canadians: The Blacks of Nova Scotia* (Don Mills, Ont.: Longman, 1973); D.R. Hughes and E. Kallen, *The Anatomy of*

Racism: Canadian Dimensions (Montreal: Harvest House, 1974); K. Ishwaran, *The Canadian Family* (Toronto: Holt, Rinehart and Winston, 1978) for research on class and ethnic group differences in family life; W.G. Marston, "Social Class Segregation within Ethnic Groups in Toronto," *CRSA* 6 (1959), pp. 66–79; K.G. O'Bryan, J.G. Reitz, and O.M. Kuplowska, *Non-Official Languages: A Study in Canadian Multiculturalism* (Ottawa: Ministry of Supply and Services, 1976); P. Pineo, "The Social Standing of Ethnic and Racial Groupings," *CRSA*, 14 (1977), pp. 147 57; J. Porter, "Dilemmas and Contradictions of a Multi-Ethnic Society," *Transactions of the Royal Society of Canada*, Series IV, Vol. 10 (1972), pp. 193–205; J. Porter, "Ethnic Pluralism in Canadian Perspective" in D.P. Moynihan and N. Glazer, eds., *Ethnicity* (Cambridge, Mass.: Harvard University Press, 1975), Chap. 9; J. Reitz, "Language and Ethnic Community Survival," *CRSA* (special issue: "Aspects of Canadian Society") (1974), pp. 104–22; Report of the Royal Commission on Bilingualism and Biculturalism, Book IV, *The Cultural Contribution of the Other Ethnic Groups* (Ottawa: Queen's Printer, 1969); A.H. Richmond, *Immigrants and Ethnic Groups in Metropolitan Toronto* (Ethnic Research Programme, York University, 1967); F.G. Vallee et al., "Ethnic Assimilation and Differentiation in Canada," *CJEPS*, 23 (1957), pp. 540–49; F.G. Vallee, "Multi-Ethnic Societies: The Issues of Identity and Inequality" in D. Forcese and S. Richer, eds., *Issues in Canadian Society: An Introduction to Sociology* (Scarborough: Prentice-Hall, 1975), pp. 162–202; J. White and J.S. Frideres, "Race Prejudice and Racism: A Distinction," *CRSA*, 14 (1977), pp. 81–90; R.W. Winks, *The Blacks in Canada* (New Haven: Yale University Press, 1971).

Ethnicity and Race, Native Peoples

M. Davis and J.F. Krauter, *The Other Canadians: Profiles of Six Minorities* (Toronto: Methuen, 1971); J.L. Elliott, ed., *Minority Canadians*, Vol. 1 (Scarborough: Prentice-Hall, 1971); J. Frideres, eds., *Canada's Indians: Contemporary Conflicts* (Scarborough: Prentice-Hall, 1974); J.F. Krauter and M. Davis, *Minority Canadians: Ethnic Groups* (Toronto: Methuen, 1978); E.D. Patterson II, *The Canadian Indian: A History Since 1500* (Don Mills: Collier-Macmillan, 1972); D.H. Stymeist, *Ethnics and Indians: Social Relations in a Northwestern Ontario Town* (Toronto: Peter Martin Associates, 1975); F.G. Vallee, *Kabloona and Eskimo in the Central Keewatin* (Ottawa: Canadian Research Centre for Anthropology, St. Paul's University, 1967).

Sex and Age Stratification

A.M. Ambert, *Sex Structure*, 2nd ed. (Toronto: Longman, 1975); K. Archibald, *Sex and the Public Service* (Ottawa: Information Canada, 1970); P. Armstrong and H. Armstrong, *The Double Ghetto* (Toronto: McClelland and Stewart, 1978); M. Benston, *The Political Economy of Women's Liberation* (Toronto: New Hogtown Press, 1969); G.C.A. Cook, ed., *Opportunity for Choice: A Goal for Women in Canada* (Ottawa: Statistics Canada, 1976); R. Cook and W. Mitchinson, eds., *The Proper Sphere: Women's Place in Canadian Society* (Toronto: Oxford University Press, 1969); MM Eichler, "A Review of Selected Recent Literature on Women," *CRSA*, 9 (1972), pp. 86–96; M. Eichler, "Women as Personal Dependants," D. Smith, "Women, the Family and Corporate Capitalism," and other pieces in M. Stephenson, ed., *Women in Canada* (Toronto: New Press, 1973); S.B. Kohl, *Working Together: Women and Family in Southwestern Saskatchewan* (Toronto: Holt, Rinehart and Winston, 1978); R.D. Lambert, *Sex Role Imagery in Children*, Royal Commission on the Status of Women, Study No. 6 (Ottawa: Information Canada, 1971);

P. Marchak, "Women Workers and White Collar Unions," *CRSA*, 10 (1973), pp. 187–200; S. Ostry, *The Female Worker in Canada* (Dominion Bureau of Statistics, 1968); *Report of the Royal Commission on the Status of Women in Canada* (Ottawa: Information Canada, 1970); E.M. Schreiber, "The Social Bases of Opinions on Woman's Role in Canada," *CJS*, 1 (1975), pp. 61–74; *Women at Work: Ontario 1850–1930* (Toronto: Canadian Women's Educational Press, 1974). See also *Sociologie et Societes*, Volume 6 (1974), for a number of articles on women and work. The *CRSA*, 12 (1975) is also entirely devoted to studies of women in the Canadian social structure. On age stratification see "Lowering the Boom: How the Horde of Postwar Babies Will Turn Us Into a Geriatric Society," *Weekend*, 25, 20 (1976); L. Auerback and A. Gerber, "Implications of the Changing Age Structure of the Canadian Population," *Perception* 2 (Ottawa: Service Council of Canada, 1976); D.J. Baum, *The First Plateau: The Betrayal of Our Older Citizens* (Toronto: Burns and MacEachern, 1974); M. Brownstone, *Economic Needs and Employment of the Aged* (Ottawa: Canadian Welfare Council, 1966); Economics Research Group, *State of the Art: Research on the Elderly, 1964–72* (Ottawa: Central Mortgage and Housing Corporation, 1972); J. Legare and B. Desjardins, "La Situation des Personnes Âgées au Canada," *CRSA*, 13 (1976), pp. 321–363; R.A. Lucas, "Some Dimensions of Adult Status," *CRSA*, 3 (1966), pp. 90–103; M.W. Riley et al., *A Sociology of Age Stratification*, Vol. III of *Aging and Society* (New York: Russell Sage Foundation, 1971) — theory of age stratification and cross-national research findings on correlates of age differences.

SELECTED CORRELATES AND CONSEQUENCES OF SOCIAL STRATIFICATION

Health, Illness, and Mortality

A. Billette, "Les Inégalités Sociales de Mortalité au Québec," *RS*, 18 (1977), pp. 514–30; A. Billette, "Santé, classes sociales et politiques rédistributives," *SS*, 9 (1977), pp. 76–92; D. Cook et al., "Cancer Morbidity in National-Origin Subgroups of the Ontario Population," *CJPH*, 63 (1972), pp. 120–24; K.R. Davidson, "Conceptions of Illness and Health Practices in a Nova Scotia Community," *CJPH*, 61 (1976), pp. 232–42; Government of Canada, *A New Perspective on the Health of Canadians: A Working Document* (Ottawa: Information Canada, 1974); R.W. Hetherington, R.F. Badgley, and V.L. Matthews, "Voluntary Health-Related Behaviour in Wheatville," *CJPH*, 58 (1967), pp. 109–16; C.C. Hughes et al., *People of Cove and Woodlot, The Stirling Country Study*, Vol. II (New York: Basic Books, 1960) and D.C. Leighton et al., Vol. III (New York: Basic Books, 1963) on the quality of life and physical and mental illness in rural Nova Scotia; E. Leyton, *Dying Hard: The Ravages of Industrial Carnage* (Toronto: McClelland and Stewart, 1975); J.L. Migue and G. Belanger, *The Price of Health* (Toronto: Macmillan, 1974); J. Siemiatycki, "The Distribution of Disease," *CD*, 10, 2 (1974), pp. 15–25; M. Simard, "Conditions de travail et santé des travailleurs," *SS*, 9 (1977), pp. 93–106; "Social and Mental Health Survey, Montreal" in W.E. Mann, ed., *Social Deviance in Canada* (Copp Clark, 1971); L. Tepperman, "Effects of the Demographic Transition upon Access to the Toronto Elite," *CRSA*, 14 (1977), pp. 285–93; T.F. Ward, "Immigration and Ethnic Origin in Mental Illness," *Journal of the Canadian Psychiatric Associations*, 6 (1961), pp. 329–32; J.P. Welch et al., "The Distribution of Height and Weight, and the Influence of Socio-economic Factors in a Sample of Eastern Canadian Urban School Children," *CJPH* 62 (1971), pp. 373–81.

Crime, Delinquency, and Sentencing

R. Bienvenue and A.H. Latif, "Arrests, Dispositions and Recidivism: A Comparison of Indians and Whites," *Canadian Journal of Criminology and Corrections*, 16 (1974), pp. 105–165; W.K. Greenaway and S.L. Brickey, eds., *Law and Social Control in Canada* (Scarborough: Prentice-Hall, 1978); J. Hagan, "Criminal Justice and Native People: A Study of Incarceration in a Canadian Province," *CRSA* (special edition: "Aspects of Canadian Society") (1974), pp. 220–36; J. Hogarth, *Sentencing as a Human Process* (Toronto: University of Toronto Press, 1971); R.A. Silverman and J.J. Teevan Jr., eds., *Crime in Canadian Society* (Toronto: Butterworths, 1975); L. Tepperman, *Crime Control* (Toronto: McGraw-Hill Ryerson, 1977), especially Chap. 6, "Crime and Social Inequality"; F.G. Vallee and M. Schwartz, "Report on Criminality among the Foreign-Born in Canada" in B.R. Blishen et al., *Canadian Society* (Toronto: Macmillan, 1961); E.W. Vaz, "Delinquency and the Youth Culture: Upper and Middle Class Boys," *Journal of Criminal Law, Criminology and Police Science*, 60 (1969), pp. 33–46; E.W. Vaz, "Middle-Class Adolescents, Self-Reported Delinquency and Youth Culture Activities," *CRSA*, 2 (1965), pp. 52–62; E.W. Vaz, "Self-Reported Juvenile Delinquency and Socioeconomic Status," *Canadian Journal of Corrections*, 8 (1966), pp. 20–27.

Political Behavior

G.M. Anderson, "Voting Behaviour and the Ethnic-Religious Variable: A Study of a Federal Election in Hamilton, Ontario," *CJEPS*, 33 (1966), pp. 27–97; R. Alford, "Class Voting in the Anglo-American Political Systems" in S.M. Lipset and S. Rokkan, eds., *Party Systems and Voter Alignment* (New York: Free Press, 1967), pp. 67–93; R.R. Alford, *Party and Society* (Chicago: Rand-McNally, 1963) — stratification correlates of party preference in Canada and the other Anglo-American democracies; D.J. Bercuson, "Western Labour Radicalism and the One Big Union: Myths and Realities," *JCS*, 9 (1974), pp. 3–11; S.D. Clark, "Movements of Protest in Post-War Canadian Society," *Transactions of the Royal Society of Canada*, Series IV, 8 (1970), pp. 227–37; J.E. Curtis and R.D. Lambert, "Voting, Political Interest and Age: National Survey Findings for French- and English-Canadians," *CJPS*, 9 (1976), pp. 293–307; D. Forcese and J. deVries, "Occupations and Electoral Success in Canada: The 1974 Federal Election," *CRSA*, 14 (1977), pp. 331–40; B.J. Kay, "An Examination of Class and Left-Right Party Images in Canadian Voting," *CJPS*, 10 (1977), pp. 127–44; D. Kwavinick, *Organized Labour and Pressure Politics: The Canadian Labour Congress, 1956–1968* (Montreal: McGill-Queen's University Press, 1972); R. Ogmundson, "Mass-Elite Linkages and Class Issues in Canada," *CRSA*, 13 (1976), pp. 1–12; R. Ogmundson, "On the Measurement of Party Class Positions: The Case of Canadian Federal Political Parties," *CRSA*, 12 (1977), pp. 565–76; R. Ogmundson, "On the Use of Party Image Variables to Measure the Political Distinctiveness of a Class Vote: The Canadian Case," *CJS*, 1 (1975), pp. 169–78; N. Penner, *The Canadian Left: A Critical Analysis* (Scarborough: Prentice-Hall, 1977); M. Pinard, "Poverty and Political Movements," *Social Problems*, 15 (1967), pp. 50–63; M. Pinard, *The Rise of a Third Party* (Scarborough: Prentice-Hall, 1970), pp. 80ff; M. Pinard, "Working Class Politics: An Interpretation of the Quebec Case," *CRSA*, 7 (1970), pp. 87–109; M. Pinard and R. Hamilton, "The Independence Issue and the Polarization of the Electorate: The 1973 Quebec Election," *CJPS*, 10 (1977), pp. 215–59; M. Pinard and R. Hamilton, "The Parti-Quebecois Comes to Power: An Analysis of the 1976 Quebec Election," *CJPS*, forthcoming; P. Sinclair, "Class Structure and Populist Protest: The Case of Western Canada," *CJS*, 1 (1975), pp. 1–17; P. Stevenson, "Class and Left Wing Radicalism," *CRSA*, 14 (1977), pp. 269–84; K.W. Taylor and N. Wiseman, "Class and

Ethnic Voting in Winnipeg: The Case of 1941," *CRSA*, 14 (1977), pp. 174–83; Dale C. Thomson, ed., *Quebec Society and Politics: Views from the Inside* (Toronto: McClelland and Stewart, 1973); P. Vaillancourt, "Quebec Labour and the P.Q.," *CD*, 12, 6 (1977), pp. 3–6; J. Wilson, "Politics and Social Class in Canada: The Case of Waterloo South," *CJPS*, 1 (1968), pp. 288–309.

Styles of Life and Social Participation

R. Breton, "Institutional Completeness of Ethnic Communities and the Personal Relations of Immigrants," *AJS*, 70 (1964), pp. 163–205; D.H. Clairmont and D.W. Magill, *Africville: The Life and Death of a Canadian Black Community* (Toronto: McClelland and Stewart, 1974); S.D. Clark, *The New Urban Poor* (Toronto: McGraw-Hill Ryerson, 1978); S.D. Clark, *The Suburban Society* (Toronto: University of Toronto Press, 1966); J. Curtis, "Voluntary Association Joining," *ASR*, 36 (1971), pp. 872–81; J.E. Curtis and B.G. Milton, "Social Status and the 'Active Society': National Data on Correlates of Leisure-Time Physical and Sports Activities" in R.S. Gruneau and J.G. Albinson, *Canadian Sport: Sociological Perspectives* (Don Mills, Ontario: Addison-Wesley, 1976), pp. 302–28; A. Darroch and W. Marston, "The Social Class Basis of Ethnic Residential Segregation: The Canadian Case," *AJS*, 77 (1971), pp. 491–510; F.T. Denton and P.J. George, "The Influence of Socio-Economic Variables on Family Size in Wentworth County, Ontario, 1871: A Statistical Analysis of Historical Micro-Data," *CRSA*, 10 (1973), pp. 334–45; L. Driedger and G. Church, "Residential Segregation and Institutional Completeness: A Comparison of Ethnic Minorities," *CRSA*, 11 (1974), pp. 30–52; L. Driedger and J. Peters, "Identity and Social Distance," *CRSA*, 14 (1977), pp. 158–73; G.L. Gold, *St. Pascal* (Toronto: Holt, Rinehart and Winston, 1975); R.S. Gruneau, "Class or Mass: Notes on the Democratization of Canadian Amateur Sport" in R.S. Gruneau and J.G. Albinson, *Canadian Sport: Sociological Perspectives* (Don Mills, Ontario: Addison-Wesley, 1976), pp. 108–41; D.M. Heer and L.A. Aubay Jr., "The Trend of Interfaith Marriages in Canada, 1922–72" in K. Ishwaran, ed., *The Canadian Family*, rev. ed. (Toronto: Holt, Rinehart and Winston, 1976), pp. 408–17; A. Listiak, "Legitimate Deviance and Social Class: Bar Behaviour during Grey Cup Week," *Sociological Focus*, 7 (1974), pp. 13–44; J. Lorimer and M. Phillips, *Working People: Life in a Downtown City Neighbourhood* (Toronto: James Lewis and Samuel, 1971); R.A. Lucas, *Minetown, Milltown, Railtown: Life in Canadian Communities of Single Industry* (Toronto: University of Toronto Press, 1971); W.E. Mann, "Culture and Social Organization in the Lower Ward" in S.D. Clark, ed., *Urbanism and the Changing Canadian Society* (Toronto: University of Toronto Press, 1961); R. Matthews, *"There's No Better Place than Here": Social Change in Three Newfoundland Communities* (Toronto: Peter Martin Associates, 1976); A. Metcalfe, "Organized Sport and Social Stratification in Montreal" in R.S. Gruneau and J.G. Albinson, *Canadian Sport: Sociological Perspectives* (Don Mills, Ontario: Addison-Wesley, 1976), pp. 77–102; A.D. Ross, "Philanthropic Activity and the Business Career," *Social Forces*, 32 (1954), pp. 274–80; J. Seeley et al., *Crestwood Heights* (Toronto: University of Toronto Press, 1956); W.E. Mann, ed., *The Underside of Toronto* (Toronto: McClelland and Stewart, 1970); L. Tepperman, "Effects of the Demographic Transition upon Access to the Toronto Elite," *CRSA*, 14 (1977), pp. 285–93; S.F. Wise, "Sport and Class Values in Old Ontario and Quebec" in W.H. Heick and R. Graham, eds., *His Own Man: Essays in Honour of A.R.M. Lower* (Montreal: McGill and Queen's University Press, 1974).

Attitude, Belief, and Value Correlates

C. Anderson and A.D.J. Cote, "Belief Dissonance as a Source of Disaffection between Ethnic Groups," *Journal of Personality and Social Psychology*, 4 (1966), pp. 447-53; W.P. Archibald, *Social Psychology as Political Economy* (Toronto: McGraw-Hill Ryerson, 1978); J.W. Berry and G.J.S. Wilde, eds., *Social Psychology: The Canadian Case* (Toronto: McClelland and Stewart, 1972); A. Cameron and T. Storm, "Achievement Motivation in Canadian Indian, Middle and Working-Class Children," *Psychological Reports*, 16 (1965), pp. 459-63; C. Carisse, "Cultural Orientation in Marriages between French and English Canadians" in J.L. Elliott, ed., *Minority Canadians*, Vol. 2 (Scarborough: Prentice-Hall, 1971), pp. 191-206; R.A. Clifton, "Self-Concept and Attitudes: A Comparison of Canadian Indian and Non-Indian Students," *CRSA*, 12 (1975), pp. 577-84; D. Coburn and V.L. Edwards, "Objective and Subjective Socio-Economic Status: Intercorrelations and Consequences," *CRSA*, 13 (1976), pp. 178-88; C.J. Cuneo, "Education, Language and Multi-dimensional Continentalism," *CJPS*, 7 (1974), pp. 536-50; C.J. Cuneo, "The Social Basis of Political Continentalism in Canada," *CRSA*, 13 (1976), pp. 55-70; C.J. Cuneo and J.E. Curtis, "Quebec Separatism: An Analysis of Determinants within Social Class Levels," *CRSA*, 11 (1974), pp. 1-29; J.E. Curtis and R.D. Lambert, "Educational Status and Reactions to Social and Political Heterogeneity," *CRSA*, 13 (1976), pp. 189-203; J.E. Curtis and R.D. Lambert, "Status Dissatisfaction and Out-Group Rejection: Cross-Cultural Comparisons within Canada," 12 (1975), pp. 178-92; J. Goyder and P. Pineo, "The Accuracy of Self-Assessments of Social Status," *CRSA*, 14 (1977), pp. 235-46; E.G. Grabb, "Canada's Lower Middle Class," *CJS*, 1 (1975), pp. 295-312; F.E. Jones and W.E. Lambert, "Occupational Rank and Attitudes toward Immigrants," *Public Opinion Quarterly*, 29 (1965), pp. 137-44; R.D. Lambert and J.E. Curtis, "Social Stratification and Canadians' Reactions to American Cultural Influence: Theoretical Problems and Trend Analyses," *International Journal of Comparative Sociology*, forthcoming; W.E. Lambert el al., "Child Training Values of English Canadian and French Canadian Parents," *Canadian Journal of Behavioural Science*, 3 (1971), pp. 217-36; Rick Ogmundson, "Two Modes of Interpretation of Survey Data: A Comment on Schreiber," *Social Forces*, 55 (1977), pp. 809-11; R.M. Pike and E. Zuriek, eds., *Socialization and Values in Canadian Society*, Vol. 2, *Socialization, Social Stratification and Ethnicity* (Toronto: McClelland and Stewart, 1975); S. Richer and P. Laporte, "Culture, Cognition and English-French Competition" in J. Elliott, ed., *Minority Canadians*, Vol. 2 (Scarborough: Prentice-Hall, 1971), pp. 141-50; J.W. Rinehart and I.P. Okraku, "A Study of Class Consciousness," *CRSA*, 11 (1974), pp. 181-96; M. Rioux, "Conscience ethnique et conscience de classe au Québec," *RS*, 7 (1965), pp. 23-35; I. Rootman, "Social Class and Attitudes Towards Mental Illness," *CRSA*, 9 (1972), pp. 21-32; H. Roseborough and R. Breton, "Perceptions of the Relative Economic and Political Advantages of Ethnic Groups in Canada" in B.R. Blishen et al., *Canadian Society* (Toronto: Macmillan, 1968); E.M. Schreiber, "Cultural Changes between Occupational Categories: The Case of Canada," *Social Forces*, 55 (1976), pp. 16-29; P. Sheriff, "Preferences Valeurs et Differentiation Intraprofessionalle Salon L'origine Ethnique," *CRSA*, 11 (1974), pp. 125-37; R. Usmiani, "Canadian Radio Drama: Aspects of the Two Cultures," *Canadian Review of Comparative Literature*, 2 (1975), pp. 47-71; H. Zentner, "Religion Affiliation, Social Class and Achievement-Aspiration: Relationships among Male High School Students," *Alberta Journal of Educational Research* II (1965), pp. 233-248.

DOMINANT AND COUNTER STRATIFICATION IDEOLOGIES

B. Baldus and V. Tribe, "The Development of Perceptions and Evaluations of Social Inequality among School Children," *CRSA*, 15 (1978), pp. 50–60; D.V.J. Bell and L. Tepperman, *Canada's Political Cultures* (Toronto: McClelland and Stewart, forthcoming); W. Christian and C. Campbell, *Political Parties and Ideologies in Canada* (Toronto: McGraw-Hill Ryerson, 1974); W. Clement, *The Canadian Corporate Elite* (Toronto: McClelland and Stewart, 1975); C. Crawford and J. Curtis, "English Canadian-American Differences in Value Orientations," *Studies in Comparative International Development*, forthcoming; J.E. Curtis, M. Kuhn, and R.D. Lambert, "Education and the Pluralist Perspective" in R.A. Carlton, L.A. Colley, and N.J. MacKennon, eds., *Education, Change, and Society* (Toronto: Gage, 1976); H. Hardin, *A Nation Unaware: The Canadian Economic Culture* (Vancouver: J.J. Douglas, 1974); B. Finnigan, *Making It: The Canadian Dream* (Toronto: McClelland and Stewart, 1972); G. Horowitz, "Conservatism, Liberalism and Socialism in Canada: An Interpretation," *CJEPS*, 32 (1966), pp. 327–59; G. Horowitz, "Notes on 'Conservatism, Liberalism and Socialism in Canada,'" *CJPS*, 11 (1978), pp. 383–400; I.L. Horowitz, "The Hemispheric Connection," *Queen's Quarterly*, 80 (1973), pp. 327–59; J.C. Johnstone, "Definitions of Canadian Society," *Studies of the Royal Commission on Bilingualism and Biculturalism*, No. 2 (Ottawa: Information Canadan 1969), pp. 1–36; S.M. Lipset, "Canada and the United States — A Comparative View," *CRSA*, 1 (1964), pp. 173–85; A. MacLeod, "Nationalism and Social Class: The Unresolved Dilemma of the Quebec Left," *JCS*, 8 (1973), pp. 3–15; M.P. Marchak, *Ideological Perspectives on Canada* (Toronto: McGraw-Hill Ryerson, 1975); G. McDiarmid and D. Pratt, *Teaching Prejudice* (Toronto: Ontario Institute for Studies in Education, 1971); S.R. Mealing, "The Concept of Social Class and the Interpretation of Canadian History," *Canadian Historical Review*, 46 (1965), pp. 201–18; J. Porter, *The Vertical Mosaic* (Toronto: University of Toronto Press, 1965), Chaps. 15–16; R.L. McDougall, "The Dodo and the Cruising Auk: Class in Canadian Literature," *Canadian Literature*, 18 (1963), pp. 6–20, and 20 (1964), pp. 77–80; R. Howard and J. Scott, "International Unions and the Ideology of Class Collaboration" in G. Teeple, ed., *Capitalism and the National Question* (Toronto: University of Toronto Press, 1972), pp. 43–66; S.B. Ryerson, "Quebec: Concepts of Class and Nation" in G. Teeple, ed., *Capitalism and the National Question* (Toronto: University of Toronto Press, 1972), pp. 211–288; G. Bourque and N. Laurin-Frenette, "Social Classes and National Ideologies in Quebec, 1760–1970" in G. Teeple, ed., *Capitalism and the National Question* (Toronto: University of Toronto Press, 1972), pp. 185–210; P. Resnick, *The Land of Cain: Class and Nationalism in English Canada 1945–1975* (Vancouver: New Star, 1977); C.J. Richardson, "Education and Social Mobility: Changing Conceptions of the Role of the Educational System," *CJS*, 4 (1977), pp. 417–34; M. Rioux, "The Development of Ideologies in Quebec" in G.L. Gold and M.A. Tremblay, eds., *Communities and Culture in French-Canada* (Toronto: Holt, Rinehart and Winston, 1973), pp. 260–79; A. Rotstein and G. Lax, eds., *Getting It Back: A Program for Canadian Independence* (Toronto: Clarke, Irwin, 1974); T. Truman, "A Critique of Seymour M. Lipset's Article: Value Differences, Absolute or Relative," *CJPS*, 4 (1971), pp. 497–575.